A THEMATIC DI
MODERN F

Now available in paperback, *A Thematic Dictionary of Modern Persian* is a reference work unique in the history of English-Persian lexicography. It offers a considerably extended guide to modern everyday Persian vocabulary, arranged by theme. With approximately 25,000 Persian headwords in over seventy themed sections, it covers every conceivable vocabulary need: from everyday topics such as food or the weather, to more in-depth topics such as astronomy, psychology or international relations. Supplementary wordlists cover verbs, adjectives and parts of speech, while a special section on Persian simple and compound verbs will appeal to all learners of Persian. An easy-to-use index of English words, with over 20,000 items of vocabulary, completes the work and gives it the look and feel of a regular two-way bilingual dictionary.

Invaluable for vocabulary building, essay-writing and specialised translation, *A Thematic Dictionary of Modern Persian* caters for all your Persian language needs in one volume, and is designed to make word learning a pleasure rather than a chore.

Colin Turner is a Reader in Islamic Thought at the University of Durham, UK. His main research areas include Islamic theology and philosophy; Sufism; Shi'ism; The Qur'an and Qur'anic exegesis; Persian language and literature. Some of his previous publications are *Islam: The Basics* (2005) and *The Koran* (2004), also published by Routledge.

A THEMATIC DICTIONARY OF MODERN PERSIAN

Colin Turner

Routledge
Taylor & Francis Group

LONDON AND NEW YORK

First published 2004
Paperback edition first published 2010
by Routledge
2 Park Square, Milton Park, Abingdon, Oxon OX14 4RN

Simultaneously published in the USA and Canada
by Routledge
711 Third Avenue, New York, NY 10017

Routledge is an imprint of the Taylor & Francis Group, an informa business

© 2004, 2010 Colin Turner

British Library Cataloguing in Publication Data
A catalogue record for this book is available from the British Library

Library of Congress Cataloging in Publication Data
A catalog record has been requested for this book

ISBN10: 0–7007–0458–2 (hbk)
ISBN10: 0–415–56780–7 (pbk)
ISBN10: 0–203–85260–5 (ebk)

ISBN13: 978–0–7007–0458–3 (hbk)
ISBN13: 978–0–415–56780–0 (pbk)
ISBN13: 978–0–203–85260–6 (ebk)

CONTENTS

Preliminary Pages

Themed Sections

Supplementary Lists

Acknowledgments

I owe an enormous debt of gratitude to everyone who has helped me to bring this project to fruition, be it with practical help, such as word gathering, list-making or the provision of source material, or with kind words of encouragement and moral support. The constraints of time and space do not allow me to mention everyone individually. There are however a number of people I feel I am duty bound to mention by name - people without whose sterling support and assistance this book would never have got off the ground, let alone reach the rarefied air of the library and bookshop shelves.

Special thanks must go to my brother-in-law Bahman Shoraka, for his tireless word-gathering during the early days of the project; to Abulfazl Mirjalili, for supplying me on a regular basis with newspapers, magazines and journals, all of which were an invaluable source of lexicographical material; to my good friend Dr Reza Jamshidiha, for his kind and inestimably useful gift of a whole range of Persian specialist dictionaries – an invaluable source of headwords for the themed sections; to Ali Arpanahi, for help with the section on education and also the issue of language change; to Hossein Turner, for help with the identification of crucial additions to the word base for various sections, particularly computing and the natural sciences; to Sara Turner, whose advice on the music section was particularly welcome, and for help with word-checking; to Ali Turner, Andrea James and Maia Turner, for their love, encouragement and support; to Declan O'Sullivan, for provision of Persian software; to Mehdi Shalchi, Asif Syed and Mohammad Dadgar, without whose friendship and encouragement my life would be much poorer; to my good friend and colleague Dr Ali Ansari, for moral support and trips to the cinema whenever the going got tough; to my teacher and friend Dr Paul Luft, whose love of Persian and the culture and history of Iran is inspirational; to Professor Anoush Ehteshami, for reviving Persian at IMEIS and fighting its corner for the past decade, and without whose foresight and generosity of spirit I would not be working in Durham and this dictionary would probably never have been written; to Ali Pedram, for help with the checking of Persian headwords and also for his invaluable advice on the endlessly fascinating phenomenon that is the world of Persian slang; to Malcolm Campbell at Curzon Press, for his seemingly endless stock of patience and unfailing good humour; and, last but certainly not least, to my wife Mahshid, who, despite having lived with this project for longer than either of us cares to remember, has sustained me, body and soul, with her spirit – a spirit which, more than anything else, reminds me that when love is present, all things are possible.

This book is dedicated to her, and to lovers of the Persian language everywhere.

Foreword

Farsi shekar ast – Persian is like sugar – is the phrase often repeated by Iranians to non-native speakers of Persian. To discover exactly what is sweet about this ancient language, however, will take several years of intensive language training, a deep dive into the fascinating world of Persian/Iranian literature, and a good dictionary. To be able to relate to the nuances of Farsi verse, the prose of Iran's great writers, and the vocabulary of modern Iranians is no easy undertaking. And the whole enterprise will have become even harder since the Revolution. Iran's Islamic Revolution in 1979 has had a very direct impact on the vocabulary of Farsi, and on the turn of phrase of virtually every Iranian. Not only have some old-fashioned religiously-derived words crept into the language, but as a result of a subtle process of Persianisation of Farsi, itself fuelled by a national desire to be 'authentic' and less reliant on 'imported' Western words and phrases, there has been a frantic effort to find – even invent – words for the modern vocabulary of a globalised economy and political system. There are therefore two parallel evolutionary currents to be identified in the development of Farsi since the Iranian revolution.

It is an almost impossible task to be able to keep track of the linguistic changes of Farsi today, even while sitting in Tehran, particularly as new words are introduced into the language on a regular basis. To be able to do so – to research, catalogue and identify words which make up modern Persian – as Colin Turner has done, must surely be regarded as a major achievement. Dr Turner's new dictionary is therefore something of a landmark.

The dictionary has approximately 70 themed sections (from astronomy to weather, through politics, IR, religion, philosophy, the house, trees, animals, greetings, clothes, computing, farming, psychology...) and as such is a goldmine of information and commentary in its own right. But Dr Turner has complemented this rich database of words and phrases with a detailed 15,000 word English index, sections on simple and compound verbs and other parts of speech, and a whole section on Persian slang, including choice little phrases used in everyday discourse. The data sets are so comprehensive, the entries so detailed and the related information so enlightening that I would suggest anyone with an interest in Iran should start by thumbing through this treasure-trove of a dictionary!

Professor Anoush Ehteshami
Durham, February 2003

Introduction

The seed for this book was planted way back in the mid-Nineties following a throwaway comment by a former language student of mine. Frustrated by his inability to learn a vocabulary list for a forthcoming test, he took a piece of chalk and, during a tea-break, wrote in large letters on the board: "Alphabetical order is actually no order at all, and all dictionaries should be burned."

While unable to share his sentiments with regard to dictionaries, I was fascinated by his opening phrase. The vocabulary list I had given them was indeed ordered alphabetically; naively I had assumed that the perennially laborious and universally disliked task of learning vocabulary would somehow be made easier if it had some kind of order. It only gradually dawned on me that the difficulty in learning a long list of lexical items lay not in the list's lack of structural order, but in the fact that the items were unrelated in meaning. When you come to think about it, there is no semantic reality in alphabetical order: on the contrary, alphabetical order destroys semantic structure, keeping apart lexemes that should belong together (such as *mother* and *father*, or *tall* and *short*). Quite understandably, my student had problems learning items that were mostly unrelated in sense, and was attacking the poor dictionary simply because the dictionary, with its strict alphabetical structure, compounds the problem.

It was at this point that I realised a change was necessary, and that I as language teacher needed to develop an alternative conception of vocabulary acquisition, one based on the simple human intuition which says that groups of lexemes are related in sense. From that point onwards, translation passages were designed with the learning of thematically-linked lexical items in mind. And what better to complement the new teaching method but a two-way English-Persian dictionary structured according to the same principles: a thematic dictionary, no less, and the first of its kind in Persian lexicographical history.

My aim had been to compile a slim, pocket-sized thematic dictionary for the use of undergraduate learners of Persian, yet once the project got underway, it soon became clear that my constituency of potential user-readers was far wider than I might have imagined at the outset. Student friends in the Iranian postgraduate community, most of them involved in the natural sciences, bemoaned the fact that ordinary bilingual pocket dictionaries covered everyday conversational vocabulary but lacked the kind of lexical items crucial to their areas of expertise. Thus the plot was hatched to broaden the original remit and cover, thematically, as many of the specialist language areas as would be workable within one handy, but increasingly not so slim, volume. Thus it was that the number of themed sections ballooned from an initial twenty to well over seventy, servicing practically every area in the average university curriculum.

Discussions with friends and colleagues as the work progressed made it clear that the dictionary would serve far more than just those with purely academic needs. An Iranian friend living in the UK convinced me that such a dictionary would, provided that it incorporated a foolproof pronunciation guide, prove invaluable to the countless thousands of second-generation Iranian expatriates born after the 1979 Revolution and brought up in Europe or the USA. It was for this particular demographic that the transliteration system used in the dictionary was devised, primarily as a guide to pronunciation but also as an alternative Romanised Persian alphabet, for use in applications such as electronic mail.

As the original parameters of the project expanded, and more and more expert opinions were sought, the dictionary began to take on a wholly different shape to that first envisaged back in the classroom all those years ago. From an inchoate collection of vocabulary lists covering several different conversational themes it gradually evolved into what it is today: a fully-fledged bilingual dictionary with over seventy themed sections, examples and phrases to illustrate constructions and usage, and a huge index of English words with page references pointing to their Persian equivalents.

A dictionary of this kind has been needed for as long as learners of Persian have grappled with semantically unrelated wordlists, which is indeed as long as have people have endeavoured to learn Persian. While trusty tomes such as Professor Lambton's once groundbreaking *Persian Vocabulary* undoubtedly still have a place on the library shelf, the future lies, I believe, with the linguistically more authentic themed lexicon. Time – and, in the case of this particular offering, lovers of Persian – will tell.

Colin Turner
Durham, March 2003

Guide to Transliteration

Consonants

Persian letter	Transliteration
ب	b
پ	p
ت ث	t
ث	s
ج	j
چ	ch
ح	h
خ	kh
د	d
ذ	z
ر	r
ز	z
ژ	zh
س	s
ش	sh
ص	s
ض	z
ط	t
ظ	z
ع	'
غ	q
ف	f
ق	q
ک	k
گ	g
ل	l
م	m
ن	n
و	v
ه	h
ی	y

Vowels, diphthongs and other markers

Persian letter	Transliteration
آ	aa
	a
	e
ی	i
	o
و	u
ای	ey
او	ow
ء	'
	an
	doubles the consonant bearing it

A note on transliteration

Transliteration is always a problematic issue: there is no universally accepted system, the received wisdom being that so long as one is consistent, one may use the scheme one feels most comfortable with. My choice was made simpler for me by the limitations of the software I was using: the absence of macrons, cedillas and other diacritic markers meant that I had to devise my own scheme, which is more or less an adaptation of the Harvard system – with a few obvious differences! Nevertheless, I have since grown rather fond of the transliteration scheme you see here, and am convinced that it is far more reader-friendly than others. I leave it to users of this dictionary to judge!

There are a few anomalies to watch out for, but nothing which detracts from the book's usability.

(i)   Words ending in silent *h* (e.g. *khaaneh*) are transliterated without the *h* when they are followed by an *ezaafeh*, e.g. *khaane-ye man*, or by the plural article *haa*, e.g. *khaane-haa*.

(ii)   In the transliteration of words which include an *s* followed by a voiced *h*, e.g. *es-haal*, the *s* and *h* are separated by a dash, to avoid being confused with *sh*, which is the transliteration of ش

(iii)   The plural particle *haa* is always written separately from the word which it qualifies, e.g. *dast-haa, tup-haa, dars-haa*, thus preventing misidentification with English letter pairs, particularly th, ph and sh.

Guide to Pronunciation

Consonants

Transliteration		*Pronunciation*
b	as	b in boy
p	as	p in part
t	as	t in tap
s	as	s in sink
j	as	j in jam
ch	as	ch in chin
h	as	h in hot
kh	as	the Scottish ch in loch
d	as	d in dog
z	as	z in zoo
r	as	the trilled Spanish or Italian r
zh	as	s in pleasure
sh	as	sh in shop
'	as	a glottal stop
q		
f	as	f in fine
k	as	k in park
g	as	g in go
l	as	l in look
m	as	m in more
n	as	n in no
v	as	v in very
y	as	y in yes

Vowels and Diphthongs

Transliteration		*Pronunciation*
aa	as	a in father
a	as	a in cat
e	as	e in jet
i	as	ee in feel
o	as	o in gore
u	as	oo in food
ow	as	ow in low
ey	as	ai in mail

Abbreviations

a.	adjective	Isl.	Islam
Anat.	anatomy	Lit.	literature
Bot.	botany	Math.	mathematics
Chem.	chemistry	Med.	medicine
Comp.	computing	Mil.	military
Econ.	economics	Mus.	music
Educ.	education	n.	noun
fig.	figurative	Phys.	physics
Geog.	geography	Rel.	religion
Gram.	grammar	sl.	slang

Air Travel

سفر هوائی

travel agency	aazhaans-e mosaaferati	آژانس مسافرتی
luggage label	etiket	اتیکت
height; altitude	ertefaa'	ارتفاع
excess luggage	ezaafeh baar	اضافه بار
information	ettelaa'aat	اطلاعات
transfer; connection	enteqaal	انتقال
luggage	baar	بار
hand luggage	baar-e dasti	بار دستی
porter	baarbar	باربر
check-in desk	baazrasi-ye baar	بازرسی بار
wing	baal	بال
ascent	baalaa ravi	بالاروی
runway	baand	باند
temporary runway	baand-e movaqqat	باند موقت
information desk	bakhsh-e ettelaa'aat	بخش اطلاعات
control tower	borj-e moraaqebat	برج مراقبت
plan; timetable	barnaameh	برنامه
flight timetable	barnaame-ye parvaaz-haa	برنامه پروازها
take-off	boland shodan	بلند شدن
ticket	belit	بلیط
one-way ticket	belit-e dow sareh	بلیط دو سره
return ticket	belit-e yek sareh	بلیط یک سره
flight	parvaaz	پرواز
airmail	post-e havaa'i	پست هوائی
escalator	pelleh barqi	پله برقی
reservation	pishgereft	پیشگرفت
arrivals/departures board	taablow-ye saa'aat-e parvaaz	تابلوی ساعات پرواز
taxi	taaksi	تاکسی
departure lounge	taalaar-e rahsepaaraan	تالار رهسپاران
air sickness	tahavvo' dar havaapeymaa	تهوع در هواپیما
reduction; discount	takhfif	تخفیف
terminal	terminaal	ترمینال
air turbulence	talaatom-e havaa	تلاطم هوا
toilet	tovaalet	توالت
stop-over; transit	tavaqqof	توقف
black box	ja'be-ye siyaah	جعبه سیاه

parachute	chatr-e nejaat	چتر نجات
runway lights	cheraaq-e baand	چراغ باند
luggage trolley	charkh-e baarbari	چرخ باربری
suitcase	chamedaan	چمدان
flight crew	khadame-ye havaapeymaa	خدمه هواپیما
pilot	khalabaan	خلبان
sound barrier	divaar-e sowti	دیوار صوتی
radar	raadaar	رادار
exit	raah-e khoruji	راه خروجی
emergency exit	raah-e khoruji-ye ezteraari	راه خروجی اضطراری
moving walkway	raah-e motaharrek	راه متحرک
entrance	raah-e vorud	راه ورود
clock; hour	saa'at	ساعت
speed	sor'at	سرعت
passenger	sarneshin	سرنشین
air crash	soqut-e havaa'i	سقوط هوائی
boarding	savaari	سواری
airline	sherkat-e havaapeymaa'i	شرکت هواپیمائی
number	shomaareh	شماره
ascent	so'ud	صعود
reserved seat; reservation	sandali-ye rezerv shodeh	صندلی رزرو شده
aeroplane	tayyaareh	طیاره
air disaster	faaje'e-ye havaa'i	فاجعه هوائی
descent; landing	forud	فرود
emergency landing	forud-e ezteraari	فرود اضطراری
seat belt; safety belt	kamarband-e imani	کمربند ایمنی
air traffic control	kontrol-e aamad o shod-e parvaazi	کنترل آمد و شد پروازی
bag	kif	کیف
passport	gozarnaameh	گذرنامه
customs	gomrok	گمرک
air traffic controller	ma'mur-e kontrol-e parvaaz-ha	مامور کنترل پروازها
customs officer	ma'mur-e gomrok	مامور گمرک
traveller; passenger	mosaafer	مسافر
travel; trip; journey	mosaaferat	مسافرت
duty-free	mo'aaf az 'avaarez-e gomroki	معاف از عوارض گمرکی
destination	maqsad	مقصد
propeller	malakh	ملخ
steward; stewardess	mehmaandaar	مهماندار

map	naqsheh	نقشه
entrance	vorud	ورود
shuttle	vasile-ye shod aamad	وسیله شد آمد
helicopter	helikupter	هلی کوپتر
air; sky	havaa	هوا
aeroplane	havaapeymaa	هواپیما
cargo plane	havaapeymaa-ye baarbari	هواپیمای باربری
jet plane	havaapeymaa-ye jet	هواپیمای جت
passenger plane	havaapeymaa-ye mosaaferbari	هواپیمای مسافربری
air (adj.); aviation	havaa'i	هوائی

OTHER WORDS AND PHRASES CONNECTED WITH AIR TRAVEL

air travel مسافرت هوائی   airport فرودگاه   to go on a journey مسافرت کردن   to travel سفر کردن

return flight پرواز رفت و برگشت   direct flight پرواز مستقیم   air journey سفر هوائی

flight 219 from London to Tehran پرواز شماره ۲۱۹ از لندن به تهران   my flight is delayed پرواز من تاخیر دارد

what time does your flight leave? آن پرواز شما ساعت چند حرکت می کند؟   that flight arrived late آن پرواز دیر رسید

which terminal do we have to go to? به کدام ترمینال باید برویم؟   where is the waiting area? سالن انتظار کجاست؟

I'm scared of travelling by air من از سفر هوائی می ترسم   I'm scared of crashing از سقوط هواپیما می ترسم

which airline are you travelling with? با کدام شرکت هوائی مسافرت می کنید؟   safety record سابقه ایمنی

where do we have to check our luggage in? کجا باید بارهایمان را تحویل بدهیم   information desk باجه اطلاعات

can you help me please? لطفا میتوانید به من کمک کنید؟   I can't find .... نمی توانم .... را پیدا کنم

could you please guide me/show me the way to .... لطفا می توانید مرا به .... راهنمائی کنید؟

excuse me, where is .... ببخشید ، .... کجاست؟   the nearest toilet نزدیکترین توالت

I got on the plane سوار هواپیما شدم   we got off the plane از هواپیما پیاده شدیم   the plane took off هواپیما بلند شد

the plane ascended هواپیما صعود کرد   the plane landed هواپیما فرود آمد   the plane landed هواپیما نشست

the plane hit an air pocket هواپیما به چاه هوائی خورد   our plane hit some turbulence هواپیمای ما دچار تلاطم هوا شد

estimated time of arrival زمان تقریبی ورود   estimated time of departure زمان تقریبی عزیمت

to pass through customs آیا چیزی برای اعلام کردن به همراه دارید؟   do you have anything to declare? از گمرک رد شدن

refuelling سوخت گیری مجدد   the aeroplane entered Iranian air space هواپیما وارد آسمانهای ایران شد

supersonic aircraft هواپیمای فراصوتی   sound barrier دیوار صوتی   air-hijacking هواپیماربائی

Concorde broke the sound barrier هواپیمای کنکرد دیوار صوتی را شکست   jump jet هواپیمای عمودرو

domestic flight پرواز داخلی   international flight پرواز بین المللی   long-haul flight پرواز دوربرد

please fasten your safety belts لطفا کمربند ایمنی خود را ببندید   No Smoking سیگار کشیدن ممنوع

◄◄►►

3

Animals

حیوانات

watering place	aabkhorgaah	آبخورگاه
armadillo	aarmaadil	آرمادیل
experiment	aazmaayesh	آزمایش
deer	aahu	آهو
doe	aahu-ye maadeh	آهوی ماده
duck	ordak	اردک
horse	asb	اسب
hippopotamus	asb-e aabi	اسب آبی
horse racing	asb davaani	اسب دوانی
pony	asb-e kuchek	اسب کوچک
stallion	asb-e nar	اسب نر
reins	afsaar	افسار
zoo	baaq-e vahsh	باغ وحش
tiger	babr	ببر
tigress	babr-e maadeh	ببر ماده
fox cub	bacheh rubaah	بچه روباه
lion cub	bacheh shir	بچه شیر
baby elephant	bacheh fil	بچه فیل
wolf cub	bacheh gorg	بچه گربه
goat	boz	بز
antelope	boz-e kuhi	بز کوهی
she-goat	boz-e maadeh	بز ماده
slug	bid-e halazuni	بید حلزونی
panda	paandaa	پاندا
bird	parandeh	پرنده
udder; breast	pestaan	پستان
mammal	pestaandaar	پستاندار
wool; fur; coat	pashm	پشم
leopard	palang	پلنگ
panther	palang-e siyaah	پلنگ سیاه
claw; paw	panjeh	پنجه
penguin	pangu'an	پنگوئن
nose (of dog); mouth; snout	puzeh	پوزه
pussycat	pishi	پیشی
gallop	taakht	تاخت
alligator	temsaah	تمساح

4

puppy	tuleh sag	توله سگ
creature	jaanvar	جانور
jaguar	jaagvaar	جگوار
porcupine	jujeh tiqi	جوجه تیغی
duckling	jujeh morqaabi	جوجه مرغابی
rodent	javandeh	جونده
snail	halazun	حلزون
animal	heyvaan	حیوان
pet	heyvaan-e khaanegi	حیوان خانگی
pet shop	heyvan-forushi	حیوانفروشی
spines (of hedgehog)	khaar	خار
hedgehog	khaarposht	خارپشت
donkey	khar	خر
bear	khers	خرس
sloth	khers-e tanbal	خرس تنبل
polar bear	khers-e qotbi	خرس قطبی
trunk	khortum	خرطوم
rabbit	khargush	خرگوش
hare	khargush-e sahra'i	خرگوش صحرائی
rat	kharmush	خرموش
reptile	khazandeh	خزنده
characteristic	khosusiyyat	خصوصیت
bat	khoffaash	خفاش
flying bat	khoffaash-e parandeh	خفاش پرنده
hibernation	khaab-e zemestaani	خواب زمستانی
pig	khuk	خوک
aardvark	khuk-e khaaki	خوک خاکی
sow	khuk-e maadeh	خوک ماده
dolphin	dolfin	دلفین
tail	dom	دم
tusk	dandaan-e 'aaj	دندان عاج
fang	dandaan-e nish	دندان نیش
amphibian	dow-zist	دوزیست
mouth	dahaan	دهان
weasel	raasu	راسو
skunk	raasu-ye gandnaak	راسوی گندناک
racoon	raakoon	راکون
hindquarters	raan	ران

fox	rubaah	روباه
leech	zaalu	زالو
giraffe	zaraafeh	زرافه
saddle	zin	زین
venom	zahr	زهر
grass snake	sabzeh maar	سبزه مار
dog	sag	سگ
beaver	sag-e aabi	سگ آبی
greyhound	sag-e taazi	سگ تازی
bitch	sag-e maadeh	سگ ماده
hoof	som	سم
otter	samur-e aabi	سمور آبی
squirrel	sanjaab	سنجاب
flying squirrel	sanjaab-e parandeh	سنجاب پرنده
crocodile	susmaar	سوسمار
lynx	siyaah gush	سیاه گوش
horn; antler	shaakh	شاخ
chimpanzee	shaampaanzeh	شامپانزه
camel	shotor	شتر
dromedary	shotor-e yek kuhaaneh	شتر یک کوهانه
ostrich	shotormorq	شترمرغ
jackal	shoqaal	شغال
lion	shir	شیر
sea lion	shir-e daryaa'i	شیر دریائی
puma	shir-e kuhi	شیر کوهی
lioness	shir-e maadeh	شیر ماده
Tasmanian devil	sheytaan-e taasmaani	شیطان تاسمانی
centipede	sad paa	صدپا
prey	to'meh	طعمه
stable	tavileh	طویله
baboon	antar	عنتر
seal	fok	فک
elephant	fil	فیل
mule	qaater	قاطر
cage	qafas	قفس
ram	quch	قوچ
frog	qurbaaqeh	قورباغه
kangaroo	kaanguru	کانگورو

6

rhinoceros	kargadan	کرگدن
worm	kerm	کرم
foal	korreh asb	کره اسب
hyena	kaftaar	کفتار
koala bear	kuaalaa	کوالا
hump	kuhaaneh	کوهانه
pouch	kiseh	کیسه
cow	gaav	گاو
bull; ox	gaav-e nar	گاو نر
bullfighting	gaavbaazi	گاوبازی
buffalo	gaavmish	گاومیش
wild boar	goraaz	گراز
cat	gorbeh	گربه
wildcat	gorbe-ye vahshi	گربه وحشی
wolf	gorg	گرگ
Tasmanian wolf	gorg-e taasmaani	گرگ تاسمانی
she-wolf	gorg-e maadeh	گرگ ماده
gorilla	goril	گریل
zebra	gur-e khar	گورخر
badger	gurkan	گورکن
deer	gavazn	گوزن
reindeer	gavazn-e shomaali	گوزن شمالی
calf	gusaaleh	گوساله
sheep	gusfand	گوسفند
ewe	gusfand-e maadeh	گوسفند ماده
shell	laak	لاک
tortoise	laakposht	لاک پشت
lemur	lemur	لمور
flying lemur	lemur-e parandeh	لمور پرنده
mare	maadyaan	مادیان
female	maadeh	ماده
snake	maar	مار
anaconda	maar-e aanaakondaa	مار آناکندا
adder	maar-e ja'fari	مار جعفری
puff adder	maar-e damandeh	مار دمنده
rattlesnake	maar-e zanguleh daar	مار زنگوله دار
lizard	maarmulak	مارمولک
fish	maahi	ماهی

7

duck	*morqaabi*	مرغابی
hair; coat; fur	*mu*	مو
anteater	*murcheh khaar*	مورچه خوار
mouse	*mush*	موش
ferret	*mush-e khormaa*	موش خرما
shrew	*mush-e shabgard*	موش شبگرد
field mouse	*mush-e sahraa'i*	موش صحرانی
mole	*mush-e kur*	موش کور
rat	*mush-e vahshi*	موش وحشی
racecourse	*meydaan-e asbdavaani*	میدان اسب دوانی
monkey	*meymun*	میمون
male	*nar*	نر
orang-utan	*nasnaas*	نسناس
horseshoe	*na'l-e asb*	نعل اسب
mongoose	*nams*	نمس
teat	*nuk-e pestaan*	نوک پستان
whale	*nahang*	نهنگ
vole	*vol*	ول
millipede	*hezaar-paa*	هزارپا
mane	*yaal*	یال
cheetah	*yuzpalang*	یوزپلنگ

دوست داشتن to like نفرت داشتن to hate ترجیح دادن to prefer گربه دوست دارم I like cats

از سگ نفرت دارم I hate dogs من خرگوش ترجیح می دهم I prefer rabbits حیوان محبوبم my favourite animal

حیوانات خانگی pets نگه داشتن to keep همسایه من مار نگه می دارد my neighbour keeps snakes

حیوانات وحشی wild animals حیوانات اهلی tame animals; domesticate animals

بزرگ big کوچک small چاق fat لاغر thin بدبو smelly پشمالو hairy; furry

زشت ugly زیبا beautiful باهوش intelligent حیوانات زبان بسته dumb animals

سگ پارس می کند the dog barks گوسفند بع بع می کند the sheep bleats گربه میو میو می کند the cat meows

حیوانات خطرناک dangerous animals حیوانات کمیاب rare animals انواع تحت حمایت protected species

توی قفس گذاشتن to put in a cage در قرنطین گذاشتن to put in quarantine مار زهری poisonous snake

شکار کردن to hunt کشتن to kill غرش کردن to roar (e.g. lion) زوزه کشیدن to howl (e.g. wolf)

گاز گرفتن to bite نیش زدن to sting زنبور مرا نیش زد the bee stung me جانور دست آموز pet

گوسفند دست آموز pet lamb آزمایش کردن to experiment آزمایش روی حیوانات animal experiments

حقوق جانوران animal rights مدافعین از حقوق جانوران animal rights supporters

تربیت شده house-trained تربیت کردن to train رام کردن to tame; to break in در محیط آزاد in the wild

نوع رو به انقراض endangered species در اسارت in captivity خشونت به حیوانات cruelty to animals

در فقه اسلامی ، سگ و خوك نجس محسوب می شود in Islamic law, dogs and pigs are considered unclean

خواب زمستانی داشتن to hibernate نمایشگاه سگ dog show روانشناسی حیوانی animal psychology

ببر در هندوستان رو به انقراض است in India, the tiger is becoming extinct به دام انداختن to trap; to ensnare

سگ دوست dog-lover می گویند ملت انگلیس سگ دوستی است they say that the English are a nation of dog-lovers

❰❮❯❱

9

Art and Architecture

هنر و معماری

water colour	aabrang	آبرنگ
aqueduct	aabgozar	آبگذر
sun-dried brick	aajor-e zir-e aaftaab khoshk shodeh	آجر زیر آفتاب خشک شده
concrete block	aajor-e simaani	آجر سیمانی
brickwork	aajorkaari	آجرکاری
glazed tile	aajor-e kaashi	آجر کاشی
tracery	aazin-e turi	آذین توری
mausoleum	aaraamgaah	آرامگاه
cartouche	aaraayesh-e tumaari	آرایش طوماری
skyscraper	aasemaan kharaash	آسمانخراش
solarium	aaftaab khaaneh	آفتابخانه
acanthus	aakaantus	آکانتوس
acropolis	aakropulis	آکروپلیس
gazebo	aalaachiq	آلاچیق
amphitheatre	aamfi te'aatr	آمفی تئاتر
art school	aamuzeshgaah-e honari	آموزشگاه هنری
futurism	aayandeh garaa'i	آینده گرائی
iron	aahan	آهن
cast-iron	aahan-e rikhteh	آهن ریخته
wrought-iron	aahan-e narm	آهن نرم
wrought-iron	aahan-e varzideh	آهن ورزیده
dimensions	ab'aad	ابعاد
room; chamber	otaaq	اتاق
craftsmanship	ostaadkaari	استادکاری
expressionism	ekspresiyunism	اکسپرسیونیسم
impressionism	ampresiyunism	امپرسیونیسم
size; dimension	andaazeh	اندازه
vaulted hall; iwan; loggia	eyvaan	ایوان
portico	eyvaan-e sotundaar	ایوان ستون دار
wood cut	baasme-ye chubi	باسمه چوبی
gallery	baalaa khaaneh	بالاخانه
entablature	baalaa sotun	بالاستون
gallery; balcony	baalkon	بالکن
roof	baam	بام
concrete	botun	بتون
reinforced concrete	botun-e mosallah	بتون مسلح

pendentive	bakhsh-e seh gush-e zir-e gonbad	بخش سه گوش زیر گنبد
tower	borj	برج
pylon	borj-e darvaazeh	برج دروازه
(castle) keep	borj-e defaa'i	برج دفاعی
campanile	borj-e naaqus	برج ناقوس
belfry	borj-e naaqus-e kelisaa	برج ناقوس کلیسا
barbican	borj o baaru	برج و بارو
bas-relief	barjasteh kaari	برجسته کاری
relief	barjasteh namaa'i	برجسته نمائی
pinnacle	borjak	برجک
impressionism	bardaasht garaa'i	برداشت گرائی
enceinte	borun baaru	برون بارو
joint	bast	بست
joint	bandkeshi	بند کشی
pagoda	paagowdaa	پاگودا
column; pillar; base	paayeh	پایه
bracket	paaye-ye nasb	پایه نصب
roof	posht-e baam	پشت بام
buttress	poshtband	پشتبند
flying buttress	poshtband-e shamshiri	پشتبند شمشیری
flying buttress	poshtband-e mo'allaq	پشتبند معلق
bracket	poshtaar-e gusheh daar	پشتار گوشه دار
buttress	poshtvaareh	پشتواره
viaduct	pol-e paayeh boland	پل پایه بلند
viaduct	pol-e darreh gozar	پل دره گذر
cantilever bridge	pol-e dow aaseh	پل دو آسه
oriel	panjere-ye pish aamadeh	پنجره پیش آمده
dormer window	panjere-ye shirvaani	پنجره شیروانی
rose window	panjere-ye goldis	پنجره گلدیس
lancet window	panjere-ye neyze'i	پنجره نیزه ای
bastion	pishraftegi-ye divaar-e dezh	پیشرفتگی دیوار دژ
sculpture; statue; statuette	peykareh	پیکره
sculpting	peykareh saazi	پیکره سازی
circus	pahneh	پهنه
keystone	taaj sang	تاج سنگ
darkroom	taarik khaaneh	تاریکخانه
chamber; hall; gallery; atrium	taalaar	تالار
art gallery	taalaar-e aasaar-e honari	تالار آثار هنری

11

destruction; demolition	takhrib	تخریب
texture	tarkib	ترکیب
decoration	tazyin	تزیین
ornamental	tazyini	تزیینی
artifice; mannerism	tasanno'	تصنع
drawing; picture; portrait	tasvir	تصویر
baptistery	ta'midgaah	تعمیدگاه
symmetry	taqaaron	تقارن
fortified	taqviyat shodeh	تقویت شده
monotype	tak ru gereft	تک رو گرفت
sculpture	tandis	تندیس
recess; niche	tu raftegi	تورفتگی
rib	tir-e 'arzi	تیر عرضی
trabeated	tirdaar	تیردار
cusp	tire-ye jenaaq	تیزه جناغ
casemate	jaan panaah	جان پناه
pier	jerz	جرز
antefix	jelow band	جلوبند
aisle	jenaah	جناح
ink	jowhar	جوهر
lithography	chaap-e sangi	چاپ سنگی
cast-iron	chodan	چدن
Latin cross	chalipaa-ye laatin	چلیپای لاتین
multi-storey	chand tabaqeh	چند طبقه
circus	chahaar raah	چهار راه
frieze	haashiye-ye tazyini	حاشیه تزیینی
expressionism	haalat namaa'i	حالت نمائی
patron	haami	حامی
Cubism	hajm garaa'i	حجم گرائی
tatami	hasir-e zhaaponi	حصیر ژاپنی
parapet	hefaaz	حفاظ
carved	hakkaaki shodeh	حکاکی شده
baths	hammaam	حمام
courtyard	hayaat	حیاط
atrium	hayaat-e asli	حیاط اصلی
inlaid work	khaatam kaari	خاتم کاری
clay	khaak-e ros	خاک رس
caravanserai	khaan	خان

ruins	kharaabeh	خرابه
calligraphy	khattaati	خطاطی
self-portrait	khod negaareh	خودنگاره
arcade	daalaan	دالان
portcullis	dar-e aavizaan	در آویزان
portcullis	dar-e aahani-ye keshowi	در آهنی کشوئی
postern	darvaaze-ye posht	دروازه پشت
interior	darun	درون
donjon	darun-e dezh	درون دژ
fenestration	daricheh gozaari	دریچه گذاری
fortification	dezh	دژ
crenellation	dandaaneh	دندانه
camera	durbin	دوربین
bailey	divaar-e biruni-ye kaakh	دیوار بیرونی کاخ
curtain wall	divaar-e naazok	دیوار نازک
bracket	divaarkub	دیوارکوب
fresco; wall painting	divaar negaari	دیوارنگاری
screen	divaareh	دیواره
counterscarp	divaare-ye khaareji-ye khandaq	دیواره خارجی خندق
rood screen	divaare-ye salibdaar	دیواره صلیب دار
grille	divaare-ye moshabbak	دیواره مشبک
nave	raahrow-ye markazi-ye kelisaa	راهروی مرکزی کلیسا
corridor; aisle	raahrow	راهرو
ambulatory; cloisters	raahrow-ye sar pushideh	راهرو ی سرپوشیده
cornice	rokhbaam	رخبام
drawing	rasm	رسم
column; pillar	rokn	رکن
rococo	rokowkow	رکوکو
Renaissance	ronesaans	رنسانس
tempera	rang-e bi jalaa	رنگ بی جلا
oil paint	rang-e rowqani	رنگ روغنی
portico; cloisters	ravaaq	رواق
fenestration	rowzan gozini	روزن گزینی
lunette	rowzane-ye helaali shekl	روزنه هلالی شکل
stucco	rukaar-e simaani	روکار سیمانی
wainscot	rukesh-e chubi	روکش چوبی
Romanticism	rumaantism	رومانتیسم
gilded	zarandud	زر اندود

13

tympanum	zamine-ye santuri	زمینه سنتوری
ziyada	ziyaadeh	زیاده
undercroft	zir-e zamin-e kelisaa	زیرزمین کلیسا
impost	zir taaqi	زیرطاقی
ziggurat	ziguraat	زیگورات
structure; texture	saakhtaar	ساختار
building (n.)	saakhtemaan	ساختمان
architectural; building (a.)	saakhtemaani	ساختمانی
stucco	saaruj pushi	ساروج پوشی
pavilion	saayebaan	سایبان
chiaroscuro	saayeh rowshan	سایه روشن
style	sabk	سبک
Ionic	sabk-e iyunik	سبک ایونیک
Baroque	sabk-e baaruk	سبک باروك
Tuscan	sabk-e tuskaan	سبک توسکان
Doric	sabk-e durik	سبک دوریک
Corinthian	sabk-e korinti	سبک کرینتی
Classical	sabk-e kelaasik	سبک کلاسیک
The Orders (of classical architecture)	sabk-haa-ye me'maari-ye kelaasik	سبک های معماری کلاسیک
pillar	sotun	ستون
pier	sotun-e pol	ستون پل
hypostyle	sotundaar	ستون دار
cantilever	sotun-e sar aazaad	ستون سر آزاد
pilaster	sotun namaa	ستون نما
obelisk	sotun-e herami	ستون هرمی
colonnade	sotunegaan	ستونگان
engaged columns	sotun-haa-ye tu divaari	ستونهای تو دیواری
pavilion	saraayeh	سرایه
vault; cellar	sardaabeh	سردابه
capital	sar sotun	سرستون
volute	sar sotun-e tumaari	سرستون طوماری
composite	sar sotun-e mokhtalet	سرستون مختلط
hall; corridor; anteroom	sarsaraa	سرسرا
narthex	sarsaraa-ye kelisaa	سرسرای کلیسا
facade; exterior	sath-e khaareji	سطح خارجی
ceramic	sofaal	سفال
terracotta	sofaalineh	سفالینه
podium	saku	سکو

symbolism	sambulism	سمبولیسم
pediment	santuri	سنتوری
voussoir	sang-e taaq-e zarbi	سنگ طاق ضربی
stonemason	sang kaar	سنگ کار
masonry	sang kaari	سنگ کاری
stone-carving	sangtaraashi	سنگتراشی
breastwork	sangar-e istaadeh	سنگر ایستاده
surrealism	sur re'aalism	سور رئالیسم
embrasure	suraakh-e baaru	سوراخ بارو
machicolation	suraakh-e saqf-e dezh	سوراخ سقف دژ
easel	seh paaye-ye naqqaashi	سه پایه نقاشی
base; keystone	shaaludeh	شالوده
architrave; purlin	shaah tir	شاه تیر
fluted	shiyaar daar	شیاردار
stained glass	shishe-ye rangi	شیشه رنگی
roundel	shishe-ye gerd	شیشه گرد
martyrium	shahaadatgaah	شهادتگاه
quadrangle; mosque courtyard	sahn	صحن
Greek cross	salib-e yunaani	صلیب یونانی
acrylic resin	samq-e akrilik	صمغ اکریلیک
arch	taaq-e zarbi	طاق ضربی
arch	taaq-e qowsi	طاق قوسی
horseshoe arch	taaq-e na'l-e asbi	طاق نعل اسبی
lancet arch	taaq-e neyze'i	طاق نیزه ای
niche	taaqcheh	طاقچه
storey	tabaqeh	طبقه
turbe; tombtower	torbeh	طربه
triglyph	tarh-e seh tarak	طرح سه ترک
fluting	tarh-e shiyaari	طرح شیاری
fluting	tarh-e qaashoqi	طرح قاشقی
lens	'adasi	عدسی
pavilion	qorfeh	غرفه
faience	faayenz	فاینز
tapestry	farshineh	فرشینه
bay; recess	foru raftegi-ye divaar	فرورفتگی دیوار
frieze	feriz	فریز
fountain	favvaareh	فواره
steel	fulaad	فولاد

15

panelling	qaab bandi	قاب بندی
qibla	qebleh	قبله
cupola; dome	qobbeh	قبه
pinnacle	qobbe-ye poshtband	قبه پشتبند
cornice	qorniz	قرنیز
palace; chateau	qasr	قصر
fortress; fortification	qal'eh	قلعه
acropolis	qal'e-ye shahr	قلعه شهر
brush	qalam	قلم
etching	qalam zani	قلم زنی
castle; fortification	kaakh	کاخ
caravanserai	kaarvaansaraa	کاروانسرا
caryatid	kaaryaatid	کاریاتید
terracotta	kaashi-ye bi lo'aab	کاشی بی لعاب
tilework	kaashi kaari	کاشی کاری
canvas	karbaas	کرباس
pastel	kam rang	کم رنگ
enceinte	kamarband-e padaafandi	کمربند پدافندی
minimalism	kamineh garaa'i	کمینه گرائی
carved	kandeh kaari shodeh	کنده کاری شده
battlement	kongore-ye baaru	کنگره بارو
scalloped	kongoreh daar	کنگره دار
Cubism	kubism	کوبیسم
belvedere; pavilion; kiosk	kushk	کوشک
plaster	gach	گچ
fillet	gach bori-ye baarik	گچ بری باریک
arcade	gozargaah-e taaqdaar	گذرگاه طاقدار
sketch	garteh	گرته
cupola	gerdbaam	گردبام
finial	gorzeh	گرزه
caldarium	garmaabeh daan	گرمابه دان
minaret	goldasteh	گلدسته
dome; cupola	gonbad	گنبد
lantern; small cupola	gonbadak	گنبدك
gouache	govaash	گواش
squinch	gushe-ye taaq	گوشه طاق
eaves	labe-ye baam	لبه بام
enamel	lo'aab	لعاب

16

sculpture; statue	mojassameh	مجسمه
art collection	majmu'e-ye aasaar-e honari	مجموعه آثار هنری
mihrab; prayer niche	mehraab	محراب
chancel	mehraab-e kelisaa	محراب کلیسا
agora	mahal-e tajammo'	محل تجمع
choir	mahal-e saraayandegaan	محل سرایندگان
portal	madkhal-e mozayyan	مدخل مزین
seminary; medresa	madraseh	مدرسه
restoration work (on paintings etc.)	marammat kaari	مرمت کاری
marble	marmar	مرمر
martyrium	mash-had	مشهد
place of worship; temple; shrine	ma'bad	معبد
naos	ma'bad-e baastaani	معبد باستانی
stupa	ma'bad-e budaa'i	معبد بودائی
mosaic	mo'arraq kaari	معرق کاری
architect	me'maar	معمار
architecture	me'maari	معماری
railed enclosure	maqsureh	مقصوره
minaret	menaar	منار
turret	menaarcheh	منارچه
wood engraving	monabbat kaari	منبت کاری
pulpit	manbar	منبر
abacus	monhani-ye aabaak	منحنی آباک
corbel	menqaareh	مِنقاره
mosaic	muzaa'ik	موزائیک
mezzanine	miyaan ashkub	میان اشکوب
entasis	miyaan kuzhi	میانکوژی
metope	mitup	میتوپ
piazza; square	meydaan-e shahr	میدان شهر
amphitheatre	meydaan-e nabard	میدان نبرد
architectural legacy	miraas-e me'maari	میراث معماری
in-focus (photography)	mizaan	میزان
enamel work	minaa kaari	مینا کاری
architect	mohandes-e saakhtemaan	مهندس ساختمان
out of focus (photography)	naa mizaan	نامیزان
balustrade	narde-ye eyvaan	نرده ایوان
painting	naqqaashi	نقاشی
airbrush technique	naqqaashi-ye baa afshaangar	نقاشی با افشانگر

landscape painting	naqqaashi-ye manzareh	نقاشی منظره
pattern	naqsh	نقش
etching	naqsh andaazi	نقش اندازی
etched	naqsh andaazi shodeh	نقش اندازی شده
tracery	naqsh-e tur baaft	نقش تور بافت
intaglio	naqsh-e foru rafteh	نقش فرو رفته
motif	naqsh-e mokarrar	نقش مکرر
arabesque	naqsh o negaar be sabk-e 'arabi	نقش و نگار به سبک عربی
geometric patterns	naqsh-haa-ye hendesi	نقش های هندسی
pointillism	noqteh chin kaari	نقطه چین کاری
negative (of photographs)	negaativ	نگاتیو
art gallery	negaar khaaneh	نگارخانه
facade; exterior	namaa	نما
symbolism	nemaad garaa'i	نمادگرائی
neo-classicism	now kelaasisism	نو کلاسیسیسم
abutment	nim paayeh	نیم پایه
half-arch	nim taaq	نیم طاق
demolition	viraangaari	ویرانگری
villa	vilaa	ویلا
pyramid	heram	هرم
ziggurat	heram-e pelleh daar	هرم پله دار
octagon	hasht gusheh	هشت گوشه
gallery	hashti	هشتی
'seven colour' tiling	haft rangi	هفت رنگی
art	honar	هنر
Islamic art	honar-e eslaami	هنر اسلامی
Byzantine art	honar-e bizaansi	هنر بیزانسی
Mesopotamian art	honar-e beyn on-nahreyni	هنر بین النهرینی
Romanesque art	honar-e rumaanesk	هنر رومانسک
palaeolithic art	honar-e 'asr-e dirin sangi	هنر عصر دیرین سنگی
Gothic art	honar-e gutik	هنر گوتیک
pop art	honar-e mardom pasand	هنر مردم پسند
Egyptian art	honar-e mesri	هنر مصری
art nouveau	honar-e novin	هنر نوین
fine arts	honar-haa-ye zibaa	هنرهای زیبا
contemporary arts	honar-haa-ye mo'aaser	هنرهای معاصر

Astronomy

ستاره شناسی

space walker	aasemaangard	آسمانگرد
space walk	aasemaangardi	آسمانگردی
space junk	aashqaal-e fazaa'i	آشغال فضائی
super galaxy	abar kahkeshaan	ابر کهکشان
gas cloud	abr-e gaazi	ابر گازی
supernova	abar nowakhtar	ابر نو اختر
celestial objects; heavenly bodies	ajraam-e samaavi	اجرام سماوی
stellar	akhtari	اختری
parallax	ekhtelaaf-e manzar	اختلاف منظر
Draco; the Dragon	ezhdehaa	اژدها
Pegasus	asb-e bozorg	اسب بزرگ
astrolabe	ostorlaab	اسطرلاب
horizon	ofoq	افق
radio waves	amvaaj-e raadio'i	امواج رادیونی
light waves	amvaaj-e nuri	امواج نوری
apogee; zenith	owj	اوج
Uranus	uraanus	اورانوس
space station	istgaah-e fazaa'i	ایستگاه فضائی
solar wind	baad-e khorshidi	باد خورشیدی
constellation	borj-e falaki	برج فلکی
weightless	bi-vazn	بی وزن
spaceport	paayegaah-e fazaa'i	پایگاه فضائی
starry	por setaareh	پر ستاره
space flight	parvaaz-e fazaa'i	پرواز فضائی
space medicine	pezeshki-ye fazaa'i	پزشکی فضائی
Pluto	pelutow	پلوتو
precession	pishravi-ye e'tedaaleyn	پیشروی اعتدالین
solar radiation	taabeshgari-ye khorshidi	تابشگری خورشیدی
telescope	teleskowp	تلسکوپ
reflector	teleskowp-e baaztaabgar	تلسکوپ بازتابگر
refractor	teleskowp-e baazshekan	تلسکوپ بازشکن
radio telescope	teleskowp-e raadio'i	تلسکوپ رادیونی
Pleiades; the Seven Sisters	sorayyaa	ثریا
Orion	jabbaar	جبار
Capricorn	jady	جدی
atmosphere	javv	جو

rotation	charkhesh	چرخش
naked eye	cheshm-e qeyr-e mosallah	چشم غیر مسلح
perigee	haziz	حضیض
perihelion	haziz-e khorshidi	حضیض خورشیدی
rings (of Saturn, Uranus etc.)	halqeh-haa	حلقه ها
Aries	hamal	حمل
Pisces	hut	حوت
lunar eclipse	khosuf	خسوف
vacuum	khala'	خلا
sun	khorshid	خورشید
solar	khorshidi	خورشیدی
Ursa Minor	dobb-e asqar	دب اصغر
Ursa Major	dobb-e akbar	دب اکبر
luminosity; magnitude	derakhshesh	درخشش
Aquarius	dalv	دلو
Gemini	dow peykar	دوپیکر
binoculars	durbin	دوربین
visible	didpazir	دید پذیر
visibility	didpaziri	دید پذیری
Cassiopeia	zaat ol-korsi	ذات الکرسی
the Milky Way	raah-e shiri	راه شیری
observatory	rasad khaaneh	رصدخانه
space psychology	ravaanshenaasi-ye fazaa'i	روانشناسی فضائی
day	ruz	روز
sidereal day	ruz-e nojumi	روز نجومی
solar flare	zabaane-ye khorshidi	زبانه خورشیدی
Saturn	zohal	زحل
sidereal time	zamaan-e nojumi	زمان نجومی
astronomical table	zij	زیج
space biology	zist shenaasi-ye fazaa'i	زیست شناسی فضائی
sidereal year	saal-e nojumi	سال نجومی
light year	saal-e nuri	سال نوری
northern lights	sepide-ye shomaali	سپیده شمالی
stars	setaaregaan	ستارگان
fixed stars	setaaregaan-e saabet	ستارگان ثابت
star	setaareh	ستاره
astral	setaare'i	ستاره ای
shooting star	setaare-ye saaqeb	ستاره ثاقب

comet	setaare-ye donbaaleh-daar	ستاره دنباله دار
evening star	setaare-ye shab	ستاره شب
astronomy	setaareh shenaasi	ستاره شناسی
morning star	setaare-ye sobh	ستاره صبح
Pole star	setaare-ye qotbi	ستاره قطبی
stargazing	setaareh negari	ستاره نگری
neutron star	setaare-ye nutruni	ستاره نوترونی
nebula	sahaab	سحاب
nebular	sahaabi	سحابی
Cancer	sarataan	سرطان
speed	sor'at	سرعت
space travel	safar-e fazaa'i	سفر فضائی
celestial	samaavi	سماوی
space geology	sangshenaasi-ye fazaa'i	سنگ شناسی فضائی
meteorite	sang-e shahaab	سنگ شهاب
black hole	suraakh-e siyaah	سوراخ سیاه
planetoid	sayyaarak	سیارک
planet	sayyaareh	سیاره
planetary	sayyaare'i	سیاره ای
space shuttle	shaatel-e fazaa'i	شاتل فضائی
night	shab	شب
Leo	shir	شیر
meteor	shahaab	شهاب
galactic noise	sedaa-ye kahkeshaani	صدای کهکشانی
astrologer	taale'-bin	طالع بین
astrology	taale'-bini	طالع بینی
astonomical longitude	tul-e nojumi	طول نجومی
lens	'adasi	عدسی
astronomical latitude	'arz-e nojumi	عرض نجومی
Mercury	'otaared	عطارد
Scorpio	'aqrab	عقرب
astrophotography	'aksbardaari-ye fazaa'i	عکسبرداری فضائی
space science	'elm-e fazaa'i	علم فضائی
distance	faaseleh	فاصله
space probe	fazaa aazmaa	فضا آزما
spacecraft	fazaa peymaa	فضاپیما
astronautical	fazaa peymaayaaneh	فضاپیمایانه
astronaut	fazaa navard	فضا نورد

space	fazaa	فضاء
astrophysics	fizik-e fazaa'i	فیزیک فضائی
astrophysicist	fizik-e fazaa'i daan	فیزیک فضائی دان
pole	qotb	قطب
galactic poles	qotb-ha-ye kahkeshaani	قطب های کهکشانی
moon; satellite	qamar	قمر
arteficial satellite	qamar-e masnu'i	قمر مصنوعی
lunar	qamari	قمری
gravity	qove-ye jaazebeh	قوه جاذبه
Earth	kore-ye zamin	کره زمین
solar eclipse	kosuf	کسوف
spaceship	keshti-ye fazaa'i	کشتی فضائی
Sagittarius	kamaandaar	کماندار
universe; cosmos	keyhaan	کیهان
cosmonaut	keyhaan navard	کیهان نورد
cosmic	keyhaani	کیهانی
galaxy	kahkeshaan	کهکشان
elliptical galaxy	kahkeshaan-e beyzavi	کهکشان بیضوی
spiral galaxy	kahkeshaan-e maarpichi	کهکشان مارپیچی
irregular galaxy	kahkeshaan-e naamonazzam	کهکشان نامنظم
revolution	gardesh	گردش
planetarium	gardun-namaa	گردون نما
astrodome	gonbad-e setareh-namaa	گنبد ستاره نما
universe; cosmos	giti	گیتی
space suit	lebaas-e fazaa'i	لباس فضائی
sunspot	lakke-ye khorshidi	لکه خورشیدی
moon; month	maah	ماه
full moon	maah-e por	ماه پر
sidereal month	maah-e nojumi	ماه نجومی
lunarnaut	maahnavard	ماهنورد
axis	mehvar	محور
orbit	madaar	مدار
Tropic of Capricorn	madaar-e ra's ol-jadi	مدار راس الجدی
Tropic of Cancer	madaar-e ra's as-sarataan	مدار راس السرطان
Mars	merrikh	مریخ
distance	masaafat	مسافت
Jupiter	moshtari	مشتری
zodiac	manteqat al-boruj	منطقه البروج

visibility	*meydaan-e did*	میدان دید
magnetic field	*meydaan-e meqnaatisi*	میدان مغناطیسی
Libra	*mizaan*	میزان
crescent moon	*mahdaas*	مهداس
astronavigation	*naavbari-ye fazaa'i*	ناوبری فضائی
Neptune	*neptun*	نپتون
nova	*now akhtar*	نو اختر
light	*nur*	نور
light-polluted	*nuraalud*	نور آلود
southern hemisphere	*nimkore-ye jonubi*	نیمکره جنوبی
northern hemisphere	*nimkore-ye shomaali*	نیمکره شمالی
space vehicle	*vasile-ye fazaa'i*	وسیله فضائی
crescent moon	*helaal-e maah*	هلال ماه

OTHER ASTRONOMICAL WORDS AND PHRASES

the earth rotates on its own axis   زمین بر محور خود می چرخد   the earth orbits the sun   زمین به دور خورشید می چرخد

to travel in space   فضانوردی کردن   to stargaze; to look at the stars   ستاره نگری کردن   stargazing   ستاره نگری

launch-pad   پرتابگاه   to launch; to send (into space)   پرتاب کردن   to space-walk   فضا گردی کردن

yesterday the Americans launched a satellite into space   آمریکائی ها دیروز یک قمر مصنوعی به فضا پرتاب کردند

Biology

زیست شناسی

amnion	aab pardeh	آب پرده
saliva	aab-e dahaan	آب دهان
hydrotropism	aab garaa'i	آب گرائی
pregnancy	aabestani	آبستنی
gills	aabshosh	آبشش
hydrolysis	aabkaaft	آبکافت
appendix	aapaandis	آپاندیس
experiment	aazmaayesh	آزمایش
pest	aafat	آفت
pesticide	aafat koshi	آفت کشی
indicator organism	aagah saazeh	آگه‌سازه
penis	aalat-e tanaasoli-ye mard	آلت تناسلی مرد
pollution	aaludegi	آلودگی
antibody	aanti baadi	آنتی بادی
antibiotic	aanti biyutik	آنتی بیوتیک
enzyme	aanzim	آنزیم
phloem	aavand-e aabkeshi	آوند آبکشی
xylem	aavand-e chubi	آوند چوبی
aorta	abar sorkhrag	ابرسرخرگ
cerebrum	abar mokh	ابرمخ
gut	ahshaa	احشاء
urine	edraar	ادرار
sperm	esperm	اسپرم
bone	ostokhaan	استخوان
humerus	ostokhaan-e baazu	استخوان بازو
skeleton	ostokhaan bandi	استخوان بندی
clavicle	ostokhaan-e chanbar	استخوان چنبر
femur	ostokhaan-e raan	استخوان ران
scapula	ostokhaan-e ketf	استخوان کتف
ossicle	ostokhaancheh	استخوانچه
oestrogen	estruzhen	استروژن
osmosis	osmoz	اسمز
amino acid	asid-e aamineh	اسید آمینه
lactic acid	asid-e laaktik	اسید لاکتیک
nucleic acid	asid-e nukle'ik	اسید نوکلئیک
organ; body	andaam	اندام

energy	enerzhi	انرژی
insulin	ansulin	انسولین
systole	enqebaaz-e qalb	انقباض قلب
parasite	angal	انگل
effector	angiz resaan	انگیز رسان
stimulus	angizeh	انگیزه
urea	ureh	اوره
fertilization	baarvar saazi	بارورسازی
reproduction	baaz aavaresh	باز آورش
regeneration	baaz ruyesh	باز رویش
tissue	baaft	بافت
connective tissue	baaft-e hamband	بافت همبند
clone	baaftzaad	بافتزاد
bacteria	baakteri	باکتری
integument	barpush	برپوش
nitrogen fixation	barjaa'i-e ye nitruzhen	برجائی نیتروژن
epiglottis	barchaaknaay	برچاکنای
leaf	barg	برگ
exoskeleton	borun ostokhaan bandi	برون استخوان بندی
saliva	bozaaq	بزاق
vena cava	bozorg siyaah rag	بزرگ سیاهرگ
anther	basaak	بساک
joint	band	بند
ligament	bandineh	بندینه
ecosystem	bumsaazgaan	بوم سازگان
testis; testicles; gonads	beyzeh	بیضه
pathogen	bimari zaa	بیماری زا
antibodies	paad tan	پادتن
antibiotics	paad zi	پادزی
peptide	peptid	پپتید
pepsin	pepsin	پپسین
diffusion	pakhshesh	پخشش
receptivity	pazirandegi	پذیرندگی
receptor	pazirandeh	پذیرنده
seed dispersal	paraakanesh-e tokhm	پراکنش تخم
stamen	parcham	پرچم
villi	porz-haa-ye rudeh	پرز های روده
protein	perute'in	پروتئین

progesterone	peruzhesterun	پروژسترون
wilting; withering	pazhmordegi	پژمردگی
plasma	pelaasmaa	پلاسما
pasmolysis	pelaasmuliz	پلاسمولیز
plankton	pelaanktun	پلانکتون
polysaccharides	polisaakaarid	پلی ساکارید
saprophyte	pudeh zi	پوده زی
skin	pust	پوست
cuticle	pustak	پوستک
testa	pusteh	پوسته
decomposition	pusidegi	پوسیدگی
integument	push	پوش
neurone	pey-e yaakhteh	پی یاخته
bulb	piyaaz	پیاز
medulla oblongata	piyaaz-e maqz	پیاز مغز
protoplasm	pish deshteh	پیش دشته
urethra	pishaabraah	پیشابراه
root hairs	taar-e rishe'i	تار ریشه ای
heart beat	tapesh-e qalb	تپش قلب
seed	tokhm	تخم
ovary	tokhm daan	تخمدان
oviduct	tokhm raah	تخمراه
ovule; ovum	tokhmak	تخمک
ovulation	tokhmak aavari	تخمک آوری
fermentation	takhmir	تخمیر
translocation	taraajaa'i	تراجائی
transpiration	taraadamesh	ترادمش
organic compound	tarkib-e aali	ترکیب آلی
soil texture	tarkib-e khaak	ترکیب خاک
inorganic compound	tarkibaat-e ma'dani	ترکیبات معدنی
bacteria	tarkizeh	ترکیزه
condensation	taqtir	تقطیر
monocotyledon	tak lapeh	تک لپه
evolution	takaamol	تکامل
nerve impulses	takaane-ye 'asabi	تکانه عصبی
tuber	tokmeh	تکمه
lymph	tanaabeh	تنابه
competition	tanaazo'	تنازع

26

systole	*tanjesh*	تنجش
temperature regulation	*tanzim-e damaa*	تنظیم دما
respiration; breathing	*tanaffos*	تنفس
tendon	*tanud*	تنود
retina	*turineh*	تورینه
birth	*tavallod*	تولد
reproduction	*towlid-e mesl*	تولید مثل
vegetative reproduction	*towlid-e mesl az raah-e bazrafshaani*	تولید مثل از راه بذرافشانی
sexual reproduction	*towlid-e mesl az raah-e joftgiri*	تولید مثل از راه جفت گیری
asexual reproduction	*towlid-e mesl-e qeyr-e jensi*	تولید مثل غیر جنسی
family	*tireh*	تیره
gas exchange	*jaabejaa'i-ye gaaz-haa*	جابجائی گازها
assimilation	*jazb-e mavaad-e qazaa'i*	جذب مواد غذائی
placenta	*joft*	جفت
copulation	*joftgiri*	جفت گیری
cranium	*jomjomeh*	جمجمه
sternum	*jenaaq*	جناغ
genus	*jens*	جنس
shoot	*javaaneh*	جوانه
germination	*javaaneh zani*	جوانه زنی
lactic acid	*jowhar-e shir*	جوهر شیر
mutation	*jahesh*	جهش
glottis	*chaaknaay*	چاکنای
fat	*charbi*	چربی
water cycle	*charkhe-ye aab*	چرخه آب
carbon cycle	*charkhe-ye karbon*	چرخه کربن
nitrogen cycle	*charkhe-ye nitruzhen*	چرخه نیتروژن
eye	*cheshm*	چشم
multicellular	*chand yaakhte'i*	چند یاخته ای
wood	*chub*	چوب
pregnancy	*haamelegi*	حاملگی
alveolus	*hobaabak*	حبابک
diaphragm	*hejaab-e haajez*	حجاب حاجز
peristalsis	*harekat-e dudi*	حرکت دودی
sense of smell	*hess-e buyaa'i*	حس بویانی
sense of sight	*hess-e binaa'i*	حس بینانی
sense of taste	*hess-e cheshaa'i*	حس چشانی
sense of hearing	*hess-e shenavaa'i*	حس شنوانی

sense of touch	hess-e laameseh	حس لامسه
cochlea	halazun-e gush	حلزون گوش
annual ring	halqe-ye saaliyaaneh	حلقه سالیانه
earth; soil	khaak	خاك
mucus	khelt	خلط
autotrophic	khod parvar	خودپرور
autoradiograph	khod negaareh	خودنگاره
blood	khun	خون
plasma	khunaabeh	خونابه
haemolysis	khunkaavi	خونکاوی
dendrite	daarineh	دارینه
absorption	daraashaami	درآشامی
ileum	deraaz rudeh	درازروده
tibia	dorosht ney	درشت نی
implant; implantation	darkaasht	درکاشت
predator; predatory	darandeh	درنده
endoskeleton	darun ostokhaan bandi	درون استخوان بندی
medulla	darun laayeh	درون لایه
valve	daricheh	دریچه
lymphatic system	dastgaah-e tanaabe'i	دستگاه تنابه ای
circulatory system	dastgaah-e gardesh-e khun	دستگاه گردش خون
vascular bundle	daste-ye aavandi	دسته آوندی
excretion	daf'	دفع
heterotrophic	degarparvar	دگرپرور
metamorphosis	degardisi	دگردیسی
respiration; breathing	damzani	دمزنی
teeth	dandaan	دندان
dentition	dandaan aavari	دندان آوری
wisdom tooth	dandaan-e 'aql	دندان عقل
milk teeth	dandaan-haa-ye shiri	دندان های شیری
dicotyledons	dow lape'i	دولپه ای
long sight	durbini	دوربینی
hybrid	dow rageh	دورگه
gestation period	dowre-ye aabestani	دوره آبستنی
menstrual cycle	dowre-ye qaa'edegi	دوره قاعدگی
disaccharides	disaakaarid	دی ساکارید
mouth	dahaan	دهان
atrium	dehliz	دهلیز

order	raasteh	راسته
mitochondrion	raakizeh	راکیزه
osmosis	raand	راند
ligament	rebaat	رباط
phenotype	rokhmun	رخ مون
class	radeh	رده
classification	radeh bandi	رده بندی
balanced diet	rezhim-e qazaa'i-ye mota'aadel	رژیم غذائی متعادل
growth	roshd	رشد
primary growth	roshd-e avvaliyeh	رشد اولیه
secondary growth	roshd-e dovvomin	رشد درمین
vein	rag	رگ
chromosomes	rangin tan	رنگین تن
sex chromosomes	rangin tan-e jensi	رنگین تن جنسی
homologous chromosomes	rangin tan-haa-ye hamsaakht	رنگین تن های همساخت
iris	rangineh	رنگینه
epidermis	rupust	روپوست
intestine	rudeh	روده
duodenum	rude-ye esnaa 'ashar	روده اثنی عشر
large intestine	rude-ye bozorg	روده بزرگ
small intestine	rude-ye kuchek	روده کوچک
stoma	rowzaneh	روزنه
scientific method	ravand-e 'elmi	روند علمی
plumule	riz javaaneh	ریز جوانه
abscission	rizesh	ریزش
root	risheh	ریشه
radicle	rishe-ye avvaliyeh	ریشه اولیه
lungs	riyeh	ریه
genotype	zaadmun	زادمون
gamete	zaameh	زامه
birth	zaayesh	زایش
roughage	zebrineh	زبرینه
vitreous humour	zojaajiyeh	زجاجیه
bile	zardaab	زرداب
yolk	zardeh	زرده
aqueous humour	zolaaliyeh	زلالیه
rhizome	zamin saaqeh	زمین ساقه
food chain	zanjire-ye qazaa'i	زنجیره غذائی

radius	zand-e zebarin	زند زبرین
ulna	zand-e zirin	زند زیرین
life cycle	zist charkheh	زیست چرخه
biologist	zist shenaas	زیست شناس
biology	zist shenaasi	زیست شناسی
community	zist goruhi	زیست گروهی
habitat	zistgaah	زیستگاه
zygote	zigut	زیگوت
enzymes	zimaayeh	زیمایه
uterus	zehdaan	زهدان
cervix	zehdaangardan	زهدانگردن
foetus	zehsaan	زهسان
gene	zhen	ژن
dominant gene	zhen-e chireh	ژن چیره
genotype	zhenutip	ژنوتیپ
accommodation	saazegaari	سازگاری
organism	saazvaareh	سازواره
stem	saaqeh	ساقه
stolon	saaqe-ye ravandeh	ساقه رونده
rhizome	saaqe-ye zir-e zamini	ساقه زیرزمینی
chlorophyll	sabzineh	سبزینه
vertebral column	sotun-e faqaraat	ستون فقرات
sclerotic	sakhtineh	سختینه
artery	sorkhrag	سرخرگ
pulmonary vein	sorkhrag-e riyavi	سرخرگ ریوی
transpiration rate	sor'at-e taraavosh	سرعت تراوش
micropyle	soft	سفت
nervous system	selsele-ye a'saab	سلسله اعصاب
cell	selul	سلول
cellulose	seluloz	سلولز
metabolism	sukht o saaz	سوخت و ساز
basal metabolism	sukht o saaz paayeh	سوخت و ساز پایه
spiracle	suraakh-e tanaffos	سوراخ تنفس
tropism	su garaa'i	سوگرائی
vein	siyaah rag	سیاهرگ
phylum; branch	shaakheh	شاخه
membrane	shaaameh	شامه
retina	shabakiyeh	شبکیه

pulmonary artery	sharayaan-e riyavi	شریان ریوی
lungs	shosh	شش
pupa	shafireh	شفیره
predator; predatory	shekaargar	شکارگر
binary fission	shekaafesh-e dowgaaneh	شکافش دوگانه
abdomen	shekam	شکم
ventricle	shekamcheh	شکمچه
nitrification	shureh saazi	شوره سازی
chemotropism	shimi garaa'i	شیمی گرائی
bile	safraa	صفرا
heart beat	zarabaan-e qalb	ضربان قلب
tympanum	tabl-e gush	طبل گوش
spleen	tehaal	طحال
kingdom	'aalam	عالم
limiting factor	'aamel-e baazdaar	عامل بازدار
optic nerve	'asab-e binaa'i	عصب بینائی
auditory nerve	'asab-e shenavaa'i	عصب شنوائی
voluntary muscles	'azolaat-e eraadi	عضلات ارادی
muscle	'azoleh	عضله
suspensory muscles	'azole-ye darvaaygar	عضله دروایگر
intercostal muscles	'azole-ye miyaan dande'i	عضله میان دنده ای
organ	'ozv	عضو
response; reaction	'aks ol-'amal	عکس العمل
genetics	'elm-e zhenetik	علم ژنتیک
reflex action	'amal-e qeyr-e eraadi	عمل غیر ارادی
gonads	qodde-ye tanaasoli	غده تناسلی
thyroid gland	qodde-ye tiru'id	غده تیرونید
adrenal glands	qodde-ye fowq-e kolyeh	غده فوق کلیه
endocrine glands	qodde-haa-ye darunriz	غده های درونریز
pituitary gland	qodde-ye hipufiz	غده هیپوفیز
cartilage	qozruf	غضروف
bud	qoncheh	غنچه
anabolism	faraa gowharesh	فراگوهرش
soil erosion	farsaayesh-e khaak	فرسایش خاک
photosynthesis	foruq aamaa'i	فروغ آمائی
cornea	qarniyeh	قرنیه
thorax	qafase-ye sineh	قفسه سینه
heart	qalb	قلب

31

colon	qulun	قولون
patella	kaase-ye zaanu	كاسه زانو
cranium	kaase-ye sar	كاسه سر
soil depletion	kaahesh-e khaak	كاهش خاك
liver	kabed	كبد
keratin	keraatin	كراتين
carbohydrates	karbuhidraat	كربوهيدرات
chromosomes	korumuzum	كروموزوم
vacuole	koricheh	كريچه
crop rotation	kesht-e tanaavobi	كشت تناوبى
collagen	kolaazhen	كلاژن
chloroplasts	kolorupelaast	كلروپلاست
kidney	kolyeh	كليه
oxygen debt	kambud-e oksizhen	كمبود اكسيژن
compensation	kambud pushi	كمبود پوشى
pleura	kenaareh band	كناره بند
fertilizer	kud	كود
corm	kurm	كورم
embryo sac	kise-ye ruyaani	كيسه رويانى
gall bladder	kise-ye safraa	كيسه صفرا
gamete	gaamet	گامت
pollen	gardeh	گرده
platelet	gerdeh	گرده
pollination	gardeh afshaani	گرده افشانى
lymph nodes	gere-ye tanaabe'i	گره تنابه اى
natural selection	gozin-e tabi'i	گزين طبيعى
flower	gol	گل
lichen	golsang?	گلسنگ
pharynx	galu	گلو
glucose	gelukoz	گلوكز
glycogen	gelikuzhen	گليكوژن
saprophyte	gand khaar	گند خوار
digestion	govaaresh	گوارش
ear	gush	گوش
carnivore; carnivorous	gusht khaar	گوشتخوار
herbivore	giyaah khaar	گياه خوار
humus	laashbarg	لاشبرگ
cotyledon	lapeh	لپه

blood clot	lakhte-ye khun	لخته خون
pancreas	lowz ol-me'deh	لوز المعده
Eustachian tube	lule-ye estaash	لوله استاش
lipase	lipaaz	لیپاز
lipid	lipid	لیپید
mucus	lizaab	لیزاب
larva; pupa	liseh	لیسه
muscle	maahicheh	ماهیچه
ciliary muscle	maahiche-ye mozhaki	ماهیچه مژکی
bladder	masaaneh	مثانه
pulmonary vessels	majraa-haa-ye riyavi	مجرا های ریوی
urethra	majraa-ye edraar	مجرای ادرار
blood vessel	majraa-ye khun	مجرای خون
auditory canal	majraa-ye sam'i	مجرای سمعی
alimentary canal	majraa-ye govaaresh	مجرای گوارش
semi-circular canals	majraa-ye nimeh halqavi	مجرای نیمه حلقوی
solution	mahlul	محلول
environment	mohit-e zist	محیط زیست
cerebellum	mokhcheh	مخچه
faeces; excrement	madfu'	مدفوع
oesophagus	mery	مری
cilia	mozhak	مژک
stomach	me'deh	معده
brain	maqz	مغز
spinal cord	maqz-e tireh	مغز تیره
joint	mafsal	مفصل
anus; rectum	maq'ad	مقعد
normal distribution curve	monhani-ye gaaus	منحنی گاوس
monosaccharides	munusaakaarid	مونوساکارید
capillaries	muyine-haa	مویینه ها
mitosis	mituz	میتوز
ureter	miznaay	میزنای
microscope	mikruskup	میکروسکوپ
rod	mil yaakhteh	میل یاخته
fruit	miveh	میوه
vagina	mahbel	مهبل
anaerobe	naa havaazi	نا هوازی
fibula	naazok ney	نازك نی

trachea	naay	نای
bronchus	naayezheh	نایژه
spinal cord	nokhaa'	نخاع
sperm	narzaameh	نرزامه
short sight	nazdik bini	نزدیک بینی
starch	neshaasteh	نشاسته
sperm	notfeh	نطفه
blind spot	noqte-ye kur	نقطه کور
mineral salts	namak-e ma'dani	نمک معدنی
phototropism	nur garaa'i	نور گرائی
species	now'	نوع
soil type	now'-e khaak	نوع خاک
nitrification	nitraat saazi	نیترات سازی
denitrification	nitruzhen zadaa'i	نیتروژن زدائی
recessive	nahofteh	نهفته
denaturation	vaasereshti	واسرشتی
response; reaction	vaakonesh	واکنش
vacuole	vaku'ol	واکوئل
variation	vardaa'i	وردائی
vitamin	vitaamin	ویتامین
virus	virus	ویروس
secondary sexual characteristics	vizhegi-haa-ye saanaviye-ye jensi	ویژگی های ثانویه جنسی
digestion	haazemeh	هاضمه
spore	haag	هاگ
nucleus	hasteh	هسته
homeostasis	ham istaa'i	هم ایستائی
commensalism	ham parvardi	هم پروردی
symbiosis	hamzisti	همزیستی
sphincter	hamkesh	همکش
synapse	hamvar	همور
haemoglobin	hemugelubin	هموگلوبین
mutualism	hamyaari	همیاری
omnivore; omnivorous	hameh chiz khor	همه چیز خور
aerobe	havaazi	هوازی
hormone	hurmun	هورمون
sex hormone	hurmun-e jensi	هورمون جنسی
cytoplasm	yaakht deshteh	یاخت دشته
cell	yaakhteh	یاخته

white blood cell	yaakhte-ye khun-e sefid	یاخته خون سفید
red blood cell	yaakhte-ye khun-e qermez	یاخته خون قرمز
nerve cell	yaakhte-ye 'asabi	یاخته عصبی
cone	yaakhte-ye makhruti	یاخته مخروطی
guard cells	yaakhteh negahbaan	یاخته نگهبان
unicellular	yek yaakhte'i	یک یاخته ای
annual (e.g. plants)	yeksaalzi	یکسال زی

Birds and Insects

پرندگان و حشرات

sky	aasemaan	آسمان
swift	abaabil	ابابیل
duck	ordak	اردک
diver; sandgrouse	esfarud	اسفرود
budgerigar	baajerigaar	باجریگار
falcon; hawk	baaz	باز
thrush	baastarak	باسترک
sparrow hawk	baasheh	باشه
grouse	baaqerqereh	باقرقره
wing	baal	بال
quail	badbadak	بدبدک
cooing	baqbaqu	بغ بغو
nightingale	bolbol	بلبل
quail	beldarchin	بلدرچین
bittern	butimaar	بوتیمار
turkey	buqalamun	بوقلمون
clothes moth	bid	بید
flamingo	paaderaaz	پادراز
feather	par	پر
swallow	parastu	پرستو
migratory birds	parandegaan-e kuchgar	پرندگان کوچگر
bird	parandeh	پرنده
wader	parande-ye aabchar	پرنده آبچر
bird of prey	parande-ye shekaari	پرنده شکاری
ornithologist	parandeh shenaas	پرنده شناس
bird seller	parandeh forush	پرنده فروش
butterfly	parvaaneh	پروانه
mosquito; gnat	pasheh	پشه
sand fly	pashe-ye khaaki	پشه خاکی
midge	pasheh rizeh	پشه ریزه
penguin	pangu'an	پنگوئن
toucan	tukaan	توکان
partridge	teyhu	تیهو
owl	joqd	جغد
chick	jujeh	جوجه
baby bird	juje-ye parandeh	جوجه پرنده

cricket	jirjirak	جيرجيرك
blue-tit	charkh risak	چرخ ريسک
lark	chakaavak	چکاوک
swallow	chelcheleh	چلچله
claws; talons	changaal	چنگال
warbling	chahchaheh	چهچهه
insect	hashareh	حشره
insectivore; insectivorous	hashareh khaar	حشره خوار
entomologist	hashareh shenaas	حشره شناس
insecticide	hashareh kosh	حشره کش
woodlouse	khar-e khaaki	خرخاکی
bluebottle	khar magas	خرمگس
cockerel	khorus	خروس
woodpecker	daarkub	دار کوب
crane	dornaa	درنا
tail	dom	دم
wagtail	dom jonbaanak	دم جنبانک
raven; magpie	zaaq	زاغ
jay	zaaq-e kabud	زاغ کبود
jackdaw	zaaqcheh	زاغچه
kite	zaqan	زغن
bee; wasp	zanbur	زنبور
wasp	zanbur-e zard	زنبور زرد
bumblebee; honeybee	zanbur 'asal	زنبور عسل
cicada	zanjareh	زنجره
starling	saar	سار
greenfinch	sabz qabaa	سبزقبا
wren; garden warbler	sesk	سسک
gadfly	sag magas	سگ مگس
dragonfly	sanjaaqak	سنجاقک
buzzard	sonqor	سنقر
whistling	sut	سوت
beetle; cockroach	susk	سوسک
grouse	siyaah khorus	سياه خروس
robin	sineh sorkh	سينه سرخ
finch; goldfinch	sehreh	سهره
yellowhammer	sehre-ye orupaa'i	سهره اروپانی
hoopoe	shaaneh besar	شانه بسر

royal falcon	shaahbaaz	شاهباز
falcon; royal falcon	shaahin	شاهین
merlin	shaahin-e tireh faam	شاهین تیره فام
sparrow hawk	shaahin-e kuchek	شاهین کوچک
moth	shab pareh	شب پره
screech owl	shabaaviz	شباویز
nightingale	shabaahang	شباهنگ
bed bug; flea	shabgaz	شبگز
louse	shepesh	شپش
weevil	shepesheh	شپشه
ostrich	shotor morq	شترمرغ
greenfly; aphid	shateh	شته
centipede	sad paa	صدپا
bird-catcher	sayyaad-e parandeh	صیاد پرنده
peacock	taavus	طاووس
blackbird	torqeh	طرقه
parrot	tuti	طوطی
eagle	'oqaab	عقاب
spider	'ankabut	عنکبوت
goose	qaaz	غاز
kite	qalivaaj	غلیواج
cuckoo; ringdove	faakhteh	فاخته
droppings	fazleh	فضله
swarm	fowj	فوج
quack; quacking sound	qaat qaat	قات قات
squawk; squawking sound	qod qod	قدقد
pheasant	qarqaavol	قرقاول
sparrowhawk	qerqi	قرقی
honey buzzard	qareh chaaylaaq	قره چایلاق
black buzzard	qareh sonqor	قره سنقر
cormorant	qareh qaaz	قره قاز
eagle	qareh qush	قره قوش
sand grouse	qataa	قطا
cage	qafas	قفس
turtledove	qomri	قمری
canary	qanaari	قناری
swan	qu	قو
falcon; hawk	qush	قوش

cock-a-doodle-do	*qu quli qu qu*	قوقولی قرقر
crane	*kaarvaanak*	کاروانک
chaffinch	*kaah sehreh*	کاهسهره
partridge	*kabk*	کبک
pigeon; dove	*kabutar*	کبوتر
woodpigeon	*kabutar-e jangali*	کبوتر جنگلی
fantailed pigeon	*kabutar-e chatri*	کبوتر چتری
rock pigeon	*kabutar-e kuhi*	کبوتر کوهی
carrier pigeon	*kabutar-e naameh bar*	کبوتر نامه بر
dovecote	*kabutar khaaneh*	کبوترخانه
quail	*karak*	کرک
condor	*karkas-e aamrikaa'i*	کرکس آمریکائی
worm	*kerm*	کرم
silkworm	*kerm-e abrisham*	کرم ابریشم
caterpillar	*kerm-e derakht*	کرم درخت
glow-worm; firefly	*kerm-e shabtaab*	کرم شب تاب
dove; pigeon	*kaftar*	کفتر
homing pigeon	*kaftar-e laaneh yaab*	کفتر لانه یاب
ladybird	*kafshduzak*	کفشدوزک
flea	*kak*	کک
raven; crow	*kalaaq*	کلاغ
carrion crow	*kalaaq-e baqdaadi*	کلاغ بغدادی
magpie	*kalaaq jaareh*	کلاغ جاره
crane	*kolang*	کلنگ
bee hive	*kandu*	کندو
tick	*kaneh*	کنه
sparrow	*gonjeshk*	گنجشک
earwig	*gush khizak*	گوش خیزک
vulture	*laashkhor*	لاشخور
nest	*laaneh*	لانه
stork	*laqlaq*	لقلق
stork	*laklak*	لکلک
kingfisher	*maahi khorak*	ماهی خورک
bird; fowl; chicken	*morq*	مرغ
oriole	*morq-e anjir khaar*	مرغ انجیر خوار
warbler	*morq-e aavaaz khaan*	مرغ آوازخوان
plover	*morq-e baaraan*	مرغ باران
bird of paradise	*morq-e beheshti*	مرغ بهشتی

39

meadowlark	*morq-e chaman*	مرغ چمن
aviary	*morq khaaneh*	مرغ خانه
sea bird; seagull	*morq-e daryaa'i*	مرغ دریائی
lapwing	*morq-e zibaa*	مرغ زیبا
pelican	*morq-e saqqaa*	مرغ سقا
guinea fowl	*morq-e shaakhdaar*	مرغ شاخدار
heron	*morq-e maahi khaar*	مرغ ماهی خوار
humming bird	*morq-e magas khaar*	مرغ مگس خوار
mynah bird	*morq-e minaa*	مرغ مینا
seagull	*morq-e nowruzi*	مرغ نوروزی
osprey	*morq-e homaa'i*	مرغ همائی
duck	*morqaabi*	مرغابی
fly	*magas*	مگس
locust; grasshopper	*malakh*	ملخ
beak	*menqaar*	منقار
ant	*murcheh*	مورچه
termite	*muryaaneh*	موریانه
perch	*neshastangaah-e parandeh*	نشستنگاه پرنده
beak	*nuk*	نوک
snipe	*nukderaaz*	نوک دراز
buzz; buzzing sound	*vez vez*	وزوز
hoopoe	*hod hod*	هدهد
millipede	*hezaar paa*	هزارپا
hoot; hooting sound	*hu hu*	هوهو

MORE BIRD AND INSECT WORDS AND EXPRESSIONS

to shed (feathers) پر ریختن   to flap (the wings); to fly; to flutter پر زدن   to fly پریدن   to fly پرواز کردن

to flutter; to flap (the wings) بال زدن   the bird flapped its wings and flew off پرنده پر زد و پرید

egg-laying تخم گذاری   nesting لانه سازی   to build a nest لانه ساختن   to build a nest آشیانه ساختن

to lay eggs تخم گذاشتن   to sting نیش زدن   to buzz وزوز کردن   to chirp جیک جیک کردن

to put in a cage توی قفس گذاشتن   birdcage قفس پرنده   ant nest لانه مورچه   spider's web تار عنکبوت

to kill کشتن   to set free آزاد کردن   to trap; to ensnare به دام انداختن   to hunt شکار کردن

birdsong آواز پرنده   to sing آواز خواندن   to migrate کوچ کردن

⁙

The Calendar   تقویم

THE SEASONS

spring	*bahaar*	بهار
summer	*taabestaan*	تابستان
autumn	*paa'iz*	پائیز
winter	*zemestaan*	زمستان

IRANIAN MONTHS

1st month (20 March -19 April)	*farvardin*	فروردین
2nd month (20 April - 20 May)	*ordibehesht*	اردیبهشت
3rd month (21 May - 20 June)	*khordaad*	خرداد
4th month (21 June - 21 July)	*tir*	تیر
5th month (22 July - 21 August)	*mordaad*	مرداد
6th month (22 Aug - 21 September)	*shahrivar*	شهریور
7th month (22 September - 21 Oct)	*mehr*	مهر
8th month (22 Oct - 20 November)	*aabaan*	آبان
9th month (21 Nov - 20 December)	*aazar*	آذر
10th month (21 Dec - 19 January)	*dey*	دی
11th month (20 Jan - 18 February)	*bahman*	بهمن
12th month (19 February - 20 March)	*esfand*	اسفند

ARABIC / ISLAMIC MONTHS

1st month	*moharram*	محرم
2nd month	*safar*	صفر
3rd month	*rabi' al-avval*	ربیع الاول
4th month	*rabi' as-saani*	ربیع الثانی
5th month	*jamaadi al-avval*	جمادی الاول
6th month	*jamaadi as-saani*	جمادی الثانی
7th month	*rajab*	رجب
8th month	*sha'baan*	شعبان
9th month	*ramazaan*	رمضان
10th month	*shavvaal*	شوال
11th month	*ziqa'deh*	ذیقعده
12th month	*zihajjeh*	ذیحجه

WESTERN / CHRISTIAN CALENDAR

January	*zhaanviyeh*	ژانویه
February	*fevriyeh*	فوریه
March	*maars*	مارس
April	*aavril*	آوریل
May	*meh*	مه
June	*zhu'an*	ژوئن
July	*zhu'iyeh*	ژوئنیه
August	*ut*	اوت
September	*septaambr*	سپتامبر
October	*oktobr*	اکتبر
November	*novaambr*	نوامبر
December	*desaambr*	دسامبر

DAYS OF THE WEEK

Saturday	*shanbeh*	شنبه
Sunday	*yek shanbeh*	یکشنبه
Monday	*dow shanbeh*	دوشنبه
Tuesday	*seh shanbeh*	سه شنبه
Wednesday	*chahaar shanbeh*	چهارشنبه
Thursday	*panj shanbeh*	پنجشنبه
Friday	*jom'eh*	جمعه

SIGNS OF THE ZODIAC

Aries	*hamal*	حمل
Taurus	*sowr*	ثور
Gemini	*jowzaa*	جوزا
Cancer	*sarataan*	سرطان
Leo	*asad*	اسد
Virgo	*sonboleh*	سنبله
Libra	*mizaan*	میزان
Scorpio	*'aqrab*	عقرب
Sagittarius	*qows*	قوس
Capricorn	*jady*	جدی
Aquarius	*dalv*	دلو
Pisces	*hut*	حوت

OTHER CALENDAR VOCABULARY

calendar; diary	taqvim	تقویم
calendar; diary	saalnaameh	سالنامه
season	fasl	فصل
(the) seasons of the year	fasl-haa-ye saal	فصلهای سال
in spring	dar bahaar	در بهار
early summer	avaa'el-e taabestaan	اوائل تابستان
mid-autumn	avaaset-e paa'iz	اواسط پائیز
late winter	avaakher-e zemestaan	اواخر زمستان
month	maah	ماه
(the) months of the year	maah-haa-ye saal	ماههای سال
in January	dar zhaanviyeh	در ژانویه
the month of Farvardin	maah-e farvardin	ماه فروردین
the month of Farvardin	farvardin maah	فروردین ماه
day	ruz	روز
week	hafteh	هفته
(the) days of the week	ruz-haa-ye hafteh	روزهای هفته
on Saturday	shanbeh	شنبه
on Saturdays	shanbeh-haa	شنبه ها
last Saturday	shanbe-ye gozashteh	شنبه گذشته
next Saturday	shanbe-ye aayandeh	شنبه آینده
the beginning of the month	avval-e borj	اول برج
the end of the month	aakhar-e borj	آخر برج
the beginning of the month	avval-e maah	اول ماه
the end of the month	aakhar-e maah	آخر ماه
the beginning of the week	avval-e hafteh	اول هفته
the end of the week	aakhar-e hafteh	آخر هفته
the middle of the week; mid-week	vasat-e hafteh	وسط هفته
solar year	saal-e shamsi	سال شمسی
lunar year	saal-e qamari	سال قمری
solar *hegira* year	saal-e hejri-ye shamsi	سال هجری شمسی
lunar *hegira* year (A.H.)	saal-e hejri-ye qamari	سال هجری قمری
Christian year (A.D.)	saal-e milaadi	سال میلادی
leap year	saal-e kabiseh	سال کبیسه
public holiday	ta'til-e 'omumi	تعطیل عمومی

Cars and Driving

اتومبیل و رانندگی

water	aab	آب
tax disc	aarm-e maaliyaat-e shahrdaari	آرم مالیات شهرداری
theft alarm	aazhir-e zedd-e dozd	آژیر ضد دزد
driving lesson	aamuzesh-e raanandegi	آموزش رانندگی
side mirror; wing mirror	aayene-ye baqal	آینه بغل
wing mirror	aayene-ye jaanebi	آینه جانبی
front mirror	aayene-ye jelow	آینه جلو
rear-view mirror	aayene-ye 'aqab	آینه عقب
hitch-hiking	otu-estaap	اتو استاپ
motorway; expressway	otubaan	اتوبان
car; automobile	otumobil	اتومبیل
starter	estaart	استارت
ignition	afruzgar	افروزگر
driving test	emtehaan-e raanandegi	امتحان رانندگی
fork (in the road)	enshe'aab	انشعاب
parking meter	ist sanj	ایست سنج
traffic safety; road safety	imani-ye teraafik	ایمنی ترافیک
road safety	imani dar raah-haa	ایمنی در راه ها
battery	baatri	باتری
toll	baaj	باج
toll road	baajraah	باجراه
luggage rack	baarband	باربند
breathalyser	baazdam sanj	بازدم سنج
inspection	baaz rasi	بازرسی
petrol tank	baak-e benzin	باك بنزین
lane	baand	باند
chassis; body	badaneh	بدنه
windscreen wipers	barf paak kon	برف پاك کن
route plan; itinerary	barnaame-ye safar	برنامه سفر
motorway; highway; expressway	bozorgraah	بزرگراه
eight-lane highway	bozorgraah-e hasht baandi	بزرگراه هشت باندی
gas; petrol	benzin	بنزین
horn; hooter	buq	بوق
insurance	bimeh	بیمه
car insurance	bime-ye otumobil	بیمه اتومبیل
insurance policy	bimeh naameh	بیمه نامه

parking space; parking lot	*paarking*	پارکینگ
police officer	*paasebaan*	پاسبان
pedal	*pedaal*	پدال
accelerator	*pedaal-e gaaz*	پدال گاز
suspension bridge	*pol-e mo'allaq*	پل معلق
flyover	*pol-e havaa'i*	پل هوائی
registration plate	*pelaak-e maashin*	پلاک ماشین
police	*polis*	پلیس
traffic police	*polis-e raah*	پلیس راه
motorcycle police	*polis-e motor savaar*	پلیس موتورسوار
gas station; petrol station	*pomp-e benzin*	پمپ بنزین
sun roof	*panjere-ye aaftaabi*	پنجره آفتابی
sun roof	*panjere-ye taaq*	پنجره طاق
puncture; flat tyre	*panchar*	پنچر
oil can	*pit-e benzin*	پیت بنزین
bend	*pich*	پیچ
turn; bend (in the road)	*pich-e jaaddeh*	پیچ جاده
traffic sign	*taablow-ye raahnamaa'i*	تابلوی راهنمائی
tyre	*taayer*	تایر
driving offence	*takhallof-e raanandegi*	تخلف رانندگی
brakes	*tormoz*	ترمز
emergency brake	*tormoz-e ezteraari*	ترمز اضطراری
hand brake	*tormoz-e dasti*	ترمز دستی
emergency stop	*tormoz-e naagahaani*	ترمز ناگهانی
trailer	*tereyli*	تریلی
car accident	*tasaadof-e otumobil*	تصادف اتومبیل
slight accident	*tasaadof-e joz'i*	تصادف جزئی
pile-up	*tasaadof-e chand maashin*	تصادف چند ماشین
head-on collision	*tasaadof-e shaakh-be-shaakh*	تصادف شاخ به شاخ
collision	*tasaadom*	تصادم
driving licence	*tasdiq-e raanandegi*	تصدیق رانندگی
mechanic	*ta'mirkaar*	تعمیر کار
service station	*ta'mirgaah*	تعمیر گاه
oil change	*ta'viz-e rowqan*	تعویض روغن
diversion	*taqyir-e masir*	تغییر مسیر
junction; crossing	*taqaato'*	تقاطع
level crossing	*taqaato'-e hamsath*	تقاطع همسطح
speeding	*tondraani*	تندرانی

emergency stop	tavaqqof-e naagahaani	توقف ناگهانی
headrest	jaa sari	جا سری
road; highway	jaaddeh	جاده
exit road; slip road	jaadde-ye khoruji	جاده خروجی
ring road	jaadde-ye kamarbandi	جاده کمربندی
slip road	jaadde-ye vorudi	جاده ورودی
kerb	jadval	جدول
fine	jarimeh	جریمه
parking fine	jarime-ye paarking-e qeyr-e mojaaz	جریمه پارکینگ غیر مجاز
(traffic) island	jazire-ye imani	جزیره ایمنی
gear box	ja'be-ye dandeh	جعبه دنده
jack	jak	جک
direction	jahat	جهت
headlight	cheraaq-e jelow	چراغ جلو
flashing light	cheraaq-e cheshmak zan	چراغ چشمک زن
indicator	cheraaq-e raahnamaa	چراغ راهنما
tail light	cheraaq-e 'aqab	چراغ عقب
red light	cheraaq-e qermez	چراغ قرمز
traffic lights	cheraaq-haa-ye raahnamaa'i	چراغ های راهنمائی
wheel; tyre	charkh	چرخ
spare tyre	charkh-e zaapaas	چرخ زاپاس
choke	chowk	چوک
four-door	chahaar dari	چهار دری
crossroads	chahaar raah	چهار راه
after-sale services	khadamaat-e ba'd az forush	خدمات بعد از فروش
breakdown	kharaab shodan-e maashin	خراب شدن ماشین
damages	khesaarat	خسارت
dipstick	khattkesh-e baazdid-e rowqan	خطکش بازدید روغن
automobile; car; vehicle	khodrow	خودرو
road; street; avenue; lane	khiyaabaan	خیابان
main road	khiyaabaan-e asli	خیابان اصلی
one-way street	khiyaabaan-e yek tarafeh	خیابان یک طرفه
dashboard	daashburd	داشبرد
speed trap	daam-e sor'at	دام سرعت
roundabout	daayere-ye yek tarafeh	دایره یک طرفه
car door	dar-e maashin	در ماشین
theft alarm	dozdgir	دزدگیر
bump (in the road)	dastandaaz	دست انداز

breathalyser	dam sanj	دم سنج
gear	dandeh	دنده
cyclist	dowcharkheh savaar	دوچرخه سوار
fork (in the road)	dowraahi	دوراهی
diesel fuel	dizel	دیزل
crash barrier	divaareh	دیواره
car radio	raadiyo-ye otumobil	رادیوی اتومبیل
gear drive	raaneshgar-e dande-ye otumobil	رانشگر دنده اتومبیل
driving	raanandegi	رانندگی
careless driving	raanandegi baa bi-deqqati	رانندگی با بی دقتی
driver	raanandeh	راننده
careless driver	raanande-ye bi deqqat	راننده بی دقت
detour	raah-e enheraafi	راه انحرافی
starter	raah andaaz	راه انداز
traffic jam	raah bandaan	راه بندان
traffic cone	raah band-e pelaastiki	راه بند پلاستیکی
road; highway	raah showseh	راه شوسه
minor road; B road	raah-e far'i	راه فرعی
short cut	raah-e miyaanbor	راه میانبر
roadblock	raah gir	راهگیر
road map	raahnaameh	راهنامه
roadability; roadworthiness	raahvaari	راهواری
oil	rowqan	روغن
injured; casualty	zakhmi	زخمی
headrest	zir sari	زیر سری
underpass	zirgozar	زیر گذر
make (of car)	saakht	ساخت
choke	saasaat	ساسات
rush hour	saa'aat-e owj-e aamad o shod	ساعات اوج آمد و شد
overtaking	sebqat giri	سبقت گیری
bumper	separ	سپر
speed	sor'at	سرعت
speedometer	sor'at sanj	سرعت سنج
speeding	sor'at-e qeyr-e mojaaz	سرعت غیر مجاز
car theft	serqat-e otumobil	سرقت اتومبیل
MOT; annual service	servis-e saaliyaaneh	سرویس سالیانه
trip; journey	safar	سفر
valve	supaap	سوپاپ

fuel	sukht	سوخت
carburretor	sukhtaamaa	سوختاما
central locking system	sistem-e qofl-e markazi	سیستم قفل مرکزی
chassis	shaasi	شاسی
highway; motorway	shaah raah	شاهراه
acceleration	shetaab	شتاب
number	shomaareh	شماره
spark plug	sham'	شمع
chauffeur	shufer	شوفر
front windscreen	shishe-ye jelow	شیشه جلو
back windscreen	shishe-ye 'aqab	شیشه عقب
garage owner	saaheb-e gaaraazh	صاحب گاراژ
boot; trunk	sanduq-e 'aqab	صندوق عقب
de-icer	zedd-e yakh	ضد یخ
bump	zarbeh	ضربه
shock absorber	zarbeh khafekon	ضربه خفه کن
shock absorber	zarbeh gir	ضربه گیر
direction	taraf	طرف
pedestrian	'aaber-e piyaadeh	عابر پیاده
traffic sign	'alaamat-e raahnamaa'i	علامت راهنمائی
distance	faaseleh	فاصله
steering wheel	farmaan	فرمان
pressure	feshaar	فشار
car lighter	fandak-e maashin	فندک ماشین
hub cap	qaalpaaq	قالپاق
spare parts	qata'aat-e yadaki	قطعات یدکی
traffic regulations	qavaanin-e raft-o-aamad	قوانین رفت و آمد
bonnet; hood	kaaput	کاپوت
carburretor	karburaator	کاربوراتور
caravan	kaarvaan	کاروان
lorry; truck; juggernaut	kaamiyun	کامیون
killed; casualty	koshteh	کشته
clutch	kelaaj	کلاج
ignition	kelid-e afruzesh	کلید افروزش
safety belt; seat belt	kamarband-e imani	کمربند ایمنی
shock absorber	komak fanar	کمک فنر
verge; roadside	kenaar-e jaaddeh	کنار جاده
hard shoulder	kenaareh	کناره

garage	gaaraazh	گاراژ
lollipop-man; lollipop-lady	gozarbaan	گذربان
fender	gelgir	گلگیر
driving licence	govaahinaame-ye raanandegi	گواهینامه رانندگی
hole (in the road); pothole; puddle	gowdaal	گودال
tyre	laastik	لاستیک
spare parts	lavaazem-e yadaki	لوازم یدکی
litre	litr	لیتر
car	maashin	ماشین
breakdown van	maashin-e ta'mirkaari	ماشین تعمیرکاری
second-hand car	maashin-e dast-e dovvom	ماشین دست دوم
old banger	maashin-e qoraazeh	ماشین قراضه
traffic warden	ma'mur-e paarking	مامور پارکینگ
police officer	ma'mur-e polis	مامور پلیس
petrol pump attendant	motasaddi-ye pomp-e benzin	متصدی پمپ بنزین
built-up area	mahall-e por saakhtemaan	محل پر ساختمان
axle	mehvar	محور
documents; documentation	madaarek	مدارک
driving school	madrase-ye raanandegi	مدرسه رانندگی
five-door model	model-e panj dar	مدل پنج در
border	marz	مرز
distance	masaafat	مسافت
trip; journey	mosaaferat	مسافرت
route	masir	مسیر
itinerary	masir-e mosaaferat	مسیر مسافرت
petrol consumption	masraf-e benzin	مصرف بنزین
mileage	masraf-e maashin	مصرف ماشین
mechanic	mekaanik	مکانیک
area	mantaqeh	منطقه
engine; motor	motor	موتور
two-stroke engine	motor-e dow zamaaneh	موتور دو زمانه
motorcyclist	motorsiklet savaar	موتورسیکلت سوار
piston rod	mile-ye pistun	میله پیستون
camshaft	mile-ye supaap	میله سوپاپ
crash barrier	narde-ye kenaar-e jaaddeh	نرده کنار جاده
road map; A-to-Z	naqshe-ye raah-haa	نقشه راه ها
city map; A-to-Z	naqshe-ye shahr	نقشه شهر
car showroom	namaayeshgaah-e maashin	نمایشگاه ماشین

an inexperienced driver راننده ناشی   a good driver راننده خوب   to drive راندن   to drive رانندگی کردن

to pick s.o. up کسی را سوار کردن   to get out of the car از ماشین پیاده شدن   to get in the car سوار ماشین شدن

he doesn't know how to drive رانندگی بلد نیست   I gave Hasan a lift to university حسن را با ماشین به دانشگاه رساندم

to brake ترمز زدن   to go too fast زیادی تند رفتن   to go fast تند رفتن   to go slowly یواش رفتن

to turn off خاموش کردن   to switch on; to ignite روشن کردن   to stop ایستادن   ویراژ رفتن

to pick up speed سرعت گرفتن   to step on the gas; to accelerate گاز دادن   to swerve; to skid

pile-up تصادف چند ماشین   car accident تصادف ماشین   to have an accident; to crash تصادف کردن

I need petrol احتیاج به بنزین دارم   my petrol tank is empty باك بنزین من خالی است

how much is petrol per litre؟ بنزین لیتری چند است؟   where is the nearest petrol station نزدیکترین پمپ بنزین کجاست؟

the windscreen wipers don't work برف پاك کن کار نمی کند   you have to change the oil روغن را باید عوض کنید

the back door has a scratch on it در عقب خراش برداشته   I have a puncture ماشینم پنچر شده

how much do you charge for repairs؟ برای تعمیرات چقدر می گیرید؟   my car radio is broken رادیوی ماشینم خراب شده

we're lost گم شده ایم   can you direct us to the Central Bank؟ لطفا میتوانید مارا به بانک مرکزی راهنمائی کنید؟

turn left دست چپ بپیچید   turn right دست راست بپیچید   go straight ahead مستقیم بروید

No Left Turn گردش به چپ ممنوع   No Right Turn گردش به راست ممنوع   No Entry ورود ممنوع

minor offence تخلف جزئی   to fine جریمه کردن   No Parking پارك کردن ممنوع

they fined me £100 on account of a driving offence مرا بخاطر تخلف رانندگی ۱۰۰ پوند جریمه کردند

new driver نو راننده   to have driving lessons رانندگی یاد گرفتن   to get a driving licence تصدیق گرفتن

he is a dangerous driver او راننده خطرناکی است   his driving is very good رانندگیش خیلی خوب است

pull over! بزن کنار!   Hasan overtook us حسن از ما سبقت گرفت   to overtake سبقت گرفتن

to change gear دنده عوض کردن   to switch on the lights چراغ را روشن کردن   to sound the horn بوق زدن

you have to change gears now باید الان دنده عوض کنید   I went into reverse gear دنده عقب زدم

you have to take the car to the garage باید ماشین را به تعمیرگاه ببرید   are you insured؟ آیا شما بیمه هستید؟

I've had my car stolen ماشینم را دزدیدند   I parked the car on a yellow line ماشین را روی خط زرد پارك کردم

I'm taking the car to the garage for its MOT ماشینم را برای سرویس سالیانه به تعمیرگاه می برم

◄◄►►

Chemistry

شیمی

water	aab	آب
hydrogen peroxide	aab-e oksizheneh	آب اکسیژنه
limewater	aab-e aahak	آب آهک
water of crystallization	aab-e tabalvor	آب تبلور
distilled water	aab-e moqattar	آب مقطر
brine	aab-e namak	آب نمک
galvanized	aabkaari shodeh	آبکاری شده
electroplating	aabkaari-ye felezaat	آبکاری فلزات
hydrolysis	aabkaaft	آبکافت
methylated spirits	aabgune-haa-ye alkoli	آبگونه های الکلی
arsenic	aarsenik	آرسنیک
argon	aargun	آرگون
flame test	aazmaayesh-e baa sho'leh	آزمایش با شعله
aluminium	aaluminiyom	آلومینیم
alloy	aalyaazh	آلیاژ
ampere	aamper	آمپر
ammonia	aamuniyaak	آمونیاك
enthalpy	aantaalpi	آنتالپی
anode	aanod	آند
enzyme	aanzim	آنزیم
anion	aaniyun	آنیون
lime	aahak	آهک
slaked lime	aahak-e koshteh	آهک کشته
iron	aahan	آهن
ethane	etaan	اتان
ethanol	etaanul	اتانول
atom	atom	اتم
ethene	eten	اتن
ether	esir	اثیر
combustion	ehteraaq	احتراق
ozone	ozon	ازن
stalactite	estaalaagtit	استالاگتیت
stalagmite	estaalaagmit	استالاگمیت
ester	ester	استر
acid	asid	اسید
amino acid	asid-e aamineh	اسید آمینه

51

sulphuric acid	asid sulfurik	اسید سولفوریک
weak acid	asid-e za'if	اسید ضعیف
phosphoric acid	asid fosforik	اسید فسفریک
nitric acid	asid nitrik	اسید نیتریک
monobasic acid	asid-e yek arzeshi	اسید یک ارزشی
unsaturated	eshbaa' nashodeh	اشباع نشده
Le Chatelier's principle	asl-e lu shaateliyeh	اصل لوشاتلیه
oxidation	oksaayesh	اکسایش
anodizing	oksaayesh-e aanodi	اکسایش آندی
oxide	oksid	اکسید
basic oxide	oksid-e qalyaa'i	اکسید قلیائی
oxygen	oksizhen	اکسیژن
electrode	elektrud	الکترود
electrolyte	elektrulit	الکترولیت
electrolysis	elektruliz	الکترولیز
electron	elektrun	الکترون
delocalized electrons	elektrun-e qeyr-e mostaqar	الکترون غیر مستقر
electronegativity	elektru negaativi	الکترونگاتیوی
alcohol	alkol	الکل
diamond	almaas	الماس
miscibility	emtezaaj paziri	امتزاج پذیری
immiscibility	emtezaaj naapaziri	امتزاج ناپذیری
accumulator	anbaareh	انباره
energy	enerzhi	انرژی
kinetic energy	enerzhi-ye jonbeshi	انرژی جنبشی
activation energy	enerzhi-ye fa'aal saazi	انرژی فعال سازی
heat energy	enerzhi-ye garmaa'i	انرژی گرمائی
explosion	enfejaar	انفجار
uranium	uraaniyom	اورانیم
oleum	ule'um	اولئوم
isotope	izutup	ایزوتوپ
isomer	izumer	ایزومر
battery	baatri	باتری
dry cell	baatri-ye khoshk	باتری خشک
barium	baariyom	باریم
base	baaz	باز
tempering	baaz pokht	باز پخت
flask	baalun	بالون

vapour; steam	bokhaar	بخار
electrolysis	barq kaaft	برق‌کافت
bromine	berom	برم
brass	berenj	برنج
bronze	beronz	برنز
bromide	berumid	برومید
barrel	boshkeh	بشکه
conservation of mass and energy	baqaa-ye jerm va enerzhi	بقای جرم و انرژی
crystal	bolur	بلور
benzene	benzen	بنزن
petrol	benzin	بنزین
butane	butaan	بوتان
boron	bur	بور
burette	buret	بورت
bauxite	buksit	بوکسیت
anhydrous	bi aab	بی آب
amorphous	bi rikht	بی ریخت
paraffin	paaraafin	پارافین
refining	paalaayesh	پالایش
peptide	peptid	پپتید
potassium	potaasiyom	پتاسیم
petrochemical	petrushimi	پتروشیمی
diffusion	pakhsh	پخش
peroxide	peraaksid	پراکسید
X-ray	partov-e iks	پرتو ایکس
gamma-rays	partov-haa-ye gaamaa	پرتو های گاما
propane	perupaan	پروپان
protein	perute'in	پروتئین
platinum	pelaatin	پلاتین
plastic	pelaastik	پلاستیک
plutonium	polutuniyom	پلوتونیم
polyether	poli eter	پلی اتر
polyester	poli ester	پلی استر
polythene	politen	پلیتن
polymer	polimer	پلیمر
asbestos	panbe-ye nasuz	پنبه نسوز
shell	pusteh	پوسته
pipette	pipet	پیپت

pewter	peyuter	پیوتر
co-ordinate bond	peyvast-e hamaaraast	پیوست همارآست
bond	peyvand	پیوند
covalent bond	peyvand-e eshteraaki	پیوند اشتراکی
double bond	peyvand-e dowgaaneh	پیوند دوگانه
polar bond	peyvand-e qotbi	پیوند قطبی
ionic bond	peyvand-e yuni	پیوند یونی
covalent bond	peyvand-e hamgonjaa	پیوند هم گنجا
hydrogen bond	peyvand-e hidruzheni	پیوند هیدروژنی
ultraviolet radiation	taabesh-e faraa banafsh	تابش فرابنفش
radioactivity	taabeshgari	تابشگری
ion exchange	tabaadol-e yuni	تبادل یونی
evaporation	tabkhir	تبخیر
chemical change	tabdil-e shimiyaa'i	تبدیل شیمیائی
crystallization	tabalvor	تبلور
re-crystallization	tabalvor-e mojaddad	تبلور مجدد
analysis; decomposition	tajziyeh	تجزیه
volumetric analysis	tajziye-ye hajmi	تجزیه حجمی
double decomposition	tajziye-ye dowgaaneh	تجزیه دوگانه
fermentation	takhmir	تخمیر
scales; weighing machine	taraazu	ترازو
compound	tarkib	ترکیب
iron compounds	tarkibaat-e aahani	ترکیبات آهنی
homologous series	tarkibaat-e ham radeh	ترکیبات هم رده
terylene	terilen	تریلن
equilibrium	ta'aadol	تعادل
suspension	ta'liq	تعلیق
energy change	taqyir-e enerzhi	تغییر انرژی
physical change	taqyir-e fiziki	تغییر فیزیکی
distillation	taqtir	تقطیر
fractional distillation	taqtir-e joz-be-joz	تقطیر جزء به جزء
tonne	ton	تن
thermostat	tanzimgar-e garmaa	تنظیم گر گرما
respiration	tanaffos	تنفس
balance	tavaazon	توازن
litmus paper	turnesol	تورنسل
titanium	titaan	تیتان
precipitate	tah neshast	ته نشست

separation	*jodaa saazi*	جداسازی
periodic table	*jadval-e tanaavobi*	جدول تناوبی
mass	*jerm*	جرم
atomic mass	*jerm-e atomi*	جرم اتمی
current	*jaryaan*	جریان
electric current	*jaryaan-e barq*	جریان برق
solid (n.)	*jesm-e jaamed*	جسم جامد
atmosphere	*javv*	جو
boiling	*jush*	جوش
baking powder	*jush-e shirin*	جوش شیرین
sulphuric acid	*jowhar-e gugerd*	جوهر گوگرد
mercury	*jiveh*	جیوه
burner (e.g. Bunsen burner)	*cheraaq*	چراغ
water cycle	*charkhe-ye aab*	چرخه آب
carbon cycle	*charkhe-ye karbon*	چرخه کربن
nitrogen cycle	*charkhe-ye nitruzhen*	چرخه نیتروژن
malleable	*chakkosh khaar*	چکش خوار
stalactite	*chekandeh*	چکنده
stalagmite	*chekideh*	چکیده
density	*chegaali*	چگالی
allotrope	*chand shekl*	چند شکل
tetrahedron	*chahaar vajhi*	چهار وجهی
volume	*hajm*	حجم
heat; temperature	*haraarat*	حرارت
absolute temperature	*haraarat-e motlaq*	حرارت مطلق
thermal (adj.)	*haraarati*	حرارتی
Brownian motion	*harekat-e beraavni*	حرکت براونی
solubility	*hal paziri*	حل پذیری
solvent	*hallaal*	حلّال
property	*khaasiyat*	خاصیت
pure	*khaales*	خالص
vacuum	*khala'*	خلاء
neutral	*khonsaa*	خنثی
neutralization	*khonsaa saazi*	خنثی سازی
celsius	*daraje-ye selsiyus*	درجه سلسیوس
dextrose	*dekstruz*	دکستروز
temperature; heat	*damaa*	دما
thermometer	*damaa sanj*	دما سنج

55

room temperature	damaa-ye otaaq	دمای اطاق
Kelvin temperature	damaa-ye kelvin	دمای کلوین
period; cycle	dowreh	دوره
disaccharide	disaakaarid	دی ساکارید
dimer	dimer	دیمر
dynamite	dinaamit	دینامیت
alpha particles	zarraat-e aalfaa	ذرات آلفا
sub-atomic particles	zarraat-e bonyaadi-ye atom	ذرات بنیادی اتم
atom; particle	zarreh	ذره
beta particle	zarre-ye betaa	ذره بتا
fusion	zowb	ذوب
electrochemical series	radif-e elektru-shimiyaa'i	ردیف الکتروشیمیائی
conductor	resaanaa	رسانا
precipitate; residue	rosub	رسوب
dilute	raqiq	رقیق
dyes	rangine-haa	رنگینه ها
contact process	ravesh-e mojaaverati	روش مجاورتی
oil; grease	rowqan	روغن
zinc	ruy	روی
charcoal	zoqaal-e chub	زغال چوب
coal	zoqaal-e sang	زغال سنگ
period	zamaan-e tanaavob	زمان تناوب
chain	zanjir	زنجیر
xenon	zenun	زنون
enzyme	zimaa	زیما
poison	zahr	زهر
silica gel	zhel silikaa	ژل سیلیکا
joule	zhul	ژول
chlorophyll	sabzine-ye barg	سبزینه برگ
vulcanization	sakht saazi	سخت سازی
hardness of water	sakhti-ye aab	سختی آب
softening of water	sakhti zadaa'i-ye aab	سختی زدائی آب
sodium	sodiyom	سدیم
lead	sorb	سرب
rate of reaction	sor'at-e vaakonesh	سرعت واکنش
vinegar	serkeh	سرکه
cellulose	seluloz	سلولز
synthesis	santez	سنتز

titration	sanjesh-e hajmi	سنجش حجمی
limestone	sang-e aahak	سنگ آهک
rock salt	sang-e namak	سنگ نمک
fuel	sukht	سوخت
diesel fuel	sukht-e dizel	سوخت دیزل
caustic	suz aavar	سوز آور
sucrose	sukroz	سوکرز
sulphate	sulfaat	سولفات
sulphide	sulfid	سولفید
cyanide	siyaanur	سیانور
silicon	silikon	سیلیکن
cement	simaan	سیمان
lattice	shabakeh	شبکه
flame; burner	sho'leh	شعله
fission	shekaaft	شکافت
sugar	shekar	شکر
crack; cracking; fracture	shekastegi	شکستگی
efflorescence	shekoftegi	شکفتگی
ductility	shekl paziri	شکل پذیری
universal indicator	shenaasaagar-e 'omumi	شناساگر عمومی
glass	shisheh	شیشه
organic chemistry	shimi-ye aali	شیمی آلی
physical chemistry	shimi fizik	شیمی فیزیک
inorganic chemistry	shimi-ye ma'dani	شیمی معدنی
soap	saabun	صابون
saponification	saabuni shodan	صابونی شدن
filter	saafi	صافی
antifreeze	zedd-e yakh	ضد یخ
gold	talaa	طلا
valency; capacity	zarfiyat	ظرفیت
oxidizing agent	'aamel-e oksandeh	عامل اکسنده
dehydrating agent	'aamel-e aab zadaa'i	عامل آب زدائی
fixing agent	'aamel-e sobut	عامل ثبوت
reducing agent	'aamel-e kaahandeh	عامل کاهنده
insulator	'aayeq	عایق
atomic number	'adad-e atomi	عدد اتمی
mass number	'adad-e jermi	عدد جرمی
element	'onsor	عنصر

transition element	'onsor-e vaaseteh	عنصر واسطه
concentration	qelzat	غلظت
concentrated	qaliz	غلیظ
passive	qeyr-e fa'aal	غیر فعال
non-metal	qeyr-e felez	غیر فلز
insoluble	qeyr-e mahlul	غیر محلول
phase	faaz	فاز
photosynthesis	fotusantez	فتوسنتز
volatile	farraar	فرّار
Haber process	faraayand-e haaber	فرایند هابر
by-product	faraavarde-ye far'i	فرآورده فرعی
formalin	formaalin	فرمالین
formula	formul	فرمول
empirical formula	formul-e tajrebi	فرمول تجربی
structural formula	formul-e saakhtaari	فرمول ساختاری
molecular formula	formul-e mulkuli	فرمول مولکولی
photosynthesis	foruq aamaa'i	فروغ آمانی
phosphate	fosfaat	فسفات
phosphorous	fosfor	فسفر
pressure	feshaar	فشار
metal	felez	فلز
fluorine	folur	فلور
phenol	fenul	فنول
steel	fulaad	فولاد
filter	filter	فیلتر
Boyle's law	qaanun-e buyel	قانون بویل
Pascal's law	qaanun-e paaskaal	قانون پاسکال
Charle's law	qaanun-e shaarl	قانون شارل
law of constant proportions	qaanun-e nesbiyat-haa-ye saabet	قانون نسبیت های ثابت
combining power	qodrat-e tarkib	قدرت ترکیب
pole; electrode	qotb	قطب
anode	qotb-e mosbat	قطب مثبت
cathode	qotb-e manfi	قطب منفی
tin	qal'	قلع
alkali; base	qalyaa	قلیا
glucose	qand	قند
fructose	qand-e miveh	قند میوه
gas laws	qavaanin-e gaaz-haa	قوانین گازها

catalyst	*kaataalizur*	کاتالیزور
cathode	*kaatod*	کاتد
cation	*kaatiyun*	کاتیون
litmus paper	*kaaqaz-e litmusi*	کاغذ لیتموسی
ore	*kaaneh*	کانه
reduction	*kaahesh*	کاهش
cobalt	*kobaalt*	کبالت
carbon	*karbon*	کربن
carbon dating	*karbon sanji*	کربن سنجی
carbonate	*karbonaat*	کربنات
carbohydrate	*karbuhidraat*	کربوهیدرات
chrome	*kerom*	کرم
chromatography	*kerumaatugraafi*	کروماتوگرافی
krypton	*keriptun*	کریپتون
cryolite	*keriyulit*	کریولیت
coke	*kok*	کک
chlorine	*kolor*	کلر
chlorination	*kolordaar saazi*	کلردارسازی
chloride	*kolorid*	کلرید
calcium	*kalsiyom*	کلسیم
quantitative	*kammi*	کمی
fertilizer	*kud*	کود
blast furnace	*kure-ye zowb-e aahan*	کوره ذوب آهن
qualitative	*keyfi*	کیفی
kilo	*kilu*	کیلو
kilojoule	*kiluzhul*	کیلوژول
gas	*gaaz*	گاز
natural gas	*gaaz-e tabi'i*	گاز طبیعی
inert gases	*gaaz-haa-ye bi konesh*	گاز های بی کنش
noble gases	*gaaz-haa-ye najib*	گاز های نجیب
chalk	*gach*	گچ
graphite	*geraafit*	گرافیت
bleach	*gard-e bi rang konandeh*	گرد بی رنگ کننده
gramme	*geram*	گرم
pyrolosis	*garmaa kaaft*	گرما کافت
thermal (adj.)	*garmaa'i*	گرمائی
latent heat	*garmaa-ye nahaan*	گرمای نهان
centrifuge	*goriz az markaz*	گریز از مرکز

glycol	gelikul	گلیکول
disinfectant	gand zadaa	گند زدا
sulphur	gugerd	گوگرد
rubber	laastik	لاستیک
litre	litr	لیتر
lithium	litiyom	لیتیم
matter; material	maaddeh	ماده
washing agent	maadde-ye paak konandeh	ماده پاک کننده
detergent	maade-ye paaksaaz	ماده پاکساز
disinfectant	maade-ye zedd-e 'ofuni	ماده ضد عفونی
macromolecule	maakru mulkul	ماکرومولکول
maltose	maaltuz	مالتوز
liquid	maaye'	مایع
methane	metaan	متان
methanol	metaanul	متانول
group	majmu'eh	مجموعه
solution; solute	mahlul	محلول
saturated solution	mahlul-e eshbaa' shodeh	محلول اشباع شده
aqueous solution	mahlul-e aabaki	محلول آبکی
supersaturated solution	mahlul-e fowq-e eshbaa'	محلول فوق اشباع
yeast	mokhammer	مخمر
copper	mes	مس
flame; burner	mash'al	مشعل
synthetic; artificial	masnu'i	مصنوعی
equation	mo'aadeleh	معادله
aromatic	mo'attar	معطر
bronze	mefraq	مفرغ
percentage	meqdaar-e dar sad	مقدار در صد
amalgam	malqameh	ملغمه
manganese	manganez	منگنز
monomer	monumer	منومر
magnesium	maneziyom	منیزیم
mole	mul	مول
molarity	mulaariteh	مولاریته
molecule	mulkul	مولکول
linear molecules	mulkul-e khatti	مولکول خطی
monosaccharide	munusaakaarid	مونو ساکارید
condensation	mey'aan	میعان

starch	neshaasteh	نشاسته
indicator	neshaangar	نشانگر
symbol	neshaaneh	نشانه
kinetic theory	nazariye-ye jonbeshi	نظریه جنبشی
oil	naft	نفت
kerosine	naft-e sefid	نفت سفید
naphtha	naftaa	نفتا
diffusion	nofuz	نفوذ
silver	noqreh	نقره
end-point	noqte-ye paayaan	نقطه پایان
boiling point	noqte-ye jush	نقطه جوش
melting point	noqte-ye zowb	نقطه ذوب
deliquescence	nam paziri	نم پذیری
hygroscopic	namgir	نم گیر
salt	namak	نمک
acid salts	namak-e asidi	نمک اسیدی
basic salts	namak-e baazi	نمک بازی
neutron	nutrun	نوترون
neon	ne'un	نئون
nitrate	nitraat	نیترات
nitrogen	nitruzhen	نیتروژن
nitrites	nitrit	نیتریت
centrifugal force	niru-ye markaz goriz	نیروی مرکز گریز
Van der Waals' forces	niru-haa-ye vaan der vaals	نیروهای وان در والس
sucrose	neyshekar	نیشکر
nickel	nikel	نیکل
semi-conductor	nimeh resaanaa	نیمه رسانا
half-life	nimeh 'omr	نیمه عمر
unit	vaahed	واحد
reaction	vaakonesh	واکنش
substitutional reaction	vaakonesh-e estekhlaafi	واکنش استخلافی
addition reaction	vaakonesh-e afzaayeshi	واکنش افزایشی
reversible reaction	vaakonesh-e bargasht pazir	واکنش برگشت پذیر
reactivity	vaakonesh paziri	واکنش پذیری
displacement reaction	vaakonesh-e jaaneshini	واکنش جانشینی
chain reaction	vaakonesh-e zanjiri	واکنش زنجیری
chemical reaction	vaakonesh-e shimiyaa'i	واکنش شیمیایی
exothermic reaction	vaakonesh-e garmaazaa	واکنش گرمازا

endothermic reaction	vaakonesh-e garmaagir	واکنش گرماگیر
nuclear reaction	vaakonesh-e haste'i	واکنش هسته ای
homogenous reaction	vaakonesh-e hamgen	واکنش همگن
valency	vaalaans	والانس
vanadium	vaanaadiyom	واناديم
relative atomic weight	vazn-e atomi-ye nesbi	وزن اتمی نسبی
vulcanization	volkaanesh	ولكانش
vitamin	vitaamin	ويتامين
halogen	haaluzhen	هالوژن
halide	haalid	هاليد
nucleus	hasteh	هسته
methyl orange	helyaantin	هليانتين
helium	heliyom	هليم
synthesis	ham nahesht	هم نهشت
fusion	hamjushi	همجوشی
haemoglobin	hemugelubin	هموگلوبين
air	havaa	هوا
hydrate	hidraat	هيدرات
hydrogen	hidruzhen	هيدروژن
hydrogenation	hidruzhen daar saazi	هيدروژن دار سازی
hydrogen sulphide	hidruzhen sulfid	هيدروژن سولفيد
hydrogen chloride	hidruzhen kolorid	هيدروژن كلريد
hydrocarbon	hidrukarbon	هيدروكربن
ammonium hydroxide	hidruksid aamuniyaak	هيدروكسيد آمونياك
hydrolysis	hidruliz	هيدروليز
hydride	hidrid	هيدريد
cell	yaakhteh	ياخته
ice	yakh	يخ
dry ice	yakh-e khoshk	يخ خشك
cryolite	yakhsang	يخسنگ
iodine	yod	يد
iodides	yodid	يديد
ion	yun	يون
cation	yun-e mosbat	يون مثبت
hydrogen ion	yun-e hidruzhen	يون هيدروژن

Clothes لباس

lining	*aastar*	آستر
sleeve	*aastin*	آستین
changing cubicle	*otaaq-e perov*	اتاق پرو
size	*andaazeh*	اندازه
shoe size	*andaaze-ye kafsh*	اندازه کفش
uniform	*unifurm*	اونیفورم
fan	*baad bezan*	بادبزن
raincoat	*baaraani*	بارانی
blouse	*boluz*	بلوز
shoulder strap	*band-e piraahan*	بند پیراهن
garter	*band-e juraab*	بند جوراب
washing line	*band-e rakht*	بند رخت
braces	*band-e shalvaar*	بند شلوار
shoelace	*band-e kafsh*	بند کفش
topless	*bi pestaan push*	بی پستان پوش
bow tie	*paapiyun*	پاپیون
trouser bottoms	*paacheh*	پاچه
oilskin	*paarche-ye sham'i*	پارچه شمعی
dress material	*paarche-ye lebaas*	پارچه لباس
tear; rip	*paaregi*	پارگی
stiletto heels	*paashneh suzani*	پاشنه سوزنی
turn-up (in trousers)	*paakati*	پاکتی
coat; overcoat	*paaltow*	پالتو
fur coat	*paaltow-ye khez*	پالتوی خز
bra	*pestaanband*	پستانبند
pleat	*peliseh*	پلیسه
pullover	*polowver*	پلوور
boot	*putin*	پوتین
ankle boot	*putin-e saaq kutaah*	پوتین ساق کوتاه
clothes; clothing	*pushaak*	پوشاک
sequin	*pulak*	پولک
shirt; (woman's) dress	*piraahan*	پیراهن
long-sleeved shirt	*piraahan-e aastin boland*	پیراهن آستین بلند
short-sleeved shirt; T-shirt	*piraahan-e aastin kutaah*	پیراهن آستین کوتاه
(woman's) dress; long dress	*piraahan-e boland*	پیراهن بلند
cardigan	*piraahan-e pashmi*	پیراهن پشمی

63

jersey	piraahan-e keshbaaf	پیراهن کشباف
sweatshirt	piraahan-e varzeshi	پیراهن ورزشی
pyjamas	pizhaameh	پیژامه
apron	pish daaman	پیش دامن
apron	pishband	پیشبند
alteration	taqyir	تغییر
headband; hair band	tel	تل
knickers	tonbaan	تنبان
knickers	tonekeh	تنکه
hairnet	tur-e mu	تور مو
shirt tail	tah-e piraahan	ته پیراهن
clothes; clothing; outfit	jaameh	جامه
armhole	jaa-ye aastin	جای آستین
waistcoat	jeliqeh	جلیقه
knee-length socks	juraab-e boland	جوراب بلند
knee-length socks	juraab-e saaq boland	جوراب ساق بلند
ankle socks	juraab-e saaq kutaah	جوراب ساق کوتاه
tights	juraab-e shalvaari	جوراب شلواری
nylon stockings	juraab-e naaylon	جوراب نایلن
pocket	jib	جیب
veil	chaador	چادر
headscarf	chaarqad	چارقد
boot	chakmeh	چکمه
riding boot	chakme-ye savaari	چکمه سواری
walking stick	chubdasti	چوبدستی
crease; pleat	chin	چین
creases	chin o choruk	چین و چروك
dry cleaning; dry cleaner's	khoshk shu'i	خشکشونی
crease (from ironing)	khatt-e otu	خط اتو
skirt	daaman	دامن
pleated skirt	daaman-e chindaar	دامن چین دار
culottes	daaman-e shalvaari	دامن شلواری
short skirt; mini-skirt	daaman-e kutaah	دامن کوتاه
gloves	dastkesh	دستکش
handkerchief	dastmaal	دستمال
low neckline; plunging neckline	dekolteh	دکلته
button	dokmeh	دکمه
slippers; slip-ons	dampaa'i	دمپائی

dressing gown	robdeshaambr	رب دشامبر
clothes horse	rakht pahn kon	رخت پهن کن
cloak	redaa	ردا
knee patch	ruzaanu'i	رو زانوئی
ribbon	rubaan	روبان
overall; smock; uniform	rupush	روپوش
school uniform	rupush-e madraseh	روپوش مدرسه
headscarf	ru sari	روسری
zip	zip	زیپ
(trouser) flies	zip-e shalvaar	زیپ شلوار
undergarment	zir push	زیر پوش
lingerie	zir push-e zanaaneh	زیر پوش زنانه
vest	zir piraahani	زیر پیراهنی
underwear	zir jaameh	زیر جامه
underskirt	zir daamani	زیر دامنی
jacket	zhaakat	ژاکت
gaiter	saaqband	ساق بند
hem	sejaaf	سجاف
cuff	sardast-e aastin	سر دست آستین
headband	sarband	سربند
made-to-measure	sefaareshi	سفارشی
buttonhole	suraakh-e dokmeh	سوراخ دکمه
bra	sineh band	سینه بند
shawl	shaal	شال
(neck) scarf	shaal-e gardan	شال گردن
nightcap	shab kolaah	شب کلاه
shorts; underpants	short	شرت
wash; washing	shostoshu	شست وشو
trousers; slacks; pants	shalvaar	شلوار
ski pants	shalvaar-e eski	شلوار اسکی
flared trousers	shalvaar-e paacheh goshaad	شلوار پاچه گشاد
tight trousers	shalvaar-e tang	شلوار تنگ
jeans	shalvaar-e jin	شلوار جین
cycling shorts	shalvaar-e dowcharkheh savaari	شلوار دوچرخه سواری
long johns	shalvaar sheykhi	شلوار شیخی
short trousers; shorts	shalvaar-e kutaah	شلوار کوتاه
corduroy trousers	shalvaar-e makhmal kebriti	شلوار مخمل کبریتی
shawl	shenel	شنل

cloak	'abaa	عبا
skullcap	'araqchin	عرقچین
walking stick	'asaa	عصا
jacket; bomber jacket	kaapshen	کاپشن
coat	kot	کت
sports jacket	kot-e espurt	کت اسپرت
tails	kot-e donbaaleh daar	کت دنباله دار
suit; jacket and trousers	kot o shalvaar	کت و شلوار
tie	keraavaat	کراوات
garter	kesh-e juraab	کش جوراب
shoe	kafsh	کفش
saddle shoes	kafsh-e aaksfurd	کفش آکسفورد
snow shoes	kafsh-e barfi	کفش برفی
court shoes	kafsh-e bi band	کفش بی بند
high-heeled shoes	kafsh-e paashneh boland	کفش پاشنه بلند
clogs	kafsh-e chubi	کفش چوبی
slippers	kafsh-e khaaneh	کفش خانه
slippers	kafsh-e raahati	کفش راحتی
espadrilles	kafsh-e kataani	کفش کتانی
climbing shoes	kafsh-e kuhnavardi	کفش کوهنوردی
trainers	kafsh-e varzeshi	کفش ورزشی
hat	kolaah	کلاه
beret	kolaah-e bereh	کلاه بره
bowler hat	kolaah-e derbi	کلاه دربی
top hat	kolaah-e silender	کلاه سیلندر
swimming cap	kolaah-e shenaa	کلاه شنا
felt hat	kolaah-e namadi	کلاه نمدی
waist	kamar	کمر
belt	kamarband	کمربند
girdle	kamarband-e zanaaneh	کمربند زنانه
bag	kif	کیف
handbag	kif-e dasti	کیف دستی
(woman's) handbag	kif-e zanaaneh	کیف زنانه
track suit	garmkon	گرمکن
espadrilles	giveh	گیوه
clothes; clothing	lebaas	لباس
spare clothes	lebaas-e ezaafi	لباس اضافی
ball gown	lebaas-e baalmaaskeh	لباس بالماسکه

woolen garment; woolens	lebaas-e pashmi	لباس پشمی
off-the-peg clothes	lebaas-e pish dukhteh	لباس پیش دوخته
nightgown	lebaas-e khaab	لباس خواب
second-hand clothes	lebaas-e dast-e dovvom	لباس دست دوم
tailcoat; morning suit	lebaas-e rasmi	لباس رسمی
undergarments	lebaas-e zir	لباس زیر
evening dress	lebaas-e shab	لباس شب
swimming costume	lebaas-e shenaa	لباس شنا
bikini	lebaas-e shenaa-ye dow tekkeh	لباس شنای دو تکه
one-piece swimming costume	lebaas-e shenaa-ye yek tekkeh	لباس شنای یک تکه
worn-out clothes; rags	lebaas-e mondares	لباس مندرس
edge; hem; lapel	labeh	لبه
stain	lakkeh	لکه
loincloth	long	لنگ
(woman's) full-length coat	maantow	مانتو
swimming trunks	maayow	مایو
fashion	mod	مد
haute couture	mod-e sath-e baalaa	مد سطح بالا
veil	maqna'eh	مقنعه
mini-skirt	mini zhup	مینی ژوپ
badge	neshaan	نشان
fashion show	namaayesh-e lebaas	نمایش لباس
jacket; top	nim taneh	نیم تنه
uniform	hamaapush	هم آپوش
collar	yaqeh	یقه
lapel	yaqe-ye kot	یقه کت
a pair of shoes	yek joft kafsh	یک جفت کفش
a suit of clothes	yek dast lebaas	یک دست لباس

I get dressed after breakfast بعد از صبحانه لباس می پوشم   to get dressed لباس پوشیدن   to wear پوشیدن

to undress لباس درآوردن   to take off در آوردن   put your clothes on! لباس تنت کن!   to put on تن کردن

to put on (one's feet) پا کردن   Ahmad put a hat on احمد کلاه سرش کرد   to put on (one's head) سر کردن

to pull up بالا کشیدن   to roll up (sleeves etc.) بالا زدن   to put on (one's hands, e.g. gloves) دست کردن

to get undressed; to strip لخت شدن   to pull down پائین کشیدن   pull your trousers up! شلوارت را بالا بکش!

to become dirty کثیف شدن   to dirty کثیف کردن   to clean تمیز کردن   to change clothes لباس عوض کردن

a new suit of clothes یک دست لباس نو   yesterday I bought a shirt من دیروز پیراهن خریدم   to buy خریدن

when I tried it I saw it wasn't my size وقتی امتحان کردم دیدم اندازه نیست   to try; to examine امتحان کردن

you must look after your clothes باید خوب از لباسهایت نگهداری کنید   to screw up مچاله کردن   to fold تا کردن

folded تا کرده   my trousers have lost their crease شلوار من از تا افتاده   to iron; to press اطو کردن

my shirt has a grease stain پیراهنم لکه چربی دارد   I took my clothes to the dry cleaner's لباسهایم را به خشکشوئی بردم

this skirt is the latest fashion این دامن مد روز است   lastest fashion مد روز   fashionable; in fashion مد

chic شیک   Ali is a very fashionable dresser علی مرد شیک پوشی است   well-dressed خوش لباس

badly-dressed بد لباس   all of my clothes are out of fashion تمام لباسهای من از مد افتاده اند   out of fashion دمده

those trousers don't suit you at all آن شلوار اصلا به شما نمیاید   that skirt suits you آن دامن به شما میاید

shapeless بی ریخت   loose گشاد   tight تنگ   what's your foot size؟ اندازه پای شما چیست؟

to patch وصله دوختن   you're wearing your shirt inside-out پیراهنت را پشت و رو پوشیدی

long بلند   these trousers are too long این شلوار زیادی بلند است   short کوتاه   too short زیادی کوتاه

fashion designer طراح لباس   this coat is no longer of any use این کت دیگر به درد نمی خورد   threadbare نخ نما

rags لباس پاره پوره   we gave our old clothes to charity لباس های کهنه مان را به خیریه دادیم

◄◄◊►►

Colours

رنگ ها

blue	aabi	آبی
sky blue	aabi-ye aasemaani	آبی آسمانی
purple	arqavaani	ارغوانی
mauve	arqavaani-ye rowshan	ارغوانی روشن
beige	bezh	بژ
violet	banafsh	بنفش
crimson	jegari	جگری
fawn	hanaa'i	حنائی
grey	khaakestari	خاکستری
mustard	khardali	خردلی
auburn	khormaa'i	خرمائی
yellow	zard	زرد
ochre	zard-e tireh	زرد تیره
maroon	zereshki	زرشکی
green	sabz	سبز
emerald green	sabz-e zomorrodi	سبز زمردی
olive green	sabz-e zeytuni	سبز زیتونی
scarlet	sorkh	سرخ
navy blue	sorme'i	سرمه ای
white	sefid	سفید
black	siyaah	سیاه
wine-coloured	sharaabi	شرابی
pink	surati	صورتی
gold	talaa'i	طلائی
grey	tusi	طوسی
turquoise	firuze'i	فیروزه ای
red	qermez	قرمز
maroon	qermez-e aalbaalu'i	قرمز آلبالوئی
crimson	qermez-e sir	قرمز سیر
brown	qahve'i	قهوه ای
black and blue	kabud	کبود
black (of hair)	meshki	مشکی
orange	naarenji	نارنجی
silver	noqre'i	نقره ای
indigo	nili	نیلی

nicely-coloured خوش رنگ   what a lovely colour! چه رنگ قشنگی !   what colour is it? چه رنگی است ؟

rainbow رنگین کمان   black and white سیاه و سفید   colour television تلویزیون رنگی   coloured رنگی

to change colour رنگ عوض کردن   to paint رنگ زدن   to colour (with crayons or pencils) رنگ کردن

light green سبز روشن   dark green سبز تیره   (a) light colour رنگ روشن   (a) dark colour رنگ تیره

light کم رنگ   dark پر رنگ   the colour green رنگ سبز   green-coloured سبزرنگ

reddish-purple ارغوانی مایل به قرمز   reddish مایل به قرمز   light red قرمز کم رنگ   dark red قرمز پر رنگ

to turn red; to blush قرمز شدن   a black man مرد سیاه پوست   a white man مرد سفیدپوست

my friend suddenly appeared دوستم یک دفعه سبز شد   to turn green; to sprout; to appear سبز شدن

she was as white as snow او مثل برف سفید بود   as white as snow مثل برف سفید   as white as snow به سفیدی برف

colourless بی رنگ   to bruise; to turn black and blue کبود شدن   multi-coloured رنگارنگ

his colour's come back رنگش بر گشته   he's become pale; the colour has drained from his face رنگش پریده است

whiteness سفیدی   redness قرمزی   the darkness of night سیاهی شب   blackness; darkness سیاهی

the leaves are turning brown برگها قهوه ای می شوند   to turn brown قهوه ای شدن   yellowness; jaundice زردی

to make yellow; (fig.) to shit one's pants (with fear) زرد کردن   to whiten سفید کردن   to redden قرمز کردن

different colours رنگهای مختلف   azure; cobalt blue لاجورد   luxuriant; green and thriving سرسبز

various shades of yellow سایه های مختلف رنگ زرد   different hues of red گونه های مختلف قرمز

pigment رنگیزه   blue with purple tints; blue with a hint of purple آبی با ته رنگ ارغوانی   tint ته رنگ

colour scheme رنگ بندی   pale; wan; colourless رنگ باخته   colouring; coloration; variegation رنگ آمیزی

to dye; to tinge; to stain رنگ زدن   dyer رنگرز   dyeing رنگرزی   all sorts of people همه رنگ آدم

❮◈❯

70

Computing

کامپیوتر

start	*aaqaaz*	آغاز
antenna	*aanten*	آنتن
latest model; newest system	*aakharin model*	آخرین مدل
graphics adaptor	*aadaaptur-e negaareh saazi*	آداپتور نگاره سازی
array	*aaraayeh*	آرایه
computer-literate	*aashenaa baa kaampyuter*	آشنا با کامپیوتر
super computer	*abar kaampyuter*	ابر کامپیوتر
information superhighway	*abar shaahraah-e ettelaa'aati*	ابرشاهراه اطلاعاتی
storage device	*abzaar-e haafezeh*	ابزار حافظه
active device	*abzaar-e fa'aal*	ابزار فعال
authorization	*ejaazeh*	اجازه
execution	*ejraa*	اجرا
executable	*ejraa pazir*	اجراپذیر
manager	*edaareh konandeh*	اداره کننده
file manager	*edaareh konande-ye faayel*	اداره کننده فایل
merge	*edqaam*	ادغام
mail-merge	*edqaam-e posti*	ادغام پستی
line communications	*ertebaataat-e khatti*	ارتباطات خطی
data communications	*ertebaataat-e daade-haa*	ارتباطات داده ها
archive	*arshiv*	ارشیو
ASCII	*aski*	اسکی
pointer	*eshaareh gar*	اشاره گر
time-sharing	*eshteraak-e zamaani*	اشتراک زمانی
problem; glitch	*eshkaal*	اشکال
troubleshooting; debugging	*eshkaal zadaa'i*	اشکال زدائی
information	*ettelaa'aat*	اطلاعات
booster	*afzaayandeh*	افزاینده
attachment	*elsaaq*	الصاق
template	*olgu*	الگو
algorithm	*alguritm*	الگوریتم
ALGOL	*algul*	الگول
public-domain (PD)	*emtiyaaz-e 'omumi*	امتیاز عمومی
feasibility	*emkaan paziri*	امکان پذیری
size	*andaazeh*	اندازه
screen size	*andaaze-ye parde-ye namaayesh*	اندازه پرده نمایش
paper size	*andaaze-ye kaaqaz*	اندازه کاغذ

71

italics	*itaalik*	ایتالیک
file creation	*ijaad-e faayel*	ایجاد فایل
work station	*istgaah-e kaari*	ایستگاه کاری
Internet	*internet*	اینترنت
load	*baar*	بار
loader	*baar konandeh*	بار کننده
download	*baargozaari-ye ru be-paa'in*	بار گذاری رو به پائین
tab; tabulation	*baarikeh*	باریکه
decimal tab	*baarike-ye e'shaari*	باریکه اعشاری
left-aligned tab	*baarike-ye bechap*	باریکه بچپ
right-aligned tab	*baarike-ye beraast*	باریکه براست
centred tab	*baarike-ye markazi*	باریکه مرکزی
auto tab	*baarike-haa-ye khodkaar*	باریکه های خودکار
spellcheck	*baazbini-ye emlaa*	بازبینی املاء
error checking	*baazbini-ye khataa*	بازبینی خطا
recovery	*baaz saazi*	بازسازی
voice recognition	*baazshenaasi-ye goftaar*	بازشناسی گفتار
game; computer game	*baazi*	بازی
arcade game	*baazi-ye sekke'i*	بازی سکه ای
adventure game	*baazi-ye maajaraa juyaaneh*	بازی ماجراجویانه
video game	*baazi-ye vide'o'i*	بازی ویدئونی
data retrieval	*baazyaabi-ye daade-haa*	بازیابی داده ها
superscript	*baalaa nevesht*	بالانوشت
superscript	*baalaa nevis*	بالانویس
database	*baank-e ettelaa'aati*	بانک اطلاعاتی
relational database	*baank-e ettelaa'aati-ye raabete'i*	بانک اطلاعاتی رابطه ای
home banking	*baankdaari-ye khaanegi*	بانکداری خانگی
bite	*baayt*	بایت
sector; partition	*bakhsh*	بخش
fragmentation	*bakhsh bandi shodegi*	بخش بندی شدگی
malfunction	*badkaari*	بد کاری
body; chassis	*badaneh*	بدنه
equalizer	*baraabar saazi*	برابرساز
set-up	*barpaa saazi*	برپا سازی
highlighting	*barjasteh saazi*	برجسته سازی
setting; setting-up	*barqaraar saazi*	برقرارسازی
data sheet	*barge-ye raahnamaa*	برگه راهنما
spreadsheet	*barge-ye gostardeh*	برگه گسترده

programme	*barnaameh*	برنامه
programmable	*barnaameh pazir*	برنامه پذیر
programmer	*barnaameh saaz*	برنامه ساز
computer programmer	*barnaameh saaz-e kaampyuter*	برنامه ساز کامپیوتر
computer programme	*barnaame-ye kaampyuteri*	برنامه کامپیوتری
cut and paste	*boridan o chasbaandan*	بریدن و چسباندن
interactive	*barham koneshi*	برهمکنشی
frequency	*basaamad*	بسامد
package	*basteh*	بسته
speaker	*bolandgu*	بلندگو
internal speakers	*bolandgu-ye daakheli*	بلندگوی داخلی
undelete	*bi asar saazi-ye hazf*	بی اثرسازی حذف
invalid	*bi e'tebaar*	بی اعتبار
bit	*bit*	بیت
bit-map	*bit negaasht*	بیت نگاشت
ejection (of disk)	*birun andaazi*	بیرون اندازی
BASIC (computer language)	*beysik*	بیسیک
improvement; upgrade	*behbud*	بهبود
optimization	*behineh saazi*	بهینه سازی
erasable; re-usable	*paak shodani*	پاک شدنی
footer	*paa nevesht*	پانوشت
end-of-file	*paayaan-e faayel*	پایان فایل
timeout	*paayaan-e vaqt*	پایان وقت
terminal	*paayaaneh*	پایانه
processing	*pardaazesh*	پردازش
information processing	*pardaazesh-e ettelaa'aat*	پردازش اطلاعات
processor	*pardaazandeh*	پردازنده
co-processor	*pardaazande-ye komaki*	پردازنده کمکی
screen	*parde-ye namaayesh*	پرده نمایش
split screen	*parde-ye namaayesh-e chandbakhshi*	پرده نمایش چند بخشی
file	*parvandeh*	پرونده
backspace	*pasbord*	پسبرد
electronic mail (e-mail)	*post-e elektruniki*	پست الکترونیکی
feedback	*paskhord*	پسخورد
back space	*pasrow*	پسرو
backslash	*pas kaj khatt*	پس کج خط
backup	*poshtibaan*	پشتیبان
window	*panjereh*	پنجره

active window	panjere-ye fa'aal	پنجره فعال
dynamic	puyaa	پویا
scan; scanning	puyesh	پویش
scanner	puyeshgar	پویشگر
flatbed scanner	puyeshgar-e mosattah	پویشگر مسطح
e-mail	payaam negaar	پیام نگار
prompt	payaamvaareh	پیامواره
pre-programmed	pish barnaameh saazi shodeh	پیش برنامه سازی شده
foreground	pish zamineh	پیش زمینه
default	pish farz	پیش فرض
prototype	pish nemuneh	پیش نمونه
configuration	peykareh bandi	پیکره بندی
reconfiguration	peykareh bandi-ye mojaddad	پیکره بندی مجدد
wideband	pahn navaar	پهن نوار
bandwidth	pahnaa-ye navaar	پهنای نوار
control panel	taablow-ye kontrol	تابلوی کنترل
fibre optics	taar nur shenaasi	تارنور شناسی
data analysis	tahlil-e daade-haa	تحلیل داده ها
motherboard	takhte-ye asli	تخته اصلی
clipboard	takhte-ye kaar	تخته کار
circuit board	takhte-ye madaari	تخته مداری
left alignment	taraaz-e be chap	تراز بچپ
right alignment	taraaz-e be raast	تراز براست
full justification	taraaz-e kaamel	تراز کامل
centred (justification)	taraaz-e markazi	تراز مرکزی
chip	taraasheh	تراشه
silicon chip	taraashe-ye silikuni	تراشه سیلیکونی
sequence	tartib	ترتیب
sequencing	tartib bandi	ترتیب بندی
amendment	tarmim	ترمیم
facilities	tas-hilaat	تسهیلات
error correction	tas-hi-ye khataa	تصحیح خطا
image	tasvir	تصویر
image processor	tasvir pardaaz	تصویر پرداز
image processing	tasvir pardaazi	تصویر پردازی
emulation	taqlid	تقلید
information technology	teknuluzhi-ye ettelaa'aat	تکنولوژی اطلاعات
closed circuit television	televiziyun-e madaar basteh	تلویزیون مدار بسته

environment settings	tanzim-haa-ye mohiti	تنظیم های محیطی
parity	tavaazon	توازن
adaptor	tavaafoq gar	توافقگر
ability; capability	tavaanaa'i	توانائی
title bar	tirak-e 'onvaan	تیرک عنوان
jargon; 'computerese'	jaargon	جارگن
tab; tabulation	jadval bandi	جدول بندی
computer crime	jorm-e kaampyuteri	جرم کامپیوتری
search	jostoju	جستجو
search and replace	jostoju va jaaygozini	جستجو و جایگزینی
global search	jostoju-ye saraasari	جستجوی سراسری
control box	ja'be-ye kontrol	جعبه کنترل
dialogue box	ja'be-ye goftogu	جعبه گفتگو
sound effects	jelve-ye sowti	جلوه صوتی
peripheral	janbi	جنبی
printed	chaap shodeh	چاپ شده
draft printout; draft copy	chaap-e nemune-ye avval	چاپ نمونه اول
printer	chaapgar	چاپگر
impact printer	chaapgar-e barkhordi	چاپگر برخوردی
default printer	chaapgar-e pish farzi	چاپگر پیش فرضی
inkjet printer	chaapgar-e jowhar feshaan	چاپگر جوهر فشان
daisy-wheel printer	chaapgar-e charkhi	چاپگر چرخی
line printer	chaapgar-e satri	چاپگر سطری
page printer	chaapgar-e safhe'i	چاپگر صفحه ای
character printer	chaapgar-e kaaraakter	چاپگر کاراکتری
laser printer	chaapgar-e leyzeri	چاپگر لیزری
multi-programming	chand barnaameh kaari	چند برنامه کاری
multi-tasking	chand taklif kaari	چند تکلیف کاری
multi-access	chand dastyaabi	چند دستیابی
multimedia	chand resaane'i	چند رسانه ای
multicolour	chand rang	چند رنگ
screen grab	chang andaazi-ye pardeh	چنگ اندازی پرده
margin	haashiyeh	حاشیه
memory	haafezeh	حافظه
main memory; primary storage	haafeze-ye asli	حافظه اصلی
back-up memory	haafeze-ye poshtibaan	حافظه پشتیبان
random access memory (RAM)	haafeze-ye dastyaabi-ye tasaadofi	حافظه دستیابی تصادفی (رم)
read-only memory (ROM)	haafeze-ye faqat khaandani	حافظه فقط خواندنی

video memory	haafeze-ye vide'o	حافظه ویدئو
delete; deletion	hazf	حذف
file deletion	hazf-e faayel	حذف فایل
upper case; capital letters	horuf-e bozorg	حروف بزرگ
account	hesaab	حساب
data protection	hefaazat-e daade-haa	حفاظت داده ها
copyright	haqq-e chaap	حق چاپ
loop	halqeh	حلقه
infinite loop	halqe-ye naa motanaahi	حلقه نامتناهی
external	khaareji	خارجی
capacitor	khaazen	خازن
logging off	khaamush saazi-ye sistem	خاموش سازی سیستم
server	khadamaat resaan	خدمات رسان
failure	kharaabi	خرابی
hardware failure	kharaabi-ye sakht afzaar	خرابی سخت افزاری
close; exit	khoruj	خروج
output	khoruji	خروجی
printout; hard copy	khoruji-ye chaapi	خروجی چاپی
electronic shopping; e-commerce	kharid-e elektruniki	خرید الکترونیکی
font	khat	خط
error	khataa	خطا
execution error	khataa-ye ejraa	خطای اجرا
fatal error	khataa-ye goriz naapazir	خطای گریزناپذیر
syntax error	khataa-ye nahv	خطای نحو
horizontal ruler	khatkeshi-ye ofoqi	خطکش افقی
stand-alone	khod ettekaa	خود اتکا
automatic	khodkaar	خودکار
internal	daakehli	داخلی
data processing	daadeh pardaazi	داده پردازی
data entry	daadeh dahi	داده دهی
manual entry	daadeh dahi-ye dasti	داده دهی دستی
data	daade-haa	داده ها
control data	daade-haa-ye kontroli	داده های کنترلی
port	darb	درب
printer port	darb-e chaapgar	درب چاپگر
parallel port	darb-e movaazi	درب موازی
insertion	darj	درج
tree	derakht	درخت

macro	dorosht dastur	درشت دستور
port; gateway	dargaah	درگاهی
image sensor	daryaaftgar-e tasvir	دریافتگر تصویر
software piracy	dozdi-ye narmafzaar	دزدی نرم افزار
joystick	dastaaneh	دستانه
device; machine	dastgaah	دستگاه
communications device	dastgaah-e ertebaati	دستگاه ارتباطی
peripheral device	dastgaah-e janbi	دستگاه جنبی
device driver	dastgaah raan	دستگاه ران
audio system; sound system	dastgaah-e sowti	دستگاه صوتی
order; command	dastur	دستور
instruction	dastur ol-'amal	دستور العمل
access	dastyaabi	دستیابی
remote access	dastyaabi az dur	دستیابی از دور
shared access	dastyaabi-ye eshteraaki	دستیابی اشتراکی
disk access	dastyaabi be-disk	دستیابی به دیسک
accessibility	dastyaabi paziri	دستیابی پذیری
serial access	dastyaabi-ye seri	دستیابی سری
rapid access	dastyaabi-ye sari'	دستیابی سریع
direct access	dastyaabi-ye mostaqim	دستیابی مستقیم
keypad	daste-ye kelid	دسته کلید
print resolution	deqqat-e chaapgar	دقت چاپگر
button	dokmeh	دکمه
binomial	dow jomle'i	دو جمله ای
binary	dow dowi	دودوئی
fax	dur matn	دورمتن
duplex	dow tarafeh	دوطرفه
disk; diskette	disk	دیسک
master disk	disk-e asli	دیسک اصلی
recovery disk; back-up disk	disk-e baazsaazi	دیسک بازسازی
head-cleaning disk	disk-e paak konande-ye hed	دیسک پاک کننده هد
fixed disk	disk-e saabet	دیسک ثابت
double-density disk	disk-e dow chegaal	دیسک دو چگال
disk drive	diskraan	دیسک ران
hard disk drive	diskraan-e sakht	دیسک ران سخت
high-density disk	disk-e ziyaad chegaal	دیسک زیاد چگال
hard disk	disk-e sakht	دیسک سخت
compact disk	disk-e feshordeh	دیسک فشرده

magnetic disk	disk-e meqnaatisi	دیسک مغناطیسی
floppy disk	disk-e narm	دیسک نرم
laser optical disk	disk-e nuri	دیسک نوری
diskette	disket	دیسکت
coded-decimal	dahdahi-ye ramz shodeh	دهدهی رمز شده
data storage	zakhire-ye daade-haa	ذخیره داده ها
run	raanesh	رانش
test run	raanesh-e aazmaayeshi	رانش آزمایشی
driver	raaneshgar	رانشگر
computer	raayaaneh	رایانه
printer driver	raah andaaz-e chaapgar	راه انداز چاپگر
start-up; boot	raah andaazi	راه اندازی
re-boot	raah andaazi-ye mojaddad	راه اندازی مجدد
help (file)	raahnamaa	راهنما
user manual	raahnamaa-ye kaarbar	راهنمای کاربر
graph plotter	rassaam-e negaare-haa	رسام نگاره ها
media	resaane-haa	رسانه ها
string	reshteh	رشته
digit	raqam	رقم
digital	raqami	رقمی
digitized	raqami shodeh	رقمی شده
database record	rekurd-e baank-e ettelaa'aati	رکورد بانک اطلاعاتی
code	ramz	رمز
error code	ramz-e khataa	رمز خطا
instruction code	ramz-e dastur ol-'amal	رمز دستورالعمل
access code	ramz-e dastyaabi	رمز دستیابی
binary code	ramz-e dowdowi	رمز دودوئی
character code	ramz-e kaaraakter	رمز کاراکتر
computer code	ramz-e kaampyuteri	رمز کامپیوتری
machine code	ramz-e maashin	رمز ماشین
encoder	ramzgozaar	رمزگذار
decoding	ramzgoshaa'i	رمزگشائی
screen dump	rubardaasht-e pardeh	روبرداشت پرده
laptop	ruzaanu'i	روزانوئی
updating	ruzaamad saazi	روزآمدسازی
brightness	rowshani	روشنی
overwrite; overwriting	ru-ye ham nevisi	روی هم نویسی
microprocessor	riz pardaazandeh	ریزپردازنده

microchip	riz taraasheh	ریزتراشه
microfiche	riz fish	ریزفیش
microfilm	riz film	ریزفیلم
microcomputer	riz kaampyuter	ریز کامپیوتر
macro language	zabaan-e dorosht dastur pazir	زبان درشت دستور پذیر
low-level language	zabaan-e sath-e paa'in	زبان سطح پائین
C (computer language)	zabaan-e si	زبان سی
subscript	zirnevis	زیرنویس
software development	saakht-e narm afzaar	ساخت نرم افزار
format	saakhtaar	ساختار
hacker	saareq-e ettelaa'aat	سارق اطلاعات
IBM-compatible	saazegaar baa aay bi em	سازگار با آی بی ام
compatibility	saazegaari	سازگاری
hardware compatibility	saazegaari-ye sakht afzaar	سازگاری سخت افزار
developer	saazandeh	سازنده
overflow	sar rizi	سر ریزی
header	sar-e safheh	سر صفحه
decryption	serr goshaa'i	سرّگشائی
refresh rate	sor'at-e baazniru dehi	سرعت بازنیرودهی
baud rate	sor'at-e baaowd	سرعت باود
clock rate	sor'at-e saa'at	سرعت ساعت
hacking; piracy	serqat-e ettelaa'aat	سرقت اطلاعات
series; serial	seri	سری
encryption	serri saazi	سرّی سازی
data encryption	serri saazi-ye daade-haa	سرّی سازی داده ها
command line	satr-e farmaan	سطر فرمان
hierarchical	selseleh maraatebi	سلسه مراتبی
document	sanad	سند
source document	sanad-e asl	سند اصل
computer literacy	savaad-e kaampyuteri	سواد کامپیوتری
CD	si di	سی دی
open system	sistem-e baaz	سیستم باز
interactive system	sistem-e barhamkoneshi	سیستم برهمکنشی
single-user system	sistem-e tak kaarbari	سیستم تک کاربری
multi-access system	sistem-e chand dastyaabi	سیستم چند دستیابی
expert system	sistem-e khobreh	سیستم خبره
knowledge-based system	sistem-e daanesh-e bonyaad	سیستم دانش بنیاد
operating system	sistem-e 'aamel	سیستم عامل

computer system	*sistem-e kaampyuteri*	سیستم کامپیوتری
directory	*shaakheh*	شاخه
default directory	*shaakhe-ye pish farzi*	شاخه پیش فرضی
hexadecimal	*shaanzdah shaanzdahi*	شانزده شانزدهی
network	*shabakeh*	شبکه
local area network (LAN)	*shabake-ye pushesh-e mahalli*	شبکه پوشش محلی
networking	*shabakeh saazi*	شبکه سازی
flight simulator	*shabih saaz-e parvaaz*	شبیه ساز پرواز
simulation	*shabih saazi*	شبیه سازی
computer simulation	*shabih saazi-ye kaampyuteri*	شبیه سازی کامپیوتری
slot	*shekaaf*	شکاف
expansion slot	*shekaaf-e gostaresh*	شکاف گسترش
file format	*shekl-e parvandeh*	شکل پرونده
sprite	*sheklak*	شکلک
serial number	*shomare-ye seryaal*	شماره سریال
numbering	*shomaareh gozaari*	شماره گذاری
web page; home page	*safhe-ye interneti*	صفحه اینترنتی
repagination	*safheh bandi-ye mojaddad*	صفحه بندی مجدد
title page	*safhe-ye 'onvaan*	صفحه عنوان
keyboard	*safhe-ye kelid*	صفحه کلید
computer industry	*san'at-e kaampyuter*	صنعت کامپیوتر
sonic; sound (adj.)	*sowti*	صوتی
toggle	*zaamen*	ضامن
computer-aided design	*tarraahi be komak-e kaampyuter*	طراحی به کمک کامپیوتر
layout	*tarh bandi*	طرح بندی
system design	*tarh-e sistem*	طرح سیستم
keyboard layout	*tarh-e safhe-ye kelid*	طرح صفحه کلید
scrolling	*tumaar namaa'i*	طومارنمائی
idle	*'aatel*	عاطل
random number	*'adad-e tasaadofi*	عدد تصادفی
computer science	*'elm-e kaampyuter*	علم کامپیوتر
troubleshooting	*'eyb yaabi*	عیب یابی
inactive	*qeyr-e fa'aal*	غیر فعال
write-protected	*qeyr-e qaabel-e neveshtan*	غیر قابل نوشتن
space; space bar	*faaseleh*	فاصله
line spacing	*faasele-ye miyaan satri*	فاصله میان سطری
file	*faayel*	فایل
master file; source file	*faayel-e asli*	فایل اصلی

random-access file	faayel-e dastyaabi-ye tasaadofi	فایل دستیابی تصادفی
batch file	faayel-e daste'i	فایل دسته ای
help file	faayel-e raahnamaa	فایل راهنما
records file	faayel-e rekord-haa	فایل رکوردها
file handling; filing	faayel gardaani	فایل گردانی
text file	faayel-e matni	فایل متنی
hidden file	faayel-e makhfi	فایل مخفی
command	farmaan	فرمان
edit command	farmaan-e viraayesh	فرمان ویرایش
read-only	faqat khaandani	فقط خواندنی
technical	fanni	فنی
font	funt	فونت
directory	fehrest	فهرست
file directory	fehrest-e faayel-haa	فهرست فایل ها
subdirectory	fehrest-e far'i	فهرست فرعی
inventory	fehrest-e mowjudi	فهرست موجودی
ability; capacity	qaabeliyat	قابلیت
format	qaaleb	قالب
formatting	qaaleb bandi	قالب بندی
unformatted	qaaleb bandi nashodeh	قالب بندی نشده
bad sector	qetaa'-e kharaab	قطاع خراب
power failure	qat'-e barq	قطع برق
line break	qat'-e khat	قطع خط
page break	qat' kardan-e safheh	قطع کردن صفحه
segment	qat'eh	قطعه
lock	qofl	قفل
light pen	qalam-e nuri	قلم نوری
domain	qalamrow	قلمرو
analogue	qiyaasi	قیاسی
cable	kaabl	کابل
task; work	kaar	کار
character	kaaraakter	کاراکتر
start-up; boot	kaarandaazi	کاراندازی
logging on	kaarandaazi-ye sistem	کاراندازی سیستم
user	kaarbar	کاربر
user-friendly	kaarbar pasand	کاربرپسند
use; usage	kaarbord	کاربرد
office use	kaarbord-e edaari	کاربرد اداری

cartridge	kaartrij	کارتریج
cassette drive	kaaset raan	کاست ران
computer	kaampyuter	کامپیوتر
office computer	kaampyuter-e edaari	کامپیوتر اداری
dedicated computer	kaampyuter-e tak manzureh	کامپیوتر تک منظوره
portable computer	kaampyuter-e haml pazir	کامپیوتر حمل پذیر
home computer	kaampyuter-e khaanegi	کامپیوتر خانگی
palmtop computer	kaampyuter-e dasti	کامپیوتر دستی
laptop computer	kaampyuter-e ru zaanu'i	کامپیوتر روزانونی
desktop computer	kaampyuter-e ru mizi	کامپیوتر رومیزی
personal computer	kaampyuter-e shakhsi	کامپیوتر شخصی
notebook computer	kaampyuter-e ketaabi	کامپیوتر کتابی
central computer; mainframe	kaampyuter-e markazi	کامپیوتر مرکزی
computerization	kaampyuteri saazi	کامپیوتری سازی
channel	kaanaal	کانال
manual	ketaab-e raahnamaa	کتاب راهنما
handbook	ketaab-e marja'	کتاب مرجع
password	kalame-ye ramz	کلمه رمز
key	kelid	کلید
exit key	kelid-e paayaan	کلید پایان
space bar	kelid-e faaseleh	کلید فاصله
escape key	kelid-e goriz	کلید گریز
shift key	kelid-e mobaddeleh	کلید مبدله
return key	kelid-e vaaredsaazi	کلید واردسازی
keyword	kelid vaazheh	کلید واژه
control	kontrol	کنترل
console	konsul	کنسول
COBOL	kobol	کوبول
acronym	kutah nevesht	کوته نوشت
high-specification	keyfiyat-e baalaa	کیفیت بالا
kilobyte	kilubaayt	کیلوبایت
kilohertz	kiluherts	کیلوهرتز
bus	gozargaah	گذرگاه
graphics	geraafik	گرافیک
address bus	gozargaah-e neshaani	گزرگاه نشانی
options	gozine-haa	گزینه ها
speech synthesizer	goftaar saaz	گفتارساز
memory capacity	gonjaayesh-e haafezeh	گنجایش حافظه

data capture	girandaazi-ye daade-haa	گیراندازی داده ها
gigabyte	gigaabaayt	گیگابایت
necessities; consumables	lavaazem	لوازم
matrix	maatris	ماتریس
dot matrix	maatris-e noqte'i	ماتریس نقطه ای
machine-readable	maashin khaandani	ماشین خواندنی
mouse	maaus	ماوس
mouse-driver	maaus gardaan	ماوس گردان
mouse-driven	maaus gardaandani	ماوس گرداندنی
italic	maayel	مایل
shift	mobaddeleh	مبدله
animation	motaharrek saazi	متحرک سازی
computer animation	motaharrek saaz-e kaampyuteri	متحرک سازی کامپیوتری
computer operator	motasaddi-ye kaampyuter	متصدی کامپیوتر
global variable	motaqayyer-e saraasari	متغیر سراسری
colour pallette	majmu'e-ye rang-haa	مجموعه رنگها
character set	majmu'e-ye kaaraakter-haa	مجموعه کاراکترها
(mathematical) computing	mohaasebeh	محاسبه
local	mahalli	محلی
environment	mohit	محیط
telecommunications	mokhaaberaat	مخابرات
coordinates	mokhtasaat	مختصات
display mode	mod-e namaayesh	مد نمایش
integrated circuit	madaar-e mojtama'	مدار مجتمع
parallel circuit	madaar-e movaazi	مدار موازی
programme manager	modir-e barnaame-haa	مدیر برنامه ها
memory management	modiriyat-e haafezeh	مدیریت حافظه
computer centre	markaz-e kaampyuter	مرکز کامپیوتر
data path	masir-e daade-haa	مسیر داده ها
re-route	masirdahi-ye mojaddad	مسیردهی مجدد
shareware	moshtarak afzaar	مشترک افزار
user-friendly	moshtari pasand	مشتری پسند
customization	moshtari pasand saazi	مشتری پسند سازی
specifications	moshakhasaat	مشخصات
categorization	maquleh bandi	مقوله بندی
memory location	makaan-e haafezeh	مکان حافظه
cursor	makaan namaa	مکان نما
megabyte	megaabaayt	مگابایت

83

megahertz	megaaherts	مگاهرتز
data source	manba'-e daade-haa	منبع داده ها
drop-down menu	menu-ye birun paraandani	منوی بیرون پراندنی
pull-down menu	menu-ye birun keshidani	منوی بیرون کشیدنی
engine; motor	motor	موتور
modem	mowdem	مودم
buffer	miyaangir	میانگیر
microphone	mikrufun	میکروفون
software engineer	mohandes-e narm afzaar	مهندس نرم افزار
incompatibility	naasaazegaari	ناسازگاری
name	naam	نام
nickname	naam-e saakhtegi	نام ساختگی
unjustified	naahamtaraaz	ناهمتراز
language syntax	nahv-e zabaan	نحو زبان
software	narm afzaar	نرم افزار
communications software	narm afzaar-e ertebaataat	نرم افزار ارتباطات
business software/application	narm afzaar-e tejaari	نرم افزار تجاری
accounting software	narm afzaar-e hesaabdaari	نرم افزار حسابداری
bundled software	narm afzaar-e ru-ye kaampyuter	نرم افزار روی کامپیوتر
integrated software	narm afzaar-e mojtama'	نرم افزار مجتمع
graphics software	narm afzaar-e negaareh saazi	نرم افزار نگاره سازی
backup copy	noskhe-ye poshtiban	نسخه پشتیبان
hard copy	noskhe-ye chaapi	نسخه چاپی
pirated copy	noskhe-ye qeyr-e mojaaz	نسخه غیر مجاز
digital signal	neshaanak-e raqami	نشانک رقمی
mouse	neshaangar-e mushvaareh	نشانگر موشواره
address	neshaani	نشانی
icon	neshaaneh	نشانه
benchmark	neshaane-ye me'yaar	نشانه معیار
desk-top publishing	nashr-e ru mizi	نشر رومیزی
installation	nasb	نصب
on-board	nasb shodeh	نصب شده
mapping	naqsheh namaa'i	نقشه نمائی
graph; graphics	negaareh	نگاره
graphic (adj.)	negaare'i	نگاره ای
computer graphics	negaareh saazi-ye kaampyuteri	نگاره سازی کامپیوتری
save; saving (of a file)	negaahdaari	نگاهداری
maintenance	negahdaasht	نگهداشت

icon	nemaad	نماد
display; demonstration	namaayesh	نمایش
screen display	namaayesh-e tasviri	نمایش تصویری
monitor; display	namaayeshgar	نمایشگر
colour display	namaayeshgar-e rangi	نمایشگر رنگی
video display	namaayeshgar-e vide'o	نمایشگر ویدئو
on-screen	namaayeshi	نمایشی
pie chart	nemudaar-e daayere'i	نمودار دایره ای
bar chart	nemudaar-e mile'i	نمودار میله ای
tape; cartridge ribbon	navaar	نوار
magnetic tape	navaar-e meqnaatisi	نوار مغناطیسی
oscillation	navasaan	نوسان
programmer; writer	nevisandeh	نویسنده
central processing unit (CPU)	vaahed-e pardaazesh-e markazi	واحد پردازش مرکزی
visual-display unit (VDU)	vaahed-e namaayeshgar-e didaari	واحد نمایشگر دیداری
word processor	vaazheh pardaaz	واژه پرداز
word processing	vaazheh pardaazi	واژه پردازی
virtual reality	vaaqe'iyat-e majaazi	واقعیت مجازی
conversion	vaagardaani	واگردانی
input	vorudi	ورودی
input/output (I/O)	vorudi khoruji	ورودی خروجی
voice input	vorudi goftaari	ورودی گفتاری
online	vasl khat	وصل خط
high-resolution	vozuh-e baalaa	وضوح بالا
low-resolution	vozuh-e paa'in	وضوح پائین
display resolution	vozuh-e namaayeshgar	وضوح نمایشگر
editor	viraastaar	ویراستار
editing	viraayesh	ویرایش
computer virus	virus-e kaampyuter	ویروس کامپیوتر
print head	hed-e chaap	هد چاپ
video conferencing	hamaayesh-e vide'o'i	همایش ویدئونی
World Wide Web (WWW)	hambaaf-e jahaani	همباف جهانی
justification	hamtaraaz saazi	همترازسازی
justified	hamtaraaz shodeh	همترازشده
compression	hamfeshaari	همفشاری
data compression	hamfeshaari-ye daade-haa	همفشاری داده ها
general-purpose; all-purpose	hameh manzureh	همه منظوره
artificial intelligence	hush-e masnu'i	هوش مصنوعی

hologram	hologeraam	هولوگرام
identity	hoveyyat	هویت
mnemonic	yaad aavar	یادآور
search and replace	yaaftan va jaaygozin saakhtan	یافتن و جایگزین ساختن

MORE COMPUTER TERMINOLOGY

to turn on; switch on روشن کردن   to turn off; switch off خاموش کردن   to boot; to start up راه اندازی کردن

to reboot راه اندازی مجدد کردن   to cut off; to abort قطع کردن   to enter (data etc.); to insert وارد کردن

to write نوشتن   to write a programme برنامه نوشتن   to design طرح کردن   to make; to build ساختن

to exit خارج شدن   to enter داخل شدن   to save ذخیره کردن   to type ماشین کردن   to type تایپ زدن

to edit ویرایش کردن   to copy نسخه برداری کردن   to correct تصحیح کردن   to open باز کردن

to close بستن   to find پیدا کردن   to press فشار دادن   to connect وصل کردن   to be connected وصل شدن

to be disconnected قطع شدن   to word-process واژه پردازی کردن   to e-mail پیام الکترونیکی فرستادن

to load بار کردن   to print چاپ کردن   to scan پویش کردن   to troubleshoot عیب یابی کردن

WORD-PROCESSING COMMANDS AND TERMINOLOGY

command فرمان   menu فهرست   triple line spacing فاصله میان سطری بزرگ

double line spacing فاصله میان سطری متوسط   single line spacing فاصله میان سطری معمولی

right column edge نشانه حاشیه گذار راست   right alignment نشانه تراز براست   left alignment نشانه تراز بچپ

right aligned tab نشانه باریکه براست   left aligned tab نشانه باریکه بچپ   decimal tab نشانه باریکه اعشاری

centred tab نشانه باریکه مرکزی   left margin marker نشانه حاشیه گذار چپ   file پرونده   edit ویرایش

new جدید   open... گشایش   save... بایگانی   save as... بایگانی جدید   delete... حذف پرونده

print... چاپ   page setup... صفحه آرائی   environment محیط   exit ترک   undo لغو   cut برش

copy کپی   paste جایگذاری   clear پاکسازی   export copy صدور کپی   restore بازگردان

move حرکت بده   size اندازه   minimize کوچک کن   maximize بزرگ کن   close خروج

switch to... برو به   find... یابش   find and replace یابش و جایگزینی   go to page... گشایش صفحه

character حرف   paragraph پاراگراف   section بخش   header سرورقی   footer پاورقی

insert section جایگذاری بخش   insert page break جایگذاری صفحه   insert page number شماره گذاری

style سبک   plain ساده   bold سنگین   underline زیرخط تاکید   italic مایل   font size اندازه خط

⟨⟨⟩⟩

Countries of the World

کشورهای جهان

Azerbaijan	aazarbaayjaan	آذربایجان
Argentina	aarzhaantin	آرژانتین
Albania	aalbaani	آلبانی
Germany	aalmaan	آلمان
Antigua and Barbuda	aantigvaa va baarbudaa	آنتیگوا و باربودا
Andorra	aanduraa	آندورا
Angola	aangulaa	آنگولا
Austria	otrish	اتریش
Ethiopia	etiyupi	اتیوپی
Jordan	ordon	اردن
Armenia	armanestaan	ارمنستان
Uruguay	orugu'eh	اروگوئه
Eritrea	eritreh	اریتره
Uzbekistan	ozbekestaan	ازبکستان
Spain	espaanyaa	اسپانیا
Australia	ostraaliyaa	استرالیا
Estonia	estuni	استونی
Israel	esraa'il	اسرائیل
Slovakia	esluvaaki	اسلواکی
Slovenia	esluveni	اسلوونی
South Africa	efriqaa-ye jonubi	افریقای جنوبی
Afghanistan	afqaanestaan	افغانستان
Ukraine	okraayn	اکراین
Ecuador	ekvaadur	اکوادور
Algeria	aljazaa'er	الجزائر
El Salvador	elsaalvaadur	السالوادور
United Arab Emirates	emaaraat-e mottahede-ye 'arabi	امارات متحده عربی
Indonesia	andunezi	اندونزی
Uganda	ugaandaa	اوگاندا
United States of America	ayaalaat-e mottahede-ye aamrikaa	ایالات متحده آمریکا
Italy	itaalyaa	ایتالیا
Iran	iraan	ایران
Ireland	irland	ایرلند
Iceland	island	ایسلند
Barbados	baarbaadus	باربادوس
Bahamas	baahaamaa	باهاما

Bahrein	bahreyn	بحرین
Brazil	berzil	برزیل
Burundi	borundi	بروندی
Brunei	berune'i	برونئی
Great Britain	britaaniyaa-ye kabir	بریتانیای کبیر
Belarus	belaarus	بلاروس
Belgium	belzhik	بلژیک
Bulgaria	bolqaarestaan	بلغارستان
Belize	beliz	بلیز
Bangladesh	banglaadesh	بنگلادش
Benin	benin	بنین
Bhutan	butaan	بوتان
Botswana	butsvaanaa	بوتسوانا
Burkina Faso	burkinaa faasu	بورکینا فاسو
Bosnia	busni	بوسنی
Bolivia	bulivi	بولیوی
Paraguay	paaraagu'eh	پاراگونه
Pakistan	paakestaan	پاکستان
Palau	paalaa'u	پالائو
Panama	paanaamaa	پاناما
Portugal	portaqaal	پرتغال
Peru	peru	پرو
Tajikistan	taajikestaan	تاجیکستان
Tanzania	taanzaaniyaa	تانزانیا
Thailand	taayland	تایلند
Taiwan	taayvaan	تایوان
Turkmenistan	torkmenestaan	ترکمنستان
Turkey	torkiyeh	ترکیه
Trinidad and Tobago	trinidaad va tubaagu	ترینیداد و توباگو
Togo	towgow	توگو
Tunisia	tunes	تونس
Tonga	tungaa	تونگا
Tuvalu	tuvaalaa	توالا
Jamaica	jaamaa'ikaa	جامائیکا
Solomon Islands	jazaa'er-e soleymaan	جزائر سلیمان
Marshall Islands	jazaa'er-e maarshaal	جزائر مارشال
Central African Republic	jomhuri-ye efriqaa-ye markazi	جمهوری افریقای مرکزی
Czech Republic	jomhuri-ye chek	جمهوری چک

Democratic Republic of Congo	jomhuri-ye demukraatik-e kongu	جمهوری دموکراتیک کنگو
Dominican Republic	jomhuri-ye duminikan	جمهوری دومینیکن
Djibouti	jibuti	جیبوتی
Chad	chaad	چاد
China	chin	چین
Denmark	daanmaark	دانمارك
Cape Verde	damaaqe-ye sabz	دماغه سبز
Dominica	duminikaa	دومینیکا
Rwanda	ruvaandaa	رواندا
Russia	rusiyeh	روسیه
Romania	rumaani	رومانی
Zambia	zaambiyaa	زامبیا
New Zealand	zelaand-e now	زلاند نو
Zimbabwe	zimbaabveh	زیمبابوه
Japan	zhaapon	ژاپن
Ivory Coast	saahel-e 'aaj	ساحل عاج
Western Samoa	saamvaa-ye qarbi	ساموای غربی
Sri Lanka	serilaankaa	سریلانکا
San Marino	san maarinu	سن مارینو
St. Kitts and Nevis	sant kit va nevis	سنت کیت و نویس
St. Lucia	sant lusiyaa	سنت لوسیا
St. Vincent and the Grenadines	sant vinsent va gerenaadin	سنت وینسنت و گرنادین
Singapore	sangaapur	سنگاپور
Senegal	senegaal	سنگال
Swaziland	sevaaziland	سوازیلند
Sudan	sudaan	سودان
Surinam	surinaam	سورینام
Syria	suriyeh	سوریه
Somalia	sumaali	سومالی
Sweden	su'ed	سوند
Switzerland	su'is	سوئیس
Sierra Leone	siraa le'un	سیرالئون
Seychelles	seyshel	سیشل
Chile	shili	شیلی
Iraq	'eraaq	عراق
Saudia Arabia	'arabestaan-e sa'udi	عربستان سعودی
Oman	'omaan	عمان
Ghana	qanaa	غنا

France	faraanseh	فرانسه
Palestine	felestin	فلسطین
Finland	fanlaand	فنلاند
Fiji	fiji	فیجی
Philippines	filipin	فیلیپین
Kirghizstan	qerqizestaan	قرقیزستان
Kazakhstan	qazzaaqestaan	قزاقستان
Qatar	qatar	قطر
Costa Rica	kaastaarikaa	کاستاریکا
Cambodia	kaambuj	کامبوج
Cameroon	kaamerun	کامرون
Canada	kaanaadaa	کانادا
Croatia	korvaasi	کرواسی
South Korea	kore-ye jonubi	کره جنوبی
North Korea	kore-ye shomaali	کره شمالی
Colombia	kolombiyaa	کلمبیا
Congo	kongu	کنگو
Kenya	kenyaa	کنیا
Cuba	kubaa	کوبا
Comoros	kumur	کومور
Kuwait	koveyt	کویت
Kiribati	kiribaati	کیریباتی
Gabon	gaabon	گابن
Gambia	gaambiyaa	گامبیا
Georgia	gorjestaan	گرجستان
Grenada	grenaadaa	گرنادا
Guatemala	gvaatamaalaa	گواتمالا
Guyana	guyaan	گویان
Guinea	gineh	گینه
Equatorial Guinea	gine-ye estevaa'i	گینه استوائی
Guinea-Bissau	gineh bisaa'u	گینه بیسائو
Papua New Guinea	gineh now paapvaa	گینه نو پاپوا
Latvia	laatvi	لاتوی
Laos	laa'us	لانوس
Lebanon	lobnaan	لبنان
Lesotho	lesutu	لسوتو
Luxembourg	lukzaamburg	لوکزامبورگ
Liberia	liberiyaa	لیبریا

Libya	libi	لیبی
Lithuania	litvaani	لیتوانی
Liechtenstein	likhtenshtaayn	لیخت انشتاین
Poland	lahestaan	لهستان
Madagascar	maadaagaaskaar	ماداگاسگار
Malawi	maalaavi	مالاوی
Malta	maalt	مالت
Maldives	maaldiv	مالدیو
Malaysia	maalezi	مالزی
Mali	maali	مالی
Hungary	majaarestaan	مجارستان
Morocco	maraakesh	مراکش
Egypt	mesr	مصر
Mongolia	moqulestaan	مغولستان
Macedonia	maqduniyeh	مقدونیه
Mexico	mekzik	مکزیک
Mauritania	muritaani	موریتانی
Mauritius	muris	موریس
Mozambique	muzaambik	موزامبیک
Moldavia	muldaavi	مولداوی
Monaco	munaaku	موناکو
Myanmar (Burma)	miyaanmaar	میانمار
Micronesia	mikrunezi	میکرونزی
Namibia	naamibiyaa	نامیبیا
Nauru	naa'uru	نانورو
Nepal	nepaal	نپال
Norway	norvezh	نروژ
Niger	nijer	نیجر
Nigeria	nijeriyeh	نیجریه
Nicaragua	nikaaraagu'eh	نیگاراگونه
Vatican City	vaatikaan siti	واتیکان سیتی
Vanuatu	vaanuaatu	وانواتو
Venezuela	venezu'elaa	ونزونلا
Vietnam	viyetnaam	ویتنام
Haiti	haa'iti	هائیتی
Netherlands	holand	هلند
India	hend	هند
Honduras	honduraas	هندوراس

Yemen	*yaman*	یمن
Yugoslavia	*yugoslaavi*	یوگسلاوی
Greece	*yunaan*	یونان

SOME RULES CONCERNING COUNTRIES AND NATIONALITIES

By adding ی to most of the countries in the list on the preceding pages, the adjective denoting nationality can be formed; by adding ی together with the indefinite article یک , the noun denoting a national of the country in question is formed. For example, adding ی to the word آلمان (Germany) gives آلمانی , i.e. 'German' , while یک آلمانی means 'a German' . Below are some examples, followed by a few exceptions to this rule.

زبان ایتالیائی the Italian language   زن ایرانی an Iranian woman   ماشین آمریکائی an American car

غذای یونانی Greek food   پارچه بلژیکی Belgian cloth   یک نروژی a Norwegian   یک دانمارکی a Dane

(When countries in Persian end in the letter ی (e.g. اندونزی , or Indonesia) the adjectival ی is not added to the word to make the nationality. There are, in fact, no strict guidelines as to what one should do in such cases: for some, the word اندونزی is used to denote both 'Indonesia' and 'Indonesian', while others add ائی to solve the problem, thus giving اندونزیائی . There are no hard and fast rules).

Exceptions to the above rules are few; below are the most salient examples:

یک ارمنی an Armenian	ارمنی Armenian	ارمنستان Armenia
یک ازبک an Uzbek	ازبک Uzbeki	ازبکستان Uzbekistan
یک بلغار a Bulgar	بلغاری Bulgarian	بلغارستان Bulgaria
یک عرب an Arab	عربی Arabic; Arabian	عربستان Arabia
یک انگلیسی an English man / woman	انگلیسی English	انگلستان England
یک ترک a Turk	ترکی Turkish	ترکیه Turkey
یک روس a Russian	روسی Russian	روسیه Russia
یک فرانسوی a French man / woman	فرانسوی French	فرانسه France
یک مغول a Mongol	مغولی Mongolian	مغولستان Mongolia
یک هندی an Indian	هندی Indian	هندوستان India

《◊》

In the Countryside

در دشت و صحرا

waterfall	aabshaar	آبشار
mill	aasyaab	آسیاب
hut	aalunak	آلونک
camping	ordu	اردو
province	ostaan	استان
market	baazaar	بازار
swamp; mire; bog	baatlaaq	باطلاق
thatched roof	baam-e gaali push	بام گالی پوش
bush	boteh	بته
tower	borj	برج
harvest	bardaasht	برداشت
grape harvest	bardaasht-e angur	برداشت انگور
wheat harvest	bardaasht-e gandom	برداشت گندم
pond	berkeh	برکه
leaf	barg	برگ
countryside; country	borun shahr	برون شهر
country (adj.)	borun shahri	برون شهری
desert; heath; countryside	biyaabaan	بیابان
countryside	birun-e shahr	بیرون شهر
thicket; coppice; grove	bisheh	بیشه
hedge	parchin	پرچین
walking; rambling	piyaadeh ravi	پیاده روی
picnic	pik nik	پیک نیک
signpost	taablow	تابلو
hill	tappeh	تپّه
snare; trap; noose	taleh	تله
torrent	tondaab	تنداب
tourist	turist	توریست
shooting	tirandaazi	تیر اندازی
telegraph pole	tir-e telefon	تیر تلفن
road; way; path	jaaddeh	جاده
asphalted road	jaadde-ye esfaalteh	جاده اسفالته
dirt road; dirt track	jaadde-ye khaaki	جاده خاکی
jungle; forest; wood	jangal	جنگل
forestation; forestry	jangalkaari	جنگل کاری
hunting permit	javaaz-e shekaar	جواز شکار

93

fishing permit	*javaaz-e maahigiri*	جواز ماهیگیری
tourist	*jahaangard*	جهانگرد
tent	*chaador*	چادر
ditch; puddle	*chaaleh*	چاله
pasture; meadow; grazing ground	*charaagaah*	چراگاه
spring (of water)	*cheshmeh*	چشمه
boot; walking shoe	*chakmeh*	چکمه
grass	*chaman*	چمن
field; pasture; lawn	*chamanzaar*	چمنزار
wood; stick	*chub*	چوب
walking stick	*chub dasti*	چوب دستی
fence; hedge	*hesaar*	حصار
thorn; bramble	*khaar*	خار
plain; heath	*khaardasht*	خاردشت
heath	*khaarestaan*	خارستان
earth; soil; dirt; dust	*khaak*	خاك
farmhouse	*khaane-ye dehqaan*	خانه دهقان
summer house; holiday home	*khaane-ye yeylaaqi*	خانه ییلاقی
ruins	*kharaabeh*	خرابه
youth hostel	*khaabgaah-e javaanaan*	خوابگاه جوانان
road; avenue	*khiyaabaan*	خیابان
cattle	*daam*	دام
door; gate	*dar*	در
tree	*derakht*	درخت
wood; grove; bower; thicket	*derakhtzaar*	درختزار
wood; grove; plantation	*derakhtestaan*	درختستان
gate; gateway	*darvaazeh*	دروازه
lake	*daryaacheh*	دریاچه
valley; glen	*darreh*	دره
fortress; castle	*dezh*	دژ
pothole	*dastandaaz*	دست انداز
plain; desert; heath	*dasht*	دشت
countryside	*dasht o sahraa*	دشت و صحرا
view; vista; panorama	*durnamaa*	دورنما
village	*deh*	ده
villages; countryside	*dehaat*	دهات
villager; peasant	*dehaati*	دهاتی
farmer	*dehqaan*	دهقان

hamlet	dehkadeh	دهکده
road; path; way	raah	راه
pathway	raah baarikeh	راه باریکه
dirt track	raah-e khaaki	راه خاکی
river	rudkhaaneh	رودخانه
village	rustaa	روستا
villager	rustaa neshin	روستانشین
villager; rural	rustaa'i	روستائی
farmer	zaare'	زارع
farming; agriculture	zeraa'at	زراعت
ground; earth	zamin	زمین
country woman	zan-e rustaa'i	زن روستائی
country life	zendegi-ye rustaa'i	زندگی روستائی
gendarme	zhaandaarm	ژاندارم
coast; riverbank	saahel	ساحل
inhabitant	saaken	ساکن
source	sar cheshmeh	سرچشمه
slope; incline	sar baalaa'i	سربالائی
noise	sar o sedaa	سرو صدا
stone; rock	sang	سنگ
pebble	sangrizeh	سنگریزه
hole	suraakh	سوراخ
barbed wire	sim-e khaardaar	سیم خاردار
hunting	shekaar	شکار
poaching	shekaar-e qeyr-e mojaaz	شکار غیر مجاز
hunter	shekaarchi	شکارچی
desert; plain; heath	sahraa	صحرا
rock	sakhreh	صخره
peace	solh o safaa	صلح و صفا
fodder; hay	'olufeh	علوفه
cave	qaar	غار
plateau	felaat	فلات
village	qaryeh	قریه
castle; palace	qasr	قصر
plot (of land)	qavaareh	قواره
castle	kaakh	کاخ
caravanserai	kaarvaansaraa	کاروانسرا
farmer	keshaavarz	کشاورز

95

farming; agriculture	keshaavarzi	کشاورزی
field (of crops)	keshtzaar	کشتزار
hut	kolbeh	کلبه
side; riverbank	kenaar	کنار
narrow path	kureh raah	کوره راه
(salt) desert	kavir	کویر
mountain	kuh	کوه
mountain dweller	kuh neshin	کوه نشین
foothills	kuhpaayeh	کوهپایه
mountaineering	kuhnavardi	کوهنوردی
mud	gel	گل
wild flowers	gol-haa-ye khodrow	گلهای خودرو
wheat	gandom	گندم
wheat field	gandomzaar	گندمزار
truck; van	maashin baari	ماشین باری
fisherman	maahigir	ماهیگیر
fishing	maahigiri	ماهیگیری
field; pasture; meadow	marta'	مرتع
country man	mard-e rustaa'i	مرد روستائی
lagoon; bog	mordaab	مرداب
farm	mazra'eh	مزرعه
hotel; inn; guesthouse	mosaafer khaaneh	مسافرخانه
quarry	ma'dan-e sang	معدن سنگ
estate	melk	ملک
stage (of a journey)	manzel	منزل
view	manzareh	منظره
panorama	manzare-ye tamaam namaa	منظره تمام نما
district; area	naahiyeh	ناحیه
fence; railing	nardeh	نرده
hilltop	nuk-e tappeh	نوک تپه
reed	ney	نی
stream	nahr-e aab	نهر آب
mountain stream	nahr-e kuhi	نهر کوهی
weather; air	havaa	هوا
summer residence; holiday home	yeylaaq	ییلاق

Crime and Punishment

جنایت و مجازات

fire	aatash	آتش
arsonist	aatash afruz	آتش افروز
arson	aatash afruzi	آتش افروزی
kidnapper	aadam dozd	آدم دزد
kidnapping; abduction	aadam dozdi	آدم دزدی
kidnapping; abductor	aadam robaa'i	آدم ربانی
murderer; killer	aadam kosh	آدم کش
murder; killing	aadam koshi	آدم کشی
addict	aadam-e mo'taad	آدم معتاد
murder victim	aadam-e maqtul	آدم مقتول
courtroom	otaaq-e daadgaah	اتاق دادگاه
visiting room	otaaq-e molaaqaat	اتاق ملاقات
gas chamber	otaaqak-e gaaz-e sammi	اتاقگ گاز سمی
accusation; charge	ettehaam	اتهام
fingerprint	asar-e angosht	اثر انگشت
warrant; permit	ejaazeh	اجازه
search warrant	ejaaze-ye baazrasi	اجازه بازرسی
embezzlement	ekhtelaas	اختلاس
deposition; statement	estesh-haad	استشهاد
questioning; interrogation	estentaaq	استنطاق
appeal	estinaaf	استیناف
forged banknote	eskenaas-e taqallobi	اسکناس تقلبی
statement; plea	ez-haar naameh	اظهارنامه
statement	ez-haariyeh	اظهاریه
confession	e'teraaf	اعتراف
libel; slander	efteraa	افترا
police officer	afsar-e polis	افسر پلیس
policeman; police officer	afsar-e shahrbaani	افسر شهربانی
legal proceedings	eqdaam-e qaanuni	اقدام قانونی
stolen goods	amvaal-e masruqeh	اموال مسروقه
revolution	enqelaab	انقلاب
revolutionary	enqelaabi	انقلابی
bribe	baaj-e sebil	باج سبیل
bribery; blackmail	baajgiri	باجگیر
interrogation; investigation	baazporsi	بازپرسی
cross-examination; inquiry	baazju'i	بازجونی

97

criminal investigation	baazju'i-ye jenaa'i	بازجونی جنائی
detention; custody	baazdaasht	بازداشت
police custody	baazdaasht-e polis	بازداشت پلیس
wrongful imprisonment	baazdaasht-e qeyr-e qonuni	بازداشت غیر قانونی
temporary confinement	baazdaasht-e movaqqat	بازداشت موقت
detention centre; prison	baazdaasht gaah	بازداشتگاه
child abduction	bacheh dozdi	بچه دزدی
dispute	bahs	بحث
inquiry; investigation; examination	bar resi	بررسی
delinquent	bezehkaar	بزهکار
delinquency	bezehkaari	بزهکاری
death row	band-e marg	بند مرگ
insurance policy	bimeh naameh	بیمه نامه
alibi	bahaaneh	بهانه
frame-up; set-up	paapush saazi	پاپوش سازی
policeman	paasebaan	پاسبان
police station	paasgaah	پاسگاه
patricide	pedar koshi	پدر کشی
frame-up; set-up	parvandeh saazi	پرونده سازی
appeal	pezhuhesh khaahi	پژوهش خواهی
bailiff	polis-e qazaa'i	پلیس قضائی
secret police	polis-e makhfi	پلیس مخفی
money	pul	پول
incident	pishaamad	پیشامد
acquittal	tabra'eh	تبرئه
crime; criminality	tabahkaari	تبهکاری
assault	tajaavoz	تجاوز
rape	tajaavoz-e jensi	تجاوز جنسی
rapist	tajaavozgar-e jensi	تجاوزگر جنسی
preliminary investigations	tahqiqaat-e moqaddamaati	تحقیقات مقدماتی
offence; breach; misdemeanour	takhallof	تخلف
penal offence	takhallof-e keyfari	تخلف کیفری
terrorist	terurist	تروریست
terrorism	terurism	تروریسم
demonstrator	tazaahor konandeh	تظاهر کننده
demonstration	tazaahoraat	تظاهرات
prosecution; pursuit	ta'qib	تعقیب
criminal prosecution	ta'qib-e jazaa'i	تعقیب جزائی

suspension of punishment	ta'liq-e mojaazaat	تعلیق مجازات
search	taftish	تفتیش
guilt; fault	taqsir	تقصیر
plea bargain	tavaafoq-e tarafeyn-e da'vaa	توافق طرفین دعوی
detention; custody; arrest	towqif	توقیف
spy	jaasus	جاسوس
criminal; convict	jaani	جانی
escaped convict	jaani-ye faraari	جانی فراری
reward	jaayezeh	جایزه
crime	jorm	جرم
criminology	jorm shenaas	جرم شناس
criminologist	jorm shenaasi	جرم شناسی
crime of passion	jorm-e shahvaani	جرم شهوانی
fine	jarimeh	جریمه
penalty; punishment	jazaa	جزا
corpse	jasad	جسد
forgery	ja'l	جعل
forger	ja'l konandeh	جعل کننده
forged	ja'li	جعلی
executioner	jallaad	جلاد
hearing	jalase-ye residegi	جلسه رسیدگی
criminal (adj.)	jenaa'i	جنائی
crime	jenaayat	جنایت
violent crime	jenaayat-e khoshunat aamiz	جنایت خشونت آمیز
criminal	jenaayat kaar	جنایت کار
kleptomania	jonun-e dozdi	جنون دزدی
pick-pocket	jib bor	جیب بر
knife-wielding thug	chaaqu kesh	چاقو کش
stabbing	chaaqu keshi	چاقو کشی
gallows	chube-ye daar	چوبه دار
imprisonment; detention	habs	حبس
life imprisonment	habs-e abad	حبس ابد
(imprisonment with) hard labour	habs baa a'maal-e shaaqqeh	حبس با اعمال شاقه
corrective imprisonment	habs-e ta'dibi	حبس تادیبی
solitary confinement	habs-e mojarrad	حبس مجرد
(Islamic) penalty; punishment	hadd	حد
trick; fraud; scheming	hoqqeh	حقه
trickster; con-man	hoqqeh baaz	حقه باز

ruling; sentence; decree; verdict	*hokm*	حکم
death penalty; death sentence	*hokm-e e'daam*	حکم اعدام
warrant for arrest	*hokm-e baazdaasht*	حکم بازداشت
verdict of not guilty; acquittal	*hokm-e baraa'at*	حکم برائت
search warrant	*hokm-e taftish*	حکم تفتیش
verdict	*hokm-e daadgaah*	حکم داد گاه
verdict	*hokm-e qaazi*	حکم قاضی
hanging	*halqaavizi*	حلق آویزی
attack; assault	*hamleh*	حمله
informant	*khabarkesh*	خبر کش
emergency services	*khadamaat-e ezteraari*	خدمات اضطراری
compensation; damages	*khesaaraat-e jobraani*	خسارات جبرانی
loss; damage	*khesaarat*	خسارت
violence	*khoshunat*	خشونت
petition; complaint	*daadkhaast*	دادخواست
prosecution; lawsuit	*daadkhaahi*	دادخواهی
judge; judicial investigator	*daadras*	دادرس
trial	*daadrasi*	دادرسی
public prosecutor	*daadsetaan*	دادستان
the prosecution	*daadsetaani*	دادستانی
public prosecutor's office	*daadsaraa*	دادسرا
court; tribunal	*daadgaah*	داد گاه
industrial tribunal	*daadgaah-e edaari*	داد گاه اداری
court of appeal	*daadgaah-e estinaaf*	داد گاه استیناف
revolutionary court	*daadgaah-e enqelaab*	داد گاه انقلاب
preliminary hearing	*daadgaah-e badvi*	داد گاه بدوی
court of appeal	*daadgaah-e pezhuheshi*	داد گاه پژوهشی
criminal court; crown court	*daadgaah-e jenaa'i*	داد گاه جنائی
magistrate's court	*daadgaah-e shahrbaani*	داد گاه شهربانی
kangaroo court	*daadgaah-e sahraa'i*	داد گاه صحرائی
divorce court	*daadgaah-e talaaq*	داد گاه طلاق
high court	*daadgaah-e 'aali*	داد گاه عالی
court of appeal	*daadgaah-e farjaam*	داد گاه فرجام
law court	*daadgaah-e qazaa'i*	داد گاه قضائی
military tribunal; court-martial	*daadgaah-e nezaami*	داد گاه نظامی
judiciary; administration of justice	*daadgostari*	داد گستری
(written) judgement; verdict	*daadnaameh*	دادنامه
reform school	*daar ot-ta'dib*	دار التادیب

gang	daar o dasteh	دار و دسته
dungeon	dakhmeh	دخمه
thief; robber	dozd	دزد
den of thieves	dozd baazaar	دزد بازار
theft	dozdi	دزدی
handcuffs	dastband	دستبند
criminal justice system	dastgaah-e keyfari	دستگاه کیفری
arrest	dastgiri	دستگیری
gang of thieves	daste-ye dozdaan	دسته دزدان
argument; fight; claim; litigation	da'vaa	دعوا
claim; litigation	da'vaa	دعوی
proof; reason	dalil	دلیل
pilfering; petty theft; larceny	daleh dozdi	دله دزدی
scheming; trickery	duz o kalak	دوز و کلک
highway robber	raahzan	راهزن
incident	rokhdaad	رخداد
bribe	reshveh	رشوه
criminal behaviour	raftaar-e tabahkaaraaneh	رفتار تبهکارانه
criminal psychologist	ravaanshenaas-e tabahkaari	روان شناس تبهکاری
prison governor	ra'is-e zendaan	رئیس زندان
chief of police	ra'is-e shahrbaani	رئیس شهربانی
fight; punch-up	zad o khord	زد و خورد
prison; jail	zendaan	زندان
jailer; prison guard	zendaanbaan	زندانبان
prisoner	zendaani	زندانی
gendarme	zhaandaarm	ژاندارم
gendarmerie; police station	zhaandaarmeri	ژاندارمری
criminal record	saabeqe-ye jenaa'i	سابقه جنائی
court house	saakhtemaan-e daadgostari	ساختمان دادگستری
thief	saareq	سارق
criminal organisation	saazmaan-e tabahkaari	سازمان تبهکاری
accident	saaneheh	سانحه
theft; robbery	serqat	سرقت
armed robbery	serqat-e mosallahaaneh	سرقت مسلحانه
weapon	selaah	سلاح
solitary confinement; isolation	selul-e enferaadi	سلول انفرادی
witness	shaahed	شاهد
religious law	shar'	شرع

101

lawful; legal (from Islamic viewpoint)	shar'i	شرعی
Sharia; Islamic law	shari'at	شریعت
accomplice	sharik-e jorm	شریک جرم
receiver of stolen goods	sharik-e dozd	شریک دزد
complaint	shekaayat	شکایت
torture	shekanjeh	شکنجه
torturer	shekanjeh gar	شکنجه گر
complaint	shekveh	شکوه
riot; insurrection	shuresh	شورش
crook; cheat; imposter	shayyaad	شیاد
evidence; testimony	shahaadat	شهادت
perjury	shahaadat-e doruq	شهادت دروغ
deposition; statement	shahaadat naameh	شهادت نامه
owner	saaheb	صاحب
minor	saqir	صغیر
electric chair	sandali-ye barqi	صندلی برقی
confiscation of property	zabt-e amvaal	ضبط اموال
surety; bail bond	zemaanat naameh	ضمانت نامه
justice	'edaalat	عدالت
common law	'orf	عرف
juror	'ozv-e hey'at-e monsefeh	عضو هیئت منصفه
amnesty	'afv-e 'omumi	عفو عمومی
indecent exposure	'owrat namaa'i	عورت نمائی
illegal	qeyr-e qaanuni	غیر قانونی
escape; evasion	faraar	فرار
tax evasion	faraar az pardaakht-e maaliyaat	فرار از پرداخت مالیات
fugitive	faraari	فراری
criminal culture	farhang-e tabahkaaraaneh	فرهنگ تبهکارانه
corruption; indecency; sleaze	fesaad	فساد
(Muslim) jurist; canon lawyer	faqih	فقیه
(Islamic) jurisprudence	feqh	فقه
murderer; killer	qaatel	قاتل
serial killer	qaatel-e zanjire'i	قاتل زنجیره ای
contract killer	qaatel-e qaraardaadi	قاتل قراردادی
smuggling	qaachaaq	قاچاق
smuggler	qaachaaqchi	قاچاقچی
judge	qaazi	قاضی
magistrate	qaazi-ye daadgaah-e shahrbaani	قاضی داد گاه شهربانی

law	qaanun	قانون
penal law	qaanun-e jazaa'i	قانون جزائی
criminal law	qaanun-e jenaa'i	قانون جنائی
law of the jungle	qaanun-e jangal	قانون جنگل
lawbreaker	qaanun shekan	قانون شکن
lawbreaking	qaanun shekani	قانون شکنی
law-abiding	qaanun shenaas	قانون شناس
civil law	qaanun-e madani	قانون مدنی
law and order	qaanun o nazm	قانون و نظم
lawmaker; legislator	qaanungozaar	قانونگذار
legislation	qaanungozaari	قانونگذاری
legal	qaanuni	قانونی
legality	qaaanuniyat	قانونیت
murder	qatl	قتل
premeditated murder	qatl-e 'amd	قتل عمد
manslaughter	qatl-e qeyr-e 'amd	قتل غیر عمد
murder	qatl-e nafs	قتل نفس
(law of) retribution	qesaas	قصاص
judgement; adjudication	qezaavat	قضاوت
judicial power	qove-ye qazaa'iyeh	قوه قضائیه
legislative power	qove-ye moqanneneh	قوه مقننه
uprising; revolt	qiyaam	قیام
armed uprising	qiyaam-e mosallahaaneh	قیام مسلحانه
hero	qahremaan	قهرمان
detective	kaaraagaah	کارآگاه
legal expert; jurist	kaarshenaas-e hoquqi	کارشناس حقوقی
reformatory	kaanun-e eslaah va tarbiyat	کانون اصلاح و تربیت
killing; slaughter; murder	kosht o koshtaar	کشت و کشتار
police station	kalaantari	کلانتری
con-man; trickster; crook; swindler	kolaah bardaar	کلاهبردار
attempt	kushesh	کوشش
escape bid	kushesh baraa-ye faraar	کوشش برای فرار
purse; wallet	kif-e pul	کیف پول
punishment; penalty	keyfar	کیفر
gangster	gaangester	گانگستر
criminal tendency	geraayesh be-tabahkaari	گرایش به تبهکاری
hostage	gerowgaan	گروگان
hostage-taking	gerowgaan giri	گروگان گیری

103

report	gozaaresh	گزارش
scuffle	galaavizi	گلاویزی
witness	govaah	گواه
swindle	gushbori	گوشبری
matricide	maadar koshi	مادر کشی
guillotine	maashin-e e'daam	ماشین اعدام
stolen property	maal-e serqat shodeh	مال سرقت شده
tax; taxes	maaliyaat	مالیات
police officer	ma'mur-e polis	مامور پلیس
undercover agent	ma'mur-e makhfi	مامور مخفی
acquitted	mobarraa	مبرا
accused	mottaham	متهم
punishment	mojaazaat	مجازات
death penalty; capital punishment	mojaazaat-e e'daam	مجازات اعدام
convict (n.)	mojrem	مجرم
criminality	mojremiyat	مجرمیت
trial	mohaakemeh	محاکمه
court of appeal	mahkame-ye estinaaf	محکمه استیناف
court of law	mahkame-ye qaanuni	محکمه قانونی
convict (n.); convicted; sentenced	mahkum	محکوم
conviction	mahkumiyat	محکومیت
penitentiary; penal colony	mahall-e mojaazaat	محل مجازات
evidence; document	madrak	مدرك
defendant	modda'aa 'alayh	مدعی علیه
death	marg	مرگ
dispute	moshaajereh	مشاجره
solicitor	moshaaver-e hoquqi	مشاور حقوقی
particulars; details	moshakhasaat	مشخصات
problem	moshkel	مشکل
suspended (e.g. sentence)	mo'allaq	معلق
clerk of the court	monshi-ye daadgaah	منشی دادگاه
drugs; narcotics	mavaad-e mokhaddereh	مواد مخدره
crime rate	mizaan-e jenaayaat	میزان جنایات
bailiff	naazem-e jalaseh	ناظم جلسه
rescue	nejaat	نجات
scuffle; set-to; quarrel; 'aggro'	nezaa'	نزاع
(prison) guard	negahbaan	نگهبان
criminal intent	niyyat-e jorm	نیت جرم

break-in	vorud-e be-'onf	ورود به عنف
Ministry of Justice	vezaarat-e daadgostari	وزارت دادگستری
lawyer	vakil-e daadgostari	وکیل دادگستری
criminal lawyer	vakil-e keyfari	وکیل کیفری
defence lawyer; barrister	vakil-e modaafe'	وکیل مدافع
revolver	haft tir	هفت تیر
accomplice	hamdast	همدست
air hijacking	havaapeymaa robaa'i	هواپیما ربائی
identity	hoveyyat	هویت
voyeur; peeping Tom	hiznegar	هیزنگر
hung jury	hey'at-e daavaraan-e mo'allaq	هینت داوران معلق
jury	hey'at-e monsefeh	هینت منصفه
rebel; mutineer	yaaqi	یاغی
legal assistance; legal aid	yaavari-ye hoquqi	یاوری حقوقی

SOME OTHER TERMS AND PHRASES CONNECTED WITH LAW AND ORDER

to kill کشتن   he stole money from me! از من پول دزدید!   to steal دزدی کردن   to steal دزدیدن

to detain بازداشت کردن   hands up! دستها بالا!   to arrest دستگیر کردن   to murder; to kill به قتل رساندن

to imprison زندانی کردن   to sentence; to convict محکوم کردن   to try (in court) محاکمه کردن

they gave me five years in jail برای من پنج سال زندانی بریدند   to be imprisoned زندانی شدن

to execute اعدام کردن   to torture شکنجه دادن   to punish مجازات کردن   to escape فرار کردن

house-arrest بازداشت منزل   to bear witness شهادت دادن   to take an oath قسم خوردن

to go to court دادخواهی کردن   to go to court به دادگاه رجوع کردن   to appear in court در دادگاه حاضر شدن

he was charged with murder او را به آدم کشی متهم کردند   what were the charges against him? اتهامات علیه او چه بود؟

he was acquitted او تبرئه شد   Ali appealed to a higher court علی به دادگاه بالائی درخواست پژوهش کرد

he was acquitted on all charges از کلیه اتهامات مبرا شد   his appeal was not granted پژوهش خواهی او مردود شناخته شد

they freed him from prison او را از زندان آزاد کردند   the court dismissed the charges دادگاه اتهامات وارده را رد کرد

the police searched his house but found no clues پلیس خانه او را جستجو کرد ولی مدرکی به دست نیاورد

a lawyer pleaded his case وکیل دعوی او را اقامه کرد   to plead guilty اتهام وارده را پذیرفتن

to question; to cross-examine بازجوئی کردن   the cross-examination lasted two hours بازجوئی دو ساعت طول کشید

escaped convicts زندانیان فراری   the police cross-examined the murderer پلیس از قاتل بازجوئی کردند

a series of abductions یک سری آدم دزدی   a series of mysterious killings یک سری آدم کشی اسرار آمیز

the jury is still out هینت منصفه هنوز رای نداده است   he pleaded 'not guilty' خودش را بی گناه اعلام کرد

to be held in custody تحت بازداشت بودن   he was sentenced to ten years in prison به ده سال زندان محکوم شد

he was freed on bail با قرار تامین آزاد شد   the sentence was ten years حکم دادگاه مبنی بر ده سال زندان بود

he is being held by the police او تحت بازداشت پلیس است   crime is on the increase جنایت رو به افزایش است

105

advertising agency	aazhaans-e tabliqaati	آژانس تبلیغاتی
advertisement	aagahi	آگهی
economic targets	aamaaj-haa-ye eqtesaadi	آماج های اقتصادی
notification	eblaaq	ابلاغ
advice	eblaaqiyeh	ابلاغیه
trades union	ettehaadiye-ye asnaaf	اتحادیه اصناف
lease; hire; rent; charter	ejaareh	اجاره
charterer	ejaareh konandeh	اجاره کننده
completion; execution	ejraa	اجراء
completion of contract	ejraa-ye qaraardaad	اجرای قرارداد
credit department	edaare-ye e'tebaaraat	اداره اعتبارات
financial administration	edaare-ye omur-e maali	اداره امور مالی
administrator	edaareh konandeh	اداره کننده
claim	edde'aa	ادعا
compensation claim	edde'aa-ye khesaarat	ادعا ی خسارت
insurance claim	edde'aa-ye akhz-e bimeh	ادعای اخذ بیمه
foreign currency	arz	ارز
hard currency	arz-e mohkam	ارز محکم
hard currency	arz-e mo'tabar	ارز معتبر
value; worth	arzesh	ارزش
nominal value	arzesh-e esmi	ارزش اسمی
surrender value	arzesh-e baazkharid	ارزش بازخرید
commercial value	arzesh-e tejaari	ارزش تجاری
capitalized value	arzesh-e sarmaaye'i	ارزش سرمایه ای
face value	arzesh-e zaaheri	ارزش ظاهری
customs value	arzesh-e gomroki	ارزش گمرکی
devaluation	arzkaahi	ارزکاهی
assessment	arzyaabi	ارزیابی
loss assessment	arzyaabi-ye mizaan-e khesaarat	ارزیابی میزان خسارت
dispatch; consignment	ersaal	ارسال
sales figures	arqaam-e forush	ارقام فروش
memorandum of association	asaasnaame-ye sherkat	اساسنامه شرکت
standard	estaandaard	استاندارد
reimbursement	esterdaad	استرداد
capital recovery	esterdaad-e sarmaayeh	استرداد سرمایه
depreciation	estehlaak	استهلاک

bank note	eskenaas-e baanki	اسکناس بانکی
documents	asnaad	اسناد
shipping documents	asnaad-e haml	اسناد حمل
excess; extra	ezaafi	اضافی
information; data	ettelaa'aat	اطلاعات
bill of entry	ez-haar naame-ye vorudi	اظهارنامه ورودی
credit	e'tebaar	اعتبار
open credit	e'tebaar-e baaz	اعتبار باز
commercial credit	e'tebaar-e baazargaani	اعتبار بازرگانی
bank credit	e'tebaar-e baanki	اعتبار بانکی
trade credit	e'tebaar-e tejaarat	اعتبار تجارت
bail credit	e'tebaar-e taht-e zemaanatnaameh	اعتبار تحت ضمانت نامه
investment credit	e'tebaar-e sarmaayeh gozaari	اعتبار سرمایه گذاری
personal credit	e'tebaar-e shakhsi	اعتبار شخصی
revolving credit	e'tebaar-e qaabel-e tajdid	اعتبار قابل تجدید
consumer credit	e'tebaar-e masrafi	اعتبار مصرفی
letter of credit; credentials	e'tebaarnaameh	اعتبارنامه
strike	e'tesaab	اعتصاب
acknowledgement of receipt	e'laam-e vosul	اعلام وصول
statement	e'laamiyeh	اعلامیه
delivery notice	e'laamiye-ye tahvil	اعلامیه تحویل
announcement	e'laan	اعلان
economic surplus	afzune-ye eqtesaadi	افزونه اقتصادی
economy; economics	eqtesaad	اقتصاد
market economy	eqtesaad-e baazaar	اقتصاد بازار
free market economy	eqtesaad-e baazaar-e aazaad	اقتصاد بازار آزاد
planned economy	eqtesaad-e barnaame'i	اقتصاد برنامه ای
money economy	eqtesaad-e puli	اقتصاد پولی
econometrics	eqtesaad sanji	اقتصاد سنجی
economist	eqtesaad daan	اقتصاد دان
economic	eqtesaadi	اقتصادی
action	eqdaam	اقدام
compulsory	elzaami	الزامی
trustee	amaanat daar	امانت دار
signature	emzaa	امضا
signatory	emzaa konandeh	امضا کننده
completion of contract	emza-ye qaraardaad	امضای قرارداد
capital assets	amvaal-e sarmaaye'i	اموال سرمایه ای

bonded warehouse	anbaar-e gomrok	انبار گمرک
stock keeper	anbaar daar	انباردار
transfer of goods	enteqaal-e kaalaa	انتقال کالا
monopoly	enhesaar	انحصار
liquidation	enhelaal	انحلال
expiry	enqezaa	انقضا
securities	owraaq-e bahaadaar	اوراق بهادار
bearer securities	owraaq-e bahaadaar-e binaam	اوراق بهادار بی نام
government securities	owraaq-e bahaadaar-e dowlati	اوراق بهادار دولتی
gilt-edged securities	owraaq-e bahaadaar-e momtaaz	اوراق بهادار ممتاز
grace period	ayyaam-e mohlat	ایام مهلت
creation of capital	ijaad-e sarmaayeh	ایجاد سرمایه
cargo; load	baar	بار
general cargo	baar-e motafarreqeh	بار متفرقه
bill of lading	baarnaameh	بارنامه
railway bill of lading	baarnaame-ye raah-e aahan	بارنامه راه آهن
clean bill of lading	baarnaame-ye saadeh	بارنامه ساده
bill of lading	baarnaame-ye keshti	بارنامه کشتی
market	baazaar	بازار
credit market	baazaar-e e'tebaar	بازار اعتبار
securities market	baazaar-e owraaq-e bahaadaar	بازار اوراق بهادار
free market; open market	baazaar-e aazaad	بازار آزاد
money market	baazaar-e pul	بازار پول
foreign market	baazaar-e khaarej	بازار خارج
domestic market	baazaar-e daakheli	بازار داخلی
capital market	baazaar-e sarmaayeh	بازار سرمایه
stock market	baazaar-e sahaam	بازار سهام
dumping	baazaar shekani	بازارشکنی
yield	baazdeh	بازده
commercial	baazargaani	بازرگانی
remainder	baaqimaandeh	باقیمانده
bank	baank	بانک
remitting bank	baank-e ersaal konandeh	بانک ارسال کننده
paying bank	baank-e pardaakht konandeh	بانک پرداخت کننده
savings bank	baank-e pasandaaz	بانک پس انداز
mortgage bank	baank-e rahni	بانک رهنی
issuing bank	baank-e saader konandeh	بانک صادر کننده
national bank	baank-e melli	بانک ملی

banking	baankdaari	بانکداری
economic sector	bakhsh-e eqtesaadi	بخش اقتصادی
debtor	bedehkaar	بدهکار
debt; debit	bedehi	بدهی
absolute liability	bedehi-ye motlaq	بدهی مطلق
ad valorem	bar hasb-e arzesh	بر حسب ارزش
bill; draft	baraat	برات
credit bill	baraat-e e'tebaari	برات اعتباری
banker's bill	baraat-e baankdaar	برات بانکدار
clean bill	baaraat-e bedun-e zamimeh	برات بدون ضمیمه
bill holder	baraat daar	برات دار
sight draft	baraat-e didaari	برات دیداری
drawer	baraat kesh	برات کش
drawee	baraat gir	برات گیر
advance bill	baraat-e mosaa'edeh	برات مساعده
inspection; checking; survey	bar resi	بررسی
market survey	bar resi-ye baazaar	بررسی بازار
checking of goods; quality control	bar resi-ye kaalaa	بررسی کالا
remittance slip	barg-e hesaab-e vajh-e ersaali	برگ حساب وجه ارسالی
invoice	barg-e forush	برگ فروش
debenture	barg o sanad-e qarzeh	برگ و سند قرضه
turnover	bargasht	برگشت
debit note	barge-ye bedehi	برگه بدهی
credit note	barge-ye bestaankaar	برگه بستانکار
cover note	barge-e vasiqeh	برگه وثیقه
economic plan; economic policy	barnaame-ye eqtesaadi	برنامه اقتصادی
economic planning	barnaameh rizi-ye eqtesaadi	برنامه ریزی اقتصادی
creditor	bestaankaar	بستانکار
remainder	baqiyeh	بقیه
long-term	boland moddat	بلند مدت
building society; real estate agency	bongaah-e mo'aamelaat-e amlaaki	بنگاه معاملات املاکی
budget	budjeh	بودجه
stock exchange	burs	بورس
stock market	burs-e sahaam-e arz	بورس سهام ارز
insurance	bimeh	بیمه
joint insurance	bime-ye eshteraaki	بیمه اشتراکی
cargo insurance	bime-ye baar	بیمه بار
underwriter	bimeh gar	بیمه گر

insurance policy	bimeh naameh	بیمه نامه
all-risks insurance policy	bimeh naame-ye tamaam khatar	بیمه نامه تمام خطر
spot rate	bahaa-ye baazaar	بهای بازار
interest	bahreh	بهره
bank interest	bahre-ye baanki	بهره بانکی
simple interest	bahre-ye saadeh	بهره ساده
bonus	paadaash	پاداش
payment	pardaakht	پرداخت
arrears	pardaakht-haa-ye mo'avvaq	پرداخت های معوق
export licence	parvaane-ye saaderaat	پروانه صادرات
savings	pasandaaz	پس انداز
recession; economic decline	pasraft-e eqtesaadi	پسرفت اقتصادی
cover	poshtvaaneh	پشتوانه
cover	pushesh	پوشش
money; currency	pul	پول
debt money	pul-e bedehi	پول بدهی
legal tender	pul-e qaanuni	پول قانونی
economic forecast	pishbini-ye eqtesaadi	پیش بینی اقتصادی
sales forecast	pishbini-ye forush	پیش بینی فروش
advance payment	pish pardaakht	پیش پرداخت
pre-dated	pish taarikh shodeh	پیش تاریخ شده
bid	pishnahaad-e kharid	پیشنهاد خرید
bidder	pishnahaad dahandeh	پیشنهاد دهنده
sealed bid	pishnahaad-e laak o mohr shodeh	پیشنهاد لاک و مهر شده
contractor	peymaankaar	پیمانکار
sub-contractor	peymaankaar-e far'i	پیمانکار فرعی
delay	ta'khir	تاخیر
date	taarikh	تاریخ
expiry date	taarikh-e enqezaa	تاریخ انقضاء
delivery date	taarikh-e tahvil	تاریخ تحویل
shipment date	taarikh-e haml	تاریخ حمل
date of maturity	taarikh-e sar resid	تاریخ سررسید
acceptance date	taarikh-e qabuli	تاریخ قبولی
cover	ta'min	تامین
confirmation	ta'yid	تایید
advertising	tabliq	تبلیغ
hard advertising; hard sell	tabliqaat-e tahaajomi	تبلیغات تهاجمی
trade; commerce	tejaarat	تجارت

foreign trade	tejaarat-e khaareji	تجارت خارجی
commercial	tejaarati	تجارتی
delivery	tahvil	تحویل
delivered	tahvil shodeh	تحویل شده
discount	takhfif	تخفیف
special discount	takhfif-e makhsus	تخفیف مخصوص
estimate of costs	takhmin-e makhaarej	تخمین مخارج
balance of payments	taraaz-e pardaakht-haa	تراز پرداخت ها
balance of trade	taraaz-e tejaarat	تراز تجارت
balance of foreign trade	taraaz-e tejaarat-e khaareji	تراز تجارت خارجی
balance sheet	taraaznaameh	ترازنامه
accumulation of capital	taraakom-e sarmaayeh	تراکم سرمایه
clearance	tarkhis	ترخیص
customs clearance	tarkhis az gomrok	ترخیص از گمرک
credit facilities	tas-hilaat-e e'tebaari	تسهیلات اعتباری
customs formalities	tashrifaat-e gomroki	تشریفات گمرکی
accident	tasaadof	تصادف
liquidation	tasfiyeh	تصفیه
average adjustment	tasfiye-ye khesaarat	تصفیه خسارت
devaluation	taz'if-e arzesh-e pul	تضعیف ارزش پول
money-back guarantee	tazmin-e baaz pardaakht	تضمین بازپرداخت
stock adjustment	ta'dil-e mowjudi	تعدیل موجودی
tariff	ta'refeh	تعرفه
customs tariff	ta'refe-ye gomroki	تعرفه گمرکی
commitment; agreement	ta'ahhod	تعهد
warranty; agreement; contract	ta'ahhod naameh	تعهدنامه
profit margin	tafaavot-e sud	تفاوت سود
demand	taqaazaa	تقاضا
payment demand	taqaazaa-ye pardaakht	تقاضای پرداخت
all-risks	tamaam khataraat	تمام خطرات
discount	tanzil	تنزیل
bank discount	tanzil-e baank	تنزیل بانک
cash discount	tanzil-e pul-e naqd	تنزیل پول نقد
trade discount	tanzil-e tejaari	تنزیل تجاری
arbitration agreement	tavaafoq bar hakamiyat	توافق بر حکمیت
inflation	tavarrom	تورم
stagflation	tavarrom-e rokudi	تورم رکودی
galloping inflation	tavarrom-e savaareh	تورم سواره

hyper-inflation	*tavarrom-e shadid*	تورم شدید
reflation	*tavarrom-e 'amdi*	تورم عمدی
economic development	*towse'e-ye eqtesaadi*	توسعه اقتصادی
appeal to arbitration	*tavassol be daavari*	توسل به داوری
gross domestic product (GDP)	*towlid-e naakhaales-e daakheli*	تولید ناخالص داخلی
gross national product (GNP)	*towlid-e naakhaales-e melli*	تولید ناخالص ملی
receipt counterfoil	*tah barg-e resid*	ته برگ رسید
cheque stub	*tah chek*	ته چک
handling	*jaabejaa'i*	جابجائی
handling of goods	*jaabejaa'i-ye kaalaa*	جابجائی کالا
compensation	*jobraan-e khesaarat*	جبران خسارت
tariff schedule	*jadval-e ta'refeh*	جدول تعرفه
cash flow	*jariyaan-e naqdi*	جریان نقدی
forgery	*ja'l*	جعل
permit; licence	*javaaz*	جواز
cheque	*chek*	چک
bounced cheque	*chek-e bargashti*	چک برگشتی
crossed cheque	*chek-e basteh*	چک بسته
dishonoured cheque	*chek-e bi mahal*	چک بی محل
stale cheque	*chek-e gozashteh*	چک گذشته
crossed cheque	*chek-e masdud*	چک مسدود
open cheque	*chek-e ma'muli*	چک معمولی
post-dated cheque	*chek-e va'deh daar*	چک وعده دار
accident; occurrence	*haadeseh*	حادثه
deletion	*hazf*	حذف
sale; clearance sale	*harraaj*	حراج
account	*hesaab*	حساب
savings account	*hesaab-e pasandaaz*	حساب پس انداز
current account	*hesaab-e jaari*	حساب جاری
deposit account	*hesaab-e sepordeh*	حساب سپرده
capital account	*hesaab-e sarmaayeh*	حساب سرمایه
sales account	*hesaab-e forush*	حساب فروش
auditor	*hesaabras*	حسابرس
audit	*hesaabresi*	حسابرسی
dues; fee; duty	*haqq*	حق
fee	*haqq oz-zahmeh*	حق الزحمه
commission	*haqq ol-'amal*	حق العمل
commission agent	*haqq ol-'amalkaar*	حق العمل کار

insurance premium	haqq-e bimeh	حق بیمه
option (to buy)	haqq-e kharid	حق خرید
brokerage; broker's fees	haqq-e dallaali	حق دلالی
road haulage	haqq-e 'obur	حق عبور
sole selling rights	hoquq-e forush-e enhesaari	حقوق فروش انحصاری
customs duties	hoquq-e gomroki	حقوق گمرکی
shipper; carrier	haml konandeh	حمل کننده
transport	haml o naql	حمل و نقل
combined transport	haml o naql-e tarkibi	حمل و نقل ترکیبی
multimodal transport	haml o naql-e chand now'eh	حمل و نقل چند نوعه
domestic transport	haml o naql-e daakheli	حمل و نقل داخلی
money transfer; money order	havaale-ye pul	حواله پول
delivery note	havaale-ye tahvil	حواله تحویل
overdraft	havaale-ye zaa'ed	حواله زائد
retail	khordeh forushi	خرده فروشی
purchase	kharid	خرید
buyer	kharidaar	خریدار
treasury	khazaaneh	خزانه
damages	khesaaraat	خسارات
damage; loss	khesaarat	خسارت
damage in transit	khesaarat dar hengaam-e teraanzit	خسارت در هنگام ترانزیت
general average (g/a)	khesaarat-e kolli	خسارت کلی
risk; danger	khatar	خطر
owner's risk	khatar-e ehtemaali-ye maalek	خطر احتمالی مالک
third party risks	khataraat-e shakhs-e saales	خطرات شخص ثالث
hedge; hedging	daad o setad-e ta'mini	داد و ستد تامینی
asset; assets	daaraa'i	دارائی
invisibles	daaraa'i-ye e'laam nashodeh	دارائی اعلام نشده
equity	daaraa'i-ye khaales	دارائی خالص
capital net worth	daaraa'i-ye khaales-e sarmaaye'i	دارائی خالص سرمایه ای
capital asset	daaraa'i-ye sarmaaye'i	دارائی سرمایه
assets	daaraa'i-haa	دارائی ها
assets and liabilities	daaraa'i-haa va bedehi-haa	دارائی ها و بدهی ها
fixed assets	daaraa'i-haa-ye saabet	دارائی های ثابت
current assets	daaraa'i-haa-ye jaari	دارائی های جاری
liquid assets	daaraa'i-haa-ye naqdi	دارائی های نقدی
real assets	daaraa'i-haa-ye vaaqe'i	دارائی های واقعی
(insurance) policy holder	daarande-ye bimeh naameh	دارنده بیمه نامه

bond holder	daarande-ye zemaanat naameh	دارنده ضمانت نامه
bona fide holder	daarande-ye mojaaz	دارنده مجاز
arbitration	daavari	داوری
income	daraamad	در آمد
inland revenue	daraamad-e daakheli	درآمد داخلی
national income	daraamad-e melli	درآمد ملی
gross income	daraamad-e naakhaales	در آمد ناخالص
gross national income	daraamad-e naakhaales-e melli	در آمد ناخالص ملی
appeal for tenders	darkhaast-e mozaayedeh	درخواست مزایده
collection of goods	daryaaft-e kaalaa	دریافت کالا
warranty of payment	dastur-e pardaakht	دستور پرداخت
forwarding instructions	dasturaat-e haml	دستورات حمل
audit office	daftar-e hesaabresi	دفتر حسابرسی
invoice book	daftar-e kharid	دفتر خرید
book-keeping	daftardaari	دفتر داری
receipts book	daftar-e daryaafti-haa	دفتر دریافتی ها
stock book	daftar-e zakhire-ye mowjudi	دفتر ذخیره موجودی
customs office	daftar-e gomrok	دفتر گمرک
broker; middleman	dallaal	دلال
money broker	dallaal-e pul	دلال پول
floor broker	dallaal-e taalaar-e burs	دلال تالار بورس
commission broker	dallaal-e haqq ol-'amalkaar	دلال حق العمل کار
customs broker	dallaal-e gomrok	دلال گمرک
brokerage	dallaali	دلالی
payback period	dowre-ye bargasht-e sarmaayeh	دوره برگشت سرمایه
delivery period	dowre-ye tahvil	دوره تحویل
demurrage	dir kard	دیر کرد
capital reserve	zakhire-ye sarmaayeh	ذخیره سرمایه
beneficiary	zinaf'	ذینفع
arbitration award	ra'y-e daavari	رای داوری
free of charge; gratis	raayegaan	رایگان
mortgager	raahen	راهن
interest	rebh	ربح
compound interest	rebh-e morakkab	ربح مرکب
receipt	resid	رسید
growth	roshd	رشد
economic growth	roshd-e eqtesaadi	رشد اقتصادی
bribe	reshveh	رشوه

consent	*rezaayat*	رضایت
competition; rivalry	*reqaabat*	رقابت
recession	*rokud*	رکود
bull (market)	*ru be-taraqqi*	رو به ترقی
bear (market)	*ru be-nozul*	رو به نزول
customs procedure	*ravesh-e gomroki*	روش گمرکی
market trends	*ravand-haa-ye baazaar*	روند های بازار
mortgage	*rahn*	رهن
leasehold mortgage	*rahn-e ejaare'i*	رهن اجاره ای
closed-end mortgage	*rahn baa moddat-e mo'ayyan*	رهن با مدت معین
blanket mortgage	*rahn-e 'omumi*	رهن عمومی
hypothecation	*rahngozaari*	رهن گذاری
loss	*ziyaan*	زیان
capital loss	*ziyaan-e sarmaayeh*	زیان سرمایه
non-profit organisation	*saazmaan-e qeyr-e entefaa'i*	سازمان غیر انتفاعی
financial year	*saal-e maali*	سال مالی
deposit	*sepordeh*	سپرده
demand deposit	*seporde-ye didaari*	سپرده دیداری
depositor	*sepordeh gozaar*	سپرده گذار
expiry date	*sar resid*	سر رسید
capital	*sarmaayeh*	سرمایه
borrowed capital	*sarmaaye-ye esteqraaz shodeh*	سرمایه استقراض شده
nominal capital	*sarmaaye-ye esmi*	سرمایه اسمی
registered capital	*sarmaaye-ye be-sabt resideh*	سرمایه به ثبت رسیده
fixed capital	*sarmaaye-ye saabet*	سرمایه ثابت
authorized capital	*sarmaaye-ye sabt shodeh*	سرمایه ثبت شده
capitalist	*sarmaayeh daar*	سرمایه دار
capitalism	*sarmaayeh daari*	سرمایه داری
working capital	*sarmaayeh dar gardesh*	سرمایه در گردش
capitalization	*sarmaayeh saazi*	سرمایه سازی
investor	*sarmaayeh gozaar*	سرمایه گذار
investment	*sarmaayeh gozaari*	سرمایه گذاری
foreign investment	*sarmaayeh gozaari-ye khaareji*	سرمایه گذاری خارجی
equity capital	*sarmaaye-ye maali*	سرمایه مالی
order	*sefaaresh*	سفارش
promissory note	*safteh*	سفته
stock jobber	*safteh baaz*	سفته باز
deed; document; bill	*sanad*	سند

deed of transfer	sanad-e enteqaal	سند انتقال
indemnity bond	sanad-e pardaakht-e qaraamat	سند پرداخت غرامت
waybill	sanad-e haml	سند حمل
forgery	sanadsaazi	سند سازی
bill of sale	sanad-e forush	سند فروش
bond; debenture	sanad-e qarzeh	سند قرضه
debenture bond	sanad-e qarze-ye bi tazmin	سند قرضه بی تضمین
government bond	sanad-e qarze-ye dowlati	سند قرضه دولتی
mortgage bond	sanad-e qarze-ye rahni	سند قرضه رهنی
public bond	sanad-e qarze-ye 'omumi	سند قرضه عمومی
profit	sud	سود
dividend	sud-e sahaam	سود سهام
year-end dividend	sud-e sahaam-e paayan-e saal	سود سهام پایان سال
stock dividend	sud-e sahaam-e sarmaayeh	سود سهام سرمایه
extra dividend	sud-e sahaam-e fowq ol-'aadeh	سود سهام فوق العاده
stock dividend	sud-e sahm	سود سهم
profit and loss	sud o ziyaan	سود و زیان
economic policy	siyaasat-e eqtesaadi	سیاست اقتصادی
fiscal policy	siyaasat-e maali	سیاست مالی
invoice	siyaaheh	سیاهه
monetary system	sistem-e puli	سیستم پولی
shares	sahaam	سهام
ordinary shares	sahaam-e 'aadi	سهام عادی
stocks	sahaam-e maal ot-tejaareh	سهام مال التجاره
preference shares	sahaam-e momtaaz	سهام ممتاز
deferred shares	sahaam-e mo'akhar	سهام موخر
shareholder	sahaamdaar	سهامدار
stock; share	sahm	سهم
guaranteed stock	sahm-e tazmin shodeh	سهم تضمین شده
fully-paid stock	sahm-e tamaam pardaakht shodeh	سهم تمام پرداخت شده
authorized stock	sahm-e sabt shodeh	سهم ثبت شده
bonus stock	sahm-e jaayezeh	سهم جایزه
bond holder	sahmdaar	سهم دار
voting stock	sahm-e ra'y daar	سهم رای دار
capital stock	sahm-e sarmaaye'i	سهم سرمایه ای
inactive stock	sahm-e qeyr-e fa'aal	سهم غیر فعال
classified stock	sahm-e far'i	سهم فرعی
active stock	sahm-e fa'aal	سهم فعال

116

debenture stock	sahm-e qarzeh	سهم قرضه
cumulative preference shares	sahm-e momtaaz-e anbaashtani	سهم ممتاز انباشتنی
quota	sahmiyeh	سهمیه
index	shaakhes	شاخص
retail price index	shaakhes-e bahaa-ye khordeforushi	شاخص بهای خرده فروشی
cost of living index	shaakhes-e hazine-ye zendegi	شاخص هزینه زندگی
third party	shakhs-e saales	شخص ثالث
partnership	sheraakat	شراکت
credit terms	sharaa'et-e e'tebaar	شرائط اعتبار
clause; condition	shart	شرط
waiver clause	shart-e esqaat-e haqq	شرط اسقاط حق
escalation clause	shart-e afzaayesh-e bahaa	شرط افزایش بها
escape clause	shart-e ta'allol	شرط تعلل
arbitration clause	shart-e hakamiyat	شرط حکمیت
forfeiture clause	shart-e zarar	شرط ضرر
cancellation clause	shart-e faskh	شرط فسخ
escape clause	shart-e goriz	شرط گریز
company	sherkat	شرکت
parent company	sherkat-e asli	شرکت اصلی
insurance company	sherkat-e bimeh	شرکت بیمه
multi-national company	sherkat-e chand melliyati	شرکت چند ملیتی
shipping company	sherkat-e keshtiraani	شرکت کشتیرانی
parent company	sherkaat-e maadar	شرکت مادر
articles of association	sherkat naameh	شرکت نامه
sleeping partner; backer	sharik-e qeyr-e fa'aal	شریک غیر فعال
branch	sho'beh	شعبه
complaint	shekaayat	شکایت
stock holder	saaheb-e sahm	صاحب سهم
exports	saaderaat	صادرات
invisible exports	saaderaat-e naa aashkaar	صادرات نا آشکار
bond issue	sodur-e owraaq-e qarzeh	صدور اوراق قرضه
pension fund	sanduq-e baazneshastegi	صندوق بازنشستگی
bill; invoice	surat hesaab	صورتحساب
bunker adjustment factor	zarib-e ta'dil-e sukht	ضریب تعدیل سوخت
guarantee; warranty	zemaanat	ضمانت
bank bond	zemaanat-e baanki	ضمانت بانکی
performance guarantee	zemaanat-e hosn-e anjaam-e kaar	ضمانت حسن انجام کار
contract guarantee	zemaanat-e qaraardaad	ضمانت قرارداد

bail bond	zemaanat naameh	ضمانت نامه
addendum	zamimeh	ضمیمه
terms and conditions	zavaabet o sharaa'et	ضوابط و شرایط
claim	talab	طلب
creditor	talabkaar	طلبکار
load	zarfiyat	ظرفیت
endorsement	zahrnevisi	ظهرنویسی
factor; agent	'aamel	عامل
factoring	'aameliyat	عاملیت
traffic	'obur o morur	عبور و مرور
transit (adj.)	'oburi	عبوری
insolvency	'ajz dar pardaakht-e doyun	عجز در پرداخت دیون
failure to pay	'adam-e tavaanaa'i-ye pardaakht	عدم توانائی پرداخت
supply and demand	'arzeh va taqaazaa	عرضه و تقاضا
trade mark	'alaamat-e tejaari	علامت تجاری
wholesale	'omdeh forushi	عمده فروشی
dues	'avaarez	عوارض
berthage	'avaarez-e eskeleh	عوارض اسکله
wharfage; dockage	'avaarez-e baarandaazi	عوارض باراندازی
customs duties	'avaarez-e gomroki	عوارض گمرکی
defect	'eyb	عیب
compensation; indemnity	qaraamat	غرامت
non-negotiable	qeyr-e qaabel-e mo'aameleh	غیر قابل معامله
perishable	faased shodani	فاسد شدنی
duty-free	faaqed-e hoquq-e gomroki	فاقد حقوق گمرکی
tax evasion	faraar az pardaakht-e maaliyaat	فرار از پرداخت مالیات
sender	ferestandeh	فرستنده
wear and tear	farsudegi va saa'idegi	فرسودگی و سانیدگی
vendor; seller	forushandeh	فروشنده
loading space; loading bay	fazaa-ye qaabel-e baargiri	فضای قابل بارگیری
inventory	fehrest-e mowjudi	فهرست موجودی
negotiable	qaabel-e mo'aameleh	قابل معامله
statute of limitation	qaa'ede-ye morur-e zamaan	قاعده مرور زمان
law	qaanun	قانون
commercial law	qaanun-e tejaarat	قانون تجارت
law of contract	qaanun-e qaraardaad	قانون قرارداد
borrower's note	qabz-e bedehkaari	قبض بدهکاری
acknowledgement of debt	qabul-e bedehi	قبول بدهی

admission of liability	qabul-e ta'ahhodaat	قبول تعهدات
acceptance	qabuli	قبولی
contract	qaraardaad	قرارداد
sales contract	qaraardaad-e forush	قرارداد فروش
loan; debt	qarz	قرض
bearer bond	qarz-e bedun-e naam	قرض بدون نام
national debt	qarz-e melli	قرض ملی
debt	qarzeh	قرضه
national debt	qarze-ye melli	قرضه ملی
debt items	qalam-e bedehkaar	قلم بدهکار
trade restrictions; trade barrier	qeyd o band-e tejaarati	قید و بند تجارتی
price; cost	qeymat	قیمت
standard price	qeymat-e estaandaard	قیمت استاندارد
offering price	qeymat-e pishnahaadi	قیمت پیشنهادی
cost price	qeymat-e tamaam shodeh	قیمت تمام شده
fixed selling price	qeymat-e saabet-e forush	قیمت ثابت فروش
retail price	qeymat-e khordeh forushi	قیمت خرده فروشی
buying price	qeymat-e kharid	قیمت خرید
invoice price	qeymat-e siyaaheh	قیمت سیاهه
wholesale price	qeymat-e 'omdeh forushi	قیمت عمده فروشی
sale price	qeymat-e forush	قیمت فروش
fixed price	qeymat-e maqtu'	قیمت مقطوع
cost and freight	qeymat o hazine-ye haml	قیمت و هزینه حمل
entrepreneur	kaaraafarin	کار آفرین
cartel	kaartel	کارتل
broker	kaargozaar	کارگزار
commission	kaarmozd	کارمزد
commodity; goods	kaalaa	کالا
merchandise	kaalaa-ye tejaarati	کالای تجارتی
business goods	kaalaa-ye towlidi	کالای تولیدی
goods in transit	kaalaa-ye dar raah	کالای در راه
capital goods	kaalaa-ye sarmaaye'i	کالای سرمایه ای
smuggled goods; contraband	kaalaa-ye qaachaaq	کالای قاچاق
consumer goods	kaalaa-ye masrafi	کالای مصرفی
trade gap; trade deficit	kasri-ye tejaarati	کسری تجارتی
elasticity of demand	keshesh-e taqaazaa	کشش تقاضا
home country	keshvar-e asli	کشور اصلی
forwarding country	keshvar-e ferestandeh	کشور فرستنده

host nation	keshvar-e mizbaan	کشور میزبان
shortage	kambud	کمبود
subsidies	komak-haa-ye maali	کمک های مالی
arbitration committee	komite-ye daavari	کمیته داوری
exchange control	kontrol-e arzi	کنترل ارزی
credit control	kontrol-e e'tebaar	کنترل اعتبار
marketing audit	kontrol-e daakheli	کنترل داخلی
checks and balances	kontrol o moqaabeleh	کنترل و مقابله
consortium	konsorsiyum	کنسرسیوم
bank consortium	konsorsiyum-e baanki	کنسرسیوم بانکی
short-term	kutaah moddat	کوتاه مدت
flow; circulation; turnover	gardesh	گردش
capital turnover	gardesh-e sarmaayeh	گردش سرمایه
invested turnover	gardesh-e sarmaayeh gozaari shodeh	گردش سرمایه گذاری شده
labour turnover	gardesh-e kaar	گردش کار
merchandise turnover	gardesh-e kaalaa-haa-ye tejaari	گردش کالاهای تجاری
turnover	gardesh-e mo'aamelaat	گردش معاملات
inventory turnover	gardesh-e mowjudi	گردش موجودی
cash flow	gardesh-e vojuh	گردش وجوه
financial statement	gozaaresh-e maali	گزارش مالی
customs	gomrok	گمرک
customs	gomrokaat	گمرکات
certificate	govaahi	گواهی
probate	govaahi-ye enhesaar-e veraasat	گواهی انحصار وراثت
certificate of inspection	govaahi-ye baazresi	گواهی بازرسی
insurance certificate	govaahi-ye bimeh	گواهی بیمه
debenture certificate	govaahi-ye qarzeh	گواهی قرضه
certificate of origin	govaahi-ye mabda'	گواهی مبداء
certificate of weight	govaahi-ye vazn	گواهی وزن
certificate of receipt	govaahi-ye vosul	گواهی وصول
recipient; addressee; consignee	girandeh	گیرنده
cancellation; annulment	laqv	لغو
clause (in a contract)	maaddeh	ماده
ownership	maalekiyat	مالکیت
tax; taxes	maaliyaat	مالیات
surcharge	maaliyaat-e ezaafi	مالیات اضافی
inheritance tax; probate duty	maaliyaat-e bar ers	مالیات بر ارث
value-added tax (VAT)	maaliyaat-e bar arzesh afzudeh	مالیات بر ارزش افزوده

income tax	maaliyaat-e bar daraamad	مالیات بر در آمد
balance	maandeh	مانده
debit balance	maande-ye bedehkaar	مانده بدهکار
credit balance	maande-ye bestaankaar	مانده بستانکار
balance on current account	maande-ye hesaab-e jaari	مانده حساب جاری
exchange; barter	mobaadeleh	مبادله
shipper	mobaasher-e haml	مباشر حمل
amount; sum	mablaq	مبلغ
deductible (amount)	mablaq-e qaabel-e kasr	مبلغ قابل کسر
actuary	motakhasses-e bimeh	متخصص بیمه
forwarder	motasaddi-ye haml o naql	متصدی حمل و نقل
applicant	motaqaazi	متقاضی
license; permit	mojavvez	مجوز
time limit	mahdudiyat-e zamaani	محدودیت زمانی
product	mahsul	محصول
loading bay	mahall-e baargiri	محل بار گیری
sales outlet	mahall-e forush	محل فروش
load; consignment; shipment	mahmuleh	محموله
return cargo	mahmule-ye bargashti	محموله برگشتی
backload	mahmule-ye moraaje'at	محموله مراجعت
expenses	makhaarej	مخارج
porterage	makhaarej-e baarbari	مخارج باربری
freight charges	makhaarej-e haml	مخارج حمل
credit term	moddat-e e'tebaar	مدت اعتبار
document	madrak	مدرك
claimant	modda'i	مدعی
debted; in debt	madyun	مدیون
mortgagee	mortahen	مرتهن
customs frontier	marz-e gomrok	مرز گمرك
tender; bidding	mozaayedeh	مزایده
haul; shipping distance	masaafat-e haml	مسافت حمل
partnership	moshaarekat	مشارکت
adviser	moshaaver	مشاور
customer	moshtari	مشتری
act of God	mashiyat-e elaahi	مشیت الهی
consumer	masraf konandeh	مصرف کننده
debt claims	motaalebaat	مطالبات
exemption	mo'aafiyat	معافیت

transactions; dealings	mo'aamelaat	معاملات
transaction; dealing	mo'aameleh	معامله
credit transaction	mo'aamele-ye nesyeh	معامله نسیه
faulty	ma'yub	معیوب
tariff regulations	moqarraraat-e ta''refeh bandi	مقررات تعرفه بندی
customs regulations	moqarraraat-e gomroki	مقررات گرکی
annuities	moqarrari-ye saalaaneh	مقرری سالانه
debted; in debt	maqruz	مقروض
destination	maqsad	مقصد
monetarism	maktab-e pul garaa'i	مکتب پول گرائی
capital gains	manaafe'-e sarmaayeh	منافع سرمایه ای
tender	monaaqeseh	مناقصه
stoppage of trade	man'-e mo'aamelaat	منع معاملات
capital gain	manfa'at-e sarmaayeh	منفعت سرمایه
provisions; clauses	mavaad	مواد
balance	movaazeneh	موازنه
balance of trade	movaazene-ye tejaarati	موازنه تجارتی
(written) agreement	mo'aafeqat naameh	موافقتنامه
commercial agreement	mo'aafeqat naame-ye tejaarati	موافقتنامه تجارتی
available; in stock	mowjud	موجود
stock (of goods)	mowjudi-ye anbaar	موجودی انبار
(goods in) stock	mowjudi-ye kaalaa	موجودی کالا
discount house	mo'assase-ye tanzil	موسسه تنزیل
commission house	mo'assase-ye haqq ol-'amalkari	موسسه حق العمل کاری
carrier	mo'assase-ye haml o naql	موسسه حمل و نقل
deadline	mow'ed	موعد
medium-term	miyaan moddat	میان مدت
credit rating	mizaan-e e'tebaar	میزان اعتبار
rate of inflation	mizaan-e tavarrom	میزان تورم
brand name	naam-e tejaarati	نام تجارتی
covering letter	naame-ye towzihi	نامه توضیحی
procedure; method	nahve-ye 'amal	نحوه عمل
rate	nerkh	نرخ
(currency) exchange rate	nerkh-e arz	نرخ ارز
rate of return	nerkh-e baazdeh	نرخ بازده
bank rate	nerkh-e baanki	نرخ بانکی
interest rate	nerkh-e bahreh	نرخ بهره
conversion rate	nerkh-e tabdil	نرخ تبدیل

rate of inflation	nerkh-e tavarrom	نرخ تورم
general cargo rates	nerkh-e haml-e baar-e motafarreqeh	نرخ حمل بار متفرقه
growth rate	nerkh-e roshd	نرخ رشد
flat rate	nerkh-e saadeh	نرخ ساده
floating rate of exchange	nerkh-e shenaavar-e arz	نرخ شناور ارز
turnover rate	nerkh-e gardesh	نرخ گردش
average purchasing rate	nerkh-e motavasset-e kharid	نرخ متوسط خرید
freight rate	nerkh-e hazine-ye haml	نرخ هزینه حمل
usury	nozul khaari	نزول خواری
credit sale; hire purchase	nesyeh	نسیه
customs control	nezaarat-e gomroki	نظارت گمرکی
gold standard	nezaam-e paaye-e talaa	نظام پایه طلا
capitalism	nezaam-e sarmaayeh daari	نظام سرمایه داری
benefit	naf'	نفع
cash	naqd	نقد
liquidity	naqdinegi	نقدینگی
defect	naqs	نقص
breach of contract	naqz-e qaraardaad	نقض قرارداد
storage; holding	negahdaari	نگهداری
agency	namaayandegi	نمایندگی
representative	namaayandeh	نماینده
commercial representative	namaayande-ye baazargaani	نماینده بازرگانی
forwarding agent	namaayande-ye haml o naql	نماینده حمل و نقل
customs agent	namaayande-ye gomroki	نماینده گمرکی
debt collecting agency	namaayande-ye vosul-e motaalebaat	نماینده وصول مطالبات
economic fluctuation	navasaan-e eqtesaadi	نوسان اقتصادی
shipping unit	vaahed-e haml	واحد حمل
imports	vaaredaat	واردات
middleman; broker; go-between	vaaseteh	واسطه
customs broker	vaasete-ye omur-e gomroki	واسطه امور گمرکی
insurance broker	vaasete-ye bimeh	واسطه بیمه
commission broker	vaasete-ye 'amal	واسطه عمل
debt; loan	vaam	وام
deposit loan	vaam-e sepordeh	وام سپرده
fiduciary loan	vaam-e sheraafati	وام شرافتی
public debt	vaam-e 'omumi	وام عمومی
borrower	vaam girandeh	وام گیرنده
pledge	vasiqeh	وثیقه

pledger	vasiqeh dahandeh	وثیقه دهنده
pledgee	vasiqeh girandeh	وثیقه گیرنده
contingency fund	vojuh-e ehtiyaati	وجوه احتیاطی
emergency fund	vojuh-e ezteraari	وجوه اضطراری
reserve fund	vojuh-e andukhteh	وجوه اندوخته
fund	vajh	وجه
remittance	vajh-e ersaali	وجه ارسالی
remittance	vajh-e vaagozaari	وجه واگذاری
bankruptcy	varshekastegi	ورشکستگی
bankrupt	varshekasteh	ورشکسته
arrival	vorud	ورود
inflow of foreign funds	vorud-e vojuh-e khaareji	ورود وجوه خارجی
Board of Trade; Ministry of Trade	vezaarat-e baazargaani	وزارت بازرگانی
collection	vosul	وصول
executor	vasi	وصی
credit status	vaz'-e e'tebaari	وضع اعتباری
financial status	vaz'-e maali	وضع مالی
endowment	vaqf	وقف
power of attorney	vekaalat naameh	وکالت نامه
goal; target	hadaf	هدف
cost	hazineh	هزینه
surcharge; excess charge	hazine-ye ezaafi	هزینه اضافی
packaging cost	hazine-ye basteh bandi	هزینه بسته بندی
charges prepaid	hazine-ye pish pardaakht shodeh	هزینه پیش پرداخت شده
carriage; shipping costs	hazine-ye haml	هزینه حمل
lump sum freight	hazine-ye haml-e maqtu'	هزینه حمل مقطوع
travel costs	hazine-ye safar	هزینه سفر
operating cost	hazine-ye 'amaliyaati	هزینه عملیاتی
collection charges	hazine-ye vosul	هزینه وصول
overheads	hazine-haa-ye baalaasari	هزینه های بالاسری
customs charges	hazine-haa-ye gomrok	هزینه های گمرک

to borrow; to take out a loan قرض گرفتن   to borrow قرض کردن   to sell فروختن   to buy خریدن

to write / draw a cheque چک کشیدن   to loan; to give a loan وام دادن   to take out a loan وام گرفتن

چک نقد کردن to cash a cheque   چک او برگشت his cheque bounced   پرداخت کردن to pay

بازپرداخت کردن to repay   واریز کردن to pay in (to an account)   در آوردن to take out

هزار دلار به حسابم واریز کردم I put $1000 into my account   بیمه کردن to insure (something)

ورشکسته شدن to go bankrupt   وارد کردن to import   صادر کردن to export   بازخرید کردن to buy back

نسیه خریدن to buy on credit   نسیه نمی دهیم we don't sell on credit   باید نقد بدهید you have to pay cash

میتوانید چک بدهید you can pay by cheque   میتوانید بوسیله کارت اعتباری بپردازید you can pay by credit card

موجودی حساب من چقدر است ؟ how much do I have in my account?   پول پس انداز کردن to save money (in the bank)

صرفه جوئی کردن to economise   سرمایه گذاری کردن to invest   تجارت کردن to trade; to engage in commerce

مبادله کالا exchange of goods   نفت را با ماشین آلات مبادله کردند they exchanged oil for machinery

سرمایه گذاریهای خارجی foreign investments   بازار کساد است the market is dull   تخفیف دادن to give discount

شرکت ما چند کالای جدید به بازار عرضه کرده است our company has marketed a number of new products

مطابق با ارزش ad valorem   شرکت با مسئولیت محدود limited liability company   شرکت خصوصی private company

سیاست مضیقه و محدودیت اعتبار credit squeeze   ظهرنویسی کردن to endorse   تایید کردن to confirm

بیمه نامه مشترک عمر joint life insurance policy   بیمه نامه عمر life policy   بیمه تمام عمر whole life insurance

رسیگی به موجودی stock taking   سازمان حمایت از مصرف کنندگان consumer protection organisation

قراردادی را محترم نشمردن to dishonour a contract   قرارداد را اجراء کردن to fulfil a contract

قراردادی را محترم شمردن to honour a contract   لغو کردن to cancel; to annul   کنسل کردن to cancel

پیش پرداخت کردن to pay in advance   اقساط پرداختن to pay in instalments   قابل پیش پرداخت payable in advance

❯❮❯

laboratory	aazmaayeshgaah	آزمایشگاه
cookery; domestic studies	aashpazi	آشپزی
teaching; training; education; learning	aamuzesh	آموزش
education	aamuzesh o parvaresh	آموزش و پرورش
remedial education	aamuzesh-e vizheh	آموزش ویژه
teacher; instructor; trainer	aamuzgaar	آموزگار
teaching; training	aamuzgaari	آموزگاری
school bus	otubus-e madraseh	اتوبوس مدرسه
literature	adabiyaat	ادبیات
classical literature	adabiyaat-e kelaasik	ادبیات کلاسیک
continuous assessment	arzyaabi-ye daa'em	ارزیابی دائم
spelling	espel	اسپل
university lecturer; teacher	ostaad	استاد
doctoral supervisor	ostaad-e raahnamaa	استاد راهنما
swimming pool	estakhr	استخر
computer room	otaaq-e kaampyuter	اطاق کامپیوتر
study room	otaaq-e motaale'eh	اطاق مطالعه
economics	eqtesaad	اقتصاد
theological studies	elaahiyaat	الهیات
examination	emtehaan	امتحان
re-sit examination	emtehaan-e tajdidi	امتحان تجدیدی
doctoral examination; viva	emtehaan-e defaa'i	امتحان دفاعی
oral examination	emtehaan-e shafaahi	امتحان شفاهی
written examination	emtehaan-e katbi	امتحان کتبی
entrance examination	emtehaan-e vorudi	امتحان ورودی
spelling	emlaa	املاء
anthropology	ensaan shenaasi	انسان شناسی
essay	enshaa	انشاء
English	engelisi	انگلیسی
commerce	baazargaani	بازرگانی
school kid; child of school age	bache-ye madrase'i	بچه مدرسه ای
illiterate	bi savaad	بی سواد
clean copy; final draft	paaknevis	پاک نویس
professor	perufesur	پروفسور
research	pezhuhesh	پژوهش
researcher	pezhuheshgar	پژوهشگر

school boy	pesar-e madrase'i	پسر مدرسه ای
regression	pasraft	پسرفت
progress	pishraft	پیشرفت
history	taarikh	تاریخ
re-sit (i.e. an exam)	tajdidi	تجدیدی
studies	tahsilaat	تحصیلات
elementary studies	tahsilaat-e ebtedaa'i	تحصیلات ابتدائی
higher studies	tahsilaat-e 'aali	تحصیلات عالی
instruction; teaching	tadris	تدریس
education; nurturing	tarbiyat	تربیت
translation	tarjomeh	ترجمه
term; trimester	term	ترم
doctoral thesis	tez-e doktoraa	تز دکترا
test	test	تست
summer vacation	ta'tilaat-e taabestaani	تعطیلات تابستانی
civics	ta'limaat-e madani	تعلیمات مدنی
homework; assignment	taklif	تکلیف
information technology	teknuluzhi-ye ettelaa'aat	تکنولوژی اطلاعات
exercise	tamrin	تمرین
registration	sabt-e naam	ثبت نام
school or university term	sols	ثلث
sociology	jaame'eh shenaasi	جامعه شناسی
prize	jaayezeh	جایزه
algebra	jabr	جبر
geography	joqraafiyaa	جغرافیا
sentence	jomleh	جمله
first draft (of a piece of writing)	cherk nevis	چرک نویس
roll call	haazer qaayebi	حاضر غایبی
law	hoquq	حقوق
school yard; playground	hayaat-e madraseh	حیاط مدرسه
oriental studies	khaavar shenaasi	خاور شناسی
cramming	khar khaani	خرخوانی
dormitory	khaabgaah	خوابگاه
studying; reading	khaandan	خواندن
self-taught	khod aamukhteh	خود آموخته
pharmacology	daaru saazi	داروسازی
veterinary science	daampezeshki	دامپزشکی
student; pupil	daanesh aamuz	دانش آموز

university student	daaneshju	دانشجو
exchange student	daaneshju-ye mobaadele'i	دانشجوی مبادله ای
college; (university) department	daaneshkadeh	دانشکده
university	daaneshgaah	دانشگاه
associate professor	daaneshyaar	دانشیار
encyclopaedia	daa'erat-ol-ma'aaref	دائرة المعارف
primary school; grade school	dabestaan	دبستان
secondary school; high school	dabirestaan	دبیرستان
school girl	dokhtar-e madrase'i	دختر مدرسه ای
lesson	dars	درس
studious	darskhaan	درسخوان
grammar	dastur-e zabaan	دستور زبان
exercise book; office	daftar	دفتر
doctorate	doktoraa	دکترا
dentistry	dandaanpezeshki	دندانپزشکی
course; period	dowreh	دوره
pre-university course	dowre-ye pish daaneshgaahi	دوره پیش دانشگاهی
middle school (9-13); junior high	dowre-ye raahnamaa'i	دوره راهنمائی
training; apprenticeship	dowre-ye kaaraamuzi	دوره کارآموزی
bilingual	dow zabaaneh	دوزبانه
sewing	duzandegi	دوزندگی
friend; mate	dust	دوست
diploma	diplom	دیپلم
middle school	raahnamaa'i	راهنمائی
cloakroom	rakht kani	رخت کنی
subject; field	reshteh	رشته
field of study; subject	reshte-ye darsi	رشته درسی
behaviour	raftaar	رفتار
mate; friend	rafiq	رفیق
psychiatry	ravaan pezeshki	روانپزشکی
psychology	ravaan shenaasi	روانشناسی
Russian	rusi	روسی
math; mathematics	riyaazi	ریاضی
applied mathematics	riyaazi-ye kaarbordi	ریاضی کاربردی
languages	zabaan	زبان
geology	zamin shenaasi	زمین شناسی
break; playtime	zang-e tafrih	زنگ تفریح
biology	zist shenaasi	زیست شناسی

year	saal	سال
first year of primary school	saal-e avval-e dabestaan	سال اول دبستان
academic year	saal-e tahsili	سال تحصیلی
second year of secondary school	saal-e dovvom-e dabirestaan	سال دوم دبیرستان
third year of middle school	saal-e sevvom-e raahnamaa'i	سال سوم راهنمائی
sports hall; gymnasium	saalon-e varzesh	سالن ورزش
astronomy	setaareh shenaasi	ستاره شناسی
pupil	shaagerd	شاگرد
first in one's class; top of the class	shaagerd-e avval	شاگرد اول
first in one's class or year	shaagerd-e momtaaz	شاگرد ممتاز
examination conditions	sharaa'et-e emtehaan	شرانط امتحان
poetry	she'r	شعر
fees	shahriyeh	شهریه
chemistry	shimi	شیمی
handicrafts	sanaaye' dasti	صنایع دستی
Arabic	'arabi	عربی
computer science	'elm-e kaampyuter	علم کامپیوتر
social sciences	'olum-e ensaani	علوم انسانی
sciences	'olum-e tajrebi	علوم تجربی
political science	'olum-e siyaasi	علوم سیاسی
natural sciences	'olum-e tabi'i	علوم طبیعی
absence (from class)	qeybat	غیبت
Persian	faarsi	فارسی
graduation; graduate	faareq ot-tahsil	فارغ التحصیل
French	faraansavi	فرانسوی
philosophy	falsafeh	فلسفه
associate diploma	fowq-e diplom	فوق دیپلم
master's degree	fowq-e lisaans	فوق لیسانس
physics	fizik	فیزیک
applied physics	fizik-e kaarbordi	فیزیک کاربردی
teaching staff	kaadr-e aamuzeshi	کادر آموزشی
work; assignment; task	kaar	کار
trainee; apprentice	kaaraamuz	کارآموز
training; apprenticeship	kaaraamuzi	کارآموزی
college	kaalej	کالج
self-study book	ketaab-e khodaamuz	کتاب خودآموز
text book	ketaab-e darsi	کتاب درسی
library	ketaab khaaneh	کتابخانه

class	*kelaas*	كلاس
university entrance examination	*konkur*	كنكور
kindergarten	*kudakestaan*	كودكستان
report	*gozaaresh*	گزارش
Latin	*laatin*	لاتين
degree	*lisaans*	ليسانس
monitor	*mobser*	مبصر
pupil; student	*mohassel*	محصل
qualifications	*madaarek-e tahsili*	مدارك تحصيلى
instructor; teacher	*modarres*	مدرس
school	*madraseh*	مدرسه
private school	*madrase-ye khosusi*	مدرسه خصوصى
girls' school	*madrase-ye dokhtaraaneh*	مدرسه دخترانه
state school	*madrase-ye dowlati*	مدرسه دولتى
boarding school	*madrase-ye shabaaneh ruzi*	مدرسه شبانه روزى
qualification	*madrak*	مدرك
headmaster; headmistress	*modir-e madraseh*	مدير مدرسه
management	*modiriyat*	مديريت
studies	*motaale'aat*	مطالعات
distance learning	*motaale'eh az raah-e dur*	مطالعه از راه دور
Islamic studies	*ma'aaref-e eslaami*	معارف اسلامى
religious studies	*ma'aaref-e dini*	معارف دينى
exemption from examination	*mo'aafiyat az emtehaan*	معافيت از امتحان
teacher; instructor	*mo'allem*	معلم
teaching	*mo'allemi*	معلمى
architecture	*me'maari*	معمارى
school regulations	*moqarraraat-e madraseh*	مقررات مدرسه
examiner	*momtahen*	ممتحن
educational institution	*mo'assase-ye aamuzeshi*	موسسه آموزشى
music	*musiqi*	موسيقى
kindergarten; playschool	*mahd-e kudak*	مهد كودك
engineering	*mohandesi*	مهندسى
school supervisor	*naazem*	ناظم
(university) refectory	*naahaarkhori-ye daaneshgaah*	ناهارخورى دانشگاه
result	*natijeh*	نتيجه
woodwork; carpentry	*najjaari*	نجارى
number; score	*nomreh*	نمره
term; semester	*nimsaal*	نيمسال

sport; exercise; games	*varzesh*	ورزش
examination paper	*varaqe-ye emtehaan*	ورقه امتحان
lunch time	*vaqt-e naahaar*	وقت ناهار
geometry	*hendeseh*	هندسه
fine arts	*honar-haa-ye zibaa*	هنرهای زیبا
meteorology	*havaa shenaasi*	هواشناسی
board of examiners	*hey'at-e momtaheneh*	هیئت ممتحنه

OTHER EDUCATIONAL WORDS AND EXPRESSIONS

درس خواندن to study   درس دادن to teach   حسن سخت درس می خواند Hasan is studying hard

علی در دبیرستان فیزیک درس می دهد Ali teaches physics in high school   یاد گرفتن to learn

من دارم فرانسوی یاد می گیرم I am learning French   یاد دادن to teach   فرا گرفتن to learn

بلد بودن to know   او فارسی بلد نیست he doesn't know Persian   امتحان دادن to take an examination

قبول شدن to pass (an exam)   رد شدن to fail (an exam)   نمره آوردن to score (a mark in an exam)

سخت difficult; hard   آسان easy   خسته کننده boring; tiring   وقت گیر time-consuming

مشکل difficult   جالب interesting   سخت گیر strict   معلم ما خیلی سخت گیر است our teacher is very strict

آسان گیر easy-going   مطالعه کردن to study (e.g. a book)   تدریس کردن to teach; to instruct

تعلیم دادن to teach; to instruct   دوره کردن to revise   خواندن to read; to study   فیزیک می خوانم I study physics

حسن در سال سوم دانشگاه تهران زبان می خواند Hasan is studying languages in the third year of Tehran University

در سال چندم هستید؟ which year are you in?   امسال فارغ التحصیل می شوم I graduate this year

تحقیق کردن to research   پژوهش کردن to carry out research   آزمایش کردن to experiment

علی امسال شاگرد اول شد Ali came top of the class this year   حسن از مدرسه اخراج شد Hasan was expelled from school

صحیح کردن to correct; to mark   وارد دانشگاه شدن to enter university   عزیز کرده معلم teacher's pet

شاگرد باهوش a bright pupil   شاگرد با استعداد a talented pupil   درسخوان studious

لیسانس ادبیات a degree in literature   شاگرد تنبل a lazy pupil   نمره های خوب good marks

◀◇▶

131

The Environment   محیط زیست

water	aab	آب
weather; climate	aab o havaa	آب و هوا
irrigation	aabyaari	آبیاری
damage	aasib	آسیب
rubbish; refuse	aashqaal	آشغال
dumping ground; refuse tip	aashqaaldaani	آشغال دانی
pesticide	aafat kosh	آفت کش
contamination	aalaayesh	آلایش
decontamination	aalaayesh zadaa'i	آلایش زدائی
pollution	aaludegi	آلودگی
polluted	aaludeh	آلوده
aluminium	aaluminiyom	آلومینیم
future	aayandeh	آینده
greenhouse effect	asar-e golkhaane'i	اثر گلخانه ای
news	akhbaar	اخبار
aerosol; spray; deodorant	esperey	اسپری
aerosol	afshaaneh	افشانه
ocean	oqyaanus	اقیانوس
energy; power	enerzhi	انرژی
solar energy	enerzhi-ye khorshidi	انرژی خورشیدی
extinction	enqeraaz	انقراض
rain	baaraan	باران
acid rain	baaraan-e asidi	باران اسیدی
radioactive fallout	baaresh-e raadiyo-aktiv	بارش رادیواکتیو
recycling	baazyaabi	بازیابی
crisis	bohraan	بحران
town and country planning	barnaameh rizi-ye shahr o rustaa	برنامه ریزی شهر و روستا
discharge; leakage	borun rikht	برون ریخت
bottle	botri	بطری
petrol	benzin	بنزین
ecosystem	bum saazgaan	بوم سازگان
desert	biyaabaan	بیابان
anti-pollutant	paad aaludegi	پاد آلودگی
organic; natural	paak aavard	پاک آورد
purification; cleansing	paaksaazi	پاکسازی
purification	paalaayesh	پالایش

waste	*pasmaandeh*	پسمانده
beach	*pelaazh*	پلاژ
washing powder	*pudr-e rakhtshu'i*	پودر رختشونی
radiation; radioactivity	*taabeshgari*	تابشگری
atomic radiation	*taabeshgari-ye atomi*	تابشگری اتمی
anti-pollution measures	*tadaabir-e zedd-e aaludegi*	تدابیر ضد آلودگی
leakage	*taraavosh*	تراوش
discharge; leakage	*tarashoh*	ترشح
purification	*tasfiyeh*	تصفیه
vegetable waste	*tofaaleh*	تفاله
biodegradable	*talaashi pazir*	تلاشی پذیر
wildlife	*jaanvaraan-e vahshi*	جانوران وحشی
island	*jazireh*	جزیره
population	*jam'iyyat*	جمعیت
forest; jungle	*jangal*	جنگل
tropical rainforest	*jangal-e estevaa'i*	جنگل استوائی
world	*jahaan*	جهان
wood	*chub*	چوب
the Green Party	*hezb-e sabz-haa*	حزب سبزها
insecticide	*hashareh kosh*	حشره کش
conservation; preservation	*hefaazat*	حفاظت
conservation; protection	*hefz*	حفظ
energy conservation	*hefz-e enerzhi*	حفظ انرژی
danger; hazard	*khatar*	خطر
dangerous; hazardous	*khatarnaak*	خطرناک
scientists	*daaneshmandaan*	دانشمندان
trees	*derakhtaan*	درختان
sea	*daryaa*	دریا
lake	*daryaacheh*	دریاچه
warmth; temperature	*damaa*	دما
smoke	*dud*	دود
catalytic converter	*dudgir*	دودگیر
Friends of the Earth	*dustaan-e zamin*	دوستان زمین
government	*dowlat*	دولت
diesel	*dizel*	دیزل
coal	*zoqaal sang*	ذغال سنگ
solution	*raah-e hal*	راه حل
colour; colouring; paint	*rang*	رنگ

newspaper	*ruznaameh*	روزنامه
detergent	*zadaayesh gar*	زدایش گر
food chain	*zanjire-ye qazaa'i*	زنجیره غذائی
harmfulness	*ziyaan*	زیان
ecologist	*zist bum shenaas*	زیست بوم شناس
ecology	*zist bum shenaasi*	زیست بوم شناسی
environmentalist	*zist bum nikdaar*	زیست بوم نیکدار
coast	*saahel*	ساحل
inhabitants	*saakenaan*	ساکنان
vegetables	*sabzijaat*	سبزیجات
poison	*samm*	سم
pesticide	*samm-e daf'-e aafaat*	سم دفع آفات
fuel	*sukht*	سوخت
hole	*suraakh*	سوراخ
glass	*shisheh*	شیشه
desert	*sahraa*	صحرا
sound pollution	*sedaa aaludegi*	صدا آلودگی
natural; organic	*tabi'i*	طبیعی
animal kingdom	*'aalam-e jaanvaraan*	عالم جانوران
plant kingdom	*'aalam-e nabaataat*	عالم نباتات
food	*qazaa*	غذا
catastrophe	*faaje'eh*	فاجعه
sewage	*faazelaab*	فاضلاب
erosion	*farsudegi*	فرسودگی
breakdown of matter	*forupaashi-ye maaddeh*	فروپاشی ماده
waste matter	*fozulaat*	فضولات
continent	*qaareh*	قاره
underground water channel	*qanaat*	قنات
factory	*kaarkhaaneh*	کارخانه
canal	*kaanaal*	کانال
the earth; the planet	*kore-ye zamin*	کره زمین
country	*keshvar*	کشور
CFCs; chlorofluorocarbons	*koloru-folurow-karbon*	کلروفلورو کربن
fertilizer	*kud*	کود
animal fertilizer	*kud-e heyvaani*	کود حیوانی
chemical fertilizer	*kud-e shimyaa'i*	کود شیمیائی
gas	*gaaz*	گاز
carbon monoxide	*gaaz-e karbonik*	گاز کربنیک

greenhouse gases	gaaz-haa-ye golkhaane'i	گازهای گلخانه ای
global warming	garm shodan-e jahaani	گرم شدن جهانی
warmth; heat	garmaa	گرما
flowers	gol	گل
effluent	gandaab row	گنداب رو
plants	giyaahaan	گیاهان
ozone layer	laaye-ye ozon	لایه ازن
additive	maadde-ye afzudani	ماده افزودنی
pollutant	maadde-ye aaludeh konandeh	ماده آلوده کننده
noxious substance; poison	maadde-ye sammi	ماده سمی
deodorant	maadde-ye zedd-e bu	ماده ضد بو
detergent	maadde-ye zarfshu'i	ماده ظرفشوئی
cars	maashin-haa	ماشین ها
tax	maaliyaat	مالیات
fish	maahi	ماهی
magazine	majalleh	مجله
product	mahsul	محصول
landfill site	mahall-e dafn-e zobaaleh	محل دفن زباله
environment	mohit-e zist	محیط زیست
issue; question	mas'aleh	مسئله
energy consumption	masraf-e enerzhi	مصرف انرژی
standard(s)	me'yaar	معیار
natural resources	manaabe'-e tabi'i	منابع طبیعی
zone; area	mantaqeh	منطقه
industrial waste	mavaad-e zaa'ed-e san'ati	مواد زائد صنعتی
nuclear waste	mavaad-e zaa'ed-e haste'i	مواد زائد هسته ای
chemicals	mavaad-e shimiyaa'i	مواد شیمیائی
fruit	miveh	میوه
smog	mah dud	مه دود
region; area	naahiyeh	ناحیه
subsidence	neshast-e zamin	نشست زمین
oil	naft	نفت
light pollution	nur aaludegi	نورآلودگی
nuclear power station	nirugaah-e haste'i	نیروگاه هسته ای
wind power	niru-ye baadi	نیروی بادی
conservation	nikdaasht	نیکداشت
nuclear reactor	vaakoneshgar-e haste'i	واکنشگر هسته ای

135

polluted air هوای آلوده   to pollute the environment محیط زیست را آلوده کردن   to pollute آلوده کردن

there is a hole in the ozone layer در طبقه ازن سوراخ ایجاد شده   the sea is polluted دریا آلوده است

to consume مصرف کردن   to be contaminated آلایش پیدا کردن   to be damaged آسیب دیدن

we must cut back on our consumption of energy در مصرف انرژی باید صرفه جوئی کنیم

newspaper recycling بازیابی روزنامه   to recycle بازیابی کردن   on the verge of extinction رو به انقراض

to leak; to discharge تراوش کردن   to decontaminate آلایش زدائی کردن   to purify; to cleanse پاکسازی کردن

to conserve; to preserve; to save حفظ کردن   water purification تصفیه آب   to purify تصفیه کردن

to find a solution راه حل پیدا کردن   we must all endeavour to conserve energy همه باید در حفظ انرژی بکوشیم

environment-friendly محیط زیست پسند   unleaded petrol بنزین بدون سرب   organic طبیعی

wind power انرژی بادی   green سبز   ozone-friendly ازن پسند

The Family   خانواده

person	aadam	آدم
retired person	aadam-e baaz neshasteh	آدم بازنشسته
ancestors; forefathers	ajdaad	اجداد
inheritance	ers	ارث
marriage	ezdevaaj	ازدواج
name	esm	اسم
family name; surname	esm-e khaanevaadegi	اسم خانوادگی
nickname; pet name	esm-e khodemaani	اسم خودمانی
family name; surname	esm-e faamil	اسم فامیل
daddy; papa	baabaa	بابا
virgin	baakereh	باکره
child; baby	bacheh	بچه
unweaned baby	bache-ye shir khaareh	بچه شیرخواره
small child; small baby	bache-ye kuchek	بچه کوچک
brother	baraadar	برادر
older brother	baraadar-e bozorgtar	برادر بزرگتر
foster brother	baraadar khaandeh	برادر خوانده
foster brother	baraadar-e rezaa'i	برادر رضاعی
brother-in-law (i.e. wife's brother)	baraadar-e zan	برادر زن
brother-in-law (i.e. husband's brother)	baraadar-e showhar	برادر شوهر
step-brother; half-brother	baraadar-e naatani	برادر ناتنی
eldest	bozorgtarin	بزرگترین
adult	bozorgsaal	بزرگسال
dependents	bastegaan	بستگان
virginity	bekaarat	بکارت
widow	biveh zan	بیوه زن
widower	biveh mard	بیوه مرد
father	pedar	پدر
stepfather	pedar andar	پدر اندر
godfather	pedar-e imaani	پدر ایمانی
grandfather	pedar-e bozorg	پدر بزرگ
great-grandfather	pedar-e pedar-e bozorg	پدر پدر بزرگ
godfather	pedar-e ta'midi	پدر تعمیدی
godfather; foster father	pedar khaandeh	پدر خوانده
father-in-law (i.e. wife's father)	pedar-e zan	پدر زن
father-in-law (i.e. husband's father)	pedar-e showhar	پدر شوهر

great-grandfather	*pedar-e maadar-e bozorg*	پدر مادر بزرگ
father and mother; parents	*pedar o maadar*	پدر و مادر
forefathers; ancestors	*pedaraan*	پدران
fatherly; paternal	*pedaraaneh*	پدرانه
son; boy	*pesar*	پسر
godson	*pesar-e imaani*	پسر ایمانی
nephew (i.e. brother's son)	*pesar-e baraadar*	پسر برادر
godson	*pesar-e ta'midi*	پسر تعمیدی
cousin (i.e. maternal aunt's son)	*pesar-e khaaleh*	پسر خاله
godson	*pesar khaande-ye ruhaani*	پسر خوانده روحانی
nephew (i.e. sister's son)	*pesar-e khaahar*	پسر خواهر
cousin (i.e. paternal uncle's son)	*pesar-e amu*	پسر عمو
cousin (i.e. paternal aunt's son)	*pesar-e ammeh*	پسر عمه
great-grandson	*pesar-e naveh*	پسر نوه
cousin (i.e. maternal uncle's son)	*pesar-e daa'i*	پسردائی
quintuplets	*panj qolu*	پنج قلو
spinster; old maid	*pir dokhtar*	پیر دختر
old woman	*pir-e zan*	پیر زن
old man	*pir-e mard*	پیر مرد
old age	*piri*	پیری
tie; connection	*peyvand*	پیوند
newly-wed	*taazeh ezdevaaj kardeh*	تازه ازدواج کرده
newly-wed (bridegroom)	*taazeh daamaad*	تازه داماد
newly-wed (bride)	*taazeh 'arus*	تازه عروس
polygamy	*ta'addod-e zowjaat*	تعدد زوجات
baptismal	*ta'midi*	تعمیدی
last born; youngest child	*tah toqaari*	ته تغاری
youngsters; young people	*javaanaan*	جوانان
dowry	*jahizeh*	جهیزه
polygamy	*chand zani*	چند زنی
quadruplets	*chahaar qolu*	چهارقلو
bastard; illegitimate child	*haraamzaadeh*	حرامزاده
aunt (i.e. mother's sister)	*khaaleh*	خاله
great-aunt	*khaale-ye bozorg*	خاله بزرگ
lady; Mrs; Miss; Ms	*khaanom*	خانم
family (adj.)	*khaanevaadegi*	خانوادگی
family (n.)	*khaanevaadeh*	خانواده
one-parent family	*khaanevaade-ye tak sarparast*	خانواده تک سرپرست

nuclear family	khaanevaade-ye haste'i	خانواده هسته ای
older sister	khaahar-e bozorgtar	خواهر بزرگتر
foster sister	khaahar khaandeh	خواهر خوانده
foster sister	khaahar-e rezaa'i	خواهر رضاعی
sister-in-law (i.e. husband's sister)	khaahar-e showhar	خواهر شوهر
step-brother	khaahar-e naatani	خواهر ناتنی
relations; relatives	khishaan	خویشان
relations; relatives	khishaavandaan	خویشاوندان
distant relatives	khishaavandaan-e dur	خویشاوندان دور
close relatives	khishaavandaan-e nazdik	خویشاوندان نزدیک
blood relatives	khishaavandaan-e hamkhun	خویشاوندان هم خون
son-in-law; bridegroom	daamaad	داماد
uncle (i.e. mother's brother)	daa'i	دائی
great-uncle	daa'i-ye bozorg	دائی بزرگ
wet-nurse; nanny	daayeh	دایه
daughter; girl	dokhtar	دختر
unmarried woman	dokhtar-e ezdevaaj nakardeh	دختر ازدواج نکرده
niece (i.e. brother's daughter)	dokhtar-e baraadar	دختر برادر
god-daughter	dokhtar-e ta'midi	دختر تعمیدی
cousin (i.e. maternal aunt's daughter)	dokhtar-e khaaleh	دختر خاله
niece (i.e. sister's daughter)	dokhtar-e khaahar	دختر خواهر
cousin (i.e.maternal uncle's daughter)	dokhtar-e daa'i	دختر دائی
cousin (i.e. paternal uncle's daughter)	dokhtar-e 'amu	دختر عمو
cousin (i.e. paternal aunt's daughter)	dokhtar-e 'ammeh	دختر عمه
great grand-daughter	dokhtar-e naveh	دختر نوه
twins	dow qolu	دوقلو
connection; relationship	raabeteh	رابطه
ties; connections	reshte-haa	رشته ها
sister-in-law (i.e. brother's wife)	zan-e baraadar	زن برادر
stepmother	zan-e pedar	زن پدر
daughter-in-law	zan-e pesar	زن پسر
young woman	zan-e javaan	زن جوان
housewife	zan-e khaaneh daar	زن خانه دار
second wife	zan-e dovvom	زن دوم
husband and wife; couple	zan o showhar	زن و شوهر
adultery	zenaa	زنا
marriage; married life	zanaashu'i	زناشونی
incest	zenaa-ye baa mahaarem	زنای با محارم

couple	zowj	زوج
custody; guardianship	sarparasti	سرپرستی
age	senn	سن
triplets	seh qolu	سه قلو
person; individual	shakhs	شخص
birth certificate; identity card	shenaasnaameh	شناسنامه
husband	showhar	شوهر
stepfather	showhar-e maadar	شوهر مادر
child	tefl	طفل
divorce	talaaq	طلاق
dependents	'aa'eleh	عائله
bride; daughter-in-law	'arus	عروس
uncle (i.e. father's brother)	'amu	عمو
great-uncle	'amu bozorg	عمو بزرگ
aunt (i.e. father's sister)	'ammeh	عمه
great-aunt	'ammeh bozorg	عمه بزرگ
baptism; christening	qosl-e ta'mid	غسل تعمید
family	faamil	فامیل
child; offspring	farzand	فرزند
godchild	farzand khaandeh	فرزند خوانده
foster child	farzand-e rezaa'i	فرزند رضاعی
great-grandchild	farzand-e naveh	فرزند نوه
family; relatives; relations	qowm o khish	قوم و خویش
child; baby	kudak	کودک
nursery; creche; kindergarten	kudakestan	کودکستان
nickname	laqab	لقب
unmarried mother	maadar-e ezdevaaj nakardeh	مادر ازدواج نکرده
stepmother	maadar andar	مادر اندر
godmother	maadar-e imaani	مادر ایمانی
grandmother	maadar-e bozorg	مادر بزرگ
godmother	maadar-e ta'midi	مادر تعمیدی
godmother; foster mother	maadar khaandeh	مادر خوانده
foster mother	maadar-e rezaa'i	مادر رضاعی
mother-in-law (i.e. wife's mother)	maadar-e zan	مادر زن
mother-in-law (i.e. husband's mother)	maadar-e showhar	مادر شوهر
great-grandmother	maadar-e maadar-e bozorg	مادر مادر بزرگ
motherly; maternal	maadaraneh	مادرانه
great-grandmother	maadar-e pedar-e bozorg	مادر پدر بزرگ

mummy	*maamaan*	مامان
married	*mota'ahhel*	متاهل
wedding ceremony	*maraasem-e 'arusi*	مراسم عروسی
man	*mard*	مرد
young man	*mard-e javaan*	مرد جوان
man of the family	*mard-e khaanevaadeh*	مرد خانواده
bachelor	*mard-e mojarrad*	مرد مجرد
people	*mardom*	مردم
pensioner	*mostamarri begir*	مستمری بگیر
creche	*mahd-e kudak*	مهد کودک
stepfather	*naapedari*	ناپدری
stepmother	*naamaadari*	نامادری
fiancee	*naamzad (zan)*	نامزد (زن)
fiance	*naamzad (mard)*	نامزد (مرد)
illegitimate	*naamashru'*	نامشروع
breadwinner	*naanaavar*	نان آور
dependent	*naankhor*	نان خور
great-grandchild	*nabireh*	نبیره
next of kin	*nazdiktarin khishaavand*	نزدیکترین خویشاوند
alimony; maintenance	*nafaqeh*	نفقه
teenager	*nowjavaan*	نوجوان
grandchild	*naveh*	نوه
grandson	*nave-ye pesari*	نوه پسری
granddaughter	*nave-ye dokhtari*	نوه دختری
ancestors; forefather	*niyaakaan*	نیاکان
relationship; tie	*vaabastegi*	وابستگی
heir	*vaares*	وارث
parents	*vaaledeyn*	والدین
neighbour	*hamsaayeh*	همسایه
spouse	*hamsar*	همسر
marriage	*hamsari*	همسری
co-wife	*havu*	هوو
orphan	*yatim*	یتیم
orphanage	*yatim khaaneh*	یتیمخانه

to die مردن   to live زندگی کردن   I was born in Tehran من در تهران به دنیا آمدم   to be born به دنیا آمدن

my mother is dead مادر من مرده است   he was born in 1980 در سال ۱۹۸۰ متولد شد   to be born متولد شدن

Susan is not yet married سوسن هنوز ازدواج نکرده است   she passed away last year او پارسال در گذشت

to get married ازدواج کردن   my aunt is a widow خاله من بیوه است   Ali is still a bachelor علی هنوز مجرد است

alive زنده   do you have brothers and sisters? خواهر و برادر دارید؟   to get divorced طلاق گرفتن

I have one brother and two sisters یک برادر و دو تا خواهر دارم   my grandfather is still alive پدر بزرگم هنوز زنده است

to grow up بزرگ شدن   I'm the only child in the family من تنها بچه خانواده هستم   the only child تنها بچه

unmarried ازدواج نکرده   my mother raised five children مادرم پنج تا بچه بزرگ کرد   to rear; to raise بزرگ کردن

younger کوچکتر   my brother is older than I am برادرم از من بزرگتر است   unmarried mothers مادرهای ازدواج نکرده

to get pregnant حامله شدن   she has just given birth to a child او تازه بچه زائیده است   to give birth زائیدن

to have a miscarriage بچه انداختن   she is on the Pill او قرص ضد حاملگی می خورد   to get pregnant آبستن شدن

who looks after the children? کی از بچه ها نگهداری می کند؟   my mother goes out to work مادرم کار می کند

to grow old پیر شدن   old age دوره پیری   youth دوره جوانی   the youth of today جوانان امروز

divorcee زن طلاق گرفته   my father has remarried پدرم دوباره زن گرفته است   to take a wife زن گرفتن

Susan doesn't want to get married سوسن نمیخواهد شوهر کند   to take a husband شوهر کردن

Ali and Susan have separated علی و سوسن از هم جدا شده اند   Ali and Susan got engaged علی و سوسن نامزد شدند

family relationships روابط خانوادگی   Hasan has severed relations with his brother حسن با برادرش ترک رابطه کرده است

to make up آشتی کردن   to argue دعوا کردن   Hasan made up with his brother حسن با برادرش آشتی کرد

to respect احترام گذاشتن   my relationship with my family is not very good رابطه من با خانواده ام خیلی خوب نیست

disrespect بی احترامی   one must respect the older members of the family باید به بزرگان خانواده احترام گذاشت

Hasan inherited $100,000 from his father حسن صد هزار دلار از پدرش به ارث برد   to inherit ارث بردن

my ancestors were from Afghanistan اجداد من اهل افغانستان بودند   my late father پدر مرحوم من

paternal feelings احساسات پدرانه   maternal instincts غریزه های مادرانه   a family man مرد عیال وار

the family circle حلقه خانوادگی   the institution of the family کانون خانواده   family life زندگی خانوادگی

◄◄►►

Farming

		كشاورزى
trough	aabeshkhor	آبشخور
irrigation	aabyaari	آبیارى
trough	aakhur	آخور
windmill	aasyaab baadi	آسیاب بادى
miller	aasyaabaan	آسیابان
sheep fold	aaqel-e gusfand	آغل گوسفند
pesticide	aafat kosh	آفت کش
fallow	aayesh	آیش
blacksmith	aahangar	آهنگر
shed; hut	otaaqak	اتاقک
farm animals	ahshaam	احشام
duck	ordak	اردك
millet	arzan	ارزن
horse	asb	اسب
mule	astar	استر
loft	otaaq-e baalaa-ye tavileh	اطاق بالاى طویله
donkey	olaaq	الاغ
store; barn	anbaar	انبار
barn	anbaar-e kaah	انبار کاه
the wheat market	baazaar-e gandom	بازار گندم
crop; yield	baazdeh	بازده
orchard	baaq-e miveh	باغ میوه
sheaf	baafeh	بافه
piglet	bache-ye khuk	بچه خوك
seed	bazr	بذر
seed merchant	bazr forush	بذرفروش
seedsman	bazr kaar	بذرکار
harvest	bardaasht	برداشت
wheat harvest	bardaasht-e gandom	برداشت گندم
pond	berkeh	برکه
countryside	borun shahr	برون شهر
lamb	barreh	برّه
goat	boz	بز
goatherd	bozcheraan	بزچران
kid	bozqaaleh	بزغاله
turkey	buqalamun	بوقلمون

143

fish farm	*parvareshgaah-e maahi*	پرورشگاه ماهی
shearing	*pashm chini*	پشم چینی
vine	*taak*	تاك
vineyard	*taakestaan*	تاكستان
foot and mouth disease	*tab-e barfaki*	تب برفكی
hill	*tappeh*	تپه
seed	*tokhm*	تخم
tractor	*teraaktur*	تراكتور
pile; heap	*tal*	تل
pile; heap	*tudeh*	توده
haystack	*tude-ye kaah*	توده كاه
animal	*jaandaar*	جاندار
mating	*joft giri*	جفت گیری
forest; wood; jungle	*jangal*	جنگل
barley	*jow*	جو
oats	*jow-e dow sar*	جو دوسر
chick	*jujeh*	جوجه
ditch; puddle	*chaaleh*	چاله
rye	*chaavdaar*	چاودار
well	*chaah*	چاه
pasture; meadow	*charaagaah*	چراگاه
lawn; meadow; field	*chamanzaar*	چمنزار
shepherd	*chupaan*	چوپان
cattle	*chahaar paayaan*	چهارپایان
insecticide	*hashareh kosh*	حشره كش
fence	*hesaar*	حصار
farmyard	*hayaat-e khaane-ye keshaavarz*	حیاط خانه كشاورز
animal	*heyvaan*	حیوان
domestic animals; tame animals	*heyvaanaat-e ahli*	حیوانات اهلی
earth; soil	*khaak*	خاك
farmhouse	*khaane-ye keshaavarz*	خانه كشاورز
donkey	*khar*	خر
cockerel	*khorus*	خروس
fodder	*khoraak-e daam*	خوراك دام
pig	*khuk*	خوك
pigsty	*khukdaani*	خوكدانی
sickle	*daas*	داس
cattle	*daam*	دام

cattle breeding	daamparvari	دامپروری
animal husbandry	daamdaari	دامداری
seed; grain	daaneh	دانه
door; gate	dar	در
gate	darvaazeh	دروازه
plough	dastgaah-e shokhm zani	دستگاه شخم زنی
milking machine	dastgaah-e shir dushi	دستگاه شیردوشی
bunch; sheaf; bundle	dasteh	دسته
countryside; wilderness	dasht o sahraa	دشت و صحرا
village	deh	ده
villager; peasant	dehaati	دهاتی
farmer	dehqaan	دهقان
corn; maize	zorrat	ذرت
hops	raazak	رازک
village	rustaa	روستا
villager; peasant; rural (adj.)	rustaa'i	روستائی
farmer	zaare'	زارع
agriculture; farming	zeraa'at	زراعت
earth; ground	zamin	زمین
arable land	zamin-e mazru'i	زمین مزروعی
farmer's wife	zan-e dehqaan	زن دهقان
bucket; pail	satl	سطل
dog	sag	سگ
slaughterhouse	sallaakh khaaneh	سلاخ خانه
pesticide	samm-e daf'-e aafaat	سم دفع آفات
crop-dusting; crop spraying	sammpaashi	سمپاشی
ploughman	shokhm zan	شخم زن
ploughing	shokhm zani	شخم زنی
furrow	sheyaar	شیار
barn	tavileh	طویله
byre	tavile-ye gaav	طویله گاو
meadow; pasture	'alafzaar	علفزار
fodder	'olufeh	علوفه
hay	'olufe-ye khoshk	علوفه خشک
goose	qaaz	غاز
grain; seed	qalleh	غله
mating season	fasl-e joft giri	فصل جفت گیری
ram	quch	قوچ

agriculturist	kaarshenaas-e keshaavarzi	کارشناس کشاورزی
dairy worker	kaargar-e labaniyaati	کارگر لبنیاتی
farmhand	kaargar-e mazra'eh	کارگر مزرعه
hay; straw	kaah	کاه
hayloft	kaah anbaar	کاه انبار
heap; pile	koppeh	کپه
churn	kareh gir	کره گیر
foal	korre-ye asb	کرهٔ اسب
farmer	keshaavarz	کشاورز
tenant farmer	keshaavarz-e mosta'jer	کشاورز مستاجر
farmer	keshaavarz	کشاورزی
mixed farming	keshaavarzi-ye chand mahsuli	کشاورزی چند محصولی
crop rotation	kesht-e tanaavobi	کشت تناوبی
slaughterhouse; abattoir	koshtaargaah	کشتارگاه
field; meadow	keshtzaar	کشتزار
cornfield	keshtzaar-e zorrat	کشتزار ذرت
plantation	kalaan keshtzaar	کلان کشتزار
hut; cottage	kolbeh	کلبه
combine harvester	kombaayn	کمباین
fertilizer; manure	kud	کود
animal fertilizer	kud-e heyvaani	کود حیوانی
chemical fertilizer	kud-e shimiyaa'i	کود شیمیائی
pile; heap	kumeh	کومه
cow	gaav	گاو
cowherd	gaavcheraan	گاو چران
byre	gaavsaraa	گاو سرا
bull; ox	gaav-e nar	گاو نر
milk cows	gaav-haa-ye shirdeh	گاوهای شیرده
herd	galeh	گله
wheat	gandom	گندم
calf	gusaaleh	گوساله
sheep	gusfand	گوسفند
dairy	labaniyaat saazi	لبنیات سازی
mare	maadiyaan	مادیان
female	maadeh	ماده
scarecrow	matarsak	مترسک
plantation	mojtama'-e keshaavarzi	مجتمع کشاورزی
crop	mahsul	محصول

seed crop	*mahsul-e bazri*	محصول بذری
cereal crops	*mahsulaat-e qallaati*	محصولات غلاتی
farmyard	*mahvate-ye keshtgaah*	محوطه کشتگاه
field	*marta'*	مرتع
chicken; hen	*morq*	مرغ
laying hen	*morq-e tokhm gozaar*	مرغ تخم گذار
hen house	*morq khaaneh*	مرغ خانه
guinea fowl	*morq-e shaakhdaar*	مرغ شاخدار
duck	*morqaabi*	مرغابی
field; meadow; pasture	*marqzaar*	مرغزار
farm	*mazra'eh*	مزرعه
cattle farm; dairy farm	*mazra'e-ye gaavdaari*	مزرعه گاوداری
groom	*mehtar*	مهتر
district	*naahiyeh*	ناحیه
male	*nar*	نر
ladder	*nardeh baan*	نرده بان
van	*vaanet*	وانت

MORE FARMING WORDS AND PHRASES

to plant; to sow   کاشتن   to till the land   زمین را زراعت کردن   to farm; to cultivate   زراعت کردن

to sow or scatter seeds   تخم پاشیدن   to sow or scatter seeds   بذر پاشیدن   to plough; to till; to furrow   شخم زدن

the farmer was milking the cows   زارع گاوها را می دوشید   to milk   دوشیدن   to reap; to harvest   درو کردن

horse breeding   پرورش اسب   to nurture; to raise; to breed   پرورش دادن   I work on a farm   من در مزرعه کار می کنم

cotton crop   محصولات پنبه   farmers take their produce to market   کشاورزان محصولات خود را به بازار می برند

staple; staple crop   محصول عمده   the country's wheat crop has doubled   محصول گندم کشور دو برابر شده است

stud farm   پرورشگاه اسب تخمی   underground water channel (traditional in Iran)   قنات

Feelings and Relationships

احساسات و روابط

relief; calm; peace and quiet	aasaayesh	آسایش
abuse	ejhaaf	اجحاف
self-respect	ehteraam-e be-khod	احترام به خود
feeling	ehsaas	احساس
loneliness	ehsaas-e tanhaa'i	احساس تنهائی
feelings	ehsaasaat	احساسات
difference; disagreement	ekhtelaaf	اختلاف
difference of opinion	ekhtelaaf-e nazar	اختلاف نظر
self-alienation	az khod bigaanegi	از خود بیگانگی
blunder; gaffe	eshtebaah-e ahmaqaaneh	اشتباه احمقانه
self-confidence	e'temaad-e be-nafs	اعتماد به نفس
revenge	enteqaam	انتقام
disgust	enzejaar	انزجار
grudge; bad intention	bad khaahi	بد خواهی
verbal abuse	bad dahani	بد دهنی
abuse	bad raftaari	بد رفتاری
clash	barkhord	برخورد
impatience	bi sabri	بی صبری
unfaithfulness	bi vafaa'i	بی وفائی
self-hatred	bizaari az khish	بیزاری از خویش
alienation	bigaanegi	بیگانگی
strangeness	bivaaregi	بیوارگی
astonishment	boht zadegi	بهت زدگی
audacity	por ru'i	پر روئی
prejudice	pishdaavari	پیشداوری
ecstasy; elation	tab o taab	تب و تاب
abuse; rape	tajaavoz	تجاوز
pity	tarahhom	ترحم
trepidation	tars o larz	ترس و لرز
obsessive fear	tars-e vasvaas angiz	ترس وسواس انگیز
break-up	tark-e raabeteh	ترک رابطه
prejudice	ta'assob	تعصب
insult	towhin	توهین
attraction; attractiveness	jazzaabiyat	جذابیت
sexuality	jensiyat	جنسیت
rival	harif	حریف

148

shame; shyness; bashfulness	khejaalat	خجالت
violence; abuse; aggressiveness	khoshunat	خشونت
self-image	khod engaareh	خود انگاره
self-awareness; self-consciousness	khod aagaahi	خود آگاهی
self-aggrandizement	khod bozorg bini	خود بزرگ بینی
self-dependence	khod poshtvaani	خود پشتوانی
selfishness	khod khaahi	خود خواهی
self-control	khod daari	خود داری
self-love	khod dusti	خود دوستی
self-criticism	khod sanji	خود سنجی
self-knowledge	khod shenaasi	خود شناسی
self-deception	khod faribi	خود فریبی
self-doubt	khod naabaavari	خود ناباوری
self-destruction	khod viraangari	خود ویرانگری
happiness	khosh haali	خوشحالی
self-belief	khishtan baavari	خویشتن باوری
irritation; pain-in-the-neck	dard-e sar	درد سر
enmity	doshmani	دشمنی
argument	da'vaa	دعوا
grudge	deqq-e deli	دق دلی
relief	del aasaa'i	دل آسائی
pity	delsuzi	دلسوزی
exhilaration; happiness	delshaadi	دلشادی
anxiety; alarm	delvaapasi	دلواپسی
dread	delhoreh	دلهره
friend; companion	dust	دوست
boyfriend	dust-e pesar	دوست پسر
girlfriend	dust-e dokhtar	دوست دختر
close friend; intimate	dust-e samimi	دوست صمیمی
close friend	dust-e nazdik	دوست نزدیک
friendship	dusti	دوستی
relationship	raabeteh	رابطه
love affair	raabete-ye 'eshqi	رابطه عشقی
illicit affair	raabete-ye naa mashru'	رابطه نامشروع
comfort	raahati	راحتی
friendship; comradeship	refaaqat	رفاقت
friend; comrade	rafiq	رفیق
rival	raqib	رقیب

resentment	ranjesh	رنجش
standing on ceremony; bashfulness	rudar beyisti	رودربایستی
adultery	zenaa	زنا
ecstasy	sarmasti	سرمستی
disorientation	sardargomi	سردرگمی
disorientation	sargashtegi	سرگشتگی
misunderstanding	su'-e tafaahom	سوء تفاهم
bad intention	su'-e niyyat	سوء نیت
self-respect	sheraafat-e nafs	شرافت نفس
shame	sharm	شرم
wonder; awe	shegefti	شگفتی
elation	showq o sha'f	شوق و شعف
patience	sabr	صبر
intimacy	samimiyat	صمیمیت
divorce	talaaq	طلاق
lover	'aasheq	عاشق
lovers; lovebirds	'aasheq o ma'shuq	عاشق و معشوق
enmity	'adaavat	عداوت
conflict	'adam-e tavaafoq	عدم توافق
love; passion	'eshq	عشق
love triangle; eternal triangle	'eshq-e seh jaanebeh	عشق سه جانبه
pride	qorur	غرور
sadness; sorrow	qam	غم
conflict; clash; struggle	keshmakesh	کشمکش
exhilaration	keyf	کیف
rancour	kineh	کینه
vengeance	kineh ju'i	کینه جوئی
audacity; rudeness	gostaakhi	گستاخی
gay	gey	گی
attraction; attractiveness	giraa'i	گیرائی
flirting	laas zani	لاس زنی
nickname	laqab	لقب
bone of contention	maaye-ye nefaaq	مایه نفاق
split; break-up	motaarekeh	متارکه
annoyance; irritation	mozaahemat	مزاحمت
(male) lover	ma'shuq	معشوق
(female) lover; mistress	ma'shuqeh	معشوقه
tenderness	molaatefat	ملاطفت

sexual desire; libido	*meyl-e jensi*	میل جنسی
tenderness; kindness	*mehr*	مهر
nickname; pet name	*naam-e mehraamiz*	نام مهرآمیز
hatred	*nefrat*	نفرت
anxiety; worry	*negaraani*	نگرانی
terror; horror; dread	*vahshat*	وحشت
obsession	*vasvaas-e fekri*	وسواس فکری
faithfulness	*vafaadaari*	وفاداری
alarm; panic; fear	*haraas*	هراس
homosexual	*hamjens baaz*	همجنس باز
passing fancy; whim	*havas*	هوس
panic	*howl*	هول
friend; companion; mate	*yaar*	یار

MORE WORDS AND EXPRESSIONS CONNECTED WITH FEELINGS AND RELATIONSHIPS

to dislike دوست نداشتن   I like you; I love you تو را دوست دارم   to like; to love دوست داشتن

to fall in love خاطرخواه شدن   to fall in love عاشق شدن   I hate him از او نفرت دارم   to hate نفرت داشتن

to annoy; to upset ناراحت کردن   Hasan has fallen in love with Susan حسن عاشق سوسن شده

to annoy; to vex; to hurt; to bother اذیت کردن   to become upset; to be annoyed ناراحت شدن

to be embarrassed خجالت کشیدن   to lie دروغ گفتن   to betray خیانت کردن   to be jealous of حسادت کردن

Susan and Ali have just separated / broken up سوسن و علی تازه از هم جدا شده اند   shame on you! خجالت بکش!

to break off a relationship قطع رابطه کردن   to feel regret; to feel remorse پشیمان شدن

to make up آشتی کردن   to kiss بوسیدن   to lose a friend دوست از دست دادن   to find friends دوست پیدا کردن

to have sexual intercourse جماع کردن   to make love عشق بازی کردن   to quarrel دعوا کردن

to feel guilty احساس گناه کردن   I have a clear conscience وجدان من راحت است

to make friends with someone با کسی طرح دوستی ریختن   to treat someone badly با کسی بدرفتاری کردن

《◇》

Festivals and Commemorations

جشن و يادبود

fire; bonfire	aatash	آتش
fireworks	aatash baazi	آتش بازی
ceremony	aayin	آيين
marriage	ezdevaaj	ازدواج
Father Christmas	baabaa no'el	بابا نوئل
retirement	baaz neshastegi	بازنشستگی
bazaar; fair	baazaar	بازار
annual fair	baazaar-e saalaneh	بازار سالانه
commemoration (of an individual)	bozorgdaasht	بزرگداشت
national flag	parcham-e melli	پرچم ملی
coffin	taabut	تابوت
(funeral) wreath; garland	taaj-e gol	تاج گل
coronation	taajgozaari	تاجگذاری
date; history	taarikh	تاريخ
ceremony; proceedings	tashrifaat	تشريفات
national holiday	ta'til-e 'omumi	تعطيل عمومی
holidays	ta'tilaat	تعطيلات
baptism; christening	ta'mid	تعميد
birth	tavallod	تولد
ceremony; party; festival	jashn	جشن
birthday party	jashn-e tavallod	جشن تولد
engagement party	jashn-e naamzadi	جشن نامزدی
festivities	jashn o sorur	جشن و سرور
commemoration; memorial	jashn-e yaadbud	جشن يادبود
film festival	jashnvaare-ye film	جشنواره فيلم
music festival	jashnvaare-ye musiqi	جشنواره موسيقی
funeral lights (traditional in Iran)	chelcheraaq	چلچراغ
(Iranian) ritual of bonfire lighting on the last Wednesday of the year, hailing the advent of Now Ruz.	chahaarshanbeh suri	چهارشنبه سوری
burial	khaak sepaari	خاك سپاری
party given to celebrate the circumcision of a baby boy.	khatneh suraan	ختنه سوران
marriage proposal	khaastegaari	خواستگاری
death; passing	dar gozasht	درگذشت
stall	dakkeh	دکه

bicentenary	devistomin saalgard	دویستمین سالگرد
death; passing	rehlat	رحلت
(commemoration of) the death of the Prophet Muhammad.	rehlat-e peyqambar	رحلت پیغمبر
march; procession	rezheh	رژه
dance	raqs	رقص
Fathers' Day	ruz-e pedar	روز پدر
Mothers' Day	ruz-e maadar	روز مادر
best man; bridesmaid	saaqdush	ساقدوش
anniversary	saalruz	سالروز
anniversary	saalgard	سالگرد
wedding anniversary	saalgard-e ezdevaaj	سالگرد ازدواج
anniversary of martyrdom	saalgard-e shahaadat	سالگرد شهادت
anniversary of death (of Imam)	saalgard-e vafaat	سالگرد وفات
anniversary of birth (of Imam)	saalgard-e velaadat	سالگرد ولادت
New Year	saal-e now	سال نو
speech	sokhanraani	سخنرانی
graveside	sar-e qabr	سر قبر
national anthem	sorud-e melli	سرود ملی
mourning	sugvaari	سوگواری
circus	sirk	سیرک
the 13th day of Farvardin, the first month of the Iranian year, which is customary for all families to spend out in the open.	sizdah bedar	سیزده بدر
wedding night	shab-e zefaaf	شب زفاف
eve of the third day after someone's death, marked in Iran by prayers and readings from the Koran.	shab-e sevvom	شب سوم
(Iranian) New Year's Eve	shab-e 'eyd	شب عید
the 'night of power', towards the end of the month of Ramadan, when it is alleged that the Koran was first revealed.	shab-e qadr	شب قدر
Christmas Eve	shab-e kerismas	شب کریسمس
eve of the seventh day after someone's death, marked in Iran by prayers and readings from the Koran.	shab-e haftom	شب هفتم

153

midwinter; (traditional Iranian) celebration of winter solstice.	*shab-e yaldaa*	شب يلدا
martyrdom	*shahaadat*	شهادت
churchyard	*sahn-e kelisaa*	صحن كليسا
float (in procession)	*sahne-ye motaharrek*	صحنه متحرك
centenary	*sadomin saal*	صدمين سال
funeral procession (of people)	*saff-e moshaaye'in-e jenaazeh*	صف مشايعين جنازه
commemoration of the martydrom of the third Shi'ite Imam, Hossein b. Ali.	*'aashuraa*	عاشورا
wedding	*'arusi*	عروسی
ritual conducted after childbirth in which a sheep is slaughtered and alms are given.	*'aqiqeh*	عقيقه
Easter	*'eyd-e paak*	عيد پاك
New Year	*'eyd-e saal-e now*	عيد سال نو
festival celebrated on the occasion of Ali b. Abi Taleb being appointed successor to the Prophet.	*'eyd-e qadir-e khom*	عيد غدير خم
the festival at the end of the fasting month of Ramadan.	*'eyd-e fetr*	عيد فطر
the festival at the end of the pilgrimage to Mecca.	*'eyd-e qorbaan*	عيد قربان
Christmas	*'eyd-e kerismas*	عيد كريسمس
(Iranian) New Year	*'eyd-e nowruz*	عيد نو روز
new year's gift	*'eydi*	عيدی
fair; fairground	*faanfaar*	فانفار
lantern	*faanus*	فانوس
festive season	*fasl-e jashn o sorur*	فصل جشن و سرور
grave	*qabr*	قبر
graveyard	*qabrestaan*	قبرستان
acceptance; pass (in exams, etc.)	*qabuli*	قبولی
raffle	*qor'eh keshi*	قرعه کشی
cortege (of cars)	*qataar-e otumobil*	قطار اتومبيل
present; gift	*kaadow*	كادو
carnival	*kaarnaavaal*	كارناوال
honeymoon	*maah-e 'asal*	ماه عسل
registry office	*mahzar*	محضر
ceremony	*maraasem*	مراسم

closing ceremony	maraasem-e ekhtetaamiyeh	مراسم اختتامیه
opening ceremony	maraasem-e eftetaahiyeh	مراسم افتتاحیه
graduation ceremony	maraasem-e faareq ot-tahsili	مراسم فارغ التحصیلی
deceased; the deceased	marhum	مرحوم
cremation	mordeh suzi	مرده سوزی
death	marg	مرگ
tomb	maqbareh	مقبره
guest	mehmaan	مهمان
party; get-together; banquet	mehmaani	مهمانی
host	mizbaan	میزبان
engagement	naamzadi	نامزدی
confetti	noql o nabaat	نقل و نبات
fireworks display	namaayesh-e aatash baazi	نمایش آتش بازی
death; passing	vafaat	وفات
death of (an) Imam	vafaat-e emaam	وفات امام
wedding banquet	valimeh	ولیمه
present; gift	hediyeh	هدیه
millennium	hezaareh	هزاره
commemoration; remembrance	yaadbud	یادبود
centenary	yek sad saaleh	یک صد ساله

MORE WORDS AND PHRASES INVOLVING FESTIVALS AND COMMEMORATIONS

to have a birthday party جشن تولد گرفتن   to celebrate; to hold a celebration; to commemorate جشن گرفتن

to give a party; to throw a party; to entertain مهمانی دادن   to give presents; to give a gift هدیه دادن

مهمانی چای tea party   dinner party مهمانی شام   evening party; soiree شب نشینی   to invite دعوت کردن

to be invited دعوت شدن   I've invited Ali to my birthday party علی را به جشن تولدم دعوت کرده ام

به خاک سپردن to bury (i.e. the dead)   they're burying Ali's father tomorrow فردا پدر علی را به خاک می سپارند

در تشییع جنازه شرکت کردن to take part in a funeral   funeral ceremonies; mourning rites مراسم سوگواری

سوگواری کردن to mourn; to lament   mourning clothes لباس عزاداری   to mourn عزاداری کردن

Fish

ماهی

saltwater	*aab-e shur*	آب شور
freshwater	*aab-e shirin*	آب شیرین
aquatic	*aabzi*	آبزی
salmon trout	*aazaad maahi*	آزادماهی
fishing tackle	*abzaar-e maahigiri*	ابزار ماهیگیری
pike	*ordak maahi*	اردك ماهی
sawfish	*arreh maahi*	اره ماهی
seahorse	*asb-e daryaa'i*	اسب دریائی
seahorse	*asb maahi*	اسب ماهی
scallop	*eskaalup*	اسکالوپ
fin	*baaleh*	باله
tadpole	*bacheh qurbaaqeh*	بچه قورباغه
mullet	*boz maahi*	بزماهی
skate	*partov maahi-ye bozorg*	پرتو ماهی بزرگ
ray	*partov maahi*	پرتوماهی
oyster bed	*parvareshgaah-e sadaf-e khoraaki*	پرورشگاه صدف خوراکی
plaice	*pelaays*	پلایس
scale	*pulak*	پولک
sturgeon	*taas maahi*	تاس ماهی
lobster pot	*tale-ye laabster giri*	تله لابستر گیری
tench	*tench*	تنچ
sea urchin	*tutiyaa-ye daryaa'i*	توتیای دریائی
fishing net	*tur-e maahigiri*	تور ماهیگیری
loach	*tiyaan*	تیان
shellfish	*jaanvaraan-e sadafdaar*	جانوران صدفدار
jellyfish	*chatr-e daryaa'i*	چتر دریائی
crayfish	*changaareh*	چنگاره
swordfish	*khaar maahi*	خارماهی
crab	*kharchang*	خرچنگ
oyster crab	*kharchang-e sadafzi*	خرچنگ صدف زی
seafood	*khuraak-e daryaa'i*	خوراك دریائی
porpoise	*khuk maahi*	خوك ماهی
sea cucumber	*khiyaar-e daryaa'i*	خیار دریائی
aquatic; marine; sea (adj.)	*daryaa'i*	دریائی
dolphin	*dolfin*	دلفین
devilfish	*div maahi*	دیو ماهی

electric ray	rakhsh maahi	رخش ماهی
torpedo fish	ra'd maahi	رعدماهی
river	rudkhaaneh	رودخانه
barbel	rishak maahi	ریشک ماهی
skink	rig maahi	ریگماهی
jellyfish	zheleh maahi	ژله ماهی
sardine	saardin	ساردین
creel	sabad-e maahi	سبد ماهی
brill	separ maahi	سپرماهی
starfish	setaareh maahi	ستاره ماهی
flatfish	sofreh maahi	سفره ماهی
cuttlefish	sefidaaj	سفیداج
dogfish	sag maahi	سگ ماهی
zander	suf	سوف
cuttlefish	sibiyaa	سیبیا
mullet; herring	shaah maahi	شاه ماهی
sea anemone	shaqaayeq-e daryaa'i	شقایق دریائی
swordfish	shamshir maahi	شمشیر ماهی
siren fish	shir maahi	شیرماهی
fisheries	shilaat	شیلات
clam; shell	sadaf	صدف
razor clam	sadaf-e tiqi	صدف تیغی
oyster; pearl	sadaf-e khuraaki	صدف خوراکی
oyster catcher	sadaf gir	صدف گیر
pearl fisher	sayyad-e sadaf	صیاد صدف
oyster catcher	sayyad-e sadaf-e khuraaki	صیاد صدف خوراکی
lobsterman	sayyad-e laabster	صیاد لابستر
bait	to'meh	طعمه
scorpion fish	'aqrab maahi	عقرب ماهی
sperm whale	'anbar maahi	عنبرماهی
angel fish	fereshteh maahi	فرشته ماهی
seal	fok	فک
scales	feles	فلس
trout	qezel aalaa	قزل آلا
brown trout	qezel aalaa-ye tireh	قزل آلای تیره
sea trout	qezel aalaa-ye daryaa'i	قزل آلای دریائی
brook trout	qezel aalaa-ye nahri	قزل آلای نهری
cod	kaad	کاد

freshwater carp	kapur-e aab-e shirin	کپور آب شیرین
maggot	kermak	کرمک
fishing boat; fishing vessel	keshti-ye maahigiri	کشتی ماهیگیری
tadpole	kafcheh lizak	کفچه لیزك
shark	kuseh	کوسه
basking shark	kuse-ye aasudgar	کوسه آسودگر
thresher shark	kuse-ye domkub	کوسه دمکوب
hammerhead shark	kuse-ye sar chakkoshi	کوسه سر چکشی
white shark	kuse-ye sefid	کوسه سفید
mackerel shark	kuse-ye maakrel	کوسه ماکرل
spiny dogfish	kuseh maahi-ye khaardaar	کوسه ماهی خاردار
dugong	gaav maahi	گاوماهی
catfish	gorbeh maahi	گربه ماهی
lobster	laabster	لابستر
spiny lobster	laabster-e khaardaar	لابستر خاردار
perch	luti maahi	لوتی ماهی
eel	maar maahi	مارماهی
mussel	maasel	ماسل
mackerel	maakrel	ماکرل
fish	maahi	ماهی
salmon	maahi-ye aazaad	ماهی آزاد
flying fish	maahi-ye parandeh	ماهی پرنده
sea bream	maahi-ye purgi	ماهی پورگی
flatfish	maahi-ye pahn	ماهی پهن
tuna	maahi-ye ton	ماهی تن
sole	maahi-ye halvaa	ماهی حلوا
tank; aquarium	maahi khaaneh	ماهی خانه
sturgeon	maahi-ye khaavyaar	ماهی خاویار
bleak	maahi-ye dorosht-e qanaat	ماهی درشت قنات
cod	maahi-ye rowqan	ماهی روغن
gudgeon	maahi-ye riz-e qanaat	ماهی ریز قنات
burbot	maahi-ye rishdaar	ماهی ریشدار
whiting	maahi-ye sefid	ماهی سفید
bream	maahi-ye sim	ماهی سیم
carp	maahi-ye kapur	ماهی کپور
gudgeon	maahi-ye gubi	ماهی گوبی
dab	maahi-ye limaand	ماهی لیماند
squid	maahi-ye morakkab	ماهی مرکب

lamprey	*maahi-ye mekandeh*	ماهی مکنده
angler; fisherman	*maahigir*	ماهیگیر
fishing; angling	*maahigiri*	ماهیگیری
jellyfish	*meduz*	مدوز
prawn; shrimp	*meygu*	میگو
semi-aquatic	*nimeh daryaa'i*	نیمه دریانی
stream	*nahr*	نهر
halibut	*haalibut*	هالیبوت
haddock	*hadaak*	هداك
octopus	*hasht paa*	هشت پا
hake	*heyk*	هیک

MORE FISHY TERMS AND EXPRESSIONS!

to go fishing ماهیگیری کردن   to catch (a) fish ماهی گرفتن   to swim in the water در آب شنا کردن

to cast a net تور انداختن   fish hook قلاب ماهیگیری   fishing صید ماهی   to fish; to hunt صید کردن

I don't like seafood خوراك دریائی دوست ندارم   fish bait طعمه ماهی   to fish with a net با تور ماهی گرفتن

Flowers and Plants

گل و گیاه

watering can; sprinkler	aab paash	آب پاش
watering	aab paashi	آب پاشی
irrigation	aabyaari	آبیاری
gardening tools	abzaar-e baaqbaani	ابزار باغبانی
juniper	ors	ارس
orchid	orkideh	ارکیده
azalea	azaaliyeh	ازالیه
lavender	ostuqodus	استوقدوس
foxglove	angoshtaaneh	انگشتانه
rain	baaraan	باران
large garden; orchard	baaq	باغ
landscape gardener	baaq aaraa	باغ آرا
landscape gardening	baaq aaraa'i	باغ آرائی
gardener	baaqbaan	باغبان
gardening	baaqbaani	باغبانی
garden	baaqcheh	باغچه
layout of flower beds or garden	baaqcheh bandi	باغچه بندی
parkway	baaqraah	باغراه
gardens; grounds	baaqestaan	باغستان
bush	boteh	بته
guelder-rose; dog elder	bodaaq	بداغ
carpel	barcheh	برچه
leaf	barg	برگ
belladonna	belaadon	بلادن
pansy	banafsheh	بنفشه
primrose	paamchaal	پامچال
stamen	parcham	پرچم
hedge	parchin	پرچین
butterfly	parvaaneh	پروانه
flower growing; horticulture	parvaresh-e gol	پرورش گل
nursery	parvareshgaah-e gol	پرورشگاه گل
digitalis; foxglove	panje-ye 'ali	پنجه علی
cyclamen	panje-ye maryam	پنجه مریم
pennyroyal	puneh	پونه
honeysuckle	pich-e amin-od-dowleh	پیچ امین الدوله
passion-flower	pich-e saa'ati	پیچ ساعتی

ivy	pichak	پیچک
grafting	peyvand	پیوند
seed	tokhm	تخم
seed pod	tokhmdaan	تخمدان
gentian	jentiyaana	جنتیانا
wheelbarrow	charkh-e dasti	چرخ دستی
grass	chaman	چمن
lawn	chamanzaar	چمنزار
border	haashiyeh	حاشیه
fence	hesaar	حصار
pond	howz	حوض
thorn	khaar	خار
soil; earth	khaak	خاك
oleander	khar zahreh	خرزهره
Syrian mallow	khatmi-ye derakhti	خطمی درختی
hollyhock	khatmi-ye farangi	خطمی فرنگی
hawthorn	khancheh	خنچه
sun	khorshid	خورشید
seed	daaneh	دانه
tree	derakht	درخت
sapling; shrub	derakhtcheh	درختچه
shrubbery	derakhtcheh zaar	درختچه زار
bunch of flowers	daste-ye gol	دسته گل
path	raah baarikeh	راه باریکه
root	risheh	ریشه
ground; earth	zamin	زمین
stalk	saaqeh	ساقه
shade; shadow	saayeh	سایه
vegetables	sabzijaat	سبزیجات
greenery; grass; foliage	sabzeh	سبزه
grass; meadow; verdure	sabzeh zaar	سبزه زار
hyacinth	sonbol	سنبل
stone	sang	سنگ
stone garden	sang baaq	سنگ باغ
pebble; gravel	sang rizeh	سنگ ریزه
meadow-saffron	surenjaan	سورنجان
automatic sprinkler system	sistem-e aabpaashi-ye khodkaar	سیستم آبپاشی خودکار
dew	shabnam	شبنم

161

anemone; corn poppy	shaqaayeq	شقایق
anemone	shaqaayeq-e no'maan	شقایق نعمان
in bloom	shokufaa	شکوفا
flowering; blooming	shokufaa'i	شکوفانی
blossom	shokufeh	شکوفه
clover	shabdar	شبدر
geranium	sham'daani	شمعدانی
hose pipe	shilang	شیلنگ
scent	'atr	عطر
grass; weeds	'alaf	علف
bud	qoncheh	غنچه
dandelion	qaasedak	قاصدک
cutting	qalameh	قلمه
secateurs	qeychi-ye baaqbaani	قیچی باغبانی
sepal	kaasbarg	کاسبرگ
worm	kerm	کرم
manure; fertiliser	kud	کود
dahlia	kowkab	کوکب
pollen	gardeh	گرده
pollination	gardeh afshaani	گرده افشانی
greenhouse; glasshouse	garmkhaaneh	گرمخانه
stinging nettle	gazaneh	گزنه
flower	gol	گل
sunflower	gol-e aaftaab gardaan	گل آفتاب گردان
buttercup	gol-e aalaaleh	گل آلاله
fuchsia	gol-e aaviz	گل آویز
zinnia	gol-e aahaar	گل آهار
acacia	gol-e abrisham	گل ابریشم
hydrangea	gol-e edris	گل ادریس
Judas tree flower	gol-e arqavaan	گل ارغوان
campanula	gol-e estekaani	گل استکانی
calendula	gol-e ashrafi	گل اشرفی
petunia	gol-e atlasi	گل اطلسی
locust flower; acacia	gol-e aqaaqiyaa	گل آقاقیا
chamomile	gol-e baabuneh	گل بابونه
lily-of-the-valley	gol-e barf	گل برف
hybrid tea-rose	gol-e bamba'i	گل بمبئی
pink; sweet-william	gol-e buqalamun	گل بوقلمون

162

mallow	*gol-e panirak*	گل پنيرك
bindweed	*gol-e pichak*	گل پيچک
columbine	*gol-e taaj ol-moluk*	گل تاج الملوك
woody nightshade	*gol-e taajrizi*	گل تاجريزی
cockscomb; love-lies-bleeding	*gol-e taaj-e khorus*	گل تاج خروس
French marigold	*gol-e ja'fari*	گل جعفری
tea rose	*gol-e chaay*	گل چای
autumn crocus; meadow saffron	*gol-e hasrat*	گل حسرت
garden balsam; touch-me-not	*gol-e hanaa*	گل حنا
bramble	*gol-e khaar*	گل خار
hollyhock	*gol-e khatmi*	گل خطمی
chrysanthemum; ox-eye daisy	*gol-e daavudi*	گل داودی
Arabian jasmine	*gol-e raazeqi*	گل رازقی
rose	*gol-e roz*	گل رز
China aster	*gol-e ra'naa zibaa*	گل رعنا زيبا
delphinium	*gol-e zabaan dar qafaa*	گل زبان در قفا
yellow rose	*gol-e zard*	گل زرد
crocus	*gol-e za'feraan*	گل زعفران
iris; white lily	*gol-e zanbaq*	گل زنبق
passionflower	*gol-e saa'at*	گل ساعت
rose; red rose	*gol-e sorkh*	گل سرخ
sweetbriar	*gol-e sefid*	گل سفيد
lichen	*gol-e sang*	گل سنگ
lily	*gol-e susan*	گل سوسن
verbena	*gol-e shaah pasand*	گل شاه پسند
stock; wallflower	*gol-e shab bu*	گل شب بو
corn poppy; corn rose	*gol-e shaqaayeq*	گل شقايق
trumpet flower	*gol-e sheypuri*	گل شيپوری
hundred-leafed rose	*gol-e sad barg*	گل صد برگ
peony	*gol-e sad tumaani*	گل صدتومانی
broom flower	*gol-e taavusi*	گل طاووسی
jonquil	*gol-e 'anbari*	گل عنبری
phlox	*gol-e foluks*	گل فلوکس
dandelion	*gol-e qaasedi*	گل قاصدی
Damascus rose	*gol-e golaab*	گل گلاب
blue cornflower	*gol-e gandom*	گل گندم
fuchsia	*gol-e gushvaareh*	گل گوشواره
nasturtium	*gol-e laadan*	گل لادن

163

Damascus rose	gol-e mohammadi	گل محمدی
daisy	gol-e morvaarid	گل مروارید
tuberose	gol-e maryam	گل مریم
musk-rose	gol-e meshkin	گل مشکین
Venus fly-trap	gol-e magas gir	گل مگس گیر
snapdragon	gol-e meymun	گل میمون
aster	gol-e minaa	گل مینا
sweetpea	gol-e nokhud shirin	گل نخود شیرین
narcissus	gol-e narges	گل نرگس
lilac	gol-e yaas	گل یاس
marigold	gol-e hamisheh bahaar	گل همیشه بهار
gladiolus	galaayol	گلایل
petal; rose leaf	golbarg	گلبرگ
flower-picking	golchini	گلچینی
greenhouse	golkhaaneh	گلخانه
vase; flower pot	goldaan	گلدان
flower bed; rose garden	golzaar	گلزار
rose garden; flower garden	golestaan	گلستان
flower garden	golshan	گلشن
rosebud; flower bud	golqoncheh	گلغنچه
florist	golforush	گلفروش
florist's shop	golforushi	گلفروشی
floriculturist	golkaar	گلکار
flower work; flower bed	golkaari	گلکاری
pomegranate blossom	golnaar	گلنار
wistaria	gelisiyen	گلیسین
plant; shrub	giyaah	گیاه
house plant	giyaah-e khaanegi	گیاه خانگی
grove; thicket; copse; grassy place	giyaah zaar	گیاه زار
botanist; herbalist	giyaah shenaas	گیاه شناس
botany	giyaah shenaasi	گیاه شناسی
flowering plant	giyaah-e gol aavar	گیاه گل آور
tulip	laaleh	لاله
poppy	laale-ye biyaabaani	لاله بیابانی
marvel-of-Peru	laale-ye 'abbaasi	لاله عباسی
pistil	maadegi	مادگی
lawnmower	maashin-e chaman zani	ماشین چمن زنی
celandine	maamiraan	مامیران

forget-me-not	*maraa faraamush nakon*	مرا فراموش نکن
magnolia	*magnuliyaa*	مگنولیا
carnation	*mikhak*	میخک
sweet william	*mikhak-e shaa'er*	میخک شاعر
mimosa	*mimuzaa*	میموزا
ladder	*nardeh baan*	نرده بان
narcissus	*narges*	نرگس
daffodil	*narges-e zard*	نرگس زرد
sweetbriar; eglantine	*nastaran*	نسترن
flower show	*namaayeshgaah-e gol*	نمایشگاه گل
morning-glory	*nilufar*	نیلوفر
water-lily	*nilufar-e aabi*	نیلوفر آبی
bench	*nimkat*	نیمکت
honeysuckle; woodbine	*visheh*	ویشه
lilac	*yaas*	یاس
jasmine	*yaasaman*	یاسمن
Virginia creeper	*yaasaman-e zard*	یاسمن زرد

OTHER WORDS AND PHRASES CONNECTED WITH FLOWERS

to plant trees or shrubs درختکاری کردن   to plant flowers گلکاری کردن   to plant کاشتن

آب دادن to water   to irrigate آبیاری کردن   I watered the flowers گلهارا آب دادم   to water آبپاشی کردن

چمن را زدن to cut the grass   to prune سر شاخه زدن   to pick چیدن   don't pick the flowers! گلهارا نچین!

باغبانی کردن to garden; to do the gardening   پدر من از باغبانی لذت می برد my father enjoys gardening

گل دادن to flower   این گیاه هر سال گل می دهد this plant flowers every year   شکوفه دادن to blossom

این درخت هر بهار شکوفه قرمزی می دهد this tree gives a red blossom every spring   شکوفا شدن to blossom

کود ریختن to apply fertilizer   پای درختچه کود ریختم I applied fertilizer at the base of the shrub

خاک توی گلدان ریختم I put some soil in the flower pot   تخم پاشیدن to scatter seeds

در سرتاسر باغچه تخم لاله بیابانی پاشید he scattered poppy seeds all over the garden

آن گیاه را از گلدان به باغچه انتقال دادم I transferred that plant from the plant pot to the garden

165

Food and Drink

خوردنی و آشامیدنی

(Note that names of fruits, vegetables and fish are not listed here; they appear in their own separate sections)

water	*aab*	آب
lemon juice	*aab-e limu*	آب لیمو
fruit juice	*aab-e miveh*	آب میوه
brine; salted water	*aab-e namak*	آب نمک
beer	*aab-e jow*	آبجو
a thick Iranian soup/stew, combining meat, potatoes, pulses and spices.	*aabgusht*	آبگوشت
mixed nuts	*aajil*	آجیل
chewing gum	*aadams*	آدامس
flour	*aard*	آرد
rice flour	*aard-e berenj*	آرد برنج
wheat flour	*aard-e gandom*	آرد گندم
a thick soup/stew made from pulses and herbs, meat and vegetables; many different varieties exist.	*aash*	آش
pomegranate *aash*	*aash-e anaar*	آش انار
plum *aash*	*aash-e aalu*	آش آلو
rice *aash*	*aash-e berenj*	آش برنج
barley *aash*	*aash-e jow*	آش جو
a type of *aash* that combines herbs, meatballs and vermicelli.	*aash-e reshteh*	آش رشته
a type of *aash* which combines spinach with either vinegar or orange juice.	*aash-e saak*	آش ساک
a type of *aash* that combines a wide variety of herbs and pulses, including rice and split peas.	*aash-e sholeh qalamkaar*	آش شله قلمکار
a type of *aash* eaten with dried whey.	*aash-e kashk*	آش کشک
a type of *aash* that includes yoghourt.	*aash-e maast*	آش ماست
cook; chef	*aashpaz*	آشپز
cooking	*aashpazi*	آشپزی
steamed white rice with morello cherries.	*aalbaalu polow*	آلبالو پلو
spices	*adviyeh*	ادویه
bone	*ostokhaan*	استخوان
tea glass	*estekaan*	استکان

pepper steak	*esteyk-e felfel*	استیک فلفل
appetite	*eshtehaa*	اشتها
a type of broth made from flour, water, oil, onions, herbs and, occasionally, eggs.	*eshkeneh*	اشکنه
eating and drinking	*akl o shorb*	اکل و شرب
omelette	*omlet*	املت
almond	*baadam*	بادام
peanut	*baadaam-e zamini*	بادام زمینی
peanut brittle	*baadaam-e sukhteh*	بادام سوخته
sugared almonds	*baadaam-e qandi*	بادام قندی
cashew nuts	*baadaam-e hendi*	بادام هندی
steamed white rice with broad beans	*baaqalaa polow*	باقلا پلو
baklava	*baaqlavaa*	باقلوا
bay leaf	*barg-e bu*	برگ بو
dried fruit	*bargeh*	برگه
(uncooked) white rice	*berenj*	برنج
ice-cream	*bastani*	بستنی
ice lolly	*bastani-ye chubi*	بستنی چوبی
ice-cream cone	*bastani-ye qifi*	بستنی قیفی
plate	*boshqaab*	بشقاب
pulses	*bonshan*	بنشن
name given to a number of dishes which combine particular vegetables with herbs fried in oil, and often eaten with yoghourt.	*buraani*	بورانی
spinach *buraani*	*buraani-ye esfenaaj*	بورانی اسفناج
aubergine *buraani*	*buraani-ye baadenjaan*	بورانی بادنجان
courgette *buraani*	*buraani-ye kadu*	بورانی کدو
carrot *buraani*	*buraani-ye havij*	بورانی هویج
turkey	*buqalamun*	بوقلمون
biscuit	*bisku'it*	بیسکویت
steak	*biftek*	بیفتک
Iranian dessert made from threads of iced vermicelli in sugar and chilled lemon juice.	*paaludeh*	پالوده
portion	*pors*	پرس
pistachio	*pesteh*	پسته

candyfloss	*pashmak*	پشمک
Iranian sweetmeat made from egg white, sugar and pistachio kernels.	*pofak*	پفک
cooked white rice	*polow*	پلو
cheese	*panir*	پنیر
Iranian cheese (similar to Feta)	*panir-e iraani*	پنیر ایرانی
grated cheese	*panir-e randeh kardeh*	پنیر رنده کرده
Feta cheese	*panir-e fetaa*	پنیر فتا
mashed potato	*pure-ye sib-e zamini*	پوره سیب زمینی
lemon peel	*pust-e limu*	پوست لیمو
pizza	*pitzaa*	پیتزا
type of sweet or savoury doughnut	*piraashki*	پیراشکی
starters; hors d'oeuvres	*pish qazaa*	پیش غذا
a stew made from potatoes, meat, onions, tomatoes and dried limes.	*taas kabaab*	تاس کباب
sunflower seeds	*tokhm-e aaftaab gardaan*	تخم آفتاب گردان
pumpkin seeds	*tokhm-e kadu*	تخم کدو
egg	*tokhm-e morq*	تخم مرغ
boiled egg	*tokhm-e morq-e aab paz*	تخم مرغ آب پز
scrambled egg	*tokhm-e morq-e qaati shodeh*	تخم مرغ قاطی شده
fried egg	*tokhm-e morq-e nimru*	تخم مرغ نیمرو
melon seeds	*tokhm-e hendavaaneh*	تخم هندوانه
pickle	*torshi*	ترشی
pickled onions	*torshi-ye piyaaz*	ترشی پیاز
pickled garlic	*torshi-ye sir*	ترشی سیر
mixed pickle	*torshi-ye liteh*	ترشی لیته
herbs and vegetables	*tareh baar*	تره بار
toast	*tost*	تست
thirst	*teshnegi*	تشنگی
tamarind	*tamr-e hendi*	تمر هندی
nibbles; snack food	*tanaqqolaat*	تنقلات
a dish of lamb steamed in white rice, egg and yoghourt.	*tah chin*	ته چین
the crunchy crust at the bottom of the pan after rice has been steamed.	*tah dig*	ته دیگ
liver	*jegar*	جگر
chicken kebab	*jujeh kabaab*	جوجه کباب
nutmeg	*jowz-e hendi*	جوز هندی

relish; sauce; seasoning; dressing	*chaashni*	چاشنی
knife	*chaaqu*	چاقو
tea	*chaay*	چای
fat (i.e. of meat)	*charbi*	چربی
popcorn (lit. "elephant's fart")	*chos-e fil*	چس فیل
cooked white rice	*chelow*	چلو
cooked white rice with lamb kebab, braised tomato and sumac; usually revered as the Iranian 'national dish'.	*chelow kabaab*	چلو کباب
fork	*changaal*	چنگال
potato chips; potato crisps	*chips*	چیپس
pulses; grains	*hobubaat*	حبوبات
halwa	*halvaa*	حلوا
a type of halwa made with pistachios	*halvaa ardeh*	حلوا ارده
a sweet and sticky type of halwa	*halvaa-ye shirin*	حلوای شیرین
a type of porridge made from wheat and meat.	*halim*	حلیم
a type of scrambled eggs	*khaagineh*	خاگینه
cream	*khaameh*	خامه
caviar	*khaaviyaar*	خاویار
mustard	*khardal*	خردل
breadcrumbs	*khorde-ye naan*	خرده نان
date	*khormaa*	خرما
dried fruit and nuts	*khoshkbaar*	خشکبار
toothpick	*khelaal-e dandaan*	خلال دندان
dough	*khamir*	خمیر
yeast	*khamir torsh*	خمیر ترش
food; stew	*khoraak*	خوراک
food; edible	*khordani*	خوردنی
a thick sauce, different varieties of which combine meat, pulses, fruit and/or vegetables, used as an accompaniment to boiled or steamed white rice. Nearest English equivalent for translation purposes is 'stew'.	*khoresht*	خورشت
spinach stew	*khoresht-e esfenaaj*	خورشت اسفناج
aubergine stew	*khoresht-e baadenjaan*	خورشت بادنجان
okra stew	*khoresht-e baamiyeh*	خورشت بامیه

rhubarb stew	*khoresht-e rivaas*	خورشت ریواس
apple stew	*khoresht-e sib*	خورشت سیب
duck, walnut and pomegranate stew	*khoresht-e fesenjaan*	خورشت فسنجان
green herb stew	*khoresht-e qormeh sabzi*	خورشت قرمه سبزی
lamb and split-pea stew	*khoresht-e qeymeh*	خورشت قیمه
aubergine, lamb and split-pea stew	*khoresht-e qeymeh baadenjaan*	خورشت قیمه بادنجان
courgette stew	*khoresht-e kadu*	خورشت کدو
celery stew	*khoresht-e karafs*	خورشت کرفس
gherkin	*khiyaar shur*	خیار شور
cinnamon	*daarchin*	دارچین
meatloaf	*dastpich*	دست پیچ
dessert; pudding	*deser*	دسر
heart (e.g. sheep's heart)	*del*	دل
stuffed aubergine	*dolme-ye baadenjaan*	دلمه بادنجان
stuffed pepper	*dolme-ye felfel*	دلمه فلفل
stuffed cabbage	*dolme-ye kalam*	دلمه کلم
stuffed tomato	*dolme-ye gowjeh farangi*	دلمه گوجه فرنگی
a type of cooked rice, usually steamed with broad beans.	*dami*	دمی
yoghourt drink	*duq*	دوغ
Turkish delight	*raahat ol-holqum*	راحت الحلقوم
concentrate; puree	*robb*	رب
pomegranate puree	*robb-e anaar*	رب انار
tomato puree	*robb-e gowjeh farangi*	رب گوجه فرنگی
restaurant	*rasturaan*	رستوران
steamed white rice with vermicelli	*reshteh polow*	رشته پلو
food colouring	*rang-e khoraaki*	رنگ خوراکی
Iranian dessert made from flour, sugar, dates, pistachio kernels and spices.	*ranginak*	رنگینک
oil	*rowqan*	روغن
sunflower oil	*rowqan-e aaftaab gardaan*	روغن آفتاب گردان
olive oil	*rowqan-e zeytun*	روغن زیتون
soya oil	*rowqan-e suyaa*	روغن سویا
fish oil	*rowqan-e maahi*	روغن ماهی
vegetable oil	*rowqan-e nabaati*	روغن نباتی
Iranian cream pastry, similar to Swiss roll.	*rulet*	رولت
table cloth	*ru mizi*	رومیزی

turmeric	zardchubeh	زردچوبه
steamed white rice with barberries	zereshk polow	زرشک پلو
saffron	za'feraan	زعفران
ginger	zanjabil	زنجبیل
cumin	zireh	زیره
ham	zhaambun	ژامبون
gelatine	zhelaatin	ژلاتین
oven-cooked fillet of lamb, beef or venison.	zhigu	ژیگو
salad	saalaad	سالاد
Iranian delicacy made from boiled eggs, chicken, potatoes, gherkins and mayonnaise.	saalad oliviyeh	سالاد الویه
sandwich	saandvich	ساندویچ
toasted sandwich	saandvich-e tost shodeh	ساندویچ تست شده
herbs	sabzi	سبزی
rice steamed with herbs	sabzi polow	سبزی پلو
herb rice with fish (usually eaten to celebrate the Iranian New Year).	sabzi polow maahi	سبزی پلو ماهی
dried herbs	sabzi-ye khoshk	سبزی خشک
fresh herbs	sabzi khordan	سبزی خوردن
vegetables	sabzijaat	سبزیجات
head chef	sar aashpaz	سر آشپز
bottle top	sar-e botri	سر بطری
vinegar	serkeh	سرکه
sauce	sos	سس
salad dressing	sos-e saalad	سس سالاد
white sauce	sos-e sefid	سس سفید
tomato sauce; ketchup	sos-e gowjeh farangi	سس گوجه فرنگی
a kind of sherbet made from syrup and vinegar.	sekanjabin	سکنجبین
sumac	somaaq	سماق
soup	sup	سوپ
barley soup	sup-e jow	سوپ جو
chicken soup	sup-e morq	سوپ مرغ
sausage	susis	سوسیس
a type of hard sweet made from flour and honey.	sowhaan 'asal	سوهان عسل

boiled potatoes	sib-e zamini-ye aab paz	سیب زمینی آب پز
fries; chips	sib-e zamini-ye sorkh kardeh	سیب زمینی سرخ کرده
garlic	sir	سیر
dinner; evening meal	shaam	شام
wine	sharaab	شراب
cider	sharaab-e sib	شراب سیب
sherbet; squash	sharbat	شربت
chocolate	shokolaat	شکلات
tripe	shekambeh	شکمبه
a pottage of rice, pulses and spices	sholeh	شله
a traditional dessert made with rice, sugar and saffron.	sholeh zard	شله زرد
white rice steamed with dill	shevid polow	شوید پلو
rice pudding	shir berenj	شیر برنج
rice steamed with currants, orange peel and sugar.	shirin polow	شیرین پلو
cakes; pastries; sweetmeats	shirini	شیرینی
moist or cream-filled pastries	shirini-ye tar	شیرینی تر
dry pastries	shirini-ye khoshk	شیرینی خشک
syrup	shireh	شیره
a type of lamb or beef kebab	shishlik	شیشلیک
breakfast	sobhaaneh	صبحانه
bill (in restaurant)	surat hesaab	صورتحساب
taste; flavour	ta'm	طعم
dish; bowl; pan	zarf	ظرف
lentil	'adas	عدس
Iranian stew made of lamb and lentils, and sometimes with aubergine.	'adasi	عدسی
booze; spirits; arrak; cordial	'araq	عرق
peppermint cordial	'araq-e na'naa'	عرق نعناع
honey	'asal	عسل
essence; extract	'osaareh	عصاره
vanilla essence	'osaare-ye vaanil	عصاره وانیل
afternoon tea	'asraaneh	عصرانه
aroma; perfume	'atr	عطر
food	qazaa	غذا
cooked food	qazaa-ye pokhteh	غذای پخته
fast food	qazaa-ye haazeri	غذای حاضری

172

frozen food	qazaa-ye yakhzadeh	غذای یخزده
a type of custard	fereni	فرنی
pepper	felfel	فلفل
cup; mug	fenjaan	فنجان
hazelnut	fandoq	فندق
fillet of lamb or beef	fileh	فیله
mushroom	qaarch	قارچ
spoon	qaashoq	قاشق
cloves	qaranfol	قرنفل
crust (of bread)	qeshr	قشر
an Iranian sweetmeat made from flour, sugar, eggs, oil, rosewater and pistachio kernels.	qottaab	قطاب
kidney	qolveh	قلوه
tin	quti	قوطی
coffee	qahveh	قهوه
curry	kaari	کاری
dish; bowl	kaaseh	کاسه
cafeteria	kaafeh	کافه
cocoa	kaakaa'u	کاکائو
salami	kaalbaas	کالباس
kebab	kabaab	کباب
lamb kebab	kabaab-e barg	کباب برگ
liver kebab	kabaab-e jegar	کباب جگر
mincemeat kebab	kabaab-e kubideh	کباب کوبیده
chicken kebab	kabaab-e morq	کباب مرغ
cutlet	kotlet	کتلت
a type of cooked white rice	kateh	کته
butter	kareh	کره
dried whey	kashk	کشک
an Iranian dish made of fried aubergines and dried whey.	kashk-e baadenjaan	کشک بادنجان
currants	keshmesh	کشمش
rice steamed with currants	keshmesh polow	کشمش پلو
sultanas	keshmesh-e sabz	کشمش سبز
rice steamed with cabbage	kalam polow	کلم پلو
sheep's head and trotters	kalleh paacheh	کله پاچه
tin; tinned food	konserv	کنسرو

173

meatball	*kufteh*	کوفته
special type of meatball stuffed with boiled eggs and dates	*kufte-ye tabrizi*	کوفته تبریزی
small meatballs	*kufteh rizeh*	کوفته ریزه
small meatballs	*kufteh qelqeli*	کوفته قلقلی
type of thick omelette with various fillings	*kuku*	کوکو
aubergine *kuku*	*kuku-ye baadenjaan*	کوکوی بادنجان
herb *kuku*	*kuku-ye sabzi*	کوکوی سبزی
potato *kuku*	*kuku-ye sib zamini*	کوکوی سیب زمینی
tea bag(s)	*kise-ye chaay*	کیسه چای
cake	*keyk*	کیک
cream cake	*keyk-e khaame'i*	کیک خامه ای
chocolate cake	*keyk-e shokolaati*	کیک شکلاتی
currant cake	*keyk-e keshmeshi*	کیک کشمشی
powdered dried lime	*gard-e limu*	گرد لیمو
walnut	*gerdu*	گردو
hunger	*gorosnegi*	گرسنگی
Iranian dish made of spinach and eggs	*gol dar chaman*	گل در چمن
rosewater	*golaab*	گلاب
meat	*gusht*	گوشت
horse meat	*gusht-e asb*	گوشت اسب
venison	*gusht-e aahu*	گوشت آهو
lamb	*gusht-e barreh*	گوشت بره
fatty meat	*gusht-e charb*	گوشت چرب
minced meat	*gusht-e charkh kardeh*	گوشت چرخ کرده
pork	*gusht-e khuk*	گوشت خوک
leg (meat)	*gusht-e raan*	گوشت ران
breast (meat)	*gusht-e sineh*	گوشت سینه
camel meat	*gusht-e shotor*	گوشت شتر
beef	*gusht-e gaav*	گوشت گاو
neck (meat)	*gusht-e gardan*	گوشت گردن
veal	*gusht-e gusaaleh*	گوشت گوساله
mutton	*gusht-e gusfand*	گوشت گوسفند
lean meat	*gusht-e lokhm*	گوشت لخم
dairy foods	*labaniyaat*	لبنیات
boiled beetroot	*labu*	لبو
split peas	*lapeh*	لپه

rice steamed with green beans	lubiyaa polow	لوبیا پلو
black-eyed peas	lubiyaa-ye cheshm bolboli	لوبیای چشم بلبلی
haricot beans	lubiyaa chiti	لوبیای چیتی
kidney beans	lubiyaa-e ye qermez	لوبیای قرمز
wine list	list-e sharaab	لیست شراب
dried lime	limu-ye 'omaani	لیموی عمانی
lemonade	limunaad	لیموناد
marmalade	maarmaalaad	مارمالاد
yoghurt	maast	ماست
strained yoghurt	maast-e chekideh	ماست چکیده
plain yoghurt	maast-e saadeh	ماست ساده
yoghurt with shallots	maast-e musir	ماست موسیر
fruit yoghurt	maast-e mive'i	ماست میوه ای
pasta	maakaaruni	ماکارونی
fish	maahi	ماهی
rice steamed with fish	maahi polow	ماهی پلو
smoked fish	maahi-ye dudi	ماهی دودی
jam	morabbaa	مربا
fried or braised chicken	morq-e bereshteh shodeh	مرغ برشته شده
duck	morqaabi	مرغابی
taste; flavour	mazeh	مزه
customer	moshtari	مشتری
drink; alcohol; booze	mashrub	مشروب
alcoholic drinks	mashrubaat-e alkoli	مشروبات الکلی
non-alcoholic drinks; soft drinks	mashrubaat-e qeyr-e alkoli	مشروبات غیر الکلی
brains	maqz	مغز
marrow	maqz-e ostokhaan	مغز استخوان
guest	mehmaan	مهمان
host	mizbaan	میزبان
prawns; shrimps	meygu	میگو
appetite; desire	meyl	میل
fruit	miveh	میوه
desiccated coconut	naargil-e khoshk	نارگیل خشک
bread	naan	نان
baguette	naan-e baaget	نان باگت
type of traditional Iranian bread	naan-e barbari	نان بربری
toast	naan-e bereshteh	نان برشته
rice cakes	naan-e berenji	نان برنجی

pitta bread	naan-e pitaa	نان پیتا
traditional type of Iranian bread	naan-e taaftun	نان تافتون
barley bread	naan-e jow	نان جو
profiteroles	naan-e khaame'i	نان خامه ای
sliced bread	naan-e saandvich	نان ساندویچ
sliced (white) bread	naan-e sefid	نان سفید
traditional type of Iranian bread, cooked on hot pebbles.	naan-e sangak	نان سنگک
French toast	naan-e sukhaari	نان سوخاری
sweet type of bread	naan-e qandi	نان قندی
wholemeal bread; bread made from wheat flour.	naan-e gandom	نان گندم
traditional type of Iranian bread	naan-e lavaash	نان لواش
mass-produced bread	naan-e maashini	نان ماشینی
type of sweetmeat made from crushed chickpeas.	naan-e nokhudchi	نان نخودچی
lunch	naahaar	ناهار
refectory; dining room	naahaar khori	ناهارخوری
chickpea	nokhudchi	نخودچی
starch	neshaasteh	نشاسته
saucer	na'lbaki	نعلبکی
salt	namak	نمک
drink	nushaabeh	نوشابه
straw (to drink through)	ney	نی
fried egg	nimru	نیمرو
vanilla	vaanil	وانیل
cardamom	hel	هل
beefburger; hamburger	hamberger	همبرگر
rice steamed with carrots	havij polow	هویج پلو
traditional Iranian dessert made from sugar, rice flour, rosewater and pistachio kernels, eaten cold.	yakh dar behesht	یخ در بهشت
type of Iranian stew	yakhni	یخنی

MORE WORDS AND PHRASES INVOLVING FOOD AND COOKING

to swallow قورت دادن — to drink آشامیدن — to drink نوشیدن — to eat; to drink خوردن

to chew جویدن — to bite گاز زدن — to lick لیس زدن — to lick لیسیدن — to taste مزه کردن

to boil (tr.) جوشاندن — to cook; to do the cooking آشپزی کردن — to cook (something) پختن

to bring to the boil به جوش آوردن — the water is boiling آب میجوشد — to boil (intr.) جوشیدن

to fry; to be fried سرخ شدن — to fry (tr.) سرخ کردن — to simmer به دل جوشیدن — to come to the boil جوش آمدن

to roast; to toast برشته کردن — to boil; to poach آبپز کردن — to warm; to heat گرم کردن

on a low heat روی شعله کم — to put in the oven توی فر گذاشتن — to be roasted; to be toasted برشته شدن

to chop into small pieces ریز ریز قطعه کردن — to chop into pieces قطعه قطعه کردن — to slice قاچ کردن

to cut to pieces; to grind خرد کردن — to pound کوبیدن — to grate رنده کردن — to cut بریدن

to pour; to spill ریختن — to take out of the oven از فر در آوردن — to mix; to blend مخلوط کردن

to dish up the food غذا کشیدن — to drain the water from something آب چیزی را کشیدن — to strain صاف کردن

different kinds of food انواع و اقسام غذاها — to prepare food غذا تهیه کردن — to prepare تهیه کردن

to prepare; to make ready حاضر کردن — to prepare; to make ready آماده کردن — to sprinkle پاشیدن

to wash the dishes ظرف شستن — last night I made dinner دیشب من شام درست کردم — to make درست کردن

bittersweet ملس — bitter تلخ — sour ترش — sweet شیرین — savoury شورمزه — salty شور

tasty خوشمزه — lacking in salt; tasteless بی نمک — hot (i.e. spicy) تند — astringent گس

the food has gone (ice-) cold غذا یخ کرده! — hot داغ — warm گرم — cold سرد — bad-tasting بدمزه

to go bad; to spoil خراب شدن — this bread has gone mouldy این نان کپک زده است — to go mouldy کپک زدن

frozen vegetables سبزیجات یخ زده — fresh vegetables سبزیجات تازه — fresh تازه — rotten فاسد

you have to put it in the fridge باید آن را توی یخچال بگذارید — you have to defrost it باید یخش را باز کنید

this food doesn't agree with me این غذا بمن نمیسازد — a hearty breakfast صبحانه مفصل

hungry گرسنه — I have indigestion سوء هاضمه دارم — this food made me feel sick این غذا حال مرا بهم زد

glutton شکمو — I have no appetite اشتها ندارم — I'm full سیر شدم — full سیر — thirsty تشنه

‹‹◊››

177

fireworks	aatash baazi	آتش بازی
weekend	aakhar-e hafteh	آخر هفته
ace (in cards)	aas	آس
cooking	aashpazi	آشپزی
advertisement	aagahi	آگهی
singing	aavaaz khaani	آواز خوانی
opera	operaa	اپرا
news	akhbaar	اخبار
television news	akhbaar-e televiziyun	اخبار تلویزیون
tourist camp; holiday camp	ordugaah-e turisti	اردوگاه توریستی
blind-man's-buff (children's game)	az-man-daari	از من داری
horse riding	asb savaari	اسب سواری
toy	asbaab-e baazi	اسباب بازی
swimming pool	estakhr	استخر
rest; relaxation	esteraahat	استراحت
notice	ettelaa'iyeh	اطلاعیه
kite	baad baadak	باد بادك
balloon	baad konak	بادکنک
game; playing	baazi	بازی
darts	baazi-ye tir paraani	بازی تیرپرانی
computer game	baazi-ye kaampyuter	بازی کامپیوتر
club	baashgaah	باشگاه
night club	baashgaah-e shabaaneh	باشگاه شبانه
community centre	baashgaah-e mahalleh	باشگاه محله
sports club	baashgaah-e varzeshi	باشگاه ورزشی
gardening	baaqbaani	باغبانی
knitting	baafandegi	بافندگی
hot-air ballooning	baalun savaari	بالون سواری
television programme	barnaame-ye televiziyun	برنامه تلویزیون
radio programme	barnaame-ye raadiyo	برنامه رادیو
ticket	belit	بلیط
queen (in cards)	bibi	بیبی
park	paark	پارك
leisure park; amusement park	paark-e tafrihi	پارك تفریحی
jigsaw puzzle	paazel	پازل
bird-watching	parandeh bini	پرنده بینی

pocket money	pul-e tu jibi	پول تو جیبی
e-mail	payaam-e elektruniki	پیام الکترونیکی
scout; girl guide	pishaahang	پیشاهنگ
spades (in cards)	pik	پیک
picnic	pik nik	پیک نیک
art gallery	taalaar-e aasaar-e honari	تالار آثار هنری
dance hall	taalaar-e raqs	تالار رقص
publicity	tabliqaat	تبلیغات
skateboard	takhte-ye eskeyt	تخته اسکیت
chess board	takhte-ye shatranj	تخته شطرنج
backgammon	takhteh nard	تخته نرد
weekend	ta'tilaat-e aakhar-e hafteh	تعطیلات آخر هفته
enjoyment; amusement; fun	tafrih	تفریح
telephone	telefon	تلفن
physical exercise	tamrin-e badani	تمرین بدنی
ball game; playing ball	tup baazi	توپ بازی
theatre	te'aatr	تئاتر
places of interest	jaa-haa-ye didani	جاهای دیدنی
crossword	jadval	جدول
touring; travelling	jahaangardi	جهانگردی
parachuting	chatr baazi	چتر بازی
merry-go-round	charkh o falak	چرخ و فلک
draughts; checkers	chekerz	چکرز
diamonds (in cards)	khaaj	خاج
shopping	kharid	خرید
reading	khaandan	خواندن
singer	khaanandeh	خواننده
enjoyment; having a good time	khoshgozaraani	خوشگذرانی
serialised story	daastaan-e donbaaleh daar	داستان دنباله دار
story-writing	daastaan nevisi	داستان نویسی
video recorder	dastgaah-e vide'o	دستگاه ویدئو
hearts (in cards)	del	دل
cycling	dow charkheh savaari	دو چرخه سواری
camera; binoculars	durbin	دوربین
sewing	duzandegi	دوزندگی
friend	dust	دوست
boyfriend	dust-e pesar	دوست پسر
girlfriend	dust-e dokhtar	دوست دختر

visiting (i.e. friends and family)	*did o baazdid*	دید و بازدید
meeting	*didaar*	دیدار
compact disk (CD)	*disk-e feshordeh*	دیسک فشرده
radio	*raadiyo*	رادیو
driving	*raanandegi*	رانندگی
walking; rambling; hiking	*raahnavardi*	راهنوردی
dance; dancing	*raqs*	رقص
novel	*romaan*	رمان
police novel	*romaan-e polisi*	رمان پلیسی
spy novel	*romaan-e jaasusi*	رمان جاسوسی
detective novel	*romaan-e kaaraagaahi*	رمان کاراگاهی
thriller	*romaan-e mohayyej*	رمان مهیج
painting; colouring	*rangzani*	رنگزنی
newspaper	*ruznaameh*	روزنامه
playground	*zamin-e baazi*	زمین بازی
beekeeping	*zanburdaari*	زنبور داری
film star	*setaare-ye sinamaa*	ستاره سینما
hobby; pastime	*sargarmi*	سرگرمی
jack (in cards)	*sarbaaz*	سرباز
slide	*sorsoreh*	سرسره
series	*seri*	سری
serial	*seryaal*	سریال
trip; journey	*safar*	سفر
drive; car journey	*safar-e baa maashin*	سفر با ماشین
outing; pleasure trip	*safar-e tafrihi*	سفر تفریحی
circus	*sirk*	سیرک
cinema	*sinamaa*	سینما
king (in cards)	*shaah*	شاه
evening; night	*shab*	شب
betting (e.g. on a horse)	*shartbandi*	شرطبندی
chess	*shatranj*	شطرنج
hunting	*shekaar*	شکار
swimming	*shenaa*	شنا
record	*safheh*	صفحه
long-playing record (LP)	*safhe-ye si o seh dowr*	صفحه ۳۳ دور
single	*safhe-ye chehel o panj dowr*	صفحه ۴۵ دور
tape recorder	*zabt-e sowt*	ضبط صوت
skipping	*tanaab baazi*	طناب بازی

member (i.e. of a club)	'ozv	عضو
photography	'akkaasi	عکاسی
photograph	'aks	عکس
interest	'alaaqeh	علاقه
brothel	faahesheh khaaneh	فاحشه خانه
fortune teller	faalgir	فالگیر
funfair	faanfaar	فانفار
leisure activities	fa'aaliyat-haa-ye tafrihi	فعالیت های تفریحی
sports activities	fa'aaliyat-haa-ye varzeshi	فعالیت های ورزشی
table football	futbaal-e dasti	فوتبال دستی
film	film	فیلم
camera film	film-e durbin	فیلم دوربین
video film	film-e vide'o'i	فیلم ویدئونی
storyteller	qesseh gu	قصه گو
gambling	qomaar baazi	قمار بازی
casino	qomaar khaaneh	قمارخانه
cabaret; night club	kaabaareh	کاباره
cartoon	kaartun	کارتون
cassette	kaaset	کاست
cafe	kaafeh	کافه
personal computer	kaampyuter-e shakhsi	کامپیوتر شخصی
youth club	kaanun-e javaanaan	کانون جوانان
book	ketaab	کتاب
library	ketaabkhaaneh	کتابخانه
collection	koleksiyun	کلکسیون
collector	koleksiyuner	کلکسیونر
concert	konsert	کنسرت
record player; stereo system	geraamaafun	گرامافون
collector	gerdaavar	گرد آور
collection	gerdaavard	گرد آورد
stamp collecting	gerdaavari-ye tambr	گرد آوری تمبر
walk; ramble; hike	gardesh	گردش
pinball machine	maashin-e pinbaal	ماشین پین بال
slot machine	maashin-e sekkeh pazir	ماشین سکه پذیر
fishing	maahigiri	ماهیگیری
comic	majalle-ye fokaahi	مجله فکاهی
illustrated magazine	majalle-ye mosavvar	مجله مصور
competition	mosaabeqeh	مسابقه

181

drinking; boozing	mashrub khori	مشروب خوری
meeting	molaaqaat	ملاقات
drugs	mavaad-e mokhaddereh	مواد مخدره
museum	muzeh	موزه
pop music	musiqi-ye paap	موسیقی پاپ
classical music	musiqi-ye kelaasik	موسیقی کلاسیک
pub; tavern	meykhaaneh	میخانه
party	mehmaani	مهمانی
letter	naameh	نامه
letter writing	naameh negaari	نامه نگاری
painting	naqqaashi	نقاشی
art gallery	negaar khaaneh	نگار خانه
baby sitting	negahdaari-ye bacheh	نگهداری بچه
show; exhibition	namaayesh	نمایش
sound and light show	namaayesh-e sedaa va nur	نمایش صدا و نور
exhibition centre	namaayeshgaah	نمایشگاه
stage play	namaayesh naameh	نمایشنامه
tape	navaar	نوار
small ads; want ads	niyaazmandi-haa	نیازمندیها
personal stereo; Walkman	vaakman	واکمن
sports stadium	varzeshgaah	ورزشگاه
game of cards	varaq baazi	ورق بازی
free time	vaqt-e aazaad	وقت آزاد
free time	vaqt-e feraaqat	وقت فراغت
killing time	vaqt koshi	وقت کشی
acting	honar namaa'i	هنرنمائی
yoga	yowgaa	یوگا

to be interested in; to enjoy; to like   علاقه داشتن   what do you do to pass the time?   وقتت را چطور می گذرانی؟

I enjoy swimming   از شنا لذت می برم   to enjoy   لذت بردن   I'm interested in sport; I like sport   به ورزش علاقه دارم

to read   خواندن   I watch television   تلویزیون تماشا می کنم   I go out with my friends   با دوستهایم بیرون می روم

I go for a walk   پیاده روی می روم   I read the newspaper   روزنامه می خوانم   I read books   کتاب می خوانم

my favourite hobby is chess   سرگرمی محبوبم شطرنج است   I have lots of hobbies   سرگرمی زیاد دارم

I go to the cinema   به سینما می روم   to swim   شنا کردن   to play chess   شطرنج بازی کردن   to play   بازی کردن

to sleep   خوابیدن   to rest   استراحت کردن   to stay at home   خانه ماندن   to play cards   ورق بازی کردن

whenever I get bored...   هر وقت حوصله ام سر می رود ...   to play the piano   پیانو زدن   to play the guitar   گیتار زدن

enjoyable   لذت بخش   great; cool; neat   باحال   funny   خنده دار   boring   خسته کننده   exciting   هیجان انگیز

what day?   چه روزی؟   when shall we meet?   کی هم دیگر را ببینیم؟   where shall we meet?   کجا هم دیگر را ببینیم؟

let's make (it) a date   قراری بگذاریم   give me a ring   بمن یک زنگی بزنید   I'll ring you   به شما زنگ می زنم

I don't have time   وقت ندارم   you've wasted my time   وقت مرا تلف کردی   to waste time   وقت تلف کردن

I don't have enough money   به اندازه کافی پول ندارم   I can't go out tonight   امشب نمی توانم بیرون بروم

I'm busy this evening   امشب کار دارم   I'm bored   حوصله ام سررفته   I can't be bothered   حوصله ندارم

I don't have time to go out   وقت بیرون رفتن را ندارم   to kill time   وقت کشی کردن   some other time   یک وقت دیگر

183

Fruit

میوه

plum	aalu	آلو
prune	aalu bokhaaraa	آلو بخارا
yellow plum; eggplum	aalu zard	آلو زرد
black cherry	aalubaalu	آلوبالو
damson	aalucheh	آلوچه
pineapple	aanaanaas	آناناس
avocado	aavokaadow	آوکادو
medlar	azgil	ازگیل
pomegranate	anaar	انار
mango	anbeh	انبه
fig	anjir	انجیر
grape(s)	angur	انگور
gooseberry	angur-e farangi	انگور فرنگی
almond	baadaam	بادام
peanut	baadaam-e zamini	بادام زمینی
cashew	baadaam-e hendi	بادام هندی
orchard	baaq-e miveh	باغ میوه
citron	baalang	بالنگ
bush	botteh	بته
bilberry	bilberi	بیل بری
quince	beh	به
papaya	paapaayaa	پاپایا
orange	portaqaal	پرتقال
pistachio	pesteh	پسته
skin; peel	pust	پوست
vineyard	taakestaan	تاکستان
tamarind	tamr-e hendi	تمر هندی
raspberry	tameshk	تمشک
blackberry	tameshk-e siyaah	تمشک سیاه
mulberry	tut	توت
strawberry	tut-e farangi	توت فرنگی
pink grapefruit	tusorkh	توسرخ
gooseberry	khaartut	خارتوت
honeydew melon	kharbozeh	خربزه
papaya	kharboze-ye derakhti	خربزه درختی
date	khormaa	خرما

persimmon	*khormaalu*	خرمالو
bunch of grapes	*khushe-ye angur*	خوشه انگور
grapefruit	*daaraabi*	دارابی
pip; stone	*daaneh*	دانه
fruit tree	*derakht-e miveh*	درخت میوه
breadfruit (tree)	*derakht-e naan*	درخت نان
grove; plantation	*derakhtestaan*	درختستان
variety of small melon	*dastanbu*	دستنبو
dogberry	*zoqaal akhteh*	ذغال اخته
rhubarb	*rivaas*	ریواس
wild plum	*zaalzaalak*	زالزالک
apricot	*zardaalu*	زرد آلو
olive	*zeytun*	زیتون
apple	*sib*	سیب
chestnut	*shaah balut*	شاه بلوط
black mulberry	*shaah tut*	شاه توت
nectarine	*shalil*	شلیل
cranberry	*keraan beri*	کران بری
kiwi fruit	*kivi*	کیوی
walnut	*gerdu*	گردو
cantaloupe melon	*garmak*	گرمک
pear	*golaabi*	گلابی
guava	*guaavaa*	گواوا
prune	*gowjeh baraqaani*	گوجه برقانی
cherry	*gilaas*	گیلاس
lychee	*lichi*	لیچی
lemon	*limu*	لیمو
lime	*limu-ye sabz*	لیموی سبز
sweet lemon	*limu-ye shirin*	لیموی شیرین
banana	*mowz*	موز
coconut	*naargil*	نارگیل
bitter (Seville) orange	*naarenj*	نارنج
tangerine; Satsuma; clementine	*naarangi*	نارنگی
date palm	*nakhl-e khormaa*	نخل خرما
palm grove	*nakhlestaan*	نخلستان
pip; stone	*hasteh*	هسته
peach	*holu*	هلو
watermelon	*hendavaaneh*	هندوانه

پر آب juicy   آبدار juicy   رسیده ripe   نارس unripe   شیرین sweet   ترش sour   تلخ bitter

گس astringent   لهیده squashed; squishy   هسته دار containing pips   خوش بو aromatic

پوست کلفت thick-skinned   پوست نازك thin-skinned   پوست کرده peeled   پوست کردن to peel

پوست کندن to peel   زیادی رسیده over-ripe   میوه دادن to bear fruit   میوه کاری fruit growing

به عمل آمدن to grow   آناناس در انگلستان به عمل نمیاید pineapples do not grow in England

کدام میوه را از همه بیشتر دوست دارید؟ which fruit do you like best of all?   خوش مزه tasty

آن میوه ها میشود با پوست خورد those fruits can be eaten with their skins   بدون هسته seedless

انواع و اقسام میوه ها different kinds of fruits   آن درخت میوه نمی دهد that tree doesn't bear fruit

بیشتر از صد نوع آلو در انگلستان به عمل میاید more than fifty varieties of plum grow in England

پنبه ای woody (lit. 'like cotton wool')   این سیب ها خشک و پنبه ای اند these apples are dry and woody

خرمالوی نارس خیلی گس است unripe persimmons are very astringent   میوه های نرم soft fruits

میوه ای fruit (adj.)   ماست میوه ای fruit yoghourt   آب میوه fruit juice   میوجات fruits

دانه seed   فصل انار است it is the pomegranate season   خارج از فصل out of season   فصلی seasonal

مرکبات citrus fruits   مازندران به باغ های مرکبات معروف است Mazanderan is famous for its citrus orchards

میوه جزء مهمی از رژیم غذائی سالم است fruit is an important part of a healthy diet   درخت میوه دار fruit-bearing tree

مغذی nutritious   پوست آن میوه از خود میوه مغذی تر است the skin of that fruit is more nutritious than the fruit itself

سرشار از ویتامین full of vitamins   مرکبات سرشار از ویتامین ث است citrus fruits are rich in vitamin C

میوه دلم my darling; my sweetheart (lit. 'fruit of my heart')   ثمر fruit   ثمربخش fruitful

کار ثمربخش a fruitful undertaking   اقدامات ثمربخش fruitful ventures   بی ثمر futile; fruitless

186

Geographical Features

ویژگی های جغرافیانی

watershed	aab pakhshaan	آب پخشان
fjord	aabdarreh	آبدره
waterway	aabraah	آبراه
reef	aabsang	آبسنگ
waterfall	aabshaar	آبشار
geyser	aabfeshaan	آبفشان
ravine	aabkand	آبکند
volcano	aatashfeshaan	آتشفشان
steppe	estep	استپ
ocean	oqiyaanus	اقیانوس
swamp	baatlaaq	باتلاق
quicksand	baatlaaq-e sheni	باتلاق شنی
desert	biyaabaan	بیابان
avalanche	bahman	بهمن
cliff; precipice	partgaah	پرتگاه
hinterland	paskaraaneh	پسکرانه
sand dune	tape-ye sheni	تپه شنی
gorge	tangdarreh	تنگدره
gorge	tangraah	تنگراه
strait	tangeh	تنگه
tundra	tundraa	توندرا
island	jazireh	جزیره
jungle; forest	jangal	جنگل
brook	juybaar	جویبار
spring	cheshmeh	چشمه
equator	khatt-e estevaa	خط استواء
gulf	khalij	خلیج
sea	daryaa	دریا
lake	daryaacheh	دریاچه
valley	darreh	دره
plain	dasht	دشت
moor; heath	dasht-e por tiq	دشت پر تیغ
delta	deltaa	دلتا
crater	dahaane-ye aatashfeshaan	دهانه آتشفشان
delta	rudbaar	رودبار
river	rudkhaaneh	رودخانه

landslide	*rizesh-e zamin*	ریزش زمین
earthquake	*zelzeleh*	زلزله
earth tremor	*zamin larzeh*	زمین لرزه
coast	*saahel*	ساحل
hinterland	*sarzamin-e doruni*	سر زمین درونی
mountain range	*selseleh jebaal*	سلسله جبال
rock	*sang*	سنگ
swamp	*siyaah aab*	سیاه آب
gully	*seylaab darreh*	سیلاب دره
tributary	*shaakhaabeh*	شاخابه
peninsula	*shebh-e jazireh*	شبه جزیره
abyss	*shekaaf-e zharf*	شکاف ژرف
sand dune	*shenposhteh*	شن پشته
shifting sands	*shenhaa-ye laqzandeh*	شنهای لغزنده
desert	*sahraa*	صحرا
rock	*sakhreh*	صخره
cave	*qaar*	غار
plateau	*felaat*	فلات
continent	*qaareh*	قاره
summit; peak	*qolleh*	قله
desert	*kavir*	کویر
mountain	*kuh*	کوه
iceberg	*kuh-e yakh*	کوه یخ
mountainside	*kuhpaayeh*	کوهپایه
lava	*godaazeh*	گدازه
mountain pass	*gardaneh*	گردنه
archipelago	*majma' ol-jazaa'er*	مجمع الجزائر
marsh	*mordaab*	مرداب
watercourse	*masir-e aab*	مسیر آب
estuary	*masabb*	مصب
stream	*nahr*	نهر
oasis	*vaaheh*	واحه
chasm	*varteh gaah*	ورطه گاه
ice flow	*yakhpaareh*	یخ پاره
ice cap	*yakhpahneh*	یخپهنه
glacier	*yakhrud*	یخرود
ice field	*yakhzaar*	یخزار
crevasse	*yakhshekaaf*	یخشکاف

Geology

زمین شناسی

corrosion; water erosion	*aab saa'i*	آب سانی
alluvium	*aabraft*	آبرفت
basin	*aabgir*	آبگیر
pyroclastic	*aazar aavari*	آذر آوری
marl	*aahak-e ros*	آهک رس
iron	*aahan*	آهن
epidote	*epidut*	اپی دوت
Iceland spar	*espaar-e islandi*	اسپار ایسلندی
stalactite	*estaalaagtit*	استالاگتیت
stalagmite	*estaalaagmit*	استالاگمیت
elaterite	*elaaterit*	الاتریت
alexandrite	*aleksaandrit*	الکساندریت
diamond	*almaas*	الماس
olivine	*olivin*	الیوین
xenolith	*anir sang*	انیر سنگ
loess	*baadraft*	باد رفت
deflation; wind erosion	*baad farsaa'i*	باد فرسائی
outlier	*borun heshteh*	برون هشته
bedding plane	*bastareh*	بستره
crystal	*bolur*	بلور
bort	*burt*	بورت
bauxite	*buksit*	بوکسیت
bitumen	*bitumen*	بیتومن
rock	*paareh sang*	پاره سنگ
shale	*paalmeh sang*	پالمه سنگ
podsol	*podzol*	پدزل
pegmatite	*pegmaatit*	پگماتیت
slate	*polmeh sang*	پلمه سنگ
alluvial fan	*panje-ye aabrafti*	پنجه آبرفتی
geode	*puk sang*	پرک سنگ
lepidolite	*pulak sang*	پولک سنگ
pitchblende	*pichbelend*	پیچ بلند
fool's gold; pyrite	*pirit*	پیریت
anticline	*taaqdis*	تاقدیس
concretion	*tahajjor*	تحجر
rock; boulder	*takhte-ye sang*	تخته سنگ

permeability	taraavaa'i	تراوائی
fracture	tarak	ترك
tripoli	teripuli	تریپولی
deformation	taqyir-e shekl	تغییر شكل
culm	tofaale-ye zoqaal-e sang	تفاله زغال سنگ
peat	turb	تورب
tourmaline	turmaalin	تورمالین
tufa	tufaa	توفا
tundra	tundraa	توندرا
alluvium	tah neshin	ته نشین
abstraction	jodaa saazi	جدا سازی
lustre	jalaa	جلا
gems; precious stones; jewels	javaaher	جواهر
composite; conglomerate	jush sang	جوش سنگ
cinnabar	jiveh sulfid-e qermez	جیوه سولفید قرمز
artesian well	chaah-e khod jush	چاه خود جوش
chert	chert	چرت
stalactite	chekandeh sang	چكنده سنگ
stalagmite	chekideh sang	چكیده سنگ
fold	chin	چین
moonstone	hajr ol-qamar	حجر القمر
soil; earth	khaak	خاك
pedalfer	khaak-e aahan	خاك آهن
china clay	khaak-e chini	خاك چینی
adobe	khaak-e kheshti	خاك خشتی
clay	khaak-e ros	خاك رس
chernozem	khaak-e siyaah	خاك سیاه
loam	khaak-e goldaani	خاك گلدانی
fire clay	khaak-e nasuz	خاك نسوز
argillaceous rocks	khaak-haa-ye ros maanand	خاك های رس مانند
ash	khaakestar	خاكستر
detritus	khordeh sang	خرده سنگ
creep	khazesh	خزش
cairngorm	dorr-e kuhi	در كوهی
joint	darzeh	درزه
incretion	darun rizeh	درونریزه
inclusion	darun gireh	درونگیره
metamorphism	degarguni	دگرگونی

dolomite	dulumit	دولومیت
diatomite	diyaatumit	دیاتومیت
diorite	diyurit	دیوریت
fulgurite	rakhsheh sang	رخشه سنگ
porous	rekhneh pazir	رخنه پذیر
ball clay	ros-e kuzeh gari	رس کوزه گری
deposit	rosub	رسوب
vein; layer; stratum	rageh	رگه
dendritic	rageh daar	رگه دار
overburden	rubaar	روبار
rutile	rutil	روتیل
flowage	ravandesh	روندش
granule	rizeh	ریزه
gravel	rig	ریگ
topaz	zabarjad	زبرجد
peridot	zabarjad-e sabz	زبرجد سبز
zircon	zargun	زرگون
coal	zoqaal-e sang	زغال سنگ
earthquake	zelzeleh	زلزله
emerald	zomorrod	زمرد
aquamarine	zomorrod-e kabud	زمرد کبود
geologist	zamin shenaas	زمین شناس
geology	zamin shenaasi	زمین شناسی
earth tremor	zamin larzeh	زمین لرزه
geosyncline	zamin-e naavdis	زمین ناودیس
zeolite	ze'ulit	زئولیت
subsoil	zir khaak	زیر خاک
batholith	zharf sakhreh	ژرف صخره
columnar structure	saakhtaar-e sotuni	ساختار ستونی
abrasion	saayesh	سایش
ablation	saayidegi	ساییدگی
neck	sotun-e sang-haa-ye aazarin	ستون سنگ های آذرین
hard-pan	sakht laayeh	سخت لایه
nodule	sakhtgaah	سختگاه
hardness	sakhti	سختی
galena	sorb-e gugerdi	سرب گوگردی
asthenosphere	sost koreh	سست کره
cleavage plane	sath-e shekaaf	سطح شکاف

water table	sofre-ye aab	سفره آب
celestite	selestit	سلستیت
rock; stone; boulder	sang	سنگ
acid rock	sang-e asidi	سنگ اسیدی
chert	sang-e aatash zaneh	سنگ آتش زنه
sill	sang-e aazarin-e feshordeh	سنگ آذرین فشرده
clastic rock	sang-e aavaari	سنگ آواری
limestone	sang-e aahak	سنگ آهک
black-band ironstone	sang-e aahan-e navaar siyaah	سنگ آهن نوار سیاه
basalt	sang-e baazaalt	سنگ بازالت
breccia	sang-e beresh	سنگ برش
country rock	sang-e borungir	سنگ برونگیر
pumice	sang-e paa	سنگ پا
tor	sang tal	سنگ تل
flint	sang-e chakhmaaq	سنگ چخماق
granite	sang-e khaaraa	سنگ خارا
corundum	sang-e sonbaadeh	سنگ سنباده
hornstone	sang-e shaakhi	سنگ شاخی
soapstone	sang-e saabun	سنگ صابون
gypsum	sang-e gach	سنگ گچ
lapis lazuli; ultramarine	sang-e laajavard	سنگ لاجورد
touchstone	sang-e mahak	سنگ محک
halite	sang-e namak	سنگ نمک
gneiss	sang-e nis	سنگ نیس
semi-precious stone	sang-e nimeh bahaadaar	سنگ نیمه بها دار
chalcedony	sang-e yamaani	سنگ یمانی
igneous rocks	sang-haa-ye aazarin	سنگ های آذرین
extrusive rocks	sang-haa-ye borun raandi	سنگ های برون راندی
metamorphic rocks	sang-haa-ye degardisi	سنگ های دگردیسی
sedimentary rocks	sang-haa-ye rosubi	سنگ های رسوبی
arenacious rocks	sang-haa-ye sheni	سنگ های شنی
basic rock	sang-haa-ye qalyaa'i	سنگ های قلیائی
precious stones; gems	sang-haa-ye geraanbahaa	سنگ های گرانبها
plutonic rocks	sang-haa-ye moqaaki	سنگ های مغاکی
concretion	sangaal	سنگال
cobble	sangpaareh	سنگپاره
detritus; pebble; granule; gravel	sangrizeh	سنگریزه
fossil	sangvaareh	سنگواره

silica	silikaa	سیلیکا
kieselguhr	silikaa zhel	سیلیکا ژل
silicates	silikaat	سیلیکات
syenite	siyenit	سینیت
cleavage; fracture	shekaaf	شکاف
sand; grit	shen	شن
oil shale	shen-e naft daar	شن نفت دار
schist	shist	شیست
obsidian	shisheh sang	شیشه سنگ
glassy	shisheh maanand	شیشه مانند
rock; stone	sakhreh	صخره
dyke	sakhreh divaar	صخره دیوار
gold	talaa	طلا
talc	talq	طلق
agate; opal	'aqiq	عقیق
sardonyx	'aqiq-e raah raah	عقیق راه راه
chrysoprase	'aqiq-e sabz	عقیق سبز
onyx	'aqiq-e soleymaani	عقیق سلیمانی
amorphous	qeyr-e motabalver	غیر متبلور
ablation; erosion	farsaayesh	فرسایش
leaching	foru shost	فروشست
cataclastic	foru shekan	فروشکن
fossil	fosil	فسیل
feldspar	feldespaar	فلدسپار
fluorite	folurit	فلوریت
fuchsite	fuksit	فوکسیت
turquoise	firuzeh	فیروزه
boulder	qolveh sang	قلوه سنگ
bitumen	qir-e ma'dani	قیر معدنی
karst	kaarst	کارست
cassiterite	kaasiterit	کاسی تریت
chondrites	kaandrit	کاندریت
mineral (adj.)	kaani	کانی
ore	kaaneh	کانه
elaterite	kaa'uchu-ye ma'dani	کائوچوی معدنی
kaolin	kaa'ulin	کائولین
carbonate	karbonaat	کربنات
chromite	kerumit	کرومیت

chalcocite	kalsusit	كلسوسيت
chalcopyrite	kalkupirit	كلكوپريت
chlorite	kolurit	كلوريت
quartz	kvaartz	كوارتز
rock crystal	kvaartz-e bolurin	كوارتز بلورين
citrine	kvaartz-e zard	كوارتز زرد
rose quartz	kvaartz-e sorkh	كوارتز سرخ
cuprite	kuprit	كوپريت
corundum	kuraandom	كوراندم
orogeny	kuh zaa'i	كوه زائى
horst	kuheh	كوهه
chiastolite	kiyaastulit	كياستوليت
kyanite	kiyaanit	كيانيت
kimberlite	kimberlit	كيمبرليت
amber	kahrobaa	كهربا
jet	kahrobaa-ye siyaah	كهرباى سياه
gaabro	gaabrow	گابرو
natural gas	gaaz-e tabi'i	گاز طبيعى
ganister	gaanister	گانيستر
chalk	gach	گچ
lava	godaazeh	گدازه
intrusion	godaazeh raani	گدازه رانى
rhyolite	godaazeh sang	گدازه سنگ
graphite	geraafit	گرافيت
hade	gosal shib	گسل شيب
fault	gosaleh	گسله
mud	gel	گل
mudstone	gelsang	گلسنگ
salt dome	gonbad-e namak	گنبد نمک
humus	giyaah khaak	گياه خاك
labradorite	laabraadurit	لابرادوريت
laterite	laaterit	لاتريت
humus	laashbarg	لاشبرگ
aquifer	laaye-ye aabzaa	لايه آبزا
lamination	laaye-ye naazok	لايه نازك
silt	lajan	لجن
garnet	la'l	لعل
spinel	la'l-e badakhshaan	لعل بدخشان

limonite	limunit	لیمونیت
mineral (n.)	maadde-ye ma'dani	ماده معدنی
sandstone	maaseh sang	ماسه سنگ
magma	maagmaa	ماگما
magnetite	maagnetit	ماگنتیت
malachite	maalaashit	مالاشیت
monzonite	maanzunit	مانزونیت
moonstone	maah sang	ماه سنگ
porous	motakhalkhal	متخلخل
coral	marjaan	مرجان
epicentre	markaz-e zamin larzeh	مرکز زمین لرزه
marble	marmar	مرمر
onyx marble	marmar-e abri	مرمر ابری
basalt	marmar-e siyaah	مرمر سیاه
muscovite	mosgovit	مسگویت
mine	ma'dan	معدن
quarry	ma'dan-e sang	معدن سنگ
magnesite	magnezit	مگنزیت
mica	mikaa	میکا
oil	naft	نفت
impervious	nofuz naapazir	نفوذ ناپذیر
silver	noqreh	نقره
salt	namak	نمک
hemicrystalline	nimeh boluri	نیمه بلوری
deposit	nahesht	نهشت
mineral deposits	nahesht kaani	نهشت کانی
wolframite	volfraamit	ولف رامیت
haematite	hemaatit	هماتیت
convergence	hamgaraa'i	همگرائی
weathering	havaazadegi	هوازدگی
amethyst	yaaqut-e arqavaani	یاقوت ارغوانی
chrysolite	yaaqut-e sabz	یاقوت سبز
ruby	yaaqut-e sorkh	یاقوت سرخ
sapphire	yaaqut-e kabud	یاقوت کبود
erratic	yakhrafteh	یخرفته
jasper	yashm	یشم
bloodstone	yashm-e khataa'i	یشم خطائی
jade	yashm-e sabz	یشم سبز

Grammar   دستور زبان

blend	*aamikhteh*	آمیخته
epicene	*episin*	اپی سین
declarative; indicative	*akhbaari*	اخباری
contraction	*ekhtesaari*	اختصار
particle	*adaat*	ادات
suppletion	*ertebaat-e takmili*	ارتباط تکمیلی
anaphora	*erjaa'*	ارجاع
imperfect; continuous; progressive	*estemraari*	استمراری
noun	*esm*	اسم
collective noun	*esm-e jam'*	اسم جمع
proper noun; name	*esm-e khaas*	اسم خاص
common noun; generic noun	*esm-e 'aam*	اسم عام
gerund; verbal noun	*esm-e fe'l*	اسم فعل
nominal	*esmi*	اسمی
demonstrative	*eshaare'i*	اشاره ای
derivation	*eshteqaaq*	اشتقاق
paradigm	*olgu-ye sarfi*	الگوی صرفی
imperative	*amri*	امری
regular	*baa qaa'edeh*	با قاعده
reflexive	*baaztaabi*	بازتابی
segmentation	*bakhsh bakhsh saazi*	بخش بخش سازی
partitive	*bakhshi*	بخشی
restrictive	*bar aayandi*	بر آیندی
iterative	*basaayand namaa*	بسایند نما
simple	*basit*	بسیط
stem	*bon*	بن
clause	*band*	بند
main clause	*band-e asli*	بند اصلی
relative clause	*band-e mowsuli*	بند موصولی
subordinate clause	*band-e vaabasteh*	بند وابسته
coordinate clause	*band-e hampaayeh*	بند همپایه
irregular	*bi qaa'edeh*	بی قاعده
question	*porsesh*	پرسش
rhetorical question	*porsesh-e badihi*	پرسش بدیهی
indirect question	*porsesh-e qeyr-e mostaqim*	پرسش غیر مستقیم
postposition	*pas aayand*	پس آیند

suffix	*pasvand*	پسوند
enclitic	*pey bast*	پی بست
proclitic	*pish bast*	پیش بست
antecedent	*pish vaazheh*	پیش واژه
prefix	*pishvand*	پیشوند
connective	*peyvandi*	پیوندی
intensifier	*ta'kidi*	تأکیدی
dual	*tasniyeh*	تثنیه
parsing	*tajziyeh*	تجزیه
declension; inflection	*tasrif*	تصریف
diminutive	*tasqiri*	تصغیری
comparative	*tafzili*	تفضیلی
morpheme	*takvaazh*	تکواژ
optative	*tamannaa'i*	تمنائی
inversion	*jaabejaa saazi*	جابجاسازی
animate	*jaandaar*	جاندار
plural	*jam'*	جمع
sentence	*jomleh*	جمله
complex sentence	*jomle-ye morakkab*	جمله مرکب
clause	*jomleh vaareh*	جمله واره
main clause	*jomleh vaare-ye asli*	جمله واره اصلی
independent clause	*jomleh vaare-ye naavaabasteh*	جمله واره ناوابسته
dependent clause	*jomleh vaare-ye vaabasteh*	جمله واره وابسته
aspect	*janbe-ye fe'l*	جنبه فعل
gender	*jens*	جنس
enclitic	*chasbaaneh*	چسبانه
case	*haalat*	حالت
instrumental	*haalat-e abzaari*	حالت ابزاری
locative	*haalat-e andaari*	حالت اندری
nominative	*haalat-e faa'eli*	حالت فاعلی
accusative	*haalat-e maf'uli*	حالت مفعولی
dative	*haalat-e maf'ul-e baa vaaseteh*	حالت مفعول با راسطه
genitive	*haalat-e melki*	حالت ملکی
vocative	*haalet-e nedaa*	حالت ندا
preposition	*harf-e ezaafeh*	حرف اضافه
article	*harf-e ta'rif*	حرف تعریف
conjunction	*harf-e rabt*	حرف ربط
subordinating conjunction	*harf-e rabt-e vaabasteh saaz*	حرف ربط وابسته ساز

correlative conjunction	*harf-e rabt-e hambasteh*	حرف ربط همبسته
exclamation	*harf-e nedaa*	حرف ندا
predicate	*khabar*	خبر
indicative	*khabari*	خبری
degree	*darajeh*	درجه
grammar	*dastur-e zabaan*	دستور زبان
grammatical	*dasturi*	دستوری
reduplication	*dowgaan saazi*	دوگانسازی
concrete	*zaat*	ذات
substantive	*zaati*	ذاتی
root	*risheh*	ریشه
tense	*zamaan*	زمان
future tense	*zamaan-e aayandeh*	زمان آینده
present tense	*zamaan-e haal*	زمان حال
perfect (tense)	*zamaan-e kaamel*	زمان کامل
past tense	*zamaan-e gozashteh*	زمان گذشته
morphology	*saakht shenaasi-ye vaazhgaani*	ساخت شناسی واژگانی
constituent	*saazeh*	سازه
causative	*sababi*	سببی
stem	*setaak*	ستاک
person	*shakhs*	شخص
conditional	*sharti*	شرطی
inceptive	*shoru'i*	شروعی
countable	*shomaaresh pazir*	شمارش پذیر
conjugation; declension; inflection	*sarf*	صرف
finite	*sarf shodani*	صرف شدنی
adjective	*sefat*	صفت
adjunct	*sefat-e far'i*	صفت فرعی
gerundive	*sefat-e fe'li*	صفت فعلی
predicate adjective	*sefat-e gozaare'i*	صفت گزاره ای
possessive adjective	*sefat-e melki*	صفت ملکی
form	*siqeh*	صیغه
subjunctive	*siqe-ye sharti*	صیغه شرطی
pronoun	*zamir*	ضمیر
demonstrative pronoun	*zamir-e eshaareh*	ضمیر اشاره
exclusive	*zamir-e enhesaari*	ضمیر انحصاری
possessive pronoun	*zamir-e melki*	ضمیر ملکی
relative pronoun	*zamir-e mowsuli*	ضمیر موصولی

pronominal	*zamiri*	ضميرى
generic	*'aam*	عام
clause; phrase	*'ebaarat*	عبارت
prepositional phrase	*'ebaarat-e qeydi*	عبارت قيدى
apposition	*'atf-e bayaan*	عطف بيان
impersonal	*qeyr-e shakhsi*	غير شخصى
oblique	*qeyr-e faa'eli*	غير فاعلى
subject	*faa'el*	فاعل
compound subject	*faa'el-e morakkab*	فاعل مركب
government	*farmaanesh*	فرمانش
verb	*fe'l*	فعل
inceptive	*fe'l-e aaqaazgar*	فعل آغازگر
irregular verb	*fe'l-e bi qaa'edeh*	فعل بى قاعده
copula	*fe'l-e rabt*	فعل ربط
auxiliary verb	*fe'l-e komaki*	فعل كمكى
phrasal verb	*fe'l-e morakkab*	فعل مركب
rule	*qaa'edeh*	قاعده
adverb	*qeyd*	قيد
adverbial	*qeydi*	قيدى
word	*kalameh*	كلمه
clipping; abbreviation	*kutah saazi*	كوته سازى
preterite; past tense	*gozashteh*	گذشته
pluperfect	*gozashte-ye kaamel*	گذشته كامل
phrase; predicate	*gozaareh*	گزاره
intransitive	*laazem*	لازم
preterite; past tense	*maazi*	ماضى
pluperfect	*maazi-ye ba'id*	ماضى بعيد
past narrative; perfect tense	*maazi-ye naqli*	ماضى نقلى
subject and predicate	*mobtadaa va khabar*	مبتداء و خبر
transitive	*mota'addi*	متعدى
affirmative	*mosbat*	مثبت
passive	*majhul*	مجهول
closed	*makhtum be-harf-e bi sedaa*	مختوم به حرف بى صدا
antecedent	*marja'*	مرجع
complement	*mosnad*	مسند
infinitive	*masdar*	مصدر
split infinitive	*masdar-e gosasteh*	مصدر گسسته
concord; agreement	*motaabeqat*	مطابقت

definite	mo'arrefeh	معرفه
active	ma'lum	معلوم
single	mofrad	مفرد
object; passive	maf'ul	مفعول
indirect object	maf'ul-e baa vaaseteh	مفعول با واسطه
direct object	maf'ul-e bi vaaseteh	مفعول بی واسطه
ablative	maf'ul-on-beh	مفعول به
direct object	maf'ul-e mostaqim	مفعول مستقیم
notional	mafhumi	مفهومی
possessive	melki	ملکی
negative	manfi	منفی
infix	miyaanvand	میانوند
discontinuous	naapeyvasteh	ناپیوسته
indefinite	naashenaakhteh	ناشناخته
defective	naaqes	ناقص
hypotaxis	naahampaayegi	ناهمپایگی
syntax	nahv	نحو
syntactic	nahvi	نحوی
tagmeme	naqsh gir	نقش گیر
indirect speech	naql-e qowl-e qeyr-e mostaqim	نقل قول غیر مستقیم
indefinite (article)	nakareh	نکره
dependent	vaabasteh	وابسته
determiner	vaabaste-ye esm	وابسته اسم
subordinator	vaabasteh saaz	وابسته ساز
subordination	vaabasteh saazi	وابسته سازی
qualifier	vaabaste-ye vasfi	وابسته وصفی
root	vaaj paayeh	واج پایه
modification	vaazh degaresh	واژ دگرش
morpheme	vaazhak	واژک
word	vaazheh	واژه
word order	vaazheh pardaazi	واژه پردازی
interrogative	vaazhe-ye porseshi	واژه پرسشی
hybrid	vaazhe-ye peyvandi	واژه پیوندی
formative	vaazheh saaz	واژه ساز
word formation	vaazheh saazi	واژه سازی
interjection	vaazhe-ye shegeft namaa	واژه شگفت نما
form; mood	vajh	وجه
indicative mood	vajh-e akhbaari	وجه اخباری

imperative mood	vajh-e amri	وجه امری
subjunctive mood	vajh-e sharti	وجه شرطی
modal	vajh namaa	وجه نما
participle	vajh-e vasfi	وجه وصفی
past participle	vajh-e vasfi-ye majhul	وجه وصفی مجهول
present participle	vajh-e vasfi-ye ma'lum	وجه وصفی معلوم
attributive	vasfi	وصفی
affix; particle	vand	وند
head	haste-ye asli	هسته اصلی
correlative	hambasteh saaz	همبسته ساز
coordination; parataxis	hampaayegi	همپایگی
coordinate	hampaayeh	همپایه
coordinator	hampaayeh saaz	همپایه ساز

Greetings and Interjections

خوش آمد گونی و واژه های شگفت نما

GREETINGS

hello! (said both as initial greeting and response)	*salaam*	سلام!
hello! (lit. 'peace be with you')	*salaam 'aleykom*	سلام علیکم!
hello! (response to above; lit. 'and peace be with you too')	*'aleykom as-salaam*	علیکم السلام!
good morning!	*sobh bekheyr*	صبح بخیر!
good day!	*ruz bekheyr*	روز بخیر!
how are you?	*haal-e shomaa chetowreh?*	حال شما چطوره؟
fine, thanks	*khubeh, mersi*	خوبه، مرسی
not bad, thanks	*bad nist, mersi*	بد نیست، مرسی
how are you?	*chetowrid?*	چطورید؟
I'm fine, thanks	*khubam, mersi*	خوبم، مرسی
what's new?	*che khabar?*	چه خبر؟
pleased to meet you	*az aashenaa'iyetaan kheyli khoshvaqtam*	از آشنائیتان خیلی خوشوقتم
hello (on the telephone)	*alo*	الو
good evening; good night	*shab bekheyr*	شب بخیر!
see you tomorrow!	*fardaa mibinamet*	فردا می بینمت!
goodbye	*khodaa haafez*	خدا حافظ!
hope to see you soon	*be-omid-e didaar*	به امید دیدار!
take care! (lit. may God protect you)	*khodaa negahdaar*	خدا نگهدار!
good night; sweet dreams	*shab khosh*	شب خوش!

BEST WISHES

happy birthday!	*tavallod-e shomaa mobaarak*	تولد شما مبارك!
happy New Year! (Iranian)	*'eyd-e shomaa mobaarak*	عید شما مبارك!
congratulations!	*tabrik 'arz mikonam*	تبریک عرض می کنم!
congratulations! (said when admiring a new acquisition)	*mobaarak baasheh*	مبارك باشه!
bon appetit!	*nush-e jaan*	نوش جان!
good luck!	*mo'affaq baashid*	موفق باشید!
bless you! (after a sneeze)	*'aafiyat baasheh*	عافیت باشه!
cheers!	*salaamati*	سلامتی!
bon voyage!	*safar bekheyr*	سفر بخیر!

SURPRISE

oh God!	ey khodaa	ای خدا!
well...	khob	خُب ...
what was that? what happened?	chi shod	چی شد؟
really?	jeddi	جدّی؟
really? no kidding?	raast migu'i	راست می گوئی ؟
really?	vaaq'an	واقعا ؟
what a lot of ...	cheh	چه ...
how ...	cheqadr	چقدر ...
you're kidding!	shukhi mikoni	شوخی می کنی!
get away with you!	boro baabaa	برو بابا!
what luck!	'ajab shaansi	عجب شانسی!

POLITENESS

please	lotfan	لطفاً
please	khaahesh mikonam	خواهش می کنم
thankyou	motashakkeram	متشکرم
thankyou	mersi	مرسی
thankyou very much	kheyli mamnun	خیلی ممنون
excuse me	bebakhshid	ببخشید
please forgive me	ma'zerat mikhaaham	معذرت می خواهم
please (have a seat; start eating; come in, etc.)	befarmaa'id	بفرمائید
no thankyou	nah mersi	نه مرسی
no thankyou	nah motashakkeram	نه متشکرم
yes please	baleh lotfan	بلی لطفاً
not at all; don't mention it	khaahesh mikonam	خواهش می کنم!
of course	albatteh	البته
with pleasure	baa kamaal-e meyl	با کمال میل
it's no problem	mas'ale'i nist	مسئله ای نیست
say hello to him from me	salaam-e maraa be-u beresaanid	سلام مرا به او برسانید
thankyou (lit. 'may your hand not hurt')	dast-e shomaa dard nakoneh	دست شما درد نکنه
not at all (lit. 'may your head not hurt')	sar-e shomaa dard nakoneh	سر شما درد نکنه
thankyou (lit. 'may I be your sacrifice')	qorbaan-e shomaa	قربان شما!

AGREEMENT

yes	baleh	بلی
no	nah	نه
of course; naturally	albatteh	البته
okay	baasheh	باشه
agreed?	qabul	قبول؟
do you agree?	mo'aafeq hastid	موافق هستید؟
exactly; that's just it	hamin	همین!
so much the better	cheh behtar	چه بهتر
I don't mind; it's all the same to me	baraa-ye man farqi nemikoneh	برای من فرقی نمی کنه

DISAGREEMENT

no	nah	نه
no; not at all	nakheyr	نخیر
yes (contradicting a negative statement)	cheraa	چرا!
of course not	albatteh keh nah	البته که نه
never! not on your life!	nah baabaa	نه بابا!
not at all	aslan	اصلأ
never	abadan	ابدأ
on the contrary	bar 'aks	بر عکس
what a cheek!	'ajab ru'i	عجب روئی!
what's it got to do with you?	be-to cheh	به تو چه؟
mind your own business	kaar-e khodet-raa bokon	کار خودترا بکن!
it's none of your business	be-shomaa marbut nist	به شما مربوط نیست
what business is it of yours?	be-shomaa cheh marbut?	به شما چه مربوط؟
it depends	bastegi daarad	بستگی دارد
down with.... ; death to....	marg bar	مرگ بر...

DISTRESS

help!	komak	کمک!
fire!	aatash	آتش!
ouch!	aakh	آخ!
I'm sorry	mota'assefam	متاسفم
excuse me	bebakhshid	ببخشید
excuse me; forgive me	ma'zerat mikhaaham	معذرت می خواهم

204

please accept my condolences	tasliyat 'arz mikonam	تسلیت عرض می کنم
what a shame!	heyf	حیف!
I'm bored	howselam sar rafteh	حوصله ام سر رفته
I'm fed up; I'm tired	khasteh shodam	خسته شدم
I can't stand it any longer	digar tahammol nadaaram	دیگر تحمل ندارم
what a shambles!	'ajab khar tu khari	عجب خر تو خری!
no! what a shame!	ey baabaa	ای بابا!
how awful!	che bad	چه بد!
what am I to do?	che kaar konam	چه کار کنم؟
what point is there?	che faayede'i daarad	چه فایده ای دارد؟
there's no point	faayedeh nadaarad	فایده ندارد

ORDERS

watch out!; be careful!	movaazeb baash	مواظب باش!
stop!	vaastaa	واستا!
go!	boro	برو!
get lost!	boro gom show	برو گم شو!
shhh	his	هیس!
that's enough!	baseh digeh	بسه دیگه!
calm down!	araam begir	آرام بگیر!
be quiet!	saaket baash	ساکت باش!
shut up!	khafeh show	خفه شو!
go to hell!	boro jahannam	برو جهنم!
come!	biyaa	بیا!
don't!	nakon	نکن!
don't speak!	harf nazan	حرف نزن!

OTHERS

maybe; perhaps	shaayad	شاید
so what?	khub chi	خوب چی؟
I'm coming!	aamadam	آمدم!
listen!	gush kon	گوش کن!
don't rush (into things)!	'ajaleh nakon	عجله نکن!
make yourself at home!	raahat baash	راحت باشید!
it's not worth it	nemiyarzeh	نمی ارزه
poor thing!	bichaareh	بیچاره!
well done!	maashaallaah	ماشاء الله!
bravo!	aafarin	آفرین!

God forbid!	khodaa nakoneh	خدا نکنه !
in no way	be-hich vajh	به هیچ وجه
God willing	enshaallaah	انشاء الله
(I swear) on your life	be jaan-e to	به جان تو
may God have mercy on him	khodaa rahmatesh koneh	خدا رحمتش کنه
don't go to any trouble	zahmat nakeshid	زحمت نکشید
by the way...	raasti	راستی

206

hydrotherapy	aab darmaani	آب درمانی
dehydration	aab zadaa'i	آب زدائی
glaucoma	aab-e siyaah	آب سیاه
cataract	aab-e morvaarid	آب مروارید
ectopic pregnancy	aabestani-ye khaarej-e rahem	آبستنی خارج رحم
abscess	aabseh	آبسه
smallpox	aabeleh	آبله
chickenpox	aabeleh morqaan	آبله مرغان
disabled person	aadam-e ma'lul	آدم معلول
sedative	aaraam bakhsh	آرامبخش
test; examination; screening; smear	aazmaayesh	آزمایش
urine test	aazmaayesh-e edraar	آزمایش ادرار
skin test	aazmaayesh-e pust	آزمایش پوست
blood test	aazmaayesh-e khun	آزمایش خون
aspirin	aasperin	آسپرین
asthma	aasm	آسم
pathology	aasib shenaasi	آسیب شناسی
osteopathy	aasib shenaasi-ye ostokhaan	آسیب شناسی استخوان
sunburn	aaftaab sukhtegi	آفتاب سوختگی
allergy	aalerzhi	آلرژی
swelling; inflammation	aamaas	آماس
appendicitis	aamaas-e aapaandis	آماس آپاندیس
duodenitis	aamaas-e esnaa 'ashar	آماس اثنی عشر
phalangitis	aamaas-e band-e angosht	آماس بند انگشت
orchitis	aamaas-e beyzeh	آماس بیضه
meningitis	aamaas-e parde-haa-ye maqz	آماس پرده های مغز
urethritis	aamaas-e pishaabraah	آماس پیشابراه
gastroenteritis	aamaas-e shekam	آماس شکم
neuritis	aamaas-e 'asab	آماس عصب
gingivitis	aamaas-e laseh	آماس لثه
tonsillitis	aamaas-e lowze-haa	آماس لوزه ها
cystitis	aamaas-e masaaneh	آماس مثانه
encephalitis	aamaas-e maqz	آماس مغز
ambulance	aambulaans	آمبولانس
injection	aampul	آمپول
emphysema	aamfizem	آمفیزم

antibiotic	*aanti biutik*	آنتی بیوتیک
angina	*aanzhin*	آنژین
influenza	*aanflu aanzaa*	آنفلوانزا
aneurysm	*aanurism*	آنوریسم
Ayurveda	*aayur vedaa*	آیور ودا
waiting room	*otaaq-e entezaar*	اتاق انتظار
operating theatre	*otaaq-e jarraahi*	اتاق جراحی
HIV	*ech aay vi*	اچ آی وی
convulsion	*ekhtelaaj*	اختلاج
stomach upset	*ekhtelaal-e me'deh*	اختلال معده
urine	*edraar*	ادرار
orthodontics	*artaa dandaanpezeshki*	ارتادندانپزشکی
orthotics	*artaa saazi*	ارتاسازی
throat spray	*esperey-e galu*	اسپری گلو
spina bifida	*espenaa bifidaa*	اسپنا بیفیدا
bone	*ostokhaan*	استخوان
orthopaedics	*ostokhaan pezeshki*	استخوان پزشکی
steroids	*esteru'id*	استرونید
dropsy	*estesqaa*	استسقاء
vomiting	*estefraaq*	استفراغ
schizophrenia	*eskizufreni*	اسکیزوفرنی
diarrhoea	*es-haal*	اسهال
dysentery	*es-haal-e khuni*	اسهال خونی
X-rays	*asha'e-ye iks*	اشعه ایکس
radiotherapy	*asha'eh darmaani*	اشعه درمانی
addiction	*e'tiyaad*	اعتیاد
alcoholism	*e'tiyaad be-alkol*	اعتیاد به الکل
drug addiction	*e'tiyaad be-mavaad-e mokhaddereh*	اعتیاد به مواد مخدره
depression	*afsordegi*	افسردگی
eczema	*egzemaa*	اگزما
inflammation	*eltehaab*	التهاب
laryngitis	*eltehaab-e hanjareh*	التهاب حنجره
enteritis	*eltehaab-e rudeh*	التهاب روده
peritonitis	*eltehaab-e sefaaq*	التهاب صفاق
colitis	*eltehaab-e qulun*	التهاب قولون
renal diseases	*amraaz-e kolyavi*	امراض کلیوی
blood transfusion	*enteqaal-e khun*	انتقال خون
artificial limb	*andaam-e masnu'i*	اندام مصنوعی

premature ejaculation	enzaal-e mani-ye zudras	انزال منی زودرس
anthropology	ensaan shenaasi	انسان شناسی
insulin	ansulin	انسولین
parasitology	angal shenaasi	انگل شناسی
urology	uruluzhi	اورولوژی
mumps	ureyyun	اوریون
immunisation	ijaad-e imani	ایجاد ایمنی
Aids	eydz	ایدز
cardiac arrest	ist-e qalbi	ایست قلبی
immunity	imani	ایمنی
immunology	imani shenaasi	ایمنی شناسی
barbiturates	baarbituraat	باربیتورات
in vitro fertilization (IVF)	baarvari saazi-ye aazmaayeshgaahi	باروری سازی آزمایشگاهی
stenosis	baarik shodegi	باریک شدگی
histopathology	baaft aasib shenaasi	بافت آسیب شناسی
biopsy	baaft bardaari	بافت برداری
histology	baaft shenaasi	بافت شناسی
histochemistry	baaft shimi	بافت شیمی
infarct	baaft margi	بافت مرگی
bacteria	baakteri	باکتری
test-tube baby	bache-ye lule-ye aazmaayeshi	بچه لوله آزمایشی
department; ward	bakhsh	بخش
outpatients' department	bakhsh-e bimaaraan-e sarpaa'i	بخش بیماران سرپائی
casualty department; A&E	bakhsh-e savaaneh va tasaadofaat	بخش سوانح و تصادفات
intensive care department	bakhsh-e moraaqebat-e vizheh	بخش مراقبت ویژه
sutures; stitches	bakhiyeh	بخیه
malignant	bad khim	بد خیم
stretcher	beraankaar	برانکار
tomography	boresh negari	برش نگاری
thrush	barfak	برفک
electrocution	barq gereftegi	برق گرفتگی
bronchitis	berunshit	برونشیت
hospital bed	bastar	بستر
bed-sore	bastar zakhm	بستر زخم
piles; haemorrhoids	bavaasir	بواسیر
bulimia	bulimiyaa	بولیمیا
endemic	bum gir	بوم گیر
anorexia nervosa	bi eshtehaa'i-ye 'asabi	بی اشتهائی عصبی

209

arrhythmia	*bi nazmi-ye zarabaan-e qalb*	بی نظمی ضربان قلب
ill; sick; unwell	*bimaar*	بیمار
hospital	*bimaarestaan*	بیمارستان
illness; sickness	*bimaari*	بیماری
endemic	*bimaari-ye bumi*	بیماری بومی
Parkinson's Disease	*bimaari-ye paarkinsun*	بیماری پارکینسون
venereal disease; STD	*bimaari-ye moqaarebati*	بیماری مقاربتی
pandemic	*bimaari-ye vaagir*	بیماری واگیر
Hodgkin's lymphoma	*bimaari-ye haajkin*	بیماری هاجکین
epidemic	*bimaari-ye hameh gir*	بیماری همه گیر
outpatients	*bimaar-haa-ye sarpaa'i*	بیمارهای سرپائی
rhinology	*bini shenaasi*	بینی شناسی
general anaesthetic	*bihushi-ye kaamel*	بیهوشی کامل
local anaesthetic	*bihushi-ye mowze'i*	بیهوشی موضعی
recovery	*behbud*	بهبود
hygiene	*behdaasht*	بهداشت
hygienic	*behdaashti*	بهداشتی
chiropodist	*paa pezeshk*	پا پزشک
chiropody	*paa pezeshki*	پا پزشکی
paraplegia	*paa falaji*	پا فلجی
antiserum	*paad peymaab*	پاد پیماب
antibody; antitoxin	*paad tan*	پادتن
antibiotic	*paad zi*	پادزی
antidote	*paad zahr*	پادزهر
antigen	*paad gan*	پادگن
bandage; dressing	*paansemaan*	پانسمان
menorrhagia	*por dashtaani*	پر دشتانی
radiotherapy	*partov darmaani*	پرتو درمانی
radiobiology	*partov zist shenaasi*	پرتو زیست شناسی
radiology	*partov shenaasi*	پرتو شناسی
radiograph	*partov negaar*	پرتو نگار
nurse	*parastaar*	پرستار
peritonitis	*peritunit*	پریتونیت
doctor; physician	*pezeshk*	پزشک
general practitioner (GP)	*pezeshk-e amraaz-e 'omumi*	پزشک امراض عمومی
gynaecologist	*pezeshk-e zanaan*	پزشک زنان
paediatrician	*pezeshk-e kudak*	پزشک کودک
medicine (i.e. the discipline)	*pezeshki*	پزشکی

preventative medicine	pezeshki-ye pishgiri	پزشکی پیشگیری
forensic medicine	pezeshki-ye qaanuni	پزشکی قانونی
afterbirth	pas zaayeh	پس زایه
reflex	pas konesh	پس کنش
decline; regression	pasraft	پسرفت
ointment	pomaad	پماد
cotton wool	panbeh	پنبه
eczema	pust afrukhtegi	پوست افروختگی
dermatology	pust pezeshki	پوست پزشکی
plaster cast	pushesh-e gachi	پوشش گچی
condom	pushineh	پوشینه
osteoporosis	puki-ye ostokhaan	پوکی استخوان
polyp	pulip	پولیپ
geriatrics	piri pezeshki	پیری پزشکی
gerontology	piri shenaasi	پیری شناسی
vitiligo	pisi	پیسی
prolapse	pish oft	پیش افت
prognosis	pish shenaakht	پیش شناخت
diuretic	pishaab aavar	پیشاب آور
prevention; prophylaxis	pishgiri	پیشگیری
callus	pineh	پینه
transplant; graft	peyvand	پیوند
heart transplant	peyvand-e qalb	پیوند قلب
laparotomy	pahlu shekaafi	پهلو شکافی
blister	taaval	تاول
fever; high temperature	tab	تب
rheumatic fever	tab-e rumaatism	تب روماتیسم
yellow fever	tab-e zard	تب زرد
prickly heat	tab-e 'araq gaz	تب عرق گز
hay fever	tab-e yunjeh	تب یونجه
cold sore	tabkhaal	تبخال
herpes simplex	tabkhaal-e saadeh	تبخال ساده
bed	takhtekhaab	تختخواب
phobia	tars-e bimaar guneh	ترس بیمار گونه
bacteria	tarkizeh	ترکیزه
bacteriology	tarkizeh shenaasi	ترکیزه شناسی
thrombosis	terombuz	ترمبوز
injection	tazriq	تزریق

211

diagnosis	*tashkhis-e bimaari*	تشخیص بیماری
sclerosis	*tasallob*	تصلب
arteriosclerosis	*tasallob-e sharaayin*	تصلب شرایین
booster (injection)	*talqih-e tavaan afzaa*	تلقیح توان افزا
artificial insemination	*talqih-e masnu'i*	تلقیح مصنوعی
physiotherapist	*tan darmaangar*	تن درمانگر
physiotherapy	*tan darmaani*	تن درمانی
lymph	*tanaabeh*	تنابه
health	*tandorosti*	تندرستی
family planning	*tanzim-e khaanevaadeh*	تنظیم خانواده
artificial respiration	*tanaffos-e masnu'i*	تنفس مصنوعی
shock	*tankub*	تنکوب
breathlessness; dyspnoea	*tangi-ye nafas*	تنگی نفس
prosthetics	*jaanahesht shenaasi*	جانهشت شناسی
scar	*jaa-ye zakhm*	جای زخم
goitre	*jakhsh*	جخش
leprosy	*jozaam*	جذام
leper	*jozaami*	جذامی
surgeon	*jarraah*	جراح
wound	*jeraahat*	جراحت
surgery	*jaraahi*	جراحی
plastic surgery	*jaraahi-ye pelaastik*	جراحی پلاستیک
reconstructive surgery	*jaraahi-ye tarmimi*	جراحی ترمیمی
thoracic surgery	*jaraahi-ye sineh*	جراحی سینه
heart surgery	*jaraahi-ye qalb*	جراحی قلب
brain surgery	*jaraahi-ye maqz*	جراحی مغز
neurosurgery	*jaraahi-ye maqz o a'saab*	جراحی مغز و اعصاب
scabies	*jarab*	جرب
afterbirth; placenta	*joft*	جفت
contraception	*jelowgiri az haamelegi*	جلوگیری از حاملگی
blackhead	*jush-e sar siyaah*	جوش سرسیاه
pimple; spot	*jush-e surat*	جوش صورت
obesity	*chaaqi-ye shadid*	چاقی شدید
pus; mucus	*cherk*	چرک
ear wax	*cherk-e gush*	چرک گوش
eye specialist	*cheshm pezeshk*	چشم پزشک
ophthalmology	*chesm pezeshki*	چشم پزشکی
incontinence	*chakmizaki*	چکمیزکی

crutches	chubdasti	چوبدستی
nausea	haalat-e tahavvo'	حالت تهوع
peristalsis	harekat-e dudi	حرکت دودی
involuntary movement; tic; twitch	harekat-e qeyr-e eraadi	حرکت غیر ارادی
sensitivity; allergy	hassaasiyat	حساسیت
typhoid fever	hasbeh	حصبه
narcolepsy	hamle-ye khaab	حمله خواب
scratch	kharaashidegi	خراشیدگی
laryngitis	khorusak	خروسک
incubator	khosbaangar	خسبانگر
tiredness; fatigue	khastegi	خستگی
laryngology	khoshk naay shenaasi	خشک نای شناسی
phlegm	khelt	خلط
expectorant	khelt aavar	خلط آور
scrofula	khanaazir	خنازیر
hypnotherapy	khaab darmaani	خواب درمانی
hypochondriac	khod bimaar engaar	خود بیمار انگار
hypochondria	khod bimaar engaari	خود بیمار انگاری
leprosy	khoreh	خوره
benign	khosh khim	خوش خیم
blood	khun	خون
nosebleed	khun damaaq	خون دماغ
haematology	khun shenaasi	خون شناسی
haemolysis	khun kaavi	خون کاوی
serum	khunaabeh	خونابه
bleeding; haemorrhage	khunrizi	خونریزی
medicine; drugs	daaru	دارو
chemist's shop; pharmacy	daaru khaaneh	داروخانه
pharmacology	daaru shenaasi	دارو شناسی
pharmacist	daaru saaz	داروساز
apothecary; chemist	daarugar	داروگر
anaesthetic	daaru-ye bihushi	داروی بیهوشی
sedative; tranquilliser	daaru-ye mosakken	داروی مسکن
tonic; pick-me-up	daru-ye moqavvi	داروی مقوی
cautery	daaq zani	داغ زنی
delirium tremens	daa ol-khamr	داء الخمر
chorea; St. Vitus dance	daa or-raqs	داء الرقص
psoriasis	daa os-sadaf	داء الصدف

213

elephantiasis	daa ol-fil	داء الفیل
sleeping sickness	daa on-nowm	داء النوم
removal (e.g. of organ)	dar aavardan	در آوردن
dislocation	dar raftegi	در رفتگی
pain; ache	dard	درد
neuralgia	dard-e a'saab	درد اعصاب
painkiller	dardkosh	درد کش
acromegaly	dorosht sari	درشت سری
implant	darkaasht	در کاشت
cure; remedy; treatment	darmaan	درمان
iatrogenic	darmaan zaad	درمان زاد
therapeutics	darmaan shenaasi	درمان شناسی
healer	darmaan bakhsh	درمانبخش
clinic	darmaangaah	درمانگاه
endocrinology	darun riz shenaasi	درون ریز شناسی
endoscope	darun namaa	درون نما
electrocardiograph	dastgaah-e navaar-e qalb	دستگاه نوار قلب
boil; abscess	domal	دمل
toothache	dandaan dard	دندان درد
dentist	dandaan pezeshk	دندانپزشک
dentistry	dandaan pezeshki	دندانپزشکی
medicine; drug	davaa	دوا
incubation period	dowraan-e kamun	دوران کمون
course of treatment	dowre-ye darmaan	دوره درمان
dialysis	diyaaliz	دیالیز
pleurisy	zaat ol-janb	ذات الجنب
pneumonia	zaat or-riyeh	ذات الریه
nephritis	zaat ol-kolyeh	ذات الکلیه
diet	rezhim-e qazaa'i	رژیم غذائی
growth	roshd	رشد
phlebitis	rag afrukhtegi	رگ افروختگی
aneurysm	rag aamaaseh	رگ آماسه
embolism	rag bastegi	رگ بستگی
tourniquet	rag band	رگ بند
sprain	rag-be-rag shodegi	رگ به رگ شدگی
colour blindness	rang kuri	رنگ کوری
psychiatry	ravaan pezeshki	روان پزشکی
psychotherapy	ravaan darmaani	روان درمانی

neurosis	ravaan ranjuri	روان رنجوری
schizophrenia	ravaan gosikhtegi	روان گسیختگی
psychology	ravaanshenaasi	روانشناسی
psychoanalysis	ravaankaavi	روانکاوی
rheumatism	rumatism	روماتیسم
rheumatology	rumaatism shenaasi	روماتیسم شناسی
rheumatoid arthritis	rumaatism-e mafaasel	روماتیسم مفاصل
embryology	ruyaan shenaasi	رویان شناسی
hair loss	rizesh-e mu	ریزش مو
childbirth	zaayemaan	زایمان
obstetrics	zaayemaan shenaasi	زایمان شناسی
wound; ulcer	zakhm	زخم
stomach ulcer	zakhm-e me'deh	زخم معده
sting	zakhm-e nish	زخم نیش
jaundice	zardi	زردی
chill; cold	zokaam	زکام
wart	zegil	زگیل
gynaecology	zan pezeshki	زن پزشکی
premature	zud ras	زودرس
shingles; herpes zoster	zownaa	زونا
biology	zist shenaasi	زیست شناسی
neurobiology	zist shenaasi-ye 'asab	زیست شناسی عصب
biophysics	zist fizik	زیست فیزیک
cervical	zehdaan gardani	زهدانگردنی
poison; toxin	zahr	زهر
toxaemia	zahr-e khuni	زهر خونی
toxicology	zahr shenaasi	زهر شناسی
genetics	zhen shenaasi	ژن شناسی
accident	saaneheh	سانحه
cyst	sakht baaft	سخت بافت
ankylosis	sakhti-ye mafaasel	سختی مفصل
rubella; German measles	sorkhcheh	سرخچه
measles	sorkhak	سرخک
cancer	sarataan	سرطان
skin cancer	sarataan-e pust	سرطان پوست
leukaemia	sarataan-e khun	سرطان خون
cancer of the uterus	sarataan-e rahem	سرطان رحم
lung cancer	sarataan-e riyeh	سرطان ریه

carcinogen	sarataan zaa	سرطان زا
cervical cancer	sarataan-e zehdaan gardani	سرطان زهدانگردنی
breast cancer	sarataan-e sineh	سرطان سینه
liver cancer	sarataan-e kabed	سرطان کبد
kidney cancer	sarataan-e kolyeh	سرطان کلیه
cough	sorfeh	سرفه
vertigo; giddiness	sargijeh	سرگیجه
(intravenous) drip	serom	سرم
blood serum	serom-e khun	سرم خون
cryo-surgery	sarmaa jaraahi	سرما جراحی
(common) cold	sarmaa khordegi	سرما خوردگی
chilblain; frostbite	sarmaa zadegi	سرما زدگی
syringe	sorang	سرنگ
myasthenia	sosti-ye maahicheh	سستی ماهیچه
syphilis	seflis	سفلیس
abortifacient	seqt aavar	سقط آور
miscarriage	seqt-e jenin	سقط جنین
heart attack	sekte-ye qalbi	سکته قلبی
stroke	sekte-ye maqzi	سکته مغزی
hiccough	seksekeh	سکسکه
tuberculosis	sel	سل
health	salaamat	سلامت
syndrome	sandrom	سندرم
gall stone	sang-e safraa	سنگ صفراء
kidney stone	sang-e kolyeh	سنگ کلیه
metabolism	sukht o saaz	سوخت و ساز
burn	sukhtegi	سوختگی
gonorrhoea	suzaak	سوزاك
heartburn	suzesh-e me'deh	سوزش معده
pins and needles	suzan suzan shodegi	سوزن سوزن شدگی
heart murmur	sufl-e qalbi	سوفل قلب
malnutrition	su'e taqziyeh	سوء تغذیه
sciatica	siyaatik	سیاتیک
anthrax	siyaah zakhm	سیاه زخم
whooping cough	siyaah sorfeh	سیاه سرفه
jugular vein	siyaah rag-e gardan	سیاهرگ گردن
cirrhosis	siruz	سیروز
sinusitis	sinuzit	سینوزیت

pneumonia	sineh pahlu	سینه پهلو
head lice	shepesh	شپش
severe; acute	shadid	شدید
syrup	sharbat	شربت
fracture; break	shekastegi	شکستگی
shock	shok	شوک
chemotherapy	shimi darmaani	شیمی درمانی
hoarseness; loss of voice	sedaa gereftegi	صدا گرفتگی
damage	sadameh	صدمه
brain damage	sadame-ye maqzi	صدمه مغزی
epilepsy	sar'	صرع
wheelchair	sandali-ye charkh daar	صندلی چرخ دار
antispasmodic	zedd-e espaasm	ضد اسپاسم
antidepressant	zedd-e afsordegi	ضد افسردگی
anticoagulant	zedd-e en'eqaad-e khun	ضد انعقاد خون
anticonvulsant	zedd-e tashannoj	ضد تشنج
anti-emetic	zedd-e tahavvo'	ضد تهوع
disinfectant	zedd-e 'ofuni	ضد عفونی
trauma	zarbe-ye jesmi	ضربه جسمی
concussion	zarbe-ye maqzi	ضربه مغزی
senility	za'f-e piri	ضعف پیری
poultice	zemaad	ضماد
baldness	taasi	طاسی
plague	taa'un	طاعون
traditional medicine	tebb-e sonnati	طب سنتی
acupuncture	tebb-e suzani	طب سوزنی
nuclear medicine	tebb-e haste'i	طب هسته ای
naturopathy	tab'iyat darmaani	طبیعت درمانی
nerve	'asab	عصب
neurology	'asab shenaasi	عصب شناسی
strained muscle	'azole-ye rag-be-rag shodeh	عضله رگ به رگ شده
artificial limb	'ozv-e masnu'i	عضو مصنوعی
aromatherapy	'atr darmaani	عطر درمانی
infection	'ofunat	عفونت
septicaemia; sepsis	'ofunat-e khun	عفونت خون
ear infection	'ofunat-e gush	عفونت گوش
X-ray	'aks bardaari	عکس برداری
cure; remedy	'alaaj	علاج

symptom	'alaamat	علامت
genetics	'elm-e zhenetik	علم ژنتیک
medicine (i.e. the discipline)	'elm-e tebb	علم طب
surgical operation	'amal-e jaraahi	عمل جراحی
Caesarian section	'amal-e sezaariyen	عمل سزارین
relapse	'ud	عود
gland; lump; tumour	qoddeh	غده
lachrymal gland	qodde-ye ashki	غده اشکی
exocrine gland	qodde-ye borun riz	غده برون ریز
salivary gland	qodde-ye bozaaqi	غده بزاقی
thyroid gland	qodde-ye tiru'id	غده تیرونید
endocrine gland	qodde-ye darun riz	غده درون ریز
lymph gland	qodde-ya lanfaavi	غده لنفاوی
oncology	qoddeh shenaasi	غده شناسی
fainting; blackout	qash	غش
hernia	fatq	فتق
hiatus hernia	fatq-e hejaab-e haajez	فتق حجاب حاجز
ultrasound	faraavaa darmaani	فراوادرمانی
hypertension	fozun tanesh	فزون تنش
hyperactivity	fozun kaari	فزون کاری
hyperthermia	fozun garmaa'i	فزون گرمانی
blood pressure	feshaar-e khun	فشار خون
stress; nervous tension	feshaar-e 'asabi	فشار عصبی
spastic paralysis	falaj-e espaasmi	فلج اسپاسمی
polio	falaj-e atfaal	فلج اطفال
multiple sclerosis	falaj-e chandgaaneh	فلج چندگانه
physiology	fiziuluzhi	فیزیولوژی
menstruation	qaa'edegi	قاعدگی
dysmenorrhoea	qaa'edegi-ye dardnaak	قاعدگی دردناک
gangrene	qaanqaariyaa	قانقاریا
tolerance	qodrat-e tahammol	قدرت تحمل
tablet; pill	qors	قرص
sleeping tablet	qors-e khaab	قرص خواب
birth-control pill	qors-e zedd-e haamelegi	قرص ضد حاملگی
lozenge	qors-e mekidani	قرص مکیدنی
eye drops	qatre-ye cheshm	قطره چشم
ear drops	qatre-ye gush	قطره گوش
cardiology	qalb shenaasi	قلب شناسی

cardiac	qalbi	قلبی
lump	qolombeh shodegi	قلمبه شدگی
'stitch' (in one's side)	qulenj-e pahlu	قولنج پهلو
vomit; vomiting	qey	قی
emetic	qey aavar	قی آور
sickness and diarrhoea	qey o es-haal	قی و اسهال
condom	kaaput	کاپوت
anatomy	kaalbod shenaasi	کالبد شناسی
chiropractic	kaayruperaaktik	کایروپراکتیک
reduction; remission	kaahesh	کاهش
bruise	kabud shodegi	کبود شدگی
black eye	kabudi-ye cheshm	کبودی چشم
capsule	kapsul	کپسول
pharmacopoeia	ketaab-e raahnamaa-ye daaru'i	کتاب راهنمای داروئی
worm	kerm	کرم
caries; tooth decay	kerm khordegi-e ye dandaan	کرم خوردگی دندان
chorea	koreh	کره
tetanus	kozaaz	کزاز
scoliosis	kazh poshti	کژپشتی
clinic	kelinik	کلینیک
renal	kolyavi	کلیوی
kidney	kolyeh	کلیه
nephritis	kolyeh afrukhtegi	کلیه افروختگی
nephrology	kolyeh shenaasi	کلیه شناسی
anaemia	kam khuni	کم خونی
hypoglycaemia	kam qand-e khuni	کم قند خونی
hypothermia	kam garmaa'i	کم گرمائی
lack; deficiency	kambud	کمبود
vitamin deficiency	kambud-e vitaamin	کمبود ویتامین
lumbar	kamari	کمری
auxiliary nurse	komak parastaar	کمک پرستار
first aid	komak-haa-ye avvaliyeh	کمک های اولیه
mentally defective	kond zehn	کند ذهن
paediatrics	kudak pezeshki	کودک پزشکی
abortion	kurtaazh	کورتاژ
boil; abscess	kurak	کورک
bruise	kuftegi	کوفتگی
cyst	kist	کیست

219

sling	gardan aaviz	گردن آویز
lumbar	gerde'i	گرده ای
cramp	gereftegi	گرفتگی
spasm; cramp	gereftegi-ye 'azoleh	گرفتگی عضله
scabies	gari	گری
otolaryngology	galubini shenaasi	گلو بینی شناسی
sore throat	galu dard	گلو درد
polyp	gandomeh	گندمه
goitre	guvaatr	گواتر
ear ache	gush dard	گوش درد
otology	gush shenaasi	گوش شناسی
mumps	gushak	گوشک
leucocyte	guyche-ye sefid	گویچه سفید
herbalism	giaapezeshki	گیا پزشکی
laryngitis	laarenzhit	لارنزیت
thrombosis	lakhtaaki	لختاکی
clot; thrombus	lakhteh	لخته
blood clot	lakhte-ye khun	لخته خون
thrombus	lakhteh shodegi	لخته شدگی
lymph	lanf	لنف
squint	luchi-ye cheshm	لوچی چشم
disinfectant	maadde-ye zedd-e 'ofuni	ماده ضد عفونی
narcotics	maadde-ye mokhaddereh	ماده مخدره
massage	maasaazh	ماساژ
malaria	maalaariyaa	مالاریا
midwife	maamaa	ماما
inoculation	maayeh kubi	مایه کوبی
specialist	motakhasses	متخصص
heart specialist; cardiologist	motakhasses-e qalb	متخصص قلب
treatment	modaavaa	مداوا
faeces	madfu'	مدفوع
intensive care	moraaqebat-e vizheh	مراقبت ویژه
proctology	morz shenaasi	مرز شناسی
venereology	morzesh shenaasi	مرزش شناسی
illness; disease	maraz	مرض
incurable illness	maraz-e bi darmaan	مرض بیدرمان
genito-urinary disease	maraz-e tanaasoli-edraari	مرض تناسلی ادراری
acute illness	maraz-e haad	مرض حاد

220

pathology	maraz shenaasi	مرض شناسی
diabetes	maraz-e qand	مرض قند
chronic illness	maraz-e mozmen	مرض مزمن
venereal disease; STD	maraz-e moqaarebati	مرض مقاربتی
contagious disease	maraz-e vaagirdaar	مرض واگیردار
morphine	morfin	مرفین
brain death	marg-e maqzi	مرگ مغزی
hospital	marizkhaaneh	مریضخانه
illness; sickness	marizi	مریضی
ointment; dressing; poultice	marham	مرهم
dressing; bandage	marham-e zakhm	مرهم زخم
sedative; tranquillizer	mosakken	مسکن
poisoning	masmumiyat	مسمومیت
laxative	mos-hel	مسهل
(possible) side effects	mozerraat-e ehtemaali	مضرات احتمالی
doctor's surgery	matab-e pezeshk	مطب پزشک
medical examination	mo'aayene-ye tebbi	معاینه طبی
gastro-enterology	me'deh o rudeh shenaasi	معده و روده شناسی
disabled; handicapped	ma'lul	معلول
disability; handicap	ma'luliyat	معلولیت
the disabled	ma'lulin	معلولین
meningitis	meninzhit	منینژیت
glandular fever	munu nukle'uz-e 'ofuni	مونو نوکلئوز عفونی
corn	mikhcheh	میخچه
ureter	miznaay	میزنای
microbe	mikrub	میکروب
migraine	migren	میگرن
bio-engineering	mohandesi-ye zist shenaasi	مهندسی زیست شناسی
blind	naabinaa	نا بینا
blindness	naabinaa'i	نابینائی
physical disability	naatavaani-ye jesmi	ناتوانی جسمی
illness	naakhoshi	ناخوشی
amenorrhoea	naamaahegi	ناماهگی
pulse	nabz	نبض
rickets	narmi-ye ostokhaan	نرمی استخوان
prescription	noskheh	نسخه
syndrome	neshaangaan	نشانگان
sign; symptom	neshaaneh	نشانه

nephritis	nefrit	نفریت
convalescence	neqaahat	نقاهت
gout	neqres	نقرس
bandage	navaar-e zakhm bandi	نوار زخم بندی
(insect) sting	nish zadegi	نیش زدگی
hemiplegia	nimeh falaj	نیمه فلج
varicose veins	vaaris	واریس
diagnosis	vaa shenaakht	واشناخت
vaccine	vaaksan	واکسن
vaccination	vaaksan zani	واکسن زنی
cholera	vabaa	وبا
swelling; oedema	varam	ورم
mastitis	varam-e pestaan	ورم پستان
ovaritis	varam-e tokhmdaan	ورم تخمدان
peritonitis	varam-e sefaaq	ورم صفاق
splenitis	varam-e tehaal	ورم طحال
hepatitis	varam-e kabed	ورم کبد
gastritis	varam-e me'deh	ورم معده
gastroenteritis	varam-e me'deh o rude-haa	ورم معده و روده ها
arthritis	varam-e mafaasel	ورم مفاصل
osteoarthritis	varam-e mafaasel o ostokhaan	ورم مفاصل و استخوان
conjunctivitis	varam-e moltahemeh	ورم ملتحمه
spondylitis	varam-e mohre-haa-ye posht	ورم مهره های پشت
appointment	vaqt-e molaaqaat	وقت ملاقات
virus	virus	ویروس
virology	virus shenaasi	ویروس شناسی
rabies	haari	هاری
hepatitis	hepaatit	هپاتیت
herpes	herpiz	هرپیز
heroin	heru'in	هروئین
anastomosis	ham dahaanegi	هم دهانگی
haemophilia	hemufili	هموفیلی
sleeping sickness	hamisheh khaabi	همیشه خوابی
epidemiology	hameh gir shenaasi	همه گیر شناسی
hypnotism	hipnutizm	هیپنوتیزم
pituitary gland	hipufiz	هیپوفیز
cell	yaakhteh	یاخت
cytogenetics	yaakhteh zaad shenaasi	یاخته زاد شناسی

cytology	yaakhteh shenaasi	یاخته شناسی
constipation	yobusat	یبوست
jaundice	yaraqaan	یرقان

MORE WORDS AND PHRASES CONNECTED WITH HEALTH AND ILLNESS

Susan feels unwell سوسن احساس ناخوشی می کند   Hasan is unwell حسن ناخوش است   I'm ill مریض هستم

Hasan is really sick حال حسن خیلی خراب است   I'm ill حالم بد است   I'm not well حالم خوب نیست   I'm cold سردم است

I keep going hot and cold هی گرما سرما می شوم   I'm warm/hot گرمم است

I've got sickness and diarrhoea قی و اسهال دارم   I'm shivering دارم میلرزم   I feel sick/nauseous حالت تهوع دارم

my throat hurts گلوی من درد می کند   to hurt درد کردن   to throw up بالا آوردن   to vomit استفراغ کردن

I've got stomach ache شکم درد دارم   my stomach aches شکم من درد می کند   I've got a sore throat گلو درد دارم

I feel giddy سرم گیج میرود   to sneeze عطسه زدن   to cough سرفه کردن   I can't sleep نمی توانم بخوابم

I'm out of breath نفس تنگی دارم   to bleed خونریزی کردن   to get fat چاق شدن   to lose weight وزن کم کردن

his arm is broken دستش شکسته   to be injured زخمی شدن   to be injured مجروح شدن

it's swollen ورم کرده   I've sprained my ankle مچ پای من رگ به رگ شده   I've burnt my hand دستم را سوزانده ام

I fainted غش کردم   she's had a heart attack سکته قلبی کرده   he's had a stroke سکته مغزی کرده

Susan is 6 months pregnant سوسن شش ماه حامله است   my mother's blood pressure is up فشار خون مادرم بالاست

to regain consciousness به هوش آمدن   to become unconscious از هوش رفتن   he's in a coma در حالت اغما است

deep breath نفس عمیق   he can hardly breathe نفس او به سختی بر میاید   to become out of breath از نفس افتادن

abnormal غیر عادی   normal عادی   to breath normally بطور عادی نفس کشیدن   to breathe نفس کشیدن

in sound health صحیح و سالم   unhealthy ناسالم   health سالم   unnatural غیر طبیعی   natural طبیعی

to make an appointment وقت ملاقات گرفتن   you'd better see a doctor بهتر است پیش دکتر بروید

he examined my stomach شکم را معاینه کرد   he looked in my ears توی گوشم نگاه کرد   to examine معاینه کردن

test tube لوله آزمایشی   they tested my urine ادرارم را آزمایش کردند   he took blood from me از من خون گرفت

to take tablets قرص خوردن   you must rest باید استراحت کنید   what do you diagnose? چی تشخیص می دهید؟

I have a cold سرماخوردگی دارم   afflicted with Aids مبتلاء به ایدز   I've caught a cold سرما خورده ام

❮❮❮❯❯

223

Herbs and Vegetables

سبزی و سبزیجات

garden thyme; oregano	aavishan	آویشن
sweet basil	esparqam	اسپرغم
spinach	esfenaaj	اسفناج
rosemary	eklil-e kuhi	اکلیل کوهی
aubergine; eggplant	baadenjaan	بادنجان
broad bean	baaqelaa	باقلا
okra; lady's fingers	baamiyeh	بامیه
bay leaf	barg-e bu	برگ بو
corn on the cob	balaal	بلال
onion	piyaaz	پیاز
chives	piyaaz-e kuhi	پیاز کوهی
spring onion	piyaazcheh	پیازچه
horseradish	torob-e kuhi	ترب کوهی
radish	torobcheh	تربچه
cress	tartizak	ترتیزک
tarragon	tarkhun	ترخون
sorrel	torshak	ترشک
chives	tareh	تره
leek	tareh farangi	تره فرنگی
parsley	ja'fari	جعفری
chervil	ja'fari-ye farangi	جعفری فرنگی
beetroot	choqondar	چغندر
cardoon	kharshuf	خرشوف
purslane	khorfeh	خرفه
cucumber	khiyaar	خیار
sweetcorn	zorrat	ذرت
fennel	raaziyaaneh	رازیانه
samphire	raaziyaane-ye aabi	رازیانه آبی
basil	reyhaan	ریحان
ginger	zanjabil	زنجبیل
herbs	sabzi	سبزی
vegetables	sabzijaat	سبزیجات
potato	sib zamini	سیب زمینی
Jerusalem artichoke	sib zamini torshi	سیب زمینی ترشی
sweet potato	sib zamini-ye shirin	سیب زمینی شیرین
yam	sib zamini-ye hendi	سیب زمینی هندی

garlic	sir	سیر
rocket	shaabaanak	شابانک
watercress	shaahi-ye aabi	شاهی آبی
turnip	shalqam	شلغم
swede; rutabaga	shalqam-e rowqani	شلغم روغنی
fenugreek	shanbalileh	شنبلیله
salsify	sheng-e tare'i	شنگ تره ای
dill	shevid	شوید
pepper; capsicum	felfel	فلفل
chilli pepper	felfel tond	فلفل تند
mushroom	qaarch	قارچ
truffle	qaarch-e donbalaan	قارچ دنبلان
chicory	kaasni	کاسنی
endive	kaasni-ye farangi	کاسنی فرنگی
lovage	kaashan	کاشن
lettuce	kaahu	کاهو
marrow; courgette	kadu	کدو
pumpkin	kadu tanbal	کدو تنبل
celery	karafs	کرفس
cabbage	kalam	کلم
Brussels sprout	kalam dogme'i	کلم دگمه ای
kohlrabi	kalam qomri	کلم قمری
prickly artichoke	kangar	کنگر
artichoke	kangar-e farangi	کنگر فرنگی
coriander	geshniz	گشنیز
cauliflower	gol-e kalam	گل کلم
tomato	gowjeh farangi	گوجه فرنگی
mustard	giyaah-e khardal	گیاه خردل
bean	lubiyaa	لوبیا
asparagus	maarchubeh	مارچوبه
marjoram	marzangush	مرزنگوش
savory	marzeh	مرزه
sage	maryam goli	مریم گلی
shallot	musir	موسیر
garden pea; green pea	nokhud sabz	نخود سبز
mint	na'naa'	نعناع
carrot	havij	هویج
parsnip	havij farangi	هویج فرنگی

fire	aatash	آتش
elevator; lift	aasaansur	آسانسور
chef; cook	aashpaz	آشپز
luggage	asbaab	اسباب
swimming pool	estakhr	استخر
room	otaaq	اطاق
family room	otaaq-e khaanevaadegi	اطاق خانوادگی
double room	otaaq-e dow nafareh	اطاق دو نفره
single room	otaaq-e yek nafareh	اطاق یک نفره
stay; residence	eqaamat	اقامت
luggage; bar	baar	بار
porter	baarbar	باربر
elevator	baalaabar	بالابر
balcony	baalkon	بالکن
bed and breakfast	bastar o sobhaaneh	بستر و صبحانه
page (boy)	paadow	پادو
boarding house; guesthouse	paansiyun	پانسیون
hotel reception	paziresh-e hotel	پذیرش هتل
receptionist	pazireshgar	پذیرشگر
escalator	pelle-ye barqi	پله برقی
stairs	pelle-haa	پله ها
deposit	pish pardaakht	پیش پرداخت
booking	pish gozini	پیش گزینی
waiter; waitress	pish khedmat	پیشخدمت
reservation	pish gereft	پیشگرفت
date	taarikh	تاریخ
double bed	takht-e khaab-e dow nafareh	تخت خواب دونفره
single bed	takht-e khaab-e yek nafareh	تخت خواب یک نفره
discount	takhfif	تخفیف
facilities	tas-hilaat	تسهیلات
leisure facilities	tas-hilaat-e refaahi	تسهیلات رفاهی
sports facilities	tas-hilaat-e varzeshi	تسهیلات ورزشی
tariff	ta'refeh	تعرفه
telephone	telefon	تلفن
television	televiziyun	تلویزیون
gents' toilet	tovaalet-e mardaaneh	توالت مردانه

cheque	chek	چک
suitcase	chamedaan	چمدان
minimum price	hadd-e aqqal qeymat	حد اقل قیمت
maximum price	hadd-e aksar qeymat	حداکثر قیمت
bathroom; bath	hammaam	حمام
waiter	khedmatkaar	خدمتکار
doorman	darbaan	دربان
comfort	raahati	راحتی
fire escape	raah-e faraar az aatash suzi	راه فرار از آتش سوزی
restaurant	rasturaan	رستوران
receipt	resid	رسید
day	ruz	روز
dining room	saalon-e qazaakhori	سالن غذاخوری
head waiter	sar khedmatkaar	سر خدمتکار
noise	sar o sedaa	سر و صدا
per person	saraaneh	سرانه
head chef	sar aashpaz	سرآشپز
No Smoking	sigaar keshidan mamnu'	سیگار کشیدن ممنوع
dinner	shaam	شام
sommelier; wine waiter	sharaabdaar	شرابدار
complaint	shekaayat	شکایت
room number	shomaare-ye otaaq	شماره اطاق
breakfast	sobhaaneh	صبحانه
bill	surat hesaab	صورتحساب
floor; storey	tabaqeh	طبقه
ground floor	tabaqe-ye hamkaf	طبقه همکف
food; meal	qazaa	غذا
price; cost	qeymat	قیمت
fixed price	qeymat-e maqtu'	قیمت مقطوع
credit card	kaart-e e'tebaari	کارت اعتباری
guide book	ketaab-e raahnamaa	کتاب راهنما
key	kelid	کلید
(electrical) switch	kelid-e barq	کلید برق
passport	gozarnaameh	گذرنامه
hotel resident	maandegaar	ماندگار
satellite	maahvaareh	ماهواره
manager	modir	مدیر
hotel; guesthouse; inn	mosaafer khaaneh	مسافرخانه

customer	*moshtari*	مشتری
hotel regulations	*moqarraraat-e hotel*	مقررات هتل
waiter	*mizdaar*	میزدار
guest; resident	*mehmaan*	مهمان
hotel; guesthouse	*mehmaan khaaneh*	مهمان خانه
hospitality	*mehmaan navaazi*	مهمان نوازی
guesthouse; inn	*mehmaan saraa*	مهمانسرا
lunch	*naahaar*	ناهار
hotel	*hotel*	هتل
four-star hotel	*hotel-e chahaar setaareh*	هتل چهار ستاره
hotelier	*hoteldaar*	هتلدار

MORE HOTEL WORDS AND EXPRESSIONS

we only have single room   فقط اطاق یک نفره داریم   I'd like a double room please   لطفاً اطاق دو نفره میخواهم

we have no rooms   اطاق نداریم   we stayed in a four-star hotel   در هتل چهار ستاره ماندیم   luxury hotel   هتل لوکس

a room with a bath; en-suite   اطاق با حمام   I'd like to reserve a room   میخواهم یک اطاق رزرو کنم

do you have any means of identification   وسیله شناسائی دارید؟   please fill in this form   این فرم را پر کنید لطفاً

a passport will do   گذرنامه کافی است   please give me your ID card   شناسنامه لطف کنید

let me show you the room   بفرمائید اطاق را به شما نشان بدهم   please sign here   لطفاً همینجا امضاء کنید

bed, breakfast and evening meal   بستر ، صبحانه و شام   a room overlooking the sea   اطاقی که پنجره اش رو به دریا باشد

the elevator isn't working   آسانسور کار نمی کند   we took our luggage up   بارهایمان را بالا بردیم

will you please wake us up at seven o'clock in the morning?   لطفاً صبح ساعت هفت مارا بیدار می کنید؟

to rest   استراحت کردن   to eat breakfast   صبحانه خوردن   to wake up   بیدار شدن   to sleep   خوابیدن

to break (down)   خراب شدن   the heating doesn't work   شوفاژ کار نمی کند   my room is dirty   اطاق من کثیف است

to open   باز کردن   the window won't close   پنجره بسته نمی شود   my room is too hot   اطاق من زیادی گرم است

could you send someone to clean our room, please?   لطفاً می توانید یک کسی را بفرستید اطاقمان را نظافت کند؟

there's no hot water   آب گرم نیست   there's no soap   صابون نیست   there's a lot of noise   سر و صدا زیاد است

the food is inedible   غذا غیر قابل خوردن است   I want to make an official complaint   می خواهم رسماً شکایت کنم

how much is a room?   اطاق چند است؟   how many nights would you like to stay?   چند شب میخواهید بمانید؟

do you have any letters for me?   نامه برای من هست؟   will you park my car, please?   لطفاً ماشین مرا پارک می کنید؟

the phone isn't working   تلفن کار نمی کند   has anyone left a message for me?   کسی برای من پیغام گذاشته؟

what time does it close?   ساعت چند می بندد؟   what time does the restaurant open?   رستوران ساعت چند باز می شود؟

The House　　　　　　　　　　　　　　　　　　　　　خانه

water	aab	آب
running water	aab-e jaari	آب جاری
gutter	aab gozar	آب گذر
water heater; boiler	aab garmkon	آب گرم کن
apartment; flat	aapaartamaan	آپارتمان
two-bedroomed apartment	aapaartamaan-e dow otaaq khaabeh	آپارتمان دو اطاق خوابه
council flat	aapaartamaan-e saazmaani	آپارتمان سازمانی
furnished apartment	aapaartamaan-e mobleh	آپارتمان مبله
bedsit; one-roomed apartment	aapaartamaan-e yek otaaqeh	آپارتمان یک اطاقه
fire	aatash	آتش
adaptor	aadaaptur	آداپتور
fire alarm	aazhir-e aatash suzi	آژیر آتش سوزی
elevator; lift	aasaansur	آسانسور
skyscraper	aasemaan kharaash	آسمان خراش
coffee grinder	aasiyaab-e qahveh	آسیاب قهوه
kitchen	aashpazkhaaneh	آشپزخانه
rubbish; refuse	aashqaal	آشغال
shed	aalunak	آلونک
antenna	aanten	آنتن
mirror	aayeneh	آینه
full-length mirror	aayene-ye tamaam qad	آینه تمام قد
sponge	abr	ابر
bath sponge	abr-e hammaam	ابر حمام
gardening tools	abzaar-e baaqbaani	ابزار باغبانی
room	otaaq	اتاق
bedroom	otaaq-e khaab	اتاق خواب
utility room; washroom	otaaq-e rakhtshu'i	اتاق رختشوئی
attic	otaaq-e zir-e shirvaani	اتاق زیر شیروانی
janitor's room	otaaq-e seraayedaar	اتاق سرایدار
utility room	otaaq-e zarfshu'i	اتاق ظرفشوئی
rented room	otaaq-e keraaye'i	اتاق کرایه ای
study	otaaq-e motaale'eh	اتاق مطالعه
guest room	otaaq-e mehmaan	اتاق مهمان
dining room	otaaq-e naahaarkhori	اتاق نهارخوری
sitting room; living room	otaaq-e neshiman	تاق نشیمن
shower room; shower cubicle	otaaqak-e dush	اتاقک دوش

229

furniture	asaasiyeh	اثاثیه
rent; renting; lease	ejaareh	اجاره
rent (to pay)	ejaare-ye khaaneh	اجاره خانه
tenant	ejaareh neshin	اجاره نشین
cooker	ojaaq	اجاق
household items	asbaab-e khaaneh	اسباب خانه
cupboard	eshkaaf	اشکاف
valuables	ashyaa-ye qeymati	اشیای قیمتی
store; pantry	anbaar	انبار
work station	istgaah-e kaari	ایستگاه کاری
intercom	interkaam	اینترکام
balcony; patio	eyvaan	ایوان
garden	baaqcheh	باغچه
elevator; lift	baalaabar	بالابر
pillow	baalesh	بالش
balcony; verandah	baalkon	بالکن
heater	bokhaari	بخاری
brush	beros	برس
electricity	barq	برق
lightning rod	barq gir	برق گیر
estate agent's; real estate agency	bongaah-e mo'aamelaat-e melki	بنگاه معاملات ملکی
foundations	bonyaan	بنیان
bidet	bideh	بیده
outside	birun	بیرون
doormat	paadari	پا دری
parking area	paarking	پارکینگ
landing	paagardaan	پاگردان
blanket; duvet	patu	پتو
electric blanket	patu-ye barqi	پتوی برقی
hedge	parchin	پرچین
curtain	pardeh	پرده
power point	periz	پریز
cupboard	pastu	پستو
walk-in cupboard	pastu-ye jaadaar	پستوی جادار
roof	posht-e baam	پشت بام
house number	pelaak	پلاک
stairs; steps	pelleh	پله
doorstep	pelle-ye jelow-ye dar	پله جلوی در

stairs	pelle-haa	پله ها
window	panjereh	پنجره
fanlight	panjere-ye dom kaftari	پنجره دم کفتری
skylight	panjere-ye ru-be-baam	پنجره رو به بام
washing powder	pudr-e rakhtshu'i	پودر رختشوی
poster	powster	پوستر
(roof) slate	pahnak	پهنک
skylight	taabraan	تابران
picture; painting	taablow-ye naqqaashi	تابلوی نقاشی
ledge; shelf	taaqcheh	تاقچه
headboard	takhte-ye baalaa takhti	تخته بالاتختی
scales	taraazu	ترازو
crack	tarak	ترک
decoration; decor	tazyinaat	تزیینات
basin	tasht	تشت
picture; screen	tasvir	تصویر
television	televiziyun	تلویزیون
microwave	tondpaz	تندپز
toilet; WC	tovaalet	توالت
beam	tir	تیر
ventilation	tahviyeh	تهویه
air conditioning	tahviye-ye matbu'	تهویه مطبوع
soapdish	jaa saabuni	جا صابونی
coat peg	jaa lebaasi	جا لباسی
broom	jaaru	جارو
vacuum cleaner	jaaru-ye barqi	جاروی برقی
light; lamp	cheraaq	چراغ
view; vista	cheshmandaaz	چشم انداز
bolt	cheft-e dar	چفت در
lawn	chamanzaar	چمنزار
parquet flooring	chubfarsh	چوب فرش
coat hanger	chub lebaasi	چوب لباسی
central heating	haraarat-e markazi	حرارت مرکزی
fence	hesaar	حصار
bathroom	hammaam	حمام
hand towel	howle-ye dasti	حوله دستی
yard; courtyard	hayaat	حیاط
back yard; back garden	hayaat-e posht-e manzel	حیاط پشت منزل

family	khaanevaadeh	خانواده
house	khaaneh	خانه
rented accommodation	khaane-ye ejaare'i	خانه اجاره ای
country house; manor	khaane-ye arbaabi	خانه اربابی
detached house	khaane-ye mojazaa	خانه مجزا
semi-detached house	khaane-ye nimeh mojazaa	خانه نیمه مجزا
summer residence; holiday home	khaane-ye yeylaaqi	خانه ییلاقی
toothpaste	khamir-e dandaan	خمیر دندان
food processor	khoraak khord kon	خوراك خرد كن
air freshener	khosh bu konande-ye havaa	خوش بو کننده هوا
road; street	khiyaabaan	خیابان
inside	daakhel	داخل
corridor; hallway	daalaan	دالان
cellar	dakhmeh	دخمه
front door	dar-e jelow	در جلو
back door	dar-e hayaat	در حیاط
entrance	dar-e vorudi	در ورودی
doorway	dargaah	درگاه
sink	dast shu'i	دستشونی
stereo system	dastgaah-e esteriyow	دستگاه استریو
air conditioner	dastgaah-e tahviye-ye matbu'	دستگاه تهویه مطبوع
coffee grinder	dastgaah-e qahveh khord kon	دستگاه قهوه خرد کنی
video recorder	dastgaah-e vide'o	دستگاه ویدنو
handle	dastgireh	دستگیره
handkerchief	dastmaal	دستمال
bunch of keys	daste-ye kelid	دسته کلید
decoration; decor	dekur	دکور
smoke	dud	دود
smoke alarm	dudyaab	دود یاب
shower	dush	دوش
pressure cooker	dig-e zud paz	دیگ زود پز
wall	divaar	دیوار
screen	divaareh	دیواره
comfort	raahati	راحتی
radiator	raadiyaatur	رادیاتور
stairway	rah pelleh	راه پله
corridor	raah row	راهرو
clothes dryer; tumble dryer	rakht khoshk kon	رخت خشک کن

bedding; bedclothes	rakhtekhaab	رختخواب
bedspread	rupush-e takhtekhaab	روپوش تختخواب
pillowcase	rukesh-e motakkaa	روکش متکا
tablecloth	ru mizi	رومیزی
mortgage	rahn	رهن
ground; floor	zamin	زمین
housewife	zan-e khaaneh daar	زن خانه دار
place mat	zir boshqaabi	زیر بشقابی
stool	zirpaa'i	زیر پانی
cellar	zir-e zamin	زیر زمین
ashtray	zir sigaari	زیر سیگاری
building	saakhtemaan	ساختمان
block of flats	saakhtemaan-e aapaartamaan	ساختمان آپارتمان
canopy	saayebaan	سایبان
fireguard	separ-e jelow-ye shumineh	سپر جلوی شومینه
canopy; portal	sar dar	سر در
janitor; caretaker	saraayedaar	سرایدار
porch	sarpush	سرپوش
cellar	sardaab	سرداب
rubbish bin	satl-e khaakrubeh	سطل خاکروبه
waste paper bin	satl-e kaaqaz baateleh	سطل کاغذ باطله
ceiling	saqf	سقف
pumice stone	sang-e paa	سنگ پا
flagstone	sang-e sangfarshi	سنگ سنگفرشی
paving	sangfarsh	سنگفرش
spy-hole	suraakh-e didzani	سوراخ دیدزنی
keyhole	suraakh-e kelid	سوراخ کلید
tray	sini	سینی
telephone number	shomaare-ye telefon	شماره تلفن
candle	sham'	شمع
candlestick	sham'daan	شمعدان
central heating	shufaazh-e markazi	شوفاژ مرکزی
fireplace	shumineh	شومینه
house husband	shuhar-e khaaneh daar	شوهر خانه دار
tap; faucet	shir-e aab	شیر آب
double glazing	shishe-ye dow jedaareh	شیشه دو جداره
city; town	shahr	شهر
owner	saaheb	صاحب

233

landlord; landlady	saaheb khaaneh	صاحبخانه
walk-in cupboard; closet	sanduq khaaneh	صندوق خانه
tape recorder	zabt-e sowt	ضبط صوت
canopy	taaq-e kaazeb	طاق کاذب
mantelpiece	taaqche-ye ru bokhaari	طاقچه رو بخاری
pot; pan; dish	zarf	ظرف
pots and pans; dishes	zoruf	ظروف
soundproofing	'aayeq-e zedd-e sedaa	عایق ضد صدا
picture; photograph	'aks	عکس
carpet	farsh	فرش
water filter	filter-e aab	فیلتر آب
fuse	foyuz	فیوز
panelling	qaab bandi	قاب بندی
saucepan	qaablemeh	قابلمه
carpet	qaali	قالی
rug	qaalicheh	قالیچه
electricity cut	qat' shodan-e barq	قطع شدن برق
lock	qofl	قفل
cafetiere; coffee percolator	qahveh jush	قهوه جوش
dish; bowl	kaaseh	کاسه
lodging; cottage; nest; haven	kaashaaneh	کاشانه
tiling	kaashi kaari	کاشی کاری
wallpaper	kaaqaz divaari	کاغذ دیواری
fire extinguisher	kapsul-e aatash neshaani	کپسول آتش نشانی
mould	kapak	کپک
kettle	ketri	کتری
blinds	kerkereh	کرکره
hearth	kaf-e shumineh	کف شومینه
lino	kafpush	کفپوش
doormat	kafsh paak kon	کفش پاک کن
hut; shed	kolbeh	کلبه
key	kelid	کلید
wardrobe	komod	کمد
street; alley; lane	kucheh	کوچه
street; alley; lane	kuy	کوی
bath flannel	kiseh	کیسه
hot water bottle	kise-ye aab-e jush	کیسه آب جوش
garage	gaaraazh	گاراژ

gas	*gaaz*	گاز
record player	*geraamaafun*	گرامافون
duster	*gard gir*	گرد گیر
feather duster	*gard gir-e pardaar*	گرد گیر پردار
greenhouse; hothouse	*garmkhaaneh*	گرمخانه
greenhouse; glasshouse	*golkhaaneh*	گلخانه
vase; flower pot	*goldaan*	گلدان
window box	*goldaan-e panjereh*	گلدان پنجره
mud-remover (for shoes)	*gelgir*	گلگیر
lamp; bulb	*laamp*	لامپ
edge; rim; (window) ledge	*labeh*	لبه
quilt	*lahaaf*	لحاف
duvet; eiderdown	*lahaaf-e narmpar*	لحاف نرم پر
bowl	*lagan*	لگن
valuables	*lavaazem-e qeymati*	لوازم قیمتی
hinge	*lowlaa*	لولا
pipe	*luleh*	لوله
flannel; sponge	*lif*	لیف
mothballs	*maadde-ye zedd-e bid*	ماده ضد بید
microwave	*maaykruveyv*	مایکروویو
frying pan	*maahitaabeh*	ماهیتابه
furniture	*moblemaan*	مبلمان
pillow	*motakkaa*	متکا
accommodation	*mahall-e sokunat*	محل سکونت
district; quarter; neighbourhood	*mahalleh*	محله
tenant	*mosta'jer*	مستاجر
toilet; WC	*mostaraah*	مستراح
sheet	*malaafeh*	ملافه
fitted sheet	*malaafe-ye keshdaar*	ملافه کش دار
house; home	*manzel*	منزل
view; vista	*manzareh*	منظره
fitted carpet	*muket*	موکت
mezzanine	*miyaan ashkub*	میان اشکوب
ironing board	*miz-e otu*	میز اتو
towel rack	*mile-ye howleh*	میله حوله
veranda	*mahtaabi*	مهتابی
drainpipe; guttering	*naavdaan*	ناودان
fence; rail	*nardeh*	نرده

address	neshaani	نشانی
leak (of water, gas etc.)	nasht	نشت
cleaner	nezaafatchi	نظافتچی
silverware	noqreh aalaat	نقره آلات
house move; moving house	naql-e makaan	نقل مکان
facade; front	namaa	نما
lighting	nur resaani	نور رسانی
bath tub	vaan	وان
villa; summer house	vilaa	ویلا
hall; hallway	haal	هال
vestibule	hashti	هشتی
neighbour	hamsaayeh	همسایه
air vent; cooker hood	havaakesh	هواکش
ventilation	havaa resaani	هوارسانی

MORE WORDS AND PHRASES CONCERNING THE HOUSE

من در آپارتمان زندگی می کنم I live in an apartment   به طبقه بالا رفتن to go upstairs   طبقه پائین downstairs

حسن (در) منزل است Hasan is at home   از پنجره بیرون نگاه کردن to look out of the window

نقل مکان کردن to move house   مستقر شدن to settle in   جا افتادن to settle in   اجاره کردن to rent; to hire

خانه ساختن to build a house   خانه خریدن to buy a house   جمع و جور کردن to tidy up   مرتب کردن to tidy up   to tidy

اطاقتان را مرتب کنید ! tidy up your room!   بوی نم میدهد it smells stuffy / damp   خانه رفتن to go home

در زدن to knock at the door   زنگ زدن to ring (the bell)   حمام کردن to have a bath   دوش گرفتن to shower

کار خانه را انجام دادن to do the housework   آشپزی کردن to do the cooking   پختن to cook (something)

تلویزیون تماشا کردن to watch television   گردگیری کردن to dust; to do the dusting   ظرف شستن to do the dishes

چراغ را روشن کردن to switch on the light   خاموش کردن to switch off   در را باز کردن to open the door

در را بستن to close the door   پرده ها را باز کردن to open the curtains   پرده ها را کشیدن to close the curtains

چیزی را در سطل آشغال انداختن to throw something in the dustbin   به برق وصل کردن to connect to the electricity

جارو کشیدن to sweep   جارو برقی کشیدن to hoover   اتوکشی کردن to do the ironing   میز اتو ironing-board

تمیز کردن to clean   شستن to wash   آویزان کردن to hang (up)   واکس زدن to polish

رنگ زدن to paint   لامپ عوض کردن to change a bulb   خانه تکانی کردن to spring-clean

باغبانی کردن to do the gardening   تامیر کردن to repair   وارد خانه شدم I went into the house

از خانه بیرون آمدم I came out of the house   خانه را فروختن to sell the house   خانه بغلی the house next door

آدرش شما چیست؟ what's your address   کجا زندگی می کنید؟ where do you live?

236

Household Furniture

اسباب خانه

mirror	aayeneh	آینه
devices; appliances	abzaar	ابزار
furniture; furnishings	asaasiyeh	اثاثیه
furniture	asbaab-e khaaneh	اسباب خانه
cupboard; sideboard	eshkaaf	اشکاف
room	otaaq	اطاق
workstation	istgaah-e kaari	ایستگاه کاری
cushion	baalesh	بالش
heater	bokhaari	بخاری
curtain	pardeh	پرده
closet; cupboard	pastu	پستو
fan	pankeh	پنکه
answering machine	payaam gir	پیام گیر
chest	taaqche-ye dardaar	تاقچه دردار
bed	takhtekhaab	تختخواب
cot	takhtekhaab-e bacheh	تختخواب بچه
fold-up bed	takhtekhaab-e taashow	تختخواب تاشو
four-poster bed	takhtekhaab-e chahaar deyraki	تختخواب چهار دیرکی
bunk bed	takhtekhaab-e dow tabaqe'i	تختخواب دو طبقه ای
travel bed; fold-up bed	takhtekhaab-e safari	تختخواب سفری
scales	taraazu	ترازو
mattress	toshak	تشک
picture	tasvir	تصویر
telephone	telefon	تلفن
cordless telephone; mobile	telefon-e bedun-e sim	تلفن بدون سیم
television	televiziyun	تلویزیون
armrest	jaa dasti	جا دستی
bookcase	jaa ketaabi	جا کتابی
coat rack	jaa lebaasi	جا لباسی
vacuum cleaner	jaaru barqi	جارو برقی
light; lamp	cheraaq	چراغ
standard lamp	cheraaq-e paayeh daar	چراغ پایه دار
wall lamp; wall light	cheraaq-e divaari	چراغ دیواری
chandelier	chelcheraaq	چلچراغ
lampshade	hobaab-e cheraaq	حباب چراغ
house	khaaneh	خانه

appliance; device; machine	*dastgaah*	دستگاه
heater	*dastgaah-e garmaayeshi*	دستگاه گرمایشی
CD player	*dastgaah-e lowh gardaan*	دستگاه لوح گردان
video recorder	*dastgaah-e vide'o*	دستگاه ویدئو
armrest	*daste-ye sandali*	دسته صندلی
mattress	*doshak*	دشک
camcorder	*durbin-e filmbardaari-ye vide'o*	دوربین فیلمبرداری ویدئو
remote control	*dur farmaan*	دورفرمان
screen	*divaareh*	دیواره
folding screen	*divaare-ye taashow*	دیواره تاشو
radiator	*raadiyaatur*	رادیاتور
radio	*raadiyo*	رادیو
clock radio	*raadiyo-ye saa'at daar*	رادیوی ساعت دار
bedding; bedclothes	*rakhtekhaab*	رختخواب
footstool	*zir paa'i*	زیر پائی
clock	*saa'at*	ساعت
chair; seat	*sandali*	صندلی
armchair	*sandali-ye dasteh daar*	صندلی دسته دار
armchair; easy chair	*sandali-ye raahati*	صندلی راحتی
reclining chair	*sandali-ye lamidani*	صندلی لمیدنی
chest; trunk	*sanduq*	صندوق
walk-in cupboard; closet	*sanduq khaaneh*	صندوق خانه
tape recorder	*zabt-e sowt*	ضبط صوت
coffee table; small table	*'asali*	عسلی
curling tongs	*fer zani*	فر زنی
frame	*qaab*	قاب
carpet	*qaali*	قالی
rug	*qaalicheh*	قالیچه
bookcase	*qafase-ye ketaab*	قفسه کتاب
chest of drawers	*qafase-ye keshow daar*	قفسه کشو دار
chandelier	*qandil*	قندیل
wallpaper	*kaaqaz-e divaari*	کاغذ دیواری
computer	*kaampyuter*	کامپیوتر
sofa; couch; settee	*kaanapeh*	کاناپه
blinds	*kerkereh*	کرکره
drawer	*keshow*	کشو
wardrobe	*komod*	کمد
stereo system; music centre	*geraamaafun*	گرامافون

sideboard; cupboard	ganjeh	گنجه
kitchen dresser	ganje-ye zarf	گنجه ظرف
cradle	gahvaareh	گهواره
tumble-dryer; spin-dryer	maashin-e rakht khoshk koni	ماشین رخت خشک کنی
washing machine	maashin-e rakhtshu'i	ماشین رختشوئی
furniture	mobl	مبل
pouffe	mobl-e kusani	مبل کوسنی
linen cupboard	malaafeh daan	ملافه دان
hair-dryer	mu khoshk kon	مو خشک کن
fitted carpet	muket	موکت
table	miz	میز
coffee table	miz-e pishdasti	میز پیشدستی
writing table; writing bureau; desk	miz-e tahrir	میز تحریر
dressing table	miz-e tuvaalet	میز توالت
bedside table	miz-e kenaar takhti	میز کنار تخت
painting	naqqaashi	نقاشی
divan; bench	nimkat	نیمکت
device; appliance	vasileh	وسیله
fridge	yakhchaal	یخچال
piece of furniture	yek 'adad mobl	یک عدد مبل

MORE FURNITURE WORDS AND PHRASES

four-bedroomed apartment آپارتمان چهار اطاق خوابه furnished apartment آپارتمان مبله

second-hand furniture مبل دست دوم to buy furniture اثاثیه خریدن four-roomed چهار اطاقه

antique furniture مبل عتیقه furniture shop مبل فروشی we bought the furniture new مبل را نو خریدیم

to polish واکس زدن to polish روغن جلا زدن to make the bed تخت خواب را مرتب کردن

to dust گردگیری کردن to lay the tablecloth سفره پهن کردن to set the table میز را چیدن

to put; to place گذاشتن to take out در آوردن to close بستن to open the drawer کشو را باز کردن

to paint رنگ زدن to put down (on the floor) (روی) زمین گذاشتن to pick up بلند کردن

please, sit down! بفرمائید بنشینید! I built the cupboard myself اشکاف را خودم ساختم

The Human Body

بدن انسان

appendix	aapaandis	آپاندیس
elbow	aarenj	آرنج
burp; belch	aaruq	آروغ
female reproductive organ; vagina	aalat-e tanaasoli-ye zan	آلت تناسلی زن
male reproductive organ; penis	aalat-e tanaasoli-ye mard	آلت تناسلی مرد
penis	aalat-e mardi	آلت مردی
aorta	aa'urt	آنورت
aorta	abar sorkhrag	ابرسرخرگ
eyebrow	abru	ابرو
guts	ahshaa'	احشاء
features	asbaab-e surat	اسباب صورت
bone	ostokhaan	استخوان
humerus	ostokhaan-e baazu	استخوان بازو
bone structure; skeleton	ostokhaan bandi	استخوان بندی
sternum	ostokhaan-e jenaaq-e sineh	استخوان جناغ سینه
clavicle	ostokhaan-e chanbar	استخوان چنبر
sacrum	ostokhaan-e khaaji	استخوان خاجی
tibia	ostokhaan-e dorosht ney	استخوان درشت نی
femur	ostokhaan-e raan	استخوان ران
shoulder bone	ostokhaan-e shaaneh	استخوان شانه
shin bone	ostokhaan-e qalam-e paa	استخوان قلم پا
shoulder blade	ostokhaan-e ketf	استخوان کتف
collar bone	ostokhaan-e gardan	استخوان گردن
cheek bone	ostokhaan-e guneh	استخوان گونه
hip bone	ostokhaan-e lagan	استخوان لگن
fibula	ostokhaan-e naazok ney	استخوان نازك نی
skeleton	eskelet	اسکلت
measurement; size	andaazeh	اندازه
body; organ; limb	andaam	اندام
reproductive organs	andaam-haa-ye tanaasoli	اندامهای تناسلی
endocrine organs	andaam-haa-ye darun riz	اندامهای درون ریز
finger	angosht	انگشت
ring finger	angosht-e angoshtar	انگشت انگشتر
toe	angosht-e pa	انگشت پا
ring finger	angosht-e dovvom	انگشت دوم
index finger	angosht-e sabaabeh	انگشت سبابه

little finger	*angosht-e kuchek*	انگشت کوچک
middle finger	*angosht-e vasat*	انگشت وسط
arm; upper arm	*baazu*	بازو
body	*badan*	بدن
joint	*band*	بند
ligament	*bandineh*	بندینه
testicle	*beyzeh*	بیضه
sight; seeing	*binaa'i*	بینائی
nose	*bini*	بینی
foot; leg	*paa*	پا
heel	*paashne-ye paa*	پاشنه پا
hymen	*parde-ye bekaarat*	پرده بکارت
eardrum	*parde-ye gush*	پرده گوش
nape of the neck	*pas-e gardan*	پس گردن
breast	*pestaan*	پستان
back	*posht*	پشت
eyelid	*pelk-e cheshm*	پلک چشم
skin	*pust*	پوست
foreskin	*pish pust*	پیش پرست
forehead	*pishaani*	پیشانی
side	*pahlu*	پهلو
vocal chords	*taar-haa-ye aavaa'i*	تارهای آوائی
pupil	*tokhm-e cheshm*	تخم چشم
ovary	*tokhmdaan*	تخمدان
breathing; respiration	*tanaffos*	تنفس
tendon	*tanud*	تنود
spine	*tire-ye posht*	تیره پشت
scar	*jaa-ye zakhm*	جای زخم
plastic surgery	*jarraahi-ye pelaastik*	جراحی پلاستیک
liver	*jegar*	جگر
lung	*jegar-e sefid*	جگر سفید
skull	*jomjomeh*	جمجمه
movement	*jonbesh*	جنبش
embryo	*jenin*	جنین
digestive system	*jahaaz-e haazemeh*	جهاز هاضمه
dimple	*chaal*	چال
chin	*chaaneh*	چانه
eye	*cheshm*	چشم

diaphragm	*hejaab-e haajez*	حجاب حاجز
movement	*harekat*	حرکت
sense of smell	*hess-e buyaa'i*	حس بویائی
sense of sight	*hess-e binaa'i*	حس بینائی
sense of taste	*hess-e cheshaa'i*	حس چشائی
sense of hearing	*hess-e shenavaa'i*	حس شنوائی
sense of touch	*hess-e laameseh*	حس لامسه
larynx	*hanjareh*	حنجره
five senses	*havaas-e panjgaaneh*	حواس پنجگانه
itching	*khaaresh*	خارش
testicle	*khaayeh*	خایه
scratch	*kharaashidegi*	خراشیدگی
trachea	*kherkhereh*	خرخره
larynx	*khoshk naay*	خشک نای
blood	*khun*	خون
ileum	*deraaz rudeh*	درازروده
epiglottis	*dariche-ye naay*	دریچه نای
hand; arm	*dast*	دست
urinary system	*dastgaah-e pishaabi*	دستگاه پیشابی
lymphatic system	*dastgaah-e tanaabe'i*	دستگاه تنابه ای
respiratory system	*dastgaah-e tanaffosi*	دستگاه تنفسی
circulatory system	*dastgaah-e gardesh-e khun*	دستگاه گردش خون
nose	*damaaq*	دماغ
coccyx	*donbaalcheh*	دنبالچه
tooth	*dandaan*	دندان
molar	*dandaan-e aasyaab*	دندان آسیاب
pre-molar	*dandaan-e pish korsi*	دندان پیش کرسی
incisor	*dandaan-e pishin*	دندان پیشین
milk tooth	*dandaan-e shiri*	دندان شیری
wisdom tooth	*dandaan-e 'aql*	دندان عقل
false teeth	*dandaan-e masnu'i*	دندان مصنوعی
canine tooth	*dandaan-e nish*	دندان نیش
rib	*dandeh*	دنده
menstrual cycle	*dowre-ye qaa'edegi*	دوره قاعدگی
mouth	*dahaan*	دهان
thigh	*raan*	ران
ligament	*rebaat*	رباط
vein	*rag*	رگ

large intestine	*rude-ye bozorg*	روده بزرگ
small intestine	*rude-ye kuchek*	روده کوچک
lungs	*riyeh*	ریه
knee	*zaanu*	زانو
tongue	*zabaan*	زبان
scar	*zakhmgaah*	زخمگاه
scar	*zakhmneshaan*	زخمنشان
wart	*zegil*	زگیل
radius	*zand-e zebarin*	زند زبرین
ulna	*zand-e zirin*	زند زیرین
armpit	*zir-e baqal*	زیر بغل
uterus	*zehdaan*	زهدان
foetus	*zehsaan*	زهسان
gene	*zhen*	ژن
forearm	*saa'ed*	ساعد
calf	*saaq-e paa*	ساق پا
spinal column	*sotun-e faqaraat*	ستون فقرات
head	*sar*	سر
hip bone	*sar ostokhaan-e raan*	سر استخوان ران
artery	*sorkhrag*	سرخرگ
chilblain	*sarmaa zadegi*	سرمازدگی
palate	*saqf-e dahaan*	سقف دهان
hiccough	*seksekeh*	سکسکه
nervous system	*selsele-ye a'saab*	سلسله اعصاب
nostril	*suraakh-e damaaq*	سوراخ دماغ
chest; breast	*sineh*	سینه
shoulder	*shaaneh*	شانه
jugular vein	*shaahrag*	شاهرگ
artery	*sheryaan*	شریان
thumb	*shast*	شست
lungs	*shosh*	شش
big toe	*shast-e paa*	شست پا
temple	*shaqiqeh*	شقیقه
abdomen; belly	*shekam*	شکم
hearing	*shenavaa'i*	شنوائی
voice	*sedaa*	صدا
face	*surat*	صورت
spleen	*tehaal*	طحال

243

nerve	'asab	عصب
thyroid gland	qodde-ye tiru'id	غده تیرونید
adrenal glands	qodde-haa-ye fowq-e kolyavi	غده های فوق کلیوی
pituitary gland	qodde-ye hipufiz	غده هیپوفیز
cartilage	qozruf	غضروف
jaw	fakk	فک
nape of the neck	qafaa	قفاء
ribcage	qafase-ye dandeh	قفسه دنده
heart	qalb	قلب
foreskin	qalafeh	قلفه
shin	qalam-e paa	قلم پا
cramp	qulenj	قولنج
colon	qulun	قولون
kneecap; patella	kaase-ye zaanu	کاسه زانو
bruise; bruising	kabud shodegi	کبودشدگی
bruise; bruising	kabudi	کبودی
groin	keshaale-ye raan	کشاله ران
sole	kaf-e paa	کف پا
palm	kaf-e dast	کف دست
buttocks; bottom	kafal	کفل
kidney	kolyeh	کلیه
arch of the eyebrow	kamaan-e abru	کمان ابرو
waist	kamar	کمر
pectoral girdle	kamarband-e sine'i	کمربند سینه ای
gall bladder	kise-ye safraa	کیسه صفراء
pelvic girdle	gardaan-e lagani	گردان لگنی
neck	gardan	گردن
cramp	gereftegi-ye 'azoleh	گرفتگی عضله
throat	galu	گلو
ear	gush	گوش
flesh; meat	gusht	گوشت
cheek	guneh	گونه
lip	lab	لب
cheek	lop	لپ
gum	laseh	لثه
pelvis	lagan	لگن
pancreas	lowz ol me'deh	لوز المعده
tonsils	lowzateyn	لوزتین

bronchial tubes	lule-haa-ye naayezheh	لوله های نایژه
muscle	maahicheh	ماهیچه
biceps	maahiche-ye dow sar	ماهیچه دوسر
bladder	masaaneh	مثانه
urethra	majraa-ye pishaab	مجرای پیشاب
alimentary canal	majraa-ye govaaresh	مجرای گوارش
ankle	moch-e paa	مچ پا
wrist	moch-e dast	مچ دست
eyelash	mozheh	مژه
fist	mosht	مشت
stomach	me'deh	معده
brain	maqz	مغز
joint	mafsal	مفصل
anus	maq'ad	مقعد
semen	mani	منی
hair	mu	مو
pubic hair	mu-ye zehaar	موی زهار
vagina	mahbel	مهبل
vertebra	mohreh	مهره
nail	naakhon	ناخن
navel	naaf	ناف
trachea	naay	نای
pulse	nabz	نبض
ear lobe	narme-ye gush	نرمه گوش
bottom	neshastgaah	نشستگاه
breath	nafas	نفس
nipple	nuk-e pestaan	نوک پستان
body; form; figure	heykal	هیکل

standing ایستاده   sitting نشسته   lying down دراز کشیده   to breathe نفس کشیدن   to feel حس کردن

to think فکر کردن   to see دیدن   to hear شنیدن   to touch; to feel لمس کردن   to listen گوش دادن

to smell (trans.) بو کردن   to smell (of something) بو دادن   his breath smells دهانش بو می دهد

to sneeze عطسه زدن   to yawn خمیازه کشیدن   to laugh خندیدن   to cry گریه کردن   to smile لبخند زدن

to talk حرف زدن   to hum زمزمه کردن   to cough سرفه کردن   to sniff فخ فخ کردن   to shiver لرزیدن

to ache; to hurt درد کردن   my ear aches گوشم درد می کند   to open one's mouth دهان را باز کردن

to close one's mouth دهان را بستن   to swallow بلعیدن   to swallow قورت دادن   to eat; to drink خوردن

to wink چشمک زدن   to stare خیره شدن   why are you staring at me? چرا به من خیره شدی؟

to lick لیس زدن   to suck مکیدن   to chew جویدن   to hiccough سکسکه کردن   to spit تف کردن

to kick لگد زدن   to punch مشت زدن   to hit; to strike زدن   to sweat عرق کردن   to sweat عرق ریختن

blind نابینا   deaf ناشنوا   dumb لال   handicapped معلول   lame; crippled چلاق

I cut my hand دستم را بریدم   you hurt my hand دستم را درد آوردی   I sprained my wrist مچ دستم رگ به رگ شد

bleeding خونریزی   my hand is bleeding دستم خونریزی می کند   my nose is bleeding از دماغ من خون میاید

to answer the call of nature; to relieve oneself رفع حاجت کردن   urine ادرار   to urinate ادرار کردن

piss شاش   to piss شاشیدن   faeces مدفوع   shit گه   to shit ریدن   to burp; to belch آروغ زدن

to vomit بالا آوردن   to throw up بالا آوردن   snot عن دماغ   ear wax چرک گوش   dirt; pus چرک

to masturbate استمناء کردن   semen منی   ejaculation انزال منی   to have sexual intercourse جماع کردن

to pass wind باد شکم دادن   fart گوز   to fart گوز دادن   (silent) fart چس   to fart (silently) چس دادن

strong قوی   well-built قوی هیکل   weak ضعیف   tall قد بلند   short قد کوتاه   fat چاق

thin لاغر   beautiful زیبا   pretty خوشگل   ugly زشت   handsome خوش تیپ

wrinkles چین و چروک   to look نگاه کردن   to glance نگاه انداختن   to touch دست زدن

to mess with; to fiddle with ور رفتن به   she keeps fiddling with her hair هی به موهایش ور میرود

long hair موی بلند   short hair موی کوتاه   yesterday I had my hair cut دیروز موهایم را زدم

sweet-smelling خوش بو   smelly; bad-smelling بدبو   big; fat گنده   the five senses حواس پنجگانه

from head to foot از سر تا پا   in the twinkling of an eye در یک چشم بهم زدن   heartbeat تپش قلب

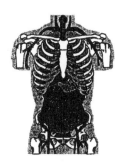

246

Industry and Development

صنعت و توسعه

statistics	aamaar	آمار
completion; implementation	ejraa	اجراء
construction; production; erection	ehdaas	احداث
industrial merger	edqaam-e sanaaye'	ادغام صنایع
lands; estates	araazi	اراضی
foreign currency	arz	ارز
export value	arzesh-e saaderaati	ارزش صادراتی
mining; extraction	estekhraaj	استخراج
borrowing; loan	esteqraaz	استقراض
dock; wharf; landing bay; jetty	eskele-ye takhliyeh va baargiri	اسکله تخلیه و بارگیری
floating platform	eskele-ye shenaavar	اسکله شناور
credit	e'tebaar	اعتبار
medium-term credit	e'tebaar-e miyaan moddat	اعتبار میان مدت
opening; launch	eftetaah	افتتاح
increase	afzaayesh	افزایش
industrial action	eqdaam-e kaargari	اقدام کارگری
new discoveries	ekteshaafaat-e jadid	اکتشافات جدید
transportation of oil	enteqaal-e naft	انتقال نفت
repayments	baaz pardaakht-haa	باز پرداخت ها
currency market	baazaar-e arz	بازار ارز
free market	baazaar-e aazaad	بازار آزاد
consumer market	baazaar-e masraf	بازار مصرف
market survey; assessment	baazaaryaabi	بازاریابی
inspection	baazdid	بازدید
reconstruction	baaz saazi	بازسازی
national bank	baank-e melli	بانک ملی
economic crisis	bohraan-e eqtesaadi	بحران اقتصادی
private sector	bakhsh-e khosusi	بخش خصوصی
public sector	bakhsh-e dowlati	بخش دولتی
agricultural sector	bakhsh-e keshaavarzi	بخش کشاورزی
setting-up; erection; establishment	barpaa'i	برپائی
electrification	barq keshi	برقکشی
plan; programme	barnaameh	برنامه
five-year plan	barnaame-ye panj saaleh	برنامه پنجساله
planning	barnaameh rizi	برنامه ریزی
development planning	barnaameh rizi-ye 'omraani	برنامه ریزی عمرانی

development programme	barnaame-ye 'omraani	برنامه عمرانی
highway	bozorgraah	بزرگراه
barrel	boshkeh	بشکه
use; implementation; application	bekaar giri	بکارگیری
port	bandar	بندر
budget	budjeh	بودجه
development budget	budje-ye 'omraani	بودجه عمرانی
Tehran Stock Exchange	burs-e Tehraan	بورس تهران
price	bahaa	بها
amelioration; improvement	behsaazi	بهسازی
industrial park	paark-e san'ati	پارک صنعتی
refinery	paalaayeshgaah	پالایشگاه
potential	potaansiyel	پتانسیل
payment	pardaakht	پرداخت
development project	pruzhe-ye 'omraani	پروژه عمرانی
research centre	pezhuhesh kadeh	پژوهشکده
progress; development	pishraft	پیشرفت
contractor	peymaankaar	پیمانکار
sub-contractor	peymaankaar-e far'i	پیمانکار فرعی
merchant; trader	taajer	تاجر
installation; establishment; founding	ta'sis	تاسیس
merchants; traders	tojjaar	تجار
equipment	tajhizaat	تجهیزات
research	tahqiqaat	تحقیقات
transit of goods	teraanzit-e kaalaa	ترانزیت کالا
communication facilities	tas-hilaat-e ertebaati	تسهیلات ارتباطی
new facilities	tas-hilaat-e jadid	تسهیلات جدید
road-widening	ta'riz-e jaaddeh	تعریض جاده
financial commitments	ta'ahhodaat-e maali	تعهدات مالی
technology	teknuluzhi	تکنولوژی
development	towse'eh	توسعه
industrial development	towse'e-ye san'ati	توسعه صنعتی
undeveloped	towse'eh nayaafteh	توسعه نیافته
developed	towse'eh yaafteh	توسعه یافته
production	towlid	تولید
mass production	towlid-e anbuh	تولید انبوه
products	towlidaat	تولیدات
natural wealth	servat-e tabi'i	ثروت طبیعی

multi-functional	chand manzureh	چند منظوره
industrial law	hoquq-e san'ati	حقوق صنعتی
ringroad	halqe-ye teraafiki	حلقه ترافیکی
transport of cargo	haml-e baar	حمل بار
foreign purchases	kharid-haa-ye khaareji	خریدهای خارجی
production line	khat-e towlid	خط تولید
pipeline	khat-e luleh	خط لوله
gas pipeline	khat-e lule-ye gaaz	خط لوله گاز
assembly line	khat-e muntaazh	خط مونتاژ
self-sufficiency	khod kafaa'i	خود کفائی
vehicle	khod row	خودرو
oil income	daraamad-e nafti	در آمد نفتی
oil reserves	zakhaa'er-e nafti	ذخائر نفتی
setting-up; inception; launch	raah andaazi	راه اندازی
highway	raah shuseh	راه شوسه
competition; rivalry	reqaabat	رقابت
recession; economic decline	rokud-e eqtesaadi	رکود اقتصادی
economic relations	ravaabet-e eqtesaadi	روابط اقتصادی
industrial relations	ravaabet-e san'ati	روابط صنعتی
infrastructure	zir banaa	زیربنا
make; structure	saakht	ساخت
made in Iran	saakht-e iraan	ساخت ایران
Planning and Budget Organisation	saazmaan-e barnaameh va budjeh	سازمان برنامه و بودجه
Ports and Shipping Organisation	saazmaan-e banaader va keshtiraani	سازمان بنادر و کشتیرانی
Environmental Protection Agency	saazmaan-e hefaazat-e mohit-e zist	سازمان حفاظت محیط زیست
current year	saal-e jari	سال جاری
hardware	sakht afzaar	سخت افزار
investment	sarmaayeh gozaari	سرمایه گذاری
level of quality	sath-e keyfi	سطح کیفی
order	sefaaresh	سفارش
consumption ceiling	saqf-e masraf	سقف مصرف
multifunctional system; multimedia	sistem-e chand kaarbordi	سیستم چند کاربردی
transport network	shabake-ye haml o naql	شبکه حمل و نقل
computer network	shabake-ye kaampyuteri	شبکه کامپیوتری
company	sherkat	شرکت
cooperative company	sherkat-e ta'aavoni	شرکت تعاونی
multinational company	sherkat-e chand melliyati	شرکت چند ملیتی
trade partner	sharik-e tejaari	شریک تجاری

floating (e.g. currency or oil-rig)	shenaavar	شناور
roadway; highway; causeway	shuseh	شوسه
fisheries	shilaat	شیلات
town council	shahrdaari	شهرداری
industrial park	shahrak-e san'ati	شهرك صنعتی
exports	saaderaat	صادرات
non-oil exports	saaderaat-e qeyr-e nafti	صادرات غیر نفتی
saving; thrift; economy	sarfeh ju'i	صرفه جوئی
industries	sanaaye'	صنایع
handicrafts	sanaaye'-e dasti	صنایع دستی
industry	san'at	صنعت
nuclear industry	san'at-e atomi	صنعت اتمی
car industry	san'at-e otumobil saazi	صنعت اتومبیل سازی
petrochemical industry	san'at-e petrushimi	صنعت پتروشیمی
clothing industry	san'at-e pushaak	صنعت پوشاك
leather industry	san'at-e charm	صنعت چرم
transport industry	san'at-e haml o naql	صنعت حمل و نقل
pharmaceutical industry	san'at-e daaru'i	صنعت داروئی
chemical industry	san'at-e shimiyaa'i	صنعت شیمیائی
food industry	san'at-e qazaa'i	صنعت غذائی
carpet industry	san'at-e farsh	صنعت فرش
space industry	san'at-e fazaa'i	صنعت فضائی
computer industry	san'at-e kaampyuter	صنعت کامپیوتر
farming industry	san'at-e keshaavarzi	صنعت کشاورزی
shipbuilding industry	san'at-e keshti saazi	صنعت کشتی سازی
industrialist	san'at gar	صنعت گر
industrialism	san'atgaraa'i	صنعت گرائی
textile industry	san'at-e nassaaji	صنعت نساجی
oil industry	san'at-e naft	صنعت نفت
aviation industry	san'at-e havaapeymaa'i	صنعت هواپیمائی
industrial	san'ati	صنعتی
industrialization	san'ati saazi	صنعتی سازی
regulations	zavaabet	ضوابط
design	tarh	طرح
capacity	zarfiyat	ظرفیت
annual production capacity	zarfiyat-e towlid-e saalaaneh	ظرفیت تولید سالانه
revenues; earnings; gains	'aayedaat	عایدات
supply and demand	'arzeh va taqaazaa	عرضه و تقاضا

250

operations	'amaliyaat	عملیات
duties; dues; fees	'avaarez	عوارض
product; by-product	faraavardeh	فراورده
job opportunity	forsat-e shoqli	فرصت شغلی
green belt	fazaa-ye sabz	فضای سبز
technique; skill; technology	fan	فن
industrial arts	fonun-e san'ati	فنون صنعتی
steel	fulaad	فولاد
capability; worth; ability	qaabeliyat	قابلیت
contract	qaraardaad	قرارداد
the underclass	qeshr-e mostaz'af	قشر مستضعف
parts	qate'aat	قطعات
accessories	qate'aat-e monfaseleh	قطعات منفصله
item (e.g. of merchandise)	qalam	قلم
horse power	qove-ye asb	قوه اسب
competitive prices	qeymat-haa-ye qaabel-e reqaabat	قیمت های قابل رقابت
factory	kaarkhaaneh	کارخانه
tank-building factory	karkhaane-ye taanksaazi	کارخانه تانکسازی
factory owner; industrialist	kaarkhaaneh daar	کارخانه دار
industrialist	kaarsaalaar-e san'ati	کارسالار صنعتی
expert	kaarshenaas	کارشناس
employees	kaarkonaan	کارکنان
workshop	kaargaah	کارگاه
industrial worker	kaargar-e san'ati	کارگر صنعت
workers	kaargaraan	کارگران
goods; merchandise	kaalaa	کالا
basic goods	kaalaa-ye asaasi	کالای اساسی
reduction	kaahesh	کاهش
advanced nations	keshvar-haa-ye pishrafteh	کشورهای پیشرفته
undeveloped nations	keshvar-haa-ye towse'eh nayaafteh	کشورهای توسعه نیافته
developed nations	keshvar-haa-ye towse'eh yaafteh	کشورهای توسعه یافته
developing nations	keshvar-haa-ye dar haal-e towse'eh	کشورهای در حال توسعه
green belt	kamarband-e sabz	کمربند سبز
price control	kontrol-e qeymat	کنترل قیمت
quality of goods	keyfiyat-e kaalaa-haa	کیفیت کالاها
natural gas	gaaz-e tabi'i	گاز طبیعی
report	gozaaresh	گزارش
export licence	govaahinaame-ye saaderaati	گواهینامه صادراتی

251

machinery; machine tools	maashin abzaar	ماشین ابزار
industrial machinery	maashin aalaat-e san'ati	ماشین آلات صنعتی
expert; specialist	motakhasses	متخصص
industrial complex	mojtama'-e san'ati	مجتمع صنعتی
products; produce	mahsulaat	محصولات
industrial products	mahsulaat-e san'ati	محصولات صنعتی
agricultural produce	mahsulaat-e keshaavarzi	محصولات کشاورزی
project manager	modir-e pruzheh	مدیر پروژه
managing director	modir-e 'aamel	مدیر عامل
negotiations; talks	mozaakeraat	مذاکرات
opening ceremony; launch	maraasem-e raah andaazi	مراسم راه اندازی
(good) quality	marqubiyat	مرغوبیت
farms; fields	mazaare'	مزارع
economic issues	masaa'el-e eqtesaadi	مسائل اقتصادی
customer	moshtari	مشتری
oil derivatives; oil by-products	moshtaqqaat-e nafti	مشتقات نفتی
economic problems	moshkelaat-e eqtesaadi	مشکلات اقتصادی
environmental problems	moshkelaat-e mohit-e zist	مشکلات محیط زیست
annual consumption (rate)	masraf-e saraaneh	مصرف سرانه
exemption	mo'aafiyat	معافیت
customs exemption	mo'aafiyat-e gomroki	معافیت گرکی
officials	maqaamaat	مقامات
human resources	manaabe'-e ensaani	منابع انسانی
water resources	manaabe'-e aabi	منابع آبی
national resources	manaabe'-e melli	منابع ملی
deprived areas	manaateq-e mahrum	مناطق محروم
industrial area	mantaqe-ye san'ati	منطقه صنعتی
raw materials	mavaad-e avvaliyeh	مواد اولیه
organisation; institute; foundation	mo'asseseh	موسسه
oil field	meydaan-e naft	میدان نفت
foreign debt rate	mizaan-e bedehi-ye khaareji	میزان بدهی خارجی
level of production; rate of production	mizaan-e towlid	میزان تولید
engineer	mohandes	مهندس
fleet; navy	naavgaan-e daryaa'i	ناوگان دریانی
installation; setting-up; fixing	nasb	نصب
crude oil	naft-e khaam	نفت خام
mapping; surveying	naqsheh bardaari	نقشه برداری
exhibition centre	namaayeshgaah	نمایشگاه

price fluctuation	navasaan-e qeymat-haa	نوسان قیمت ها
manpower	niru-ye ensaani	نیروی انسانی
institution	nahaad	نهاد
government institutions	nahaad-haa-ye dowlati	نهادهای دولتی
dependence	vaabastegi	وابستگی
dependence on oil	vaabastegi be-naft	وابستگی به نفت
unit	vaahed	واحد
imports	vaaredaat	واردات
non-oil imports	vaaredaat-e qeyr-e nafti	واردات غیر نفتی
Ministry of Commerce	vezaarat-e baazargaani	وزارت بازرگانی
Ministry of Telecommunications	vezaarat-e post o telegraaf o telefon	وزارت پست و تلگراف و تلفن
Ministry of Transport	vezaarat-e raah o taraabari	وزارت راه و ترابری
Ministry of Heavy Industries	vezaarat-e sanaaye'-e sangin	وزارت صنایع سنگین
Ministry of Mines and Steel	vezaarat-e ma'aaden o felezaat	وزارت معادن و فلزات
Ministry of Power	vezaarat-e niru	وزارت نیرو
ministry	vezaarat khaaneh	وزارتخانه
means of transport	vasaa'et-e naqliyeh	وسائط نقلیه
cost	hazineh	هزینه
industrial complex	hamtaaft-e san'ati	همتافت صنعتی
economic cooperation	hamkaari-ye eqtesaadi	همکاری اقتصادی
board of directors	hey'at-e modireh	هیئت مدیره

to carry out اجراء كردن   to require; to ask for درخواست كردن   to sign a contract قرارداد بستن

to build ساختن   to design طرح كردن   to set up راه انداختن   to establish; to set up تاسيس كردن

to decrease كاهش يافتن   to increase; to be increased افزايش پيدا كردن   to construct; to build احداث كردن

the factory was made operational كارخانه راه اندازی شد   the ship was launched كشتی به آب انداخته شد

to be set up بر پا شدن   to export صادر كردن   to import وارد كردن   to purchase خريداری كردن

the plan was put into effect طرح به مرحله اجراء در آمد   the exhibition was set up نمايشگاه بر پا شد

to be built ساخته شدن   to produce توليد كردن   to advance; to progress پيشرفت كردن

to use; to put to work بكار گرفتن   the use of new techniques بكارگيری تكنيك های جديد   use بكارگيری

the setting up of a new industrial complex برپائی يک مجتمع صنعتی جديد   setting up; establishment برپائی

to report گزارش دادن   advanced technology تكنولوژی پيشرفته   to mine; to extract استخراج كردن

on the decrease رو به كاهش   on the increase رو به افزايش   to order سفارش دادن

the new car was launched ماشين جديد روانه بازار شد   to be put on the market; to be launched روانه بازار شدن

new discoveries اكتشافات جديد   to invent اختراع كردن   to discover كشف كردن

method of production شيوه توليد   new methods شيوه های جديد   new inventions اختراعات جديد

the production line is able to build 500 engines a year خط توليد قادر است ساليانه ۵۰۰ دستگاه موتور بسازد

254

subscription	aabunmaan	آبونمان
subscriber; subscribed	aabuneh shodeh	آبونه شده
lost property office	edaare-ye ashiyaa-ye gomshodeh	اداره اشیای گم شده
foreign currency	arz-e khaareji	ارز خارجی
forwarding; sending; delivery	ersaal	ارسال
bank note	eskenaas-e banki	اسکناس بانکی
name	esm	اسم
mistake	eshtebaah	اشتباه
subscription	eshteraak	اشتراك
information	ettelaa'aat	اطلاعات
signature	emzaa	امضاء
credit transfer	enteqaal-e e'tebaar	انتقال اعتبار
emergency services	urzhaans	اورژانس
return	baazgasht	بازگشت
bank	baank	بانک
computer banking	baankdaari-ye kaampyuteri	بانکداری کامپیوتری
explanatory leaflet	barge-ye ettelaa'aat	برگه اطلاعات
brochure	berowshur	بروشور
parcel; package	basteh	بسته
ticket	belit	بلیط
dialling tone	buq-e aazaad	بوق آزاد
engaged tone	buq-e eshqaal	بوق اشغال
continuous tone	buq-e daa'em	بوق دائم
price; rate	bahaa	بها،
licence fee	bahaa-ye govaahinaameh	بهای گواهینامه
envelope	paakat-e naameh	پاکت نامه
payment	pardaakht	پرداخت
post	post	پست
poste restante	post restaant	پست رستانت
surface mail	post-e zamini	پست زمینی
airmail	post-e havaa'i	پست هوائی
post office	postkhaaneh	پستخانه
telephone line rental fee	pul-e ejaare-ye khat-e telefon	پول اجاره خط تلفن
scanner	puyeshgar	پویشگر
electronic mail	payaam-e elektruniki	پیام الکترونیکی
e-mail	payaam negaar	پیام نگار

counter	pishkhaan	پیشخوان
reduction (in price); discount	takhfif	تخفیف
telephone	telefon	تلفن
(telephone) operator	telefonchi	تلفن چی
long distance call	telefon-e raah-e dur	تلفن راه دور
local call	telefon-e shahri	تلفن شهری
telegraph	telegraaf	تلگراف
telegram	telegraam	تلگرام
phone call	tamaas-e telefoni	تماس تلفنی
stamp	tambr	تمبر
tuman (unit of Iranian currency)	tumaan	تومان
cheque stub	tah chek	ته چک
reward; prize	jaayezeh	جایزه
answer; reply; response	javaab	جواب
cheque	chek	چک
initials	horuf-e avval-e esm	حروف اول اسم
capitals; upper case	horuf-e bozorg	حروف بزرگ
lower case (letters)	horuf-e kuchek	حروف کوچک
savings account	hesaab-e pasandaaz	حساب پس انداز
current account	hesaab-e jaari	حساب جاری
money order	havaaleh	حواله
services	khadamaat	خدمات
postal services	khadamaat-e posti	خدمات پستی
biro; automatic	khodkaar	خودکار
instructions; directions for use	dastur ol-'amal	دستور العمل
telephone directory	daftar-e raahnamaa-ye telefon	دفتر راهنمای تلفن
cheque book	daftarche-ye chek	دفترچه چک
fax machine	durnevis	دورنویس
free; gratis	raayegaan	رایگان
receipt	resid	رسید
visa	ravaadid	روادید
rial (10 rials = 1 tuman)	riyaal	ریال
bell	zang	زنگ
ringing (of telephone)	zang-e telefon	زنگ تلفن
token (for telephone etc.)	zhetun	ژتون
the speaking clock	saa'at-e guyaa	ساعت گویا
deposit	sepordeh	سپرده
expiry	sar resid	سر رسید

acronym	sarnaam	سرنام
coin	sekkeh	سکه
slot; hole	suraakh	سوراخ
number	shomaareh	شماره
ID card; birth certificate	shenaas naameh	شناسنامه
bureau de change	sarraafi	صرافی
cash register	sanduq	صندوق
postbox; PO box	sanduq-e post	صندوق پست
bill; invoice	surat hesaab	صورتحساب
passport photograph	'aks-e paaspurti	عکس پاسپورتی
fax	faaks	فاکس
sender	ferestandeh	فرستنده
form	form	فرم
loan	qarz	قرض
price	qeymat	قیمت
credit card	kaart-e e'tebaar	کارت اعتبار
bank card	kaart-e baanki	کارت بانکی
postcard	kaart postaal	کارت پستال
telephone card	kaart-e telefon	کارت تلفن
wrapping paper	kaaqaz-e basteh bandi	کاغذ بسته بندی
writing paper	kaaqaz-e tahrir	کاغذ تحریر
post code	kod-e posti	کد پستی
city code (i.e. part of phone number)	kod-e shahr	کد شهر
purse; wallet	kif-e pul	کیف پول
phone booth	kiusk-e telefon	کیوسک تلفن
photo-booth	kiusk-e 'aks-e fowri	کیوسک عکس فوری
passport	gozarnaameh	گذرنامه
bank statement	gozaaresh-e baanki	گزارش بانکی
(telephone) receiver	gushi	گوشی
receiver (e.g. of a letter)	girandeh	گیرنده
tax	maaliyaat	مالیات
expenses	makhaarej	مخارج
abbreviation	mokhaffaf	مخفف
means of identification	madaarek-e shenaasaa'i	مدارک شناسائی
tourist information centre	markaz-e ettelaa'aat-e jahaangardi	مرکز اطلاعات جهانگردی
information desk; information point	maqar-e ettelaa' resaani	مقر اطلاع رسانی
surname	naam-e khaanevaadegi	نام خانوادگی
first name	naam-e kuchek	نام کوچک

delivery (of letters)	naameh resaani	نامه رسانی
registered letter	naame-ye sefaareshi	نامه سفارشی
airmail letter	naame-ye havaa'i	نامه هوائی
rate	nerkh	نرخ
address	neshaani	نشانی
home address	neshaani-ye manzel	نشانی منزل
printed matter	nashriyaat	نشریات
visa	vizaa	ویزا
cost; charge	hazineh	هزینه
extra cost; extra charge	hazine-ye ezaafi	هزینه اضافی
postal charges	hazine-ye post	هزینه پست

OTHER WORDS AND EXPRESSIONS

English	Persian
to telephone	تلفن کردن
to ring	زنگ زدن
I want to ring my father	می خواهم به پدرم زنگ بزنم
to pick up the receiver	گوشی را برداشتن
to dial the number	شماره را گرفتن
wrong number	شماره اشتباه
there's no dialling tone	بوق آزاد نیست
the line is busy	خط اشغال است
no-one is answering	کسی جواب نمی دهد
please hold the line	لطفا گوشی دستتان باشد
please hang up the receiver	لطفا گوشی را بگذارید
we were suddenly cut off	خط یک دفعه قطع شد
try again in half an hour	نیم ساعت دیگر سعی کنید
to send a telex	تلکس زدن
to fax; to send a fax	فاکس زدن
to leave a message	پیغام گذاشتن
to ask for information	درخواست اطلاع کردن
to ask for help	کمک خواستن
to guide; to direct	راهنمائی کردن
could you please direct me to the nearest bank?	لطفا می توانید مرا به نزدیکترین بانک راهنمائی کنید؟
I want to post a letter	می خواهم نامه پست کنم
I want to cash a cheque	می خواهم چک نقد کنم
I want to e-mail him	می خواهم برای او پیام الکترونیکی بفرستم
where can I buy stamps?	کجا می شود تمبر خرید؟
to apply	تقاضا دادن
to fill in	پر کردن
you have to fill in this form	باید این فرم را پر کنید
to sign	امضاء کردن
write your name in block letters	اسمتان را با حروف بزرگ بنویسید
what's your address?	آدرس شما چیست؟
how do you spell that?	آن را چه جوری اسپل می کنند؟
how do I get to the post office?	پستخانه از کدام طرفه؟
straight on	مستقیم
to / on the right	دست راست
to / on the left	دست چپ
opposite; facing	روبرو
it's opposite the bank	روبروی بانک است
behind	پشت
it's behind the town hall	پشت شهرداری است
in front (of)	جلو (ی)
next (to)	پهلو (ی)
in the direction of	به طرف
north	شمال
south	جنوب
east	شرق
west	غرب
I don't know where it is	نمی دانم کجاست
I've lost my wallet	کیف پولم را گم کرده ام
to find	پیدا کردن
to ask	سوال کردن
to ask	پرسیدن
to answer	جواب دادن
to help	کمک کردن
I'm sorry, I can't help you	متاسفانه نمی توانم به شما کمک کنم
I have no information; I don't know	اطلاع ندارم

روابط بین المللی

international waterways	aabraah-haa-ye beyn ol-mellali	آبراههای بین المللی
free waters	aab-haa-ye aazaad	آبهای آزاد
international waters	aab-haa-ye beyn ol-mellali	آبهای بین المللی
territorial waters	aab-haa-ye sar zamini	آبهای سرزمینی
attache	aataasheh	آتاشه
freedom of the (high) seas	aazaadi-ye daryaa-haa	آزادی دریاها
Americanization	aamrikaa'i saazi	آمریکانی سازی
displaced persons	aavaaregaan	آوارگان
superpowers	abar qodrat-haa	ابرقدرتها
new superpowers	abar qodrat-haa-ye jadid	ابرقدرتهای جدید
unity; coalition; union	ettehaad	اتحاد
customs union	ettehaadiye-ye gomroki	اتحادیه گمرکی
alliance; agreement	ettefaaq	اتفاق
alien; foreign; foreigner	ajnabi	اجنبی
recall	ehzaar	احضار
letter of recall	ehzaar naameh	احضارنامه
international dispute	ekhtelaaf-e beyn ol-mellali	اختلاف بین المللی
extradition of criminals	esterdaad-e mojremin	استرداد مجرمین
colonialism	este'maar	استعمار
decolonization	este'maar zadaa'i	استعمار زدائی
letter of credentials	ostovaar naameh	استوارنامه
diplomatic documents	asnaad-e diplomaatik	اسناد دیپلماتیک
sovereign immunity	asl-e masuniyat-e ra'is-e keshvar	اصل مصونیت رئیس کشور
members of the consular post	a'zaa-ye post-e konsuli	اعضای پست کنسولی
members of the mission	a'zaa-ye ma'muriyat	اعضای ماموریت
joint declaration; joint statement	e'laamiye-ye moshtarak	اعلامیه مشترک
unilateral declaration (independence)	e'laamiye-ye yekjaanebe-ye esteqlaal	اعلامیه یک جانبه استقلال
domicile	eqaamatgaah	اقامتگاه
international economics	eqtesaad-e beyn ol-mellali	اقتصاد بین المللی
accession; adhesion	elhaaq	الحاق
abolitionism	elqaagari	الغاگری
consular premises	amaaken-e konsuli	اماکن کنسولی
cultural imperialism	amperyaalism	امپریالیسم
cultural imperialism	amperyaalism-e farhangi	امپریالیسم فرهنگی
capitulations	emtiyaazaat-e vizhe-ye bigaanegaan	امتیازات ویژه بیگانگان
international security	amniyat-e beyn ol-mellali	امنیت بین المللی

collective security	amniyat-e jam'i	امنیت جمعی
internationalism	anternaasiyunaalism	انترناسیونالیسم
cultural transmission	enteqaal-e farhangi	انتقال فرهنگی
isolationism	enzevaa talabi	انزواطلبی
annexation	enzemaam	انضمام
Balkanization	baalkaanizeh kardan	بالکانیزه کردن
boycott	baaykut	بایکوت
diplomatic archives	baayegaani-ye diplomaatik	بایگانی دیپلماتیک
consular archives	baayegaani-ye konsuli	بایگانی کنسولی
quid pro quo	bedeh bestaan	بده بستان
military parity	baraabari-ye nezaami	برابری نظامی
'clash of civilisations'	barkhord-e tamaddon-haa	برخورد تمدنها
bloc	boluk	بلوک
impasse	bonbast	بن بست
stateless	bi taabe'iyat	بی تابعیت
statelessness	bi taabe'iyati	بی تابعیتی
joint declaration	bayaaniye-ye moshtarak	بیانیه مشترک
neutralization	bitaraf saazi	بیطرف سازی
alien; foreign	bigaaneh	بیگانه
xenophobia	bigaaneh haraasi	بیگانه هراسی
international	beyn ol-mellali	بین المللی
international institution	bonyaad-e beyn ol-mellali	بنیاد بین المللی
gold standard	paaye-ye talaa	پایه طلا
consular post	post-e konsuli	پست کنسولی
voluntary refugees	panaahandegaan-e daavtalab	پناهندگان داوطلب
territorial asylum	panaahandegi-ye dorunmarzi	پناهندگی درونمرزی
political asylum	panaahandegi-ye siyaasi	پناهندگی سیاسی
asylum seeker; refugee	panaahandeh	پناهنده
economic refugee	panaahande-ye eqtesaadi	پناهنده اقتصادی
political asylum seeker	panaahande-ye siyaasi	پناهنده سیاسی
diplomatic courier	peyk-e diplomaatik	پیک دیپلماتیک
alliance; treaty; pact; confederacy	peymaan	پیمان
general alliance	peymaan-e ettehaad-e 'omumi	پیمان اتحاد عمومی
non-aggression pact	peymaan-e 'adam-e tajaavoz	پیمان عدم تجاوز
adhesion	peyvastegi	پیوستگی
legislative graft	peyvand-e taqnini	پیوند تقنینی
dual nationality	taabe'iyat-e dowgaaneh	تابعیت دوگانه
international cultural propaganda	tabliqaat-e farhangi-ye beyn ol-mellali	تبلیغات فرهنگی بین المللی

free trade	tejaarat-e aazaad	تجارت آزاد
rapprochement	tajdid-e ravaabet-e dustaaneh	تجدید روابط دوستانه
sanctions	tahrim	تحریم
economic sanctions	tahrim-e eqtesaadi	تحریم اقتصادی
arms embargo	tahrim-e taslihaati	تحریم تسلیحاتی
diplomatic representation	tazakkor-e diplomaatik	تذکر دیپلماتیک
international terrorism	terurism-e beyn ol-mellali	تروریسم بین المللی
approval; ratification	tasvib	تصویب
conflict of laws	ta'aaroz-e qavaanin	تعارض قوانین
moratorium	ta'liq	تعلیق
delimitation	ta'yin-e hodud	تعیین حدود
entente	tafaahom	تفاهم
divide and rule	tafraqe-ye biyandaaz o hokumat kon	تفرقه بینداز و حکومت کن
demarcation	tafkik-e hodud	تفکیک حدود
reprisal	talaafi	تلافی
territorial integrity	tamaamiyat-e arzi	تمامیت ارضی
accord; agreement; consensus	tavaafoq	توافق
cultural invasion	tahaajom-e farhangi	تهاجم فرهنگی
espionage	jaasusi	جاسوسی
international society	jaame'e-ye beyn ol-mellali	جامعه بین المللی
world community	jaame'e-ye jahaani	جامعه جهانی
international crime	jorm-e beyn ol-mellali	جرم بین المللی
expatriation	jalaa-ye vatan	جلای وطن
banana republic	jomhuri-ye mowz	جمهوری موز
non-alignment movement	jonbesh-e 'adam-e ta'ahhod	جنبش عدم تعهد
cold war	jang-e sard	جنگ سرد
First World	jahaan-e avval	جهان اوّل
free world	jahaan-e aazaad	جهان آزاد
Fourth World	jahaan-e chahaarom	جهان چهارم
Second World	jahaan-e dovvom	جهان دوّم
globalism	jahaan saalaari	جهان سالاری
Third World	jahaan-e sevvom	جهان سوّم
cosmopolitanism	jahaan vatani	جهان وطنی
globalization	jahaani saazi	جهانی سازی
constructive presence	hozur-e mo'asser	حضور موثر
right of asylum	haqq-e panaahandegi	حق پناهندگی
right of self-determination	haqq-e khod mokhtaari	حق خودمختاری
universal international law	hoquq-e beyn ol-mellali-ye jahaani	حقوق بین الملل جهانی

261

general international law	hoquq-e beyn ol-mellal-e 'aam	حقوق بین الملل عام
international criminal law	hoquq-e beyn ol-mellal-e keyfari	حقوق بین الملل کیفری
particular international law	hoquq-e beyn ol-mellal-e vizheh	حقوق بین الملل ویژه
refugee law	hoquq-e panaahandegi	حقوق پناهندگان
law of state succession	hoquq-e jaaneshini-ye dowlat	حقوق جانشینی دولت
maritime law	hoquq-e daryaa'i	حقوق دریائی
law of the sea	hoquq-e daryaa-haa	حقوق دریاها
diplomatic law	hoquq-e diplomaatik	حقوق دیپلماتیک
space law	hoquq-e fazaa	حقوق فضا
consular law	hoquq-e konsuli	حقوق کنسولی
peaceful settlement (of disputes)	hall-e mosaalemat aamiz	حل مسالمت آمیز
diplomatic protection	hemaayat-e diplomaatik	حمایت دیپلماتیک
free trade area	howze-ye tejaarat-e aazaad	حوزه تجارت آزاد
ad hoc arbitration	daavari-ye khaas	داوری خاص
secretary-general	dabir-e kol	دبیر کل
secretariat	dabir khaaneh	دبیرخانه
intervention	dekhaalat	دخالت
humanitarian intervention	dekhaalat-e ensaandustaaneh	دخالت انساندوستانه
legitimate defence	defaa'-e mashru'	دفاع مشروع
counterforce doctrine	doktrin-e paadkonesh	دکترین پادکنش
act of state doctrine	doktrin-e haakemiyat-e dowlat	دکترین حاکمیت دولت
receiving state	dowlat-e pazirandeh	دولت پذیرنده
vassal state	dowlat-e kharaajgozaar	دولت خراجگزار
sending state	dowlat-e ferestandeh	دولت فرستنده
sovereign state	dowlat-e mostaqel	دولت مستقل
dependent state	dowlat-e vaabasteh	دولت وابسته
diplomat	diplomaat	دیپلمات
diplomacy	diplomaasi	دیپلماسی
imperialist diplomacy	diplomaasi-ye amperyaalisti	دیپلماسی امپریالیستی
preventative diplomacy	diplomaasi-ye baazdaarandeh	دیپلماسی بازدارنده
shirt-sleeve diplomacy	diplomaasi-ye bedun-e tashrifaat	دیپلماسی بدون تشریفات
basic diplomacy	diplomaasi-ye bonyaadi	دیپلماسی بنیادی
shuttle diplomacy	diplomaasi-ye parvaazi	دیپلماسی پروازی
open diplomacy	diplomaasi-ye dar-haa-ye baaz	دیپلماسی درهای باز
dollar diplomacy	diplomaasi-ye dolaar	دیپلماسی دلار
democratic diplomacy	diplomaasi-ye demukraatik	دیپلماسی دموکراتیک
summit diplomacy	diplomaasi-ye saraan	دیپلماسی سران
secret diplomacy	diplomaasi-ye serri	دیپلماسی سری

international criminal court	divaan-e beyn ol-mellali-ye keyfari	دیوان بین المللی کیفری
bad debts	doyun-e manfur	دیون منفور
global village	dehkade-ye jahaani	دهکده جهانی
veto	ra'y-e manfi	رای منفی
adjudication	residegi-ye qazaa'i	رسیدگی قضائی
reciprocity	raftaar-e motaqaabel	رفتار متقابل
international relations	ravaabet-e beyn ol-mellali	روابط بین المللی
diplomatic relations	ravaabet-e diplomaatik	روابط دیپلماتیک
consular relations	ravaabet-e konsuli	روابط کنسولی
no-man's land	zamin-e bi maalek	زمین بی مالک
geopacifics	zhe'u paasifik	ژئوپاسیفیک
geopolitics	zhe'u pulitik	ژئوپولیتیک
international organization	saazmaan-e beyn ol-mellali	سازمان بین المللی
supranational organizations	saazmaan-haa-ye faraa melli	سازمانهای فراملی
containment of Communism	sadd-e nofuz-e komunism	سد نفوذ کمونیسم
boundary	sar hadd	سرحد
territory	sarzamin	سرزمین
abandoned territory	sarzamin-e rahaa shodeh	سرزمین رها شده
enclave	sarzamin-e mohaat	سرزمین محاط
non-self governing territories	sarzamin-haa-ye qeyr-e khod mokhtar	سرزمینهای غیر خودمختار
overseas territories	sarzamin-e maavaraa-ye behaar	سرزمین ماورای بحار
consul-general	sar konsul	سر کنسول
consulate-general	sar konsulgari	سر کنسولگری
embassy	sefaarat	سفارت
embassy	sefaarat khaaneh	سفارتخانه
ambassador	safir	سفیر
ambassador accredite	safar-e akrediteh	سفیر اکردیته
roving ambassador	safir-e sayyaar	سفیر سیار
ambassador extraordinary	safir-e fowq ol-'aadeh	سفیر فوق العاده
appeasement	siyaasat-e erzaa	سیاست ارضاء
international politics	siyaasat-e beyn ol-mellali	سیاست بین المللی
geopolitics	siyaasat-e joqraafiyaa'i	سیاست جغرافیانی
big-stick policy	siyaasat-e chomaaq-e bozorg	سیاست چماق بزرگ
foreign policy	siyaasat-e khaareji	سیاست خارجی
bipartisan foreign policy	siyaasat-e khaareji-ye dow hezbi	سیاست خارجی دوحزبی
open door policy	siyaasat-e dar-haa-ye baaz	سیاست درهای باز
power politics	siyaasat-e zur	سیاست زور
principality	shaahzaadeh neshin	شاهزاده نشین

international personality	shakhsiyat-e beyn ol-mellali	شخصیت بین المللی
multinational corporation	sherkat-e chand melliyati	شرکت چند ملیتی
de facto recognition	shenaasaa'i-ye belfe'l	شناسائی بالفعل
recognition of government	shenaasaa'i-ye hokumat	شناسائی حکومت
recognition of state	shenaasaa'i-ye dowlat	شناسائی دولت
tacit recognition	shenaasaa'i-ye zemni	شناسائی ضمنی
de jure recognition	shenaasaa'i-ye qaanuni	شناسائی قانونی
cold peace	solh-e sard	صلح سرد
anti-colonialism	zedd-e este'maar	ضد استعمار
counter-espionage	zedd-e jaasusi	ضد جاسوسی
arc of crisis	taaq-e bohraan	طاق بحران
consular classes	tabaqaat-e konsuli	طبقات کنسولی
non-alignment	'adam-e ta'ahhod	عدم تعهد
non-intervention	'adam-e dekhaalat	عدم دخالت
international custom	'orf-e beyn ol-mellali	عرف بین المللی
unfriendly act	'amal-e qeyr-e dustaaneh	عمل غیر دوستانه
reparations	qaraamat-e jang	غرامت جنگ
Westernization	qarbi shodan	غربی شدن
envoy	ferestaadeh	فرستاده
envoy extraordinary ·	ferestaade-ye fowq ol-'aadeh	فرستاده فوق العاده
special envoy	ferestaade-ye vizheh	فرستاده ویژه
consular commission	farmaan-e konsuli	فرمان کنسولی
governor-general	farmaandaar-e koll	فرماندار کل
acculturation	farhang paziri	فرهنگ پذیری
cannon shot rule	qaa'ede-ye tir ras-e tup	قاعده تیررس توپ
international law	qaanun-e beyn ol-mellali	قانون بین المللی
bargaining power	qodrat-e chaaneh zani	قدرت چانه زنی
modus vivendi	qaraar-e mo'aafeqat	قرار موافقت
arrangement	qaraar o madaar	قرار و مدار
bilateral agreement	qaraardaad-e dow jaanebeh	قرارداد دوجانبه
breaking-off of diplomatic relations	qat'-e ravaabet-e diplomaatik	قطع روابط دیپلماتیک
cartel	kaartel	کارتل
charge d'affaires	kaardaar	کاردار
charge d'affaires ad interim	kaardaar-e movaqqat	کاردار موقت
members of the consular staff	kaarkonaan-e konsuli	کارکنان کنسولی
international functionary	kaarmand-e beyn ol-mellali	کارمند بین المللی
consular employee	kaarmand-e konsuli	کارمند کنسولی
members of the diplomatic staff	kaarmandaan-e diplomaatik	کارمندان دیپلماتیک

ad referendum	kasb-e taklif	کسب تکلیف
international conflict	keshmakesh-e beyn ol-mellali	کشمکش بین المللی
country; state	keshvar	کشور
blend country	keshvar-e tarkibi	کشور ترکیبی
buffer state	keshvar-e haa'el	کشور حائل
great powers	keshvar-haa-ye bozorg	کشورهای بزرگ
developing countries	keshvar-haa-ye dar haal-e towse'eh	کشورهای در حال توسعه
micro-powers	keshvar-haa-ye zarre'i	کشورهای ذره ای
emerging countries	keshvar-haa-ye sar bar aavardeh	کشورهای سربرآورده
backwarded countries	keshvar-haa-ye 'aqab oftaadeh	کشورهای عقب افتاده
non-aligned countries	keshvar-haa-ye qeyr-e mota'ahhed	کشورهای غیر متعهد
small powers	keshvar-haa-ye kuchek	کشورهای کوچک
foreign aid	komak-e khaareji	کمک خارجی
high commissioner	komiser-e 'aali	کمیسر عالی
high commission	komisiyun-e 'aali	کمیسیون عالی
consul	konsul	کنسول
consulate	konsulgari	کنسولگری
diplomatic bag	kise-ye diplomaatik	کیسه دیپلماتیک
duty passport	gozarnaame-ye khedmat	گذرنامه خدمت
diplomatic passport	gozarnaame-ye diplomaatik	گذرنامه دیپلماتیک
conference; meeting	gerdehamaa'i	گردهمائی
vested interests; interested parties	goruh-haa-ye zinaf'	گروه های ذینفع
discourse; discussion	goftaar	گفتار
diplomatic list	list-e diplomaatik	لیست دیپلماتیک
diplomatic agent	ma'mur-e diplomaatik	مامور دیپلماتیک
consular officer	ma'mur-e konsuli	مامور کنسولی
honorary consular officer	ma'mur-e konsuli-ye eftekhaari	مامور کنسولی افتخاری
mission	ma'muriyat	ماموریت
diplomatic mission	ma'muriyat-e diplomaatik	ماموریت دیپلماتیک
extraordinary mission	ma'muriyat-e fowq ol-'aadeh	ماموریت فوق العاده
special mission; ad hoc mission	ma'muriyat-e vizheh	ماموریت ویژه
diplomatic manoeuvres	maanovr-haa-ye diplomaatik	مانورهای دیپلماتیک
allies	mottafeqin	متفقین
axis	mehvar	محور
intervention	modaakheleh	مداخله
negotiation; talks	mozaakereh	مذاکره
border; boundary; frontier	marz	مرز
international boundary	marz-e beyn ol-mellali	مرز بین المللی

diplomatic privileges	*mazaayaa-ye diplomaatik*	مزایای دیپلماتیک
consular privileges	*mazaayaa-ye konsuli*	مزایای کنسولی
assistance	*mosaa'edat*	مساعدت
colony	*mosta'mareh*	مستعمره
crown colony	*mosta'mare-ye farmaangozaar*	مستعمره فرمانگزار
dominion	*mostamlak*	مستملک
international responsibility	*mas'uliyat-e beyn ol-mellali*	مسئولیت بین المللی
immunity	*masuniyat*	مصونیت
inviolability	*masuniyat az ta'arroz*	مصونیت از تعرض
immunity from jurisdiction	*masuniyat az salaahiyat*	مصونیت از صلاحیت
diplomatic immunity	*masuniyat diplomaatik*	مصونیت دیپلماتیک
consular immunity	*masuniyat-e konsuli*	مصونیت کنسولی
diplomatic correspondence	*mokaatebaat-e diplomaatik*	مکاتبات دیپلماتیک
debtor nation	*mellat-e bedehkaar*	ملت بدهکار
country	*mamlekat*	مملکت
vital interests	*manaafe'-e hayaati*	منافع حیاتی
international dispute	*monaaqeshe-ye beyn ol-mellali*	مناقشه بین المللی
charter	*manshur*	منشور
exclusive economic zone	*mantaqe-ye enhesaari-ye eqtesaadi*	منطقه انحصاری اقتصادی
free trade zone	*mantaqe-ye aazaad-e tejaari*	منطقه آزاد تجاری
contiguous zone	*mantaqe-ye mojaaver*	منطقه مجاور
sphere of influence	*mantaqe-ye nofuz*	منطقه نفوذ
balance of power	*movaazene-ye qodrat*	موازنه قدرت
balance of terror	*movaazene-ye vahshat*	موازنه وحشت
agreement; convention	*mo'aafeqat naameh*	موافقتنامه
associated status	*mowqe'iyat-e vaabasteh*	موقعیت وابسته
mediation	*miyaanjigari*	میانجیگری
covenant	*misaaq*	میثاق
migration	*mohaajerat*	مهاجرت
international migration	*mohaajerat-e beyn ol-mellali*	مهاجرت بین المللی
dual containment	*mahaar-e dow jaanebeh*	مهار دوجانبه
exchange control	*nezaarat-e arzi*	نظارت ارزی
international system	*nezaam-e beyn ol-mellali*	نظام بین المللی
bipolar system; bipolarity	*nezaam-e dow qotbi*	نظام دوقطبی
mandate system	*nezaam-e sarparasti*	نظام سرپرستی
trusteeship system	*nezaam-e qeymumat*	نظام قیمومت
colonial system	*nezaam-e mosta'maraati*	نظام مستعمراتی
new world order	*nezaam-e novin-e jahaani*	نظام نوین جهانی

end of history theory	nazariye-ye paayaan-e taarikh	نظریه پایان تاریخ
risk theory	nazariye-e khatar	نظریه خطر
domino theory	nazariye-ye duminu	نظریه دومینو
consular agency	namaayandegi-ye konsuli	نمایندگی کنسولی
permanent representative	namaayande-ye daa'emi	نماینده دائمی
consular agent	namaayande-ye konsuli	نماینده کنسولی
dependence	vaabastegi	وابستگی
interdependence	vaabastegi-ye motaqaabel	وابستگی متقابل
dependency; attache	vaabasteh	وابسته
commercial attache	vaabaste-ye baazargaani	وابسته بازرگانی
press attache	vaabaste-ye matbu'aati	وابسته مطبوعاتی
military attache	vaabaste-ye nezaami	وابسته نظامی
cession	vaagozaari	واگذاری
foreign loan	vaam-e khaareji	وام خارجی
ministry of foreign affairs	vezaarat-e omur-e khaarejeh	وزارت امور خارجه
minister plenipotentiary	vazir-e mokhtaar	وزیر مختار
minister resident	vazir-e moqim	وزیر مقیم
mediation	vesaatat	وساطت
consular functions	vazaa'ef-e konsuli	وظایف کنسولی
transit visa	vizaa-ye 'oburi	ویزای عبوری
peaceful coexistence	hamzisti-ye mosaalemat aamiz	همزیستی مسالمت آمیز
assimilation	hamsaan gardi	همسان گردی
cooperation	hamkaari	همکاری
regional integration	hamgaraa'i-ye mantaqe'i	همگرائی منطقه ای
plebiscite	hameh porsi	همه پرسی
diplomatic corps	hey'at-e diplomaatik	هیئت دیپلماتیک
consular corps	hey'at-e konsuli	هیئت کنسولی

〈〈◇〉〉

Islam

اسلام

Adam and Eve	aadam o havvaa	آدم و حوا
verses of the Koran; 'signs' of God	aayaat	آیات
verse of the Koran; 'sign' of God	aayeh	آیه
Abraham	ebraahim	ابراهیم
the devil; Satan	eblis	ابلیس
independent analysis or interpretation of Islamic law.	ejtehaad	اجتهاد
consensus of the Muslim scholarly community, a source of Islamic law.	ejmaa'	اجماع
Prophetic Traditions	ahaadis	احادیث
The Muslim Brotherhood	ekhvaan-e moslemin	اخوان مسلمین
apostasy	ertedaad	ارتداد
the 'Pillars of Islam'	arkaan-e eslaam	ارکان اسلام
Islam	eslaam	اسلام
political Islam	eslaam-e siyaasi	اسلام سیاسی
Ishmael	esmaa'il	اسماعیل
Isma'ili	esmaa'ili	اسماعیلی
The 'beautiful names' of God	esmaa' ol-hosnaa	اسماء الحسنی
Divine names	esmaa'-e elaahi	اسماء الهی
reform	eslaah	اصلاح
the fundamentals of religion	osul-e din	اصول دین
principles of jurisprudence.	osul-e feqh	اصول فقه
breaking the fast at Ramadan	eftaar	افطار
atheism	elhaad	الحاد
Allah; God	allaah	الله
the cry "God is great!"	allaho akbar	الله اکبر!
Friday prayer leader	emaam jom'eh	امام جمعه
the 'Lord of the Age', i.e. the Mahdi	emaam-e zamaan	امام زمان
imamate	emaamat	امامت
the Islamic community	ommat	امت
Islamic revolution	enqelaab-e eslaami	انقلاب اسلامی
belief; faith	imaan	ایمان
Job (the prophet)	ayyub	ایوب
innovation; heresy; deviation from Islamic tradition.	bed'at	بدعت
purgatory	barzakh	برزخ

the appointment of Muhammad to prophethood.	*be'sat*	بعثت
to 'abide in God', the Sufi state that follows the stage of self-annihilation.	*baqaa*	بقاء
Islamic fundamentalism	*bonyaadgaraa'i-ye eslaami*	بنیادگرائی اسلامی
heaven	*behesht*	بهشت
purdah	*pardeh*	پرده
prophet	*payaambar*	پیامبر
Sufi master	*pir*	پیر
prayer leader	*pishnamaaz*	پیشنماز
prophet	*peyqambar*	پیغمبر
renewal; revival of Islam	*tajdid*	تجدید
prayer beads similar to rosary	*tasbih*	تسبیح
Sunnism	*tasannon*	تسنن
Shi'ism	*tashayyo'*	تشیع
Sufism	*tasavvof*	تصوف
polygamy	*ta'addod-e zowjaat*	تعدد زوجات
the Shi'ite 'passion play', commemorating the martyrdom of Imam Hossein.	*ta'ziyeh*	تعزیه
the unquestioning following of Islamic tradition; the 'emulation', in Shi'ism, by lay Shi'ites of a learned scholar.	*taqlid*	تقلید
dissimulation in the face of danger, especially in Shi'ism.	*taqiyyeh*	تقیه
the practice of declaring someone an unbeliever; 'excommunication'.	*takfir*	تکفیر
repentance	*towbeh*	توبه
Divine unity; monotheism	*towhid*	توحید
prayer mat	*jaa namaaz*	جا نماز
the 'Age of Ignorance' prior to the advent of Islam.	*jaaheliyat*	جاهلیت
the 'poll-tax' on non-Muslims	*jaziyeh*	جزیه
the Islamic Republic	*jomhuri-ye eslaami*	جمهوری اسلامی
jinn	*jenn*	جن
defensive war against unbelievers	*jehaad*	جهاد
hell	*jahannam*	جهنم
veil	*chaador*	چادر

polygamy	chand zani	چند زنی
Haji, i.e. someone who has performed the pilgrimage to Mecca.	haaji	حاجی
the pilgrimage to Mecca	hajj	حج
modest dress	hejaab	حجاب
Koranic penalty for crimes such as theft, adultery etc.	hadd	حد
Prophetic Tradition	hadis	حدیث
prohibited; unlawful	haraam	حرام
the 'party of God'	hezbollaah	حزب الله
Islamic government	hokumat-e eslaami	حکومت اسلامی
permitted; lawful	halaal	حلال
belonging to the Hanbali school of jurisprudence	hanbali	حنبلی
belonging to the Hanafi school of jusrisprudence	hanafi	حنفی
Koranic term for pre-Islamic monotheists adhering neither to Christianity nor Judaism	hanif	حنیف
circumcision	khatneh	ختنه
God	khodaa	خدا
sermon	khotbeh	خطبه
caliphate	khelaafat	خلافت
the 'abode of peace', i.e. wherever Islam rules	daar ol-eslaam	دار الاسلام
the 'abode of war', i.e. wherever Islam is suppressed	daar ol-harb	دار الحرب
David	daavud	داود
the Antichrist	dajjaal	دجال
invocation; prayer	do'aa	دعا
the call to Islam; proselytizing	da'vat	دعوت
the 12 Imams	davaazdah emaam	دوازده امام
religion	din	دین
'remembrance'; the Sufi practice of repeating God's names to become more aware of the Divine presence.	zekr	ذکر
non-Muslim citizen of Muslim state	zemmi	ذمی
personal (legal) opinion	ra'y	رای

usury	rebaa	ربا
prophethood (lit. 'mission')	resaalat	رسالت
prophet; apostle	rasul	رسول
a unit of canonical prayer, consisting of standing, bowing, prostrating, etc.	rak'at	ركعت
bowing in prayer	roku'	ركوع
Ramadan	ramazaan	رمضان
narration; Shi'ite Tradition	revaayat	روايت
the 'clergy', i.e. Shi'ite scholars	olamaa	علما
fasting	ruzeh	روزه
annual alms tax	zakaat	زكات
annual alms tax (alternative spelling)	zakaat	زكوة
adultery	zenaa	زنا
visiting an Imam's shrine	ziyaarat	زيارت
place of pilgrimage	ziyaaratgaah	زيارتگاه
Zaydi	zeydi	زيدى
prayer rug	sajjadeh	سجاده
prostration (in prayer)	sajdeh	سجده
the meal taken before fasting	sahari	سحرى
Solomon	soleymaan	سليمان
the normative practice of the Prophet	sonnat	سنت
Sunnite	sonni	سنى
the ritual beating of the chest during the Shi'ite commemoration of the martyrdom of Imam Hossein	sineh zani	سينه زنى
'temporary' wife (allowed in Shi'ism)	siqeh	صيغه
an adherent of the Shafi'ite law of jurisprudence	shaafe'i	شافعى
polytheism; associating other gods with God	sherk	شرك
Islamic law	shari'at	شريعت
consultation	shuraa	شورا
head of a tribe; Sufi leader; elder or learned scholar	sheykh	شيخ
Satan	sheytaan	شيطان
Twelver Shi'ism	shi'e-ye esnaa 'ashari	شيعه اثنى عشرى
martyrdom	shahaadat	شهادت
martyr	shahid	شهيد

the Companions of the Prophet	sahaabeh	صحابه
alms	sadaqeh	صدقه
the Divine attributes	sefaat-e elaahi	صفات الهى
canonical prayer	salaat	صلات
canonical prayer (alternative spelling)	salaat	صلوة
Sufi	sufi	صوفى
Sufi brotherhood	tariqeh	طريقه
tyranny; oppression	zolm	ظلم
Ashura, the day on which Shi'ites commemorate the martyrdom of Imam Hossein	'aashuraa	عاشورا
worship	'ebaadat	عبادت
justice	'edaalat	عدالت
mysticism; gnosis	'erfaan	عرفان
mourning	'azaadaari	عزادارى
religious scholars; 'clergy'	'olamaa	علما
the lesser pilgrimage to Mecca, which can be performed at any time	'omreh	عمره
the 'festival of breaking the fast', marking the end of Ramadan	'eyd-e fetr	عيد فطر
the 'festival of sacrifice', marking the end of the pilgrimage to Mecca	'eyd-e qorbaan	عيد قربان
Jesus	'isaa	عيسى
full ritual ablution	qosl	غسل
sinner; someone who is corrupt	faaseq	فاسق
fatwa, or religious edict	fatvaa	فتوا
Pharaoh	fer'own	فرعون
sect; faction	ferqeh	فرقه
sin; corruption; decadence	fesq	فسق
Sufi mendicant; someone who has renounced worldly goods	faqir	فقير
jurist; expert in jurisprudence	faqih	فقيه
jurisprudence	feqh	فقه
Islamic philosophy	falsafe-ye eslaami	فلسفه اسلامى
Sufi notion of annihilation of the self in God	fanaa	فناء
judge	qaazi	قاضى
direction of prayer, i.e. facing Mecca	qebleh	قبله

compass used to determine the direction of Mecca	qebleh namaa	قبله نما
Koran	qoraan	قران
recitation of the Koran	qeraa'at-e qoraan	قرائت قرآن
juristic reasoning by use of analogy	qiyaas	قیاس
unbeliever; infidel	kaafar	کافر
the cube-shaped shrine in the middle of Mecca; the focal point of canonical prayer and pilgrimage	ka'beh	کعبه
unbelief	kofr	کفر
theology	kalaam	کلام
sin	gonaah	گناه
sinner	gonaah kaar	گناهکار
dome of a mosque	gonbad	گنبد
adherent of the Maleki school of jurisprudence	maaleki	مالکی
permitted; allowed	mobaah	مباح
'soldier of God'; someone who exerts effort for the sake of God	mojaahed	مجاهد
one who practices *ejtehaad* (see above)	mojtahed	مجتهد
'renewer'; one who brings about the renewal of Islam	mojadded	مجدد
'niche' in the wall of a mosque, indicating the direction of Mecca	mehraab	محراب
Islamic college or seminary faculty of theology; theological seminary	madraseh	مدرسه
Medina	madineh	مدینه
school of law; rite of jurisprudence	maz-hab	مذهب
apostate	mortadd	مرتد
lit. 'source of emulation', i.e. learned Shi'ite jurist whom lay Shi'ites emulate in matters of jurisprudence	marja'-e taqlid	مرجع تقلید
Mary (mother of Jesus)	maryam	مریم
word used to describe acts which are encouraged by Islamic law, but which are not obligatory	mostahab	مستحب

273

mosque	masjed	مسجد
Muslim	mosalmaan	مسلمان
polytheist	moshrek	مشرك
the resurrection and re-creation of man in the world to come	ma'aad	معاد
Islamic laws (i.e. civil, criminal, family) which govern social relationships	mo'aamelaat	معاملات
jurist; canon lawyer	mofti	مفتی
a word used to describe acts which are discouraged but not forbidden	makruh	مكروه
Mecca	makkeh	مكه
mulla; local religious leader or scholar	mollaa	ملا
atheist	molhed	ملحد
minaret	menaareh	مناره
the rites of pilgrimage to Mecca	manaasek-e hajj	مناسک حج
hypocrite	monaafeq	منافق
pulpit	menbar	منبر
Moses	musaa	موسی
believer	mowmen	مومن
the birth of the Prophet	milaad-e nabi	میلاد نبی
the Mahdi	mahdi	مهدی
tablet of clay on which some Shi'ites prefer to prostrate during prayer	mohr	مهر
prophethood	nabovvat	نبوت
ritually unclean	najes	نجس
system; regime	nezaam	نظام
canonical prayer	namaaz	نماز
congregational prayer	namaaz-e jamaa'at	نماز جماعت
night prayer	namaaz-e shab	نماز شب
morning prayer	namaaz-e sobh	نماز صبح
mid-day prayer	namaaz-e zohr	نماز ظهر
late evening prayer	namaaz-e 'eshaa	نماز عشاء
afternoon prayer	namaaz-e 'asr	نماز عصر
Noah	nuh	نوح
invocation; prayer	niyaayesh	نیایش
obligatory (act)	vaajeb	واجب
lit. the 'unity of existence', a notion held by some Sufis	vahdat-e vojud	وحدت وجود

ablution (taken before prayer)	*vozu'*	وضوء
religious endowment	*vaqf*	وقف
'rule of the jurist'; the notion, in Shi'ism, of government by an expert in Shi'ite jurisprudence.	*velaayat-e faqih*	ولایت فتیه
the migration of Muhammad and his followers from Mecca to Medina in A.D. 622, marking the beginning of the Muslim calendar.	*hejrat*	هجرت
Jacob	*ya'qub*	یعقوب
Joseph	*yusof*	یوسف
Jonah	*yunos*	یونس

MORE WORDS AND EXPRESSIONS CONCERNING ISLAM

to pray دعا کردن   to pray (five times a day) نماز خواندن   to become Muslim مسلمان شدن

to believe اعتقاد داشتن   to sin گناه کردن   to go on a pilgrimage به زیارت رفتن   to fast روزه گرفتن

to change religion دین عوض کردن   to preach; to give a sermon خطبه خواندن   I believe in God به خدا اعتقاد دارم

to take ablutions وضوء گرفتن   to become an apostate مرتد شدن   to have faith; to have belief ایمان داشتن

to give alms صدقه دادن   to read the Koran قرآن خواندن   to go to the mosque به مسجد رفتن

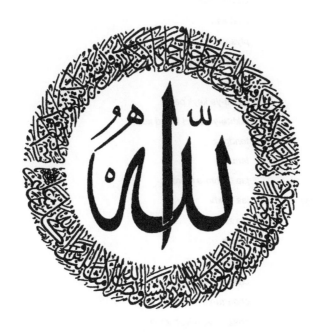

In the Kitchen

در آشپزخانه

lemon squeezer	aab-e limu gir	آب لیمو گیر
juicer; fruit juice extractor	aab-e miveh gir	آب میوه گیر
colander	aabkesh	آبکش
spice mill	aasiyaab-e adviyeh	آسیاب ادویه
pepper mill	aasiyaab-e felfel	آسیاب فلفل
kitchen	aashpazkhaaneh	آشپزخانه
cooking	aashpazi	آشپزی
cooking utensils	abzaar-e aashpazkhaaneh	ابزار آشپزخانه
electric cooker	ojaaq-e barqi	اجاق برقی
gas cooker	ojaaq-e gaazi	اجاق گازی
utensils; devices; tools	asbaab	اسباب
teacup; tea glass	estekaan	استکان
pantry; larder; storeroom	anbaari	انباری
plate; dish	boshqaab	بشقاب
dish	boshqaab-e tah gowd	بشقاب ته گرد
dessert plate	boshqaab-e deser khori	بشقاب دسرخوری
rice cooker	polow paz	پلوپز
(potato) masher	pureh saaz	پوره ساز
peeler	pust kan	پوست کن
cup	piyaaleh	پیاله
soup cup	piyaale-ye sup khori	پیاله سوپ خوری
pan	taabeh	تابه
cake pan	taave-ye keyk pazi	تاوه کیک پزی
chopping board	takhte-ye sabzi khord kon	تخته سبزی خرد کنی
microwave	tondpaz	تندپز
oven; furnace; clay oven	tanur	تنور
egg cup	jaa tokhm-e morqi	جا تخم مرغی
freezer compartment; ice tray	jaa yakhi	جا یخی
draining rack; cupboard	jaa zarfi	جاظرفی
box; container	ja'beh	جعبه
knife	chaaqu	چاقو
carving knife	chaaqu-ye gusht bori	چاقوی گوشت بری
fish knife	chaaqu-ye maahi khori	چاقوی ماهی خوری
fruit knife	chaaqu-ye miveh khori	چاقوی میوه خوری
tea-strainer	chaay saaf kon	چای صاف کن
cooker; stove	cheraaq-e khoraak pazi	چراغ خوراک پزی

mincer; meat grinder	charkh-e gusht	چرخ گوشت
fork	changaal	چنگال
kitchen towel; paper towel	howle-ye kaaqazi	حوله کاغذی
food processor	khord kon	خرد کن
food processor	khoraak khord kon	خوراک خرد کن
can opener	dar-e quti baaz kon	در قوطی باز کن
oven gloves	dastkesh-e aashpazi	دستکش آشپزی
appliance; machine	dastgaah	دستگاه
fruit juicer	dastgaah-e aab-e miveh giri	دستگاه آب میوه گیری
ice-cream maker	dastgaah-e bastani saazi	دستگاه بستنی سازی
vegetable chopper	dastgaah-e sabzi khord koni	دستگاه سبزی خرد کنی
pepper mill	dastgaah-e felfel khord koni	دستگاه فلفل خرد کنی
yoghourt maker	dastgaah-e maastbandi	دستگاه ماست بندی
handle	dastgireh	دستگیره
handle	dasteh	دسته
pestle	daste-ye haavan	دسته هاون
pantry	dulaab	دولاب
pot; casserole	dizi	دیزی
pot; pan	dig	دیگ
steamer	dig-e bokhaar	دیگ بخار
stewpot	dig-e dasteh deraaz	دیگ دسته دراز
slow cooker	dig-e dirpaz	دیگ دیرپز
pressure cooker	dig-e zudpaz	دیگ زودپز
grater	randeh	رنده
timer	zamaan sanj	زمان سنج
cleaver; chopper	saatur	ساطور
timer	saa'at-e aashpazi	ساعت آشپزی
bottle opener	sar-e shisheh baaz kon	سر شیشه باز کن
tea urn; samovar	samaavar	سماور
roasting spit	sikh	سیخ
sugar bowl	shekardaan	شکردان
milk jug	shirkhori	شیرخوری
colander; sieve	saafi	صافی
coffee filter	saafi-ye qahveh	صافی قهوه
pan; pot; plate; dish	zarf	ظرف
dinner plate	zarf-e khoraak khori	ظرف خوراک خوری
dessert plate	zarf-e deser	ظرف دسر
gravy boat; sauce boat	zarf-e sos	ظرف سس

soup tureen	zarf-e supkhori-ye dar daar	ظرف سوپ خوری در دار
butter dish	zarf-e kareh	ظرف کره
kitchenware	zoruf-e aashpazkhaaneh	ظروف آشپزخانه
cookware	zoruf-e khoraak pazi	ظروف خوراک پزی
rolling pin	qaltak-e khamir	غلتک خمیر
oven	fer	فر
freezer	ferizer	فریزر
pepper pot	felfeldaan	فلفل دان
teacup; cup; mug	fenjaan	فنجان
nutcrackers	fandoq shekan	فندق شکن
saucepan	qaablemeh	قابلمه
teaspoon	qaashoq-e chaaykhori	قاشق چایخوری
dessert spoon	qaashoq-e deserkhori	قاشق دسرخوری
soup spoon	qaashoq-e supkhori	قاشق سوپ خوری
tablespoon	qaashoq-e qazaakhori	قاشق غذاخوری
cookie-cutter	qaaleb-e shirini pazi	قالب شیرینی پزی
cake tin	qaaleb-e keyk pazi	قالب کیک پزی
cupboard	qafaseh	قفسه
kitchen cupboard	qafase-ye aashpazkhaaneh	قفسه آشپزخانه
(lump) sugar bowl	qand daan	قند دان
teapot	quri	قوری
coffee pot	qahveh jush	قهوه جوش
coffee grinder	qahveh khord kon	قهوه خرد کن
knife	kaard	کارد
knives and forks	kaard o changaal	کارد و چنگال
bowl; dish	kaaseh	کاسه
salad bowl	kaase-ye saalaad	کاسه سالاد
soup bowl	kaase-ye supkhori	کاسه سوپ خوری
fruit bowl	kaase-ye miveh	کاسه میوه
kettle	ketri	کتری
spatula	kafgir	کفگیر
dishcloth	kohne-ye zarfshu'i	کهنه ظرفشوئی
tinfoil	kaaqaz-e aaluminiyom	گاغذ آلومینیم
kitchen cupboard	ganjeh	گنجه
meat cleaver	gusht khord kon	گوشت خرد کن
meat pounder	gusht kub	گوشت کوب
wine glass	gilaas	گیلاس
tableware	lavaazem-e miz	لوازم میز

278

glass	livaan	لیوان
mug	livaan-e dasteh daar	لیوان دسته دار
microwave oven	maaykruveyv	مایکروویو
frying pan	maahitaabeh	ماهیتابه
ladle	malaaqeh	ملاقه
food processor	mulineks	مولینکس
table	miz	میز
saucer	na'lbaki	نعلبکی
salt cellar	namakdaan	نمکدان
rolling pin	navard	نورد
kitchen utensils	vasaa'el-e aashpazkhaaneh	وسائل آشپزخانه
household appliances	vasaa'el-e khaanegi	وسائل خانگی
utensil; appliance	vasileh	وسیله
mortar	haavan	هاون
corer	hasteh gir	هسته گیر
whisk	hamzan	همزن
electric whisk	hamzan-e barqi	همزن برقی
cooker hood	havaakesh	هواکش
utensil	yaarafzaar	یارافزار
fridge	yakhchaal	یخچال

N.B. FOOD AND COOKING PHRASES
CAN BE FOUND ON PAGE 177.

information; awareness	aagaahi	آگاهی
informant	aagaahi dahandeh	آگاهی دهنده
articulator	aavaa saaz	آوا ساز
phonetics	aavaa shenaasi	آوا شناسی
Spoonerism	aavaa laqzaani	آوا لغزانی
phonetic	aavaa'i	آوائی
obsolescent	az pasand oftaadani	از پسند افتادنی
imagery; metaphor	este'aareh	استعاره
hypocorism	esm-e khodemaani	اسم خودمانی
pseudonym; anonym	esm-e mosta'aar	اسم مستعار
deictic	eshaaratgar	اشارتگر
solecism	eshtebaah-e dasturi	اشتباه دستوری
slip of the tongue; malapropism	eshtebaah-e lopi	اشتباه لپی
expression	estelaah	اصطلاح
linguistic atlas	atlas-e zabaan shenaasi	اطلس زبان شناسی
dialect atlas	atlas-e guyeshi	اطلس گویشی
circumlocution	etnaab	اطناب
hyperbole	eqraaq	اغراق
linguistic minority	aqalliyat-e zabaani	اقلیت زبانی
alphabet	alefbaa	الفبا
paradigm	olgu	الگو
paradigmatic	olgudaar	الگودار
imperative; command	amr	امر
spelling	emlaa	املاء
phonetic spelling	emlaa-ye aavaa'i	املای آوانی
misspelling	emlaa-ye qalat	املای غلط
heterography	emlaa-ye qeyr-e mota'aaref	املای غیر متعارف
deviation	enheraaf	انحراف
coherence	ensejaam	انسجام
regular	baa qaa'edeh	با قاعده
semantic load	baar-e ma'naa'i	بار معنانی
component	bakhsh	بخش
pejorative	bad cham	بد چم
cacography	bad khati	بد خطی
pejorative	bad ma'ni	بد معنی
excrescent	bar afzaayesh	بر افزایش

semantic interpretation	bardaasht-e ma'naa'i	برداشت معنائی
epigraph	bar negaasht	برنگاشت
epigraphy	bar negaasht shenaasi	برنگاشت شناسی
extra-linguistic	borun zabaani	برون زبانی
purism	bonyaad garaa'i	بنیاد گرائی
patois	bum guyesh	بوم گویش
irregular	bi qaa'edeh	بی قاعده
paragraph	paaraagraaf	پاراگراف
oxytone	paayaan feshordeh	پایان فشرده
paraphrase	par engaasht	پرانگاشت
expressive	por ma'ni	پر معنی
paralanguage	paraa zabaan	پرازبان
distribution	paraakandegi	پراکندگی
back formation	pas andaakht	پس انداخت
linguistic ontogeny	peydaayesh shenaasi-ye zabaan	پیدایش شناسی زبان
catenation	peyvand	پیوند
acronym	taarak naam	تارک نام
emphasis	ta'kid	تاکید
alliteration	tajaanos-e aavaa'i	تجانس آوائی
literal	taht ol-lafzi	تحت اللفظی
discourse analysis	tahlil-e goftaar	تحلیل گفتار
pseudonym; pen-name	takhallos	تخلص
transliteration	taraa nevisi	ترانویسی
translation	tarjomeh	ترجمه
free translation	tarjome-ye aazaad	ترجمه آزاد
machine translation	tarjome-ye maashini	ترجمه ماشینی
construction	tarkib	ترکیب
exegesis	tafsir	تفسیر
monolingual	tak zabaaneh	تک زبانه
monologue	tak gu'i	تک گوئی
emphasis; accent	tekyeh	تکیه
accentual	tekyeh daar	تکیه دار
pronunciation	talaffoz	تلفظ
cross-sectional	tamaam boreshi	تمام برشی
dissonance	tanaafor-e vaake'i	تنافر واکه ای
competence	tavaanaa'i	توانائی
communicative competence	tavaanaa'i-ye resaaneshi	توانائی رسانشی
linguistic competence	tavaanaa'i-ye zabaani	توانائی زبانی

description	*towsif*	توصیف
metathesis	*jaabejaa'i*	جابجائی
speech community	*jaame'e-ye zabaani*	جامعه زبانی
alternation; substitution	*jaaygozini*	جایگزینی
semantic distinction	*jodaagaanegi-ye ma'naa'i*	جداگانگی معنائی
linguistic geography	*joqraafiyaa-ye zabaani*	جغرافیای زبانی
sentence	*jomleh*	جمله
pun	*jenaas*	جناس
chrestomathy	*jong-e zabaan aamuz*	جُنگ زبان آموز
agglutination	*chasbaanesh*	چسبانش
agglutinative	*chasbaaneshi*	چسبانشی
poly-alphabetic	*chand alefbaa'i*	چند الفبائی
deletion	*hazf*	حذف
consonant	*harf-e bi-sedaa*	حرف بی صدا
expletive	*harf-e zesht*	حرف زشت
vowel	*harf-e sedaa daar*	حرف صدا دار
tautology	*hashv-e qabih*	حشو قبیح
area	*howzeh*	حوزه
cliche	*khoshkeh 'ebaarat*	خشکه عبارت
dash	*khatt-e tireh*	خط تیره
handwriting; calligraphy	*khattaati*	خطاطی
creativity	*khallaqiyat*	خلاقیت
euphony	*khosh sedaa'i*	خوش صدائی
pleonasm	*deraaz gu'i*	دراز گوئی
longitudinal	*deraaz moddat*	دراز مدت
orthoepy	*dorost gu'i*	درست گوئی
comprehension	*dark-e matlab*	درک مطلب
intuition	*darun yaaft*	درون یافت
grammar	*dastur-e zabaan*	دستور زبان
transformational grammar	*dastur-e gashtaari*	دستور گشتاری
holograph	*dastineh*	دستینه
heteronym	*degar cham*	دگر چم
allomorph	*degar chehreh*	دگر چهره
semantic change; semantic shift	*degarguni-ye ma'naa'i*	دگر گونی معنائی
bilingual	*dow zabaaneh*	دو زبانه
colon	*dow noqteh*	دو نقطه
duality of structure	*dowgaanegi-ye saakhtaar*	دوگانگی ساختار
substantive	*zaati*	ذاتی

mentalistic	zehngaraayaaneh	ذهنگرایانه
dash	rajeh	رجه
level	radeh	رده
stratification	radeh bandi	رده بندی
convention	rasm	رسم
orthography	rasm ol-khat	رسم الخط
behaviourism	raftaar garaa'i	رفتار گرائی
cipher; code	ramz	رمز
decipherment	ramz goshaa'i	رمز گشائی
cryptography	ramz negaari	رمز نگاری
cryptanalysis	ramz yaabi	رمز یابی
encipher	ramzi kardan	رمزی کردن
calque	ru bardaasht	رو برداشت
surface grammar	ru dastur	رو دستور
fluency	ravaani	روانی
redundant	zaa'ed	زائد
generative	zaayandeh	زاینده
language	zabaan	زبان
sign language	zabaan-e eshaareh	زبان اشاره
baby language	zabaan-e bachegaaneh	زبان بچگانه
body language	zabaan-e tan	زبان تن
slang	zabaan-e khodemaani	زبان خودمانی
cant	zabaan-e zargari	زبان زرگری
linguist	zabaan shenaas	زبان شناس
linguistics	zabaan shenaasi	زبان شناسی
statistical linguistics	zabaan shenaasi-ye aamaari	زبان شناسی آماری
educational linguistics	zabaan shenaasi-ye aamuzeshi	زبان شناسی آموزشی
linguistic prehistory	zabaan shenaasi-ye pish taarikhi	زبان شناسی پیش تاریخی
historical linguistics; philology	zabaan shenaasi-ye taarikhi	زبان شناسی تاریخی
comparative linguistics	zabaan shenaasi-ye tatbiqi	زبان شناسی تطبیقی
geographical linguistics	zabaan shenaasi-ye joqraafiyaa'i	زبان شناسی جغرافیائی
microlinguistics	zabaan shenaasi-ye khord	زبان شناسی خرد
diachronic linguistics	zabaan shenaasi-ye zamaan sepaar	زبان شناسی زمان سپار
structural linguistics	zabaan shenaasi-ye saakhtaari	زبان شناسی ساختاری
ethnolinguistics	zabaan shenaasi-ye farhangi	زبان شناسی فرهنگی
applied linguistics	zabaan shenaasi-ye kaarbordi	زبان شناسی کاربردی
macro-linguistics	zabaan shenaasi-ye kalaan	زبان شناسی کلان
synchronic linguistics	zabaan shenaasi-ye hamzamaani	زبان شناسی همزمانی

inflecting language	zabaan-e sarfi	زبان صرفی
natural language	zabaan-e tabi'i	زبان طبیعی
jargon; technical language	zabaan-e fanni	زبان فنی
mother tongue; first language	zabaan-e maadari	زبان مادری
machine language	zabaan-e maashini	زبان ماشینی
source language	zabaan-e mabda'	زبان مبداء
artificial language	zabaan-e masnu'i	زبان مصنوعی
object language; target language	zabaan-e maqsad	زبان مقصد
lingua franca	zabaan-e miyaanji	زبان میانجی
tone language	zabaan-e navaakhti	زبان نواختی
linguistic; language (adj.)	zabaani	زبانی
tense	zamaan	زمان
syntagmatic	zanjiri	زنجیری
hierarchy	zineh bandi	زینه بندی
deep grammar	zharf dastur	ژرف دستور
deep structure	zharf saakhtaar	ژرف ساختار
morphology	saakht shenaasi-e ye vaazhgaani	ساخت شناسی واژگانی
structure	saakhtaar	ساختار
structuralism	saakhtaar garaa'i	ساختار گرائی
semantic compatibility	saazegaari-ye ma'naa'i	سازگاری معنائی
systemic	saazgaani	سازگانی
semantic constituent	saaze-ye ma'naa'i	سازه معنائی
stylistics	sabk shenaasi	سبک شناسی
base	setaak	ستاك
discourse; speech	sokhan	سخن
phatic	sokhan vaar	سخن وار
cursive	sar-e ham	سر هم
petroglyph	sang negaasht	سنگ نگاشت
syllable	silaab	سیلاب
semantic feature	simaa-ye ma'naa'i	سیمای معنائی
acrostic	she'r-e ramzi	شعر رمزی
cursive	shekasteh	شکسته
consonantal	saametdaar	صامتدار
correctness	sehhat	صحت
cacophony	sedaa-ye naahanjaar	صدای ناهنجار
declension	sarf-e esm	صرف اسم
linguistic economy	sarfeh ju'i-ye zabaani	صرفه جوئی زبانی
linguistic form	surat-e zabaani	صورت زبانی

bound form	*surat-e vaabasteh*	صورت وابسته
proverb; saying	*zarb ol-masal*	ضرب المثل
taxonomy	*tabaqeh bandi*	طبقه بندی
elecution	*tarz-e bayaan*	طرز بیان
epigram	*tanzcheh*	طنزچه
colloquial; slang	*'aamiyaaneh*	عامیانه
exclamation mark	*'alaamat-e ta'ajjob*	علامت تعجب
question mark	*'alaamat-e so'aal*	علامت سئوال
interpersonal function	*'amal-e miyaan fardi*	عمل میان فردی
performance	*'amalkard*	عملکرد
functional	*'amali*	عملی
expletive	*fohsh*	فحش
apostrophe	*faraaz vek*	فراز وک
meta-language	*faraa zabaan*	فرازبان
cliche	*farsudeh vaazheh*	فرسوده واژه
formulaic	*formuldaar*	فرمولدار
lexicography	*farhang nevisi*	فرهنگ نویسی
concordance; glossary	*fehrest-e vaazhe-haa*	فهرست واژه ها
acceptable	*qaabel-e qabul*	قابل قبول
analogy	*qarineh saazi*	قرینه سازی
function	*kaar*	کار
usage	*kaar bord*	کار برد
archaism	*kaarbord-e qadimi*	کاربرد قدیمی
functional	*kaar kardi*	کار کردی
epigraph	*katibeh*	کتیبه
concordance	*kashf ol-loqaat*	کشف اللغات
brackets	*kamaanak*	کمانک
linguistic performance	*konesh-e zabaani*	کنش زبانی
aphorism	*kutah kalaam*	کوته کلام
archaism	*kohneh vaazheh*	کهنه واژه
chronogram	*gaah negaareh*	گاه نگاره
grammar	*geraamer*	گرامر
speculative grammar	*geraamer-e nazari*	گرامر نظری
analects	*gozide-haa-ye adabi*	گزیده های ادبی
transformation	*gashtaar*	گشتار
discourse; speech	*goftaar*	گفتار
direct speech	*goftaar-e mostaqim*	گفتار مستقیم
speech science	*goftaar shenaasi*	گفتارشناسی

utterance	gofteh	گفته
dialect	guyesh	گویش
dialectology	guyesh shenaasi	گویش شناسی
idiolect	guyesh-e fardi	گویش فردی
epigram	latifeh	لطیفه
epithet	laqab	لقب
text	matn	متن
textual analysis	matn kaavi	متن کاوی
figurative; metaphorical	majaazi	مجازی
corpus	majmu'eh	مجموعه
environment	mohit	محیط
active	ma'lum	معلوم
semanteme	ma'naa paayeh	معنا پایه
semanticist	ma'naa shenaas	معنا شناس
semantics	ma'naa shenaasi	معنا شناسی
semantic	ma'naa'i	معنائی
contrast	moqaayeseh	مقایسه
semantic category	maqule-ye ma'naa'i	مقوله معنائی
linguistic nationalism	mellat baavari-ye zabaani	ملت باوری زبانی
appropriate	monaaseb	مناسب
topic	mowzu'	موضوع
linguistic field	meydaan-e zabaani	میدان زبانی
semantic field	meydaan-e ma'naa'i	میدان معنائی
purism	naab garaa'i	ناب گرائی
paradox	naasaazeh	ناسازه
eponym	naam dahandeh	نام دهنده
full stop; period	noqteh	نقطه
punctuation	noqteh gozaari	نقطه گذاری
semi-colon	noqteh virgul	نقطه ویرگول
patronymic	namaayeshgar-e nasab-e pedari	نمایشگر نسب پدری
neologism	now vaazheh	نو واژه
euphony	nik aavaa'i	نیک آوائی
euphemism	nik vaazheh	نیک واژه
hyphen	nim rajeh	نیم رجه
semi-colon	nim vek	نیم وك
phoneme	vaaj	واج
phonology	vaajaavaa shenaasi	واج آوا شناسی
phonologist	vaaj shenaas	واج شناس

phonemics	vaaj shenaasi	واج شناسی
variant	vaajguneh	واجگونه
phonological	vaaji	واجی
linguistic unit	vaahed-e zabaani	واحد زبانی
palindrome	vaaru khaaneh	وارو خوانه
irony	vaarun pendaasht	وارون پنداشت
anagram	vaaru vaazheh	وارووارژه
diction	vaazhgu'i	واژگونی
compound	vaazhe-ye morakkab	واژه مرکب
glossary; dictionary	vaazheh naameh	واژه نامه
dialect borrowing	vaamgiri-ye guyesh	وام گیری گویش
form	vajh	وجه
medium; means	vasileh	وسیله
comma	vek	وك
affixation	vandafzaa'i	وند افزانی
comma	virgul	ویرگول
apostrophe	virgul-e baalaa	ویرگول بالا
feature; characteristic	vizhegi	ویژگی
argot	vizheh guyesh	ویژه گویش
syllable	hejaa	هجا
homonym	hamaavaa	هم آوا
context	ham baaft	هم بافت
homograph	ham neviseh	هم نویسه
ellipsis	hamaanand zani	همانند زنی
conjunct	hambasteh	همبسته
semantic complex	hamtaaft-e ma'naa'i	همتافت معنانی
agglutinative	hamchasbeshi	همچسبشی
apposition	hamneshini	همنشینی
sememe	yekaan-e ma'naa'i	یکان معنانی

287

Literature

ادبیات

blurb	*aagahi-ye ta'rif aamiz*	آگهی تعریف آمیز
song	*aavaaz*	آواز
onomatopoeia	*aavaa naam*	آوانام
jingle	*aahang-e tabliqaati*	آهنگ تبلیغاتی
libretto	*operaa naameh*	اپرانامه
pastiche	*asar-e taqlidi*	اثر تقلیدی
enjambment	*edaame-ye jomleh*	ادامه جمله
mime	*adaa namaayesh*	ادانمایش
literary	*adabi*	ادبی
literature; belles-lettres	*adabiyaat*	ادبیات
comparative literature	*adabiyaat-e moqaayese'i*	ادبیات مقایسه ای
imagery; metaphor	*este'aareh*	استعاره
myth	*ostureh*	اسطوره
pen-name; pseudonym	*esm-e mosta'aar*	اسم مستعار
solecism	*eshtebaah-e dasturi*	اشتباه دستوری
idiom; saying	*estelaah*	اصطلاح
hyperbole	*eqraaq*	اغراق
legend; fable	*afsaaneh*	افسانه
expressionism	*expresiyunism*	اکسپرسیونیسم
essay	*enshaa*	انشاء
essayist	*enshaa nevis*	انشاء نویس
climax	*owj*	اوج
cast; dramatis personae	*baazigaraan*	بازیگران
ballad	*baalaad*	بالاد
discourse	*bahs*	بحث
section; episode; segment	*bakhsh*	بخش
rhetoric	*badi'*	بدیع
paraphrase	*baraa negaasht*	برانگاشت
paragraph	*band*	بند
manifesto	*bayaaniyeh*	بیانیه
couplet	*beyt*	بیت
oxymoron	*paad aamizeh*	پاد آمیزه
paragraph	*paaraagraaf*	پاراگراف
colophon	*payaan negaasht*	پایان نگاشت
act (of a play)	*pardeh*	پرده
rhetorical question	*porsesh-e badihi*	پرسش بدیهی

flashback	*pas namaa*	پس نما
didacticism	*pand aamizi*	پندآمیزی
avant-garde	*pishgaam*	پیشگام
foreword; prologue; preface	*pishgoftaar*	پیشگفتار
pathos	*ta'assor*	تاثر
annals	*taarikhcheh*	تاریخچه
emphasis; stress	*ta'kid*	تاکید
alliteration	*tajaanos-e aavaa'i*	تجانس آوائی
alliteration	*tajaanos-e khatti*	تجانس خطی
pen-name; pseudonym	*takhallos*	تخلص
fantasy; imagination	*takhayyol*	تخیل
tragedy	*teraazhedi*	تراژدی
song	*taraaneh*	ترانه
translation	*tarjomeh*	ترجمه
oxymoron	*tarkib-e motazaad*	ترکیب متضاد
thesis	*tez*	تز
simile	*tashbih*	تشبیه
artifice	*tasanno'*	تصنع
description	*ta'rif*	تعریف
commitment	*ta'ahhod*	تعهد
exegesis; hermeneutics	*tafsir*	تفسیر
scansion	*taqti'*	تقطیع
mimesis	*taqlid*	تقلید
lampoon (n.)	*taqlid-e moz-hek*	تقلید مضحک
monologue; soliloquy	*tak gu'i*	تک گوئی
repetition	*tekraar*	تکرار
technique	*teknik*	تکنیک
stress; emphasis	*tekyeh*	تکیه
abridgement	*talkhis*	تلخیص
theme	*tem*	تم
allegory	*tamsil*	تمثیل
caption	*towzih-e zir-e 'aks*	توضیح زیر عکس
pamphlet	*jozveh*	جزوه
pun	*jenaas*	جناس
zeitgeist	*javv-e fekri*	جو فکری
edition; printing	*chaap*	چاپ
abstract; digest	*chekideh*	چکیده
episodic	*chand bakhshi*	چندبخشی

annotator	*haashiyeh nevis*	حاشیه نویس
annotation; gloss	*haashiyeh nevisi*	حاشیه نویسی
ellipsis	*hazf-e be-qarineh*	حذف به قرینه
double entendre	*harf-e dow pahlu*	حرف دو پهلو
action (in a novel or play)	*harakaat va raftaar*	حرکات و رفتار
tautology	*hashv-e qabih*	حشو قبیح
copyright	*haqq-e chaap*	حق چاپ
anecdote; story	*hekaayat*	حکایت
parable; morality tale	*hekaayat-e akhlaaqi*	حکایت اخلاقی
parable	*hekaayat-e pand aamiz*	حکایت پندآمیز
epic	*hamaaseh*	حماسه
stream of consciousness	*khaater namaa'i*	خاطرنمائی
sermon	*khotbeh*	خطبه
abridgement	*kholaaseh*	خلاصه
abridged	*kholaaseh shodeh*	خلاصه شده
autobiography	*khod zistnaameh*	خودزیستنامه
autobiographer	*khod zistnaameh negaar*	خودزیستنامه نگار
euphony	*khosh sedaa'i*	خوش صدائی
story; narrative; fiction	*daastaan*	داستان
fairy story	*daastaan-e jenn o pari*	داستان جن و پری
love story	*daastaan-e 'aasheqaaneh*	داستان عاشقانه
short story	*daastaan-e kutaah*	داستان کوتاه
short story writer	*daastaan-e kutaah nevis*	داستان کوتاه نویس
narrator	*daastaan gu*	داستان گو
omniscient narrator	*daastaan gu-ye hameh chiz daan*	داستان گوی همه چیز دان
story writer	*daastaan nevis*	داستان نویس
fiction (adj.); narrative (adj.)	*daastaani*	داستانی
encyclopaedia	*daa'erat ol-ma'aaref*	دائرة المعارف
periphrasis	*deraaz gu'i*	درازگونی
drama	*deraam*	درام
episode	*darun daastaan*	درون داستان
episodic	*darun daastaan daar*	درون داستان دار
plagiarism	*dozdi-ye adabi*	دزدی ادبی
vade-mecum	*dast yaavar*	دست یاور
diary; journal	*daftar-e khaateraat*	دفتر خاطرات
cycle	*dowre-ye kaamel*	دوره کامل
duologue	*dow gu'i*	دوگونی
preface	*dibaacheh*	دیباچه

quatrain	robaa'i	رباعی
saga	razm naameh	رزمنامه
treatise; tract	resaaleh	رساله
pathos	reqqat	رقت
novel	romaan	رمان
experimental novel	romaan-e aazmaayeshi	رمان آزمایشی
police novel	romaan-e polisi	رمان پلیسی
historical novel	romaan-e taarikhi	رمان تاریخی
psychological novel	romaan-e ravaanshenaakhti	رمان روانشناختی
detective novel	romaan-e kaaraagaahi	رمان کارآگاهی
novella	romaan-e kutaah	رمان کوتاه
epistolary novel	romaan-e mokaatebaati	رمان مکاتباتی
novelist	romaan nevis	رمان نویس
cipher	ramz	رمز
picaresque novel	rend naameh	رند نامه
Renaissance	ronesaans	رنسانس
zeitgeist	ruh-e zamaan	روح زمان
newspaper; journal	ruznaameh	روزنامه
journalism	ruznaameh negaari	روزنامه نگاری
Enlightenment	rowshangari	روشنگری
chronicle	ruydaad naameh	رویدادنامه
action (i.e. in novel); events	ruydaad-haa	رویدادها
realism	re'aalism	رئالیسم
slang	zabaan-e khodemaani	زبان خودمانی
linguistics	zaban shenaasi	زبان شناسی
vernacular; dialect	zabaan-e mahalli	زبان محلی
diatribe	zakhm-e zabaan	زخم زبان
biography	zendegi naameh	زندگی نامه
biographer	zendegi naameh nevis	زندگی نامه نویس
aesthetics	zibaa'i shenaasi	زیبائی شناسی
subtext	zircham	زیرچم
subplot	zirdaastaan	زیرداستان
annotation	zirnevisi	زیرنویسی
biography	zistnaameh	زیست نامه
parallelism	saakht-e hamgun	ساخت همگون
structure	saakhtaar	ساختار
structuralism	saakhtaar garaa'i	ساختار گرائی
sonnet	saanet	سانت

Bowdlerization	saansur-e akhlaaqi	سانسور اخلاقی
genre; style	sabk	سبک
colloquialism	sabk-e goftaari	سبک گفتاری
hagiography	sepentaa negaasht	سپنتانگاشت
rhetoric	sokhan sanji	سخن سنجی
caption	sar-e safheh	سر صفحه
line	satr	سطر
taste	saliqeh	سلیقه
symbol	sambol	سمبل
symbolism	sambolism	سمبلیسم
tradition; custom	sonnat	سنت
surrealism	sur re'aalism	سوررئالیسم
epitaph	sowg naameh	سوگ نامه
poet	shaa'er	شاعر
poetic	shaa'eraaneh	شاعرانه
poetaster	shaa'erak	شاعرک
poetaster; pseudo-poet	shaa'ernamaa	شاعرنما
first-person (narrative)	shakhs-e avval	شخص اول
third-person (narrative)	shakhs-e sevvom	شخص سوم
character; individual	shakhsiyat	شخصیت
protagonist	shakhsiyat-e avval	شخصیت اول
characterization	shakhsiyat pardaazi	شخصیت پردازی
exposition	sharh	شرح
poetry; verse	she'r	شعر
free verse	she'r-e aazaad	شعر آزاد
doggerel	she'r-e band-e tonbaani	شعر بند تنبانی
blank verse	she'r-e bi qaafiyeh	شعر بی قافیه
doggerel	she'r-e bi maayeh	شعر بی مایه
gnomic verse	she'r-e pandaamiz	شعر پند آمیز
jingle	she'r-e tabliqaati	شعر تبلیغاتی
narrative verse	she'r-e daastaani	شعر داستانی
acrostic	she'r-e ramzi	شعر رمزی
blank verse	she'r-e sepid	شعر سپید
light verse	she'r-e tanzi	شعر طنزی
lyric	she'r-e qenaa'i	شعر غنائی
light verse; comic verse	she'r-e fokaahi	شعر فکاهی
nursery rhyme	she'r-e kudakaaneh	شعر کودکانه
prose poem	she'r-e mansur	شعر منثور

prosody	she'r negaari	شعرنگاری
heroine	shirzan	شیرزن
scene	sahneh	صحنه
formalism	surat garaa'i	صورت گرائی
anti-climax	zedd-e owj	ضد اوج
anti-hero	zedd-e qahremaan	ضد قهرمان
proverb; aphorism; maxim; saying	zarb ol masal	ضرب المثل
poetic licence	zarurat-e shaa'eraaneh	ضرورت شاعرانه
addendum; appendix	zamimeh	ضمیمه
irony	ta'neh	طعنه
satire	tanz	طنز
epigram	tanzcheh	طنزچه
poetic justice	'edaalat-e shaa'eraaneh	عدالت شاعرانه
prosody	'aruz	عروض
science fiction	'elmi-takhayyuli	علمی تخیلی
lyric poem; ghazal; ode	qazal	غزل
fantasy	faantezi	فانتزی
surrealism	faraa raasti garaa'i	فراراستی گرائی
form	form	فرم
formalism	formaalism	فرمالیسم
dictionary; lexicon	farhang	فرهنگ
gazetteer	farhang-e joqraafiyaa'i	فرهنگ جغرافیائی
folklore	farhang-e 'aameh	فرهنگ عامه
periodical; quarterly (publication)	fasl naameh	فصلنامه
atmosphere	fazaa	فضاء
technique	fan	فن
film script	filmnaameh	فیلمنامه
index	fehrest	فهرست
bibliography	fehrest-e maraaje'	فهرست مراجع
concordance	fehrest-e vaazhe-haa	فهرست واژه ها
rhyme	qaafiyeh	قافیه
sprung rhythm	qaafiye-ye taabdaar	قافیه تاب دار
lexicon	qaamus	قاموس
imagination	qodrat-e takhayyul	قدرت تخیل
episode; part; section	qesmat	قسمت
ode	qasideh	قصیده
story; tale; yarn	qesseh	قصه
folio	qat'-e rahli	قطع رحلی

hero; heroine	qahremaan	قهرمان
character	kaaraakter	کاراکتر
caricature	kaarikaatur	کاریکاتور
almanac	ketaab-e saal	کتاب سال
bibliography	ketaabshenaasi	کتابشناسی
bibliography	ketaabnaameh	کتابنامه
chorus	kor	کر
classical	kelaasik	کلاسیک
play on words; pun	kalameh baazi	کلمه بازی
canon; collected works	kolliyaat	کلیات
cliche	kelisheh	کلیشه
black comedy	komedi-ye siyaah	کمدی سیاه
synopsis	kutahvaar	کوتهوار
discourse	goftaar	گفتار
euphuism	goftaar-e por tasanno'	گفتار پر تصنع
dialogue	goftogu	گفتگو
anthology	golchin-e adabi	گلچین ادبی
epitaph	gurnegaasht	گورنگاشت
dialect	guyesh	گویش
poetic diction	lahn-e shaa'eraaneh	لحن شاعرانه
philology	loqatshenaasi	لغت شناسی
dictionary	loqatnaameh	لغتنامه
limerick	limerik	لیمریک
synonym	motaraadef	مترادف
translator	motarjem	مترجم
text	matn	متن
philology	matn shenaasi	متن شناسی
adage	masal	مثل
mathnawi; couplet poem	masnavi	مثنوی
metaphor	majaaz	مجاز
magazine; journal	majalleh	مجله
cycle	majmu'eh	مجموعه
canon; collected works	majmu'e-ye aasaar	مجموعه آثار
elegy	marsiyeh	مرثیه
documentary (adj.)	mostanad	مستند
hemistich	mesraa'	مصراع
prologue	matla'	مطلع
riddle; puzzle	mo'ammaa	معما

article; essay	*maqaaleh*	مقاله
introduction; preface; prologue	*moqaddameh*	مقدمه
poet laureate	*malek ash-sho'araa*	ملک الشعراء
melodrama	*meludraam*	ملودرام
verse (adj.)	*manzum*	منظوم
naturalism	*naaturaalism*	ناتورالیسم
paradox	*naasaazeh*	ناسازه
anonymous	*naashenaas*	ناشناس
eponymous	*naamdeh*	نام ده
letter; epistle	*naameh*	نامه
moral	*natije-ye akhlaaqi*	نتیجه اخلاقی
prose (n.)	*nasr*	نثر
syntax	*nahv*	نحو
manuscript	*noskhe-ye khatti*	نسخه خطی
symbol	*neshaaneh*	نشانه
semiotics	*neshaaneh shenaasi*	نشانه شناسی
journal; publication	*nashriyeh*	نشریه
verse	*nazm*	نظم
versification	*nazm nevisi*	نظم نویسی
criticism	*naqd*	نقد
literary criticism	*naqd-e adabi*	نقد ادبی
literary critic	*naqdgar-e adabi*	نقدگر ادبی
review	*naqdnaameh*	نقدنامه
point of view	*noqte-ye nazar*	نقطه نظر
parody	*naqizeh*	نقیضه
literary critic	*naqqaad-e adabi*	نقاد ادبی
lampoon (n.)	*nekuhesh naameh*	نکوهش نامه
symbol	*namaad*	نماد
symbolism	*namaad garaa'i*	نماد گرائی
play	*namaayesh*	نمایش
morality play	*namaayesh-e akhlaaqi*	نمایش اخلاقی
revue	*namaayesh-e aamikhteh*	نمایش آمیخته
stage play	*namaayesh-e sahne'i*	نمایش صحنه ای
mime	*namaayesh-e laalbaazi*	نمایش لال بازی
passion play; mystery play	*namaayesh-e maz-habi*	نمایش مذهبی
stage play	*namaayesh naameh*	نمایشنامه
dramatic; theatrical	*namaayeshi*	نمایشی
modernism	*now garaa'i*	نو گرائی

neologism	now vaazheh	نو واژه
writing; authorship	nevisandegi	نویسندگی
writer; author	nevisandeh	نویسنده
ghost writer; anonymous author	nevisande-ye majhul	نویسنده مجهول
neoclassical	ne'u kelaasik	ننوکلاسیک
euphony	nikaavaa'i	نیک آوائی
euphemism	nikvaazheh	نیک واژه
hemistich	nim beyt	نیم بیت
assonance	nim qaafiyeh	نیم قافیه
irony	vaarun pendaasht	وارون پنداشت
anagram	vaaru vaazheh	وارووارژه
glossary; lexicon	vaazheh naameh	واژه نامه
synonym	vaazhe-ye ham ma'ni	واژه هم معنی
deconstruction	vaasaazi	واسازی
realism	vaaqe' garaa'i	واقع گرائی
social realism	vaaqe' garaa'i-ye ejtemaa'i	واقع گرائی اجتماعی
meter	vazn	وزن
chronicle	vaqaaye' naameh	وقایع نامه
edition	viraayesh	ویرایش
monograph	vizheh negaasht	ویژه نگاشت
expurgation	harzeh zadaa'i	هرزه زدائی
pornography	harzeh negaari	هرزه نگاری
synthesis	ham nahesht	هم نهشت
tautology	hamaangu'i	همانگونی
antagonist	hamaavard	هماورد
literary review	honarsanji-ye adabi	هنرسنجی ادبی
memoirs	yaadnaameh	یادنامه
euphuism	yufyuzgu'i	یوفیوزگونی

Materials

مواد و اجناس مختلف

gold-plated	*aab talaa kaari shodeh*	آب طلا کاری شده
silver-plated	*aab noqreh shodeh*	آب نقره شده
ebony	*aabnus*	آبنوس
brick	*aajor*	آجر
acrylic	*aakril*	آکریل
aluminium	*aaluminyom*	آلومینیم
alloy	*aalyaazh*	آلیاژ
lime	*aahak*	آهک
iron	*aahan*	آهن
ironware	*aahan aalaat*	آهن آلات
tin; tinplate	*aahan-e sefid*	آهن سفید
wrought iron	*aahan-e kubideh*	آهن کوبیده
silk	*abrisham*	ابریشم
asphalt	*esfaalt*	اسفالت
foam rubber	*esfanj-e laastiki*	اسفنج لاستیکی
satin	*atlas*	اطلس
concrete	*botun*	بتون
putty	*botuneh*	بتونه
brass	*berenj*	برنج
bronze	*beronz*	برنز
crystal	*bolur*	بلور
petrol	*benzin*	بنزین
paraffin	*paaraafin*	پارافین
woollen cloth; wool	*paarche-ye pashmi*	پارچه پشمی
denim	*paarche-ye jin*	پارچه جین
towelling; terry-towelling	*paarche-ye howle'i*	پارچه حوله ای
wool	*pashm*	پشم
fibre glass	*pashm-e shisheh*	پشم شیشه
platinum	*pelaatin*	پلاتین
plastic	*pelaastik*	پلاستیک
cotton wool	*panbeh*	پنبه
pigskin	*pust-e khuk*	پوست خوک
sheepskin	*pust-e gusfand*	پوست گوسفند
tarmac	*taarmak*	تارمک
plywood	*takhte-ye chand laa*	تخته چند لا
suede	*jir*	جیر

cast iron	chodan	چدن
leather	charm	چرم
imitation leather	charm-e masnu'i	چرم مصنوعی
glue	chasb	چسب
wood	chub	چوب
cork	chub panbeh	چوب پنبه
mahogany	chub-e maahun	چوب ماهون
chintz	chit	چیت
china; porcelain	chini	چینی
wickerwork	hasir saazi	حصیرسازی
tin	halabi	حلبی
granite	khaaraa	خارا
fur	khaz	خز
paper pulp	khamir-e kaaqaz	خمیر کاغذ
rattan; bamboo	kheyzaraan	خیزران
diesel	dizel	دیزل
coal	zoqaal-e sang	ذغال سنگ
raffia	raafiyaa	رافیا
oil; grease	rowqan	روغن
rough; coarse; hard	zebar	زبر
emerald	zomorrod	زمرد
lead	sorb	سرب
earthenware; terracotta	sofaalineh	سفالینه
limestone	sang-e aahak	سنگ آهک
pumice stone	sang-e paa	سنگ پا
flint	sang-e chakhmaaq	سنگ چخماق
sandstone	sang maaseh	سنگ ماسه
ore	sang-e ma'dan	سنگ معدن
wire	sim	سیم
cement	simaan	سیمان
sand	shen	شن
mother-of-pearl	sadaf-e morvaarid	صدف مروارید
gold	talaa	طلا
rope	tanaab	طناب
earthenware	zoruf-e sofaali	ظروف سفالی
ivory	'aaj	عاج
tweed	faastuni	فاستونی
metal	felez	فلز

steel	fulaad	فولاد
stainless steel	fulaad-e zang nazan	فولاد زنگ نزن
scrap iron	qoraaze-ye aahan	قراضه آهن
nugget	qat'e-ye felez	قطعه فلز
tin	qal'	قلع
paper	kaaqaz	کاغذ
sandpaper	kaaqaz-e sonbaadeh	کاغذ سنباده
straw	kaah	کاه
cotton; flax	kataan	کتان
canvas	karbaas	کرباس
jet	kahrobaa-ye siyaah	کهربای سیاه
gas	gaaz	گاز
plaster; chalk	gach	گچ
clay	gel-e kuzeh gari	گل کوزه گری
sulphur	gugerd	گوگرد
rubber	laastik	لاستیک
material	maaddeh	ماده
liquid	maaye'	مایع
velvet	makhmal	مخمل
corduroy	makhmal-e kebriti	مخمل کبریتی
marble	marmar	مرمر
copper	mes	مس
pewter	mesvaar	مسوار
cardboard	moqavvaa	مقوا
muslin	malmal	ململ
materials	mavaad	مواد
wax	mum	موم
enamel	minaa	مینا
nylon	naaylun	نایلون
cotton (n.); thread	nakh	نخ
cotton (adj.)	nakhi	نخی
oil	naft	نفت
silver	noqreh	نقره
felt	namad	نمد
condition	vaz'	وضع
vinyl	vinil	وینیل
lace	yaraaq	یراق
jasper; jade	yashm	یشم

to be used; to be incorporated in به کار رفتن   to use ..... از ..... استفاده کردن

golden; gold (adj.) طلائی   gold has been used (in the making of) this watch در این ساعت طلا به کار رفته

a satin shawl شال اطلسی   satin (adj.) اطلسی   an iron table میز آهنی   iron (adj.) آهنی   brickwork آجرکاری

crystal (adj.) بلورین   brasswork برنج کاری   a brass vase گلدان برنجی   brass (adj.) برنجی

cotton-wool (adj.) پنبه ای   plastic (adj.) پلاستیکی   woollen clothing; woollens لباس پشمی   woollen پشمی

wooden spoon قاشق چوبی   wooden; wood (adj.) چوبی   leather jacket کاپشن چرمی   leather (adj.) چرمی

this hinge has rusted این لولا زنگ زده است   to rust زنگ زدن   oily; greasy روغنی   fur coat پوست خز

cement (adj.) سیمانی   to lay electric wires سیم کشی کردن   electric wire سیم برق   to wire سیم کشیدن

metalwork فلزکاری   metal (adj.) فلزی   sand castle قصر شنی   sand (adj.); sandy شنی

cotton (adj.) کتانی   paper handkerchief; paper tissue دستمال کاغذی   paper (adj.) کاغذی

gas (adj.) گازی   amber necklace گردنبند کهربائی   amber (adj.) کهربائی   canvas (adj.) کرباسی

velvet skirt دامن مخملی   velvet (adj.) مخملی   rubber ball توپ لاستیکی   rubber (adj.) لاستیکی

cardboard box جعبه مقوائی   cardboard (adj.) مقوائی   copper bowl کاسه مسی   copper (adj.) مسی

cotton (adj.) نخی   nylon stockings جوراب نایلونی   nylon (adj.) نایلونی   enamel work مینا کاری

silver (adj.) نقره ای   oil revenue درآمد نفتی   oil (adj.) نفتی   cotton shirt پیراهن نخی

felt hat کلاه نمدی   felt (adj.) نمدی   silverwork نقره کاری   silverware نقره آلات

Mathematics

ریاضی

algebraic identity	*ettehaad-e jabri*	اتحاد جبری
union	*ejtemaa'*	اجتماع
diagonal; slant; oblique	*orib*	اُریب
cylinder	*ostovaaneh*	استوانه
natural numbers	*a'daad-e tabi'i*	اعداد طبیعی
decimal	*e'shaari*	اعشاری
increase	*afzaayesh*	افزایش
horizontal	*ofoqi*	افقی
improper integral	*antegraal-e naasareh*	انتگرال ناسره
size; measurement	*andaazeh*	اندازه
measurement; measuring	*andaazeh giri*	اندازه گیری
divisor; factor	*bakhsh yaab*	بخشیاب
face (e.g. of a cube)	*bar*	بر
equal	*baraabar*	برابر
numerator	*barkheh shomaar*	برخه شمار
denominator	*barkheh yaab*	برخه یاب
vector	*bordaar*	بردار
cross-section	*boresh-e 'arzi*	برش عرضی
plus	*be'alaaveh*	بعلاوه
height	*bolandi*	بلندی
node	*band*	بند
integration	*bondak giri*	بندك گیری
element	*bonyaad*	بنیاد
infinity	*bi nehaayat*	بی نهایت
icosahedron	*bist vajhi*	بیست وجهی
ellipse; oval	*beyzi*	بیضی
quotient	*bahr*	بهر
segment	*paareh*	پاره
pentagon	*panj zel'i*	پنج ضلعی
pentagon	*panj gusheh*	پنج گوشه
circumference; perimeter	*piraamun*	پیرامون
width; breadth	*pahnaa*	پهنا
function	*taabe'*	تابع
algebraic function	*taabe'-e jabri*	تابع جبری
logarithmic function	*taabe'-e logaaritm*	تابع لگاریتم
exponential function	*taabe'-e namaa'i*	تابع نمائی

301

tangent	taanzhaant	تانژانت
transformation	tabdil	تبدیل
arithmetical progression	tasaa'od-e hesaabi	تصاعد حسابی
arithmetical progression	tasaa'od-e 'adadi	تصاعد عددی
geometrical progression	tasaa'od-e hendesi	تصاعد هندسی
equilibrium	ta'aadol	تعادل
subtraction	tafriq	تفریق
symmetry	taqaaron	تقارن
symmetrical	taqaaroni	تقارنی
division	taqsim	تقسیم
square (i.e. to the power of 2)	tavaan-e dovvom	توان دوم
cube (i.e. to the power of 3)	tavaan-e sevvom	توان سوم
power of 3; cube	tavaan-e seh	توان سه
permutation	jaaygasht	جایگشت
algebra	jabr	جبر
chart; table	jadval	جدول
multiplication table(s)	jadval-e zarb	جدول ضرب
square root	jazr	جذر
element; member (of set)	joz'	جزء
member of a set	joz'-e majmu'eh	جزء مجموعه
even (number)	joft	جفت
addition; total	jam'	جمع
addition and subtraction	jam' o tafriq	جمع و تفریق
sine	jeyb	جیب
cosine	jeyb-e tamaam	جیب تمام
rotation	charkhesh	چرخش
polygon	chand zel'i	چند ضلعی
spherical polygon	chand zel'i-ye koravi	چند ضلعی کروی
polygon	chand gush	چند گوش
polyhedron	chand vajhi	چند وجهی
quadrilateral	chahaar zel'i	چهار ضلعی
square	chahaar gush	چهار گوش
quadrilateral; tetrahedron	chahaar vajhi	چهار وجهی
sum	haasel-e jam'	حاصل جمع
product	haasel-e zarb	حاصل ضرب
volume	hajm	حجم
minimum	hadd-e 'aqqal	حد اقل
maximum	hadd-e aksar	حد اکثر

integral calculus	hesaab-e jaame'eh	حساب جامعه
differential calculus	hesaab-e faazeleh	حساب فاضله
calculus	hesaabaan	حسابان
solution	hall	حل
diagonal line	khatt-e orib	خط اریب
edge; straigh line	khatt-e raast	خط راست
axis	khatt-e sanjesh	خط سنجش
perpendicular (n.)	khatt-e 'amud	خط عمود
algebraic curve	kham-e jabri	خم جبری
properties	khavaas	خواص
circle	daayereh	دایره
percentage	dar sad	در صد
length	deraazaa	درازا
degree	darajeh	درجه
decimal system	dastgaah-e dahdahi	دستگاه ده دهی
sequence	donbaaleh	دنباله
binomial	dow jomle'i	دو جمله ای
dodecagon	davaazdah zel'i	دوازده ضلعی
dodecahedron	davaazdah vajhi	دوازده وجهی
binary (scale)	dowgaan	دوگان
differential	diferaansiyel	دیفرانسیل
decimal	dahdahi	ده دهی
decagon	dah zel'i	ده ضلعی
decagon	dah gusheh	ده گوشه
denary (scale)	dahgaaneh	دهگانه
trapezium	zowzanaqe-ye naamovaazi	ذوزنقه ناموازی
radian	raadiyaan	رادیان
apex; vertex	ra's	راس
vertex of an angle	ra's-e zaaviyeh	راس زاویه
apex of a triangle	ra's-e mosallas	راس مثلث
compound interest	rebh-e morakkab	ربح مرکب
quadrant	rob' daayereh	ربع دایره
digit; number	raqam	رقم
union	raman	رمن
mathematics	riyaazi	ریاضی
pure mathematics	riyaazi-ye khaales	ریاضی خالص
mathematician	riyaazi daan	ریاضی دان
applied mathematics	riyaazi-ye kaarbordi	ریاضی کاربردی

root	risheh	ریشه
simple root	rishe-ye basit	ریشه بسیط
square root	rishe-ye dovvom	ریشه دوم
cube root	rishe-ye sevvom	ریشه سوم
angle	zaaviyeh	زاویه
acute angle	zaaviye-ye haaddeh	زاویه حاده
vertical angle	zaaviye-ye ra's	زاویه راس
right angle	zaaviye-ye qaa'emeh	زاویه قائمه
spherical angle	zaaviye-ye koravi	زاویه کروی
angle of a circle	zaaviye-ye mohaati	زاویه محاطی
plane angle	zaaviye-ye mostavi	زاویه مستوی
angle of convergence	zaaviye-ye hamgaraa'i	زاویه همگرائی
time	zamaan	زمان
adjacent angles	zavaayaa-ye mojaaver	زوایای مجاور
even (number)	zowj	زوج
sub-set	zir majmu'eh	زیر مجموعه
column	sotun	ستون
speed; velocity	sor'at	سرعت
relative velocity	sor'at-e nesbi	سرعت نسبی
geometric series	seri-ye hendesi	سری هندسی
surface	sath	سطح
plane	sath-e mostavi	سطح مستوی
arithmetic scale	sanje-ye hesaabi	سنجه حسابی
profit	sud	سود
decimal system	sistem-e e'shaari	سیستم اعشاری
sine	sinus	سینوس
solid; three-dimensional	seh bo'di	سه بعدی
parabola	sahmi	سهمی
network	shabakeh	شبکه
acceleration	shetaab	شتاب
hexagon	shesh zel'i	شش ضلعی
hexagon	shesh gusheh	شش گوشه
radius	sho'aa'	شعاع
shape	shekl	شکل
number	shomaareh	شماره
numerator	surat	صورت
coefficient	zarib	ضریب
gradient	zarib-e zaaviyeh	ضریب زاویه

side	zel'	ضلع
odd (number)	taaq	طاق
pattern	tarh	طرح
geometric pattern	tarh-e hendesi	طرح هندسی
length	tul	طول
capacity	zarfiyat	ظرفیت
number; digit; numeral	'adad	عدد
cardinal number	'adad-e 'asli	عدد اصلی
prime number	'adad-e avval	عدد اول
whole number	'adad-e taam	عدد تام
ordinal number	'adad-e tartibi	عدد ترتیبی
algebraic number	'adad-e jabri	عدد جبری
whole number	'adad-e sahih	عدد صحیح
natural number	'adad-e tabi'i	عدد طبیعی
mixed number; fractional number	'adad-e kasri	عدد کسری
irrational number	'adad-e gong	عدد گنگ
finite number	'adad-e motanaahi	عدد متناهی
positive number	'adad-e mosbat	عدد مثبت
complex number	'adad-e mokhtalet	عدد مختلط
compound number	'adad-e morakkab	عدد مرکب
abstract number	'adad-e motlaq	عدد مطلق
negative number	'adad-e manfi	عدد منفی
irrational number	'adad-e naaguyaa	عدد ناگویا
breadth; width; ordinate	'arz	عرض
plus sign	'alaamat-e be'alaaveh	علامت بعلاوه
multiplication	'amal-e zarb	عمل ضرب
vertical	'amudi	عمودی
differential	faazeleh	فاضله
intersection	fasl-e moshtarek	فصل مشترک
rule; base (of triangle etc.)	qaa'edeh	قاعده
value	qadr	قدر
Pythagoras's theorem	qaziye-ye fisaaqures	قضیه فیثاغورث
sector	qetaa'	قطاع
diameter; thickness; diagonal	qotr	قطر
conic section	qat'-e makhruti	قطع مخروطی
segment	qat'eh	قطعه
arc	qows	قوس
polygon	kasir ol-azlaa'	کثیر الاضلاع

brackets	*korusheh*	کروشه
sphere	*koreh*	کره
fraction	*kasr*	کسر
proper fraction	*kasr-e sareh*	کسر سره
vulgar fraction	*kasr-e mota'aarefi*	کسر متعارفی
cosine	*kosinus*	کسینوس
cube root	*ka'b*	کعب
capacity	*gonjaayesh*	گنجایش
right angle	*gushe-ye raast*	گوشه راست
edge	*labeh*	لبه
logarithm	*logaritm*	لگاریتم
rhombus	*lowzi*	لوزی
matrix	*maatris*	ماتریس
base (e.g. base 2)	*mabda'*	مبدا
sum; amount (of money)	*mablaq*	مبلغ
concurrent	*motaqaate'*	متقاطع
parallelogram	*motavaazi ol-azlaa'*	متوازی الاضلاع
positive	*mosbat*	مثبت
triangle	*mosallas*	مثلث
Pascal's triangle	*mosallas-e paaskaal*	مثلث پاسکال
spherical triangle	*mosallas-e koravi*	مثلث کروی
equilateral triangle	*mosallas-e motasaavi ol-azlaa'*	مثلث متساوی الاضلاع
isosceles triangle	*mosallas-e motasaavi os-saaqeyn*	مثلث متساوی الساقین
scalene triangle	*mosallas-e mokhtalef ol-azlaa'*	مثلث مختلف الاضلاع
trigonometry	*mosallasaat*	مثلثات
spherical trigonometry	*mosallasaat-e koravi*	مثلثات کروی
square	*majzur*	مجذور
set	*majmu'eh*	مجموعه
universal set	*majmu'e-ye 'aam*	مجموعه عام
ordinate set	*majmu'e-ye 'arzi*	مجموعه عرضی
sub-set	*majmu'e-ye far'i*	مجموعه فرعی
calculation	*mohaasebeh*	محاسبه
axis	*mehvar*	محور
co-ordinate axes	*mehvar-haa-ye mokhtassaat*	محور های مختصات
co-ordinates	*mokhtassaat*	مختصات
denominator	*makhraj*	مخرج
cone	*makhrut*	مخروط
improper conic	*makhruti-ye naasareh*	مخروطی ناسره

square	morabba'	مربع
centre	markaz	مركز
area	masaahat	مساحت
surface area	masaahat-e sath	مساحت سطح
equal	mosaavi	مساوی
rectangle	mostatil	مستطیل
hexagon	mosaddas	مسدس
problem	mas'aleh	مسئله
logarithmic differentiation	moshtaq giri-ye logaritm	مشتق گیری لگاریتم
multiple	mazrab	مضرب
equation	mo'aadeleh	معادله
vector equation	mo'aadele-ye bordaari	معادله برداری
quadratic equation	mo'aadele-ye darajeh dovvom	معادله درجه دوم
value	meqdaar	مقدار
intersection of sets	maqta'-e majmu'e-haa	مقطع مجموعه ها
cube	moka'ab	مکعب
cuboid	moka'ab maanand	مکعب مانند
tangent	momaas	مماس
graph; curve; arc; parabola	monhani	منحنی
plane curve	monhani-ye mostavi	منحنی مستوی
prism	manshur	منشور
negative	manfi	منفی
minus	menhaa	منها
parallel	movaazi	موازی
diagonal	mo'arrab	مورب
average; mean	miyaangin	میانگین
geometric mean	miyaangin-e hendesi	میانگین هندسی
median	miyaaneh	میانه
ratio	nesbat	نسبت
exponential	namaa'i	نمائی
graph; chart; diagram	nemudaar	نمودار
bar chart	nemudaar-e khatti	نمودار خطی
pie chart	nemudaar-e gerd	نمودار گرد
Venn diagram	nemudaar-e ven	نمودار ون
semi-circle	nim daayereh	نیم دایره
hemisphere	nim koreh	نیم کره
bisector	nimsaaz	نیمساز
nonagon	noh zel'i	نه ضلعی

nonagon	noh gusheh	نه گوشه
arithmetic mean	vaasete-ye 'adadi	واسطه عددی
chord; hypotenuse	vatar	وتر
face; surface; side	vajh	وجه
weight	vazn	وزن
hyperbola	hazluli	هذلولی
rectangular hyperbola	hazluli-ye mostatil	هذلولی مستطیل
pyramid	heram	هرم
octagon	hasht zel'i	هشت ضلعی
octagon	hasht gusheh	هشت گوشه
octahedron	hasht vajhi	هشت وجهی
heptagon	haft zel'i	هفت ضلعی
heptagon	haft gusheh	هفت گوشه
isometric; equivalent	ham andaazeh	هم اندازه
congruent	hamaayand	همایند
symmetrical	hamdush	همدوش
concurrent	hamres	همرس
geometric	hendesi	هندسی
geometry	hendeseh	هندسه
co-ordinate geometry	hendese-ye aaraasteh	هندسه آراسته
analytic geometry	hendese-ye tahlili	هندسه تحلیلی
plane geometry	hendese-ye mostavi	هندسه مستوی
plane geometry	hendese-ye mosattah	هندسه مسطح
parabolic geometry	hendese-ye hazluli	هندسه هذلولی

The Media رسانه ها

subscription	aabunmaan	آبونمان
logo	aarm	آرم
freedom of the press	aazaadi-ye matbu'aat	آزادی مطبوعات
advertisement	aagahi	آگهی
TV commercial	aagahi-ye televiziyuni	آگهی تلویزیونی
obituary	aagahi-ye dargozasht	آگهی درگذشت
hoarding	aagahi-ye divaari	آگهی دیواری
classified ad	aagahi-ye sotuni	آگهی های ستونی
audience ratings	aamaargiri-ye binandegaan	آمارگیری بینندگان
front page news	akhbaar-e safhe-ye avval	اخبار صفحه اول
sports news	akhbaar-e varzeshi	اخبار ورزشی
editorial office	edaare-ye sar dabir	اداره سر دبیر
recording studio	otaaq-e pakhsh	اطاق پخش
newsroom	otaaq-e khabar	اطاق خبر
recording studio	otaaq-e zabt	اطاق ضبط
press release	ettelaa'iye-ye rasmi	اطلاعیه رسمی
mass market	baazaar-e 'omumi	بازار عمومی
market research	baazaar pezhuheshi	بازارپژوهشی
programme	barnaameh	برنامه
repeat (programme)	barnaame-ye tekraari	برنامه تکراری
viewer	binandeh	بیننده
broadcast	pakhsh-e barnaameh	پخش برنامه
poster	powster	پوستر
preview	pish namaayesh	پیش نمایش
billboard; sign	taablow	تابلو
advertising	tabliqaat	تبلیغات
renewal of subscription	tajdid-e aabunmaan	تجدید آبونمان
satellite television	televiziyun-e maahvaare'i	تلویزیون ماهواره ای
caption	towzih-e zir nevis	توضیح زیرنویس
circulation	tiraazh	تیراژ
daily newspapers	jaraayed-e yowmiyeh	جراید یومیه
edition	chaap	چاپ
reprint	chaap-e mojaddad	چاپ مجدد
new edition	chaap-e now	چاپ نو
royalties	haqq ot-ta'lif	حق التالیف
newscaster	khabar resaan	خبر رسان

309

scoop	khabar-e dast-e avval	خبر دست اول
newsflash	khabar-e kutaah va daaq	خبر کوتاه و داغ
TV journalism	khabar paraakani-ye televiziyuni	خبرپراکنی تلویزیونی
news agency	khabar gozaari	خبرگزاری
journalist	khabar negaar	خبرنگار
radio journalist	khabar negaar-e raadiyo	خبرنگار رادیو
journalism	khabar negaari	خبرنگاری
news gathering	khabaryaabi	خبریابی
news summary	kholaase-ye akhbaar	خلاصه اخبار
story	daastaan	داستان
quality fiction	daastaan nevisi-ye keyfiyat-daar	داستان نویسی کیفیت دار
pulp fiction	daastaan nevisi-ye mobtazal	داستان نویسی مبتذل
editor	dabir-e bakhsh	دبیر بخش
disinformation	doruq paraakani	دروغ پراکنی
sequel	donbaaleh	دنباله
radio	raadiyo	رادیو
mass media	resaane-haa-ye goruhi	رسانه های گروهی
public media	resaane-haa-ye hamegaani	رسانه های همگانی
newspaper; daily	ruznaameh	روزنامه
newspaper writer; journalist	ruznaameh negaar	روزنامه نگار
journalism	ruznaameh negaari	روزنامه نگاری
daily newspaper	ruznaame-ye yowmiyeh	روزنامه یومیه
censorship	saansur	سانسور
journalese; journalistic	sabk-e ruznaame'i	سبک روزنامه ای
column	sotun	ستون
columnist	sotun nevis	ستون نویس
broadcasting	sokhan paraakani	سخن پراکنی
editor-in-chief	sar dabir	سردبیر
editorial	sar maqaaleh	سر مقاله
editorial writer	sar maqaaleh nevis	سر مقاله نویس
series	seri	سری
serial	seryaal	سریال
tabloid	shaaye'eh naameh	شایعه نامه
caption	sharh	شرح
slogan	sho'aar	شعار
listener	shenavandeh	شنونده
page one; front page	safhe-ye avval	صفحه اول
recording	zabt	ضبط

title; caption	onvaan	عنوان
headline	'onvaan-e maqaaleh	عنوان مقاله
periodical	fasl naameh	فصلنامه
advertising campaign	fa'aaliyat-e tabliqaati	فعالیت تبلیغاتی
serial film	film-e chand bakhshi	فیلم چند بخشی
documentary film	film-e mostanad	فیلم مستند
editorial staff	kaarmandaan-e daftar-e sardabiri	کارمندان دفتر سردبیری
channel	kaanaal	کانال
press conference	konferaans-e matbu'aati	کنفرانس مطبوعاتی
royalties	kiyaabahr	کیابهر
report	gozaaresh	گزارش
special report; 'exclusive'	gozaaresh-e vizheh	گزارش ویژه
reporter; correspondent	gozaareshgar	گزارشگر
economic correspondent	gozaareshgar-e eqtesaadi	گزارشگر اقتصادی
announcer; presenter	guyandeh	گوینده
news presenter	guyande-ye akhbaar	گوینده اخبار
monthly (n.)	maahnaameh	ماهنامه
press officer	motasaddi-ye tabliqaat	متصدی تبلیغات
compere; presenter	mojri-ye barnaameh	مجری برنامه
magazine; journal	majalleh	مجله
comic	majalle-ye fokaahi	مجله فکاهی
illustrated magazine	majalle-ye mosavvar	مجله مصور
the press	matbu'aat	مطبوعات
copy	matlab-e qaabel-e darj	مطلب قابل درج
article	maqaaleh	مقاله
critic	montaqed	منتقد
music critic	montaqed-e musiqi	منتقد موسیقی
television critics	montaqedin-e televiziyun	منتقدین تلویزیون
publisher	naasher	ناشر
publishing	nashr	نشر
publication; journal	nashriyeh	نشریه
best-selling author	nevisande-ye por forush	نویسنده پرفروش
classifieds; want-ads	niyaazmandi-haa	نیازمندیها
video	vide'o	ویدئو
weekly (adj.)	haftegi	هفتگی
weekly (n.)	hafteh naameh	هفته نامه
theatre review	honarsanji-e te'aatr	هنرسنجی تئاتر
film review	honarsanji-e film	هنرسنجی فیلم

to write نوشتن   مقاله نوشتن to write articles   حسن برای روزنامه مقاله می نویسد Hasan writes articles for the paper

پخش کردن to broadcast   آن برنامه را دیشب پخش کردند they broadcast that programme last night

آن برنامه را زنده پخش کردند they broadcast that programme live   برنامه پیش ضبط شده pre-recorded programme

پخش اخبار news broadcasting   گزارش دادن to report   بنا به گزارش اخبار according to the news report

ضبط کردن to record   برنامه ضبط کردن to record a programme   فیلم برداری کردن to film

تجدید آبونمان کردن to renew one's subscription   تماشا کردن to view; to watch   گوش دادن to listen

چاپ کردن to print; to publish   این روزنامه امروز صبح چاپ شد this newspaper was printed this morning

چاپ امروز today's edition   آن مجله هنوز بیرون نیامده that magazine hasn't come out yet

روزنامه کیهان چاپ لندن the London edition of the *Kayhan* (newspaper)   سرویس خبری news service

فاش کردن to reveal   روزنامه گاردین امروز فاش کرد که... today the *Guardian* revealed that.....

بنا به گزارش ..... according to the report.....   سانسور کردن to censor   درج کردن to include

312

Military Affairs

امور نظامی

fire; shooting	aatash	آتش
ceasefire	aatash bas	آتش بس
truce	aatash bas-e movaqqat	آتش بس موقت
anti-aircraft battery	aatashbaar-e padaafand-e havaa'i	آتشبار پدافند هوائی
adjutant	aajudaan	آجودان
adjutant general	aajudaan-e kol	آجودان کل
air-raid siren	aazhir-e zedd-e hamle-ye havaa'i	آژیرضد حمله هوائی
truce; reconciliation	aashti	آشتی
offensive (n.)	aafand	آفند
rules of engagement	aayin-e jang	آیین جنگ
strategic defence initiative (SDI)	ebtekaar-e defaa'-e estraatezhik	ابتکار دفاع استراتژیک
international dispute	ekhtelaaf-e beyn-ol-mellali	اختلاف بین المللی
army; troops; the armed forces	artesh	ارتش
militarism	artesh garaa'i	ارتش گرائی
marshall (army)	arteshbod	ارتشبد
camp	ordugaah	اردوگاه
prisoner-of-war camp	ordugaah-e asiraan	اردوگاه اسیران
torpedo	azhdar	اژدر
fortifications	estehkaamaat	استحکامات
strategy	estraatezhi	استراتژی
sergeant-major	ostovaar	استوار
sergeant first class	ostovaar-e dovvom	استوار دوم
subjugation; conquest	estilaa	استیلا
prisoner of war	asir-e jangi	اسیر جنگی
occupation (of territory)	eshqaal	اشغال
declaration of war	e'laan-e jang	اعلان جنگ
flight officer; flying officer	afsar-e parvaaz	افسر پرواز
pilot officer	afsaar khalabaan	افسر خلبان
adjutant general	afsaar-e mo'aaven-e edaari	افسر معاون اداری
bombardier	afsar vazife-ye tupkhaaneh	افسر وظیفه توپخانه
warrant officer	afsaryaar	افسریار
warrant officer 1st class	afsaryaar-e darajeh yek	افسریار درجه یک
ammunition dump	anbaar-e mohemmaat	انبار مهمات
retaliation	enteqaam	انتقام
military discipline	enzebaat-e arteshi	انضباط ارتشی
annexation	enzemaam	انضمام

war games	baazi-haa-ye jangi	بازیهای جنگی
look-out tower	borj-e dideh baani	برج دیده بانی
strategy	barnaameh rizi-ye nezaami	برنامه ریزی نظامی
mobilisation	basij	بسیج
partial mobilisation	basij-e joz'i	بسیج جزئی
general mobilisation	basij-e 'omumi	بسیج عمومی
bomb	bomb	بمب
bomber (i.e. aircraft)	bombafkan	بمب افکن
bomb bay	bomb khaaneh	بمب خانه
bombing	bombaaraan	بمباران
barracks; army camp	paadegaan	پادگان
missile base	paayegaah-e mushaki	پایگاه موشکی
airbase	paayegaah-e havaa'i	پایگاه هوائی
defence	padaafand	پدافند
flag of truce	parcham-e tark-e mokhaasemeh	پرچم ترک مخاصمه
cartridge case	pukeh	پوکه
infantry	piyaadeh nezaam	پیاده نظام
armoured infantry	piyaadeh nezaam-e zerehi	پیاده نظام زرهی
courier	peyk	پیک
peace treaty	peymaan-e solh	پیمان صلح
tank	taank	تانک
pistol	tapaancheh	تپانچه
provocation; agitation	tahrik	تحریک
suspension of arms	tark-e aslaheh	ترک اسلحه
surrender	taslim	تسلیم
unconditional surrender	taslim-e belaa shart	تسلیم بلاشرط
conquest	tasarrof	تصرف
gun	tofang	تفنگ
reprisal	talaafi	تلافی
conventional weapons	taslihaat-e mota'aaref	تلسیحات متعارف
tension	tanesh	تنش
strategic capability	tavaan-e estraatezhik	توان استراتژیک
cannon	tup	توپ
armoured artillery	tupkhaane-ye zerehi	توپخانه زرهی
use of force	tavassol-e be zur	توسل به زور
brigade	tip	تیپ
gunman; marksman	tirandaaz	تیر انداز
shooting	tirandaazi	تیر اندازی

sharp shooter	tirandaaz-e maaher	تیرانداز ماهر
invasion	tahaajom	تهاجم
nuclear threat	tahdid-e haste'i	تهدید هسته ای
front	jebheh	جبهه
bullet-proof jacket	jeliqe-ye zedd-e goluleh	جلیقه ضد گلوله
war crimes	jenaayaat-e jangi	جنایات جنگی
the peace movement	jonbesh-e solh	جنبش صلح
war	jang	جنگ
nuclear war	jang-e atomi	جنگ اتمی
undeclared war	jang-e e'laan nashodeh	جنگ اعلان نشده
electronic warfare	jang-e elektrunik	جنگ الکترونیک
war of subversion	jang-e barandaazi	جنگ براندازی
total war	jang-e taam	جنگ تام
guerrilla warfare	jang-e chariki	جنگ چریکی
civil war	jang-e daakheli	جنگ داخلی
sea warfare	jang-e daryaa'i	جنگ دریائی
psychological warfare	jang-e ravaani	جنگ روانی
submarine warfare	jang-e zirdaryaa'i	جنگ زیر دریائی
Star Wars	jang-e setaaregaan	جنگ ستارگان
Cold War	jang-e sard	جنگ سرد
chemical warfare	jang-e shimiyaa'i	جنگ شیمیائی
anti-submarine warfare	jang-e zedd-e zirdaryaa'i	جنگ ضد زیر دریائی
warmonger	jangtalab	جنگ طلب
just war	jang-e 'aadelaaneh	جنگ عادلانه
conventional warfare	jang-e 'aadi	جنگ عادی
unjust war	jang-e qeyr-e 'aadelaaneh	جنگ غیر عادلانه
war of attrition	jang-e farsaayeshi	جنگ فرسایشی
space warfare	jang-e fazaa'i	جنگ فضائی
low-intensity warfare	jang-e kam sheddat	جنگ کم شدت
spy satellite warfare	jang-e maahvaare-ye jaasusi	جنگ ماهواره جاسوسی
local war	jang-e mahalli	جنگ محلی
mechanised warfare	jang-e mekaanizeh	جنگ مکانیزه
biological warfare	jang-e mikrubi	جنگ میکروبی
catalytic war	jang-e vaasete'i	جنگ واسطه ای
nuclear war	jang-e haste'i	جنگ هسته ای
air warfare	jang-e havaa'i	جنگ هوائی
fighter	jangandeh	جنگنده
guerrilla	charik	چریک

state of war	haalat-e jang	حالت جنگ
attack; offensive; raid	hamleh	حمله
ambush	hamleh az kamingaah	حمله از کمینگاه
pre-emptive strike	hamle-ye pishdastaaneh	حمله پیشدستانه
preventive attack	hamle-ye pishgirandeh	حمله پیشگیرنده
armed attack	hamle-ye mosallahaaneh	حمله مسلحانه
air attack	hamle-ye havaa'i	حمله هوائی
curfew	khaamush baash	خاموش باش
military service	khedmat-e nezaam vazifeh	خدمت نظام وظیفه
cartridge frame	kheshaab	خشاب
disarmament	khal'-e selaah	خلع سلاح
mortar-shell	khompaareh	خمپاره
mortar	khompaareh andaaz	خمپاره انداز
dagger	khanjar	خنجر
armoured vehicle	khodrow-e zerehi	خودرو زرهی
volunteer	daavtalab	داوطلب
armed intervention	dekhaalat-e mosallahaaneh	دخالت مسلحانه
rank	darajeh	درجه
non-commissioned officer	darajeh daar	درجه دار
vice-admiral	daryaabaan	دریا بان
rear-admiral	daryaadaar	دریا دار
admiral	daryaa saalaar	دریا سالار
admiralty	daryaa saalaari	دریا سالاری
fort	dezh	دژ
defence	defaa'	دفاع
anticipatory self-defence	defaa'-e pishgiraaneh	دفاع پیشگیرانه
civil defence	defaa'-e qeyr-e nezaami	دفاع غیر نظامی
legitimate defence	defaa'-e mashru'	دفاع مشروع
ballistic missile defence	defaa'-e mushak-e baalistik	دفاع موشک بالیستیک
scout	dideh var	دیده ور
nuclear stockpiles	zakhaayer-e haste'i	ذخایر هسته ای
military strategy	razmaaraa'i	رزم آرائی
war veteran	razm dideh	رزم دیده
battle fatigue; battle stress	razm ranjuri	رزم رنجوری
parade; march	rezheh	رژه
military parade	rezhe-ye nezaami	رژه نظامی
skirmish	zad o khord	زد و خورد
conciliation	saazesh	سازش

army; corps	sepaah	سپاه
soldier; legionnaire	sepaahi	سپاهی
air chief marshall	sepahbod	سپهبد
army commander	sepahdaar	سپهدار
general staff	setaad-e koll	ستاد کل
lieutenant (army)	sotvaan	ستوان
second lieutenant	sotvaan dow	ستوان دو
first lieutenant	sotvaan yek	ستوان یک
fifth column	sotun-e panjom	ستون پنجم
soldier	sarbaaz	سرباز
infantryman	sarbaaz-e piyaadeh	سرباز پیاده
paratrooper	sarbaaz-e chatr baaz	سرباز چترباز
recruitment	sarbaazgiri	سرباز گیری
conscript	sarbaaz vazifeh	سرباز وظیفه
barracks	sarbaaz khaaneh	سربازخانه
military service	sarbaazi	سربازی
the Unknown Soldier	sarbaaz-e gomnaam	سرباز گمنام
lieutenant-general; brigadier-general	sartip	سرتیپ
corporal	sarjukheh	سر جوخه
lance-corporal	sarjukhe-ye movaqqat	سر جوخه موقت
captain	sar farmaandeh	سر فرمانده
major	sargord	سر گرد
general; air commodore	sar lashgar	سر لشگر
captain (army)	sarvaan	سروان
colonel	sarhang	سرهنگ
lieutenant-colonel	sarhang-e dovvom	سرهنگ دوم
weapon	selaah	سلاح
anti-satellite weapons	selaah-haa-ye zedd-e maahvaare'i	سلاحهای ضد ماهواره ای
strategic nuclear weapons	selaah-haa-ye haste'i-ye estraatezhik	سلاحهای هسته ای استراتژیک
tactical nuclear weapons	selaah-haa-ye haste'i-ye taaktiki	سلاحهای هسته ای تاکتیکی
fortified	sangarbandi shodeh	سنگربندی شده
cavalry	savaareh nezaam	سواره نظام
appeasement	siyaasat-e erzaa	سیاست ارضاء
sword	shamshir	شمشیر
theatre of operations	sahne-ye jang	صحنه جنگ
troop disposal	safaaraa'i-ye nezaami	صف آرائی نظامی
peace	solh	صلح
causus belli	'ellat-e jang	علت جنگ

hostilities	'amaliyaat-e jangi	عملیات جنگی
pact; treaty	'ahdnaameh	عهد نامه
treaty of neutrality	ahdnaame-ye bitarafi	عهد نامه بیطرفی
war spoils	qanimat-e jangi	غنیمت جنگی
non-combatant	qeyr-e razmi	غیر رزمی
civilian	qeyr-e nezaami	غیر نظامی
ammunition belt	faanusqeh	فانوسقه
conquest; victory	fath	فتح
deserter	faraari	فراری
commander	farmaandeh	فرمانده
squadron leader	farmaande-ye eskaadraan	فرمانده اسکادران
brigade commander	farmaande-ye tip	فرمانده تیپ
commander (navy)	farmaande-ye sevvom-e naav	فرمانده سوم ناو
commander-in-chief	farmaande-ye kol-e qovaa	فرمانده کل قوا
group captain	farmaande-ye goruh	فرمانده گروه
wing commander	farmaande-ye goruh-e havaa'i	فرمانده گروه هوائی
captain (navy); fleet commander	farmaande-ye naav	فرمانده ناو
air command	farmaandehi-ye niru-ye havaa'i	فرماندهی نیروی هوائی
arms sales	forush-e taslihaati	فروش تسلیحاتی
cartridge	feshang	فشنگ
sea power	qodrat-e daryaa'i	قدرت دریائی
military power	qodrat-e nezaami	قدرت نظامی
threshold nuclear powers	qodrat-haa-ye haste'i-ye aastaane'i	قدرت های هسته ای آستانه ای
army; troops	qoshun	قشون
armed uprising	qiyaam-e mosallahaaneh	قیام مسلحانه
war cabinet	kabine-ye jangi	کابینه جنگی
staff	kaadr	کادر
warship	keshti-ye jangi	کشتی جنگی
international conflict	keshmakesh-e beyn-ol-mellali	کشمکش بین المللی
nuclear warhead	kolaahak-e atomi	کلاهک اتمی
arms control	kontrol-e taslihaat	کنترل تسلیحات
tear gas	gaaz-e ashkaavar	گاز اشک آور
squadron	gordaan	گردان
contingent	goruh-e e'zaami	گروه اعزامی
air group; air division	goruh-e havaa'i	گروه هوائی
sergeant	goruhbaan	گروهبان
patrol	gasht zani	گشت زنی
uniform; fatigues	lebaas-e khedmat	لباس خدمت

318

foreign legion	lezhyun-e khaareji	لژیون خارجی
army; division	lashgar	لشگر
commander of a division	lashgarbod	لشگربد
armoured division	lashgar-e zerehi	لشگر زرهی
military expedition	lashgarkeshi	لشگر کشی
army camp	lashgargaah	لشگر گاه
torpedo tube	lule-ye azhdar	لوله اژدر
trigger	maasheh	ماشه
manoeuvre	maanovr	مانور
aggressor	motajaavez	متجاوز
belligerent	motahaareb	متحارب
belligerent; invader	motakhaasem	متخاصم
conscientious objector	mokhaalef-e vojdaani	مخالف وجدانی
leave; rest and relaxation	morakhasi	مرخصی
militarised frontiers	marz-haa-ye mostahkam shodeh	مرزهای مستحکم شده
arms race	mosaabeqe-ye taslihaati	مسابقه تسلیحاتی
machine gun	mosalsal	مسلسل
sub-machine gun	mosalsal-e dasti	مسلسل دستی
agressor nation	mellat-e tajaavoz kaar	ملت تجاوز کار
catapult	manjaniq	منجنیق
war zone	mantaqe-ye jangi	منطقه جنگی
missile launcher	mushak andaaz	موشک انداز
ground-to-ground missile	mushak-e zamin-be-zamin	موشک زمین به زمین
surface-to-air missile	mushak-e zamin-be-havaa	موشک زمین به هوا
air-to-ground missle	mushak-e havaa-be-zamin	موشک هوا به زمین
air-to-air missile	mushak-e havaa-be-havaa	موشک هوا به هوا
minefield	meydaan-e min	میدان مین
landmine	min-e zamini	مین زمینی
mine-laying	min gozaari	مین گذاری
mine detector	min yaab	مین یاب
invader	mohaajem	مهاجم
ammunition	mohemmat	مهمات
armed ammunition	mohemmat-e aamade-ye enfejaar	مهمات آماده انفجار
mutually assured destruction (MAD)	naabudi-ye hatmi-ye motaqaabel	نابودی حتمی متقابل
captain (navy)	naakhodaa yekom	ناخدا یکم
grenade	naarenjak	نارنجک
torpedo boat	naav-e azhdar afkan	ناو اژدر افکن
warship	naav-e jangi	ناو جنگی

319

lieutenant commander (navy)	naav sarvaan	ناو سروان
destroyer	naav shekan	ناو شکن
naval brigade; flotilla	naav goruh	ناو گروه
mine layer	naav-e min gozaar	ناو مین گذار
aircraft carrier	naav-e havaapeymaabar	ناو هواپیمابر
lieutenant (navy)	naavbaan	ناوبان
frigate	naavche-ye jangi	ناوچه جنگی
patrol boat	naavche-ye gashti	ناوچه گشتی
officers' mess	naahaar khaane-ye arteshi	ناهارخانه ارتشی
battle	nabard	نبرد
sea battle	nabard-e daryaa'i	نبرد دریائی
battleship	nabard naav	نبرد ناو
military service	nezaam vazifeh	نظام وظیفه
serviceman; military (adj.)	nezaami	نظامی
militarism	nezaamigari	نظامیگری
sentry	negahbaan	نگهبان
(new) recruit	now sarbaaz	نو سرباز
ammunition belt	navaar-e feshang	نوار فشنگ
stripe	navaareh	نواره
occupying forces	niru-haa-ye eshqaalgar	نیرو های اشغالگر
paramilitary forces	niru-haa-ye shebh-e nezaami	نیرو های شبه نظامی
rapid reaction forces	niru-ye vaakonesh-e sari'	نیروی واکنش سریع
navy	niru-ye daryaa'i	نیروی دریائی
army	niru-ye zamini	نیروی زمینی
air force	niru-ye havaa'i	نیروی هوائی
target; goal; aims	hadaf	هدف
military aims	hadaf-e nezaami	هدف نظامی
revolver	haft tir	هفت تیر
peaceful coexistence	hamzisti-ye mosaalemat aamiz	همزیستی مسالمت آمیز
accommodation	hamsaazi	همسازی
regiment	hang	هنگ
infantry regiment	hang-e piyaadeh	هنگ پیاده
fighter plane	havaapeymaa-ye jangandeh	هواپیمای جنگنده
war plane	havaapeymaa-ye jangi	هواپیمای جنگی
fighter plane	havaapeymaa-ye shekaari	هواپیمای شکاری
unit	yegaan	یگان
armoured units	yegaan-haa-ye zerehi	یگان های زرهی
armed services	yegaan-haa-ye niru-ye mosallah	یگانهای نیروی مسلح

their soldiers attacked us سربازهای آنها به ما حمله کردند to defend دفاع کردن to attack حمله کردن

to fight; to wage war جنگ کردن every country has the right to defend itself هر کشور حق دارد از خود دفاع کند

from today our country is at war از امروز کشور ما در حال جنگ است to declare war اعلان جنگ کردن

to fight; to wage war جنگیدن a running battle جنگ و گریز a battle between two ships جنگ بین دو کشتی

حسن و علی سالها با هم جنگیدند Hasan and Ali fought each other for years جنگ جهانی اول First World War

جنگ جهانی دوم Second World War در گرفتن to break out یک دفعه جنگ در گرفت war suddenly broke out

سربازگیری کردن to recruit soldiers من به خدمت نظام خوانده شدم I was called to military service; I was drafted

خدمت نظام وظیفه military service من دو سال خدمت کردم I served for two years به مرخصی رفتن to go on leave

آتش بس اعلان کردن to announce a cease-fire انتقام گرفتن to retaliate اسیر کردن to capture; to imprison

محاصره کردن to surround; to besiege محاصره آن شهر چندین سال طول کشید the siege of that city lasted many years

مجهز کردن to equip; to mobilize سپاهیان مجهزاند the troops are equipped and ready محاربه fighting; battle

امام علی در همه محاربات عمده صدر اسلام شرکت کرد Imam Ali took part in all of the major battles of early Islam

پیروز شدن to win; to be victorious شکست دادن to defeat; to beat شکست خوردن to be beaten; to be defeated

آلمان در جنگ جهانی دوم شکست خورد Germany was defeated in the Second World War بمب انداختن to bomb

بمباران کردن to bomb; to bombard هواپیماهای دشمن شهر ما را بمباران کردند enemy planes bombed our city

در اثر بمباران عده زیادی کشته شدند as a result of the bombing, many were killed زخمی شدن to be injured

مبارزه کردن to battle; to fight; to campaign; to struggle باید با دشمن مبارزه کنیم we must struggle against the enemy

اشغال کردن to occupy سربازهای دشمن شهر ما را اشغال کرده اند the enemy soldiers have occupied our town

تحریک کردن to provoke; to agitate تسلیم شدن to surrender به تصرف در آوردن to conquer; to take over

به زور متوسل شدن to use force تیراندازی کردن to shoot شلیک کردن to volley; to fire a gun

جنگ خانه به خانه house-to-house fighting کشیک دادن to keep watch; to guard کشیک کشیدن to patrol

پاس دادن to guard; to stand guard پست دیدبانی lookout (observation) post افسر کشیک the officer on duty

صف آرائی کردن to array or line up (the troops) مانور دادن to drill; to manoeuvre اعزام کردن to send; to dispatch

نیروهای اعزامی expeditionary forces مسلح کردن to arm; to equip with weapons مسلح شدن to become armed

پس زدن to beat back; to repel سربازان ما حمله دشمن را پس زد our soldiers beat back the enemy attack

گشت زدن to patrol افسر گشتی patrol officer دستور دادن to order فرمان دادن to (issue an) order

پاسداری کردن to patrol ناوگان انگلیس کرانه را پاسداری کرد the British fleet patrolled the coast

قیام کردن to rise up; to revolt بر علیه حکومت قیام کردند they rose up against the government

مینگذاری کردن to lay mines موشک پرتاب کردن to launch a missile نارنجک انداختن to throw a grenade

اصابت کردن to hit (the target) موشک زمین به هوا به هدف خود اصابت کرد the ground-to-air missile hit its target

هدف گیری کردن to aim; to take aim ماشه را کشیدن to pull the trigger تیرخوردن to be hit (by a bullet)

نیروهای نظامی ایران Iran's military forces متحدین بر علیه ژاپن جنگیدند the Allies fought against Japan

پیمان صلح بستن to conclude a peace treaty رزمدیدگان جنگ ایران و عراق veterans of the Iran-Iraq war

هواپیماهای شکاری ما دو بمب افکن دشمن را به زیر آورد our fighter planes brought down two enemy bombers

تلفات سنگین heavy casualties تلفات غیر نظامی سنگین بود civilian casualties were heavy

Music

(violin) bow	aarsheh	آرشه
accordeon	aakurde'un	آکوردئون
accordeonist	aakurde'un zan	آکوردئون زن
musical instrument	aalat-e musiqi	آلت موسیقی
alto	aaltow	آلتو
chord	aamizeh	آمیزه
song	aavaaz	آواز
singer	aavaaz khaan	آوازخوان
singing	aavaaz khaani	آوازخوانی
tune; song	aahang	آهنگ
refrain	aahang-e vaagardaan	آهنگ واگردان
composer	aahangsaaz	آهنگساز
song-writing; composition	aahangsaazi	آهنگسازی
oboe	obo	ابو
opera	operaa	اپرا
performance	ejraa-ye barnaameh	اجرای برنامه
organ	arqanun	ارغنون
orchestra	orkestr	ارکستر
organ	org	ارگ
pipe organ	org-e ostovaaneh daar	ارگ استوانه دار
harmonium	org-e kuchek	ارگ کوچک
scale	eskaalaa	اسکالا
baritone	baaritun	باریتون
bass	baas	باس
bassoon	baasun	باسون
ballad	baalaad	بالاد
lute	barbat	بربط
impresario	barnaameh riz	برنامه ریز
loudspeaker	boland gu	بلندگو
bass; low	bam	بم
bass horn	buq-e berenji	بوق برنجی
score	paartitur	پارتیتور
piano	piyaanow	پیانو
pianist	piyaanow navaaz	پیانو نواز
electric keyboard	piyaanow-ye barqi	پیانوی برقی
piccolo	pikulu	پیکولو

موسیقی

tar (Iranian guitar-like instrument)	taar	تار
opera house	taalaar-e operaa	تالار اپرا
concert hall	taalaar-e konsert	تالار کنسرت
trombone	teraambun	ترامبون
song	taraaneh	ترانه
songwriter	taraaneh saraa	ترانه سرا
chorus (of song)	tarji' band	ترجیع بند
trumpet	terumpet	ترومپت
triangle	tarizeh	تریزه
composition	tasnif	تصنیف
ballad; love song	tasnif-e 'aasheqaaneh	تصنیف عاشقانه
soloist (vocal)	tak khaan	تکخوان
solo (vocal)	tak khaani	تکخوانی
soloist (instrumental)	taknavaaz	تکنواز
solo (instrumental)	taknavaazi	تکنوازی
singing exercise	tamrin-e aavazkhaani	تمرین آوازخوانی
tambour	tanbureh	تنبوره
tenor	tenur	تنور
music theory	te'uri-ye musiqi	تنوری موسیقی
jazz	jaaz	جاز
cello	chelow	چلو
cellist	chelow zan	چلو زن
harp	chang	چنگ
lyre	chang-e dasti	چنگ دستی
harpist	chang navaaz	چنگ نواز
lyre	changcheh	چنگچه
drumstick	chub-e tabl	چوب طبل
stave	haamel	حامل
CD player	dastgaah-e lowh-e feshordeh	دستگاه لوح فشرده
quintet	daste-ye panj nafareh	دسته پنج نفره
quartet	daste-ye chahaar nafareh	دسته چهار نفره
trio	daste-ye seh nafareh	دسته سه نفره
tambourine	daf	دف
duet	dow navaazi	دو نوازی
music lover	dustdaar-e musiqi	دوستدار موسیقی
compact disk	disk-e feshordeh	دیسک فشرده
drum; kettledrum	dohol	دهل
keyboard	radif-e kelid-haa	ردیف کلید ها

conductor	rahbar	رهبر
zither	ziter	زیتر
xylophone	zilufun	زیلوفون
string	zeh	زه
instrument	saaz	ساز
instrumentation	saazaaraa'i	ساز آرائی
synthesizer	saaz-e barqi	ساز برقی
mouth organ	saaz-e dahani	ساز دهنی
instrumentalist	saaz zan	ساز زن
playing (an instrument)	saaz zani	ساز زنی
wind instruments	saaz-haa-ye baadi	ساز های بادی
brass instruments	saaz-haa-ye berenji	ساز های برنجی
string instruments	saaz-haa-ye zehi	ساز های زهی
percussion instruments	saaz-haa-ye kube'i	ساز های کوبه ای
saxophone	saaksofun	ساکسفون
sitar	setaar	ستار
choir	saraayeh	سرایه
trumpet; bugle	sornaa	سرنا
trumpet player; bugler	sornaachi	سرناچی
symphony	samfuni	سمفونی
dulcimer	santur	سنتور
cymbals	senj	سنج
soprano	supraanow	سوپرانو
string	sim	سیم
nursery rhyme	she'r-e kudakaaneh	شعر کودکانه
trumpet; horn	sheypur	شیپور
trumpet player; bugler	sheypur zan	شیپور زن
French horn	sheypur-e faraansavi	شیپور فرانسوی
(gramophone) record	safheh	صفحه
long-playing record; LP	safhe-ye si-o-seh dowr	صفحه ۳۳ دور
45-RPM record	safhe-ye chehel-o-panj dowr	صفحه ۴۵ دور
recording; taping	zabt	ضبط
beat	zarb	ضرب
drum; tomtom	tabl	طبل
bass drum	tabl-e dow tarafeh	طبل دوطرفه
drummer	tabl zan	طبل زن
lute	'ud	عود
flute	folut	فلوت

flautist	*folut zan*	فلوت زن
recorder	*folut-e hasht suraakheh*	فلوت هشت سوراخه
clarinet	*qareh ney*	قره نی
clarinettist	*qareh ney zan*	قره نی زن
piece (of music)	*qat'eh*	قطعه
solo	*qat'e-ye yek nafari*	قطعه یک نفری
French horn; choir	*kor*	کر
horn	*karnaa*	کرنا
horn player	*karnaachi*	کرناچی
clarinet	*kelaarinet*	کلارینت
key	*kelid*	کلید
bass clef	*kelid-e baas*	کلید باس
Iranian violin	*kamaancheh*	کمانچه
contralto	*kontraaltow*	کنتر آلتو
double bass	*kontor baas*	کنتر باس
concerto	*konsertow*	کنسرتو
percussion	*kube'i*	کوبه ای
drum; kettledrum	*kus*	کوس
impresario	*kaargardaan*	کارگردان
scale	*gaam*	گام
gramophone; record player	*geraamaafun*	گرامافون
(record) turntable	*garduneh*	گردونه
group	*goruh*	گروه
guitar	*gitaar*	گیتار
bass guitar	*gitaar-e baas*	گیتار باس
guitarist	*gitaar zan*	گیتار زن
lullaby	*laalaa'i*	لالائی
mandolin	*maandulin*	ماندولین
nursery rhyme	*matal*	متل
lyrics	*matn-e aavaaz*	متن آواز
composer	*mosannef*	مصنف
plectrum	*mezraab*	مضراب
musician	*motreb*	مطرب
music	*musiqi*	موسیقی
pop music	*musiqi-ye paap*	موسیقی پاپ
musicianship; music-making	*musiqi saazi*	موسیقی سازی
musicology	*musiqi shenaasi*	موسیقی شناسی
classical music	*musiqi-ye kelaasik*	موسیقی کلاسیک

musician; composer	*musiqi negaar*	موسیقی نگار
musician	*musiqi navaaz*	موسیقی نواز
(conductor's) baton	*mizaaneh*	میزانه
tune	*naqmeh*	نغمه
empty tape; empty cassette	*navaar-e khaali*	نوار خالی
playing (of an instrument)	*navaazandegi*	نوازندگی
player; performer	*navaazandeh*	نوازنده
bassist	*navaazande-ye baas*	نوازنده باس
flute	*ney*	نی
bagpipes	*neyanbaan*	نی انبان
flautist	*ney navaaz*	نی نواز
amplifier	*niru afzaa*	نیرو افزا
violin	*viyulan*	ویولن
violinist	*viyulan zan*	ویولن زن
harpsichord	*haarpsikurd*	هارپسی کورد
harpsichordist	*haarpsikurd navaaz*	هارپسی کورد نواز
harmony	*haarmuni*	هارمونی
four-part harmony	*haarmuni-ye chahaar bakhshi*	هارمونی چهار بخشی
accompanist	*hamnavaazgar*	همنوازگر
harmony	*hamaahangi*	هماهنگی
accompaniment	*hamraah navaazi*	همراه نوازی
chorus (of singers)	*hamsaraayaan*	همسرایان
accompaniment	*hamnavaazi*	همنوازی

MORE MUSICAL WORDS AND EXPRESSIONS

I love classical music   من عاشق موسیقی کلاسیک هستم   to listen to music   به موسیقی گوش دادن

I like traditional Iranian music   موسیقی سنتی ایرانی دوست دارم   I don't like pop music   از موسیقی پاپ خوشم نمیاید

to perform a programme (of music); to put on a show   برنامه اجرا کردن   to perform   اجرا کردن

to play   نواختن   to play the piano   پیانو زدن   to play the guitar   گیتار زدن   to hit; to strike; to strum; to play   زدن

to start   شروع کردن   to conduct; to lead   رهبری کردن   to play the flute   فلوت زدن   to play the violin   ویولن زدن

to compose a tune   آهنگ ساختن   to compose   تصنیف کردن   to sing a song   آواز خواندن   to sing   خواندن

to sing opera   اپرا خواندن   he has composed many tunes   او آهنگهای بسیاری تصنیف کرده است

Ali can't sing at all   علی اصلا نمی تواند آواز بخواند   Hasan has a very good voice   حسن صدای خیلی خوبی دارد

Numbers (Cardinal)

اعداد اصلی

nought; zero	۰	sefr	صفر
one	۱	yek	یک
two	۲	dow	دو
three	۳	seh	سه
four	٤	chahaar	چهار
five	٥	panj	پنج
six	٦	shesh	شش
seven	۷	haft	هفت
eight	۸	hasht	هشت
nine	۹	noh	نه
ten	۱۰	dah	ده
eleven	۱۱	yaazdah	یازده
twelve	۱۲	davaazdah	دوازده
thirteen	۱۳	sizdah	سیزده
fourteen	۱٤	chahaardah	چهارده
fifteen	۱٥	paanzdah	پانزده
sixteen	۱٦	shaanzdah	شانزده
seventeen	۱۷	hefdah	هفده
eighteen	۱۸	hejdah	هجده
nineteen	۱۹	nuzdah	نوزده
twenty	۲۰	bist	بیست
twenty-one	۲۱	bist-o-yek	بیست و یک
twenty-two	۲۲	bist-o-do	بیست و دو
twenty-three	۲۳	bist-o-seh	بیست و سه
thirty	۳۰	si	سی
thirty-one	۳۱	si-o-yek	سی و یک
thirty-two	۳۲	si-o-do	سی و دو
forty	٤۰	chehel	چهل
fifty	٥۰	panjaah	پنجاه
sixty	٦۰	shast	شصت
seventy	۷۰	haftaad	هفتاد
eighty	۸۰	hashtaad	هشتاد
ninety	۹۰	navad	نود
a/one hundred	۱۰۰	sad	صد
a/one hundred and one	۱۰۱	sad-o-yek	صد و یک

English	Numeral	Transliteration	Persian
a hundred and eighty two	۱۸۲	sad-o-hashtaad-o-dow	صد و هشتاد و دو
two hundred	۲۰۰	devist	دویست
two hundred and one	۲۰۱	devist-o-yek	دویست و یک
two hundred and two	۲۰۲	devist-o-do	دویست و دو
three hundred	۳۰۰	si sad	سیصد
four hundred	۴۰۰	chahaar sad	چهارصد
five hundred	۵۰۰	paansad	پانصد
six hundred	۶۰۰	shesh sad	ششصد
seven hundred	۷۰۰	haft sad	هفتصد
eight hundred	۸۰۰	hasht sad	هشتصد
nine hundred	۹۰۰	noh sad	نهصد
a/one thousand	۱۰۰۰	hezaar	هزار
a thousand and one	۱۰۰۱	hezaar-o-yek	هزار و یک
a thousand and two	۱۰۰۲	hezaar-o-dow	هزار و دو
two thousand	۲۰۰۰	dow hezaar	دو هزار
ten thousand	۱۰۰۰۰	dah hezaar	ده هزار
a/one hundred thousand	۱۰۰۰۰۰	sad hezaar	صد هزار
a/one million	۱۰۰۰۰۰۰	yek miliyun	یک میلیون
two million	۲۰۰۰۰۰۰	dow miliyun	دو میلیون

MORE WORDS AND EXPRESSIONS CONNECTED WITH NUMBERS

numbers; digits اعداد   odd number عدد طاق   even number عدد جفت   number عدد

شماره number   telephone number شماره تلفن   to dial (a number) شماره گرفتن

a plate of یک بشقاب   a group of یک دسته   lots of خیلی   I have lots of books خیلی کتاب دارم

lots; many زیاد   many books کتابهای زیاد   a bowl of یک کاسه   a bottle of یک شیشه

a lot of; a load of یک عالم   that man has loads of money آن مرد یک عالم پول دارد   a bit of; a piece of یک تکه

a bit of paper یک تکه کاغذ   a spoonful of یک قاشق   one book; a book یک کتاب   two books دو تا کتاب

half نصف   half a glass of نصف لیوان   half نیم   half a kilo (of) نیم کیلو

half a litre of petrol نصف لیتر بنزین   I bought half a kilo of apples نیم کیلو سیب خریدم

half a kilo نصف کیلو   half-way نصف راه   midnight نصف شب   three and a half kilos سه کیلو و نیم

half a kilo نصف کیلو   one and a half hours یک ساعت و نیم   two hours and a quarter دو ساعت و ربع

a quarter of an hour ربع ساعت   two and three quarter hours دو ساعت و سه ربع

a metre of cloth یک متر پارچه   a metre and a half یک متر و نیم   two kilometres دو کیلومتر

five and a half kilometres پنج کیلومتر و نیم   a pair of shoes یک جفت کفش   a packet of tea یک بسته چای

چند ساعت؟ how many hours?   چند کیلو؟ how many kilos?   چند تا کتاب؟ how many books

من چند تا کتاب دارم I have a few books   دو سه تا two or three   یکی دو تا one or two

یک کم شکر به من می دهید؟ will you give me a little sugar?   یک کم a little   قسمتی از a part of

یک خروار money a pile of   یک خروار پول a pile of money   مقدار amount   مقدار زیادی a large amount

تعداد number   تعداد زیادی a large number   تعداد کمی a small number   مقداری کمی a small amount

تعداد زیادی از آدمهای این شهر بیکار هستند a large number of the people in this town are unemployed

در حدود around; about   در حدود صد نفر around a hundred people   تقریباً approximately

تقریباً هزار تا لوح فشرده دارم I have approximately a thousand compact disks   حدوداً approximately

یک قاچ هندوانه a slice of melon   نصف موز half a banana   یک چهارم پرتقال a quarter of an orange

چند کیلومتر a few kilometres   یک ذره a tiny bit of   یک ذره سیب a tiny bit of apple

یک مشت a handful; a fistful   یک مشت دلار a fistful of dollars   دو سال و نیم two and a half years

پنج و سه دهم five and three tenths   یک و سه چهارم one and three quarters

329

Numbers (Ordinal) اعداد وصفی

first	yekom ; avval ; avvalin	یکم ؛ اول ؛ اولین
second	dovvom ; dovvomin	دوم؛ دومین
third	sevvom ; sevvomin	سوم ؛ سومین
fourth	chahaarom ; chahaaromin	چهارم ؛ چهارمین
fifth	panjom ; panjomin	پنجم ؛ پنجمین
sixth	sheshom ; sheshomin	ششم ؛ ششمین
seventh	haftom ; haftomin	هفتم ؛ هفتمین
eighth	hashtom ; hashtomin	هشتم ؛ هشتمین
ninth	nohom ; nohomin	نهم ؛ نهمین
tenth	dahom ; dahomin	دهم ؛ دهمین
eleventh	yaazdahom ; yaazdahomin	یازدهم ؛ یازدهمین
twelfth	davaazdahom ; davaazdahomin	دوازدهم ؛ دوازدهمین
thirteenth	sizdahom ; sizdahomin	سیزدهم ؛ سیزدهمین
fourteenth	chahaardahom ; chahaardahomin	چهاردهم ؛ چهاردهمین
fifteenth	paanzdahom ; paanzdahomin	پانزدهم ؛ پانزدهمین
sixteenth	shaanzdahom ; shaanzdahomin	شانزدهم ؛ شانزدهمین
seventeenth	hefdahom ; hefdahomin	هفدهم ؛ هفدهمین
eighteenth	hejdahom ; hejdahomin	هجدهم ؛ هجدهمین
nineteenth	nuzdahom ; nuzdahomin	نوزدهم ؛ نوزدهمین
twentieth	bistom ; bistomin	بیستم ؛ بیستمین
twenty-first	bist-o-yekom ; bist-o-yekomin	بیست ویکم ؛ بیست ویکمین
twenty-second	bist-o-dovvom ; bist-o-dovvomin	بیست ودوم ؛ بیست ودومین
thirtieth	siyom ; siyomin	سیم ؛ سیمین
thirty-first	si-o-yekom ; si-o-yekomin	سی ویکم ؛ سی ویکمین
fortieth	chehelom ; chehelomin	چهلم ؛ چهلمین
fiftieth	panjaahom ; panjaahomin	پنجاهم ؛ پنجاهمین
sixtieth	shastom ; shastomin	شصتم ؛ شصتمین
seventieth	haftaadom ; haftaadomin	هفتادم ؛ هفتادمین
eightieth	hashtaadom ; hashtaadomin	هشتادم ؛ هشتادمین
ninetieth	navadom ; navadomin	نودم ؛ نودمین
hundredth	sadom ; sadomin	صدم ؛ صدمین
hundred and first	sad-o-yekom ; sad-o-yekomin	صدویکم ؛ صدویکمین
hundred and tenth	sad-o-dahom ; sad-o-dahomin	صدودهم ؛ صدودهمین
two hundredth	devistom ; devistomin	دویستم ؛ دویستمین
three hundredth	sisadom ; sisadomin	سیصدم ؛ سیصدمین
four hundredth	chahaarsadom ; chahaarsadomin	چهارصدم ؛ چهارصدمین

five hundredth	paansadom ; paansadomin	پانصدم ؛ پانصدمین
six hundredth	sheshsadom ; sheshsadomin	ششصدم ؛ ششصدمین
seven hundredth	haftsadom ; haftsadomin	هفتصدم ؛ هفتصدمین
eight hundredth	hashtsadom ; hashtsadomin	هشتصدم ؛ هشتصدمین
nine hundredth	nohsadom ; nohsadomin	نهصدم ؛ نهصدمین
thousandth	hezaarom ; hezaaromin	هزارم ؛ هزارمین
two thousandth	dah hezaarom ; dah hezaaromin	دو هزارم ؛ دو هزارمین
millionth	milyunom ; milyunomin	میلیونم ؛ میلیونمین
two millionth	dow milyunom ; dow milyunomin	دو میلیونم ؛ دو میلیونمین

MORE NUMERICAL WORDS AND EXPRESSIONS

the Third World جهان سوم   the First World جهان اول   I came first in the competition در مسابقه اول شدم

from the first day; from day one از روز اول   man of the match مرد اول بازی   first-aid کمکهای اولیه

it's my first child بچه اول من است   today, my second lesson is physics امروز کلاس دوم من فیزیک است

this was the first book that I read اولین کتابی که خواندم این بود   the first book اولین کتاب

first days of winter اولین روزهای زمستان   no-one forgets his or her first love هیچکس اولین عشقش را فراموش نمی کند

331

ink pad	estaamp	استامپ
work station	istgaah-e kaari	ایستگاه کاری
self-seal envelope	paakat-e khod chasb	پاکت خود چسب
envelope	paakat-e naameh	پاکت نامه
pair of compasses	pargaar	پرگار
file	parvandeh	پرونده
folder; file; plastic cover	pusheh	پوشه
scanner	puyeshgar	پویشگر
board eraser; board wiper	takhteh paak kon	تخته پاك كن
white board	takhte-ye sefid	تخته سفید
black board	takhte-ye siyaah	تخته سیاه
black board eraser	takhte-ye siyaah paak kon	تخته سیاه پاك كن
diary; calendar	taqvim	تقویم
telephone	telefon	تلفن
bookmark	jaa safhe'i	جا صفحه ای
ink	jowhar	جوهر
printer	chaapgar	چاپگر
inkjet printer	chaapgar-e jowhar feshaan	چاپگر جوهرفشان
daisywheel printer	chaapgar-e suzani	چاپگر سوزنی
laser printer	chaapgar-e leyzeri	چاپگر لیزری
ruler	khatkesh	خطكش
pen; biro	khodkaar	خودكار
fountain pen	khodnevis	خودنویس
fax machine	dastgaah-e dur negaar	دستگاه دورنگار
photocopy machine	dastgaah-e fotukopi	دستگاه فتوكپی
video recorder	dastgaah-e vide'o	دستگاه ویدئو
exercise book; notebook	daftar	دفتر
diary; daily planner	daftar-e ruzaaneh	دفتر روزانه
appointments book	daftar-e sar resid	دفتر سر رسید
notebook; jotter	daftar-e yaad daasht	دفتر یادداشت
magnifying glass	zarreh bin	ذره بین
computer	raayaaneh	رایانه
tape recorder	zabt-e sowt	ضبط صوت
dictionary	farhang	فرهنگ
filing cabinet	qafase-ye baayegaani	قفسه بایگانی

pen	qalam	قلم
pencil case	qalamdaan	قلمدان
scissors	qeychi	قیچی
paper	kaaqaz	کاغذ
rough or scrap paper	kaaqaz-e baateleh	کاغذ باطله
paper cutter	kaaqaz bor	کاغذبر
scrap of paper	kaaqaz paareh	کاغذ پاره
writing paper; typing paper	kaaqaz-e tahrir	کاغذ تحریر
tracing paper	kaaqaz charbeh	کاغذ چربه
blotting paper	kaaqaz khoshk kon	کاغذ خشک کن
headed paper	kaaqaz-e sarbarg	کاغذسربرگ
graph paper	kaaqaz-e shatranji	کاغذ شطرنجی
paperweight	kaaqaz negahdaar	کاغذنگهدار
computer	kaampyuter	کامپیوتر
book	ketaab	کتاب
booklet; brochure	ketaabcheh	کتابچه
globe	kore-ye joqraafiyaa'i	کره جغرافیائی
briefcase; document case	kif-e asnaad	کیف اسناد
bag; briefcase	kif-e dasti	کیف دستی
school bag; satchel	kif-e madraseh	کیف مدرسه
chalk	gach	گچ
set square	guniyaa	گونیا
paper clip	gire-ye kaaqaz	گیره کاغذ
Tippex; correcting fluid	laak-e qalat gir	لاک غلط گیر
writing materials; stationery	lavaazem-e tahrir	لوازم تحریر
office supplies; office equipment	lavaazem-e daftari	لوازم دفتری
felt-tip pen; marker	maazhik	ماژیک
typewriter	maashin-e tahrir	ماشین تحریر
calculator	maashin-e hesaab	ماشین حساب
pocket calculator	maashin-e hesaab-e jibi	ماشین حساب جیبی
guillotine	maashin-e kaaqaz bori	ماشین کاغذبری
stapling machine	maashin-e gireh zani	ماشین گیره زنی
pencil	medaad	مداد
eraser	medaad paak kon	مداد پاک کن
pencil sharpener	medaad taraash	مداد تراش
propelling pencil	medaad-e khodnevis	مداد خودنویس
wax crayon	medaad-e sham'i	مداد شمعی
hole punch	manganeh	منگنه

table; desk	*miz*	میز
writing table; desk	*miz-e tahrir*	میز تحریر
work table; desk	*miz-e kaar*	میز کار
microscope	*mikruskup*	میکروسکوپ
microfiche	*mikrufish*	میکروفیش
microfilm	*mikrufilm*	میکروفیلم
rubber stamp	*mohr-e laastiki*	مهر لاستیکی
software	*narm afzaar*	نرم افزار
map	*naqsheh*	نقشه
fax machine	*namaabar*	نمابر
writing materials; stationery	*nevesht afzaar*	نوشت افزار
word processor	*vaazheh pardaaz*	واژه پرداز
dedicated word processor	*vaazheh pardaaz-e tak manzureh*	واژه پرداز تک منظوره
paperweight	*vazne-ye kaaqaz*	وزنه کاغذ

MORE SCHOOL AND OFFICE EQUIPMENT WORDS AND PHRASES

نوشتن to write   قرض کردن to borrow   می توانم آن مداد را قرض کنم لطفاً؟ may I borrow that pencil please?

می شود از ماژیک شما استفاده کنم لطفاً؟ could I use your felt-tip pen please?   می شود داشته باشم؟ can I have it?

یادم رفت خود کار بیاورم I forgot to bring a biro   می خواهید از مال من استفاده کنید؟ would you like to use mine?

پاک کن را کجا گذاشتی؟ where did you put the eraser?   نمی توانم آن را پیدا کنم I can't find it   گم شده it's lost

به جوهر احتیاج دارم I need ink   پاکت نامه لازم داریم we need envelopes   سفارش دادن to order

باید کاغذ سفید سفارش بدهیم we have to order some white paper   هیچی نمانده there is none left

به شرکت باید تلفن کنید you'll have to phone the company   کاغذ فتوکپی تمام شده the photocopy paper is finished

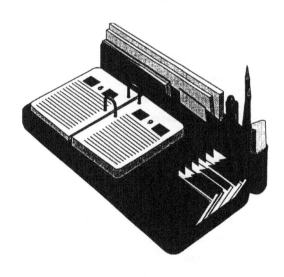

334

Personal Characteristics

ویژگی های شخصی

person	aadam	آدم
idiot; imbecile; fool	aadam-e ablah	آدم ابله
idiot; imbecile; clot	aadam-e ahmaq	آدم احمق
hard worker	aadam-e porkaar	آدم پرکار
lazy person; loafer	aadam-e tanbal	آدم تنبل
flatterer	aadam-e chaaplus	آدم چاپلوس
poser	aadam-e khodnamaa	آدم خودنما
poser	aadam-e zhesti	آدم ژستی
recluse	aadam-e gusheh gir	آدم گوشه گیر
drunkard	aadam-e mast	آدم مست
blind person	aadam-e naabinaa	آدم نابینا
deaf person	aadam-e naashenavaa	آدم ناشنوا
villain; bastard	aadam-e naakes	آدم ناکس
simpleton; fool	aadam-e haalu	آدم هالو
relaxed; calm	aaraam	آرام
peace; calm	aaraamesh	آرامش
sadist	aazaargar	آزارگر
gentlemanly	aaqaa maneshaaneh	آقا منشانه
foolish; stupid; simple	ablah	ابله
scar	asar-e zakhm	اثر زخم
sociable	ejtemaa'i	اجتماعی
stupid; foolish	ahmaq	احمق
sulky; sullen	akhmu	اخمو
talent	este'daad	استعداد
tear (i.e. from crying)	ashk	اشک
problem; difficulty	eshkaal	اشکال
self-assurance	e'temaad be nafs	اعتماد به نفس
snobbish	efaade'i	افاده ای
size	andaazeh	اندازه
body; organ; limb	andaam	اندام
polite	baa adab	با ادب
thoughtful	baa fekr	با فکر
bags under the eyes	baad kardegi-ye zir-e cheshm	باد کردگی زیر چشم
childish	bachegaaneh	بچگانه
child	bacheh	بچه
unpleasant	bad qeleq	بد قلق

335

pessimistic	badbin	بدبین
wit; good humour	bazleh gu'i	بذله گوئی
chauvinist	bartari ju	برتری جو
naked	berahneh	برهنه
adult	bozorgsaal	بزرگسال
unaffected	bi piraayeh	بی پیرایه
rude; impolite	bi tarbiyat	بی تربیت
off-hand; unthinking	bi tavajjoh	بی توجه
rude; off-hand	bi nezaakat	بی نزاکت
bare-footed	paa berahneh	پابرهنه
bitch	patiyaareh	پتیاره
clot; stupid; brainless	pakhmeh	پخمه
rude; impolite; insolent	por ru	پر رو
boy	pesar	پسر
young boy	pesar-e kuchek	پسر کوچک
lad	pesarak	پسرك
the elderly	pir-haa	پیر ها
drop-out (i.e. from education)	tark-e tahsil kardeh	ترك تحصیل کرده
lazy	tanbal	تنبل
lazy; loafer; good-for-nothing	taneh lash	تنه لش
nervous twitch; tic	tik-e 'asabi	تیک عصبی
ambitious	jaah talab	جاه طلب
serious	jeddi	جدی
attractive	jazzaab	جذاب
boldness; impertinence	jesaarat	جسارت
bold; impertinent; brave	jasur	جسور
rowdy; rebel-rouser	janjaal aafarin	جنجال آفرین
agile	chaabok	چابک
flatterer; sycophant	chaaplus	چاپلوس
fat	chaaq	چاق
dimple	chaal	چال
left-handed	chap dast	چپ دست
fringe	chatri	چتری
complexion	chordeh	چرده
nimble	chost o chaalaak	چست و چالاك
eyes	cheshm-haa	چشم ها
wrinkles	chin o choruk	چین و چروك
face	chehreh	چهره

mood	*haal*	حال
expression	*haalat*	حالت
gossip	*harf-e moft zan*	حرف مفت زن
gesture	*harekat*	حرکت
sensitive	*hassaas*	حساس
scatter-brained	*havaas part*	حواس پرت
spot; beauty spot	*khaal*	خال
beauty spot	*khaal-e zibaa'i*	خال زیبائی
tattoo	*khaalkubi*	خالکوبی
sycophant; crawler; ass-licker	*khaayeh maal*	خایه مال
embarrassment; shame	*khejaalat*	خجالت
shy	*khejaalati*	خجالتی
idiot; prat; imbecile; dumbo	*khar*	خر
dodgy; corrupted; of low morals	*kharaab*	خراب
bad quality	*kheslat-e bad*	خصلت بد
good quality	*kheslat-e khub*	خصلت خوب
sideburns	*khatt-e rish*	خط ریش
nature; temperament	*kholq*	خلق
recluse	*khalvat neshin*	خلوت نشین
humourous	*khandeh aavar*	خنده آور
funny	*khandeh daar*	خنده دار
good; nice; pleasant	*khub*	خوب
self-conscious	*khod aagaah*	خود آگاه
self-awareness	*khod aagaahi*	خود آگاهی
self-taught	*khod aamukhteh*	خود آموخته
selfish	*khod khaah*	خود خواه
reserved; quiet	*khod daar*	خود دار
self-absorbed; autistic	*khod garaa*	خود گرا
naive	*khosh baavar*	خوش باور
pleasant; genial	*khosh barkhord*	خوش برخورد
well-behaved	*khosh raftaar*	خوش رفتار
well-dressed; chic	*khosh lebaas*	خوش لباس
pleasant; affable; friendly	*khosh mashrab*	خوش مشرب
optimistic	*khoshbin*	خوشبین
handsome	*khoshtip*	خوشتیپ
happy	*khosh haal*	خوشحال
pretty	*khoshgel*	خوشگل
laid back; sanguine	*khunsard*	خونسرد

dreamer	*khiyaal baaf*	خیال‌باف
scholar; academic	*daaneshmand*	دانشمند
pimple; spot	*daaneh*	دانه
drunkard	*daa'em ol-khamr*	دائم‌الخمر
idiot	*dabang*	دبنگ
little girl	*dokhtar-e kuchek*	دختر کوچک
liar	*doruq gu*	دروغگو
introvert	*darungaraa*	درونگرا
bare-armed	*dast berahneh*	دست برهنه
clumsy	*dast o paa choloft*	دست و پا چلفت
pleasant; nice	*delpazir*	دلپذیر
charming	*delrobaa*	دلربا
seductive	*delfarib*	دلفریب
ponytail	*dom-e asbi*	دم اسبی
false teeth	*dandaan-e masnu'i*	دندان مصنوعی
mischievous	*dow beham zan*	دوبهم زن
mad	*divaaneh*	دیوانه
comfortable; relaxed	*raahat*	راحت
right-handed	*raast dast*	راست دست
truthful	*raastgu*	راستگو
behaviour	*raftaar*	رفتار
childishness	*raftaar-e bachegaaneh*	رفتار بچگانه
outspoken	*rok gu*	رک گو
colour; colouring	*rang*	رنگ
skin colour; complexion	*rang-e pust*	رنگ پوست
complexion	*rang-e chehreh*	رنگ چهره
colour-blind	*rang kur*	رنگ کور
mood; spirit	*ruhiyeh*	روحیه
hypocrite	*riyaakaar*	ریاکار
appearance	*rikht*	ریخت
beard	*rish*	ریش
bearded	*rishdaar*	ریشدار
ugly	*zesht*	زشت
ugliness	*zeshti*	زشتی
effeminate	*zan sefat*	زن صفت
rude; obnoxious; obscene	*zanandeh*	زننده
beauty	*zibaa'i*	زیبائی
simpleton; naive; fool	*saadeh lowh*	ساده لوح

adults	saalmandaan	سالمندان
moustache	sebil	سبیل
early-riser	sahar khiz	سحرخیز
bare-headed	sar berahneh	سربرهنه
superficial; casual	sat-hi	سطحی
bitch; cow; slut	seliteh	سلیته
age	senn	سن
scrounger	surcharaan	سورچران
night-owl	shab zendeh daar	شب زنده دار
likeness; similarity	shebaahat	شباهت
person; individual	shakhs	شخص
personality	shakhsiyat	شخصیت
shame	sharm	شرم
curl	shekanj	شکنج
wonderful; extraordinary	shegeft angiz	شگفت انگیز
sense of humour	shukh tab'i	شوخ طبعی
devil; devilish; naughty	sheytaan	شیطان
chic; well-dressed	shik push	شیک پوش
lifestyle	shive-ye zendegi	شیوه زندگی
bald	taas	طاس
nature	tabi'at	طبیعت
gait	tarz-e raah raftan	طرز راه رفتن
lifestyle	tarz-e zendegi	طرز زندگی
appearance	zaaher	ظاهر
habit	'aadat	عادت
great; excellent	'aali	عالی
sweat	'araq	عرق
drinker; drunkard	'araq khor	عرق خور
nervous	'asabi	عصبی
backward; slow	'aqab oftaadeh	عقب افتاده
common sense	'aql-e salim	عقل سلیم
distinguishing marks	'alaa'em-e tashkhisi	علائم تشخیصی
fault; defect	'eyb	عیب
glasses	'eynak	عینک
giant	qul peykar	غول پیکر
gossip; backbiter	qeybat gu	غیبت گو
unusual; eccentric	qeyr-e 'aadi	غیر عادی
individual	fard	فرد

nimble; quick; alert	ferz	فرز
parting (in hair)	farq	فرق
height	qad	قد
tall	qad deraaz	قد دراز
short	qad kutaah	قد کوتاه
go-getter	kaarbor	کاربر
bald	kachal	کچل
deaf and dumb	kar o laal	کر و لال
behaviour	kerdaar	کردار
freckles	kak mak	کک مک
freckled	kak maki	کک مکی
swindler; cheat	kolaah bardaar	کلاه بردار
absent-minded	kam haafezeh	کم حافظه
waist	kamar	کمر
timid	kamru	کمرو
timidity	kamru'i	کمرونی
inquisitive; curious; nosy	konjkaav	کنجکاو
dwarf; midget	kutuleh	کوتوله
small	kuchek	کوچک
thick; stupid	kowdan	کودن
boil; pimple	kurak	کورک
gypsy	kowli	کولی
quality	keyfiyat	کیفیت
insolent; rude; impudent	gostaakh	گستاخ
hunchback	guzh posht	گوژ پشت
gay (i.e. homosexual)	gey	گی
attractive	giraa	گیرا
thin	laaqar	لاغر
braggart	laafzan	لافزن
dumb	laal	لال
harelip	lab shekari	لب شکری
stubborn	lajbaaz	لجباز
naked	lokht	لخت
nickname	laqab	لقب
tic; twitch	laqveh	لقوه
birthmark; strawberry mark	lakke-ye surat	لکه صورت
accent	lahjeh	لهجه
resourceful; inventive	mobtaker	مبتکر

cheat; swindler	*motaqalleb*	متقلب
flatterer; sycophant	*modaaheneh gar*	مداهنه گر
man; guy; bloke	*mard*	مرد
forty year-old man	*mard-e chehel saaleh*	مرد چهل ساله
bachelor	*mard-e mojarrad*	مرد مجرد
one-legged man	*mard-e yek paa*	مرد یک پا
unsociable	*mardom goriz*	مردم گریز
disgusting; stomach-turning	*moshma'ez konandeh*	مشمئز کننده
famous	*mash-hur*	مشهور
biased	*moqrez*	مغرض
scrounger; hanger-on	*moft khor*	مفت خور
hair	*mu*	مو
polite	*mo'addab*	مودب
braid; plait	*mu-ye baafteh*	موی بافته
long hair	*mu-ye boland*	موی بلند
bunches (i.e. of hair)	*mu-ye dom mushi*	موی دم موشی
killjoy	*mu-ye damaaq*	موی دماغ
short hair	*mu-ye kutaah*	موی کوتاه
bun (i.e. of hair)	*mu-ye gowje'i*	موی گوجه ای
kind	*mehrabaan*	مهربان
kindness	*mehrabaani*	مهربانی
important	*mohem*	مهم
hospitable	*mehmaan navaaz*	مهمان نواز
blind	*naabinaa*	نابینا
dissatisfied; unhappy	*naaraazi*	ناراضی
deaf	*naashenavaa*	ناشنوا
villain; bastard	*naakes*	ناکس
pet name; nickname	*naam-e khodemaani*	نام خودمانی
loner; unsociable	*naa mo'aasherati*	نامعاشرتی
inhospitable	*naa mehmaan navaaz*	نامهمان نواز
nice; good; noble; pure	*najib*	نجیب
short-sighted	*nazdik bin*	نزدیک بین
racist	*nezhaad parast*	نژادپرست
double; doppelganger	*noskhe-ye dovvom*	نسخه دوم
fault; defect	*naqs*	نقص
weak point	*noqte-ye za'f*	نقطه ضعف
conscience	*vojdaan*	وجدان
terrible; awful; horrendous; hideous	*vahshat angiz*	وحشت انگیز

341

weight	vazn	وزن
seductive; alluring	vasvaseh angiz	وسوسه انگیز
means of identification	vasile-ye shenaasaa'i	وسیله شناسائی
composure	vaqaar	وقار
idler; loafer	vaqt talaf kon	وقت تلف کن
loafer	velgard	ولگرد
simpleton; fool	haalu	هالو
insolent; bad-mouthed	harzeh dahaan	هرزه دهان
octagenerian	hashtaad saaleh	هشتاد ساله
homosexual	hamjens baaz	همجنس باز
double	hamzaad	همزاد
hippy	hipi	هیپی
excited	hayejaan zadeh	هیجان زده
build; stature	heykal	هیکل
fellow; chap	yaaru	یارو

MORE WORDS AND EXPRESSIONS CONCERNING PERSONAL CHARACTERISTICS

how old are you? چند سال دارید؟   I'm forty years old من چهل سال دارم   middle-aged man مرد میانسال

middle-aged woman زن میانسال   to appear; to seem; to look به نظر رسیدن   in my opinion به نظر من

he/she looks tired خسته به نظر می رسد   he/she looks sad غمگین به نظر می رسد   they say that... می گویند که ...

they say that Hasan is a thief می گویند که حسن دزد است   it seems that... به نظر میاید که ...

what colour eyes does he/she have? چشمهایش چه رنگی است؟   what colour is your hair? موی شما چه رنگی است؟

blonde hair موی بور   black hair موی مشکی   ginger hair موی قرمز   he/she has white/grey hair موی سفید دارد

curly hair موی مجعد   long hair موی بلند   short hair موی کوتاه   Ali is going bald عل دارد کچل می شود

bald; slaphead کله طاس   what does he look like? او چه ریختی است؟   is she old or young? پیر است یا جوان؟

to smile لبخند زدن   to cry گریه کردن   to laugh خندیدن   Susan is always laughing سوسن همیشه می خندد

what weight are you? وزن شما چقدر است؟   I weigh 70 kilos وزن من هفتاد کیلو است   to lose weight وزن کم کردن

Ali has lost weight علی وزن کم کرده است   Akram has put on weight/become fat اکرم چاق شده است

to wear glasses عینک زدن   he looks like his father شبیه پدرش است   he is in a bad mood اوقاتش تلخ است

he's around seventy در حدود هفتاد سال دارد   to grow old پیر شدن   what kind of person is he? چه جور آدمی است؟

to describe توصیف کردن   they speak very highly of him; they say good things about him از او خیلی تعریف می کنند

❮❰❯❱

Personal Effects

لوازم شخصی

pendant	*aavizeh*	آویزه
mirror	*aayeneh*	آینه
eau de cologne; after-shave	*odukolon*	ادوکلن
bangle	*alangu*	النگو
ring	*angoshtar*	انگشتر
signet ring	*angoshtar-e khaatam daar*	انگشتر خاتم دار
brush	*beros*	برس
hair brush	*beros-e mu*	برس مو
envelope	*paakat-e naameh*	پاکت نامه
face powder; foundation	*pudr-e surat*	پودر صورت
powder puff; powder compact	*pudr maal*	پودرمال
money	*pul*	پول
hairspray	*taaft-e mu*	تافت مو
calendar; diary	*taqvim*	تقویم
hair band	*tel*	تل
mobile phone	*telefon-e hamraah*	تلفن همراه
stamp	*tambr*	تمبر
razor blade	*tiq-e rish taraashi*	تیغ ریش تراشی
glasses case	*jaa 'eynaki*	جا عینکی
key ring	*jaa kelidi*	جا کلیدی
box	*ja'beh*	جعبه
jewellery	*javaaher*	جواهر
wedding ring	*halqe-ye 'arusi*	حلقه عروسی
toothpaste	*khamir-e dandaan*	خمیر دندان
shaving gel; shaving cream	*khamir-e rish*	خمیر ریش
pen; biro	*khodkaar*	خودکار
bracelet	*dastband*	دستبند
handkerchief	*dastmaal*	دستمال
sanitary towel	*dastmaal-e zanaaneh*	دستمال زنانه
face flannel	*dastmaal-e surat*	دستمال صورت
paper handkerchief; tissue	*dastmaal-e kaaqazi*	دستمال کاغذی
name and address book	*daftar-e naam o neshaani*	دفتر نام و نشانی
pad; exercise book; jotter	*daftarcheh*	دفترچه
cheque book	*daftarche-ye chek*	دفترچه چک
cufflink	*dokme-ye sar dast*	دکمه سردست
rouge	*ruzh*	روژ

343

eyeliner	rimel	ريمل
chain	zanjir	زنجير
watch	saa'at	ساعت
wristwatch	saa'at-e mochi	ساعت مچی
eye shadow	saaye-ye cheshm	سايه چشم
eyeliner	sormeh	سرمه
brooch	sanjaaq-e sineh	سنجاق سينه
hair pin	sanjaaq-e mu	سنجاق مو
car keys	sevich-e maashin	سويچ ماشين
nail file	sowhaan-e naakhon	سوهان ناخن
comb	shaaneh	شانه
I.D. card; birth certificate	shenaasnaameh	شناسنامه
perfume	'atr	عطر
(cigarette) lighter	fandak	فندك
condom	kaaput	كاپوت
writing paper	kaaqaz-e tahrir	كاغذ تحرير
face cream; foundation	kerem-e surat	كرم صورت
moisturising cream	kerem-e martub konandeh	كرم مرطوب كننده
key	kelid	كليد
house key	kelid-e khaaneh	كليد خانه
purse; wallet	kif-e pul	كيف پول
make-up bag	kif-e lavaazem-e aaraayesh	كيف لوازم آرايش
passport	gozarnaameh	گذرنامه
necklace	gardanband	گردنبند
driving licence	govaahinaame-ye raanandegi	گواهينامه رانندگی
earring	gushvaareh	گوشواره
hair pin	gire-ye sar	گيره سر
nail varnish	laak	لاك
make-up	lavaazem-e aaraayesh	لوازم آرايش
personal items	lavaazem-e shakhsi	لوازم شخصی
valuables	lavaazem-e qeymati	لوازم قيمتی
lipstick	maatik	ماتيک
calculator	maashin-e hesaab	ماشين حساب
pencil	medaad	مداد
toothbrush	mesvaak	مسواك
mobile phone	mubaayel	موبايل
tweezers	muchin	موچين
nail clippers	naakhon gir	ناخنگير

Philosophy

فلسفه

idealism	*aarmaan garaa'i*	آرمان گرائی
critical idealism	*aarmaan garaa'i-ye enteqaadi*	آرمان گرائی انتقادی
empirical	*aarvini*	آروینی
doctrine; school; ideology	*aayin*	آیین
agnosticism	*aayin-e laa adriyeh*	آیین لاادریه
instrumentalism	*abzaar engaari*	ابزار انگاری
atomism	*atom garaa'i*	اتم گرائی
positivism	*esbaat garaa'i*	اثبات گرائی
sensationalism	*ehsaas garaa'i*	احساس گرائی
free-will	*ekhtiyaar*	اختیار
morals; morality; ethics	*akhlaaq*	اخلاق
applied ethics	*akhlaaq-e kaarbordi*	اخلاق کاربردی
moral; ethical	*akhlaaqi*	اخلاقی
free-will	*eraade-ye aazaad*	اراده آزاد
voluntarism	*eraadeh garaa'i*	اراده گرائی
a posteriori reasoning	*estedlaal-e enni*	استدلال انی
circular argument	*estedlaal-e dowri*	استدلال دوری
deduction	*estedlaal-e qiyaasi*	استدلال قیاسی
a priori reasoning	*estedlaal-e lemmi*	استدلال لمی
induction	*esteqraa*	استقراء
induction	*estentaaj-e estegraa'i*	استنتاج استقرائی
logical implication	*estentaaj-e manteqi*	استنتاج منطقی
illuminism; illuminationism	*eshraaq garaa'i*	اشراق گرائی
pragmatism	*esaalat-e 'amal*	اصالت عمل
principle	*asl*	اصل
principle of universal causality	*asl-e elliyat-e 'omumi*	اصل علیت عمومی
axiom	*asl-e mota'aaref*	اصل متعارف
postulate	*asl-e mowzu'*	اصل موضوع
Platonism	*aflaatun garaa'i*	افلاطون گرائی
neo-Platonism	*aflaatun garaa'i-ye now*	افلاطون گرائی نو
existentialism	*egsistaansiyaalism*	اگزیستانسیالیسم
atheism	*elhaad*	الحاد
axiom	*amr-e badihi*	امر بدیهی
abstraction	*entezaa'*	انتزاع
humanism	*ensaan garaa'i*	انسان گرائی
idealism	*engaar garaa'i*	انگار گرائی

345

a posteriori	enni	انی
first principles	avvaliyaat	اولیات
idealism	ideh aalism	ایده آلیسم
pessimism	badbini	بدبینی
self-evident	badihi	بدیهی
argument	borhaan	برهان
argument from design	borhaan-e etqaan-e son'	برهان اتقان صنع
a posteriori demonstration	borhaan-e enni	برهان انّی
argument from order	borhaan-e bar entezaam	برهان بر انتظام
first cause argument	borhaan-e bar 'ellat-e avval	برهان بر علت اول
cosmological argument	borhaan-e keyhaan shenaakhti	برهان کیهان شناختی
a priori demonstration	borhaan-e lemmi	برهان لمّی
ontological argument	borhaan-e ma'refat-e vojudi	برهان معرفت وجودی
outlook; point of view	binesh	بینش
meliorism	behbud garaa'i	بهبود گرائی
antithesis	paad nahaad	پاد نهاد
paradox	paaraaduks	پارادوکس
epiphenomenon	padidaar-e saanavi	پدیدار ثانوی
phenomenalism	padidaar shenaasi	پدیدار شناسی
phenomenalism	padideh garaa'i	پدیده گرائی
a posteriori	pasini	پسینی
illusion	pendaar	پندار
positivism	puzitivism	پوزیتیویسم
a priori	pishini	پیشینی
empirical	tajrebi	تجربی
empiricism	tajrobeh garaa'i	تجربه گرائی
abstraction	tajrid	تجرید
analysis	tajziyeh	تجزیه
philosophical research	tahqiqaat-e falsafi	تحقیقات فلسفی
synthesis	tarkib	ترکیب
thesis	tez	تز
evolutionism	tatavvor garaa'i	تطور گرائی
transcendentalism	ta'aali garaa'i	تعالی گرائی
universalizability	ta'mim paziri	تعمیم پذیری
logical paradox	tanaaqoz namaa	تناقض نما
hallucination	tavahhom	توهم
determinism; fatalism	jabr	جبر
fatalism	jabrigari	جبریگری

dialectic	*jadal*	جدل
dogmatism	*jazm garaa'i*	جزم گرائی
particular	*joz'i*	جزئی
essence	*jowhar*	جوهر
worldview; ideology	*jahaanbini*	جهان بینی
proof	*hojjat*	حجت
contingency	*hodus*	حدوث
creation ex nihilo	*hodus-e hasti az nisti*	حدوث هستی از نیستی
value judgement	*hokm-e arzeshi*	حکم ارزشی
value judgement	*hokm-e e'tebaari*	حکم اعتباری
logical analysis	*hokm-e tahlili*	حکم تحلیلی
theism	*khodaa garaa'i-ye laahuti*	خدا گرائی لاهوتی
atheism	*khodaa naabaavari*	خدا ناباوری
rationalism	*kherad garaa'i*	خرد گرائی
fallacy	*khataa*	خطا
egoism; self-worship	*khod parasti*	خود پرستی
egoism	*khod garaa'i*	خود گرائی
optimism	*khoshbini*	خوشبینی
the greatest good	*kheyr-e a'laa*	خیر اعلا
good and evil	*kheyr o sharr*	خیر و شر
sense data	*daade-haa-ye hessi*	داده های حسی
proof; reason	*dalil*	دلیل
dualism	*dowgaaneh garaa'i*	دوگانه گرائی
dialectic	*diyaalektik*	دیالکتیک
altruism	*digar garaa'i*	دیگر گرائی
essence	*zaat*	ذات
subjectivity	*zehniyat*	ذهنیت
relationship	*raabeteh*	رابطه
behavourism	*raftaar garaa'i*	رفتار گرائی
realism	*re'aalism*	رئالیسم
asceticism	*riyaazat garaa'i*	ریاضت گری
ascetic	*zaahed*	زاهد
aesthetics	*zibaa'i shenaasi*	زیبائی شناسی
asceticism	*zohd*	زهد
structuralism	*saakht garaa'i*	ساخت گرائی
sophistry	*safsateh*	سفسطه
chain of being	*selsele-ye vojud*	سلسله وجود
personalism	*shakhs garaa'i*	شخص گرائی

evil	sharr	شر
scepticism	shak garaa'i	شک گرائی
knowledge	shenaakht	شناخت
intuitionism	shohud garaa'i	شهود گرائی
concept	surat-e 'aqli	صورت عقلی
archetype	surat-e mesaali	صورت مثالی
necessary	zaruri	ضروری
naturalism	tabi'at garaa'i	طبیعت گرائی
mysticism; gnosis	'erfaan	عرفان
first intellect	'aql-e avval	عقل اول
common sense	'aql-e salim	عقل سلیم
rationalism	'aql garaa'i	عقل گرائی
efficient cause	'ellat-e faa'eli	علت فاعلی
final cause	'ellat-e nahaa'i	علت نهائی
cause and effect	'ellat o ma'lul	علت و معلول
causality	'elliyat	علیت
determinism	'elliyat garaa'i	علیت گرائی
objectivity	'eyniyat	عینیت
teleology	qaayat shenaasi	غایت شناسی
utilitarianism	faayedeh garaa'i	فایده گرائی
negative utilitarianism	faayedeh garaa'i-e ye manfi	فایده گرائی منفی
hypothetical	farzi	فرضی
hypothesis	farziyeh	فرضیه
philosopher kings	farmaan ravaayaan-e filsuf	فرمانروایان فیلسوف
philosophical	falsafi	فلسفی
philosophy	falsafeh	فلسفه
ethics	falsafe-ye akhlaaq	فلسفه اخلاق
Islamic philosophy	falsafe-ye eslaami	فلسفه اسلامی
emotivism	falsafe-ye esaalat-e 'avaatef	فلسفه اصالت عراطف
philosophy of religion	falsafe-ye din	فلسفه دین
metaphysics	falsafe-ye faraagiti	فلسفه فراگیتی
peripatetic philosophy	falsafe-ye mashaa'i	فلسفه مشائی
philosopher	filsuf	فیلسوف
verifiable	qaabel-e tasdiq	قابل تصدیق
law of contradiction	qaanun-e tanaaqoz	قانون تناقض
proposition	qaziyeh	قضیه
causal laws	qavaanin-e 'elli	قوانین علی
potentiality and actuality	qovveh va fe'l	قوه و فعل

analogy	*qiyaas*	قیاس
functionalism	*kaarkard garaa'i*	کارکرد گرائی
plurality	*kesrat*	کثرت
pluralism	*kesrat garaa'i*	کثرت گرائی
universal; general	*kolli*	کلی
universals	*kolliyaat*	کلیات
perfection	*kamaal*	کمال
alchemy	*kimiyaa*	کیمیا
cosmology; cosmogony	*keyhaan shenaasi*	کیهان شناسی
agnostic	*laa adri*	لا ادری
infinite	*laa motanaahi*	لامتناهی
hedonism	*lezzat garaa'i*	لذت گرائی
a priori	*lemmi*	لمی
materialism	*maaddeh garaa'i*	ماده گرائی
dialectical materialism	*maaddeh garaa'i-ye diyaalektiki*	ماده گرائی دیالکتیکی
essence	*maahiyat*	ماهیت
metaphysical	*metaagitik*	متاگیتیک
finite	*motanaahi*	متناهی
prime mover; first cause	*moharrek-e avval*	محرک اول
mysticism	*mazhab-e ahl-e baaten*	مذهب اهل باطن
ascetic	*mortaaz*	مرتاض
problem of evil	*mas'ale-ye sharr*	مسئله شر
pragmatism	*maslahat garaa'i*	مصلحت گرائی
absolute	*motlaq*	مطلق
absolutism	*motlaq garaa'i*	مطلق گرائی
miracle	*mo'jezeh*	معجزه
epistemology	*ma'refat shenaasi*	معرفت شناسی
paradox; puzzle	*mo'ammaa*	معما
fallacy	*moqaaleteh*	مغالطه
logical fallacy	*moqaalete-ye manteqi*	مغالطه منطقی
concept	*mafhum-e kolli*	مفهوم کلی
conceptualism	*mafhum garaa'i*	مفهوم گرائی
premises	*moqaddamaat-e qiyaas*	مقدمات قیاس
Aristotelian categories	*maqulaat-e arastu*	مقولات ارسطو
school (of thought)	*maktab*	مکتب
logic	*manteq*	منطق
Aristotelian logic	*manteq-e arastu*	منطق ارسطو
nominalism	*naam garaa'i*	نام گرائی

relativism	*nesbi garaa'i*	نسبی گرائی
moral order	*nezaam-e akhlaaqi*	نظام اخلاقی
thesis; idea	*nazar*	نظر
theory	*nazariyeh*	نظریه
falsificationism	*nazariye-ye ebtaal paziri*	نظریه ابطال پذیری
instrumentalism	*nazariye-ye esaalat-e vasileh*	نظریه اصالت وسیله
epistemology; theory of knowledge	*nazariye-ye shenaakht*	نظریه شناخت
interactionism	*nazariye-ye 'amal-e motaqaabel*	نظریه عمل متقابل
virtue theory	*nazariye-ye fazilat*	نظریه فضیلت
critique	*naqd*	نقد
antithesis	*naqiz*	نقیض
outlook	*negaresh*	نگرش
nominalism	*numinaalism*	نومینالیسم
nihilism	*nist baavari*	نیست باوری
realism	*vaaqe' garaa'i*	واقع گرائی
critical realism	*vaaqe' garaa'i-ye enteqaadi*	واقع گرائی انتقادی
representative realism	*vaaqe' garaa'i-ye baaznamaa*	واقع گرائی بازنما
causal realism	*vaaqe' garaa'i-ye 'elli*	واقع گرائی علی
ultimate reality	*vaaqe'iyat-e nahaa'i*	واقعیت نهائی
existence; being	*vojud*	وجود
existentialism	*vojud garaa'i*	وجود گرائی
unity	*vahdat*	وحدت
unity of being; pantheism	*vahdat-e vojud*	وحدت وجود
being; existence	*hasti*	هستی
pure being	*hasti-ye mahz*	هستی محض
pure being; absolute being	*hasti-ye motlaq*	هستی مطلق
synthesis	*hamnahaad*	همنهاد
panpsychism	*hame ravaan baavari*	همه روان باوری
neutral monism	*yektaa garaa'i-ye khonsaa*	یکتا گرائی خنثی
monism	*yegaaneh garaa'i*	یگانه گرائی

350

Physics

فیزیک

ampere	*aamper*	آمپر
ammeter	*aamper sanj*	آمپرسنج
enthalpy	*aantaalpi*	آنتالپی
anion	*aaniyun*	آنیون
pendulum	*aavang*	آونگ
magnet	*aahanrobaa*	آهنربا
magnetism	*aahanrobaa'i*	آهنربائی
atom	*atom*	اتم
piezoelectric effect	*asar-e pizu-elektrik*	اثر پیزوالکتریک
Doppler effect	*asar-e dupler*	اثر دوپلر
potential difference	*ekhtelaaf-e potaansiyel*	اختلاف پتانسیل
parallax	*ekhtelaaf-e manzar*	اختلاف منظر
spin	*espin*	اسپین
osmosis	*osmoz*	اسمز
saturation	*eshbaa'*	اشباع
Archimedes principle	*asl-e arshimedes*	اصل ارشیمدس
Pauli's exclusion principle	*asl-e tard-e paa'uli*	اصل طرد پائولی
gain	*afzaayesh*	افزایش
induction	*elqaa*	القاء
electrolyte	*elektrolit*	الکترولیت
electron	*elektrun*	الکترون
valence electron	*elektrun vaalaans*	الکترون والانس
electron volt	*elektrun volt*	الکترون ولت
electronic	*elektrunik*	الکترونیک
transverse waves	*amvaaj-e 'arzi*	امواج عرضی
harmonic waves	*amvaaj-e hamaahang*	امواج هماهنگ
momentum	*andaaze-ye harekat*	اندازه حرکت
energy	*enerzhi*	انرژی
kinetic energy	*enerzhi-ye jonbeshi*	انرژی جنبشی
isobar	*izubaar*	ایزوبار
isotope	*izutup*	ایزوتوپ
ohm	*ohm*	اهم
bar; charge	*baar*	بار
discharge	*baargiri*	بارگیری
reflection	*baaztaab*	بازتاب
betatron	*betaatrun*	بتاترون

351

vapour	bokhaar	بخار
vector	bordaar	بردار
magnification	bozorgnamaa'i	بزرگنمائی
frequency	basaamad	بسامد
conservation of mass and energy	baqaa-ye jerm va enerzhi	بقای جرم و انرژی
conservation of matter	baqaa-ye maaddeh	بقای ماده
dispersion	paashandegi	پاشندگی
diffusion	pakhsh	پخش
diffraction	paraash	پراش
diffractometer	paraash sanj	پراش سنج
dispersion; scattering	paraakandegi	پراکندگی
x-ray	partow-e iks	پرتو ایکس
alpha rays	partow-e aalfaa	پرتو آلفا
Becquerel rays	partow-e raadiyom	پرتو رادیم
cosmic rays	partow-haa-ye keyhaani	پرتو های کیهانی
gamma rays	partow-haa-ye gaamaa	پرتوهای گاما
infra-red rays	partow-haa-ye maadun-e sorkh	پرتوهای مادون سرخ
proton	perowton	پروتون
hysteresis	pasmaand	پسماند
plasma	pelaasmaa	پلاسما
positron	puzitrun	پوزیترون
shell	pusteh	پوسته
radiation	taabesh	تابش
ultra-violet radiation	taabesh-e faraa banafsh	تابش فرابنفش
densitometer	taari sanj	تاری سنج
decay	tabaahi	تباهی
evaporation	tabkhir	تبخیر
discharge	takhliyeh	تخلیه
interference	tadaakhol	تداخل
transistor	teraanzistur	ترانزیستور
thermodynamics	termudinaamik	ترمودینامیک
resonance	tashdid	تشدید
gain	taqviyat	تقویت
transductor	taqviyat konande-ye meqnaatisi	تقویت کننده مغناطیسی
disintegration	talaashi	تلاشی
heat pump	tolombe-ye garmaa'i	تلمبه گرمائی
power	tavaan	توان
Planck's constant	saabet-e pelaank	ثابت پلانک

gravity; gravitation	seql	ثقل
mass	jerm	جرم
atomic mass	jerm-e atomi	جرم اتمی
current	jaryaan	جریان
alternating current	jaryaan-e motanaaveb	جریان متناوب
direct current	jaryaan-e mostaqim	جریان مستقیم
laminar flow	jaryaan-e movaazi	جریان موازی
black body	jesm-e siyaah	جسم سیاه
spin; rotation	charkhesh	چرخش
density	chegaali	چگالی
allotropy	haalat-e chand shekli	حالت چندشکلی
motion; movement	harekat	حرکت
Brownian movement	harekat-e beraavni	حرکت براونی
simple harmonic motion	harekat-e hamaahang-e saadeh	حرکت هماهنگ ساده
Newton's rings	halqe-haa-ye niyutuni	حلقه های نیوتونی
capacitor	khaazen	خازن
vacuum	khala'	خلاء
machine; apparatus	dastgaah	دستگاه
rectifier	dastgaah-e saboksaaz	دستگاه سبکساز
temperature	damaa	دما
standard temperature and pressure	damaa va feshaar-e mota'aaref	دما و فشار متعارف
telescope; binoculars	durbin-e nojumi	دوربین نجومی
dielectric	diyelektrik	دی الکتریک
alpha particles	zarraat-e aalfaa	ذرات آلفا
elementary particles	zarraat-e bonyaadi	ذرات بنیادی
beta particle	zarre-ye betaa	ذره بتا
fusion	zowb	ذوب
radioactivity	raadyow aaktiviteh	رادیو آکتیویته
conductor	resaanaa	رسانا
conductivity	resaanaa'i	رسانائی
microwave	riz mowj	ریزموج
period	zamaan-e tanaavob	زمان تناوب
earth	zamin	زمین
joule	zhul	ژول
speed	sor'at	سرعت
cryogenics	sarmazaa'i	سرمازائی
free fall	soqut-e aazaad	سقوط آزاد
nuclear fuel	sukht-e haste'i	سوخت هسته ای

scintillation	*susuzani*	سوسوزنی
fluid	*sayyaal*	سیال
densitometer	*siyaahi sanj*	سیاهی سنج
cyclotron	*siklutrun*	سیکلوترون
flux	*shaar*	شار
electric flux	*shaar-e elektriki*	شار الکتریکی
lattice	*shabakeh*	شبکه
acceleration	*shetaab*	شتاب
accelerator	*shetaabgar*	شتابگر
electric field intensity	*sheddat-e meydaan-e elektriki*	شدت میدان الکتریکی
normal temperature/pressure (NTP)	*sharaa'et-e mota'aarefi*	شرائط متعارفی (دما و فشار)
fission	*shekaaft*	شکافت
nuclear fission	*shekaaft-e haste'i*	شکافت هسته ای
refraction	*shekast*	شکست
Geiger counter	*shomaarande-ye gaayger*	شمارنده گایگر
candela	*sham'*	شمع
absolute zero	*sefr-e motlaq*	صفر مطلق
sound; tone	*sowt*	صوت
anti-matter	*zedd-e maaddeh*	ضد ماده
wavelength	*tul-e mowj*	طول موج
spectrum	*tif*	طیف
absorption spectrum	*tif-e jazbi*	طیف جذبی
mass spectrometer	*tif sanj-e jerm*	طیف سنج جرم
spectrometry	*tif sanji*	طیف سنجی
visible spectrum	*tif-e mar'i*	طیف مرئی
capacity; capacitance	*zarfiyyat*	ظرفیت
conductor	*'aayeq*	عایق
atomic number	*'adad-e atomi*	عدد اتمی
Mach number	*'adad-e maakh*	عدد ماخ
lens	*'adasi*	عدسی
semi-permeable membrane	*qeshaa'-e nimeh taraavaa*	غشاء نیمه تراوا
phase	*faaz*	فاز
pitch	*faaseleh*	فاصله
ultrasonic	*faraasowti*	فراصوتی
disintegration	*forupaashi*	فروپاشی
ferromagnetism	*ferumeqnaatisi*	فرومغناطیسی
pressure	*feshaar*	فشار
barometer	*feshaar sanj*	فشارسنج

fluorescence	feluresaans	فلورسانس
supercooling	fowq-e enjemaad	فوق انجماد
superconductivity	fowq-e resaanaa'i	فوق رسانانی
physics	fizik	فیزیک
nuclear physics	fizik-e haste'i	فیزیک هسته ای
Einstein's law	qaanun-e inshtin	قانون اینشتین
Pascal's law	qaanun-e paaskaal	قانون پاسکال
pole	qotb	قطب
anode	qotb-e mosbat	قطب مثبت
cathode	qotb-e manfi	قطب منفی
polarization	qotbesh	قطبش
work	kaar	کار
efficiency	kaaraa'i	کارآنی
elasticity	keshaayandegi	کشایندگی
elasticity	keshidegi	کشیدگی
kelvin	kelvin	کلوین
galvanometer	gaalvaanumeter	گالوانومتر
fusion	godaaz	گداز
viscosity	geraanravi	گرانروی
gravitation	geraanesh	گرانش
heat	garmaa	گرما
calorimeter	garmaa sanj	گرما سنج
latent heat	garmaa-ye nehaan	گرمای نهان
atomic group	goruh-e atomi	گروه اتمی
photo-emission	gosil-e nur	گسیل نور
moment	gashtaavar	گشتاور
cathode ray tube	laamp-e partov-e kaatodi	لامپ پرتو کاتدی
inertia	lakhti	لختی
laser	leyzer	لیزر
transformer	mobaddel	مبدل
convex	mohaddab	محدب
orbit	madaar	مدار
Schrodinger's equation	mo'aadele-ye shrudinger	معادله شرودینگر
magnetism	meqnaatis	مغناطیس
resistance	moqaavemat	مقاومت
resistivity	moqaavemat-e vizheh	مقاومت ویژه
concave	moqa'ar	مقعر
Celsius scale	meqyaas-e selsiyus	مقیاس سلسیوس

Fahrenheit scale	meqyaas-e faarenhaayt	مقیاس فارنهایت
mechanics	mekaanik	مکانیک
quantum mechanics	mekaanik-e kvaantomi	مکانیک کوانتمی
prism	manshur	منشور
motor	motur	موتور
wave	mowj	موج
longitudinal wave	mowj-e tuli	موج طولی
mole	mul	مول
capillarity	muyinegi	مویینگی
electric field	meydaan-e elektriki	میدان الکتیکی
magnetic field	meydaan-e meqnaatisi	میدان مغناطیسی
microscope	mikruskup	میکروسکوپ
relativity	nesbiyyat	نسبیت
quantum theory	nazariyye-ye kvaantomi	نظریه کوانتمی
diffusion	nofuz	نفوذ
permeability	nofuz pazir	نفوذپذیری
radio-opaque	nofuz naapaziri baraaye partow	نفوذناپذیری برای پرتو
freezing point	noqte-ye enjemaad	نقطه انجماد
boiling point	noqte-ye jush	نقطه جوش
triple point	noqte-ye seh gaaneh	نقطه سه گانه
curie point	noqte-ye kuri	نقطه کوری
neutron	nutrun	نوترون
light	nur	نور
optics	nurshenaasi	نورشناسی
oscillation	navasaan	نوسان
nucleon	nukle'un	نوکلئون
force	niru	نیرو
centripetal force	niru-ye markaz-garaa	نیروی مرکزگرا
centrifugal force	niru-ye markaz-goriz	نیروی مرکزگریز
semiconductor	nimeh resaanaa	نیمه رسانا
half-life	nimeh 'omr	نیمه عمر
breeder reactor	vaakoneshgar-e zaayaa	واکنشگر زایا
weight	vazn	وزن
atomic weight	vazn-e atomi	وزن اتمی
volt	volt	ولت
hertz	herts	هرتس
nucleus	haste-ye atom	هسته اتم
atomic	haste'i	هسته ای

fusion	hamjushi	همجوشی
nuclear fusion	hamjushi-ye haste'i	همجوشی هسته ای
convection	hamraft	همرفت
isobar	hamfeshaar	همفشار
hydrodynamics	hidrudinaamik	هیدرودینامیک
rectifier	yeksu konandeh	یکسو کننده
ion	yun	یون

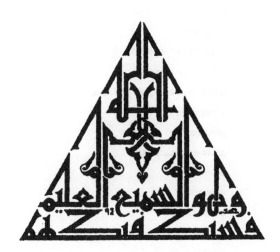

Politics

امور سیاسی

apartheid	*aapaartaayd*	آپارتاید
utopia	*aarmaanshahr (madine-ye faazeleh)*	آرمانشهر (مدینه فاضله)
aristodemocracy	*aaristu demukraasi*	آریستو دموکراسی
liberation	*aazaad saazi*	آزادسازی
freedom	*aazaadi*	آزادی
freedom of association	*aazaadi-ye ejtemaa'aat*	آزادی اجتماعات
freedom of expression	*aazaadi-ye bayaan*	آزادی بیان
political freedom	*aazaadi-ye siyaasi*	آزادی سیاسی
freedom of opinion	*aazaadi-ye 'aqideh*	آزادی عقیده
scientific freedom	*aazaadi-ye 'elmi*	آزادی علمی
individual freedom	*aazaadi-ye fardi*	آزادی فردی
freedom of the press	*aazaadi-ye matbu'aat*	آزادی مطبوعات
personal freedoms	*aazaadi-haa-ye fardi*	آزادیهای فردی
civil liberties	*aazaadi-haa-ye madani*	آزادیهای مدنی
riot; unrest; revolt	*aashub*	آشوب
rioter	*aashubgar*	آشوبگر
revolutionary consciousness	*aagaahi-ye enqelaabi*	آگاهی انقلابی
class consciousness	*aagaahi-ye tabaqaati*	آگاهی طبقاتی
false class consciousness	*aagaahi-ye tabaqaati-ye kaazeb*	آگاهی طبقاتی کاذب
alternative	*aalternaativ*	آلترناتیو
anarchy	*aanaarshism*	آنارشیسم
Caesaropapism	*aayin-e qeysar paapi*	آیین قیصرپاپی
by-law	*aayin naameh*	آیین نامه
super power	*abar qodrat*	ابر قدرت
unity; alliance	*ettehaad*	اتحاد
labour union	*ettehaadiye-ye kaargari*	اتحادیه کارگری
coercion	*ejbaar*	اجبار
community	*ejtemaa'*	اجتماع
rally (of party members)	*ejtemaa'-e hezbi*	اجتماع حزبی
session	*ejlaas*	اجلاس
consensus	*ejmaa'*	اجماع
public sentiment	*ehsaasaat-e 'omumi*	احساسات عمومی
full powers	*ekhtiyaar-e taam*	اختیار تام
libertarianism	*ekhtiyaar garaa'i*	اختیار گرائی
expulsion	*ekhraaj*	اخراج
exile; deportation	*ekhraaj az keshvar*	اخراج از کشور

administration; management	edaareh	اداره
reactionary	ertejaa'i	ارتجاعی
party organ	orgaan-e hezbi	ارگان حزبی
Eurocentrism	orupaa mehvari	اروپامحوری
statute; constitution	asaasnaameh	اساسنامه
de-Stalinization	estaalin zadaa'i	استالین زدائی
Stalinism	estaalinism	استالینیسم
provincial governor	ostaandaar	استاندار
tyranny; despotism	estebdaad	استبداد
Asiatic despotism	estebdaad-e aasyaa'i	استبداد آسیائی
oriental despotism	estebdaad-e sharqi	استبداد شرقی
authoritarianism	estebdaad talabi	استبداد طلبی
dictatorship of the proletariat	estebdaad-e kaargari	استبداد کارگری
totalitarianism	estebdaad-e faraagir	استبداد فراگیر
strategy	estraatezhi	استراتژی
eavesdropping; bugging	esteraaq-e sam'	استراق سمع
colonialism	este'maar	استعمار
independence	esteqlaal	استقلال
interpellation	estizaah	استیضاح
secret documents	asnaad-e serri	اسناد سری
classified documents	asnaad-e tabaqeh bandi shodeh	اسناد طبقه بندی شده
confidential documents	asnaad-e mahramaaneh	اسناد محرمانه
nobles; the nobility	ashraaf	اشراف
aristocrat	ashraaf zaadeh	اشراف زاده
aristocracy	ashraaf saalaari	اشراف سالاری
reform	eslaah	اصلاح
reformism	eslaah talabi	اصلاح طلبی
land reforms	eslaahaat-e arzi	اصلاحات ارضی
amendment (to a law)	eslaahiyeh	اصلاحیه
doctrinaire	osuli	اصولی
blind obedience; passive obedience	etaa'at-e kurkuraaneh	اطاعت کورکورانه
protest	e'teraaz	اعتراض
strike	e'tesaab	اعتصاب
token strike	e'tesaab-e e'laami	اعتصاب اعلامی
wild cat strike	e'tesaab-e bi poshtvaaneh	اعتصاب بی پشتوانه
strike breaker; blackleg	e'tesaab shekan	اعتصاب شکن
general strike	e'tesaab-e 'omumi	اعتصاب عمومی
unauthorised strike	e'tesaab-e qeyr-e mojaaz	اعتصاب غیر مجاز

declaration	e'laamiyeh	اعلامیه
bill of rights	e'laamiye-ye hoquq	اعلامیه حقوق
lobbying	e'maal-e nofuz	اعمال نفوذ
extremism	efraat garaa'i	افراط گرائی
muckraking	efshaa-ye fesaad	افشای فساد
public opinion	afkaar-e 'omumi	افکار عمومی
authority	eqtedaar	اقتدار
economy; economics	eqtesaad	اقتصاد
controlled economy	eqtesaad-e ershaadi	اقتصاد ارشادی
free economy	eqtesaad-e aazaad	اقتصاد آزاد
political economy	eqtesaad-e siyaasi	اقتصاد سیاسی
mixed economy	eqtesaad-e mokhtalet	اقتصاد مختلط
minority	aqalliyat	اقلیت
majority	aksariyat	اکثریت
moral majority	aksariyat-e akhlaaqi	اکثریت اخلاقی
silent majority	aksariyat-e saaket	اکثریت ساکت
relative majority	aksariyat-e nesbi	اکثریت نسبی
abolitionism	elqaagari	الغاگری
ABC of politics	alefbaa-ye siyaasi	الفبای سیاست
indoctrination	elqaa-e 'aqideh	القاء عقیده
imamate	emaamat	امامت
emperor	emperaatur	امپراتور
empire	emperaaturi	امپراتوری
imperialism	amperyaalism	امپریالیسم
neo-imperialism	amperyaalism-e jadid	امپریالیسم جدید
cultural imperialism	amperyaalism-e farhangi	امپریالیسم فرهنگی
abstentionism	emtenaa' garaa'i	امتناع گرائی
concession	emtiyaaz	امتیاز
security	amniyat	امنیت
national security	amniyat-e melli	امنیت ملی
administrative affairs	omur-e edaari	امور اداری
foreign affairs	omur-e khaareje	امور خارجه
political affairs	omur-e siyaasi	امور سیاسی
electorate; the voters	entekhaab konandegaan	انتخاب کنندگان
election(s)	entekhaabaat	انتخابات
parliamentary election	entekhaabaat-e paarlemaani	انتخابات پارلمانی
general election	entekhaabaat-e saraasari	انتخابات سراسری
by-election	entekhaabaat-e far'i	انتخابات فرعی

mid-term elections	entekhaabaat-e miyaan dowre'i	انتخابات میاندوره ای
Intifada	entefaazeh	انتفاضه
association	anjoman	انجمن
intelligence community	anjoman-e ettelaa'aati	انجمن اطلاعاتی
monopoly	enhesaar	انحصار
isolationism	enzevaa garaa'i	انزواگرائی
party discipline	enzebaat-e hezbi	انضباط حزبی
secession	enfesaal	انفصال
revolution	enqelaab	انقلاب
Islamic revolution	enqelaab-e eslaami	انقلاب اسلامی
commercial revolution	enqelaab-e baazargaani	انقلاب بازرگانی
bourgeois revolution	enqelaab-e burzhvaa'i	انقلاب بورژوائی
permanent revolution	enqelaab-e daa'em	انقلاب دائم
Green revolution	enqelaab-e sabz	انقلاب سبز
socialist revolution	enqelaab-e susyaalisti	انقلاب سوسیالیستی
political revolution	enqelaab-e siyaasi	انقلاب سیاسی
industrial revolution	enqelaab-e san'ati	انقلاب صنعتی
cultural revolution	enqelaab-e farhangi	انقلاب فرهنگی
technological revolution	enqelaab-e fannaavari	انقلاب فناوری
revolutionary	enqelaabi	انقلابی
coalition	e'telaaf	ائتلاف
altruism	isaar	ایثار
ideology	ide'uluzhi	ایدئولوژی
idealism	ideh aalism	ایده آلیسم
free market	baazaar-e aazaad	بازار آزاد
black market	baazaar-e siyaah	بازار سیاه
interrogation	baazju'i	بازجوئی
repatriation	baazgardaani be mihan	بازگردانی به میهن
Bakuninism	baakuninism	باکونینیسم
boycott	baaykut	بایکوت
Paper Tiger	babr-e kaaqazi	ببر کاغذی
debate; discussion	bahs	بحث
crisis	bohraan	بحران
economic crisis	bohraan-e eqtesaadi	بحران اقتصادی
political crisis	bohraan-e siyaasi	بحران سیاسی
private sector	bakhsh-e khosusi	بخش خصوصی
equality	baraabari	برابری
overthrow; subversion	barandaazi	براندازی

slavery	*bardeh daari*	برده داری
development plan	*barnaame-ye towse'eh*	برنامه توسعه
planning	*barnaameh rizi*	برنامه ریزی
military planning	*barnaameh rizi-ye nezaami*	برنامه ریزی نظامی
platform (in election)	*barnaame-ye kaar*	برنامه کار
Bolshevism	*bolshevism*	بلشویسم
bluffing	*boluf zani*	بلوف زنی
yes-man	*baleh qorbaan gu*	بله قربان گو
impasse	*bonbast*	بن بست
Bonapartism	*bonaapaartism*	بناپارتیسم
fundamentalism	*bonyaad garaa'i*	بنیاد گرائی
Islamic fundamentalism	*bonyaad garaa'i-ye eslaami*	بنیاد گرائی اسلامی
budget	*budjeh*	بودجه
bureaucracy	*buraakraasi*	بوراکراسی
bourgeois	*burzhvaa*	بورژوا
embourgeoisement	*burzhvaa shodan*	بورژوا شدن
bourgeoisie	*burzhvaazi*	بورژوازی
bureaucratic bourgeoisie	*burzhvaazi-ye edaari*	بورژوازی اداری
comprador bourgeoisie	*burzhvaazi-ye kompraadur*	بورژوازی کمپرادور
bureaucracy (alt. Persian spelling)	*burukraasi*	بورو کراسی
political apathy	*bi e'tenaa'i-ye siyaasi*	بی اعتنائی سیاسی
statelessness	*bi taabe'iyati*	بی تابعیتی
political instability	*bi sobaati-ye siyaasi*	بی ثباتی سیاسی
apolitical	*bi taraf dar siyaasat*	بی طرف در سیاست
manifesto	*bayaaniyeh*	بیانیه
black consciousness	*bidaari-ye siyaah*	بیداری سیاه
unemployment	*bikaari*	بیکاری
alienation	*bigaanegi*	بیگانگی
xenophobia	*bigaaneh haraasi*	بیگانه هراسی
Socialist International	*beyn-ol-mellal-e susyaalist*	بین الملل سوسیالیست
economic recovery	*behbud-e eqtesaadi*	بهبود اقتصادی
eugenics	*behnezhaadi*	بهنژادی
patrician	*paatrisyen*	پاتریسین
king; sovereign	*paadeshaah*	پادشاه
favouritism; nepotism	*paarti baazi*	پارتی بازی
parliament	*paarlemaan*	پارلمان
purge	*paaksaazi*	پاکسازی
ethnic cleansing	*paaksaazi-ye nezhaadi*	پاکسازی نژادی

362

Pan-Islamism	paan eslaamism	پان اسلامیسم
'End of History'	paayaan-e taarikh	پایان تاریخ
class status	paayegaah-e tabaqaati	پایگاه طبقاتی
patriarchy	pedar saalaari	پدرسالاری
flag	parcham	پرچم
Red Flag	parcham-e sorkh	پرچم سرخ
flag of convenience	parcham-e naf' o raahati	پرچم نفع و راحتی
perestroika	perestruykaa	پرسترویکا
proletariat	pruletaariyaa	پرولتاریا
police	polis	پلیس
secret police	polis-e makhfi	پلیس مخفی
territorial asylum	panaahandegi-ye darunmarzi	پناهندگی درونمرزی
political asylum	panaahandegi-ye siyaasi	پناهندگی سیاسی
asylum seeker; refugee	panaahandeh	پناهنده
political refugee	panaahande-ye siyaasi	پناهنده سیاسی
involuntary refugee	panaahande-ye qeyr-e daavtalab	پناهنده غیر داوطلب
group dynamics	puyesh-e goruhi	پویش گروهی
alliance; pact; confederacy	peymaan	پیمان
crown	taaj	تاج
coronation	taajgozaari	تاجگذاری
social security	ta'min-e ejtemaa'i	تامین اجتماعی
exile; ostracism	tab'id	تبعید
discrimination; segregation	tab'iz	تبعیض
racial discrimination	tab'iz-e nezhaadi	تبعیض نژادی
propaganda	tabliqaat	تبلیغات
free trade	tejaarat-e aazaad	تجارت آزاد
revisionism	tajdid-e nazar talabi	تجدیدنظرطلبی
unlawful assembly	tajammo'-e qeyr-e qaanuni	تجمع غیرقانونی
protectorate	taht ol-hemaayegi	تحت الحمایگی
agitation; provocation	tahrik	تحریک
sanction	tahrim	تحریم
economic sanctions	tahrim-e eqtesaadi	تحریم اقتصادی
analysis	tahlil	تحلیل
confidence building measures	tadaabir-e ijaad-e etminaan	تدابیر ایجاد اطمینان
balance of trade	taraaz-e baazargaani	تراز بازرگانی
balance of payments	taraaz-e pardakht-haa	تراز پرداخت ها
cabinet reshuffle	tarmim-e kaabineh	ترمیم کابینه
terror; assassination	teror	ترور

363

character assassination	*teror-e shakhsiyat*	ترور شخصیت
terrorist	*terorist*	تروریست
terrorism	*terorism*	تروریسم
state terrorism	*terorism-e dowlati*	تروریسم دولتی
dominant ideology thesis	*tez-e ide'uluzhi-ye mosallat*	تز ایدئولوژی مسلط
moral rearmament	*taslih-e akhlaaqi*	تسلیح اخلاقی
protocol; red tape	*tashrifaat*	تشریفات
organisation; institutions	*tashkilaat*	تشکیلات
underground	*tashkilaat-e zir-e zamini*	تشکیلات زیرزمینی
approval by acclamation	*tasdiq be vasile-ye kaf zadan*	تصدیق به وسیله کف زدن
purge	*tasfiyeh*	تصفیه
decision	*tasmim*	تصمیم
decision-maker	*tasmim girandeh*	تصمیم گیرنده
decision-making	*tasmim giri*	تصمیم گیری
approval; ratification	*tasvib*	تصویب
contradiction of capitalism	*tazzaad-e sarmaayeh daari*	تضاد سرمایه داری
devaluation	*taz'if-e puli*	تضعیف پولی
demonstration	*tazaahoraat*	تظاهرات
equilibrium	*ta'aadol*	تعادل
class conflict	*ta'aaroz-e tabaqaati*	تعارض طبقاتی
co-operative	*ta'aavoni*	تعاونی
checks and balances	*ta'dil o tavaazon*	تعدیل و توازن
fanaticism; prejudice	*ta'assob*	تعصب
moratorium	*ta'liq*	تعلیق
commitment; obligation	*ta'ahhod*	تعهد
divide and rule	*tafraqeh biyandaaz o hokumat kon*	تفرقه بینداز و حکومت کن
separation of powers	*tafkik-e qovaa*	تفکیک قوا
segregation (i.e. racial)	*tafkik-e nezhaadi*	تفکیک نژادی
delegation of authority	*tafviz-e ekhtiyaar*	تفویض اختیار
delegation of power	*tafviz-e qodrat*	تفویض قدرت
apportionment	*taqsim-e korsi-haa*	تقسیم کرسی ها
local divisions	*taqsimaat-e keshvari*	تقسیمات کشوری
maverick	*takrow*	تکرو
techno-diplomacy	*teknudiplomaasi*	تکنودیپلماسی
territorial integrity	*tamaamiyat-e arzi*	تمامیت ارضی
civilization	*tamaddon*	تمدن
sedition	*tamarrod*	تمرد
centralization	*tamarkoz*	تمرکز

revolutionary tension	*tanesh-e enqelaabi*	تنش انقلابی
totemism	*towtem garaa'i*	توتم گرائی
mass(es)	*tudeh*	توده
inflation	*tavarrom*	تورم
development	*towse'eh*	توسعه
economic development	*towse'e-ye eqtesaadi*	توسعه اقتصادی
political development	*towse'e-ye siyaasi*	توسعه سیاسی
expansionism	*towse'eh talabi*	توسعه طلبی
conspiracy	*towte'eh*	توطئه
cultural invasion	*tahaajom-e farhangi*	تهاجم فرهنگی
economic stability	*sobaat-e eqtesaadi*	ثبات اقتصادی
political stability	*sobaat-e siyaasi*	ثبات سیاسی
spy	*jaasus*	جاسوس
espionage	*jaasusi*	جاسوسی
society	*jaame'eh*	جامعه
open society	*jaame'e-ye baaz*	جامعه باز
mass society	*jaame'e-ye tude'i*	جامعه توده ای
political society	*jaame'e-ye siyaasi*	جامعه سیاسی
political sociology	*jaame'eh shenaasi-ye siyaasi*	جامعه شناسی سیاسی
post-industrial society	*jaame'e-ye faraa san'ati*	جامعه فراصنعتی
civil society	*jaame'e-ye madani*	جامعه مدنی
affluent society	*jaame'e-ye moraffah*	جامعه مرفه
consumer society	*jaame'e-ye masrafi*	جامعه مصرفی
economic determinism	*jabr-e eqtesaadi*	جبر اقتصادی
popular front	*jebhe-ye khalq*	جبهه خلق
united front	*jebhe-ye mottahed*	جبهه متحد
national front	*jebhe-ye melli*	جبهه ملی
separatist	*jodaa'i khaah*	جدائی خواه
separatism	*jodaa'i khaahi*	جدائی خواهی
secularism	*jodaa'i-ye siyaasat az din*	جدائی سیاست از دین
charisma; appeal	*jazabeh*	جذبه
political crime	*jorm-e siyaasi*	جرم سیاسی
dogmatism	*jazm andishi*	جزم اندیشی
political geography	*joqraafiyaa-ye siyaasi*	جغرافیای سیاسی
caucus	*jalase-ye hezbi*	جلسه حزبی
secret session	*jalase-ye makhfi*	جلسه مخفی
canvass	*jam' aavari-ye aaraa*	جمع آوری آراء
collectivism	*jam' garaa'i*	جمع گرائی

republic	*jomhuri*	جمهوری
Islamic republic	*jomhur-ye eslaami*	جمهوری اسلامی
democratic republic	*jomhuri-ye demukraatik*	جمهوری دموکراتیک
people's democratic republic	*jomhuri-ye demukraatik-e khalq*	جمهوری دموکراتیک خلق
banana republic	*jomhuri-ye mowz*	جمهوری موز
republicanism	*jomhuri khaahi*	جمهوریخواهی
left wing	*jenaah-e chap*	جناح چپ
right wing	*jenaah-e raast*	جناح راست
opposition	*jenaah-e mokhaalef*	جناح مخالف
crime against humanity	*jenaayat 'aleyh-e bashariyat*	جنایت علیه بشریت
social movement	*jonbesh-e ejtemaa'i*	جنبش اجتماعی
urban social movement	*jonbesh-e ejtemaa'i-ye shahri*	جنبش اجتماعی شهری
national liberation movement	*jonbesh-e aazaadi bakhsh-e melli*	جنبش آزادیبخش ملی
Green party movement	*jonbesh-e hezb-e sabz-haa*	جنبش حزب سبزها
peasant movement	*jonbesh-e dehqaani*	جنبش دهقانی
labour movement	*jonbesh-e kaargari*	جنبش کارگری
alarmist	*janjaal barangiz*	جنجال برانگیز
war; fight; struggle	*jang*	جنگ
ideological warfare	*jang-e 'aqidati*	جنگ عقیدتی
power struggle	*jang-e qodrat*	جنگ قدرت
residence permit	*javaaz-e eqaamat*	جواز اقامت
economic climate	*javv-e eqtesaadi*	جو اقتصادی
political climate	*javv-e siyaasi*	جو سیاسی
rationing	*jireh bandi*	جیره بندی
Third World	*jahaan-e sevvom*	جهان سوم
cosmopolitanism	*jahaan vatani*	جهان وطنی
globalization	*jahaani saazi*	جهانی سازی
Chartism	*chaartism*	چارتیسم
collective bargaining	*chaaneh zani-ye jam'i*	چانه زنی جمعی
leftism	*chap garaa'i*	چپ گرائی
new left	*chap-e now*	چپ نو
left and right	*chap o raast*	چپ وراست
urban guerrilla	*charik-e shahri*	چریک شهری
polycentrism	*chand markazi*	چند مرکزی
ruler; governor	*haakem*	حاکم
sovereignty	*haakemiyat*	حاکمیت
people's sovereignty	*haakemiyat-e khalq*	حاکمیت خلق
national sovereignty	*haakemiyat-e melli*	حاکمیت ملی

quorum	hadd-e nesaab	حد نصاب
party	hezb	حزب
hizbollah	hezbollaah	حزب الله
catch-all party	hezb-e faraagir	حزب فراگیر
Labour party	hezb-e kaargar	حزب کارگر
Communist party	hezb-e komunist	حزب کمونیست
Conservative party	hezb-e mohaafezeh kaar	حزب محافظه کار
right-wing parties	hezb-haa-ye raastgaraa	حزبهای راست گرا
self-preservation	hefz-e mowjudiyat	حفظ موجودیت
right; rights	haqq	حق
blackmail; bribe	haqq os-sokut	حق السکوت
divine right of kings	haqq-e elaahi-ye paadeshaahi	حق الهی پادشاهی
right of asylum	haqq-e panaahandegi	حق پناهندگی
right of self-determination	haqq-e khod mokhtaari	حق خودمختاری
franchise	haqq-e ra'y	حق رای
civil rights	hoquq-e ejtemaa'i	حقوق اجتماعی
administrative law	hoquq-e edaari	حقوق اداری
constitutional law	hoquq-e asaasi	حقوق اساسی
human rights	hoquq-e bashar	حقوق بشر
political rights	hoquq-e siyaasi	حقوق سیاسی
natural rights	hoquq-e tabi'i	حقوق طبیعی
common law	hoquq-e 'orfi	حقوق عرفی
government; administration; rule	hokumat	حکومت
absolutism	hokumat-e estebdaadi	حکومت استبدادی
Islamic government	hokumat-e eslaami	حکومت اسلامی
majority rule	hokumat-e aksariyat	حکومت اکثریت
representative government	hokumat-e entekhaabi	حکومت انتخابی
crisis government	hokumat-e bohraan	حکومت بحران
self-government	hokumat bar khod	حکومت بر خود
plutocracy	hokumat-e tavaangaraan	حکومت توانگران
arbitrary government	hokumat-e khodsaraaneh	حکومت خودسرانه
home rule	hokumat-e daakheli	حکومت داخلی
government-in-exile	hokumat dar tab'id	حکومت در تبعید
democratic regime	hokumat-e demukraatik	حکومت دمو کراتیک
theocracy	hokumat-e dini	حکومت دینی
presidential government	hokumat-e ra'is-e jomhuri	حکومت رئیس جمهوری
tyranny	hokumat-e setamgar	حکومت ستمگر
meritocracy	hokumat-e shaayestegaan	حکومت شایستگان

rule of law	hokumat-e qaanun	حکومت قانون
legitimate government	hokumat-e qaanuni	حکومت قانونی
cabinet government	hokumat-e kaabine'i	حکومت کابینه ای
commission government	hokumat-e komisyuni	حکومت کمیسیونی
carpetbaggers' government	hokumat-e kiseh goshaadaan	حکومت کیسه گشادان
oligarchy	hokumat-e motanaffezin	حکومت متنفذین
limited government	hokumat-e mahdud	حکومت محدود
local government	hokumat-e mahalli	حکومت محلی
central government	hokumat-e markazi	حکومت مرکزی
constitutional government	hokumat-e mashruteh	حکومت مشروطه
absolutism	hokumat-e motlaqeh	حکومت مطلقه
martial law	hokumat-e nezaami	حکومت نظامی
political patronage	hemaayatgari-ye siyaasi	حمایتگری سیاسی
area; district	howzeh	حوزه
constituency; voting area	howze-ye entekhaabaati	حوزه انتخاباتی
free trade area	howze-ye tejaarat-e aazaad	حوزه تجارت آزاد
safe seat; safe district	howze-ye motma'en	حوزه مطمئن
prestige	heysiyat	حیثیت
circumvention of the law	hile-ye qaanuni	حیله قانونی
curfew	khaamush baash	خاموش باش
dynasty	khaandaan	خاندان
military service	khedmat-e nezaam vazifeh	خدمت نظام وظیفه
sabotage; Luddism	kharaabkaari	خرابکاری
petit bourgeoisie	khordeh burzhvaazi	خرده بورژوازی
violence	khoshunat	خشونت
privatization	khosusi saazi	خصوصی سازی
line of defence	khatt-e defaa'	خط دفاع
policy	khatt-e mashy	خط مشی
caliphate	khelaafat	خلافت
people; masses	khalq	خلق
caliph	khalifeh	خلیفه
autocracy; despotism	khod kaamegi	خودکامگی
autocrat; dictator; despot	khod kaameh	خودکامه
self-sufficiency	khod kafaa'i	خودکفائی
self-determination; autonomy	khod mokhtaari	خودمختاری
junta	khuntaa	خونتا
treason	khiyaanat	خیانت
common good	kheyr-e 'omumi	خیر عمومی

parliamentary tribunal	daadsetaan-e paarlemaani	دادستان پارلمانی
revolutionary tribunal	daadgaah-e enqelaabi	دادگاه انقلابی
court-martial	daadgaah-e nezaami	دادگاه نظامی
gang; band	daar o dasteh	دار و دسته
arbitration	daavari	داوری
secretary	dabir	دبیر
humanitarian intervention	dekhaalat-e ensaandustaaneh	دخالت انساندوستانه
interventionism	dekhaalat-e dowlat dar eqtesaad	دخالت دولت در اقتصاد
government apparatus	dastgaah-e dowlati	دستگاه دولتی
administration	dastgaah-e rahbari	دستگاه رهبری
agenda	dastur-e jalaseh	دستور جلسه
faction; group	dasteh	دسته
faction; cabal	dasteh bandi	دسته بندی
challenge	da'vat be-mobaarezeh	دعوت به مبارزه
national defence	defaa'-e melli	دفاع ملی
doctrine of limited sovereignty	doktrin-e haakemiyat-e mahdud	دکترین حاکمیت محدود
social change	degarguni-ye ejtemaa'i	دگرگونی اجتماعی
catastrophic change	degarguni-ye faaje'eh aamiz	دگرگونی فاجعه آمیز
cultural change	degarguni-ye farhangi	دگرگونی فرهنگی
dogma	dogm	دگم
dogmatism	dogmaatism	دگماتیسم
democrat	demukraat	دموکرات
democratic	demukraatik	دموکراتیک
democratisation	demukraatik kardan	دموکراتیک کردن
democracy	demukraasi	دموکراسی
social democracy	demukraasi-ye ejtemaa'i	دموکراسی اجتماعی
directed democracy	demukraasi-ye ershaadi	دموکراسی ارشادی
indirect democracy	demukraasi-ye baa vaaseteh	دموکراسی با واسطه
bourgeois democracy	demukraasi-ye burzhvaa'i	دموکراسی بورژوائی
people's democracy	demukraasi-ye khalq	دموکراسی خلق
socialist democracy	demukraasi-ye susyaalisti	دموکراسی سوسیالیستی
representative democracy	demukraasi-ye qeyr-e mostaqim	دموکراسی غیر مستقیم
liberal democracy	demukraasi-ye liberaal	دموکراسی لیبرال
direct democracy	demukraasi-ye mostaqim	دموکراسی مستقیم
Christian democracy	demukraasi-ye masihi	دموکراسی مسیحی
two-party (adj.)	dow hezbi	دوحزبی
vicious circle	dowr-e baatel	دور باطل
reign	dowraan-e paadeshaahi	دوران پادشاهی

369

term (of office); period	*dowreh*	دوره
government; state	*dowlat*	دولت
police state	*dowlat-e polisi*	دولت پلیسی
social-service state	*dowlat-e khedmatgozaar-e jaame'eh*	دولت خدمتگزار جامعه
welfare state	*dowlat-e refaah-e 'omumi*	دولت رفاه عمومی
etatism	*dowlat saalaari*	دولت سالاری
corporate state	*dowlat-e senfi*	دولت صنفی
secular state	*dowlat-e qeyr-e dini*	دولت غیر دینی
etatism	*dowlat mehvari*	دولت محوری
sovereign state	*dowlat-e mostaqel*	دولت مستقل
provisional government	*dowlat-e movaqqat*	دولت موقت
city-state	*dowlatshahr*	دولتشهر
diplomat	*diplomaat*	دیپلمات
diplomacy	*diplomaasi*	دیپلماسی
people's diplomacy	*diplomaasi-ye khalq*	دیپلماسی خلق
Machiavellian diplomacy	*diplomaasi-ye maakyaaveli*	دیپلماسی ماکیاولی
stereotype	*did-e qaalebi*	دید قالبی
dictator	*diktaatur*	دیکتاتور
dictatorship	*diktaaturi*	دیکتاتوری
constitutional dictatorship	*diktaaturi-ye qaanuni*	دیکتاتوری قانونی
bureaucracy	*divaan saalaari*	دیوان سالاری
bureaucratisation	*divaani shodan*	دیوانی شدن
radical	*raadikaal*	رادیکال
rightist	*raast garaa*	راست گرا
new right	*raast-e now*	راست نو
vote	*ra'y*	رای
vote of confidence	*ra'y-e e'temaad*	رای اعتماد
voters; the electorate	*ra'y dahandegaan*	رای دهندگان
vote counting	*ra'y shomaari*	رای شماری
vote of no confidence	*ra'y-e 'adam-e e'temaad*	رای عدم اعتماد
ballot	*ra'y giri*	رای گیری
second ballot	*ra'y giri-ye dovvom*	رای گیری دوم
advisory opinion	*ra'y-e mashverati*	رای مشورتی
veto	*ra'y-e manfi*	رای منفی (وتو)
councillor	*raayzan*	رایزن
reich	*raaysh*	رایش
regime	*rezhim*	رژیم
puppet regime	*rezhim-e dast neshaandeh*	رژیم دست نشانده

authoritarian regime	rezhim-e solteh talab	رژیم سلطه طلب
political regime	rezhim-e siyaasi	رژیم سیاسی
puppet regime; puppet government	rezhim-e 'arusaki	رژیم عروسکی
fascist regime	rezhim-e faashisti	رژیم فاشیستی
political scandal	rosvaa'i-e siyaasi	رسوائی سیاسی
economic growth	roshd-e eqtesaadi	رشد اقتصادی
growth of citizenship	roshd-e shahrvandi	رشد شهروندی
consent	rezaayat	رضایت
comradeship	refaaqat	رفاقت
political behaviour	raftaar-e siyaasi	رفتار سیاسی
positive discrimination	raf'-e tab'iz	رفع تبعیض
comrades	rofaqaa	رفقا
rivalry	reqaabat	رقابت
economic depression	rokud-e eqtesaadi	رکود اقتصادی
international relations	ravaabet-e beyn ol-mellali	روابط بین المللی
public relations	ravaabet-e 'omumi	روابط عمومی
collective psychology	ravaanshenaasi-ye jam'i	روانشناسی جمعی
superstructure	rubanaa	روبنا
zeitgeist	ruh-e zamaan	روح زمان
anti-clericalism	ruhaaniyat setizi	روحانیت ستیزی
method	ravesh	روش
intelligentsia	rowshanfekraan	روشنفکران
enlightenment	rowshangari	روشنگری
confrontation	ruyaaru'i	رویارونی
the American dream	rowyaa-ye aamrikaa'i	رویای آمریکائی
president	ra'is-e jomhur	رئیس جمهور
head of state	ra'is-e dowlat	رئیس دولت
head of state	ra'is-e keshvar	رئیس کشور
speaker (in parliament)	ra'is-e majles	رئیس مجلس
hypocrisy	riyaakaari	ریاکاری
leader	rahbar	رهبر
charismatic leader	rahbar-e baa jazabeh	رهبر با جذبه
opinion leader	rahbar-e 'aqidati	رهبر عقیدتی
leadership	rahbari	رهبری
collective leadership	rahbari-ye jam'i	رهبری جمعی
political prisoner	zendaani-ye siyaasi	زندانی سیاسی
withering away of the state	zevaal-e dowlat	زوال دولت
infrastructure; substructure	zirbanaa	زیربنا

base and superstructure	zirbanaa va rubanaa	زیربنا و روبنا
environmentalism	zist mohit garaa'i	زیست محیط گرائی
structure	saakhtaar	ساختار
economic structure	saakhtaar-e eqtesaadi	ساختار اقتصادی
compromise; conciliation; adaptation	saazesh	سازش
organization; organ	saazmaan	سازمان
intelligence service	saazmaan-e ettelaa'aat	سازمان اطلاعات
disorganization	saazmaan shekani	سازمان شکنی
non-governmental organization	saazmaan-e qeyr-e dowlati	سازمان غیر دولتی
United Nations organization	saazmaan-e mellal	سازمان ملل متحد
adhocracy	saazmaan-e vizhe-ye movaqqat	سازمان ویژه موقت
front organizations	saazmaan-haa-ye zaahersaaz	سازمانهای ظاهرساز
samizdat	saamizdaat	سامیزدات
censorship	saansur	سانسور
censor	saansurchi	سانسورچی
scapegoat	separ-e balaa	سپربلا
census	sarshomaari	سرشماری
repression; oppression	sarkubgari	سرکوبگری
capitalism	sarmaayeh daari	سرمایه داری
advanced capitalism	sarmaayeh daari-ye pishrafteh	سرمایه داری پیشرفته
state capitalism	sarmaayeh daari-ye dowlati	سرمایه داری دولتی
czarism	sezaarism	سزاریسم
embassy	sefaarat	سفارت
quietism	sokut garaa'i	سکوت گرائی
denationalisation	salb-e taabe'iyat	سلب تابعیت
hierarchy	selsele-ye maraateb	سلسله مراتب
sultan; emperor	soltaan	سلطان
sultanate	soltaan neshin	سلطان نشین
monarchy	saltanat	سلطنت
elective monarchy	saltanat-e entekhaabi	سلطنت انتخابی
monarchist	saltanat talab	سلطنت طلب
legitimist	saltanat talab-e haqaani	سلطنت طلب حقانی
royalism	saltanat talabi	سلطنت طلبی
limited monarchy	saltanat-e mahdud	سلطنت محدود
constitutional monarchy	saltanat-e mashruteh	سلطنت مشروطه
hereditary monarchy	saltanat-e mowrusi	سلطنت موروثی
dominance; hegemony	solteh	سلطه
document	sanad	سند

syndicate	sandikaa	سندیکا
syndicalism	sandikaalism	سندیکالیسم
revolutionary syndicalism	sandikaalism-e enqelaabi	سندیکالیسم انقلابی
anarcho-syndicalism	sandikaalism-e aanaarshisti	سندیکالیسم آنارشیستی
barricade	sangarbandi-ye khiyaabaani	سنگربندی خیابانی
abuse of right	su estefaadeh az haqq	سوء استفاده از حق
question	so'aal	سوال
socialist	susyaalist	سوسیالیست
socialism	susyaalism	سوسیالیسم
market socialism	susyaalism-e baazaari	سوسیالیسم بازاری
developed socialism	susyaalism-e pishrafteh	سوسیالیسم پیشرفته
utopian socialism	susyaalism-e takhayyoli	سوسیالیسم تخیلی
evolutionary socialism	susyaalism-e takaamoli	سوسیالیسم تکاملی
creeping socialism	susyaalism-e khazandeh	سوسیالیسم خزنده
command socialism	susyaalism-e dasturi	سوسیالیسم دستوری
democratic socialism	susyaalism-e demukraatik	سوسیالیسم دموکراتیک
state socialism	susyaalism-e dowlati	سوسیالیسم دولتی
competitive socialism	susyaalism-e reqaabati	سوسیالیسم رقابتی
green socialism	susyaalism-e sabz	سوسیالیسم سبز
guild socialism	susyaalism-e senfi	سوسیالیسم صنفی
Marxian socialism	susyaalism-e maarksi	سوسیالیسم مارکسی
Christian socialism	susyaalism-e masihi	سوسیالیسم مسیحی
soviet	suvyet	سرویت
politics; policy	siyaasat	سیاست
linkage politics	siyaasat-e ertebaat	سیاست ارتباط
Islamic politics; Islamism	siyaasat-e eslaami	سیاست اسلامی
neutralism	siyaasat-e bitarafi	سیاست بیطرفی
criminal policy	siyaasat-e jenaa'i	سیاست جنائی
'big stick' policy	siyaasat-e chomaaq-e bozorg	سیاست چماق بزرگ
foreign policy	siyaasat-e khaareji	سیاست خارجی
domestic policy	siyaasat-e daakheli	سیاست داخلی
open door policy	siyaasat-e dar-haa-ye baaz	سیاست درهای باز
gunboat diplomacy	siyaasat-e zur	سیاست زور
policy-maker	siyaasat saaz	سیاست ساز
ostpolitik	siyaasat-e geraayesh be sharq	سیاست گرایش به شرق
dynamic policy	siyaasat-e motaharrek	سیاست متحرک
realpolitik	siyaasat-e vaaqe'i	سیاست واقعی
politician	siyaasatmadaar	سیاستمدار

political	siyaasi	سیاسی
politicization	siyaasi shodan	سیاسی شدن
rumour	shaaye'eh	شایعه
rumourmonger	shaaye'eh pardaaz	شایعه پرداز
emirate	shaahzaadeh neshin	شاهزاده نشین
authoritarian personality	shakhsiyat-e estebdaad talab	شخصیت استبدادطلب
bureaucratic personality	shakhsiyat-e moqarraraati	شخصیت مقرراتی
orientalism	sharq shenaasi	شرق شناسی
brainwashing	shostoshu-ye maqzi	شستشوی مغزی
slogan	sho'aar	شعار
defeatism	shekast paziri	شکست پذیری
torture	shekanjeh	شکنجه
torturer	shekanjeh gar	شکنجه گر
recognition of government	shenaasaa'i-ye hokumat	شناسائی حکومت
council; soviet	shuraa	شورا
council of state	shuraa-ye dowlati	شورای دولتی
town council	shuraa-ye shahr	شورای شهر
insurrection; insurgency	shuresh	شورش
cultural shock	shuk-e farhangi	شوک فرهنگی
chauvinism	shuvinism	شوونیسم
sheikhdom	sheykh neshin	شیخ نشین
Asiatic mode of production	shive-ye towlid-e aasyaa'i	شیوه تولید آسیائی
town council	shahr daari	شهرداری
citizen	shahrvand	شهروند
citizenship	shahrvandi	شهروندی
active citizenship	shahrvandi-ye fa'aal	شهروندی فعال
vested interests	saahebaan-e manaafe'	صاحبان منافع
chancellor	sadr-e a'zam	صدر اعظم
export of revolution	sodur-e enqelaab	صدور انقلاب
pacifism	solh talabi	صلح طلبی
guild	senf	صنف
corporatism	senf garaa'i	صنف گرائی
socio-economic formation	suratbandi-ye ejtemaa'i-eqtesaadi	صورتبندی اجتماعی اقتصادی
Zionist	sahyunist	صهیونیست
Zionism	sahyunism	صهیونیسم
anti-colonialism	zedd-e este'maar	ضد استعمار
counter-intelligence	zedd-e ettelaa'aat	ضد اطلاعات
counter-revolution	zedd-e enqelaab	ضد انقلاب

374

counter-revolutionary	zedd-e enqelaabi	ضد انقلابی
counter-propaganda	zedd-e tabliq	ضد تبلیغ
deflation	zedd-e tavarrom	ضد تورم
counter-espionage	zedd-e jaasusi	ضد جاسوسی
counter-insurgency	zedd-e shuresh	ضد شورش
counter-culture	zedd-e farhang	ضد فرهنگ
social class	tabaqe-ye ejtemaa'i	طبقه اجتماعی
upper class	tabaqe-ye baalaa	طبقه بالا
ruling class	tabaqe-ye haakem	طبقه حاکم
service class	tabaqe-ye khadamaati	طبقه خدماتی
cognitariat	tabaqe-ye daaneshvar	طبقه دانشور
working class	tabaqe-ye kaargar	طبقه کارگر
middle class	tabaqe-ye motavasset	طبقه متوسط
new middle class	tabaqe-ye motavasset-e jadid	طبقه متوسط جدید
rebellion	toqyaan	طغیان
Chalfont syndrome	'aareze-ye chaalfunt	عارضه چالفونت
justice	'edaalat	عدالت
decentralization	'adam-e tamarkoz	عدم تمرکز
federalism	'adam-e tamarkoz-e siyaasi	عدم تمرکز سیاسی
member	'ozv	عضو
amnesty	'afv	عفو
dogma	'aqide-ye jazmi	عقیده جزمی
determinism	'ellat garaa'i	علت گرائی
political science	'elm-e siyaasat	علم سیاست
fait accompli	'amal-e anjaam shodeh	عمل انجام شده
activism; pragmatism	'amal garaa'i	عمل گرایی
direct action	'amal-e mostaqim	عمل مستقیم
actions; operations	'amaliyaat	عملیات
rabble	'avaam on-naas	عوام الناس
demagogue	'avaam farib	عوام فریب
demagogy	'avaam faribi	عوام فریبی
populism	'avaam garaa'i	عوام گرائی
factors of production	'avaamel-e towlid	عوامل تولید
westernisation	qarbi shodan	غربی شدن
usurpation of power	qasb-e qodrat	غصب قدرت
absenteeism	qeybat az kaar	غیبت از کار
secular	qeyr-e dini	غیر دینی
secularisation	qeyr-e dini kardan	غیر دینی کردن

fascism	faashism	فاشیسم
neo-fascism	faashism-e jadid	فاشیسم جدید
clerico-fascism	faashism-e kelisaa'i	فاشیسم کلیسائی
falange	faalaanzh	فالانژ
falangism	faalaanzhism	فالانژیسم
utilitarianism	faayedeh garaa'i	فایده گرائی
intrigue; sedition	fetneh angizi	فتنه انگیزی
fatwa	fatvaa	فتوا
federation	federaasyun	فدراسیون
federal	federaal	فدرال
federalism	federaalism	فدرالیسم
co-operative federalism	federaalism-e ta'aavoni	فدرالیسم تعاونی
recall (of diplomatic staff)	faraakhaani	فراخوانی
brain drain	faraar-e maqz-haa	فرار مغزها
freemasonry	faraamaasunri	فراماسونری
process	faraayand	فرایند
opportunism	forsat talabi	فرصت طلبی
sect	ferqeh	فرقه
governor-general	farmaandar-e kol	فرماندار کل
arms sale	forush-e aslaheh	فروش اسلحه
mob; the 'great unwashed'	forumaayegaan	فرومایگان
culture	farhang	فرهنگ
political culture	farhang-e siyaasi	فرهنگ سیاسی
political corruption	fesaad-e siyaasi	فساد سیاسی
group pressure	feshaar-e goruhi	فشار گروهی
pauperisation	faqir shodan-e zahmatkeshaan	فقیر شدن زحمتکشان
political thought	fekr-e siyaasi	فکر سیاسی
technocrat	fann saalaar	فن سالار
technocracy	fann saalaari	فن سالاری
feudalism	fe'udaalism	فئودالیسم
electoral list	fehrest-e naamzad-haa	فهرست نامزدها
drug smuggling	qaachaaq-e mavaad-e mokhadder	قاچاق مواد مخدر
smuggler	qaachaaqchi	قاچاقچی
law	qaanun	قانون
constitution	qaanun-e asaasi	قانون اساسی
written constitution	qaanun-e asaasi-ye modavvan	قانون اساسی مدون
divine law	qaanun-e elaahi	قانون الهی
electoral law	qaanun-e entekhaabaat	قانون انتخابات

deputy	qaa'em maqaam	قائم مقام
power	qodrat	قدرت
productivity	qodrat-e towlid	قدرت تولید
bargaining power	qodrat-e chaaneh zani	قدرت چانه زنی
state power	qodrat-e dowlati	قدرت دولتی
political power	qodrat-e siyaasi	قدرت سیاسی
arrangement	qaraar-e tanzimi	قرار تنظیمی
accord; agreement	qaraar-e mo'aafeqat	قرار موافقت
polarization	qotb bandi	قطب بندی
resolution (e.g. UN resolution)	qat'naameh	قطعنامه
heartland	qalb-e zamin	قلب زمین
pogrom	qowm koshi	قوم کشی
judicial power	qovve-ye qazaa'i	قوه قضائی
executive power	qovve-ye mojriyeh	قوه مجریه
legislative power	qovve-ye moqanneneh	قوه مقننه
uprising; revolt	qiyaam	قیام
armed uprising	qiyaam-e mosallahaaneh	قیام مسلحانه
cabinet	kaabineh	کابینه
shadow cabinet	kaabine-ye saayeh	کابینه سایه
the White House	kaakh-e sefid	کاخ سفید
cadre	kaadr	کادر
political cadre	kaadr-e siyaasi	کادر سیاسی
work; labour	kaar	کار
work-to-rule	kaar-e motaabeq-e moqarraraat	کار مطابق مقررات
cartel	kaartel	کارتل
charge d'affaires	kaardaar	کاردار
civil servant	kaarmand-e dowlat	کارمند دولت
Castroism	kaastruism	کاستروایسم
bureaucratism; red tape	kaaqaz baazi	کاغذبازی
candidate	kaandidaa	کاندیدا
dark horse	kaandidaa-ye naashenaas	کاندیدای ناشناس
political pluralism	kesrat garaa'i-ye siyaasi	کثرت گرائی سیاسی
praxis	kerdaar-e enqelaabi	کردار انقلابی
naturalization	kasb-e taabe'iyat	کسب تابعیت
country; state; nation	keshvar	کشور
protected state; protectorate	keshvar-e taht ol-hemaayeh	کشور تحت الحمایه
federal state	keshvar-e federaal	کشور فدرال
micropowers	keshvar-haa-ye zarre'i	کشور های ذره ای

civics; administration	keshvardaari	کشورداری
non-aligned countries	keshvar-haa-ye qeyr-e mota'ahhed	کشورهای غیر متعهد
established church	kelisaa-ye rasmi	کلیسای رسمی
lack; deficit	kambud	کمبود
commune	komun	کمون
communist	komunist	کمونیست
communism	komunism	کمونیسم
Euro-communism	komunism-e orupaa'i	کمونیسم اروپائی
anarcho-communism	komunism-e aanaarshisti	کمونیسم آنارشیستی
garrison communism	komunism-e paadegaani	کمونیسم پادگانی
anti-communism	komunism setizi	کمونیسم ستیزی
committee	komiteh	کمیته
central committee	komite-ye markazi	کمیته مرکزی
commissar	komisar	کمیسر
commission	komisyun	کمیسیون
parliament commission	komisyun-e majles	کمیسیون مجلس
abdication	kenaareh giri	کناره گیری
social control	kontrol-e ejtemaa'i	کنترل اجتماعی
thought control	kontrol-e afkaar	کنترل افکار
crisis management	kontrol-e bohraan	کنترل بحران
civilian control of the military	kontrol-e qeyr-e nezaami-ye artesh	کنترل غیر نظامی ارتش
consortium	konsorsiyum	کنسرسیوم
concordat	konkurdaa	کنکوردا
congress	kongreh	کنگره
coup d'etat	kudetaa	کودتا
Comintern	kumintern	کومینترن
personality cult	kish-e shakhsiyat	کیش شخصیت
ghetto	getow	گتو
meeting	gerdehamaa'i	گردهمائی
hostage	gerowgaan	گروگان
hostage taking	gerowgaan giri	گروگانگیری
group	goruh	گروه
interest group	goruh-e zinaf'	گروه ذینفع
pressure group	goruh-e feshaar	گروه فشار
brains trust	goruh-e kaarshenaas	گروه کارشناس
ethnic group; racial group	goruh-e nezhaadi	گروه نژادی
discussion; discourse	goftaar	گفتار
discussion; debate	goftogu	گفتگو

glasnost	gelaasnust	گلاسنوست
customs	gomrok	گمرک
nest of spies; den of spies	laane-ye jaasusi	لانه جاسوسی
bill (i.e. of law)	laayeheh	لایحه
mudslinging	lajan paraakani	لجن پراکنی
Leninism	leninism	لنینیسم
lumpen proletariat	lumpen pruletaariyaa	لومپن پرولتاریا
liberal	liberaal	لیبرال
liberalism	liberaalism	لیبرالیسم
economic liberalism	liberaalism-e eqtesaadi	لیبرالیسم اقتصادی
black list	list-e siyaah	لیست سیاه
adventurism	maajeraaju'i	ماجراجویی
matriarchy	maadar saalaari	مادرسالاری
materialism	maaddeh garaa'i	ماده گرائی
dialectical materialism	maaddeh garaa'i-e ye diyaalektik	ماده گرائی دیالکتیکی
Marxism	maarksism	مارکسیسم
neo-Marxism	maarksism-e jadid	مارکسیسم جدید
dogmatic Marxism	maarksism-e jazmi	مارکسیسم جزمی
creative Marxism	maarksism-e khallaaq	مارکسیسم خلاق
Marxism-Leninism	maarksism-leninism	مارکسیسم لنینیسم
Mafia	maafiyaa	مافیا
Machiavellianism	maakiyaavelism	ماکیاولیسم
private property	maalekiyat-e khosusi	مالکیت خصوصی
sleeper (agent)	ma'mur-e khaabideh	مامور خوابیده
electoral manoeuvres	maanuvr-haa-ye entekhaabaati	مانورهای انتخاباتی
Maoism	maa'uism	مائوایسم
discussion; debate	mobaaheseh	مباحثه
struggle; campaign	mobaarezeh	مبارزه
election campaign	mobaareze-ye entekhaabaati	مبارزه انتخاباتی
class struggle	mobaareze-ye tabaqaati	مبارزه طبقاتی
progressive	motaraqqi	مترقی
military-industrial complex	mojtama'-e nezaami-san'ati	مجتمع نظامی صنعتی
assembly; parliament	majles	مجلس
upper house	majles-e faraadast	مجلس فرادست
people's assembly	majles-e khalq	مجلس خلق
senate assembly	majles-e senaa	مجلس سنا
consultative assembly	majles-e shuraa	مجلس شورا
lower house	majles-e avaam	مجلس عوام

national assembly	majles-e melli	مجلس ملی
constituent assembly	majles-e mo'assesaan	مجلس موسسان
representative assembly	majles-e namaayandegaan	مجلس نمایندگان
general assembly	majma'-e 'omumi	مجمع عمومی
self-protection	mohaafezat az khod	محافظت از خود
conservative	mohaafezeh kaar	محافظه کار
conservatism	mohaafezeh kaari	محافظه کاری
show trial	mohaakeme-ye namaayeshi	محاکمه نمایشی
parochialism	mahdudiyat-e fekri	محدودیت فکری
deprived	mahrum	محروم
gross domestic product	mahsul-e naakhaales-e daakheli	محصول ناخالص داخلی
dissident	mokhaalef	مخالف
opposition	mokhaalefat	مخالفت
think tank	makhzan-e fekri	مخزن فکری
secrecy; concealment	makhfi kaari	مخفی کاری
deschooling	madraseh zadaa'i	مدرسه زدائی
credentialism	madrak garaa'i	مدرک گرائی
authoritarian management	modiriyat-e eqtedaar talab	مدیریت اقتدارطلب
talks; negotiations	mozaakeraat	مذاکرات
negotiation	mozaakereh	مذاکره
people; the masses	mardom	مردم
centrism	markaz garaa'i	مرکزگرائی
centralism	markaziyat	مرکزیت
mercenary	mozdur	مزدور
privilege	maziyat-e vizheh	مزیت ویژه
arms race	mosaabeqe-e taslihaati	مسابقه تسلیحاتی
egalitarianism	mosaavaat talabi	مساوات طلبی
ministerial responsibility	mas'uliyat-e vezaarati	مسئولیت وزارتی
accountability	mas'uliyat-e paasokh gu'i	مسئولیت پاسخگوئی
political participation	moshaarekat-e siyaasi	مشارکت سیاسی
constitutionalism	mashruteh khaahi	مشروطه خواهی
reason of state	maslahat-e dowlat	مصلحت دولت
parliamentary immunity	masuniyat-e paarlemaani	مصونیت پارلمانی
judicial immunity	masuniyat-e qazaa'i	مصونیت قضائی
conscientious objector	mo'tarez-e akhlaaqi	معترض اخلاقی
agent provocateur	mofsedeh ju	مفسده جو
non-violent resistance	moqaavemat-e bi khoshunat	مقاومت بی خشونت
active resistance	moqaavemat-e fa'aal	مقاومت فعال

passive resistance	moqaavemat-e manfi	مقاومت منفی
curfew	moqarraraat-e man'-e raft o aamad	مقررات منع رفت و آمد
doctrine; school of thought	maktab	مکتب
monetarism	maktab-e esaalat-e pul	مکتب اصالت پول
cynicism	maktab-e badbini	مکتب بدبینی
political school	maktab-e siyaasi	مکتب سیاسی
nation	mellat	ملت
queen	malakeh	ملکه
national	melli	ملی
nationalization	melli saazi	ملی سازی
nationalism	melli garaa'i	ملی گرائی
nationality	melliyat	ملیت
class interests	manaafe'-e tabaqaati	منافع طبقاتی
national interests	manaafe'-e melli	منافع ملی
charter	manshur	منشور
region; area	mantaqeh	منطقه
regionalism	mantaqeh garaa'i	منطقه گرائی
sphere of influence	mantaqe-ye nofuz	منطقه نفوذ
picketing	man'-e e'tesaab shekani	منع اعتصاب شکنی
blockade; curfew	man'-e 'obur o morur	منع عبور و مرور
political balance	movaazene-ye siyaasi	موازنه سیاسی
agreement; convention	moaafeqat naameh	موافقتنامه
mediation	miyaanjigari	میانجیگری
moderate	miyaane row	میانه رو
round table	miz-e gerd	میز گرد
immigrant	mohaajer	مهاجر
migration; immigration	mohaajerat	مهاجرت
social unrest	naa aaraami-ye ejtemaa'i	نا آرامی اجتماعی
dissident	naaraazi	ناراضی
Nazism	naazism	نازیسم
nationalism	naasyunaalism	ناسیونالیسم
civil disobedience	naafarmaani-ye madani	نافرمانی مدنی
candidate	naamzad	نامزد
nomination	naamzad saazi	نامزدسازی
regent	naayeb os-saltaneh	نایب السلطنه
elite	nokhbegaan	نخبگان
power elite	nokhbegaan-e qodrat	نخبگان قدرت
elitism	nokhbeh garaa'i	نخبه گرائی

prime minister	nakhost vazir	نخست وزیر
racism	nezhaad parasti	نژادپرستی
genocide	nasl koshi	نسل کشی
speech	notq	نطق
system	nezaam	نظام
social system	nezaam-e ejtemaa'i	نظام اجتماعی
agrarian system	nezaam-e arzi	نظام ارضی
economic system	nezaam-e eqtesaadi	نظام اقتصادی
electoral system	nezaam-e entekhaabaati	نظام انتخاباتی
admass	nezaam-e aagahi-haa-ye tejaarati	نظام آگهی های تجارتی
multiparty system	nezaam-e chand hezbi	نظام چند حزبی
bipartism	nezaam-e dow hezbi	نظام دوحزبی
bicameralism	nezaam-e dow majlesi	نظام دومجلسی
corporate welfarism	nezaam-e refaah-e san'ati	نظام رفاه صنعتی
political system	nezaam-e siyaasi	نظام سیاسی
caesarism	nezaam-e qeysari	نظام قیصری
estate system	nezaam-e maraateb-e ejtemaa'i	نظام مراتب اجتماعی
colonial system	nezaam-e mosta'maraati	نظام مستعمراتی
new world order	nezaam-e novin-e jahaani	نظام نوین جهانی
single-party system	nezaam-e yek hezbi	نظام یک حزبی
poll	nazar khaahi	نظرخواهی
public opinion poll	nazar sanji-e 'omumi	نظرسنجی عمومی
game theory	nazariye-ye baazi-haa	نظریه بازی ها
end of ideology theory	nazariye-ye paayaan-e ide'uluzhi	نظریه پایان ایدئولوژی
fault theory	nazariye-ye taqsir	نظریه تقصیر
conspiracy theory	nazariye-ye towte'eh	نظریه توطئه
political theory	nazariye-ye siyaasi	نظریه سیاسی
self-interest	naf'-e shakhsi	نفع شخصی
influence	nofuz	نفوذ
breach of the peace	naqz-e solh	نقض صلح
proportional representation	namaayandegi-ye tanaasobi	نمایندگی تناسبی
representative	namaayandeh	نماینده
member of parliament	namaayande-ye majles	نماینده مجلس
neo-colonialism	now este'maar	نو استعمار
paramilitary forces	niru-ye shebh-e nezaami	نیروی شبه نظامی
political forces	niru-haa-ye siyaasi	نیروهای سیاسی
institution	nahaad	نهاد
governmental institutions	nahaad-haa-ye hokumati	نهادهای حکومتی

movement	nehzat	نهضت
communitarianism	nehzat-e jaame'eh garaa	نهضت جامعه گرا
enclosure movement	nehzat-e hesaar keshi	نهضت حصار کشی
resistance movement	nehzat-e moqaavemat	نهضت مقاومت
fact; reality	vaaqe'iyat	واقعیت
veto	vetu	وتو
collective conscience	vojdaan-e jam'i	وجدان جمعی
political unity	vahdat-e siyaasi	وحدت سیاسی
the 'China card'	varaq-e chin	ورق چین
ministry of foreign affairs	vezaarat-e omur-e khaarejeh	وزارت امور خارجه
ministry of the interior; home office	vezaarat-e keshvar	وزارت کشور
ministry	vezaarat khaaneh	وزارتخانه
minister	vazir	وزیر
foreign minister	vazir-e omur-e khaarejeh	وزیر امور خارجه
minister of defence	vazir-e defaa'	وزیر دفاع
minister without portfolio	vazir-e moshaaver	وزیر مشاور
state of emergency	vaz'-e ezteraari	وضع اضطراری
status quo	vaz'-e mowjud	وضع موجود
loyalist	vafaadaar be-hokumat-e vaqt	وفادار به حکومت وقت
crown prince	vali'ahd	ولیعهد
solidarity	hambastegi	همبستگی
opposite number	hamtaa	همتا
climbing aboard the bandwagon	hamrang-e jamaa'at shodan	همرنگ جماعت شدن
conformism	hamrangi baa jamaa'at	همرنگی با جماعت
assimiliation	hamsaan gardi	همسان گردی
co-operation	hamkaari	همکاری
regional integration	hamgaraa'i-ye mantaqe'i	همگرائی منطقه ای
referendum; plebiscite	hameh porsi	همه پرسی
air hijacking	havaapeymaa robaa'i	هواپیماربائی
supporter; sympathiser	havaadaar	هوادار
government supporter	havaadaar-e hokumat	هوادار حکومت
electoral college	hey'at-e entekhaab konandegaan	هیئت انتخاب کنندگان
cabinet	hey'at-e dowlat	هیئت دولت
aide memoire; note	yaad daasht	یاد داشت
anti-semitism	yahud setizi	یهود ستیزی

to join a (political) party عضو حزب شدن   to take part in elections در انتخابات شرکت کردن

my father is a member of the Labour Party پدر من عضو حزب کارگر است   to rule حکومت کردن

to reform اصلاح کردن   to protest اعتراض کردن   to go on strike اعتصاب کردن   to declare اعلام کردن

to indoctrinate القای عقیده کردن   to revolt; to stage a revolution انقلاب کردن   to stage a coup d'etat کودتا کردن

to interrogate بازجونی کردن   to debate; to discuss بحث کردن   to bluff بلوف زدن   to purge پاکسازی کردن

to discriminate (racially or otherwise) تبعیض قائل شدن   to provoke; to agitate; to incite; to stir up تحریک کردن

to form a government تشکیل دولت دادن   نخست وزیر کابینه را ترمیم کرد the prime-minister reshuffled the cabinet

to assassinate ترور کردن   to decide تصمیم گرفتن   to approve; to ratify; to sanction تصویب کردن

to plot; to conspire توطئه کردن   آنها توطئه کردند که شاه را سرنگون کنند they plotted to overthrow the king

to spy جاسوسی کردن   to be opposed مخالف بودن   من مخالف سیاست آنها هستم I am opposed to their policy

to oppose مخالفت کردن   to support حمایت کردن   to commit treason خیانت کردن   to consent رضایت دادن

to censor سانسور کردن   to torture شکنجه دادن   to imprison زندانی کردن   to set free; to liberate آزاد کردن

to legislate قانونگزاری کردن   to attain power قدرت به دست آوردن   to abdicate کناره گیری کردن

to resign استعفاء دادن   to privatize خصوصی کردن   to judge; to arbitrate داوری کردن   to vote رای دادن

to veto رای منفی دادن   to ballot رای گیری کردن   به او رای عدم اعتماد دادند they gave him a vote of no confidence

to lead رهبری کردن   او قبلاً حزب محافظه کار را رهبری می کرد he used to lead the Conservative Party

to quell; to repress; to put down سرکوب کردن   ارتش شورشیان را سرکوب کرد the army quelled the rioters

to reign سلطنت کردن   شاه اسماعیل دوم فقط یک سال سلطنت کرد Shah Ismail II reigned for one year only

to spread rumours شایعه پراکندن   to brainwash شستشوی مغزی دادن   to dupe (the people) عوام فریبی کردن

to produce a fatwa or ruling فتوا دادن   to have talks; to discuss گفتگو کردن   to debate; to discuss مباحثه کردن

to struggle; to fight; to campaign مبارزه کردن   to put on trial محاکمه کردن   to participate مشارکت کردن

to resist مقاومت کردن   to nationalize ملی کردن   دولت راه آهن را ملی کرد the government nationalised the railway

to give a speech; to talk نطق کردن   نخست وزیر الان می خواهد نطق کند the Prime Minister is about to give a speech

Psychology

روانشناسی

psychological test	aazmun-e ravaani	آزمون روانی
psychopathology	aasibshenaasi-ye ravaani	آسیب شناسی روان
anxiety	aasimegi	آسیمگی
mental confusion	aashoftegi-ye zehni	آشفتگی ذهنی
neuritis	aamaas-e 'asab	آماس عصب
guilt; sense of guilt	ehsaas-e gonaah	احساس گناه
anxiety	ezteraab	اضطراب
depression	afsordegi	افسردگی
depression	afsordeh ravaani	افسرده روانی
cyclical depression	afsordeh ravaani-ye advaari	افسرده روانی ادواری
manic-depressive	afsordeh-sheydaa	افسرده شیدا
autism	utism	اوتیسم
extroversion	borungaraa'i	برونگرانی
anorexia nervosa	bi eshtehaa'i-ye 'asabi	بی اشتهائی عصبی
apathy	bi 'alaaqegi	بی علاقگی
frigidity	bi meyli-ye jensi	بی میلی جنسی
apathy	bi vaakoneshi	بی واکنشی
alienation	bigaanegi	بیگانگی
psychosomatic illness	bimaari-ye ravaan tani	بیماری روان تنی
psychopathy; mental illness	bimaari-ye ravaani	بیماری روانی
paranoia	paaraanuyaa	پارانویا
fixation	paaybandi	پایبندی
phenomenology	padidaar shenaasi	پدیدار شناسی
mental retardation	pasmaandegi-ye zehni	پسماندگی ذهنی
mentally retarded	pasmaandeh zehn	پسمانده ذهن
phobia	tars-e bimaar guneh	ترس بیمارگونه
body language	tanvaagu'i	تن واگونی
illusion; delusion	tavahhom	توهم
psychological type	tip-e ravaani	تیپ روانی
catatonia	jomud-e khalse'i	جمود خلسه ای
mania	jonun	جنون
hebephrenia	jonun-e javaani	جنون جوانی
hypomania	jonun-e khafif	جنون خفیف
penis envy	hasrat-e bi narrinegi	حسرت بی نرینگی
boredom	khastegi-ye ruhi	خستگی روحی
superiority complex	khod bozorg bini	خود بزرگ بینی

hypochondriac	khod bimaar pendaar	خود بیمار پندار
hypochondriasis	khod bimaar pendaari	خود بیمار پنداری
inferiority complex	khod kuchek bini	خود کوچک بینی
egocentric	khod madaar	خود مدار
egoism	khod madaar engaari	خود مدار انگاری
egocentrism	khod madaari	خود مداری
autism; introversion	khod garaa'i	خودگرائی
exhibitionism	khod namaa'i	خودنمائی
neuralgia	dard-e a'saab	درد اعصاب
introversion	darun garaa'i	درون گرائی
boredom	delzadegi	دلزدگی
psychopathy	ravaan bimaari	روان بیماری
schizophrenia	ravaan paaregi	روان پارگی
schizophrenic	ravaan paareh	روان پاره
psychodynamics	ravaan puyeh shenaasi	روان پویه شناسی
trauma	ravaan tekaan	روان تکان
neurotic	ravaan ranjur	روان رنجور
neurosis	ravaan ranjuri	روان رنجوری
conversion hysteria	ravaan ranjuri-ye tabdili	روان رنجوری تبدیلی
traumatic neurosis	ravaan ranjuri-ye tekaaneshi	روان رنجوری تکانشی
obsessional neurosis	ravaan ranjuri-ye vasvaasi	روان رنجوری وسواسی
psychopath	ravaan ranjeh	روان رنجه
psychopathic	ravaan ranje'i	روان رنجه ای
psychogenic	ravaan zaad	روان زاد
psycholinguistics	ravaan zabaan shenaasi	روان زبان شناسی
developmental psychobiology	ravaan zist shenaasi-ye baalandegi	روان زیست شناسی بالندگی
psychobiological	ravaan zist shenaasik	روان زیست شناسیک
neurotic	ravaan nazhand	روان نژند
neurosis	ravaan nazhandi	روان نژندی
psychosis	ravaan parishi	روانپریشی
manic depressive psychosis	ravaanparishi-ye afsordeh-sheydaa'i	روانپریشی افسرده شیدائی
psychiatrist	ravaanpezeshk	روانپزشک
psychiatry	ravaanpezeshki	روانپزشکی
psychometrics	ravaansanji	روانسنجی
psychologist	ravaanshenaas	روانشناس
psychology	ravaanshenaasi	روانشناسی
body-centred psychology	ravaanshenaasi-ye tangaraa	روانشناسی تن گرا
behavioural psychology	ravaanshenaasi-ye raftaari	روانشناسی رفتاری

individual psychology	ravaanshenaasi-ye fardi	روانشناسی فردی
ego psychology	ravaanshenaasi-ye khod	روانشناسی خود
psychoanalyst	ravaankaav	روانکاو
psychoanalysis	ravaankaavi	روانکاوی
Freudian psychoanalysis	ravaankaavi-ye feruydi	روانکاوی فرویدی
mental; psychological; mad	ravaani	روانی
psychosexual	ravaani-jensi	روانی جنسی
dementia	zevaal-e 'aql-e pishras	زوال عقل پیش رس
frigidity	sard mezaaji	سردمزاجی
mental health	salaamat-e zehni	سلامت ذهنی
mental age	senn-e 'aqli	سن عقلی
psychomotor acceleration	shetaab-e ravaan jonbeshi	شتاب روان جنبشی
elation	showq o sha'f	شوق و شعف
mania	sheydaa'i	شیدائی
trauma	zarbe-ye ruhi	ضربه روحی
psychomotor retardation	'aqab oftaadegi-ye ravaan jonbeshi	عقب افتادگی روان جنبشی
Oedipus complex	'oqde-ye odip	عقده ادیپ
inferiority complex	'oqde-ye heqaarat	عقده حقارت
behavioural science	'elm-e raftaari	علم رفتاری
sexual exhibitionism	'owrat namaa'i	عورت نمائی
amnesia	faraamushi	فراموشی
fugue	faraamushi-ye ravaani	فراموشی روانی
depersonalisation	fardiyat zadaa'i	فردیت زدائی
implosion	forupaashi-ye ravaani	فروپاشی روانی
catatonia	kaataatuni	کاتاتونی
delusion	kazh engaari	کژانگاری
delusions of grandeur	kazh pendaasht-e khod bozorg bini	کژپنداشت خود بزرگ بینی
hypomania	kam divaanegi	کم دیوانگی
disassociation	gosastegi	گسستگی
melancholy	maalikhuliyaa	مالیخولیا
psychological environment	mohit-e ravaani	محیط روانی
ego; "I"	man	من
mental disorder	naabesaamaani-ye zehni	نابسامانی ذهنی
behavioural disorder	naabesaamaani-ye raftaari	نابسامانی رفتاری
psychogenic disorder	naabesaamaani-ye ravaanzaad	نابسامانی روان زاد
psychological disorder	naabesaamaani-ye ravaani	نابسامانی روانی
mentally handicapped	naatavaan zehn	ناتوان ذهن
impotence	naatavaani-ye jensi	ناتوانی جنسی

387

delusion	*naadorost engaari*	نادرست انگاری
mental defect	*naaresaa'i-ye zehni*	نارسانی ذهنی
amnesia	*nesyaan*	نسیان
learning theory	*nazariye-ye aamuzesh*	نظریه آموزش
hallucination	*nehaazesh*	نهازش
fixation	*vaagari*	واگری
obsession	*vasvaas-e fekri*	وسواس فکری
hebephrenia	*hebefreni*	هبفرنی
delusion	*hazyaan*	هذیان
delusions of grandeur	*hazyaan-e shokuh*	هذیان شکوه
phobia; fear	*haraas*	هراس
phobia	*haraas zadegi*	هراس زدگی
phobic	*haraas zadeh*	هراس زده
hysteria	*histeri*	هیستری

immaculate conception	aabestani-ye ma'sumaaneh	آبستنی معصومانه
fire temple	aatashkadeh	آتشکده
Arian	aaryusi	آریوسی
free will	aazaadi-ye eraadeh	آزادی اراده
irenics	aashti ju'i	آشتی جوئی
creationism	aafarinesh baavari	آفرینش باوری
first creation	aafarinesh-e nakhostin	آفرینش نخستین
celibate	aamizesh parhiz	آمیزش پرهیز
celibacy	aamizesh parhizi	آمیزش پرهیزی
Ahura Mazda	aahuraa mazdaa	آهورا مزدا
ayatollah	aayatollaah	آیت الله
rite; ceremony; creed	aayin	آیین
Brahmanism	aayin-e berahmani	آیین برهمنی
Shintoism	aayin-e shintow	آیین شینتو
sacrament; Eucharist	aayin-e 'ashaa-ye rabbaani	آیین عشای ربانی
Episcopalianism	aayin-e kelisaa-ye osqofi	آیین کلیسای اسقفی
Confucianism	aayin-e konfusiyusi	آیین کنفوسیوسی
conversion	aayin gardaani	آیین گردانی
Lamaism	aayin-e laamaa	آیین لاما
Mazdaism	aayin-e mazdaa'i	آیین مزدانی
Mazdakism	aayin-e mazdaki	آیین مزدکی
Mithraism	aayin-e mehr	آیین مهر
eternity	abad	ابد
socio-religious	ejtemaa'i-dini	اجتماعی دینی
dietary laws	ahkaam-e shar'i-ye akl o shorb	احکام شرعی اکل و شرب
(Islamic) call to prayer; adhan	azaan	اذان
God's will	eraade-ye elaahi	اراده الهی
orthodox	ortodoks	ارتدکس
articles of faith	arkaan-e imaan	ارکان ایمان
pre-eternity	azal	ازل
Israelite	esraa'ili	اسرائیلی
bishop	osqof	اسقف
episcopalism	osqof saalaari	اسقف سالاری
episcopacy	osqof neshin	اسقف نشین
Episcopal	osqofi	اسقفی
Islam	eslaam	اسلام

Divine Names	asmaa-e elaahi	اسماء الهی
ashram	ashraam	اشرام
doctrine; principles; fundamentals	osul	اصول
fundamentals of belief; creed	osul-e 'aqaa'ed	اصول عقائد
pogrom	aqalliyat koshi	اقلیت کشی
Biblical theology	elaahiyaat-e ahl-e ketaab	الاهیات اهل کتاب
god; goddess; deity	elaaheh	الاهه
atheism; non-belief	elhaad	الحاد
Allah; God	allaah	الله
divinity	oluhiyat	الوهیت
kenosis	oluhiyat zadaa'i	الوهیت زدائی
divine inspiration	elhaam	الهام
divine	elaahi	الهی
imam; (Muslim) prayer leader	emaam	امام
imamate	emaamat	امامت
New Testament; Gospel	enjil	انجیل
Synoptic Gospels	enjil-haa-ye hamnavaa	انجیل های همنوا
evangelical	enjili	انجیلی
humanism	ensaan baavari	انسان باوری
anthropomorphism	ensaanguneh engaari	انسان گونه انگاری
God	izad	ایزد
belief; faith	imaan	ایمان
practical faith	imaan-e 'amali	ایمان عملی
secular; 'this-worldly'	injahaani	اینجهانی
Ahriman	ahriman	اهریمن
Sunnis	ahl-e sonnat	اهل سنت
contemplative; Gnostic	ahl-e kashf	اهل کشف
devout; faithful	baa imaan	با ایمان
godliness	baa khodaa'i	با خدائی
Babism	baabigari	بابیگری
Baptist	baaptist	باپتیست
cargo cult	baar parasti	بارپرستی
Holy See	baargaah-e qodsi	بارگاه قدسی
Anabaptism	baaz ta'mid gari	بازتعمیدگری
virgin birth	baakereh zaadi	باکره زادی
Blessed Virgin	baakere-ye moqaddas	باکره مقدس
belief	baavar	باور
idol; graven image	bot	بت

idolater	*bot parast*	بت پرست
idolatrous	*bot parastaaneh*	بت پرستانه
idolatry; idol-worship	*bot parasti*	بت پرستی
Brahma	*berahmaa*	برهما
Brahman	*berahman*	برهمن
Agnus Dei; lamb of God	*barre-ye khodaavand*	بره خداوند
fundamentalist	*bonyaad garaa*	بنیاد گرا
fundamentalism	*bonyaad garaa'i*	بنیاد گرائی
Buddhist	*budaa'i*	بودائی
atheist	*bi khodaa*	بی خدا
atheism	*bi khodaa'i*	بی خدائی
irreligious	*bi din*	بی دین
irreligion; unbelief	*bi dini*	بی دینی
spiritual vision	*binesh-e ma'navi*	بینش معنوی
Bahai	*bahaa'i*	بهائی
heaven; paradise	*behesht*	بهشت
the Pope	*paap*	پاپ
patriarch	*paatriyaark*	پاتریارك
piety	*paarsaa'i*	پارسائی
pastor	*paastur*	پاستور
pagoda	*paagudaa*	پاگودا
pan-Islamism	*paan eslaamism*	پان اسلامیسم
Holy Father	*pedar-e moqaddas*	پدر مقدس
Church Fathers	*pedaraan*	پدران
worship	*parastesh*	پرستش
worshipper	*parastandeh*	پرستنده
Protestant	*perutestaan*	پروتستان
Protestantism	*perutestaanism*	پروتستانیسم
spiritual development	*parvaresh-e ma'navi*	پرورش معنوی
Pelagianism	*pelaagiyusi*	پلاگیوسی
sanctuary	*panaahgaah*	پناهگاه
prophet; apostle	*payaambar*	پیامبر
presbyter	*pir keshish*	پیر کشیش
presbyterate	*pir keshishi*	پیر کشیشی
pre-Christian	*pish az masihiyat*	پیش از مسیحیت
prelapsarian	*pish az hobut*	پیش از هبوط
prophet; apostle	*peyqambar*	پیغمبر
Taoist	*taa'u'ist*	تائونیست

Taoism	taa'u'ism	تائونیسم
evangelism	tabliq-e enjil	تبلیغ انجیل
Trinity	taslis	تثلیث
mystic experience	tajrobe-ye baateni	تجربه باطنی
visionary experience	tajrobe-ye shohudi	تجربه شهودی
Divine manifestation; epiphany	tajalli-ye khodaa	تجلی خدا
prayer beads; rosary	tasbih	تسبیح
Sufism	tasavvof	تصوف
baptistery	ta'midgaah	تعمیدگاه
Baptist	ta'midgar	تعمیدگر
baptismal	ta'midi	تعمیدی
exegesis	tafsir	تفسیر
holiness; sanctity; piety	taqaddos	تقدس
sanctification	taqaddos bakhshi	تقدس بخشی
consecration	taqaddos yaaftegi	تقدس یافتگی
excommunication	takfir	تکفیر
repentance	towbeh	توبه
Torah	towraat	تورات
sociology of religion	jaame'eh shenaasi-ye din	جامعه شناسی دین
eternity	jaavdaanegi	جاودانگی
eternal	jaavdaaneh	جاودانه
festival	jashnvaareh	جشنواره
congregation	jamaa'at-e kelisaa'i	جماعت کلیسائی
Immovable Mover; Prime Mover	jonbaanande-ye naajonbaa	جنباننده ناجنبا
ecumenism	jonbesh-e nazdiki-ye din-haa	جنبش نزدیکی دین ها
crusade	jang-e salibi	جنگ صلیبی
just war	jang-e mashru'	جنگ مشروع
holy war	jang-e moqaddas	جنگ مقدس
exorcism	jengiri	جنگیری
(Islamic) defensive war	jahaad	جهاد
the other world; the hereafter	jahaan-e digar	جهان دیگر
haji; pilgrim (to Mecca)	haaji	حاجی
hajj, or pilgrimage to Mecca	hajj	حج
Prophetic Tradition	hadis	حدیث
Divinely-revealed Tradition (Islam)	hadis-e qodsi	حدیث قدسی
sacrilege	hormat shekani	حرمت شکنی
Divine decree	hokm-e elaahi	حکم الهی
canon; decree	hokm-e kelisaa	حکم کلیسا

sage; philosopher	*hakim*	حکیم
doxology	*hamd khaani*	حمد خوانی
apostle; disciple	*havvaari*	حواری
apostolic	*havvaariyaaneh*	حواریانه
rabbi	*khaakhaam*	خاخام
rabbinical	*khaakhaami*	خاخامی
beatification	*khojasteh shomaari*	خجسته شماری
God	*khodaa*	خدا
theism; autotheism; belief in God	*khodaa baavari*	خداباوری
deification	*khodaa gunegi*	خدا گونگی
godlike	*khodaa guneh*	خدا گونه
atheist	*khodaa naabaavar*	خداناباور
atheism	*khodaa naabaavari*	خداناباوری
unbeliever; atheist	*khodaa nashenaas*	خدانشناس
atheism	*khodaa nashenaasi*	خدانشناسی
Lord of Hosts	*khodaavand-e lashgaryaan*	خداوند لشگریان
divinity; godhood	*khodaavandi*	خداوندی
God's will	*khaast-e khodaa*	خواست خدا
good and evil	*kheyr o sharr*	خیر و شر
inquisition	*daadgaah-e baazju'i-ye dini*	دادگاه بازجونی دینی
Taoist	*daa'u baavar*	دائو باور
Taoism	*daa'u baavari*	دائو باوری
Antichrist	*dajjaal*	دجال
tree of knowledge; forbidden fruit	*derakht-e daanesh*	درخت دانش
dervish; Sufi follower	*darvish*	درویش
the Church	*dastgaah-e dini-ye masihi*	دستگاه دینی مسیحی
prayer; invocation	*do'aa*	دعا
requiescat	*do'aa-ye aamorzesh*	دعای آمرزش
the Lord's Prayer	*do'aa-ye khodaavand*	دعای خداوند
benediction	*do'aa-ye kheyr*	دعای خیر
heterodoxy	*degar andishi*	دگراندیشی
transubstantiation	*degar gowharandegi*	دگر گوهرندگی
dogma	*dogm*	دگم
worldly; secular	*donyaa'i*	دنیائی
born-again	*dowbaareh zaad*	دوباره زاد
Christian era	*dowraan-e masihiyat*	دوران مسیحیت
monastery	*deyr*	دیر
monasticism	*deyr neshini*	دیرنشینی

monastic	deyri	دیری
religion	din	دین
Biblical religion	din-e ahl-e ketaab	دین اهل کتاب
Buddhism	din-e budaa'i	دین بودائی
religiosity	din parasti	دین پرستی
reformation	din piraa'i	دین پیرائی
secularism	din jodaa khaahi	دین جداخواهی
secularism; laicism; laicisation	din jodaa gari	دین جداگری
devotion;piety; belief	dindaari	دین داری
secularisation	dinzadaa'i	دین زدائی
Zoroastrianism	din-e zardoshti	دین زردشتی
theocracy	din saalaari	دین سالاری
anticlerical	din saalaari setiz	دین سالاری ستیز
Sikhism	din-e sik	دین سیک
Sabaism	din-e saabe'i	دین صابئی
natural religion	din-e tabi'i	دین طبیعی
convert	din gardaan	دین گردان
religious conversion	din gardaani	دین گردانی
Manichaenism	din-e maani	دین مانی
Hinduism	din-e hendu	دین هندو
devotion; religiosity	dindaari	دینداری
religious	dini	دینی
sacerdotalism	dinyaar saalaari	دینیارسالاری
devil; demon	div	دیو
Holy Office	divaan-e qodsi	دیوان قدسی
Ten Commandments	dah farmaan	ده فرمان
Supreme Being; Divine Essence	zaat-e baari ta'aalaa	ذات باری تعالی
Zen	zen	ذن
Zen Buddhist	zen budaa'i	ذن بودائی
orthodox	raast kish	راست کیش
monk	raaheb	راهب
nun	raahebeh	راهبه
nunnery; convent	raahebeh khaaneh	راهبه خانه
mission	resaalat	رسالت
catechism	resaale-ye osul-e din	رساله اصول دین
resurrection	rastaakhiz	رستاخیز
salvation	rastegaari	رستگاری
holy orders	raste-haa-ye kelisaa'i	رسته های کلیسائی

spiritual growth	roshd-e ma'navi	رشد معنوی
behaviour	raftaar	رفتار
immorality	raftaar-e khalaaf-e akhlaaq	رفتار خلاف اخلاق
spirit	ruh	روح
Holy Spirit	ruh ol-qods	روح القدس
spiritualist	ruh baavar	روح باور
animistic; spiritualistic	ruh baavaraaneh	روح باورانه
animism; spiritualism	ruh baavari	روح باوری
spiritual; holy; cleric (n.)	ruhaani	روحانی
clergy	ruhaaniyat	روحانیت
holy day; Lord's Day	ruz-e khodaavand	روز خداوند
Day of Judgement	ruz-e daavari	روز داوری
Day of Judgement	ruz-e qiyaamat	روز قیامت
holy day	ruz-e moqaddas	روز مقدس
provost	ra'is-e kelisaa	رئیس کلیسا
monkery; monasticism	rahbaaniyat	رهبانیت
Nativity	zaadmaan-e masih	زادمان مسیح
ascetic	zaahed	زاهد
Zoroastrian	zardoshti	زردشتی
Zend-Avesta	zand o avestaa	زند و اوستا
everlasting life	zendegi-ye jaavid	زندگی جاوید
pilgrimage	ziyaarat	زیارت
pilgrim	ziyaaratgar	زیارتگر
asceticism	zohd	زهد
contemplative	zharf andish	ژرف اندیش
A.D.	saal-e milaadi	سال میلادی
A.H. (Anno Hegira)	saal-e hejri	سال هجری
Sabbatarian	sabati	سبتی
Judah	sabt-e yahudaa	سبط یهودا
prayer mat	sajjaadeh	سجاده
archbishop	sar osqof	سر اسقف
archdiocese	sar osqof neshin	سر اسقف نشین
archbishopric	sar osqofi	سر اسقفی
the Promised Land	sarzamin-e mow'ud	سر زمین موعود
vicarage	saraa-ye vikaar	سرای ویکار
archdeacon	sarparast-e osqof neshin	سرپرست اسقف نشین
archpriest	sar keshish	سر کشیش
hymn; religious song	sorud-e dini	سرود دینی

beatitude	sa'aadat	سعادت
sunna (of the Prophet Muhammad)	sonnat	سنت
Sunni	sonni	سنی
Sikh	sik	سیک
Trinitarian	seh gaaneh engaar	سه گانه انگار
Trinitarianism	seh gaaneh engari	سه گانه انگاری
tritheism	seh gaaneh khodaa'i	سه گانه خدائی
Last Supper	shaam-e aakhar	شام آخر
(religiously) lawful	shar'i	شرعی
antinomian	shari'at setiz	شریعت ستیز
Law of Moses	shari'at-e musaa	شریعت موسی
icon	shamaayel	شمایل
iconolatry	shamaayel parasti	شمایل پرستی
iconoclasm	shamaayel shekani	شمایل شکنی
iconography	shamaayel negaari	شمایل نگاری
Holy Synod	shuraa-ye qodsi	شورای قدسی
Satan; the Devil	sheytaan	شیطان
Devil-worship	sheytaan parasti	شیطان پرستی
demonic; satanic	sheytaani	شیطانی
Shi'ism	shi'eh	شیعه
Shinto	shintow	شینتو
martyrdom	shahaadat	شهادت
City of God	shahr-e khodaavand	شهر خداوند
martyr	shahid	شهید
martyrolatry	shahid parasti	شهید پرستی
martyrology	shahid shenaasi	شهید شناسی
courtyard (of mosque)	sahn	صحن
church yard	sahn-e kelisaa	صحن کلیسا
alms	sadaqeh	صدقه
Divine attributes	sefaat-e elaahi	صفات الهی
cross	salib	صلیب
imago Dei	surat-e khodaa	صورت خدا
Sufi	sufi	صوفی
abbey	sowme'eh	صومعه
abbot	sowme'eh daar	صومعه دار
anti-pope	zedd-e paap	ضد پاپ
Counter Reformation	zedd-e din piraa'i	ضد دین پیرانی
antireligious	zedd-e dini	ضد دینی

gnostic	'aaref	عارف
visible world	'aalam-e shahaadat	عالم شهادت
invisible world	'aalam-e qeyb	عالم غیب
devotional	'ebaadati	عبادتی
the Divine Throne	'arsh-e elaahi	عرش الهی
gnosis	'erfaan	عرفان
Cabalism	'erfaan-e yahudi	عرفان یهودی
gnostic	'erfaani	عرفانی
Last Supper; Eucharist	'ashaa-ye rabbaani	عشای ربانی
age of faith	'asr-e imaan	عصر ایمان
First Intellect	'aql-e avval	عقل اول
belief; opinion; creed	'aqideh	عقیده
theology	'elm-e kalaam	علم کلام
Islamic theology	'elm-e kalaam-e eslaami	علم کلام اسلامی
Christian Science	'elm-e masihaa'i	علم مسیحانی
absolute knowledge	'elm-e motlaq	علم مطلق
(Muslim) scholars	'olamaa	علماء
Easter	'eyd-e rastaakhiz-e masih	عید رستاخیز مسیح
Christmas	'eyd-e milaad-e masih	عید میلاد مسیح
Jesus Christ	'isaa-ye masih	عیسی مسیح
the New Testament	'ahd-e jadid	عهد جدید
the Old Testament	'ahd-e 'atiq	عهد عتیق
baptism; christening	qosl-e ta'mid	غسل تعمید
gentile	qeyr-e yahudi	غیر یهودی
Franciscan	faraansisi	فرانسیسی
eschatology	farjaam shenaasi	فرجام شناسی
angel	fereshteh	فرشته
sect	ferqeh	فرقه
Quakerism	ferqe-ye kuveykeri	فرقه کویکری
sectarianism	ferqeh garaa'i	فرقه گرانی
jurist	faqih	فقیه
jurisprudence	feqh	فقه
juristic	feqhi	فقهی
Islamic philosophy	falsafe-ye eslaami	فلسفه اسلامی
philosophy of religion	falsafe-ye din	فلسفه دین
Vedantism	falsafe-ye vedaa'i	فلسفه ودائی
First Heaven	falak-e avval	فلک اول
'annihilation in God' (Sufism)	fanaa-ye fi allaah	فنای فی الله

Divine law; *jus divinum*	qaanun-e elaahi	قانون الهی
canon law; *shari'a law*	qaanun-e shar'	قانون شرع
law of retribution	qaanun-e qesaas	قانون قصاص
legal; lawful	qaanuni	قانونی
Cabbala	qabbaalaa	قبالا
cemetery; graveyard	qabrestaan	قبرستان
Divine determining; predestination	qadar	قدر
predestinarian; fatalist	qadari	قدری
holy; divine; spiritual	qodsi	قدسی
sanctity; holiness	qodsiyat	قدسیت
saint	qeddis	قدیس
patron saint	qeddis-e poshtibaan	قدیس پشتیبان
sanctity; sainthood	qeddisiyat	قدیسیت
sacrificial altar	qorbaangaah	قربانگاه
sacrifice	qorbaani	قربانی
cathedral	kaatedraal	کاتدرال
Catholic	kaatulik	کاتولیک
cardinal	kaardinaal	کاردینال
karma	kaarmaa	کارما
unbeliever; infidel	kaafer	کافر
pagan	kaafer kish	کافر کیش
paganism	kaafer kishi	کافر کیشی
College of Cardinals	kaalej-e kaardinaal-haa	کالج کاردینال ها
Calvinist	kaalveni	کالونی
priest (Judaism)	kaahen	کاهن
prayer book	ketaab-e do'aa	کتاب دعا
Holy Book; Bible	ketaab-e moqaddas	کتاب مقدس
Vulgate Bible	ketaab-e moqaddas-e laatini	کتاب مقدس لاتینی
Pentateuch	ketaab-haa-ye panjgaaneh	کتابهای پنجگانه
priest; vicar; clergyman	keshish	کشیش
clergy	keshishaan	کشیشان
sacerdotal	keshishaaneh	کشیشانه
vicarage	keshish saraa	کشیش سرا
priesthood	keshishi	کشیشی
blasphemy	kofr gu'i	کفرگونی
atonement; expiation	kaffaareh	کفاره
theology	kalaam	کلام
church	kelisaa	کلیسا

churchgoer	kelisaa row	کلیسارو
church attendance	kelisaa ravi	کلیساروی
churchman; ecclesiastic	kelisaa'i	کلیسانی
Russian Orthodox Church	kelisaa-ye ortodoks-e rusi	کلیسای ارتدکس روسی
Eastern Orthodox Church	kelisaa-ye ortodoks-e sharqi	کلیسای ارتدکس شرقی
Church of England	kelisaa-ye engelestaan	کلیسای انگلستان
Anglican Church	kelisaa-ye engelisi	کلیسای انگلیسی
Broad Church; Free Church	kelisaa-ye aazaadmanesh	کلیسای آزادمنش
High Church	kelisaa-ye baalaa	کلیسای بالا
Presbyterianism	kelisaa-ye pir keshishi	کلیسای پیر کشیشی
Eastern Church	kelisaa-ye sharqi	کلیسای شرقی
Low Church	kelisaa-ye forudast	کلیسای فرودست
Coptic Church	kelisaa-ye qebti	کلیسای قبطی
Roman Catholic Church	kelisaa-ye kaatulik-e rumi	کلیسای کاتولیک رومی
synagogue	kaniseh	کنیسه
kundalini	kundaalini	کوندالینی
cult	kish	کیش
sin	gonaah	گناه
confession	gonaah gozaari	گناه گزاری
original sin	gonaah-e nakhostin	گناه نخستین
lama	laamaa	لاما
Lamaistic	laamaa'i	لامائی
Levite	laavi	لاوی
secular; laic	laa'ik	لائیک
Lutheran	luteri	لوتری
Lutheranism	luteriyat	لوتریت
mantra	maantraa	مانترا
missionary	moballeq-e dini	مبلغ دینی
fanatic	mota'asseb	متعصب
Methodism	metudism	متودیسم
altar; prayer niche	mehraab	محراب
Prime Mover	moharrek-e avval	محرک اول
Mohammedan; Muslim	mohammadi	محمدی
church school	madrase-ye kelisaa'i	مدرسه کلیسانی
religion; sect; rite	mazhab	مذهب
the Shi'ite sect	mazhab-e shi'eh	مذهب شیعه
Catholicism	mazhab-e kaatulik	مذهب کاتولیک
Calvinism	mazhab-e kaalven	مذهب کالون

399

Nestorianism	mazhab-e nesturi	مذهب نسطوری
ceremony	maraasem	مراسم
requiem	maraasem-e aamorzaaneh	مراسم آمرزانه
baptism; christening	maraasem-e qosl-e ta'mid	مراسم غسل تعمید
ordination	maraasem-e keshish gomaari	مراسم کشیش گماری
man of God	mard-e khodaa	مرد خدا
spiritual guide; guru	morshed	مرشد
Mariolatry	maryam parasti	مریم پرستی
Mariology	maryam shenaasi	مریم شناسی
psalms	mazaamir	مزامیر
Mazdakist	mazdaki	مزدکی
mosque	masjed	مسجد
Muslim	mosalmaan	مسلمان
Christ	masih	مسیح
messianic	masihaa'i	مسیحائی
Christian	masihi	مسیحی
Christianity	masihiyat	مسیحیت
Divine providence	mashiyat-e elaahi	مشیت الهی
resurrection	ma'aad	معاد
temple; place of worship	ma'bad	معبد
miracle	mo'jezeh	معجزه
spiritual	ma'navi	معنوی
magi	moqaan	مغان
mufti; canon lawyer (Islam)	mofti	مفتی
episcopate	maqaam-e osqofi	مقام اسقفی
holy	moqaddas	مقدس
Cyrenaicism	maktab-e kurnaa'i	مکتب کورنائی
mullah	mollaa	ملا
mullah-ism; theocracy	mollaa saalaari	ملاسالاری
cherubim	malaa'ek-e karrubi	ملائک کروبی
unbeliever; atheist	molhed	ملحد
Kingdom of Heaven	malakut-e aasemaan	ملکوت آسمان
Kingdom of God	malakut-e khodaavand	ملکوت خداوند
celestial	malakuti	ملکوتی
benediction; prayer	monaajaat	مناجات
Menorah	menuraah	منوراه
Mormonism	murmunism	مورمونیسم
believer	mo'men	مومن

Mahdism	mahdaviyat	مهدویت
Mahdi; Hidden Imam	mahdi	مهدی
Mithraist	mehr parast	مهرپرست
archangel	mahin fereshteh	مهین فرشته
agnostic	naashenaasaa engaar	ناشناسا انگار
agnosticism	naashenaasaa engaari	ناشناسا انگاری
baptismal name	naam-e ta'midi	نام تعمیدی
profane	naa moqaddas	نامقدس
profanity	naa moqaddasi	نامقدسی
vicar	naayeb keshish	نایب کشیش
prophethood	nabovvat	نبوت
Nestorian	nesturi	نسطوری
caste system	nezaam-e kaasti	نظام کاستی
Arianism	nazariye-ye aaryus	نظریه آریوس
soul; spirit	nafs	نفس
atman	nafs-e joz'i	نفس جزئی
(Islamic) canonical prayer	namaaz	نماز
prayer room; chapel	namaaz khaaneh	نمازخانه
convert	now din	نودین
ancestor worship	niyaa parasti	نیاپرستی
supplication; prayer	niyaayesh	نیایش
psalmodist	niyaayesh saraa	نیایش سرا
liturgy; psalmody	niyaayesh saraa'i	نیایش سرائی
nirvana	nirvaanaa	نیروانا
demigod	nimeh khodaa	نیمه خدا
quasi-religion	nimeh dini	نیمه دینی
preacher	vaa'ez	واعظ
pantheism	vahdat-e vojud	وحدت وجود
pantheistic	vahdat-e vojudi	وحدت وجودی
revelation	vahy	وحی
Divine revelation	vahy-e elaahi	وحی الهی
Vedanta	vedaantaa	ودانتا
devil's advocate	vakil-e sheytaan	وکیل شیطان
sainthood	velaayat	ولایت
saint	vali	ولی
Wahhabi	vahhaabi	وهابی
Wahhabism	vahhaabi gari	وهابی گری
migration (of Mohammad to Medina)	hejrat	هجرت

ontology	hasti shenaasi	هستی شناسی
Septuagint	haftaad gaani	هفتادگانی
ecumenical	hameh kelisaa'i	همه کلیسائی
Hindu	hendu	هندو
Gog and Magog	ya'juj o ma'juj	یاجوج و ماجوج
God	yazdaan	یزدان
Jesuit	yasu'i	یسوعی
Jesuitism	yasu'iyat	یسوعیت
Unitarian	yektaa baavar	یکتاباور
Unitarianism	yektaa baavari	یکتاباوری
monotheist	yegaaneh parast	یگانه پرست
monotheism	yegaaneh parasti	یگانه پرستی
Judaic	yahudaa'i	یهودانی
Jew; Jewish	yahudi	یهودی
Judaism	yahudiyat	یهودیت
Reform Judaism	yahudiyat-e now saamaan	یهودیت نوسامان
Orthodox Judaism	yahudiyat-e sonnati	یهودیت سنتی
Yahweh; God; Jehova	yahveh	یهوه
Jehovic; Jehovist	yahve'i	یهوه ای
Yahwism	yahveh parasti	یهوه پرستی

402

At the Seaside

در کنار دریا

pier	*eskeleh*	اسکله
horizon	*ofoq*	افق
ocean	*oqyaanus*	اقیانوس
water	*aab*	آب
sunstroke	*aaftaab zadegi*	آفتاب زدگی
sunburn	*aaftaab sukhtegi*	آفتاب سوختگی
sunbathing	*aaftaab giri*	آفتاب گیری
cargo	*baar-e keshti*	بار کشتی
quay	*baar andaaz*	باراندار
port	*bandar*	بندر
harbour	*bandargaah*	بندرگاه
spade	*bil*	بیل
oar	*paaru*	پارو
coast guard	*paasdaar-e saaheli*	پاسدار ساحلی
cliff	*partgaah*	پرتگاه
flag	*parcham*	پرچم
gangway; bridge	*pol-e keshti*	پل کشتی
beach	*pelaazh*	پلاژ
picnic	*piknik*	پیک نیک
holidays	*ta'tilaat*	تعطیلات
coastal resort	*tafrihgaah-e saaheli*	تفریحگاه ساحلی
telescope	*teleskup*	تلسکوپ
sea urchin	*tutiyaa-ye daryaa'i*	توتیای دریائی
bottom (e.g. of boat, sea etc.)	*tah*	ته
current	*jaryaan*	جریان
tide	*jazr o madd*	جزر و مد
island	*jazireh*	جزیره
parasol	*chatr-e aaftaabi*	چتر آفتابی
jellyfish	*chatr-e daryaa'i*	چتر دریانی
beach umbrella	*chatr-e saaheli*	چتر ساحلی
life buoy	*halqe-ye nejaat*	حلقه نجات
crew	*khadameh*	خدمه
crab	*kharchang*	خرچنگ
coastline	*khatt-e saaheli*	خط ساحلی
lagoon	*khoftaab*	خفتاب
bay	*khalij-e kuchek*	خلیج کوچک

403

tidal wave	khizaab-e keshandi	خیزاب کشندی
sea	daryaa	دریا
seasickness	daryaa zadegi	دریازدگی
seaman; sailor	daryaa navard	دریانورد
airbed; lilo	doshak-e baadi	دشک بادی
mast	dakal	دکل
cape	damaaqeh	دماغه
funnel	dudkesh-e keshti	دودکش کشتی
slack season (i.e. tourist trade)	dowraan-e kesaadi	دوران کسادی
binoculars	durbin	دوربین
river	rudkhaaneh	رودخانه
jellyfish	zheleh maahi	ژله ماهی
coast; shore	saahel	ساحل
sunshade	saayebaan	سایبان
passenger	sarneshin	سرنشین
bucket	satl	سطل
trip	safar	سفر
holiday	safar-e tafrihi	سفر تفریحی
cruise	safar-e daryaa'i	سفر دریائی
rudder	sekaan	سکان
stone	sang	سنگ
pebble	sangrizeh	سنگریزه
inlet	shaakhrud	شاخرود
sand	shen	شن
sand dune	shen tappeh	شن تپه
swimming	shenaa	شنا
swimmer; bather	shenaagar	شناگر
coastal town	shahr-e saaheli	شهر ساحلی
deckchair	sandali-ye taashow	صندلی تاشو
sea crossing	'obur-e daryaa'i	عبور دریائی
deck	'arsheh	عرشه
sunglasses	'eynak-e aaftaabi	عینک آفتابی
lighthouse	faanus-e daryaa'i	فانوس دریائی
boat	qaayeq	قایق
pedal boat	qaayeq-e pedaali	قایق پدالی
raft	qaayeq-e tah pahn	قایق ته پهن
fishing boat	qaayeq-e maahigiri	قایق ماهیگیری
speedboat	qaayeq-e moturi	قایق موتوری

lifeboat	qaayeq-e nejaat	قایق نجات
sailing	qaayeqraani	قایقرانی
sandcastle	qasr-e sheni	قصر شنی
shore; coast	karaaneh	کرانه
fare	keraayeh	کرایه
suntan lotion	kerem-e zedd-e aaftaab sukhtegi	کرم ضد آفتاب سوختگی
ship; vessel	keshti	کشتی
steamer	keshti-ye bokhaar	کشتی بخار
shipwreck	keshti-ye shekasteh	کشتی شکسته
tide	keshand	کشند
foam	kaf	کف
seaside	kenaar-e daryaa	کنار دریا
coastguard	gaard-e saaheli	گارد ساحلی
walk	gardesh	گردش
shell	gushmaahi	گوشماهی
seaweed	giyaah-e daryaa'i	گیاه دریانی
swimwear; swimming costume	lebaas-e shenaa	لباس شنا
bikini	lebaas-e shenaa-ye dow tekkeh	لباس شنای دو تکه
anchor	langar	لنگر
marina	langargaah	لنگرگاه
swimming trunks	maayow	مایو
fisherman	maahigir	ماهیگیر
beach attendant; lifeguard	morabbi-ye nejaat qariq	مربی نجات غریق
coral	marjaan	مرجان
holidays	morakhasi-ye tafrihi	مرخصی تفریحی
seagull	morq-e daryaa'i	مرغ دریانی
traveller; passenger; holiday maker	mosaafer	مسافر
estuary	masabb	مصب
sailor	malavaan	ملوان
wave	mowj	موج
jetty	mowj shekan	موج شکن
moorings	mahaargaah	مهارگاه
fleet	naavgaan	ناوگان
hammock	nanu	ننو
navy	niru-ye daryaa'i	نیروی دریانی
sea breeze	nasim-e daryaa'i	نسیم دریانی
creek	nahr	نهر
sea air	havaa-ye daryaa'i	هوای دریانی

we went to the seaside for our holidays برای تعطیلات به کنار دریا رفتیم   to go on holiday تعطیلات رفتن

در هتل ماندن   to stay in a hotel   زیر چادر خوابیدیم we slept in a tent   خانه کرایه کردیم we rented a house

گردش کردن   to go for a walk; to go on an outing   تفریح کردن to have fun; to amuse oneself

خوشگذرانی کردن   to have a good time   به شما خوش گذشت؟ did you have a good time? ; did you enjoy yourself?

به من خوش گذشت I had a good time   گذراندن to spend (time)   دو هفته آنجا گذراندیم we spent two weeks there

پیک نیک کردن to have a picnic   شنا کردن to swim   حسن شناگر خوبی است Hasan is a good swimmer

آفتاب گیری کردن to sunbathe   آفتاب خوردن to catch the sun   قدم زدن to stroll; to promenade

دراز کشیدن to lie down   هر روز روی پلاژ دراز می کشیدم every day we would lie on the beach   خوابیدن to sleep

نشستن to sit; to sit down   در شن بازی کردن to play in the sand   قصر شنی ساختن to build sandcastles

ماهیگیری کردن   to fish; to go fishing   ماهی گرفتن to catch fish   قایق سواری کردن to go boating

علی شنا بلد نیست Ali can't swim   غرق شدن to drown   مواظب باشید غرق نشوید be careful that you don't drown

دریا خیلی آلوده است the sea is very polluted   پلاژ خیلی کثیف است the beach is very dirty   پرچم قرمز red flag

406

Shops and Shopping

sweetshop	aab nabaat forushi	آب نبات فروشی
off-licence; wine shop	aab-e jow forushi	آبجو فروشی
confectioner's	aajil forushi	آجیل فروشی
hairdresser's salon; barber's shop	aaraayeshgaah	آرایشگاه
hairdresser; barber	aaraayeshgar	آرایشگر
travel agency	aazhaans-e mosaaferati	آژانس مسافرتی
elevator; lift	aasaansur	آسانسور
ironmonger	aahan aalaat forush	آهن آلات فروش
ironmonger's	aahan aalaat forushi	آهن آلات فروشی
fitting room	otaaq-e perov	اتاق پرو
label	etiket	اتیکت
toy seller	asbaab baazi forush	اسباب بازی فروش
toyshop	asbaab baazi forushi	اسباب بازی فروشی
mistake	eshtebaah	اشتباه
delicatessen; food store	aqziyeh forushi	اغذیه فروشی
size	andaazeh	اندازه
market; shopping centre; mall	baazaar	بازار
shopping mall	baazaarcheh	بازارچه
savings bank	baank-e pasandaaz	بانک پس انداز
building society	baank-e rahni	بانک رهنی
department	bakhsh	بخش
complaints department	bakhsh-e shekaayat-haa	بخش شکایت ها
draper	bazzaaz	بزاز
drapery	bazzaazi	بزازی
packaging	basteh bandi	بسته بندی
estate agent's	bongaah-e mo'aamelaat-e melki	بنگاه معاملات ملکی
boutique	butik	بوتیک
draper	paarcheh forush	پارچه فروش
drapery	paarcheh forushi	پارچه فروشی
arcade; mall	paasaazh	پاساژ
post office	postkhaaneh	پستخانه
escalator	pelleh barqi	پله برقی
haberdasher	pushaak forush	پوشاک فروش
haberdashery; clothes shop	pushaak forushi	پوشاک فروشی
money	pul	پول
(small) change	pul-e khord	پول خرد

down payment; deposit	*pish pardaakht*	پیش پرداخت
counter	*pishkhaan*	پیشخوان
tradesman	*pisheh var*	پیشه ور
merchant; salesman	*taajer*	تاجر
commerce; business; trade	*tejaarat*	تجارت
e-commerce	*tejaarat-e elektruniki*	تجاررت الکترونیکی
reduction	*takhfif*	تخفیف
greengrocer	*tareh baar forush*	تره بار فروش
greengrocer's	*tareh baar forushi*	تره بار فروشی
stamp seller	*tambr forush*	تمبر فروش
shopping arcade	*timcheh*	تیمچه
jeweller	*javaaher forush*	جواهر فروش
jeweller's	*javaaher forushi*	جواهر فروشی
sock shop	*juraab forushi*	جوراب فروشی
shopping trolley	*charkh-e kharid*	چرخ خرید
leather shop	*charm forushi*	چرم فروشی
cheque	*chek*	چک
sale; auction	*haraaj*	حراج
bill	*hesaab*	حساب
retailer	*khordeh forush*	خرده فروش
retailer's	*khordeh forushi*	خرده فروشی
shopping; buying	*kharid*	خرید
buying and selling	*kharid o forush*	خرید و فروش
buyer; customer; shopper	*kharidaar*	خریدار
shopping	*kharidaari*	خریداری
dry-cleaner's	*khoshkshu'i*	خشکشوئی
grocer	*khaarbaar forush*	خواربار فروش
grocer's; general store	*khaarbaar forushi*	خواربارفروشی
tailor	*khayyaat*	خیاط
pharmacy; dispensing chemist's	*daarukhaaneh*	داروخانه
herbalist	*daarugiyaa forush*	داروگیا فروش
herbalist's	*daarukhaane-ye giyaahi*	داروخانه گیاهی
tobacconist	*dokhaanchi*	دخانچی
tobacconist's	*dokhaaniyaat forushi*	دخانیات فروشی
cheque book	*daftarche-ye chek*	دفترچه چک
barber's shop	*dokkaan-e salmaani*	دکان سلمانی
shop	*dokkaan*	دکان
shopkeeper	*dokkaandaar*	دکاندار

shopkeeping	dokkaandaari	دکانداری
stall	dakkeh	دکه
fruit juice stall	dakke-ye aab-e miveh	دکه آب میوه
bookmaker	dallaal-e shartbandi	دلال شرطبندی
estate agent	dallaal-e mo'aamelaat-e melki	دلال معاملات ملکی
hawker; pedlar	dowreh gard	دوره گرد
launderette	rakhtshur khaaneh	رختشورخانه
restaurant	rasturaan	رستوران
receipt	resid	رسید
paint shop	rang forushi	رنگ فروشی
newsagent	ruznaameh forush	روزنامه فروش
newsagent's	ruznaameh forushi	روزنامه فروشی
watchmaker	saa'at saaz	ساعت ساز
watchmaker's	saa'at saazi	ساعت سازی
watch seller	saa'at forush	ساعت فروش
watch seller's	saa'at forushi	ساعت فروشی
barber; barber's shop	salmaani	سلمانی
second hand goods dealer	semsaar	سمسار
second hand goods shop	semsaari	سمساری
souvenir	sowqaat	سوغات
cigarette seller	sigaar forush	سیگار فروش
tobacconist's; cigarette shop	sigaar forushi	سیگار فروشی
company; firm	sherkat	شرکت
insurance company	sherkat-e bimeh	شرکت بیمه
branch	sho'beh	شعبه
complaint	shekaayat	شکایت
confectioner's; pastry shop	shirini forushi	شیرینی فروشی
queue	saff	صف
record dealer	safheh forush	صفحه فروش
record shop	safheh forushi	صفحه فروشی
bill	surat hesaab	صورتحساب
floor; storey	tabaqeh	طبقه
basement	tabaqe-ye zir-e zamin	طبقه زیر زمین
ground floor	tabaqe-ye hamkaf	طبقه همکف
antique seller	'atiqeh forush	عتیقه فروش
antique shop	'atiqeh forushi	عتیقه فروشی
herbalist; perfumer; apothecary	'attaar	عطار
herbalist's; perfumery	'attaari	عطاری

wholesaler	'omdeh forush	عمده فروش
optician	'eynak saaz	عینک ساز
optician's	'eynak saazi	عینک سازی
department store	forushgaah	فروشگاه
hardware shop	forushgaah-e abzaar-e felezi	فروشگاه ابزار فلزی
gift shop	forushgaah-e ajnaas-e kaado'i	فروشگاه اجناس کادونی
musical instruments shop	forushgaah-e aalaat-e musiqi	فروشگاه آلات موسیقی
supermarket	forushgaah-e bozorg	فروشگاه بزرگ
department store	forushgaah-e chand bakhshi	فروشگاه چند بخشی
health shop	forushgaah-e khoraak-e behdaashti	فروشگاه خوراک بهداشتی
electrical goods shop	forushgaah-e lavaazem-e barqi	فروشگاه لوازم برقی
sports shop	forushgaah-e lavaazem-e varzeshi	فروشگاه لوازم ورزشی
salesperson	forushandeh	فروشنده
sale season	fasl-e haraaj	فصل حراج
carpet shop	qaali forushi	قالی فروشی
butcher	qassaab	قصاب
butcher's	qassaabi	قصابی
confectioner's	qannaadi	قنادی
price	qeymat	قیمت
fixed price	qeymat-e maqtu'	قیمت مقطوع
reduced prices; bargain prices	qeymat-haa-ye takhfif yaafteh	قیمت های تخفیف یافته
gift	kaadow	کادو
business; trade	kaar o kasb	کار و کسب
credit card	kaart-e e'tebaari	کارت اعتباری
(greetings) card shop	kaart-e tabrik forushi	کارت تبریک فروشی
employee; assistant	kaarmand	کارمند
trader	kaaseb	کاسب
trade; business	kaasebi	کاسبی
goods	kaalaa	کالا
computer shop	kaampyuter forushi	کامپیوتر فروشی
kebab shop; fast food shop	kabaabi	کبابی
second-hand bookshop	ketaab-e dast-e dovvom forushi	کتاب دست دوّم فروشی
book seller	ketaab forush	کتاب فروش
bookshop	ketaab forushi	کتاب فروشی
library	ketaabkhaaneh	کتابخانه
tie shop	keraavaat forushi	کراوات فروشی
cobbler	kafsh duz	کفش دوز
cobbler's	kafsh saaz	کفش ساز

shoe seller	kafsh forush	کفش فروش
shoe shop	kafsh forushi	کفش فروشی
purse; wallet	kif-e pul	کیف پول
florist	golforush	گلفروش
florist's	golforushi	گلفروشی
check-out	gishe-ye pardaakht-e pul	گیشه پرداخت پول
clothes shop	lebaas forushi	لباس فروشی
dairy; dairy food shop	labaniyaat forushi	لبنیات فروشی
second hand goods	lavaazem-e dast-e dovvom	لوازم دست دوّم
list	list	لیست
vending machine	maashin-e forush	ماشین فروش
fishmonger	maahi forush	ماهی فروش
fishmonger's	maahi forushi	ماهی فروشی
furniture shop	moblemaan forushi	مبلمان فروشی
shopping complex; shopping centre	mojtama'-e forushgaahi	مجتمع فروشگاهی
product	mahsul	محصول
manager	modir	مدیر
customer	moshtari	مشتری
wine shop; off-licence	mashrub forushi	مشروب فروشی
doctor's surgery	matab-e pezeshk	مطب پزشک
transaction; bargain	mo'aameleh	معامله
shop	maqaazeh	مغازه
shopkeeper	maqaazeh daar	مغازه دار
pub; tavern	meykhaaneh	میخانه
fruiterer	miveh forush	میوه فروش
fruit shop	miveh forushi	میوه فروشی
baker	naanvaa	نانوا
bakery	naanvaa'i	نانوائی
computer software shop	narm afzaar forushi	نرم افزار فروشی
silversmith	noqreh saaz	نقره ساز
car showroom	namaayeshgaah-e maashin	نمایشگاه ماشین
stationer	nevesht afzaar forush	نوشت افزار فروش
stationer's	nevesht afzaar forushi	نوشت افزار فروشی
deposit	vadi'eh	ودیعه
shop window; window display	vitrin-e maqaazeh	ویترین مغازه
video shop	vide'o forushi	ویدئو فروشی

MORE SHOPPING TERMS AND PHRASES

to buy; to shop خرید کردن   I bought three kilos of apples سه کیلو سیب خریدم   to buy خریدن

to purchase خریداری کردن   I want to go shopping today امروز می خواهم خرید بروم   to go shopping خرید رفتن

to be sold به فروش رفتن   do you sell stamps here? اینجا تمبر می فروشید؟   to sell فروختن

to be sold; to be marketed به فروش رسیدن   the cheapest ones have been sold ارزانترین ها به فروش رفته اند

what is the price of this book? قیمت این کتاب چند است   buying and selling خرید و فروش

how much does this come to? این چقدر می شود؟   how much do these cost? اینها چند اند؟

how expensive! چه گران!   it's too expensive زیادی گران است   it's very expensive خیلی گران است

don't haggle! چانه نزنید!   to haggle چانه زدن   don't you have anything cheaper than this? ارزانتر از این ندارید؟

cheap but of good quality ارزان ولی مرغوب   I am looking for a good pair of shoes دنبال یک جفت کفش خوب می گردم

can I try that one? می توانم آن یکی را امتحان کنم؟   can I have a look at that one? می توانم آن یکی را ببینم

hard to please مشکل پسند   its colour doesn't suit you رنگش به شما نمیاید   it's not your size اندازه شما نیست

two dollars a kilo کیلوئی دو دلار   how much are apples a kilo? سیب کیلوئی چنده؟

I'm just looking فقط دارم نگاه می کنم   I don't want to buy anything چیزی نمیخواهم بخرم

you won't find anything cheaper than this ارزانتر از این پیدا نمی شود   do you need anything else جیزی دیگر لازم دارید؟

to put down a deposit پیش قسط دادن   to pay in instalments قسطی پرداختن

they've lowered the prices قیمت ها را کم کرده اند   that department store has a sale on آن فروشگاه حراج دارد

᭤᭣᭤

جامعه شناسی

customs; conventions	aadaab o rosum	آداب و رسوم
experiment	aazmaayesh	آزمایش
psychopathology	aasib shenaasi-ye ravaani	آسیب شناسی روانی
class consciousness	aagaahi-ye tabaqaati	آگاهی طبقاتی
group consciousness	aagaahi-ye goruhi	آگاهی گروهی
statistics	aamaar	آمار
learning	aamuzesh	آموزش
social learning	aamuzesh-e ejtemaa'i	آموزش اجتماعی
education	aamuzesh o parvaresh	آموزش و پرورش
trade union	ettehaadiye-ye kaargari	اتحادیه کارگری
society	ejtemaa'	اجتماع
socialized	ejtemaa'i shodeh	اجتماعی شده
socialization	ejtemaa'i gari	اجتماعی گری
authority	ekhtiyaar	اختیار
morals; morality	akhlaaq	اخلاق
communication	ertebaat	ارتباط
social value	arzesh-e ejtemaa'i	ارزش اجتماعی
marriage; matrimony	ezdevaaj	ازدواج
living standards	estaandaard-e zendegi	استاندارد زندگی
employment	estekhdaam	استخدام
labelling	esm gozaari	اسم گذاری
social reform	eslaah-e ejtemaa'i	اصلاح اجتماعی
information	ettelaa'aat	اطلاعات
strike	e'tesaab	اعتصاب
drop-out	oft	افت
ethnic minority	aqalliyat-e qowmi	اقلیت قومی
alcoholism	alkolzadegi	الکل زدگی
alcoholism	alkolism	الکلیسم
cultural pattern	olgu-ye farhangi	الگوی فرهنگی
social security	amniyat-e ejtemaa'i	امنیت اجتماعی
elections	entekhaabaat	انتخابات
deviance; deviation	enheraaf	انحراف
revolution	enqelaab	انقلاب
social revolution	enqelaab-e ejtemaa'i	انقلاب اجتماعی
group image	engaare-ye goruhi	انگاره گروهی
social parasite	angal-e ejtemaa'i	انگل اجتماعی

fertility	*baarvari*	باروری
retirement	*baazneshastegi*	باز نشستگی
social reconstruction; social reform	*baazsaazi-ye ejtemaa'i*	بازسازی اجتماعی
social crisis	*bohraan-e ejtemaa'i*	بحران اقتصادی
social sector	*bakhsh-e ejtemaa'i*	بخش اجتماعی
equality	*baraabari*	برابری
slavery	*bardegi*	بردگی
survey; investigation	*bar resi*	بررسی
social survey	*bar resi-ye ejtemaa'i*	بررسی اجتماعی
pilot survey	*bar resi-ye pishaahang*	بررسی پیشاهنگ
cross-sectional study	*bar resi-ye tamaam boreshi*	بررسی تمام برشی
longitudinal study	*bar resi-ye tuli*	بررسی طولی
curriculum	*barnaame-ye aamuzeshi*	برنامه آموزشی
social planning	*barnaameh rizi-ye ejtemaa'i*	برنامه ریزی اجتماعی
urban planning	*barnaameh rizi-ye shahri*	برنامه ریزی شهری
environmental planning	*barnaameh rizi-ye mohiti*	برنامه ریزی محیطی
delinquency	*bezeh kaari*	بزه کاری
bureaucracy	*burukraasi*	بورو کراسی
social disorganisation	*bi saazmaani-ye ejtemaa'i*	بی سازمانی اجتماعی
neutrality; impartiality	*bi tarafi*	بی طرفی
unemployment	*bi kaari*	بی کاری
anomie	*bi hanjaari*	بی هنجاری
alienation	*bigaanegi*	بیگانگی
xenophobia	*bigaaneh haraasi*	بیگانه هراسی
health	*behdaasht*	بهداشت
group interest	*bahre-ye goruhi*	بهره گروهی
social welfare	*behzisti-ye ejtemaa'i*	بهزیستی اجتماعی
social hierarchy	*paayegaan-e ejtemaa'i*	پایگان اجتماعی
hierarchy of needs	*paayegaan-e niyaaz-haa*	پایگان نیازها
social status	*paayegaah-e ejtemaa'i*	پایگاه اجتماعی
social sanction	*paayandaan-e ejtemaa'i*	پایندان اجتماعی
phenomenology	*padidaar shenaasi*	پدیدار شناسی
social acceptance	*paziresh-e ejtemaa'i*	پذیرش اجتماعی
questionnaire; survey	*porsesh naameh*	پرسش نامه
social research	*pezhuhesh-e ejtemaa'i*	پژوهش اجتماعی
positivism	*puzitivism*	پوزیتیویسم
social dynamics	*puyeh shenaasi-ye ejtemaa'i*	پویه شناسی اجتماعی
prejudice; pre-judgement	*pishdaavari*	پیش داوری

414

self-fulfilling prophecy	pishbini-ye vaaqe'iyat bakhsh-e khish	پیش بینی واقعیت بخش خویش
profession; job	pisheh	پیشه
group affiliation	peyvand-e goruhi	پیوند گروهی
analysis	tahlil	تحلیل
social analysis	tahlil-e ejtemaa'i	تحلیل اجتماعی
decision making	tasmim giri	تصمیم گیری
polygamy	ta'addod-e zowjaat	تعدد زوجات
definition of reality	ta'rif-e vaaqe'iyat	تعریف واقعیت
prejudice; bigotry	ta'assob	تعصب
change	taqyir	تغییر
division of labour	taqsim-e kaar	تقسیم کار
culture shock	tekaan-e farhangi	تکان فرهنگی
technology	teknuluzhi	تکنولوژی
social tension	tanesh-e ejtemaa'i	تنش اجتماعی
loneliness	tanhaa'i	تنهائی
social development	towse'e-ye ejtemaa'i	توسعه اجتماعی
production	towlid	تولید
wealth	servat	ثروت
society	jaame'eh	جامعه
open society	jaame'e-ye baaz	جامعه باز
multi-cultural society	jaame'e-ye chand nezhaadeh	جامعه چند نژاده
sociologist	jaame'eh shenaas	جامعه شناس
sociology	jaame'eh shenaasi	جامعه شناسی
micro-sociology	jaame'eh shenaasi-ye khord	جامعه شناسی خرد
macro-sociology	jaame'eh shenaasi-ye kalaan	جامعه شناسی کلان
civil society	jaame'e-ye madani	جامعه مدنی
bias	jaanebdaari	جانبداری
crime	jorm	جرم
social inhibition	jelow giri-ye ejtemaa'i	جلوگیری اجتماعی
population	jam'iyat	جمعیت
demography	jam'iyat shenaasi	جمعیت شناسی
crime	jenaayat	جنایت
social movement	jonbesh-e ejtemaa'i	جنبش اجتماعی
ecumenism	jonbesh-e nazdiki-ye adyaan	جنبش نزدیکی ادیان
social mobility	jonbandegi-ye ejtemaa'i	جنبندگی اجتماعی
war	jang	جنگ
social climate	javv-e ejtemaa'i	جو اجتماعی
social orientation	jahatgiri-ye ejtemaa'i	جهتگیری اجتماعی

polyandry	chand showhari	چند شوهری
pluralism	chand gaanegi	چند گانگی
polygamy; polygyny	chand hamsari	چند همسری
profession	herfeh	حرفه
cannabis	hashish	حشیش
salary; wages	hoquq	حقوق
value judgement	hokm-e e'tebaari	حکم اعتباری
social animal	heyvaan-e ejtemaa'i	حیوان اجتماعی
family	khaanevaadeh	خانواده
one-parent family	khaanevaade-ye tak sarparast	خانواده تک سرپرست
extended family	khaanevaade-ye gostardeh	خانواده گسترده
nuclear family	khaanevaade-ye haste'i	خانواده هسته ای
social service	khedmat-e ejtemaa'i	خدمت اجتماعی
bigotry	khoshk andishi	خشک اندیشی
violence	khoshunat	خشونت
self	khod	خود
suicide	khodkoshi	خودکشی
egoistic suicide	khodkoshi-ye khodkhaahaaneh	خودکشی خودخواهانه
kinship	khishaavandi	خویشاوندی
social self	khishtan-e ejtemaa'i	خویشتن اجتماعی
social good	kheyr-e ejtemaa'i	خیر اجتماعی
data	daade-haa	داده ها
gang	daar o dasteh	دار و دسته
property	daaraa'i	دارائی
knowledge	daanesh	دانش
arbitration	daavari	داوری
cycle of disadvantage	daayere-ye mahrumiyat	دایره محرومیت
income	dar aamad	در آمد
involvement	dar aamikhtegi	در آمیختگی
involvement	dargiri	درگیری
internalisation	darunbord	درونبرد
internalisation	darunesh	درونش
achievement	dastaavard	دستاورد
bureaucracy	dastgaah-e edaari	دستگاه اداری
change	degarguni	دگرگونی
group interest	delbastegi-ye goruhi	دلبستگی گروهی
government	dowlat	دولت
perspective; point of view	didgaah	دیدگاه

416

liberationist perspective	didgaah-e aazaadgaraaneh	دیدگاه آزادگرانه
religion	din	دین
secularisation	dinzadaa'i	دین زدائی
dynamics	dinaamism	دینامیسم
bureaucracy	divaan saalaari	دیوانسالاری
social relation	raabete-ye ejtemaa'i	رابطه اجتماعی
voting	ra'y dahi	رای دهی
social category; social ranking	rade-ye ejtemaa'i	رده اجتماعی
media	resaane-haa	رسانه ها
social growth	roshd-e ejtemaa'i	رشد اجتماعی
social behaviour	raftaar-e ejtemaa'i	رفتار اجتماعی
morality; moral behaviour	raftaar-e akhlaaqi	رفتار اخلاقی
group behaviour	raftaar-e goruhi	رفتار گروهی
industrial relations	ravaabet-e san'ati	روابط صنعتی
psychology	ravaanshenaasi	روانشناسی
group psychology	ravaanshenaasi-ye goruhi	روانشناسی گروهی
methodology	ravesh shenaasi	روش شناسی
ethnomethodology	ravesh shenaasi-ye qowmi	روش شناسی قومی
quantitative methods	ravesh-e kamiyati	روش کمیتی
qualitative methods	ravesh-e keyfiyati	روش کیفیتی
intelligentsia	rowshanfekraan	روشنفکران
social trends	ravand-haa-ye ejtemaa'i	روند های اجتماعی
leadership	rahbari	رهبری
leadership	rahbariyat	رهبریت
language	zabaan	زبان
jargon	zabaan-e gong-e herfe'i	زبان گنگ حرفه ای
social background	zamine-ye ejtemaa'i	زمینه اجتماعی
feminism	zan aazaadkhaahi	زن آزادخواهی
social life	zendegi-ye ejtemaa'i	زندگی اجتماعی
subsistence levels	zistpaaye-haa	زیست پایه ها
social structure	saakht-e ejtemaa'i	ساخت اجتماعی
structuralism	saakht baavari	ساخت باوری
group structure	saakht-e goruhi	ساخت گروهی
social adaptation	saazgaari-ye ejtemaa'i	سازگاری اجتماعی
elitism	saraamad parvari	سرامد پروری
capitalism	sarmaayeh daari	سرمایه داری
politics	siyaasat	سیاست
social system	sistem-e ejtemaa'i	سیستم اجتماعی

meritocracy	shaayesteh saalaari	شایسته سالاری
individual (n.)	shakhs	شخص
personality	shakhsiyat	شخصیت
job; occupation	shoql	شغل
Asiatic mode of production	shive-ye towlid-e aasyaa'i	شیوه تولید آسیائی
restrictive practices	shive-ye 'amal-e mahdud	شیوه عمل محدود
urbanization	shahr garaa'i	شهر گرائی
industrialization	san'ati gari	صنعتی گری
social class	tabaqe-ye ejtemaa'i	طبقه اجتماعی
aristocracy	tabaqe-ye ashraaf	طبقه اشراف
upper class	tabaqe-ye baalaa	طبقه بالا
working class	tabaqe-ye kaargar	طبقه کارگر
middle class	tabaqe-ye motavasset	طبقه متوسط
divorce	talaaq	طلاق
intelligent	'aaqel	عاقل
justice	'edaalat	عدالت
opinion poll	'aqideh sanji	عقیده سنجی
politics; political science	'elm-e siyaasat	علم سیاست
social sciences	'olum-e ejtemaa'i	علوم اجتماعی
objectivity	'eyniyat	عینیت
instinct	qarizeh	غریزه
learning	faraagiri	فراگیری
affluence	faraavaani	فراوانی
social product	faraavarde-ye ejtemaa'i	فراورده اجتماعی
positive discrimination	farq gozaari-ye mosbat	فرق گذاری مثبت
sect	ferqeh	فرقه
culture	farhang	فرهنگ
youth culture	farhang-e javaanaan	فرهنگ جوانان
culture of poverty	farhang-e faqr	فرهنگ فقر
social pressure	feshaar-e ejtemaa'i	فشار اجتماعی
social space	fazaa-ye ejtemaa'i	فضای اجتماعی
poverty	faqr	فقر
feminism	feminism	فمینیسم
technocracy	fann saalaari	فن سالاری
technology	fann shenaakht	فن شناخت
management technique	fann-e modiriyat	فن مدیریت
social understanding	fahm-e ejtemaa'i	فهم اجتماعی
validity; legality	qaanuniyat	قانونیت

ethnic stratification	qeshrbandi-ye qowmi	قشربندی قومی
rules	qavaa'ed	قواعد
social work	kaar-e ejtemaa'i	کار اجتماعی
functionalism	kaarkard garaa'i	کارکردگرائی
employment	kaar gomaari	کارگماری
job satisfaction	kaamyaabi-ye shoqli	کامیابی شغلی
pluralism	kesrat	کثرت
social code	kod-e ejtemaa'i	کداجتماعی
church; the Church	kelisaa	کلیسا
social control	kontrol-e ejtemaa'i	کنترل اجتماعی
migration	kuch	کوچ
cult	kish	کیش
capital punishment	keyfar-e e'daam	کیفر اعدام
ghetto	getow	گتو
group	goruh	گروه
social group	goruh-e ejtemaa'i	گروه اجتماعی
peer group	goruh-e hamtaraaz	گروه همتراز
Gesellschaft	gezelshaft	گزلشفت
Gemeinschaft	gemaaynshaft	گماینشفت
social layer	laaye-ye ejtemaa'i	لایه اجتماعی
underclass	laaye-ye ejtemaa'i-ye zir-e tabaqaat	لایه اجتماعی زیر طبقات
social stratification	laayeh bandi-ye ejtemaa'i	لایه بندی اجتماعی
social strata	laaye-haa-ye ejtemaa'i	لایه های اجتماعی
property	maal	مال
ownership	maalekiyat	مالکیت
social ownership	maalekiyat-e ejtemaa'i	مالکیت اجتماعی
parliament	majles	مجلس
deprivation	mahrumiyat	محرومیت
social deprivation	mahrumiyat-e ejtemaa'i	محرومیت اجتماعی
social environment	mohit-e ejtemaa'i	محیط اجتماعی
educational qualifications	madaarek-e tahsili	مدارک تحصیلی
social worker	madadkaar-e ejtemaa'i	مددکار اجتماعی
social work	madadkaari-ye ejtemaa'i	مددکاری اجتماعی
deschooling	madraseh zadaa'i	مدرسه زدائی
organic model of society	model-e orgaanik-e jaame'eh	مدل ارگانیک جامعه
negotiation	mozaakereh	مذاکره
mortality	marg o mir	مرگ و میر
social problem	mas'ale-ye ejtemaa'i	مسئله اجتماعی

observation	*moshaahedeh*	مشاهده
interview	*mosaahebeh*	مصاحبه
social studies	*motaale'aat-e ejtemaa'i*	مطالعات اجتماعی
social meaning	*ma'naa-ye ejtemaa'i*	معنای اجتماعی
concept	*mafhum*	مفهوم
property	*molk*	ملک
secondary (data) sources	*manaabe'-e daade-haa-ye dovvomin*	منابع داده های دومین
slums	*mantaqe-ye faqirneshin*	منطقه فقیرنشین
inner city	*miyaanshahr*	میانشهر
social interaction	*miyaankonesh-e ejtemaa'i*	میانکنش اجتماعی
interactionism	*miyaankonesh baavari*	میانکنش باوری
symbolic interactionism	*miyaankonesh baavari-ye nemaadi*	میانکنش باوری نمادی
social field	*meydaan-e ejtemaa'i*	میدان اجتماعی
mortality	*mirandegi*	میرندگی
social scale	*mizaan-e ejtemaa'i*	میزان اجتماعی
birth rate	*mizaan-e zaad o valad*	میزان زاد و ولد
death rate	*mizaan-e marg o mir*	میزان مرگ و میر
migration; emigration; immigration	*mohaajerat*	مهاجرت
social engineering	*mohandesi-ye ejtemaa'i*	مهندسی اجتماعی
social unrest	*naa aaraami-ye ejtemaa'i*	نا آرامی اجتماعی
inequality	*naabaraabari*	نابرابری
social disorder	*naabesaamaani-ye ejtemaa'i*	نابسامانی اجتماعی
social abnormality	*naabehanjaari-ye ejtemaa'i*	نابهنجاری اجتماعی
death rate	*nerkh-e marg o mir*	نرخ مرگ و میر
race	*nezhaad*	نژاد
ethnocentrism	*nezhaad garaa'i*	نژاد گرائی
sex ratio	*nesbat-e zan o mard dar jam'iyat*	نسبت زن و مرد در جمعیت
dependency ratio	*nesbat-e vaabastegi*	نسبت وابستگی
cultural relativism	*nesbiyat-e farhangi*	نسبیت فرهنگی
social order	*nezaam-e ejtemaa'i*	نظام اجتماعی
feudal system	*nezaam-e fe'udaali*	نظام فئودالی
caste system	*nezaam-e kaasti*	نظام کاستی
social theory	*nazariye-ye ejtemaa'i*	نظریه اجتماعی
self; ego	*nafs*	نفس
role	*naqsh*	نقش
social role	*naqsh-e ejtemaa'i*	نقش اجتماعی
group image	*negaresh-e goruhi*	نگرش گروهی
symbol	*nemaad*	نماد

social indicator	namudgaar-e ejtemaa'i	نمودگار اجتماعی
case study	nemune-ye pezhuhi	نمونه پژوهی
sampling	nemuneh giri	نمونه گیری
altruism	now dusti	نوع دوستی
social need	niyaaz-e ejtemaa'i	نیاز اجتماعی
institutionalisation	nehaadineh gari	نهادینه گری
drug dependence	vaabastegi be mavaad-e mokhadder	وابستگی به مواد مخدر
social unit	vaahed-e ejtemaa'i	واحد اجتماعی
social constraint	vaadaargari-ye ejtemaa'i	وادارگری اجتماعی
reality	vaaqe'iyat	واقعیت
social reality	vaaqe'iyat-e ejtemaa'i	واقعیت اجتماعی
social being	vojud-e ejtemaa'i	وجود اجتماعی
group loyalty	vafaadaari-ye goruhi	وفاداری گروهی
social pyramid	heram-e ejtemaa'i	هرم اجتماعی
cohabitation	ham khaanegi	هم خانگی
consensus	ham ra'yi	هم رایی
solidarity	hambastegi	همبستگی
social solidarity	hambastegi-ye ejtemaa'i	همبستگی اجتماعی
homeostasis	hamtaraazmaani	همترازمانی
group cohesion	hamchasbi-ye goruhi	همچسبی گروهی
social accommodation	hamsaazi-ye ejtemaa'i	همسازی اجتماعی
conformity	hamsaani	همسانی
conflict	hamsetizi	همستیزی
class conflict	hamsetizi-ye tabaqaati	همستیزی طبقاتی
cultural conflict	hamsetizi-ye farhangi	همستیزی فرهنگی
industrial conflict	hamsetizi-ye kaargari	همستیزی کارگری
convergence; integration	hamgaraa'i	همگرائی
census questionnaire	hameh porsi-ye sar shomaari	همه پرسی سرشماری
norm	hanjaar	هنجار
intelligent	hushmand	هوشمند
positivism	yaaft baavari	یافت باوری
social integration	yekpaarchegi-ye ejtemaa'i	یکپارچگی اجتماعی
bias	yeksu garaa'i	یکسوگرائی
social unit	yegaan-e ejtemaa'i	یگان اجتماعی

❮❮❖❯❯

Sounds

صدا ها

sound	aavaa	آوا
sigh; sighing	aah	آه
chiming (of the clock)	aahang-e saa'at	آهنگ ساعت
echo	en'ekaas-e sedaa	انعکاس صدا
sound	baang	بانگ
sputtering (of an engine)	pet pet	پت پت
beating (of a heart)	tapesh	تپش
crack; cracking sound; bang	taraq	ترق
bang; banging; crack	taraq toruq	ترق تروق
knocking (on a door)	taq taq	تق تق
clatter	teleq	تلق تلق
ticking; tick-tock	tik tik	تیک تیک
shout	jaar	جار
uproar; din; racket	jaar o janjaal	جار و جنجال
jingle; jingling	jering jering	جرینگ جرینگ
sizzling	jelez o velez	جلز ولز
din; racket	janjaal	جنجال
chirp; chirping	jir jir	جیر جیر
creaking	jirvang	جیرونگ
scream	jiq	جیغ
squeak; squeaking	jik jik	جیک جیک
clink; clinking	jing	جینگ
chirp; chirping	chir chir	چیر چیر
purring; snoring	khor khor	خر خر
snoring	khor o pof	خر و پف
rustle; rustling; crackling	khesh khesh	خش خش
slap	darq	درق
jingle; jingling	deleng	دلنگ
bang; banging	dang	دنگ
banging; peal (of bells); clanging	dang dang	دنگ دنگ
buzz; buzzing	zer zer	زر زر
murmur	zemzemeh	زمزمه
howl; howling	zuzeh	زوزه
noise	sar o sedaa	سر و صدا
whistle	sut	سوت
gurgling; rushing (of water)	shor shor	شر شر

splash	shalap	شلپ
lapping; splashing	shalap shalap	شلپ شلپ
wailing	shivan	شیون
sound; voice	sedaa	صدا
scratching (sound)	sedaa-ye kharaash	صدای خراش
scraping (sound)	sedaa-ye kharaashidan	صدای خراشیدن
ringing	sedaa-ye zang	صدای زنگ
blare; bawling (of a baby)	'arr o 'arr	عر و عر
rumbling; croaking	qaar o qur	غار و غور
gurgle (of a baby)	qaan o qun	غان و غون
grumbling; murmuring; muttering	qor qor	غر غر
rumble; rumbling	qorresh	غرش
rumble of thunder	qorresh-e ra'd	غرش رعد
gargling	qarqareh	غرغره
rumble	qoronbeh	غرنبه
creaking	qezh qezh	غژ غژ
uproar	qowqaa	غوغا
screeching	qizh	غیژ
humming (of electrical appliances)	fer fer	فر فر
cry; scream; exclamation	faryaad	فریاد
cries	faryaad-haa	فریاد ها
rumpus; din	qaal o qil	قال و قیل
crunching; squelching	qerech qerech	قرچ قرچ
gurgle; gurgling	qol gol	قل قل
gurgling; gulping; lapping	qolop qolop	قلپ قلپ
clop; clopping	kolop kolop	کلپ کلپ
crackle (of leaves, gunfire etc.)	gorop gorop	گرپ گرپ
crying and moaning	geryeh o zaari	گریه و زاری
ear-splitting	gushkharaash	گوشخراش
lapping	lap lap	لپ لپ
miaouw; mewing	miyaaow miyaaow	میاو میاو
miaouw; mewing	miyow miyow	میو میو
moan; moaning	naaleh	ناله
humming	vez vez	وز وز
chuckle; chuckling	her her	هر هر
lapping; slurping	halaf halaf	هلف هلف
hooting	hu hu	هو هو
hissing	his	هیس

423

a loud noise; a loud voice صدای بلند   to make a sound صدا در آوردن   to sound; to make a sound صدا دادن

to echo صدا پیچیدن   an ear-splitting noise صدای گوشخراش   to make a noise سر و صدا کردن

soundproofing عایق ضد صدا   the sound of music echoed through the concert hall آوای موسیقی در تالار پیچید

shouting داد و فریاد   to shout out; to cry; to exlaim فریاد کشیدن   to cry out; to shout داد زدن

to chirr چیر چیر کردن   the chirping of the birds صدای جیر جیر پرندگان   to chirp جیر جیر کردن

to gurgle; to boil غل غل کردن   the chirring of the insects صدای چیر چیر حشرات

to gurgle (like a baby) غان و غون کردن   the gurgle of boiling milk صدای غل غل شیر درحال جوشیدن

the little baby was gurgling with happiness بچه کوچولو از خوشحالی غان و غون میکرد

the howl of the wolf زوزه گرگ   the bag fell to the floor with a thud کیف تالاپی به زمین افتاد

bleating صدای بع بع   to baa; to bleat بع بع کردن   the jingling of small bells صدای جرینگ جرینگ زنگوله ها

the mosquitoes were humming پشه ها وز وز میکردند   he slammed the door در را دنگی بست

to wail شیون کشیدن   he drank the water with a lapping sound با صدای لپ لپ آب میخورد

my ears are buzzing گوشهایم وز وز می کند   the splashing sound of the fountain صدای شر شر فواره

the ticking of the clock تیک تیک ساعت   I could hear the cry of 'God is great!' بانگ الله اکبر را می شنیدم

to bark عو عو کردن   the neighbour's dog was barking سگ همسایه پارس می کرد

the crackle of gunfire صدای تلق تلق تیر اندازی   the click of the key in the lock صدای تلق کلید در قفل

the rustle of the newspaper خش خش روزنامه   the billiard balls clicked together گوی های بیلیارد تق تق بهم خوردند

to go ding-dong دینگ دانگ صدا کردن   the creaking of the cart's wheels جیرینگ چرخهای گاری

the children were splashing about in the pool بچه ها در استخر شلپ شلوپ می کردند   to splash شلپ شلوپ کردن

to sputter لک لک کردن   my car engine is sputtering موتور ماشینم پت پت می کند

the ear-splitting sound of thunder صدای گوشخراش رعد   the black clouds were rumbling ابرهای سیاه غرش می کردند

the blare of the loudspeaker صدای عر و عر بلندگو   the train clattered into the station قطار تلق و تلق وارد ایستگاه شد

stop moaning! غر نزن!   the wood was crackling in the fire هیزم در آتش ترق تروق می کرد

to mutter and grumble غر ولند کردن   to moan ناله کردن   to sigh آه کشیدن   to snore خر و پف کشیدن

he made a farting sound with his hands با دستش صدای گوزمانندی در آورد   to blow a 'raspberry' شیشکی در کردن

sound barrier دیوار صوتی   sound صوت   to blow (out a candle) پف کردن   to whistle سوت کشیدن

◄◄◊►►

424

Sport

free; freestyle	aazaad	آزاد
injury	aasib didegi	آسیب دیدگی
offside	aafsaayd	آفساید
epee	epeh	اپه
Formula 1 racing	otomobilraani-ye formul-e yek	اتومبیلرانی فرمول یک
sending off; expulsion	ekhraaji	اخراجی
warning	ekhtaari	اخطاری
training camp	ordu-ye aamaadegi	اردوی آمادگی
horse racing	asb davaani	اسب دوانی
horse riding	asb savaari	اسب سواری
swimming pool	estakhr	استخر
skiing	eski	اسکی
water skiing	eski-ye ru-ye aab	اسکی روی آب
skating	eskeyt	اسکیت
snooker	esnuker	اسنوکر
point	emtiyaaz	امتیاز
relay	emdaadi	امدادی
fifth seed	omid daar-e shomaare-ye panj	امیددار شماره ۵
singles (tennis, badminton etc.)	enferaadi	انفرادی
out	owt	اوت
loss; defeat	baakht	باخت
loser	baazandeh	بازنده
game; match	baazi	بازی
delaying tactics	baazi-ye ta'khiri	بازی تاخیری
play-maker (football)	baazi saaz	بازی ساز
player	baazi kon	بازیکن
player	baazigar	بازیگر
play; playing	baazigari	بازیگری
Olympic Games	baazi-haa-ye olampik	بازیهای المپیک
club	baashgaah	باشگاه
golf club	baashgaah-e golf	باشگاه گلف
badminton	badmintun	بدمینتون
win; victory	bord	برد
winner	barandeh	برنده
basketball	basketbaal	بسکتبال
boxing	buks	بوکس

baseball	beysbaal	بیسبال
billiards	bilyaard	بیلیارد
pass	paas	پاس
throwing the hammer	partaab-e chakkosh	پرتاب چکش
throwing the discus	partaab-e disk	پرتاب دیسک
throwing the javelin	partaab-e neyzeh	پرتاب نیزه
putting the shot	partaab-e vazneh	پرتاب وزنه
shot-putter	partaabgar-e vazneh	پرتابگر وزنه
high-jump	paresh-e ertefaa'	پرش ارتفاع
horse-jumping	paresh-e baa asb	پرش با اسب
pole-vaulting	paresh-e baa neyzeh	پرش با نیزه
triple jump	paresh-e seh gaam	پرش سه گام
long-jump	paresh-e tul	پرش طول
butterfly stroke	parvaaneh	پروانه
penalty	penaalti	پنالتی
pentathlon	panjgaaneh	پنج گانه
defensive cover	pushesh-e defaa'i	پوشش دفاعی
victory; success; win	piruzi	پیروزی
leading goalscorer	pishtaaz-e golzanaan	پیشتاز گلزنان
match; fight	peykaar	پیکار
tactics	taaktik	تاکتیک
line-up; composition	tarkib	ترکیب
draw	tasaavi	تساوی
goalless draw	tasaavi-ye bedun-e gol	تساوی بدون گل
change (of players)	ta'viz	تعویض
teikwando	tekvaandow	تکواندو
team effort	talaash-e timi	تلاش تیمی
ski lift	teleski	تلسکی
spectator	tamaashaachi	تماشاچی
spectator	tamaashaagar	تماشاگر
table tennis	tenis-e ru-ye miz	تنیس روی میز
ball	tup	توپ
net	tur	تور
side netting	tur-e kenaari	تور کناری
tournament	turnament	تورنمنت
shooting; archery	tirandaazi	تیر اندازی
goalpost	tir-e darvaazeh	تیر دروازه
national team	tim-e melli	تیم ملی

home team	tim-e mizbaan	تیم میزبان
away team	tim-e mehmaan	تیم مهمان
placing (i.e. of the ball)	jaagiri	جاگیری
cup	jaam	جام
world cup	jaam-e jahaani	جام جهانی
knock-out cup; elimination	jaam-e hazfi	جام حذفی
substitute	jaaygozin	جایگزین
table (i.e. league or medals)	jadval	جدول
wing	jenaah	جناح
left wing	jenaah-e chap	جناح چپ
right wing	jenaah-e raast	جناح راست
judo	judow	جودو
ski stick	chub-e eski	چوب اسکی
polo	chowgaan	چوگان
opponent; rival	harif	حریف
score	hesaab	حساب
attack	hamleh	حمله
finishing line	khatt-e paayaan	خط پایان
attacking line	khatt-e hamleh	خط حمله
line of defense	khatt-e defaa'	خط دفاع
midfield line	khatt-e miyaani	خط میانی
foul	khataa	خطا
referee; umpire	daavar	داور
refereeing; umpiring	daavari	داوری
deflection	dekhaalat	دخالت
goal; goal mouth	darvaazeh	دروازه
goalkeeper	darvaazeh baan	دروازه بان
premier league; first division	daste-ye avval	دسته اول
defence	defaa'	دفاع
midfield defenders	defaa'-haa-ye miyaani	دفاع های میانی
remaining minutes	daqaayeq-e baaqimaandeh	دقایق باقیمانده
running; race	dow	دو
long-distance running	dow-e esteqaamat	دو استقامت
hurdles; steeplechase	dow-e baa maane'	دو با مانع
sprint	dow-e sor'at	دو سرعت
cross-country running	dow-e sahraa navardi	دو صحرانوردی
middle-distance running	dow-e nimeh esteqaamat	دو نیمه استقامت
track and field; athletics	dow o meydaan	دو و میدان

athletic; athletics	dow o meydaani	دو و میدانی
cyclist	dowcharkheh savaar	دوچرخه سوار
cycling	dowcharkeh savaari	دوچرخه سواری
third round	dowr-e sevvom	دور سوم
heyday	dowraan-e owj	دوران اوج
round	dowr	دور
semi-final	dowr-e nimeh nahaa'i	دور نیمه نهائی
final	dowr-e nahaa'i	دور نهائی
quarter-final	dowr-e yek chahaarom-e nahaa'i	دور یک چهارم نهائی
runner	davandeh	دونده
doubles (tennis etc.)	dow nafareh	دونفره
match; fixture; meeting; heat	didaar	دیدار
singles match	didaar-e enferaadi	دیدار انفرادی
final match; final round	didaar-e paayaani	دیدار پایانی
friendly match	didaar-e dustaaneh	دیدار دوستانه
doubles match	didaar-e dow nafareh	دیدار دونفره
preliminary matches	didaar-haa-ye moqaddamaati	دیدارهای مقدماتی
goalpost	deyrak	دیرک
decathlon	dahgaaneh	دهگانه
reserve	zakhireh	ذخیره
racket	raakat	راکت
rugby	raagbi	راگبی
ranking; position	radeh bandi	رده بندی
world ranking	radeh bandi-ye jahaani	رده بندی جهانی
category; field (of sport)	reshteh	رشته
rivalry; competition; match	reqaabat	رقابت
record	rekurd	رکورد
new world record	rekurd-e jadid-e jahaan	رکورد جدید جهان
boxing ring	ring-e buks	رینگ بوکس
tennis court	zamin-e tenis	زمین تنیس
gymnastics	zhimnaastik	ژیمناستیک
sabre	saabr	سابر
sports hall; sports arena	saalon-e varzesh	سالن ورزش
ice-rink	saalon-e paatinaazh	سالن پاتیناژ
gymnasium; gymnastics arena	saalon-e zhimnaastik	سالن ژیمناستیک
serve (tennis, badminton etc.)	serv	سرو
relegation	soqut	سقوط
winners' podium	saku-ye barandegaan	سکوی برندگان

dog racing	sag davaani	سگ دوانی
horse rider	savaar kaar	سوار کار
participant	sherkat konandeh	شرکت کننده
hunting	shekaar	شکار
defeat	shekast	شکست
shot (in football, rugby etc.)	shelik	شلیک
number	shomaareh	شماره
fencing	shamshir baazi	شمشیر بازی
swimming	shenaa	شنا
swimmer	shenaagar	شناگر
shot (in football, rugby etc.)	shut	شوت
diving	shirjeh	شیرجه
diver	shirjeh row	شیرجه رو
record holder	saaheb-e rekurd	صاحب رکورد
top of the table	sadr neshin	صدرنشین
counter attack	zedd-e hamleh	ضد حمله
penalty shoot-out	zarabaat-e penaalti	ضربات پنالتی
shot; kick; punch; hit; blow	zarbeh	ضربه
free kick	zarbe-ye aazaad	ضربه آزاد
header (in football)	zarbe-ye sar	ضربه سر
technical knock-out	zarbe-ye fanni	ضربه فنی
swerving shot	zarbe-ye qows daar	ضربه قوس دار
team member	'ozv-e tim	عضو تیم
winner; champion; victor	faateh	فاتح
call-up (to play for a team)	faraakhaani	فراخوانی
football; soccer	futbaal	فوتبال
indoor football	futbaal-e saaloni	فوتبال سالنی
championship football	futbaal-e qahremaani	فوتبال قهرمانی
footballer; soccer player	futbaalist	فوتبالیست
final	finaal	فینال
rowing; canoeing	qaayeqraani	قایقرانی
jogging	qadam dow	قدم دو
breast stroke	qurbaaqeh	قورباغه
champion; winner	qahremaan	قهرمان
former champion	qahremaan-e saabeq	قهرمان سابق
captain	kaapitaan	کاپیتان
team work	kaar-e goruhi	کار گروهی
karate	kaaraateh	کاراته

yellow card	kaart-e zard	کارت زرد
red card	kaart-e qermez	کارت قرمز
back stroke	kraal-e posht	کرال پشت
front crawl	kraal-e sineh	کرال سینه
corner	korner	کرنر
cricket	kriket	کریکت
free-style wrestling	koshti-ye aazaad	کشتی آزاد
Graeco-Roman wrestling	koshti-ye farangi	کشتی فرنگی
wrestler	koshti gir	کشتی گیر
wrestling	koshti giri	کشتی گیری
host nation	keshvar-e mizbaan	کشور میزبان
black belt	kamarband-e siyaah	کمربند سیاه
mountaineering	kuh navardi	کوه نوردی
age group	goruh-e senni	گروه سنی
goal	gol	گل
equalising goal	gol-e tasaavi	گل تساوی
goal scorer	golzan	گلزن
goal scoring	golzani	گلزنی
golf	golf	گلف
game (in tennis)	geym	گیم
lacrosse	laakraas	لاکراس
league	lig	لیگ
event; category	maaddeh	ماده
marathon	maaraaton	ماراتن
championship motor racing	maashin savaari-ye mosaabeqe'i	ماشین سواری مسابقه ای
fishing	maahigiri	ماهیگیری
challenge; struggle; match	mobaarezeh	مبارزه
ban (in football)	mahrumiyat	محرومیت
penalty area	mahvate-ye penaalti	محوطه پنالتی
medley (in swimming)	mokhtalet	مختلط
individual medley	mokhtalet-e enferaadi	مختلط انفرادی
defender	modaafe'	مدافع
bronze medal	medaal-e beronz	مدال برنز
gold medal	medaal-e talaa'i	مدال طلائی
silver medal	medaal-e noqre'i	مدال نقره ای
coach	morabbi	مربی
return match	marhale-ye bargasht	مرحله برگشت
first match (of two legs)	marhale-ye raft	مرحله رفت

preliminary round	*marhale-ye moqaddamaati*	مرحله مقدماتی
man of the match	*mard-e shomaare-ye yek-e meydaan*	مرد شماره یک میدان
championships	*mosaabeqaat-e qahremaani*	مسابقات قهرمانی
race	*mosaabeqe-ye dow*	مسابقه دو
goalless draw	*mosaavi-ye bedun-e goal*	مساوی بدون گل
boxer	*mosht zan*	مشت زن
boxing	*mosht zani*	مشت زنی
place; position	*maqaam*	مقام
first place	*makaan-e avval*	مکان اول
goal scoring opportunity	*mowqe'iyat-e gol*	موقعیت گل
midfield	*miyaane-ye meydaan*	میانه میدان
pitch; track; arena; ring; course	*meydaan*	میدان
race track (for horse racing)	*meydaan-e asbdavaani*	میدان اسب دوانی
running track	*meydaan-e dow*	میدان دو
attacker; striker	*mohaajem*	مهاجم
knock-out	*naak owt*	ناك اوت
runner-up	*naayeb qahremaan*	نایب قهرمان
netball	*netbaal*	نتبال
result; score	*natijeh*	نتیجه
warm-up; light exercise	*narmesh*	نرمش
penalty spot	*noqte-ye penaalti*	نقطه پنالتی
dressage	*namaayesh-e savaar kaari*	نمایش سوار کاری
representative	*namaayandeh*	نماینده
javelin	*neyzeh*	نیزه
reserve bench	*nimkat-e zakhire-haa*	نیمکت ذخیره ها
first half	*nime-ye avval*	نیمه اول
second half	*nime-ye dovvom*	نیمه دوم
half-marathon	*nimeh maaraaton*	نیمه ماراتن
water polo	*vaaterpolo*	واترپلو
volleyball	*vaalibaal*	والیبال
beach volleyball	*vaalibaal-e saaheli*	والیبال ساحلی
volleyball player	*vaalibaalist*	والیبالیست
sport; exercise	*varzesh*	ورزش
sportsman; sportswoman	*varzeshkaar*	ورزشکار
sports stadium	*varzeshgaah*	ورزشگاه
weightlifter	*vazneh bardaar*	وزنه بردار
weightlifting	*vazneh bardaari*	وزنه برداری
shot-putting	*vazneh paraani*	وزنه پرانی

extra time	vaqt-e ezaafi	وقت اضافی
injury time; extra time	vaqt-e talaf shodeh	وقت تلف شده
half-back	haafbak	هافبک
hockey	haaki	هاکی
ice hockey	haaki-ye ru-ye yakh	هاکی روی یخ
heptathlon	haft gaaneh	هفت گانه
handball	handbaal	هندبال
handball player	handbaalist	هندبالیست
supporter	havaadaar	هوادار
yoga	yowgaa	یوگا

OTHER SPORTING WORDS AND PHRASES

to hit; to strike; to kick زدن to lose باختن to win بردن to take part شرکت کردن to play بازی کردن

to meet; to be up against دیدار کردن to draw; to end in a draw مساوی شدن to score a goal گل زدن

to shoot (the ball) شوت زدن to be sent off از بازی اخراج شدن to save (a goal) مهار کردن

to be staged; to take place بر گزار شدن to stage; to put on (e.g. a tournament) بر گزار کردن

the competition was staged in the city sports arena مسابقه در ورزشگاه شهر بر گزار شد to beat شکست دادن

Iran beat America 6-1 ایران آمریکا را شش بر یک شکست داد to be defeated شکست خوردن

the national team was defeated in the World Cup تیم ملی در مسابقات جام جهان شکست خورد

France beat Italy فرانسه از ایتالیا برد Italy lost to France ایتالیا به فرانسه باخت

they will play against each other آنها با یکدیگر به رقابت می پردازند to meet in competition به رقابت پرداختن

he/she took first place من مقام دوم را تصاحب کردم I took second place مقام اول را کسب کرد

our team moved into top position in the premier league تیم ما در صدر جدول گروه اول قرار گرفت

to put the ball into play; to pass the ball توپ به تیر دروازه اصابت کرد the ball hit the post توپ را به گردش در آوردن

in yesterday's game, Ali scored two goals علی در بازی دیروز دو تا گل زد top of the league صدر نشین

the game ended in a penalty shoot-out بازی با ضربات پنالتی تمام شد a heavy defeat شکست سنگین

in the long jump, the world record was broken در پرش به طول رکورد جهانی شکسته شد record-holder رکورد دار

goalless draw بازی با نتیجه تساوی بدون گل خاتمه یافت the game ended in a goalless draw تساوی بدون گل

in the 400-metre relay, the Iranian team set a new record در چهارصد متر امدادی تیم ایران رکورد جدیدی بر پا کرد

he is the highest goalscorer in Asia او بهترین گلزن آسیا است Ahmad was sent off احمد از بازی اخراج شد

I reached the final of the tennis tournament من به دوره نهائی مسابقه تنیس رسیدم to be victorious پیروز شدن

the Iranian runner bettered the record by 0.07 seconds دونده ایرانی رکورد را به میزان هفت صدم ثانیه بهبود بخشید

will you play tennis with me tomorrow? فردا با من تنیس بازی می کنید؟ professional player بازیگر حرفه ای

Ali put the ball into the back of the net علی توپ را به تور دوخت leading goalscorer پیشتاز گلزنان

the Iranian team made two changes تیم ایران دست به دو تعویض زد the ref must be blind! داور باید کور باشه!

Iran won the Rajiv Gandhi Cup تیم میزبان بد بازی کرد the home team played badly ایران فاتح جام راجیو گاندی شد

he made the champion's cup his own (i.e. he won the title) او جام قهرمانی را به خود اختصاص داد

in swimming, Hasan won the bronze medal در شنا ، حسن صاحب مدال برنز شد

Stage and Screen

تناتر و سینما

sound effects	*aasaar-e sowti*	آثار صوتی
audition	*aazmaayesh-e honarpishegi*	آزمایش هنرپیشگی
interval; intermission	*aantraakt*	آنتراکت
sound effects	*aavaa pardaazi*	آواپردازی
opera	*operaa*	اپرا
operetta	*operet*	اپرت
stage effects	*asar-e sahneh*	اثر صحنه
performance	*ejraa*	اجراء
orchestra	*orkestr*	ارکستر
adaptation	*eqtebaas*	اقتباس
climax	*owj*	اوج
tragic climax	*owj-e teraazhik*	اوج تراژیک
actor; player; artist	*baazigar*	بازیگر
stage actor	*baazigar-e te'aatr*	بازیگر تناتر
professional actor	*baazigar-e herfe'i*	بازیگر حرفه ای
walk-on	*baazigar-e far'i*	بازیگر فرعی
cast; actors; dramatis personae	*baazigaraan*	بازیگران
amateur actors	*baazigaraan-e qeyr-e herfe'i*	بازیگران غیر حرفه ای
cast; film actors	*baazigaraan-e film*	بازیگران فیلم
ballet	*baaleh*	باله
stuntman; stand-in	*badal*	بدل
based on	*bar asaas*	بر اساس
cut	*boresh*	برش
rapid cut	*boresh-e sari'*	برش سریع
programme	*barnaameh*	برنامه
Oscar winner	*barande-ye oskaar*	برنده اسکار
award winner	*barande-ye jaayezeh*	برنده جایزه
cinema ticket	*belit-e sinamaa*	بلیط سینما
viewer	*binandeh*	بیننده
footlights	*paa cheraaq*	پاچراغ
end; ending	*paayaan*	پایان
happy ending	*paayaan-e khosh*	پایان خوش
treatment (of a subject)	*pardaakht*	پرداخت
screen; curtain; act (i.e. of a play)	*pardeh*	پرده
act one	*parde-ye avval*	پرده اول
poster	*powster*	پوستر

preview	pish namaa'i	پیش نمائی
auditorium	taalaar	تالار
editor	tadvingar	تدوینگر
Shi'ite passion play	ta'ziyeh	تعزیه
theme; subject	tem	تم
main theme	tem-e asli	تم اصلی
spectator	tamaashaachi	تماشاچی
theatre	tamaashaa khaaneh	تماشاخانه
spectator	tamaashaagar	تماشاگر
theatre goer	tamaashaagar-e te'aatr	تماشاگر تئاتر
audience; spectators	tamaashaagaraan	تماشاگران
rehearsal	tamrin	تمرین
dress rehearsal	tamrin-e nehaa'i	تمرین نهائی
film production	towlid-e film	تولید فیلم
theatre	te'aatr	تئاتر
theatre of the absurd	te'aatr-e puchi	تئاتر پوچی
children's theatre	te'aatr-e kudak	تئاتر کودک
theatre-in-the-round	te'aatr-e gerdaagerd	تئاتر گرداگرد
theatricality	te'aatr vaari	تئاترواری
theatrical	te'aatri	تئاتری
credits; titles	titraazh	تیتراژ
animation	tahye-ye kaartun	تهیه کارتون
producer	tahyeh konandeh	تهیه کننده
award; prize	jaayezeh	جایزه
film festival	jashnvaare-ye film	جشنواره فیلم
special effects	jelve-haa-ye vizheh	جلوه های ویژه
make-up artist	chehreh aaraa	چهره آرا
soundtrack	haashiye-ye sowti	حاشیه صوتی
epic	hamaaseh	حماسه
opera singer	khaanande-ye operaa	خواننده اپرا
story; plot	daastaan	داستان
main plot	daastaan-e asli	داستان اصلی
love story	daastaan-e 'aasheqaaneh	داستان عاشقانه
sub-plot	daastaan-e far'i	داستان فرعی
in rehearsal	dar haal-e tamrin	در حال تمرین
dramatist; playwright	deraam nevis	درام نویس
stagehand	dastyaar-e sahneh	دستیار صحنه
assistant stage manager	dastyaar-e sahneh gardaan	دستیار صحنه گردان

434

clown	*dalqak*	دلقک
dubbing	*dubleh*	دوبله
stationary camera	*durbin-e saabet*	دوربین ثابت
moving camera	*durbin-e sayyaar*	دوربین سیار
direction	*raahnamaa'i*	راهنمائی
stage direction	*raahnamaa-ye sahneh*	راهنمای صحنه
dress circle	*radif-e darajeh yek*	ردیف درجه یک
ballet dancer	*raqqaas-e baaleh*	رقاص باله
realism	*re'aalism*	رئالیسم
camera angle	*zaaviye-ye durbin*	زاویه دوربین
stage whisper	*zemzeme-ye namaayeshi*	زمزمه نمایشی
sub-plot	*zir daastaan*	زیرداستان
subtitles	*zir nevis*	زیرنویس
dramatic structure	*saakhtaar-e deraamaatik*	ساختار دراماتیک
shadow play	*saayeh baazi*	سایه بازی
genre; style	*sabk*	سبک
film star; cinema star	*setaare-ye sinamaa*	ستاره سینما
ending	*sar anjaam*	سرانجام
sequence	*sekaans*	سکانس
platform	*saku*	سکو
scenario	*senaariyow*	سناریو
subject	*suzheh*	سوژه
prompter	*suflur*	سوفلور
tragi-comedy	*sowg shaadmaayesh*	سوگ شادمایش
tragedy	*sowgmaayesh*	سوگمایش
cinema	*sinamaa*	سینما
film maker	*sinamaa pardaaz*	سینما پرداز
cinema goer	*sinamaa row*	سینما رو
cinematographer	*sinamaagar*	سینماگر
filmography	*sinamaa negaari*	سینمانگاری
cinema (adj.); cinematic	*sinamaa'i*	سینمائی
cinema verite	*sinamaa-ye haqiqat-namaa*	سینمای حقیقت نما
comedy	*shaadmaayesh*	شادمایش
opening night	*shab-e avval-e namaayesh*	شب اول نمایش
character	*shakhsiyat*	شخصیت
main character	*shakhsiyat-e asli*	شخصیت اصلی
secondary or minor character	*shakhsiyat-e far'i*	شخصیت فرعی
film company	*sherkat-e filmsaazi*	شرکت فیلمسازی

magician; juggler	sho'bedeh baaz	شعبده باز
financial failure	shekast-e maaddi	شکست مادی
ventriloquist	shekam gu	شکم گو
ventriloquism	shekam gu'i	شکم گوئی
scene; stage; set	sahneh	صحنه
first scene	sahne-ye avval	صحنه اول
stagecraft	sahneh aafarini	صحنه آفرینی
stage manager	sahneh gardaan	صحنه گردان
stagecraft	sahneh gari	صحنه گری
stage fright	sahneh haraasi	صحنه هراسی
sound; voice; noise	sedaa	صدا
sound recording	sedaa bardaari	صدابرداری
sound editing	sedaa gozaari	صداگذاری
stalls	sandali-haa-ye radif-e avval	صندلیهای ردیف اول
cinema industry	san'at-e sinamaa	صنعت سینما
film industry	san'at-e filmsaazi	صنعت فیلمسازی
set design	tarraahi-ye sahneh	طراحی صحنه
satire	tanz	طنز
satirical	tanz aamiz	طنز آمیز
the world of cinema	'aalam-e sinamaa	عالم سینما
filmdom	'aalam-e film	عالم فیلم
stills	'aks-haa-ye film	عکسهای فیلم
title	'onvaan	عنوان
film culture	farhang-e sinamaa'i	فرهنگ سینمائی
atmosphere	fazaa	فضا
film	film	فیلم
science fiction film	film-e afsaane-ye 'elmi	فیلم افسانه علمی
camera man	film bardaar	فیلم بردار
filming	film bardaari	فیلم برداری
shoot 'em up; Western	film-e bezan bezan	فیلم بزن بزن
full-length film	film-e boland	فیلم بلند
historical film	film-e taarikhi	فیلم تاریخی
epic film	film-e hamaasi	فیلم حماسی
foreign film	film-e khaareji	فیلم خارجی
film library	film khaaneh	فیلم خانه
newsreel	film-e khabari	فیلم خبری
feature film	film-e daastaani	فیلم داستانی
film lover	film dust	فیلم دوست

film noir	film-e siyaah	فیلم سیاه
black and white film	film-e siyaah o sefid	فیلم سیاه و سفید
film buff	film shenaas	فیلم شناس
silent film	film-e saamet	فیلم صامت
detective film	film-e kaaraagaahi	فیلم کاراگاهی
short film	film-e kutaah	فیلم کوتاه
adventure film	film-e maajaraa'i	فیلم ماجرائی
documentary film	film-e mostanad	فیلم مستند
horror film	film-e vahshat angiz	فیلم وحشت انگیز
Western	film-e vestern	فیلم وسترن
film editing	film viraa'i	فیلم ویرائی
pornographic film	film-e harzeh negaaraaneh	فیلم هرزه نگارانه
arthouse film	film-e honari	فیلم هنری
thriller	film-e hayajaan aafarin	فیلم هیجان آفرین
principal filming	filmbardaari-ye asli	فیلمبرداری اصلی
film maker	filmsaaz	فیلمساز
film making	filmsaazi	فیلمسازی
film director	filmgardaan	فیلمگردان
film script	filmnaameh	فیلمنامه
scriptwriter	filmnaameh nevis	فیلمنامه نویس
scriptwriting	filmnaameh nevisi	فیلمنامه نویسی
filmic	filmi	فیلمی
character	kaaraakter	کاراکتر
animation; cartoon	kaartun	کارتون
animator	kaartun saaz	کارتون ساز
film crew	kaarkonaan-e film	کارکنان فیلم
director (stage or screen)	kaargardaan	کارگردان
film director	kaargardaan-e film	کارگردان فیلم
theatre director	kaargardaan-e namaayeshnaameh	کارگردان نمایشنامه
directing	kaargardaani	کارگردانی
light comedy	komedi-ye sabok	کمدی سبک
romantic comedy	komedi-ye 'aasheqaaneh	کمدی عاشقانه
theatre company; theatre group	goruh-e te'aatri	گروه تئاتری
make-up	gerim	گریم
dialogue	goftogu	گفتگو
box-office	gisheh	گیشه
play script	matn-e namaayeshnaameh	متن نمایشنامه
scriptwriter	matn nevis	متن نویس

437

content	mohtavaa	محتوا
stage manager	modir-e sahneh	مدیر صحنه
director of photography	modir-e filmbardaari	مدیر فیلمبرداری
stage management	modiriyyat-e sahneh	مدیریت صحنه
ceremony	maraasem	مراسم
closing ceremony	maraasem-e ekhtetaamiyeh	مراسم اختتامیه
awards ceremony	maraasem-e e'taa-ye jaayeze-haa	مراسم اعطای جایزه ها
opening ceremony	maraasem-e eftetaahiyeh	مراسم افتتاحیه
location (for filming)	makaan-e filmbardaari	مکان فیلمبرداری
new wave	mowj-e now	موج نو
musical	muzikaal	موزیکال
film music	musiqi-ye film	موسیقی فیلم
film score	musiqi-ye matn	موسیقی متن
subject	mowzu'	موضوع
montage	muntaazh	مونتاژ
intermission; interval	miyaan pardeh	میان پرده
role	naqsh	نقش
leading role; starring role	naqsh-e avval	نقش اول
supporting role	naqsh-e dovvom	نقش دوم
shot	namaa	نما
opening shot	namaa-ye avval	نمای اول
long shot	namaa-ye baaz	نمای باز
closing shot	namaa-ye paayaani	نمای پایانی
closing shot	namaa-ye nahaa'i	نمای نهائی
play; staging; screening	namaayesh	نمایش
drama	namaayesh pardaazi	نمایش پردازی
tragi-comedy	namaayesh-e teraazhedi-komedi	نمایش تراژدی کمدی
musical show	namaayesh-e khanyaa'i	نمایش خنیائی
theatre	namaayesh saraa	نمایش سرا
stage play	namaayesh-e sahne'i	نمایش صحنه ای
musical show	namaayesh-e muzikaal	نمایش موزیکال
theatre	namaayesh khaaneh	نمایشخانه
performer; actor	namaayeshkaar	نمایشکار
theatrical	namaayeshkaaraaneh	نمایشکارانه
performer	namaayeshgar	نمایشگر
theatrics	namaayeshgari	نمایشگری
stage play	namaayeshnaameh	نمایشنامه
stage director	namaayeshnaameh gardaan	نمایشنامه گردان

playwright	namaayeshnaameh nevis	نمایشنامه نویس
theatrical	namaayeshi	نمایشی
excerpt; trailer	nemune-ye kutaah	نمونه کوتاه
lighting engineer	nur pardaaz	نورپرداز
lighting	nur pardaazi	نورپردازی
neo-realism	ne'u re'aalism	نئورئالیسم
props	vasaa'el-e sahneh	وسائل صحنه
understudy	hamvand	هموند
audition	honar aazmun	هنر آزمون
film art	honar-e filmsaazi	هنر فیلمسازی
acting	honarpishegi	هنرپیشگی
actor; player; performer	honarpisheh	هنرپیشه
extra; walk-on	honarpishe-ye afzudin	هنرپیشه افزودین
casting	honarpisheh gozini	هنرپیشه گزینی
critic	honar sanj	هنرسنج
theatre critic	honar sanj-e te'aatr	هنرسنج تئاتر
acting; performing	honar namaa'i	هنرنمائی
performing arts	honar-haa-ye ejraa'i	هنرهای اجرائی
performing arts	honar-haa-ye namaayeshi	هنرهای نمایشی

MORE STAGE AND SCREEN TERMS AND PHRASES

to play a role نقشی را بازی کردن   to act in a film در فیلم بازی کردن   to act; to play بازی کردن

to act هنرنمائی کردن   Hasan played the role of Genghis Khan in the film حسن در فیلم نقش چنگیز خان را بازی کرد

to act; to perform هنرپیشگی کردن   Susan acts in stage plays سوسن در نمایشنامه هنرنمائی می کند

to play a role نقشی را ایفا کردن   Ali has the leading role in that film علی در آن فیلم نقش اول را دارد

to be performed به اجراء در آمدن   to perform اجراء کردن   to film فیلم برداری کردن   to direct کارگردانی کردن

to be shown; to be screened به نمایش در آمدن   that play was performed last night آن نمایشنامه دیشب به اجراء در آمد

to watch; to view تماشا کردن   Kiarostami's new film was shown last night فیلم جدید کیارستمی دیشب به نمایش در آمد

did you enjoy the film? فیلم را دوست داشتید؟   to like دوست داشتن   to see دیدن   to show نشان دادن

live performance نمایش زنده   that film is an adaptation of the novel 'Blind Owl' آن فیلم اقتباسی است از رمان بوف کور

he won an Oscar for his animation of 'Aladdin' او بخاطر ساختن کارتون برای داستان علاء الدین جایزه اسکار برد

directed by... به کارگردانی ـ   several of his stories were dramatised چندین داستان او به صورت نمایش در آورده شد

Ahmad auditioned for the role of Hamlet احمد برای بازی در نقش هاملت هنرآزمائی کرد   to audition هنرآزمائی کردن

they made a film out of my novel رمان مرا به صورت فیلم در آوردند   to turn into a film به صورت فیلم در آوردن

to take part شرکت کردن   the Fajr International Film Festival (held annually in Tehran) جشواره بین المللی فیلم فجر

old black and white films فیلم های سیاه سفید قدیمی   science fiction film فیلم علمی تخیلی

Time

weekend	*aakhar-e hafteh*	آخر هفته
future	*aayandeh*	آینده
time difference	*ekhtelaaf-e saa'at*	اختلاف ساعت
equinox	*e'tedaal*	اعتدال
today	*emruz*	امروز
these days; the present; nowadays	*emruzeh*	امروزه
tonight; this evening	*emshab*	امشب
times	*owqaat*	اوقات
time (e.g. three times)	*baar*	بار
afternoon	*ba'd az zohr*	بعد از ظهر
last year	*paarsaal*	پارسال
end of the week; weekend	*paayaan-e hafteh*	پایان هفته
time warp	*paresh-e zamaani*	پرش زمانی
the day before yesterday	*pariruz*	پریروز
the night before last	*parishab*	پریشب
three days ago	*pas pariruz*	پس پریروز
three nights ago	*pas parishab*	پس پریشب
the day after tomorrow	*pas fardaa*	پس فردا
in three days time	*pasaan fardaa*	پسانفردا
the year before last	*piraarsaal*	پیرارسال
delay	*ta'khir*	تاخیر
date; history	*taarikh*	تاریخ
weekend	*ta'tilaat-e aakhar-e hafteh*	تعطیلات آخر هفته
calendar; diary	*taqvim*	تقویم
second (e.g. sixty seconds)	*saanyeh*	ثانیه
second hand (i.e. on a watch)	*saanyeh shomaar*	ثانیه شمار
time (e.g. how many times?)	*daf'eh*	دفعه
minute	*daqiqeh*	دقیقه
minute hand	*daqiqeh shomaar*	دقیقه شمار
fortnight	*dow hafteh*	دو هفته
period; age; era; epoch	*dowraan*	دوران
period; age; era; epoch; time	*dowreh*	دوره
yesterday	*diruz*	دیروز
last night; yesterday evening	*dishab*	دیشب
decade	*daheh*	دهه
quarter of an hour	*rob' saa'at*	ربع ساعت

day	ruz	روز
weekdays	ruz-haa-ye hafteh	روز های هفته
time; period; epoch; age; tense	zamaan	زمان
chronometer; chronoscope	zamaan sanj	زمان سنج
temporal; chronological	zamaani	زمانی
time; times; period	zamaaneh	زمانه
early	zud	زود
clock; watch; hour	saa'at	ساعت
water clock	saa'at-e aabi	ساعت آبی
sundial	saa'at-e aaftaabi	ساعت آفتابی
pocket watch	saa'at-e jibi	ساعت جیبی
timed	saatdaar	ساعت دار
wall clock	saa'at-e divaari	ساعت دیواری
watchmaker; clockmaker	saa'at saaz	ساعت ساز
hour hand	saa'at shomaar	ساعت شمار
alarm clock	saa'at-e shamaateh daar	ساعت شماطه دار
hourglass	saa'at-e sheni	ساعت شنی
grandfather clock	saa'at-e qaddi	ساعت قدی
wristwatch	saa'at-e mochi	ساعت مچی
stopwatch	saa'at-e vaqt negahdaar	ساعت وقت نگه دار
hourly; timed	saa'ati	ساعتی
year	saal	سال
leap year	saal-e kabiseh	سال کبیسه
yearbook; calendar	saalnaameh	سالنامه
dawn; early morning	sahar	سحر
at dawn	sahar gaah	سحرگاه
early evening	sar-e shab	سر شب
evening; night	shab	شب
morning	sobh	صبح
clock face	safhe-ye saa'at	صفحه ساعت
mid-day	zohr	ظهر
late afternoon	'asr	عصر
hand (on a watch or clock)	'aqrabeh	عقربه
interval	faasele-ye zamaani	فاصله زمانی
tomorrow	fardaa	فردا
tomorrow night	fardaa shab	فردا شب
tomorrow morning	fardaa sobh	فردا صبح
season	fasl	فصل

441

morning; before noon	qabl az zohr	قبل از ظهر
century	qarn	قرن
moment; instant	lahzeh	لحظه
month	maah	ماه
time limit	mahdude-ye zamaani	محدوده زمانی
period; duration	moddat	مدت
time (i.e. how many times)	martabeh	مرتبه
time; deadline	mow'ed	موعد
occasion; time	mowqe'	موقع
midnight	nesf-e shab	نصف شب
mid-day	nimruz	نیمروز
half an hour	nim saa'at	نیم ساعت
time	vaqt	وقت
punctual	vaqt shenaas	وقت شناس
punctuality	vaqt shenaasi	وقت شناسی
killing time	vaqt koshi	وقت کشی
millennium	hezaareh	هزاره
week	hafteh	هفته
time; season; opportunity	hengaam	هنگام

MORE TIME EXPRESSIONS

tomorrow فردا today امروز at twelve midnight دوازده نصف شب we went at mid-day ظهر رفتیم

two days ago دو روز پیش he is 22 years old او بیست و دو سال دارد yesterday دیروز

next week هفته آینده next week هفته دیگر last week هفته گذشته in two days' time دو روز دیگر

this year امسال a fortnight دو هفته one week یک هفته a week tomorrow فردا یک هفته دیگر

four years ago چهار سال پیش next year سال دیگر last year سال گذشته last year سال پیش

every day هر روز what's the date today? امروز چندم است؟ what day is it today? امروز چندشنبه است ؟

a few days ago چند روز پیش every few days هر چند روز every other day یک روز در میان

in the past در گذشته (many) years ago سالهای پیش a few years ago چند سال پیش

in the future در آینده now الان days of the week روزهای هفته right now همین الان

months of the year ماه های سال tomorrow night فردا شب tonight امشب last night دیشب

nowadays این روزها in the past decade در دهه اخیر in the twentieth century در قرن بیستم

several times چند بار in half an hour's time نیم ساعت دیگر these days; nowadays امروزه

how often do you go to Iran? چند وقت به چند وقت به ایران میروید؟ how often? چند وقت به چند وقت ؟

twice a month ماهی دو بار three times a year سالی سه بار once a year سالی یک بار

three times سه دفعه   five times a day روزی پنج بار   four times a week چهار بار   هفته ای

three days ago پس پریروز   the day before yesterday پریروز   there was a time when... ــه روزی بود که

some days ago; a few days ago چند روز پیش   some time ago چند وقت پیش   the day after tomorrow پس فردا

half past one ساعت یک و نیم   (it's) one o'clock (ساعت یک (است   what time is it? ساعت چند است؟

ten minutes to three ده دقیقه به سه   a quarter to three یک ربع به سه   a quarter past two ساعت دو و ربع

how much an hour? ساعتی چند؟   how many hours? چند ساعت؟   ten minutes past three ساعت سه و ده دقیقه

£5 an hour ساعتی پنج پوند   five hours پنج ساعت   how much an hour do you pay? ساعتی چند پول می دهید؟

to count the minutes دقیقه شماری کردن   wait a moment یک لحظه صبر کن   second by second لحظه به لحظه

my watch is fast ساعت من جلو است   my watch is slow ساعت من عقب است   at a set time در وقت معین

seven days a week هفته ای هفت روز   twenty four hours a day بیست و چهار ساعت   روزی

this job has no future این کار آینده ندارد   in the old days در قدیم   right now; at the present time در حال حاضر

to be late دیر کردن   to arrive on time سر وقت رسیدن   punctuality وقت شناسی   punctual وقت شناس

it departs on the hour سر ساعت حرکت می کند   to arrive early زود رسیدن   to arrive late دیر رسیدن

to waste time وقت تلف کردن   to waste time وقت حرام کردن   to kill time وقت کشی کردن   untimely بی وقت

free time وقت آزاد   free time; leisure time وقت فراغت   don't waste my time وقت مرا تلف نکنید

he spends all of his time sleeping تمام وقتش را صرف خوابیدن می کند   to spend time (on) وقت صرف کردن

to give an appointment; to give of one's time وقت دادن   to take up time; to get an appointment وقت گرفتن

by the time we arrive he will have gone تا وقتی که برسیم او رفته است   as long as ; by the time that; while تا وقتی که

I can never find the time to watch television من هرگز وقت نمی کنم تلویزیون تماشا کنم   to find the time وقت کردن

never هیچ وقت   some time or other یک وقتی   in season and out of season; occasionally وقت و بیوقت

rarely ندرتاً   sometimes بعضی اوقات   sometimes بعضی وقت ها   never هرگز   always همیشه

long-term دراز مدت   a long time مدت مدید   I haven't seen you for a while مدتی است شما را ندیده ام

from now on; henceforth از این زمان به بعد   it is a long time مدت ها است   short-term کوتاه مدت

during the time of Shah Abbas در زمان شاه عباس   in the beginning (of time) در ابتدای زمان

temporal; chronological; time (adj.) زمانی   time and place زمان و مکان   former times زمانهای قبل

in an instant; in the twinkling of an eye در یک لحظه   times have changed زمانه عوض شده است

443

Tools

ابزار آلات

scutch	*aajor shekan*	<div dir="rtl">آجر شکن</div>
spanner	*aachaar*	<div dir="rtl">آچار</div>
tools	*aalaat*	<div dir="rtl">آلات</div>
magnet	*aahan robaa*	<div dir="rtl">آهن ربا</div>
tools	*abzaar*	<div dir="rtl">ابزار</div>
hand tools	*abzaar dast*	<div dir="rtl">ابزار دست</div>
machine tools	*abzaar-e maashini*	<div dir="rtl">ابزار ماشینی</div>
carpentry tools	*abzaar-e najjaari*	<div dir="rtl">ابزار نجاری</div>
toolshed	*otaaqak-e abzaar*	<div dir="rtl">اتاقک ابزار</div>
saw	*arreh*	<div dir="rtl">اره</div>
hacksaw	*arre-ye aahan-bor*	<div dir="rtl">اره آهن بر</div>
compass saw	*arre-ye tiqeh baarik*	<div dir="rtl">اره تیغه باریک</div>
hand saw	*arre-ye dasti*	<div dir="rtl">اره دستی</div>
crosscut saw	*arre-ye dow sar*	<div dir="rtl">اره دوسر</div>
chainsaw	*arre-ye zanjiri*	<div dir="rtl">اره زنجیری</div>
bucksaw	*arre-ye qaabdaar*	<div dir="rtl">اره قابدار</div>
coping saw	*arre-ye kamaani*	<div dir="rtl">اره کمانی</div>
chisel	*eskeneh*	<div dir="rtl">اسکنه</div>
pliers	*anbor dast*	<div dir="rtl">انبر دست</div>
battery	*baatri*	<div dir="rtl">باتری</div>
spade	*bil*	<div dir="rtl">بیل</div>
shoehorn	*paashneh kesh*	<div dir="rtl">پاشنه کش</div>
sledgehammer	*potak*	<div dir="rtl">پتک</div>
vice	*peres*	<div dir="rtl">پرس</div>
compasses	*pargaar*	<div dir="rtl">پرگار</div>
thumbtack; drawing pin	*punez*	<div dir="rtl">پونز</div>
screw	*pich*	<div dir="rtl">پیچ</div>
lag screw	*pich-e chubi*	<div dir="rtl">پیچ چوبی</div>
set screw	*pich-e zaamen*	<div dir="rtl">پیچ ضامن</div>
screwdriver	*pich gushti*	<div dir="rtl">پیچ گوشتی</div>
nuts and bolts	*pich o mohreh*	<div dir="rtl">پیچ و مهره</div>
axe	*tabar*	<div dir="rtl">تبر</div>
hatchet	*tabarcheh*	<div dir="rtl">تبرچه</div>
wire netting	*tur-e simi*	<div dir="rtl">تور سیمی</div>
toolbox	*ja'be-ye abzaar*	<div dir="rtl">جعبه ابزار</div>
penknife; pocketknife	*chaaqu-ye jibi*	<div dir="rtl">چاقوی جیبی</div>

torch	cheraaq qoveh	چراغ قوه
glue	chasb	چسب
bolt (of door)	cheft-e dar	چفت در
hammer	chakkosh	چکش
mallet	chakkosh-e chubi	چکش چوبی
clawhammer	chakkosh-e mikh-kesh	چکش میخ کش
garden fork	changaal-e baaqbaani	چنگال باغبانی
corkscrew	chub panbeh kesh	چوب پنبه کش
scaffolding	daarbast	داربست
machine; contraption	dastgaah	دستگاه
bellows	dam	دم
plane	randeh	رنده
drawknife	rande-ye chaaqu'i	رنده چاقونی
sander	sonbaadeh kesh	سنباده کش
safety pin	sanjaaq qofli	سنجاق قفلی
anvil	sendaan	سندان
awl	suraakh-kon	سوراخ کن
needle	suzan	سوزن
pin	suzan-e tah gerd	سوزن ته گرد
file	sowhaan	سوهان
barbed wire	sim-e khaardaar	سیم خاردار
rake	shenkesh	شن کش
garden hose	shilang-e baaq	شیلنگ باغ
rope	tanaab	طناب
paint roller	qaltak-e rangzani	غلتک رنگ زنی
spring	fanar	فنر
lock; padlock	qofl	قفل
hook	qollaab	قلاب
paintbrush	qalam mu	قلم مو
tin opener	quti baaz-kon	قوطی باز کن
scissors	qeychi	قیچی
shears; secateurs	qeychi-ye baaqbaani	قیچی باغبانی
funnel	qif	قیف
do-it-yourself	kaar-e khodanjaam	کار خود انجام
workshop	kaargaah	کارگاه
handyman	kaargar-e chandkaareh	کارگر چند کاره
paper knife	kaaqaz-bor	کاغذ بر
pickaxe	kolang	کلنگ

key	kelid	کلید
pincers	gaaz anbor	گاز انبر
vice	gire-ye aahangari	گیره آهنگری
crank	leng	لنگ
plunger	luleh baaz-kon	لوله باز کن
machinery	maashin-aalaat	ماشین آلات
trowel	maaleh	ماله
drill	mateh	مته
electric drill	mate-ye barqi	مته برقی
hand drill	mate-ye dasti	مته دستی
pneumatic drill	mate-ye feshaari	مته فشاری
blow torch	mash'al-e jushkaari	مشعل جوشکاری
nail	mikh	میخ
crowbar	mikh kesh-e bozorg	میخکش بزرگ
workbench	miz-e kaar	میز کار
crankshaft	mil-e leng	میل لنگ
nut	mohreh	مهره
ladder	nardebaan	نرده بان
extension ladder	nardebaan-e taashow	نرده بان تاشو
stepladder	nardebaan-e dow tekkeh	نرده بان دو تکه
sellotape	navaar chasb	نوارچسب
rubber band	navaar-e kesh	نوار کش

MORE WORDS AND EXPRESSIONS INVOLVING TOOLS

to drill سوراخ کردن (با مته)   احمد با مته در را سوراخ کرد   Ahmad drilled a hole in the door

to chop تبر زدن   to file سوهان زدن   to tighten سفت کردن

پیچ را با پیچگوشتی سفت کردم   I tightened the screw with the screwdriver   to repair تامیر کردن

باید اشکاف خراب شده را تامیر کنید   you must repair the broken cupboard   to saw اره کردن

to plane رنده کردن   I sawed the wood چوب را اره کردم   to paint رنگ زدن

میز را دو لایه رنگ زدم   I gave the table two coats of paint   to screw پیچاندن

screw the nut on the bolt مهره را سر پیچ بپیچانید   to pound; to knock; to hit کوبیدن

to loosen شل کردن   we loosened all of the screws تمام پیچ هارا شل کردیم   to become loose شل شدن

پیچهای این صندلی شل شده اند   the screws on the chair have become loose   to dig بیل زدن

I was digging for three hours in the garden سه ساعت در باغچه بیل می زدم   to cut (with scissors) قیچی کردن

to stick; to glue چسباندن   to lock قفل کردن   to nail (something down) میخکوب کردن

to hit (something) with a hammer با چکش زدن   میخ را با چکش زدم   I hit the nail with a hammer

apartment; flat; apartment block	aapaartemaan	آپارتمان
skyscraper	aasemaan kharaash	آسمان خراش
hoarding; advertisement	aagahi-ye divaari	آگهی دیواری
air pollution	aaludegi-ye havaa	آلودگی هوا
double-decker bus	otobus-e dow tabaqeh	اتوبوس دو طبقه
office	edaareh	اداره
swimming baths; swimming pool	estakhr	استخر
information	ettelaa'aat	اطلاعات
tourist information	ettelaa'aat-e jahaangardi	اطلاعات جهانگردی
parking meter	ist sanj	ایست سنج
bus stop; bus shelter	istgaah-e otobus	ایستگاه اتوبوس
fire station	istgaah-e aatash neshaani	ایستگاه آتش نشانی
taxi rank	istgaah-e taaksi	ایستگاه تاکسی
train station	istgaah-e raah-e aahan	ایستگاه راه آهن
local resident	ahl-e mahal	اهل محل
market	baazaar	بازار
shopping mall; shopping centre	baazaarcheh	بازارچه
zoo	baaq-e vahsh	باغ وحش
bank	baank	بانک
church steeple; spire	borj-e kelisaa	برج کلیسا
brochure; leaflet; booklet; pamphlet	berowshur	بروشور
dead end; cul de sac	bon bast	بن بست
boulevard; dual-carriageway	bulvaar	بولوار
hospital	bimaarestaan	بیمارستان
park	paark	پارک
industrial estate	paark-e san'ati	پارک صنعتی
public park	paark-e 'omumi	پارک عمومی
parking lot; parking space	paarking	پارکینگ
arcade	paasaazh	پاساژ
policeman	paasebaan	پاسبان
post office	postkhaaneh	پستخانه
bridge	pol	پل
flyover	pol-e havaa'i	پل هوائی
petrol pump; gas station	pomp-e benzin	پمپ بنزین
pavement; sidewalk	piyaadeh row	پیاده رو
turning; bend	pich	پیچ

sign; notice	taablow	تابلو
taxi	taaksi	تاکسی
art gallery	taalaar-e aasaar-e honari	تالار آثار هنری
concert hall	taalaar-e konsert	تالار کنسرت
traffic	teraafik	ترافیک
junction	taqaato'	تقاطع
public toilet	tovaalet-e 'omumi	توالت عمومی
tour	tur	تور
tourist	turist	توریست
tunnel; underpass	tunel	تونل
theatre	te'aatr	تناتر
lamp post	tir-e cheraaq barq	تیر چراغ برق
place; location	jaa	جا
places of interest; sights	jaa-haa-ye didani	جا های دیدنی
island (at crossroads)	jazire-ye imani	جزیره ایمنی
crowd	jamaa'at	جماعت
population	jam'iyat	جمعیت
tourist	jahaangard	جهانگرد
tea-house; cafe	chaaykhaaneh	چایخانه
street light	cheraaq barq	چراغ برق
crossroads	chahaar raah	چهار راه
shanty town	hasiraabaad	حصیرآباد
shanty town	halabiyaabaad	حلبی آباد
suburbs	howmeh	حومه
university halls of residence	khaabgaah-e daaneshgaah	خوابگاه دانشگاه
vehicle; car	khod row	خودرو
street; avenue; road	khiyaabaan	خیابان
main road	khiyaabaan-e asli	خیابان اصلی
one-way street	khiyaabaan-e yek tarafeh	خیابان یک طرفه
university	daaneshgaah	دانشگاه
street peddler	dastforush-e dowregard	دست فروش دوره گرد
shop	dokkaan	دکان
newspaper stall	dakke-ye ruznaameh forushi	دکه روزنامه فروشی
graffiti	divaar neveshteh	دیوار نوشته
underground railway; metro	raah-e aahan-e zir-e zamini	راه آهن زیر زمینی
highway	raah shuseh	راه شوسه
traffic jam	raahbandaan	راهبندان
passer-by	raahgozar	راهگذر

restaurant	rasturaan	رستوران
street sweeper	roftegar	رفتگر
newspaper seller	ruznaameh forush	روزنامه فروش
prison	zendaan	زندان
underpass; subway	zir gozar	زیر گذر
building	saakhtemaan	ساختمان
apartment block; block of flats	saakhtemaan-e aapaartemaani	ساختمان آپارتمانی
town hall	saakhtemaan-e shahrdaari	ساختمان شهرداری
inhabitant	saaken	ساکن
sports hall	saalon-e varzesh	سالن ورزش
street sweeper	sopur	سپور
cobblestone; paving	sang farsh	سنگ فرش
graffiti	sho'aar-e divaari	شعار دیواری
town council	shuraa-ye shahr	شورای شهر
city/town dweller	shahr neshin	شهر نشین
police headquarters	shahrbaani	شهربانی
mayor	shahrdaar	شهردار
municipality; town council	shahrdaari	شهرداری
citizen	shahrvand	شهروند
queue	saff	صف
pedestrian	'aaber-e piyaadeh	عابر پیاده
roadsign	'alaamat-e raahnamaa'i	علامت راهنمائی
airport	forudgaah	فرودگاه
department store	forushgaah	فروشگاه
street vendor	forushande-ye kenaar-e khiyaabaan	فروشنده کنار خیابان
cemetery; graveyard	qabrestaan	قبرستان
part; section; district	qesmat	قسمت
palace	qasr	قصر
coffee shop; cafe	qahveh khaaneh	قهوه خانه
cathedral	kaatedraal	کاتدرال
castle	kaakh	کاخ
factory	kaarkhaaneh	کارخانه
cafe	kaafeh	کافه
library	ketaabkhaaneh	کتابخانه
church	kelisaa	کلیسا
street; lane; alley	kucheh	کوچه
lane; alley	kuy	کوی
garage	gaaraazh	گاراژ

workshop	kaargaah	کارگاه
beggar	gedaa	گدا
pedestrian crossing	gozargaah-e 'aaber-e piyaadeh	گذرگاه عابر پیاده
tour	gasht	گشت
dome (of mosque or church)	gonbad	گنبد
car; vehicle	maashin	ماشین
van; truck	maashin baari	ماشین باری
policeman	ma'mur-e polis	مامور پلیس
underground railway; metro	metrow	مترو
shopping complex	mojtama'-e forushgaahi	مجتمع فروشگاهی
statue	mojassameh	مجسمه
built-up area	mahal-e por taraakom	محل پر تراکم
area; district; quarter	mahalleh	محله
red light district	mahalle-ye faaheshe-haa	محله فاحشه ها
school	madraseh	مدرسه
town centre; downtown	markaz-e shahr	مرکز شهر
mosque	masjed	مسجد
shop	maqaazeh	مغازه
place; location	makaan	مکان
minaret	menaar	منار
museum	muzeh	موزه
square	meydaan	میدان
district; area; quarter	naahiyeh	ناحیه
art gallery	negaarkhaaneh	نگارخانه
sports stadium	varzeshgaah	ورزشگاه
hotel	hotel	هتل
fellow citizen	hamshahri	همشهری
monument; memorial	yaadmaan	یادمان

❯❮❯❮

urban living; city life شهرنشینی   urban; civic; metropolitan; municipal; town (adj.); townsman; citizen شهری

زندگی شهری capital city پایتخت   I live in the town/city من در شهر زندگی می کنم   town life; city life; urban life زندگی شهری

تهران پایتخت ایران است Tehran is the capital of Iran   heavily populated پرجمعیت   town centre مرکز شهر

پائین شهر downtown   دیروز به شهر رفتم I went into town yesterday   out of town; in the country خارج از شهر

حسن با قطار وارد شهر شد Hasan entered the city by train   من در حومه شهر زندگی می کنم I live in the suburbs

شهر را ترک کردم to go on foot پیاده رفتن   I went out of the city از شهر خارج شدم   we left the city شهر را ترک کردیم

سوار شدن to get on or in (a vehicle)   سوار ماشین شدم I got in the car   از ماشین پیاده شدم I got out of the car

از خیابان عبور کردن to cross the street   از خیابان رد شدن to cross the street   side street خیابان فرعی

he went from street to street کوچه به کوچه رفت   to go out (into the street) کوچه رفتن   back alley پس کوچه

اداره پست کجاست؟ where is the post office?   on the right-hand side دست راست   on the left دست چپ

اولین خیابان دست راست the first road on the right   دومین خیابان دست چپ the second road on the left

پیچیدن to turn; to take a turning   دست راست بپیچید turn right   go straight ahead مستقیم بروید

به ...... که رسیدید، دست راست بپیچید when you get to ...., turn right   the way to the hospital راه بیمارستان

راه بیمارستان را پرسیدم I asked the way to the hospital   بیمارستان از این طرف است؟ is this the way to the hospital?

راهنمائی کردن to guide; to direct   گم شدن to get lost   گم کردن to lose   راه را گم کردن to lose the way

بغل بانک next to the bank   نزدیک سینما near the cinema   پشت مسجد behind the mosque

بین تئاتر و ورزشگاه between the theatre and the sports stadium   جلوی فروشگاه in front of the department store

خیلی دور نیست it's not very far   نزدیک است it's near   پیاده می شود رفت؟ is it within walking distance?

کنار خیابان by the side of the road   انتهای خیابان at the end of the road   ته خیابان the end of the road

نبش خیابان at the corner of the street   وسط شهر in the middle of town   در مرکز شهر in the centre of town

مساحت شهر the area of the city   مساحت شهر صد کیلومتر مربع است the area of the city is 100 square kilometres

در آپارتمان زندگی می کنم I live in an apartment   حسن در خانه زندگی می کند Hasan lives in a house

اهل این شهر نیستم I'm not from this town   من خودم اینجا غریبه هستم I'm a stranger here myself

شهر را بر روستا ترجیح می دهم I prefer the town to the country   به شهر بزرگ عادت ندارم I'm not used to big cities

آلوده polluted   کثیف dirty   شلوق crowded   ترافیک شهر سنگین است the city traffic is heavy

پر سر و صدا noisy   خطرناك dangerous   اعصاب خرد کن stressful; nerve-shattering

Train Travel

سفر با قطار

alarm	aazhir	آژیر
driver's cabin	otaaqak-e raanandeh	اتاقک راننده
photo booth	otaaqak-e 'aks bardaari	اتاقک عکس برداری
tram; streetcar	otubus-e barqi	اتوبوس برقی
derailment	az khat khaarej shodan	از خط خارج شدن
waiting room	otaaq-e entezaar	اطاق انتظار
information; information desk	ettelaa'aat	اطلاعات
connection	enteqaal	انتقال
tip	an'aam	انعام
taxi rank	istgaah-e taaksi	ایستگاه تاکسی
train station	istgaah-e raah-e aahan	ایستگاه راه آهن
porter	baarbar	باربر
luggage rack	baarband	باربند
luggage compartment; hold	baardaani	باردانی
ticket inspector	baazras-e belit	بازرس بلیط
timetable	barnaame-ye saa'aat-e qataar	برنامه ساعات قطار
itinerary	barnaame-ye safar	برنامه سفر
ticket	belit	بلیط
season ticket	belit-e tamaam fasl	بلیط تمام فصل
return ticket	belit-e dow sareh	بلیط دوسره
return ticket	belit-e raft o bargasht	بلیط رفت و برگشت
one-way ticket	belit-e yeksareh	بلیط یکسره
buffet; station restaurant	bufeh	بوفه
bridge	pol	پل
escalator	pelle-ye barqi	پله برقی
fare	pul-e belit	پول بلیط
reservation	pishgereft	پیشگرفت
delay	ta'khir	تاخیر
taxi	taaksi	تاکسی
couchette	takhtak	تختک
reduction (in price)	takhfif	تخفیف
tram; streetcar	teraamvaa	تراموا
brakes	tormoz	ترمز
train	teren	ترن
seat reservation	ta'yin-e jaa	تعیین جا
stop; stopover	tavaqqof	توقف

departure; movement	harekat	حرکت
railway embankment	khaakrizi-ye raah-e aahan	خاکریزی راه آهن
track; railway line	khat	خط
rail; track; line	khatt-e aahan	خط آهن
main lines	khotut-e asli	خطوط اصلی
door	dar	در
exit	dar-e khoruji	در خروجی
entrance	dar-e vorudi	در ورودی
first class	darajeh yek	درجه یک
book of tickets	daste-ye belit	دسته بلیط
bicycle	dowcharkheh	دوچرخه
barrier	divaareh	دیواره
driver	raanandeh	راننده
engine driver	raanande-ye lukumutiv	راننده لوکوموتیو
railway	raah-e aahan	راه آهن
double-track railway	raah-e aahan-e dow khatti	راه آهن دو خطی
guard	raahbaan	راهبان
reservation	rezerv	رزرو
restaurant; buffet; buffet car	rasturaan	رستوران قطار
stationmaster	ra'is-e istgaah-e raah-e aahan	رئیس ایستگاه راه آهن
rail	reyl	ریل
underpass; subway	zir gozar	زیر گذر
clock	saa'at	ساعت
speed	sor'at	سرعت
passenger	sarneshin	سرنشین
trip; journey	safar	سفر
platform	saku	سکو
whistle	sut	سوت
railway network	shabake-ye raah-e aahan	شبکه راه آهن
railway company	sherkat-e raah-e aahan	شرکت راه آهن
number	shomaareh	شماره
seat	sandali	صندلی
trunk	sanduq	صندوق
direction	taraf	طرف
communication cord	tanaab-e zang	طناب زنگ
departure	'azimat	عزیمت
connection	'avaz kardan	عوض کردن
indirect	qeyr-e mostaqim	غیر مستقیم

distance	faaseleh	فاصله
train	qataar	قطار
goods train	qataar-e baari	قطار باری
steam train	qataar-e bokhaar	قطار بخار
electric train	qataar-e barqi	قطار برقی
underground train; metro	qataar-e zir-e zamini	قطار زیر زمینی
express train	qataar-e sari' os-seyr	قطار سریع السیر
passenger train	qataar-e mosaafer bari	قطار مسافربری
railwayman	kaargar-e raah-e aahan	کارگر راه آهن
fare	keraayeh	کرایه
compartment	kupeh	کوپه
bag	kif	کیف
guard	gaard	گارد
railway crossing	gozargaah-e raah-e aahan	گذرگاه راه آهن
passport	gozarnaameh	گذرنامه
customs	gomrok	گمرك
ticket office; ticket window	gisheh	گیشه
locomotive; engine	lukumutiv	لوکوموتیو
ticket machine	maashin-e belit	ماشین بلیط
customs official	ma'mur-e gomrok	مامور گمرك
metro	metrow	مترو
trainmaster	motasaddi-ye khat	متصدی خط
duration	moddat	مدت
border	marz	مرز
distance	masaafat	مسافت
traveller; passenger	mosaafer	مسافر
journey; trip; travel	mosaaferat	مسافرت
direct	mostaqim	مستقیم
destination	maqsad	مقصد
engine	motor	موتور
map; plan	naqsheh	نقشه
wagon; car (of train)	vaagon	واگن
freight car	vaagon-e baari	واگن باری
sleeping car	vaagon-e khaab	واگن خواب
dining car	vaagon-e rasturaan	واگن رستوران
arrival; entrance	vorud	ورود
fare	hazineh	هزینه
extra charge; supplement	hazine-ye ezaafeh	هزینه اضافه

مسافرت کردن to travel   بلیط خریدن to buy a ticket   صندلی رزرو کردن to reserve a seat

از سفر با قطار لذت می برم I enjoy travelling by train   با قطار رفتن to go by train   بوسیله قطار by train

قطار تاخیر دارد the train is delayed   قطار ساعت یک از تهران به اصفهان the one o'clock train from Tehran to Isfahan

قطار مشهد ساعت چند حرکت می کند؟ when does the train to Mashhad depart?   to depart حرکت کردن

قطار مشهد از کدام سکو حرکت می کند ؟ from which platform does the Mashhad train depart ?   راه افتادن to set off

ورود قطار arrival of the train   عزیمت قطار departure of the train   قطار دیر آمد the train was late

می خواهم دو تا صندلی رزرو کنم I'd like to reserve two seats   کسی اینجا نشسته؟ is this seat taken?

اینجا نمیشود سیگار کشید you can't smoke here   واگن رستوران کجاست؟ where is the dining car?

در اصفهان باید قطار عوض کنید you have to change (trains) in Isfahan   قطار را از دست دادم I missed the train

واگن ویژه استعمال دخانیات smoking compartment   سیگار کشیدن ممنوع! No Smoking!

قطار از خط خارج شد the train left the rails   تصادف قطار train crash   قطار آتش گرفت the train caught fire

توقف کردن to stop; to halt   قطار تهران به مشهد در گرگان توقف می کند the Tehran-Mashhad train stops in Gorgan

پیاده شدن to get off   وقتی به گرگان رسیدیم ما از قطار پیاده شدیم when we reached Gorgan we got off the train

به مقصد رسیدن to arrive at one's destination   قطار خراب شده the train has broken down

Means of Transport

وسائل نقلیه

ambulance	aambulaans	آمبولانس
bus; coach	otubus	اتوبوس
tram	otubus-e barqi	اتوبوس برقی
airbus	otubus-e havaa'i	اتوبوس هوائی
estate car	otumobil-e esteyshen	اتومبیل استیشن
convertible	otumobil-e koruki	اتومبیل کروکی
racing car	otumobil-e mosaabeqe'i	اتومبیل مسابقه ای
horse and carriage	asb o doroshkeh	اسب و درشکه
hot-air balloon	baalun	بالون
body; bodywork	badaneh	بدنه
small boat	balam	بلم
bulldozer	buldowzer	بولدوزر
ambulance	bimaarbar	بیماربر
back (of a vehicle)	posht	پشت
taxi	taaksi	تاکسی
air taxi	taaksi-ye havaa'i	تاکسی هوائی
tank	taank	تانک
space shuttle	taraabar-e fazaa'i	ترابر فضائی
trailer	tereyli	تریلی
service; overhaul	ta'mir	تعمیر
chairlift	teleh sizh	تله سیژ
cable car	teleh kaabin	تله کابین
steamroller	jaaddeh saaf kon	جاده صاف کن
crane	jarr-e saqil	جرثقیل
front (of a vehicle)	jelow	جلو
jeep	jip	جیپ
helicopter	charkh baal	چرخ بال
digger; excavator	khaakbardaar	خاکبردار
mobile home	khaane-ye sayyaar	خانه سیار
vehicle; car	khod row	خودرو
bicycle	dow charkheh	دوچرخه
moped	dow charkhe-ye motori	دوچرخه موتوری
armoured; armoured car	zerehi	زرهی
dugout	zowraq-e yekpaarcheh	زورق یکپارچه
canoe	zowraqcheh	زورقچه
submarine	zir daryaa'i	زیر دریائی

underground	*zir-e zamin*	زیر زمین
sled; sleigh	*surtmeh*	سورتمه
tricycle	*seh charkheh*	سه چرخه
space shuttle	*shod aamadgar-e fazaa'i*	شد آمدگر فضائی
barge	*taraad*	طراد
distance	*faaseleh*	فاصله
spaceship	*fazaa peymaa*	فضا پیما
boat	*qaayeq*	قایق
sailing boat	*qaayeq-e baadbaani*	قایق بادبانی
rowing boat	*qaayeq-e paaru'i*	قایق پارویی
yacht	*qaayeq-e tafrihi*	قایق تفریحی
speedboat	*qaayeq-e tondrow*	قایق تندرو
pontoon	*qaayeq-e tah pahn*	قایق ته پهن
barque	*qaayeq-e seh baadbaani*	قایق سه بادبانی
trimaran	*qaayeq-e seh badaneh*	قایق سه بدنه
ferry boat	*qaayeq-e gozaareh*	قایق گزاره
motor boat; speedboat	*qaayeq-e motori*	قایق موتوری
lifeboat	*qaayeq-e nejaat*	قایق نجات
train	*qataar*	قطار
freight train	*qataar-e baari*	قطار باری
steam train	*qataar-e bokhaar*	قطار بخار
underground train	*qataar-e zir-e zamini*	قطار زیرزمینی
funicular	*qataar-e kaabli*	قطار کابلی
passenger train	*qataar-e mosaaferbari*	قطار مسافربری
caravan	*kaarvaan*	کاروان
pram; pushchair	*kaleskeh*	کالسکه
lorry; truck	*kaamyun*	کامیون
livestock truck	*kaamyun-e daambari*	کامیون دامبری
articulated lorry	*kaamyun-e dow qat'eh*	کامیون دو قطعه
mobile library	*ketaabkhaane-ye sayyaar*	کتابخانه سیار
fare	*keraayeh*	کرایه
boat	*karaji*	کرجی
ship	*keshti*	کشتی
hydrofoil	*keshti-ye eski daar*	کشتی اسکی دار
hydroplane	*keshti-ye aabaaleh daar*	کشتی آباله دار
cargo vessel	*keshti-ye baari*	کشتی باری
steamer	*keshti-ye bokhaar*	کشتی بخار
schooner	*keshti-ye dow dakaleh*	کشتی دو دکله

457

spaceship	keshti-ye fazaa'i	کشتی فضائی
fishing boat; trawler	keshti-ye maahigiri	کشتی ماهیگیری
passenger ship; liner	keshti-ye mosaaferbari	کشتی مسافربری
tanker	keshti-ye naftkesh	کشتی نفتکش
airship	keshti-ye havaa'i	کشتی هوائی
safety helmet	kolaah-e imani	کلاه ایمنی
boat	kalak	کلک
cart	gaari	گاری
glider	gelaayder	گلایدر
boat	lenj	لنج
locomotive	lukumutiv	لوکوموتیو
car	maashin	ماشین
fire engine	maashin-e aatash neshaani	ماشین آتش نشانی
truck; van; goods vehicle	maashin-e baari	ماشین باری
police car	maashin-e polis	ماشین پلیس
breakdown van	maashin-e ta'mirkaari	ماشین تعمیر کاری
excavator	maashin-e haffaari	ماشین حفاری
distance	masaafat	مسافت
engine	motor	موتور
motorbike; motorcycle	motorsiklet	موتورسیکلت
motor scooter	motorsiklet-e sabok	موتورسیکلت سبک
minibus	minibus	مینی بوس
tugboat	naav-e yadak kesh	ناو یدک کش
aircraft carrier	naav-e havaapeymaa bar	ناو هواپیمابر
hearse	na'sh kesh	نعش کش
mobile medical unit	vaahed-e sayyaar-e pezeshki	واحد سیار پزشکی
van	vaagon-e baari	واگن باری
van	vaanet	وانت
means of transport	vasaa'el-e naqliyeh	وسائل نقلیه
hovercraft	haaverkeraaft	هاورکرافت
helicopter	helikupter	هلی کوپتر
aeroplane	havaapeymaa	هواپیما
passenger aircraft	havaapeymaa-ye mosaaferbari	هواپیمای مسافربری
glider	havaapeymaa-ye bi motor	هواپیمای بی موتر
seaplane	havaapeymaa-ye daryaa'i	هواپیمای دریائی
glider	havaasor	هواسر
(hot-air) balloon	havaanaav	هواناو
unicycle	yek charkheh	یک چرخه

to get on; to disembark سوار شدن   I got on the bus سوار اتوبوس شدم   to get on; to embark پیاده شدن

I waited for the bus از ماشین پیاده شدم   to wait منتظر شدن   I got out of the car منتظر اتوبوس شدم

to be delayed تاخیر داشتن   the bus was late; the bus came late اتوبوس دیر آمد   to come late دیر آمدن

to break down خراب شدن   our plane had a three-hour delay هواپیمای ما سه ساعت تاخیر داشت

repairs تعمیرات   to repair تامیر کردن   our car broke down half-way ماشین ما نصف راه خراب شد

cycling دوچرخه سواری   he doesn't know how to drive رانندگی بلد نیست   to drive رانندگی کردن

he cycles to work با دوچرخه به سرکار می رود   he goes cycling every day هر روز دوچرخه سواری می کند

to walk; to go on foot پیاده رفتن   he went by helicopter بوسیله هلیکپتر رفت   by; by means of بوسیله

to travel by plane با هواپیما سفر کردن   to travel; to go on a journey مسافرت کردن   to travel سفر کردن

chauffeur شوفر   co-driver کمک راننده   driver راننده   to drive راندن   air travel سفر هوائی

boating قایق سواری   helicopter pilot خلبان هلیکپتر   pilot خلبان   cyclist دوچرخه سوار

fare کرایه   to paddle پارو زدن   we go boating every week هر هفته قایق سواری می کنیم

price قیمت   taxi fares in this town are very high در این شهر کرایه تاکسی خیلی گران است

I bought a train ticket بلیط قطار خریدم   to buy a ticket بلیط خریدن   ticket بلیط

to reserve رزرو کردن   return ticket بلیط دوسره   how much is a one-way ticket? بلیط یکسره چند است؟

I missed the bus اتوبوس را از دست دادم   route مسیر   first class درجه یک   to reserve a seat صندلی رزرو کردن

Trees

درختان

ebony	aabnus	آبنوس
Siberian elm	aazaad derakht	آزاد درخت
beech	aalesh	آلش
oriental almond tree	arzhan	ارژن
juniper	ors	ارس
Judas tree	arqavaan	ارغوان
locust tree; false acacia	aqaaqiyaa	اقاقیا
elder	aqti	اقطی
lumber	alvaar	الوار
lumbering	alvaar saazi	الوار سازی
lumberyard	alvaar forushi	الوار فروشی
orchard	baaq-e miveh	باغ میوه
bamboo	baambu	بامبو
bush	boteh	بته
copse; thicket	boteh zaar	بته زار
leaf	barg	برگ
deciduous	barg riz	برگ ریز
Persian turpentine tree	baneh	بنه
tree stump	bikh-e derakht	بیخ درخت
weeping willow	bid-e majnun	بید مجنون
pussy willow; Egyptian willow	bid-e meshk	بید مشک
grove	bisheh	بیشه
Abraham's balm; hemp tree	panj angosht	پنج انگشت
bark	pust-e derakht	پوست درخت
vineyard	taakestaan	تاکستان
sycamore	tut anjir	توت انجیر
forest; jungle	jangal	جنگل
deforestation	jangal zadaa'i	جنگل زدائی
plane tree	chenaar	چنار
sycamore	chenaar-e farangi	چنار فرنگی
wood	chub	چوب
woodcutter	chub bor	چوب بر
hawthorn	khafcheh	خفچه
berry	daaneh	دانه
tree	derakht	درخت
maple	derakht-e afraa	درخت افرا

oak	derakht-e balut	درخت بلوط
willow	derakht-e bid	درخت بید
broad-leaved tree	derakht-e pahn barg	درخت پهن برگ
Lombardy poplar	derakht-e tabrizi	درخت تبریزی
service tree	derakht-e senjed	درخت سنجد
bay tree	derakht-e qaar	درخت غار
mangrove	derakht-e karnaa	درخت کرنا
fruit tree	derakht-e miveh	درخت میوه
elm	derakht-e naarun	درخت نارون
grove; plantation	derakhtestaan	درختستان
beech	raash	راش
root	risheh	ریشه
beech	zaan	زان
ash	zabaan gonjeshk	زبان گنجشک
rowan	zabaan gonjeshk-e kuhi	زبان گنجشک کوهی
undergrowth	zir rost	زیر رست
linden; lime tree	zirafun	زیرفون
teak	saaj	ساج
poplar	sepidaar	سپیدار
cedar	sedr	سدر
Lebanese cedar	sedr-e lobnaani	سدر لبنانی
treetop	sar-e derakht	سر درخت
yew	sorkhdaar	سرخدار
cypress	sarv	سرو
juniper	sarv-e kuhi	سرو کوهی
white poplar; aspen	sefidaar	سفیدار
mountain ash	somaaq-e kuhi	سماق کوهی
larch	siyaah kaaj	سیاه کاج
foliage	shaakh o barg	شاخ و برگ
grove; thicket	shaakhsaar	شاخسار
branch	shaakheh	شاخه
chestnut tree	shaah balut	شاه بلوط
horse chestnut tree	shaah balut-e hendi	شاه بلوط هندی
larch	sharbin	شربین
box tree	shemshaad	شمشاد
sap	shire-ye giyaahi	شیره گیاهی
spruce fir; spruce pine	sanubar	صنوبر
white spruce	sanubar-e sefid	صنوبر سفید

red spruce	sanubar-e qermez	صنوبر قرمز
cherry laurel	qaar gilaas	غار گیلاس
birch	qaan	غان
silver birch	qaan-e kaaqazi	غان کاغذی
bud	qoncheh	غنچه
pine tree	kaaj	کاج
plantation	kalaan keshtzaar	کلان کشتزار
log	kondeh	کنده
sap	giyaashir	گیاشیر
conifer	makhruti	مخروطی
beech	mars	مرس
mahogany	maqun	مغون
acorn	mive-ye balut	میوه بلوط
pine cone	mive-ye kaaj	میوه کاج
palm grove	nakhlestaan	نخلستان
sapling; shoot; twig	nehaal	نهال
tree nursery	nehaalestaan	نهالستان
white bryony	hezaar cheshaan	هزارچشان
evergreen	hamisheh sabz	همیشه سبز

climate; weather	aab o havaa	آب و هوا
equatorial climate	aab o havaa-ye estevaa'i	آب و هوای استوائی
equatorial climate	aab o havaa-ye haare'i	آب و هوای حاره ای
polar climate	aab o havaa-ye qotbi	آب و هوای قطبی
maritime climate	aab o havaa-ye keraane'i	آب و هوای کرانه ای
mountain climate	aab o havaa-ye kuhestaani	آب و هوای کوهستانی
Mediterranean climate	aab o havaa-ye meditaraane'i	آب و هوای مدیترانه ای
microclimate	aab o havaa-ye naahiyeh	آب و هوای ناحیه
St. Elmo's Fire	aatesh-e sant elmow	آتش سنت المو
lightning	aazarakhsh	آذرخش
ball lightning	aazarakhsh-e tupi	آذرخش توپی
atmospheric lightning	aazarakhsh-e javvi	آذرخش جوی
calm	aaraam	آرام
sky	aasemaan	آسمان
mackerel sky	aasemaan-e piseh	آسمان پیسه
thunderclap	aasemaan qoronbeh	آسمان غرنبه
damage	aasib	آسیب
turbulence	aashoftegi	آشفتگی
sunshine	aaftaab	آفتاب
sunny	aaftaabi	آفتابی
cloud	abr	ابر
stratocumulus cloud	abr-e estraatu-kumulus	ابر استراتو کومولوس
altostratus cloud	abr-e estraatus-e faraaz	ابر استراتوس فراز
rain cloud	abr-e baaraan	ابر باران
nimbus cloud	abr-e baaraan-zaa	ابر باران زا
altocumulus cloud	abr-e poshte'i-ye faraaz	ابر پشته ای فراز
storm cloud	abr-e tufaani	ابر توفانی
cirrus cloud	abr-e sirus	ابر سیروس
noctilucent cloud	abr-e shabtaab	ابر شب تاب
thundercloud	abr-e saa'eqedaar	ابر صاعقه دار
lenticular cloud	abr-e adasi shekl	ابر عدسی شکل
cloudlet	abr-e kuchak	ابر کوچک
cirrocumulus cloud	abr-e navaari	ابر نواری
convective cloud	abr-e hamraft	ابر همرفت
cloudy; overcast	abri	ابری
high clouds	abr-haa-ye por ertefaa'	ابرهای پر ارتفاع

nacreous clouds	abr-haa-ye taabnaak	ابرهای تابناک
mare's tail clouds	abr-haa-ye dom-e asbi	ابرهای دم اسبی
low clouds	abr-haa-ye kam ertefaa'	ابرهای کم ارتفاع
weather bureau	edaare-ye havaashenaasi	اداره هواشناسی
stratus cloud	estraatus	استراتوس
ray	asha'eh	اشعه
occlusion	ensedaad	انسداد
weather station	istgaah-e havaashenaasi	ایستگاه هواشناسی
wind	baad	باد
prevailing wind	baad-e bishvaz	باد بیش وز
Pampero (a type of wind)	baad-e paamperow	باد پامپرو
Levanter (a type of wind)	baad-e khaavari	باد خاوری
Khamsin (a type of wind)	baad-e khamsin	باد خمسین
Sirocco (a type of wind)	baad-e siruku	باد سیروکو
monsoon	baad-e mowsemi	باد موسمی
southerly winds	baad-haa-ye jonubi	بادهای جنوبی
easterly winds	baad-haa-ye sharqi	بادهای شرقی
northerly winds	baad-haa-ye shomaali	بادهای شمالی
westerly winds	baad-haa-ye qarbi	بادهای غربی
anemometer	baad sanj	بادسنج
weather vane	baad namaa	بادنما
windy	baadi	بادی
bar	baar	بار
nimbostratus	baaraapush	باراپوش
rain	baaraan	باران
rain gauge	baaraan sanj	باران سنج
downpour	baaraan-e shadid	باران شدید
rainy	baaraani	بارانی
rainfall; precipitation	baaresh	بارش
snowfall	baaresh-e barf	بارش برف
precipitation; rainfall	baarandegi	بارندگی
arid; dry	baayer	بایر
steam	bokhaar	بخار
mist	bokhaar-e zamin	بخار زمین
snow	barf	برف
snowdrift	barf-e baad aavard	برف باد آورد
frost	barfak	برفک
snowy	barfi	برفی

lightning conductor	barq gir	برق گیر
blizzard	buraan	بوران
cloudless; clear	bi abr	بی ابر
calm; still; windless	bi baad	بی باد
spring	bahaar	بهار
improvement	behbud	بهبود
autumn	paa'iz	پائیز
breezy	por nasim	پر نسیم
cumulus	poshte'i	پشته ای
cloud cover	pushesh-e abr	پوشش ابر
snow cover	pushesh-e barf	پوشش برف
weather forecast	pishbini-ye vaz'-e havaa	پیشبینی وضع هوا
summer	taabestaan	تابستان
halo (solar)	taaj-e khorshid	تاج خورشید
darkness	taariki	تاریکی
change	taqyir	تغییر
condensation	taqtir	تقطیر
hail	tagarg	تگرگ
hurricane; gale	tondbaad	تندباد
fog bank	tude-ye meh	توده مه
storm	tufaan	توفان
rainstorm	tufaan-e baaraan	توفان باران
snowstorm	tufaan-e barf	توفان برف
hailstorm	tufaan-e tagarg	توفان تگرگ
thunderstorm	tufaan-e tondori	توفان تندری
squall	tufaan-e zudgozar	توفان زودگذر
occluded front	jebhe-ye ensedaadi	جبهه انسدادی
weather front	jebhe-ye havaa	جبهه هوا
cold front	jebhe-ye havaa-ye sard	جبهه هوای سرد
warm front	jebhe-ye havaa-ye garm	جبهه هوای گرم
south	jonub	جنوب
south-east	jonub-e sharqi	جنوب شرقی
south-west	jonub-e qarbi	جنوب غربی
atmosphere	javv	جو
atmospheric	javvi	جوی
umbrella	chatr	چتر
whirlwind	charkhbaad	چرخ باد
cyclone	charkhand	چرخند

typhoon	*charkhand-e estevaa'i*	چرخند استوائی
cyclone	*charkheh baad*	چرخه باد
tropical cyclone	*charkheh tufaan-e estevaa'i*	چرخه توفان استوائی
heat; warmth	*haraarat*	حرارت
soil; earth	*khaak*	خاك
Levanter (type of wind)	*khaavarbaad*	خاورباد
destruction	*kharaabi*	خرابی
micro-climate	*khord aab o havaa*	خرد آب و هوا
halo (lunar)	*kharman-e maah*	خرمن ماه
dry; arid	*khoshk*	خشک
drought	*khoshksaali*	خشکسالی
aridity	*khoshki*	خشکی
isotherm	*khatt-e hamdamaa*	خط هم دما
isohyet	*khatt-e hambaaresh*	خط همبارش
isobar	*khatt-e hamfeshaar*	خط همفشار
cool	*khonak*	خنک
sun	*khorshid*	خورشید
parhelion	*khorshid-e kaazeb*	خورشید کاذب
hot	*daaq*	داغ
snowflake	*daane-ye barf*	دانه برف
hailstone	*daane-ye tagarg*	دانه تگرگ
degree	*darajeh*	درجه
dew point	*daraje-ye enqebaaz*	درجه انقباض
temperature	*daraje-ye havaa*	درجه هوا
flash of lightning	*derakhshesh-e barq*	درخشش برق
heat	*damaa*	دما
thermal (n.)	*damaa sotun*	دما ستون
thermometer	*damaasanj*	دما سنج
wet-bulb thermometer	*damaasanj-e tar*	دما سنج تر
smoke	*dud*	دود
smog	*dudmeh*	دودمه
cold spell	*dowraan-e havaa-ye sard*	دوران هوای سرد
warm spell	*dowraan-e havaa-ye garm*	دوران هوای گرم
humidity	*rotubat*	رطوبت
absolute humidity	*rotubat-e motlaq*	رطوبت مطلق
relative humidity	*rotubat-e nesbi*	رطوبت نسبی
thunder	*ra'd*	رعد
thunder and lightning	*ra'd o barq*	رعد و برق

shower	ragbaar	رگبار
sudden shower	ragbaar-e naagahaani	رگبار ناگهانی
scattered showers	ragbaar-haa-ye paraakandeh	رگبار های پراکنده
rainbow	rangin kamaan	رنگین کمان
day; daytime	ruz	روز
bright; clear	rowshan	روشن
drizzle	rizbaar	ریزبار
rainfall	rizesh-e baaraan	ریزش باران
snowfall	rizesh-e barf	ریزش برف
earthquake	zelzeleh	زلزله
winter	zemestaan	زمستان
dew	zhaaleh	ژاله
condensation	zhaaleh zaa'i	ژاله زائی
scud	zhiyaan abr	ژیان ابر
coast	saahel	ساحل
shadow	saayeh	سایه
whiteout	sepid gereftegi	سپید گرفتگی
dawn; daybreak	sahar	سحر
mirage	saraab	سراب
cold (n.)	sarmaa	سرما
Doldrums	sokun-e estevaa'i	سکون استوایی
cirrostratus	sirus-e boland	سیروس بلند
cirrocumulus	sirukumulus	سیرو کومولوس
flood	seyl	سیل
night; evening	shab	شب
dew	shabnam	شبنم
hoar frost	shabnam-e yakhzadeh	شبنم یخزده
conditions	sharaa'et	شرائط
east	sharq	شرق
north	shomaal	شمال
north-east	shomaal-e sharqi	شمال شرقی
north-west	shomaal-e qarbi	شمال غربی
thunderbolt	saa'eqeh	صاعقه
clear	saaf	صاف
morning	sobh	صبح
west	qarb	غرب
advection	faraabord	فرابرد
depression	forubaar	فروبار

atmospheric pressure	feshaar-e javv	فشار جو
low pressure	feshaar-e kam	فشار کم
season	fasl	فصل
seasonal	fasli	فصلی
drought	qahti	قحطی
raindrop	qatre-ye baaraan	قطره باران
icicle	qandil-e yakh	قندیل یخ
rainbow	qows o qazah	قوس و قزح
country	keshvar	کشور
draught	kuraan	کوران
blizzard	kulaak	کولاک
whirlwind	gerdbaad	گردباد
waterspout	gerdbaad-e daryaa'i	گردباد دریانی
overcast	gerefteh	گرفته
warm	garm	گرم
warmth; heat	garmaa	گرما
weather report	gozaaresh-e vaz'-e havaa	گزارش وضع هوا
puddle	gowdaal	گودال
snow plough	maashin-e barf rub	ماشین برف روب
moon; month	maah	ماه
changeable; variable	motaqayyer	متغیر
damp	martub	مرطوب
weather centre	markaz-e havaashenaasi	مرکز هواشناسی
temperate	mo'tadel	معتدل
Beaufort Scale	meqyaas-e bowfort	مقیاس بوفورت
region; district; area	mantaqeh	منطقه
heat wave	mowj-e havaa-ye garm	موج هوای گرم
seasonal; monsoon (adj.)	mowsemi	موسمی
visibility	meydaan-e did	میدان دید
annual rate of precipitation	mizaan-e baaresh-e saalyaaneh	میزان بارش سالیانه
visibility	mizaan-e did	میزان دید
millibar	milibaar	میلی بار
fog	meh	مه
foggy	meh aalud	مه آلود
fogbow	meh kamaan	مه کمان
fogbound	meh gerefteh	مه گرفته
whiteout	meh o barf	مه و برف
moonlight	mahtaab	مهتاب

468

ridge of high pressure	naahiye-ye por feshaar	ناحیه پر فشار
ridge of low pressure	naahiye-ye kam feshaar	ناحیه کم فشار
drizzle	narmeh baaraan	نرمه باران
breeze	nasim	نسیم
land breeze	nasim-e khoshki	نسیم خشکی
sea breeze	nasim-e daryaa'i	نسیم دریائی
weather map	naqshe-ye havaashenaasi	نقشه هواشناسی
freezing point	noqte-ye enjemaad	نقطه انجماد
dewpoint	noqte-ye shabnam	نقطه شبنم
nimbostratus	nimbow estraatus	نیمبو استراتوس
anticyclone	vaacharkheh	واچرخه
jet stream	vazaane-ye jet	وزانه جت
gust of wind	vazesh-e shadid-e baad	وزش شدید باد
lull	veqfeh	وقفه
Harmattan (type of wind)	haarmaataan	هارماتان
halo	haaleh	هاله
Haboob (type of wind)	habub	هبوب
convection	hamraft	همرفت
weather; air	havaa	هوا
barometer	havaa sanj	هوا سنج
meteorologist	havaashenaas	هواشناس
meteorology	havaashenaasi	هواشناسی
bad weather	havaa-ye bad	هوای بد
ice	yakh	یخ
sleet	yakhbaar	یخ بار
sleet	yakhbaaraan	یخ باران
rime	yakhbast	یخ بست
frost	yakhbandaan	یخبندان
ice storm	yakhtufaan	یخ توفان
black ice	yakh-e siyaah	یخ سیاه
thaw	yakh goshaa'i	یخ گشائی

469

the weather is cold هوا سرد است   the weather is warm هوا گرم است   what's the weather like? هوا چطور است؟

it's sunny آفتابی است   it's snowing برف میاید   it's windy باد میاید   it's raining باران میاید

هوای بارانی rainy weather   هوای بادی windy weather   snowy day روز برفی   sunny day روز آفتابی

it's stormy طوفانی است   it's drizzling نم نم باران میاید   it's pouring with rain جر جر باران میاید

to rain; to fall باریدن   it's raining باران می بارد   it's snowing برف می بارد   good weather هوای خوب

bad weather هوای بد   it depends on the weather بستگی به هوا دارد   unsettled weather هوای متغیر

what awful weather! چه هوای گندی!   the weather is very warm هوا خیلی گرم است   hot داغ

the weather here is humid هوای اینجا شرجی است   it's foggy today امروز مه آلود است

the sun has come out خورشید در آمده است   the sun went behind the clouds خورشید پشت ابر رفت

the weather is cloudy هوا ابری است   the weather is dull / overcast هوا گرفته است   it's bright روشن است

everywhere is frozen همه جا یخ بسته   the heat was unbearable گرما قابل تحمل نبود   severe cold سرمای شدید

there is thunder and lightning رعد و برق میاید   to take shelter پناه بردن   to get wet خیس شدن

the sky is full of clouds آسمان پر از ابر است   suddenly there was a shower یک دفعه رگبار آمد

take an umbrella with you! با خودتان چتر ببرید!   what is Iran's climate like? آب و هوای ایران چطور است؟

the rainfall is low میزان بارندگی کم است   the wind is blowing from the north باد از طرف شمال میاید

it's hailing تگرگ میاید   a rainbow appeared in the sky رنگین کمان در آسمان پیدا شد

the weather is cool today امروز هوا خنک است   tornadoes happen often in America در آمریکا گردباد زیاد میاید

Iran is in the grip of a heatwave ایران دچار موج هوای گرم شده است   unusual weather هوای غیر عادی

I listened to the weather report به گزارش وضع هوا گوش دادم   the roads are full of black ice خیابان پر از یخ سیاه است

a cool breeze is blowing نسیم خنکی میاید   the weather is calm هوا آرام است   what weather! عجب هوائی!

470

Work and Professions

کار و حرفه

teaboy; butler; pantryman	aabdaarchi	آبدارچی
unemployed person	aadam-e bikaar	آدم بیکار
hairdresser; barber	aaraayeshgar	آرایشگر
decorator	aaraayeh gar	آرایه گر
cook; chef	aashpaz	آشپز
future	aayandeh	آینده
blacksmith	aahangar	آهنگر
labour union	ettehaadiye-ye kaargari	اتحادیه کارگری
work permit	ejaaze-ye kaar	اجازه کار
dismissal	ekhraaj	اخراج
office	edaareh	اداره
seniority	arshadiyat	ارشدیت
university lecturer	ostaad-e daaneshgaah	استاد دانشگاه
resignation	este'faa	استعفا
strike	e'tesaab	اعتصاب
striker	e'tesaabgar	اعتصابگر
wage rise; raise	afzaayesh-e hoquq	افزایش حقوق
storeman	anbaardaar	انباردار
appointment (to a position)	entesaab	انتصاب
transfer	enteqaal	انتقال
anthropologist	ensaanshenaas	انسانشناس
wine grower	angurkaar	انگورکار
porter	baarbar	باربر
labour market	baazaar-e kaar	بازار کار
businessman	baazargaan	بازرگان
business; commerce	baazargaani	بازرگانی
archeologist	baastaanshenaas	باستانشناس
landscape gardener	baaq aaraa	باغ آرا
gardener	baaqbaan	باغبان
roofer	baamsaaz	بام ساز
banker	baankdaar	بانکدار
archivist	baayegaan	بایگان
stuntman; stand-in	badal	بدل
dismissal	barkenaari	بر کناری
electrician	barq kaar	برق کار
programmer (computers)	barnaameh nevis	برنامه نویس

471

builder; bricklayer	bannaa	بنا
unemployment	bikaari	بیکاری
paramedic	behyaar	بهیار
nepotism; string-pulling	paarti baazi	پارتی بازی
receptionist	pazireshgar	پذیرشگر
nurse	parastaar	پرستار
physician; doctor	pezeshk	پزشک
researcher	pezhuheshgar	پژوهشگر
paramedic	piraapezeshk	پیراپزشک
waiter; servant	pishkhedmat	پیشخدمت
trade	pisheh	پیشه
tradesman	pisheh var	پیشه ور
merchant; trader	taajer	تاجر
trade; business; commerce	tejaarat	تجارت
film editor	tadvingar	تدوینگر
promotion	tarfi'	ترفیع
stuntman	jaanbaaz	جانباز
usher	jaanamaa	جانما
ambition	jaah talabi	جاه طلبی
surgeon	jarraah	جراح
forester; woodsman	jangalbaan	جنگلبان
welder	jushkaar	جوشکار
joiner	chubkaar	چوبکار
governor; ruler	haakem	حاکم
profession; job; career	herfeh	حرفه
professional	herfe'i	حرفه ای
typesetter	horufchin	حروفچین
accountant	hesaabdaar	حسابدار
chartered accountant	hesaabdaar-e qasam khordeh	حسابدار قسم خورده
wages; salary	hoquq	حقوق
wage-earner	hoquq begir	حقوق بگیر
journalist	khabar negaar	خبرنگار
servant; maid	khedmatkaar	خدمتکار
pilot	khalabaan	خلبان
singer	khaanandeh	خواننده
tailor	khayyaat	خیاط
chemist	daarusaaz	داروساز
veterinary surgeon	daampezeshk	دامپزشک

volunteer	daavtalab	داوطلب
nanny; child-minder	daayeh	دایه
doorman	darbaan	دربان
wages; fee	dastmozd	دستمزد
assistant	dastyaar	دستیار
clerk	daftardaar	دفتردار
shopkeeper	dokkaandaar	دکاندار
bath attendant	dallaak	دلاک
dentist	dandaanpezeshk	دندانپزشک
cameraman	durbinchi	دوربینچی
training course	dowre-ye aamuzesh	دوره آموزش
ambulance driver	raanande-ye aambulaans	راننده آمبولانس
taxi driver	raanande-ye taaksi	راننده تاکسی
train driver	raanande-ye qataar	راننده قطار
nun	raahebeh	راهبه
usher; guide	raahnamaa	راهنما
tour guide	raahnamaa-ye tur	راهنمای تور
hierarchy	rotbeh bandi	رتبه بندی
dancer	raqqaas	رقاص
novelist	romaan nevis	رمان نویس
dyer	rangraz	رنگ رز
painter	rangzan	رنگ زن
psychologist	ravaanpezeshk	روانپزشک
psychiatrist	ravaanshenaas	روانشناس
journalist	ruznaameh negaar	روزنامه نگار
newspaper writer; journalist	ruznaameh nevis	روزنامه نویس
boss; head; chairman	ra'is	رئیس
housewife	zan-e khaaneh daar	زن خانه دار
prison warder	zendaanbaan	زندانبان
street sweeper	sopur	سپور
star	setaareh	ستاره
newspaper editor	sar dabir	سر دبیر
caretaker; janitor	saraayedaar	سرایدار
soldier	sarbaaz	سرباز
administrator	sarparast	سرپرست
museum curator	sarparast-e muzeh	سرپرست موزه
ambassador	safir	سفیر
barber	salmaani	سلمانی

stonemason	sang kaar	سنگ کار
stonecutter; stonemason	sangtaraash	سنگتراش
politician	siyaasat madaar	سیاستمدار
apprentice; trainee	shaagerd	شاگرد
company; firm	sherkat	شرکت
magician	sho'bedeh baaz	شعبده باز
job; profession; career	shoql	شغل
house husband	showhar-e khaaneh daar	شوهر خانه دار
milkman	shir forush	شیر فروش
glazier	shisheh bor	شیسه بر
restaurant owner	saaheb-e rasturaan	صاحب رستوران
ship owner	saaheb-e keshti	صاحب کشتی
garage owner	saaheb-e gaaraazh	صاحب گاراژ
cashier	sanduq daar	صندوق دار
industry	san'at	صنعت
craftsman	san'at kaar	صنعت کار
craftsman; industrialist	san'at gar	صنعتگر
archivist	zaabet	ضابط
designer	tarraah	طراح
fashion designer	tarraah-e lebaas	طراح لباس
antique seller	'atiqeh forush	عتیقه فروش
photographer	'akkaas	عکاس
bricklayer; builder	'amaleh bannaa	عمله بنا
optician	'eynak saaz	عینک ساز
diver	qavvaas	غواص
prostitute	faahesheh	فاحشه
tea-boy; office junior	farraash	فراش
salesperson; sales assistant	forushandeh	فروشنده
astronaut	fazaanavard	فضا نورد
metal worker	felezkaar	فلز کار
footballer	futbaalist	فوتبالیست
judge	qaazi	قاضی
carpet weaver	qaalibaaf	قالیباف
deputy director	qaa'em maqaam-e modir	قائم مقام مدیر
gravedigger	qabr kan	قبر کن
locksmith	qofl saaz	قفل ساز
work; job	kaar	کار
training; apprenticeship	kaar aamuzi	کار آموزی

474

voluntary work	kaar-e daavtalabaaneh	کار داوطلبانه
business	kaar o kasb	کار و کسب
factory	kaarkhaaneh	کارخانه
employer	kaarfarmaa	کارفرما
the management; the bosses	kaarfarmaayaan	کارفرمایان
workshop	kaargaah	کارگاه
worker	kaargar	کارگر
skilled worker	kaargar-e aamukhteh	کارگر آموخته
printer	kaargar-e chaapkhaaneh	کارگر چاپخانه
construction worker	kaargar-e saakhtemaani	کارگر ساختمانی
factory worker	kaargar-e kaarkhaaneh	کارگر کارخانه
steel worker	kaargar-e kaarkhaane-ye fulaad	کارگر کارخانه فولاد
film director	kaargardaan-e film	کارگردان فیلم
employee; worker	kaarmand	کارمند
office worker	kaarmand-e edaareh	کارمند اداره
bank clerk	kaarmand-e baank	کارمند بانک
post office worker	kaarmand-e postkhaaneh	کارمند پستخانه
civil servant	kaarmand-e dowlat	کارمند دولت
businessman; trader	kaaseb	کاسب
business; trade	kaasebi	کاسبی
tiler	kaashi saaz	کاشی ساز
candidate	kaandidaa	کاندیدا
librarian	ketaabdaar	کتابدار
farmer	keshaavarz	کشاورز
priest; vicar	keshish	کشیش
auxiliary nurse	komak parastaar	کمک پرستار
florist	golforush	گلفروش
announcer; presenter	guyandeh	گوینده
plumber	luleh kesh	لوله کش
adventurer	maajaraaju	ماجراجو
typist	maashin nevis	ماشین نویس
fireman	ma'mur-e aatash neshaani	مامور آتش نشانی
model	maankan	مانکن
physiotherapist	motakhasses-e tan darmaani	متخصص تن درمانی
cardiologist	motakhasses-e qalb	متخصص قلب
translator	motarjem	مترجم
administrator	motavalli	متولی
workplace	mahall-e kaar	محل کار

travel expenses	*makhaarej-e safar*	مخارج سفر
social worker	*madadkaar-e ejtemaa'i*	مددکار اجتماعی
instructor; teacher	*modarres*	مدرس
director (of company)	*modir*	مدیر
managing director	*modir-e 'aamel*	مدیر عامل
headmaster	*modir-e madraseh*	مدیر مدرسه
management	*modiriyat*	مدیریت
swimming instructor	*morabbi-ye shenaa*	مربی شنا
wage-earner	*mozdgir*	مزد گیر
counsellor	*moshaaver*	مشاور
solicitor	*moshaaver-e hoquqi*	مشاور حقوقی
interview	*mosaahebeh*	مصاحبه
miner	*ma'danchi*	معدنچی
teacher	*mo'allem*	معلم
architect	*me'maar*	معمار
contractor	*moqaate'eh kaar*	مقاطعه کار
radio mechanic	*mekaanik-e raadiyo*	مکانیک رادیو
sailor	*malavaan*	ملوان
mullah	*mollaa*	ملا
secretary	*monshi*	منشی
wage scale	*mizaan-e dastmozd*	میزان دستمزد
air steward; air stewardess	*mehmaandaar-e havaapeymaa*	مهماندار هواپیما
engineer	*mohandes*	مهندس
electrical engineer	*mohandes-e barq*	مهندس برق
civil engineer	*mohandes-e raah o saakhtemaan*	مهندس راه و ساختمان
agricultural engineer	*mohandes-e keshaavarzi*	مهندس کشاورزی
mechanical engineer	*mohandes-e mekaanik*	مهندش مکانیک
publisher	*naasher*	ناشر
candidate	*naamzad*	نامزد
carpenter	*najjaar*	نجار
prime minister	*nakhost vazir*	نخست وزیر
cleaner	*nezaafatchi*	نظافتچی
surveyor	*naqsheh bardaar*	نقشه بردار
draughtsman	*naqsheh kesh*	نقشه کش
painter	*naqqaash*	نقاش
bodyguard	*negahbaan-e shakhsi*	نگهبان شخصی
representative	*namaayandeh*	نماینده
writer	*nevisandeh*	نویسنده

workforce	niru-ye kaar	نیروی کار
work ethic	vojdaan-e kaar	وجدان کار
professional sportsman/woman	varzeshkaar-e herfe'i	ورزشکار حرفه ای
minister	vazir	وزیر
barrister	vakil	وکیل
lawyer	vakil-e daadgostari	وکیل دادگستری
editor	viraastaar	ویراستار
colleague	hamkaar	همکار
actor	honarpisheh	هنرپیشه
artist	honarmand	هنرمند
weather presenter; meteorologist	havaashenaas	هواشناس

OTHER WORDS AND PHRASES CONNECTED WITH THE WORLD OF WORK

to work کار کردن to find a job کار پیدا کردن I've started a new job کار جدید شروع کردم new job شغل جدید

to employ استخدام کردن to be employed استخدام شدن to be employed; to be in work شاغل بودن استخدام کردن

his profession is medicine شغل او پزشکی است he has a good job شغل خوبی دارد full-time job کار تمام وقت

part-time job کار نیمه وقت shift work کار شیفتی I started work yesterday دیروز شروع به کار کردم

what does Hasan do (for a living)? حسن چه کاره است to apply for a job تقاضای کار دادن applicant متقاضی

to be unemployed بیکار بودن to become unemployed بیکار شدن to resign استعفاء دادن

they fired him او را از کار بیرون کردند to make redundant از کار بیکار کردن to go on strike اعتصاب کردن

he has a good income درآمد خوبی دارد how much does he earn? حقوقش چقدر است؟ overtime اضافه کار

he earns £2000 a month حقوقش ۲۰۰۰ پوند در ماه است my wages are very low حقوق من خیلی کم است

my work is very interesting کار من خیلی جالب است humdrum routine کار یکنواخت روزمره

I have no job security امنیت کاری ندارم I don't enjoy my work از کارم لذت نمی برم hard-working سخت کار

they really make me work hard از من خیلی کار می کشند to change jobs کار عوض کردن ambitious جاه طلب

Ahmad is at work احمد سر کار است to be busy working مشغول کار بودن work hours; office hours ساعات کار

to work illegally; to moonlight بطور قاچاقی کار کردن I have no job satisfaction رضایت کاری ندارم

personnel office کارگزینی human resources منابع انسانی recruitment کارگاری curriculum vitae کارنامه

experienced کارکشته experienced; tried and tested کارآزموده inexperienced; novice کارنا آزموده

employment office; personnel agency بنگاه کاریابی personnel; workers کارکنان skill; expertise کاردانی

sedentary worker; white-collar worker پشت میز نشین expert; specialist کارشناس expertise کارشناسی

my father has just retired پدرم تازه بازنشسته شده retirement بازنشستگی retirement age سن بازنشستگی

work permit اجازه کار to take time off; to go on leave مرخصی گرفتن wage increase افزایش حقوق

promotion ارتقاء promotion ترفیع promotion ترفیع they promoted him to the rank of foreman او را به مقام سرکارگری ترفیع دادند

◀◆▶

Miscellaneous Nouns

اسم های متفرقه

respect; honour; prestige	*aaberu*	آبرو
idiot	*aadam-e ahmaq*	آدم احمق
cannibal	*aadam khor*	آدم خور
peace; tranquillity; rest; repose	*aaraamesh*	آرامش
hopes; aspirations	*aarezu-haa*	آرزوها
foretaste	*aazmaayesh-e qabli*	آزمایش قبلی
beginning; inception; start	*aaqaaz*	آغاز
advertisement	*aagahi*	آگهی
mixture; blend	*aamizeh*	آمیزه
intermission; interval	*aantraakt*	آنتراکت
fool; idiot	*ablah*	ابله
connection; junction; contiguity	*ettesaal*	اتصال
concord; unity; incident; happening	*ettefaaq*	اتفاق
effect; impression; result; trace	*asar*	اثر
meeting; crowd; society; gathering	*ejtemaa'*	اجتماع
respect; honour; reverence; regard	*ehteraam*	احترام
probability; eventuality; likelihood	*ehtemaal*	احتمال
caution; precaution; prudence	*ehtiyaat*	احتیاط
feeling; sentiment; sensation	*ehsaas*	احساس
news; information	*akhbaar*	اخبار
difference; dispute; disagreement	*ekhtelaaf*	اختلاف
warning; notification	*ekhtaar*	اخطار
politeness; courtesy; civility	*adab*	ادب
literature; belles-lettres	*adabiyaat*	ادبیات
nuisance; annoyance; trouble	*aziyat*	اذیت
value; worth; merit; usefulness	*arzesh*	ارزش
resumption; recommencement	*az sar giri*	از سر گیری
crowd; throng; swarm; multitude	*ezdehaam*	ازدحام
indication; hint; allusion; reference	*eshaareh*	اشاره
mistake; error; misconception	*eshtebaah*	اشتباه
eagerness; keenness; enthusiasm	*eshtiyaaq*	اشتیاق
difficulty; impracticability; problem	*eshkaal*	اشکال
saying; proverb; idiom; term	*estelaah*	اصطلاح
foundation; source; principal	*asl*	اصل
anxiety; anguish; fear; apprehension	*ezteraab*	اضطراب
certainty; trust; confidence; reliance	*etminaan*	اطمینان

479

statement; expression; declaration	ez-haar	اظهار
objection; protest; complaint	e'teraaz	اعتراض
self-confidence	e'temaad-e be-nafs	اعتماد بنفس
proclamation; declaration	e'laan	اعلان
opening; inauguration	eftetaah	افتتاح
pride; honour; glory	eftekhaar	افتخار
excess; overindulgence	efraat	افراط
residence; stay; sojourn	eqaamat	اقامت
economy; economics	eqtesaad	اقتصاد
copy; duplicate	almosannaa	المثنى
aid; assistance; help	emdaad	امداد
affair; order; command	amr	امر
possibility; feasibility; likelihood	emkaan	امکان
safety; security; protection	amniyat	امنیت
hope; expectation	omid	امید
crowd; throng; horde; mob	anbuh-e mardom	انبوه مردم
choice; election; selection	entekhaab	انتخاب
size; dimension; measurement	andaazeh	اندازه
sorrow; sadness; grief	anduh	اندوه
energy	enerzhi	انرژی
discipline; order; control	enzebaat	انضباط
reflection; reaction; repercussion	en'ekaas	انعکاس
disconnection; discontinuity	enqetaa'	انقطاع
revolution; upheaval; convulsion	enqelaab	انقلاب
revolutionary	enqelaabi	انقلابی
priority; preference	owlaviyat	اولویت
beginning; outset; commencement	avval	اوّل
objection; criticism	iraad	ایراد
stop; halt	ist	ایست
station	istgaah	ایستگاه
belief; faith; credence; trust	imaan	ایمان
importance; significance; primacy	ahamiyat	اهمیت
inspector	baazras	بازرس
survivor; remains	baazmaandeh	بازمانده
leftover; remainder; remnant	baaqi maandeh	باقی مانده
argument; discussion; debate	bahs	بحث
steam; vapour	bokhaar	بخار
luck; fortune; chance	bakht	بخت

share; part; section; district; ward	bakhsh	بخش
misfortune; adversity; affliction	badbakhti	بد بختی
bad luck; misfortune	badshaansi	بدشانسی
sticker	barchasp	برچسب
slavery; bondage; servitude	bardegi	بردگی
slave; bondsman	bardeh	برده
cut; cutting; incision	boresh	برش
return; regress; revocation	bargasht	برگشت
extraterrestrial	borun zamini	برون زمینی
barrel; cask; keg	boshkeh	بشکه
insight; intelligence; awareness	basirat	بصیرت
dimension	bo'd	بُعد
remains; vestiges; remnants	baqaayaa	بقایا
loudspeaker	bolandgu	بلند گو
height; elevation; loudness	bolandi	بلندی
impoliteness; rudeness; impudence	bi-adabi	بی ادبی
impatience; irritability; boredom	bi-howselegi	بی حوصلگی
cruelty; ruthlessness	bi-rahmi	بی رحمی
uselessness; futility	bi-faayedegi	بی فایدگی
anonymity	bi-naami	بی نامی
disorder; confusion	bi-nazmi	بی نظمی
weightlessness	bi-vazni	بی وزنی
expression; explanation; exposition	bayaan	بیان
vision; insight; perspicacity	binesh	بینش
improvement; recovery	behbud	بهبود
hygiene; health; sanitation	behdaasht	بهداشت
interest; profit; share; portion	bahreh	بهره
reward	paadaash	پاداش
tear; cut; slit	paaregi	پارگی
erasure	paak shodegi	پاك شدگی
end; conclusion; finish; completion	paayaan	پایان
reception; hospitality	paziraa'i	پذیرائی
acceptance; admission	paziresh	پذیرش
question; query; inquiry	porsesh	پرسش
distress; agitation; disturbance	parishaani	پریشانی
saving; savings	pasandaaz	پس انداز
regression; retrogression	pasravi	پس روی
back; rear; behind; posterior	posht	پشت

481

regret; remorse	*pashimaani*	پشیمانی
shelter; refuge; protection	*panaah*	پناه
victory; triumph; conquest	*piruzi*	پیروزی
foretaste	*pish cheshi*	پیش چشی
foreword	*pish goftaar*	پیش گفتار
foreground	*pish namaa*	پیش نما
progress; advancement	*pishraft*	پیشرفت
forerunner; pioneer; precursor	*pishrow*	پیشرو
message	*peyqaam*	پیغام
width; breadth; extent; expanse	*pahnaa*	پهنا
impression; effect; influence	*ta'sir*	تاثیر
crown	*taaj*	تاج
history; date	*taarikh*	تاریخ
darkness; gloom	*taariki*	تاریکی
freshness; novelty	*taazegi*	تازگی
newcomer	*taazeh vaared*	تازه وارد
exchange; interchange; alternation	*tabaadol*	تبادل
exile; banishment	*tab'id*	تبعید
advertisements; publicity	*tabliqaat*	تبلیغات
experience	*tajrobeh*	تجربه
imagination; fantasy	*takhayyol*	تخیل
preparations; arrangements	*tadaarokaat*	تدارکات
instruction; teaching	*tadris*	تدریس
fear; dread; fright; terror	*tars*	ترس
gratitude; thanks; appreciation	*tashakkor*	تشکر
decision; resolution	*tasmim*	تصمیم
picture; depiction; portrait; screen	*tasvir*	تصویر
surprise; wonder; astonishment	*ta'ajjob*	تعجب
adjustment; modification	*ta'dil*	تعدیل
fault; guilt; culpability; blame	*taqsir*	تقصیر
struggle; effort; endeavour; exertion	*taqallaa*	تقلا
spectator; viewer	*tamaashaachi*	تماشاچی
inclination; tendency; urge	*tamaayol*	تمایل
civilisation	*tamaddon*	تمدن
cleanliness; neatness	*tamizi*	تمیزی
respiration; breathing; break	*tanaffos*	تنفس
agreement; consent; concurrence	*tavaafoq*	توافق
attention; concentration; regard	*tavajjoh*	توجه

heap; mass; pile; accumulation	*tudeh*	توده
explanation; elucidation	*towzih*	توضيح
plot; conspiracy; machination	*towte'eh*	توطعه
stop; pause; stopover	*tavaqqof*	توقف
arrow; dart; girder; pole	*tir*	تير
bottom; end	*tah*	ته
place; space	*jaa*	جا
gravity; attraction; allure; charisma	*jaazebeh*	جاذبه
society; community	*jaame'eh*	جامعه
prize; award; trophy	*jaa'ezeh*	جانزه
ambition	*jaah talabi*	جاه طلبى
table; kerb; grid; puzzle	*jadval*	جدول
courage; daring; pluck	*jor'at*	جرات
spark; flash	*jaraqeh*	جرقه
part; section; portion; fraction	*joz'*	جزء
details; particulars	*joz'iyaat*	جزنيات
boldness; impertinence; audacity	*jesaarat*	جسارت
pair; couple	*joft*	جفت
beauty; charm	*jamaal*	جمال
population; crowd; society	*jam'iyat*	جمعيت
sentence	*jomleh*	جمله
aspect	*janbeh*	جنبه
war; battle; fight; quarrel	*jang*	جنگ
answer; response	*javaab*	جواب
joke	*jowk*	جوك
direction; aspect	*jahat*	جهت
view; perspective; outlook	*cheshmandaaz*	چشم انداز
wink	*cheshmak*	چشمک
summary; gist	*chekideh*	چكيده
thing	*chiz*	چيز
framework	*chahaar chubeh*	چهارچوبه
memory; recollection; remembrance	*haafezeh*	حافظه
state; mood; condition	*haalat*	حالت
limit; boundary; extent	*hadd*	حد
minimum	*hadd-e aqqal*	حد اقل
maximum	*hadd-e aksar*	حد اكثر
deletion; omission; cancellation	*hazf*	حذف
letter; speech; word	*harf*	حرف

483

party; faction; sect	*hezb*	حزب
feeling; sense; sensation	*hess*	حس
account; reckoning; score	*hesaab*	حساب
envy; jealousy	*hesaadat*	حسادت
presence; attendance	*hozur*	حضور
truth; reality; fact; actuality	*haqiqat*	حقیقت
stupidity; foolishness	*hemaaqat*	حماقت
amazement; bewilderment	*heyrat*	حیرت
trick; ruse; stratagem; cunning	*hileh*	حیله
end; conclusion	*khaatemeh*	خاتمه
reporter; correspondent	*khabarnegaar*	خبرنگار
embarrassment; shyness	*khejaalat*	خجالت
God	*khodaa*	خدا
service	*khedmat*	خدمت
ruin; decay; corruption; destruction	*kharaabi*	خرابی
damage; loss; injury; compensation	*khesaarat*	خسارت
violence; roughness; harshness	*khoshunat*	خشونت
danger; peril; hazard; risk	*khatar*	خطر
disarmament	*khal'-e selaah*	خلع سلاح
temper; temperament; humour	*kholq*	خُلق
sleep; dream	*khaab*	خواب
nightmare	*khaab-e tarsnaak*	خواب ترسناك
sleepwalking	*khaabgardi*	خوابگردی
reader; singer	*khaanandeh*	خواننده
good; goodness	*khubi*	خوبی
cheerfulness; happiness	*khoshdeli*	خوشدلی
happiness; joy; gladness; pleasure	*khoshi*	خوشی
assets; possessions; wealth	*daaraa'i*	دارائی
circle	*daa'ereh*	دائره
honesty; correctness; integrity	*dorosti*	درستی
battle; trouble	*dargiri*	درگیری
understatement; underestimation	*dast-e kam giri*	دست کم گیری
apparatus; device; system	*dastgaah*	دستگاه
instruction; order; grammar	*dastur*	دستور
enemy; foe	*doshman*	دشمن
allure; attractiveness	*delrobaa'i*	دلربائی
bravery; courage	*daliri*	دلیری
reason; cause; motive	*dalil*	دلیل

religion; faith; creed	din	دین
madness; insanity; lunacy	divaanegi	دیوانگی
connection; relation; link	raabeteh	رابطه
comfort; ease; convenience	raahati	راحتی
secret; mystery; enigma	raaz	راز
truth; honesty	raasti	راستی
way; road; path	raah	راه
launch; inception	raah andaazi	راه اندازی
solution	raah-e hall	راه حل
short cut	raah-e miyaanbor	راه میان بر
guide; directory	raahnamaa	راهنما
guidance; directing	raahnamaa'i	راهنمائی
footprint	radd-e paa	رد پا
custom; convention; rite	rasm	رسم
satisfaction; consent; willingness	rezaayat	رضایت
traffic; coming and going	raft o aamad	رفت و آمد
removal; elimination	raf'	رفع
soul; spirit; psyche; mind	ravaan	روان
spirit; soul; ghost; life; essence	ruh	روح
newspaper	ruznaameh	روزنامه
method; manner; way; procedure	ravesh	روش
light; brightness; illumination; daylight	rowshanaa'i	روشنائی
copy; transcript	ru-nevesht	رونوشت
event; happening; incident	ruydaad	رویداد
rhythm	ritm	ریتم
slang	zabaan-e 'aamiyaaneh	زبان عامیانه
time; period; duration; epoch; age	zamaan	زمان
field; background; backdrop	zamineh	زمینه
life; living; existence	zendegi	زندگی
alarm bell	zang-e khatar	زنگ خطر
force; power; strength; coercion	zur	زور
excess; surplus	ziyaadi	زیادی
beauty; elegance; loveliness	zibaa'i	زیبائی
precedent; past record	saabeqeh	سابقه
make; construction; structure	saakht	ساخت
structure	saakhtaar	ساختار
building; construction; composition	saakhtemaan	ساختمان
reason; cause; means	sabab	سبب

basket; hamper	*sabad*	سبد
style; fashion; mode; manner	*sabk*	سبک
lightness; frivolity	*saboki*	سبکی
thanksgiving; gratitude	*sepaas gozaari*	سپاسگزاری
star; asterisk	*setaareh*	ستاره
praise; adoration; acclamation	*setaayesh*	ستایش
column; pillar; shaft	*sotun*	ستون
difficulty; hardship; hardness	*sakhti*	سختی
talk; conversation; speech	*sokhan*	سخن
secret; mystery	*serr*	سر
supervision; guardianship; protection	*sarparasti*	سرپرستی
frontier; border; boundary	*sar hadd*	سرحد
fate; destiny	*sarnevesht*	سرنوشت
noise; fuss; commotion; uproar	*sar o sedaa*	سروصدا
series	*seri*	سری
surface; level	*sath*	سطح
order; recommendation; command	*sefaaresh*	سفارش
silence; quiet; stillness	*sokut*	سکوت
series; chain; range; dynasty	*selseleh*	سلسله
age	*senn*	سن
profit; benefit; advantage; gain	*sud*	سود
suspicion	*su'-e zann*	سوء ظن
question	*so'aal*	سئوال
politics	*siyaasat*	سیاست
slap	*sili*	سیلی
joy; happiness; gladness; cheer	*shaadmaani*	شادمانی
happiness; joy; elation	*shaadi*	شادی
luck; fortune	*shaans*	شانس
likeness; similarity	*shebaahat*	شباهت
network; grid; lattice	*shabakeh*	شبکه
bravery; courage; boldness	*shojaa'at*	شجاعت
person; individual; character	*shakhs*	شخص
personality; character; individuality	*shakhsiyat*	شخصیت
evil; mischief; naughtiness	*sharr*	شر
bet; wager; condition	*shart*	شرط
honour; dignity	*sharaf*	شرف
shame; modesty; coyness	*sharm*	شرم
partner; associate; participant	*sharik*	شریک

doubt; suspicion; skepticism	*shakk*	شک
defeat; failure; breakage	*shekast*	شکست
breakage; fracture	*shekastegi*	شکستگی
form; shape; appearance; figure	*shekl*	شکل
noise; confusion; tumult	*sholuqi*	شلوقی
number; digit	*shomaareh*	شماره
thing; object	*shey*	شیء
outbreak; spread; prevalence	*shoyu'*	شیوع
style; method; manner	*shiveh*	شیوه
fame; celebrity	*shohrat*	شهرت
lust; passion; libido	*shahvat*	شهوت
owner; master; holder; possessor	*saaheb*	صاحب
patience; forbearance	*sabr*	صبر
voice; sound; noise	*sedaa*	صدا
page; sheet	*safheh*	صفحه
peace	*solh*	صلح
face; image; form	*surat*	صورت
blow; stroke; impact; punch; knock	*zarbeh*	ضربه
classification; categorization	*tabaqeh bandi*	طبقه بندی
nature; temper; disposition	*tabi'yat*	طبیعت
manner; method; mode; way	*tarz*	طرز
way of speaking	*tarz-e goftaar*	طرز گفتار
way; road; path; means; manner	*tariq*	طریق
length; duration	*tul*	طول
elegance; grace; delicateness	*zeraafat*	ظرافت
oppression; tyranny	*zolm*	ظلم
sentiment; feeling	*'aatefeh*	عاطفه
expression; phrase	*'ebaarat*	عبارت
number; figure; numeral; digit	*'adad*	عدد
width; breadth	*'arz*	عرض
doll	*'arusak*	عروسک
resolution; determination	*'azm*	عزم
love; affection; passion	*'eshq*	عشق
anger; rage; fury; irascibility	*'asabaaniyat*	عصبانیت
era; time; epoch	*'asr*	عصر
member	*'ozv*	عضو
photograph; picture; reverse; contrary	*'aks*	عکس
sign; mark; signal; token; symbol	*'alaamat*	علامت

cause; reason	'ellat	علت
depth; profundity; intensity	'omq	عمق
title; heading; rubric; designation	'onvaan	عنوان
stranger	qaribeh	غریبه
sadness; sorrow; grief; woe	qam	غم
disaster; tragedy; calamity	faaje'eh	فاجعه
distance; interval; gap	faaseleh	فاصله
profit; benefit; use; utility	faayedeh	فایده
expletive; swear word	fohsh	فحش
leisure; rest; ease	feraaqat	فراغت
product; produce	faraavardeh	فرآورده
opportunity; respite; chance	forsat	فرصت
sect; faction; group	ferqeh	فرقه
form	form	فرم
cry; shout	faryaad	فریاد
charm; deception; enchantment	faribandegi	فریبندگی
culture; education; dictionary	farhang	فرهنگ
season; section; chapter	fasl	فصل
space; area	fazaa	فضا
activity; effort; endeavour; action	fa'aaliyat	فعالیت
lack; absence; want; shortage	feqdaan	فقدان
thought; idea; contemplation	fekr	فکر
index; list; catalogue; table	fehrest	فهرست
smuggler; bootlegger	qaachaaqchi	قاچاقچی
rule; regulation; principle	qaa'edeh	قاعده
rhyme	qaafiyeh	قافیه
grave; tomb	qabr	قبر
power; strength; might; ability	qodrat	قدرت
footstep; pace	qadam	قدم
part; portion; section; segment; fate	qesmat	قسمت
intention; purpose; resolution; aim	qasd	قصد
strength; force; power; potency	qovvat	قوّت
price; value; cost; rate	qeymat	قیمت
nightmare	kaabus	کابوس
efficiency; skill; competence	kaaraa'i	کارائی
success; prosperity	kaamyaabi	کامیابی
copy	kopi	کپی
filth; dirt; impurity; uncleanliness	kesaafat	کثافت

fare; hire; rent; rental; lease	keraayeh	کرایه
attraction; pull; traction	keshesh	کشش
discovery; detection; exploration	kashf	کشف
struggle; conflict; skirmish	keshmakesh	کشمکش
thickness; coarseness	kolofti	کلفتی
word	kalameh	کلمه
cliche; stereotype	kelisheh	کلیشه
shortage; deficit; lack	kambud	کمبود
help; aid; assistance	komak	کمک
quantity	kamiyat	کمیت
curiosity; inquisitiveness	konjkaavi	کنجکاوی
endeavour; attempt; try	kushesh	کوشش
quality	keyfiyat	کیفیت
diaper; nappy	kohne-ye bacheh	کهنه بچه
trouble; difficulty; preoccupation	gereftaari	گرفتاری
group	goruh	گروه
choice; selection	gozinesh	گزینش
speech; discourse; conversation	goftaar	گفتار
conversation; dialogue; talk	goftegu	گفتگو
anonymity; obscurity	gomnaami	گمنامی
depth; cavity	gowdi	گودی
grave; tomb	gur	گور
corner; angle; insinuation	gusheh	گوشه
kind; manner; species; type	guneh	گونه
smile; grin	labkhand	لبخند
viewpoint; regard	lahaaz	لحاظ
pleasure; enjoyment; delight	lezzat	لذت
elegance; delicateness; fineness	letaafat	لطافت
wit; witticism; joke	latifeh	لطیفه
curse; malediction	la'nat	لعنت
adventure	maajaraa	ماجرا
taxes	maaliyaat	مالیات
obstacle; hindrance; impediment	maane'	مانع
controversy; argument; debate	mobaaheseh	مباحثه
struggle; campaign; combat	mobaarezeh	مبارزه
pride; boasting	mobaahaat	مباهات
amount; sum	mablaq	مبلغ
expert; specialist; connoisseur	motakhasses	متخصص

489

example; parable	*mesaal*	مثال
altercation; dispute; squabble	*mojaadeleh*	مجادله
magazine; periodical	*majalleh*	مجله
calculation; computation	*mohaasebeh*	محاسبه
crop; product; produce; output	*mahsul*	محصول
meeting place	*mahall-e molaaqaat*	محل ملاقات
expenses; costs; expenditure	*makhaarej*	مخارج
hiding place	*makhfi gaah*	مخفی گاه
mixture; blend	*makhlut*	مخلوط
period; duration; time	*moddat*	مدت
document; certificate; evidence	*madrak*	مدرك
stage; phase	*marhaleh*	مرحله
border; frontier; boundary	*marz*	مرز
centre; headquarters; middle	*markaz*	مركز
advantage; privilege; preference	*maziyat*	مزيت
distance; span	*masaafat*	مسافت
stowaway	*mosaafer-e qaachaaq*	مسافر قاچاق
journey; trip	*mosaaferat*	مسافرت
dwelling; residence; accommodation	*maskan*	مسكن
problem; difficulty	*moshkel*	مشكل
interview	*mosaahebeh*	مصاحبه
affliction; disaster; catastrophe	*mosibat*	مصيبت
comparison	*motaabeqat*	مطابقت
contemporary	*mo'aaser*	معاصر
puzzle; riddle; enigma	*mo'ammaa*	معما
meaning; sense; definition	*ma'ni*	معنی
yardstick; criterion; gauge; standard	*me'yaar*	معيار
place; position; office; rank; status	*maqaam*	مقام
comparison	*moqaayeseh*	مقايسه
quantity; amount; sum	*meqdaar*	مقدار
scale; measure; standard	*meqyaas*	مقياس
conversation; talk; discussion	*mokaalemeh*	مكالمه
meeting	*molaaqaat*	ملاقات
annoyance; vexation; sadness	*malaalat*	ملالت
interests; benefits	*manaafe'*	منافع
scenery; landscape; view	*manzareh*	منظره
balance; equilibrium	*movaazeneh*	موازنه
attention; carefulness	*movaazebat*	مواظبت

subject; topic; issue; matter	mowzu'	موضوع
situation; circumstances	mowqe'iyat	موقعیت
measure; balance; degree; rate	mizaan	میزان
inclination; tendency; desire	meyl	میل
skill; dexterity; proficiency	mahaarat	مهارت
kindness; compassion	mehrabaani	مهربانی
district; region; area	naahiyeh	ناحیه
candidate; fiancee	naamzad	نامزد
filth; dirt; impurity	nejaasat	نجاست
exchange rate	nerkh-e tabdil-e arz	نرخ تبدیل ارز
quarrel; dispute	nezaa'	نزاع
mark; trace; sign; badge; emblem	neshaan	نشان
advice; admonition; counsel	nasihat	نصیحت
cleanliness; neatness	nezaafat	نظافت
regime; system; order; arrangement	nezaam	نظام
view; opinion; look; glance	nazar	نظر
theory; opinion	nazariyeh	نظریه
curse; imprecation	nefrin	نفرین
soul; self; essence	nafs	نفس
painting; drawing; portrait	naqqaashi	نقاشی
cash	naqd	نقد
plan; map	naqsheh	نقشه
graph	naqshe-ye hendesi	نقشه هندسی
point; dot; full stop; period	noqteh	نقطه
starting point	noqte-ye aaqaaz	نقطه آغاز
viewpoint	noqte-ye nazar	نقطه نظر
quotation	naql-e qowl	نقل قول
show; demonstration; exhibition	namaayesh	نمایش
diagram; graph; table; chart	nemudaar	نمودار
rhythm	navaakht	نواخت
turn	nowbat	نوبت
light; illumination	nur	نور
kind; sort; species; variety	now'	نوع
strength; power; force	niru	نیرو
willpower	niru-ye eraadeh	نیروی اراده
actuality; reality; truth; fact	vaaqe'iyat	واقعیت
event; occurrence; incident	vaaqe'eh	واقعه
reaction	vaakonesh	واکنش

conscience	vojdaan	وجدان
existence; being; presence	vojud	وجود
entrance; arrival	vorud	ورود
ministry	vezaarat	وزارت
weight; heaviness	vazn	وزن
middle; centre	vasat	وسط
extent; area; extent; capacity	vos'at	وسعت
means; way; medium; agency	vasileh	وسیله
clarity; clearness; lucidity	vozuh	وضوح
duty; obligation	vazifeh	وظیفه
appointment; date	va'de-ye molaaqaat	وعده ملاقات
time; occasion; opportunity	vaqt	وقت
speciality; peculiarity	vizhegi	ویژگی
expert; connoisseur	vizheh kaar	ویژه کار
goal; aim; objective	hadaf	هدف
harmony; coordination	hamaahangi	هماهنگی
souvenir; memento; reminder	yaadegaar	یادگار
chap; fellow	yaaru	یارو
help; assistance; friendship	yaari	یاری
certainty; assurance	yaqin	یقین

Miscellaneous Adjectives

صفات متفرقه

honourable; reputable	aaberumand	آبرومند
heated; passionate; furious	aatashi	آتشی
future	aati	آتی
last; most recent	aakharin	آخرین
calm; still; peaceful; quiet	aaraam	آرام
calm; calming	aaraam bakhsh	آرام بخش
free; liberated	aazaad	آزاد
easy	aasaan	آسان
lenient; easy going	aasaan gir	آسان گیر
disturbed; agitated; distressed	aashofteh	آشفته
evident; open; manifest; obvious	aashekaar	آشکار
sunny	aaftaabi	آفتابی
future	aayandeh	آینده
elementary; primary; preliminary	ebtedaa'i	ابتدائی
everlasting; eternal	abadi	ابدی
compulsory; obligatory	ejbaari	اجباری
social; sociable; societal	ejtemaa'i	اجتماعی
sentimental; emotional	ehsaasaati	احساساتی
private; exclusive; special	ekhtesaasi	اختصاصی
literary	adabi	ادبی
cheap; inexpensive	arzaan	ارزان
self-sacrificing	az jaan gozashteh	از جان گذشته
out of breath	az nafas oftaadeh	از نفس افتاده
firm; steadfast; unswerving	ostovaar	استوار
confusing; misleading	eshtebaah aavar	اشتباه آور
engaged (telephone)	eshqaal	اشغال
real; essential; original; genuine	asli	اصلی
extra; excess	ezaafi	اضافی
horizontal	ofoqi	افقی
economic; economical	eqtesaadi	اقتصادی
divine; Godly	elaahi	الهی
privileged	emtiyaazdaar	امتیازدار
possible; viable	emkaanpazir	امکان پذیر
angry; bad tempered;	owqaat talkh	اوقات تلخ
standing	istaadeh	ایستاده
tame; domesticated; native	ahli	اهلی

493

polite; civil	baa adab	با ادب
talented	baa este'daad	با استعداد
happy; joyful; joyous	baa sorur	با سرور
magnificent	baa shokuh	با شکوه
graceful; elegant	baa vaqaar	با وقار
experienced	baa tajrobeh	باتجربه
narrow; slender; slim	baarik	باریک
open	baaz	باز
classical; ancient	baastaani	باستانی
pleasant	baa safaa	باصفا
believable; credible	baavar kardani	باور کردنی
unbelievable; incredible	baavar nakardani	باور نکردنی
intelligent; clever	baahush	باهوش
controversial	bahsangiz	بحث انگیز
critical	bohraani	بحرانی
bad	bad	بد
smelly; malodorous	bad bu	بد بو
naughty; mischievous; roguish	bad zaat	بد ذات
moody; ill-tempered	bad qeleq	بد قلق
worst	badtarin	بدترین
ill-humoured; cranky; vicious	bad kholq	بدخلق
suspicious	bad gamaan	بدگمان
equal; equivalent	baraabar	برابر
shining; shiny; glittering; polished	barraaq	براق
impressive	barangizandeh	برانگیزنده
electric; electrical	barqi	برقی
bigger; elder	bozorgtar	بزرگتر
biggest; eldest	bozorgtarin	بزرگترین
cheerful; jovial; merry	bashshaash	بشاش
next; forthcoming; subsequent	ba'di	بعدی
tall; high; lofty; aloud	boland	بلند
native; indigenous	bumi	بومی
hopeless; desperate	bi omid	بی امید
endless; unlimited; infinite	bi entehaa	بی انتها
endless; interminable; limitless	bi paayaan	بی پایان
motionless; still	bi harekat	بی حرکت
carefree; thoughtless	bi khiyaal	بی خیال
impatient	bi sabr	بی صبر

useless; pointless	bi faayedeh	بی فایده
restless	bi qaraar	بی قرار
anonymous; nameless	binaam	بی نام
oppressive; cruel; tyrannical	bidaadgaraaneh	بیداد گرانه
awake; aware	bidaar	بیدار
countless; innumerable; numerous	bishomaar	بیشمار
immense; boundless	bikaraan	بیکران
alien; foreign	bigaaneh	بیگانه
better	behtar	بهتر
best	behtarin	بهترین
hygienic; health (a.)	behdaashti	بهداشتی
ripped; torn	paareh shodeh	پاره شده
down; below; low	paa'in	پائین
cooked	pokhteh	پخته
full	por	پر
respectful	por ehteraam	پر احترام
talkative; garrulous; loquacious	por harf	پر حرف
cheeky; rude; impudent; impertinent	por ru	پر رو
noisy	por sar o sedaa	پرسر و صدا
repentant; sorry; regretful; contrite	pashimaan	پشیمان
decayed; rotten; worn out; putrid	pusideh	پوسیده
rich; wealthy	puldaar	پولدار
old; aged	pir	پیر
victorious; triumphant	piruz	پیروز
advanced; progressive	pishrafteh	پیشرفته
wide; broad	pahn	پهن
wide; extensive; vast	pahnaavar	پهناور
brilliant; shining	taabnaak	تابناك
historic; historical	taarikhi	تاریخی
dark	taarik	تاریک
fresh; recent	taazeh	تازه
literal	taht ol-lafzi	تحت اللفظی
spick and span; clean and tidy	tar o tamiz	تر و تمیز
frightening	tarsnaak	ترسناك
cowardly	tarsu	ترسو
accidental; chance (a.)	tasaadofi	تصادفی
surprising	ta'ajjob aavar	تعجب آور
shocking	tekaan dahandeh	تکان دهنده

bitter; acrid	talkh	تلخ
lazy; indolent	tanbal	تنبل
fast; spicy	tond	تند
alone; lonely	tanhaa	تنها
able; capable	tavaanaa	توانا
reserved; introspective	tudaar	تودار
sharp; pointed; keen; acute	tiz	تیز
fixed; stable; constant; steadfast	saabet	ثابت
wealthy; rich	servatmand	ثروتمند
interesting	jaaleb	جالب
solid	jaamed	جامد
serious	jeddi	جدی
new; modern; up-to-date	jadid	جدید
even (numbers etc.)	joft	جفت
quarrelsome; troublesome	janjaal aafarin	جنجال آفرین
young	javaan	جوان
boiled	jushideh	جوشیده
fat	chaaq	چاق
left	chap	چپ
acute	haad	حاد
present; ready	haazer	حاظر
certain; definite	hatmi	حتمی
jealous; envious	hasud	حسود
real; true	haqiqi	حقیقی
portable	haml kardani	حمل کردنی
crucial	hayaati	حیاتی
amazing; bewildering	heyrat aavar	حیرت آور
amazed; bewildered	heyrat zadeh	حیرت زده
cunning	hileh gar	حیله گر
foreign; outside	khaareji	خارجی
extraordinary; unusual	khaareq ol-'aadeh	خارق العاده
empty	khaali	خالی
still; quiet; silent; extinguished	khaamush	خاموش
embarrassing	khejaalat aavar	خجالت آور
embarrassed	khejaalat zadeh	خجالت زده
shy	khejaalati	خجالتی
divine; God-given	khodaa'i	خدائی
tired	khasteh	خسته

tiring; tiresome; boring	khasteh konandeh	خسته کننده
shattered; knackered	khasteh o kufteh	خسته و کوفته
dry; arid	khoshk	خشک
angry; furious; exasperated	khashmgin	خشمگین
rough; rude; harsh; coarse	khashen	خشن
private; confidential; personal	khosusi	خصوصی
dangerous	khatarnaak	خطرناک
funny; humourous	khandeh aavar	خنده آور
funny	khandeh daar	خنده دار
cool; fresh; insipid	khonak	خنک
sleepy; drowsy	khaabaalud	خواب آلود
asleep	khaabideh	خوابیده
good; well; nice	khub	خوب
automatic	khodkaar	خودکار
happy; well; good; cheerful	khosh	خوش
sweet-smelling; fragrant	khosh bu	خوش بو
good-natured; good-humoured	khosh kholq	خوش خلق
well-behaved	khosh raftaar	خوش رفتار
cheerful; smiling; pleasant	khosh ru	خوش رو
picturesque	khosh manzareh	خوش منظره
handsome	khoshtip	خوشتیپ
happy; glad; delighted	khosh haal	خوشحال
pretty	khosh gel	خوشگل
kind; compassionate	khungarm	خونگرم
imaginary	khiyaali	خیالی
wet; soaking	khis	خیس
permanent; constant	daa'emi	دائمی
accessible	dar dastres	در دسترس
lying down; prostrate	deraaz keshideh	دراز کشیده
first-rate	darajeh yek	درجه یک
shining; brilliant	derakhshaan	درخشان
painful	dardnaak	دردناک
right; correct; proper	dorost	درست
honest; upright	dorostkaar	درستکار
precise; exact	daqiq	دقیق
nice; delightful; agreeable	delpazir	دلپذیر
delightful; agreeable	delpasand	دلپسند
annoyed; offended; displeased	delkhor	دلخور

happy; contented; joyous	delkhosh	دلخوش
discouraged; disheartened	delsard	دلسرد
worried; anxious; uneasy	delvaapas	دلواپس
brave; courageous	dalir	دلیر
distant; far away	dur	دور
nice; likeable	dust daashtani	دوست داشتنی
other	digar	دیگر
religious	dini	دینی
mad; insane	divaaneh	دیوانه
comfortable; easy	raahat	راحت
straight; right; correct; upright; true	raast	راست
satisfied; content; pleased	raazi	راضی
stagnant	raaked	راکد
free (of charge); gratis	raayegaan	رایگان
reserved (e.g. seat)	rezerv shodeh	رزرو شده
official	rasmi	رسمی
ripe	resideh	رسیده
pitiful; pitiable	reqqat angiz	رقت انگیز
annoying; offensive	ranjesh aavar	رنجش آور
pale; wan; pallid; faded	rang parideh	رنگ پریده
multicoloured; colourful; variegated	rangaarang	رنگارنگ
rural	rustaa'i	روستائی
bright; alight	rowshan	روشن
alight; lit	rowshan shodeh	روشن شده
bearded	rishdaar	ریشدار
bearded	rishu	ریشو
wounded	zakhmi shodeh	زخمی شده
clever; smart	zerang	زرنگ
ugly	zesht	زشت
coarse; rough; gross; harsh	zomokht	زمخت
effeminate	zan sefat	زن صفت
alive; vivid	zendeh	زنده
jovial; cheerful	zendeh del	زنده دل
offensive; repulsive; nasty	zanandeh	زننده
beautiful	zibaa	زیبا
previous	saabeq	سابق
plain; simple; easy; naive	saadeh	ساده
compromising	saazesh kaaraaneh	سازشکارانه

quiet; silent	saaket	ساكت
healthy; safe; intact; wholesome	saalem	سالم
annual	saalyaaneh	ساليانه
light; lively; frivolous; undignified	sabok	سبک
large; gross; big	sotorg	سترگ
magic; magical	sehraamiz	سحرآميز
hard; difficult	sakht	سخت
strict; severe; exacting	sakhtgir	سخت گير
confused; flustered; giddy	saraasimeh	سرآسيمه
cold; frigid; chilly; disappointed	sard	سرد
amusing; entertaining	sargarm konandeh	سرگرم كننده
quick; rapid	sari'	سريع
secret	serri	سرّی
traditional; customary	sonnati	سنتی
heavy; onerous; solemn; sober	sangin	سنگين
happy; jolly; joyful; glad; merry	shaad	شاد
juicy; succulent; fresh	shaadaab	شاداب
brave; courageous	shojaa'	شجاع
personal; private; individual	shakhsi	شخصی
possible; feasible; viable	shodani	شدنی
severe; intense; harsh; violent	shadid	شديد
neat; clean and tidy	shosteh o rofteh	شسته ورفته
brittle; fragile	shekanandeh	شكننده
crowded; busy	sholuq	شلوغ
sweet	shirin	شيرين
naughty; devilish	sheytaan	شيطان
chic; well-groomed	shik	شيک
municipal; urban; civic; metropolitan	shahri	شهری
truthful; sincere; candid	saadeqaaneh	صادقانه
pure; clear; smooth; level	saaf	صاف
patient; forbearing	sabur	صبور
right; true; correct; exact	sahih	صحيح
sound and healthy	sahih o saalem	صحيح وسالم
indispensable	sarfenazar nakardani	صرفنظر نكردنی
industrial	san'ati	صنعتی
weak	za'if	ضعيف
incidental	zemni	ضمنی
odd (number)	taaq	طاق

medical	tebbi	طبی
natural	tabi'i	طبیعی
refreshing	taraavat bakhsh	طراوت بخش
stormy; tempestuous	tufaani	طوفانی
elegant; dainty; fine; subtle	zarif	ظریف
just; fair; equitable	'aadel	عادل
ordinary; usual; normal	'aadi	عادی
loving; amorous; passionate	'aasheqaaneh	عاشقانه
excellent; superb; outstanding	'aali	عالی
strange; bizarre; weird	'ajib	عجیب
strange; bizarre; queer; weird	'ajib o qarib	عجیب و غریب
dear; darling	'aziz	عزیز
furious; angry; irate; enraged; mad	'asabaani	عصبانی
nervous; touchy	'asabi	عصبی
great; magnificent; huge	'azim	عظیم
practical	'amali	عملی
vertical	'amudi	عمودی
general; public; universal	'omumi	عمومی
deep; profound	'amiq	عمیق
wrong; incorrect; erroneous	qalat	غلط
sad; sorry; woeful; melancholic	qamgin	غمگین
sad; touching	qamnaak	غمناک
unusual; abnormal	qeyr-e 'aadi	غیر عادی
unbearable; insufferable	qeyr-e qaabel-e tahammol	غیر قابل تحمل
uncivilised	qeyr-e motamadden	غیر متمدن
impossible	qeyr-e momken	غیر ممکن
unnecessary	qeyr-e zaruri	غیرضروری
available; ready	faraaham	فراهم
worn out; exhausted; decrepit	farsudeh	فرسوده
secondary; minor; subsidiary	far'i	فرعی
cultural	farhangi	فرهنگی
active; operative; energetic	fa'aal	فعال
poor	faqir	فقیر
technical	fanni	فنی
immediate; instant	fowri	فوری
extraordinary; exceptional; unusual	fowq ol-'aadeh	فوق العاده
inflatable	qaabel-e baad kardan	قابل باد کردن
bearable; tolerable	qaabel-e tahammol	قابل تحمل

portable	qaabel-e haml	قابل حمل
tall	qad boland	قد بلند
short	qad kutaah	قد کوتاه
powerful; strong	qodratmand	قدرتمند
old; ancient; primitive; archaic	qadimi	قدیمی
pretty; lovely; nice	qashang	قشنگ
shortened; interrupted; cut off	qat' shodeh	قطع شده
definite; decisive; final; certain	qat'i	قطعی
strong; powerful	qavi	قوی
experienced; seasoned	kaar koshteh	کار کشته
complete; perfect; thorough	kaamel	کامل
successful; thriving; prosperous	kaamyaab	کامیاب
detestable; ugly; distasteful	karih	کریه
agricultural	keshaavarzi	کشاورزی
classic; classical	kelaasik	کلاسیک
massive; huge; great; enormous	kalaan	کلان
absent-minded	kam haafezeh	کم حافظه
reserved; taciturn; quiet	kam harf	کم حرف
bashful; shy; diffident; timid; modest	kam ru	کم رو
dim; shadowy; weak (light)	kam nur	کم نور
rare; scarce; uncommon	kamyaab	کمیاب
curious; inquisitive	konjkaav	کنجکاو
short; brief; low	kutaah	کوتاه
small; little; tiny	kuchek	کوچک
efficient; diligent; assiduous	kushaa	کوشا
tired; shattered; knackered	kufteh	کوفته
mountainous	kuhestaani	کوهستانی
old; worn-out; old-fashioned; stale	kohneh	کهنه
expensive; dear; costly	geraan	گران
round; circular	gerd	گرد
solemn; overcast; hoarse; gloomy	gerefteh	گرفته
warm; hot; friendly; cordial	garm	گرم
obscure; anonymous	gomnaam	گمنام
rotten; putrid	gandideh	گندیده
huge; fat	gondeh	گنده
deep; sunken; hollow; concave	gowd	گود
ear-splitting	gush kharaash	گوش خراش
different; diverse; various	gunaagun	گوناگون

confused; giddy	*gij*	گیج
confusing	*gij konandeh*	گیج کننده
attractive	*giraa*	گیرا
necessary; requisite	*laazem*	لازم
thin; slim	*laaqar*	لاغر
worthy; deserving; fit; meritorious	*laayeq*	لایق
enjoyable; delightful; pleasurable	*lezzat bakhsh*	لذت بخش
delicious; luscious; tasty; enjoyable	*laziz*	لذیذ
delicate; fine; elegant	*latif*	لطیف
slippy; slippery	*liz*	لیز
mechanical; machine-made	*maashini*	ماشینی
monthly	*maahiyaaneh*	ماهیانه
boring; anodyne; commonplace	*mobtazal*	مبتذل
progressive; advanced	*motaraqqi*	مترقی
deserted; abandoned; obsolete	*matruk*	متروک
distinguished; dignified	*motashakhkhes*	متشخص
numerous; many; manifold	*mota'added*	متعدد
cheating; dishonest; fraudulent	*motaqalleb*	متقلب
consecutive; successive; continuous	*motavaali*	متوالی
middle; average; medium	*motavasset*	متوسط
free; gratis	*majaani*	مجانی
experienced	*mojarrab*	مجرب
single; unmarried; abstract	*mojarrad*	مجرد
sumptuous; glorious; luxurious; grand	*mojallal*	مجلل
favourite; popular; beloved	*mahbub*	محبوب
cautious; prudent; careful; heedful	*mohtaat*	محتاط
honourable; respected; esteemed	*mohtaram*	محترم
secret; confidential; classified	*mahramaaneh*	محرمانه
local; native	*mahalli*	محلی
different; various; diverse	*mokhtalef*	مختلف
special; particular; specific	*makhsus*	مخصوص
continual; lasting; continuous	*modaavem*	مداوم
modern	*modern*	مدرن
civil; civic	*madani*	مدنی
religious	*maz-habi*	مذهبی
popular	*mardomi*	مردمی
dead	*mordeh*	مرده
mysterious; secret; cryptic	*marmuz*	مرموز

equal; even; equivalent; quits	mosaavi	مساوی
rectangular; oblong	mostatil	مستطیل
direct; straight	mostaqim	مستقیم
flat; level; even	mosattah	مسطح
certain; indisputable; sure; definite	mosallam	مسلم
responsible; accountable	mas'ul	مسئول
eager; avid; keen; anxious	moshtaaq	مشتاق
busy; preoccupied; occupied	mashqul	مشغول
difficult; hard; arduous	moshkel	مشکل
suspicious; doubtful; dubious	mashkuk	مشکوک
famous; celebrated; well-known	mash-hur	مشهور
artificial; synthetic; sham	masnu'i	مصنوعی
illustrated	mosavvar	مصور
funny; laughable; droll; ridiculous	moz-hek	مضحک
pleasing; desirable; desired	matlub	مطلوب
sure; certain; assured; confident	motma'en	مطمئن
obedient; submissive; compliant	moti'	مطیع
contemporary; contemporaneous	mo'aaser	معاصر
famous; well-known; renowned	ma'ruf	معروف
obvious; clear; evident	ma'lum	معلوم
usual; customary; in-vogue	ma'mul	معمول
ordinary; usual; commonplace	ma'muli	معمولی
nutritious; nourishing; wholesome	moqazzi	مغذی
proud; haughty; vain; conceited	maqrur	مغرور
singular	mofrad	مفرد
useful; beneficial; advantageous	mofid	مفید
mechanical	mekaaniki	مکانیکی
cube; cubic	moka'ab	مکعب
mild; gentle; calm; moderate	molaayem	ملایم
national	melli	ملی
excellent; superior; first-rate	momtaaz	ممتاز
possible; feasible	momken	ممکن
forbidden; prohibited; proscribed	mamnu'	ممنوع
thankful; obliged; grateful	mamnun	ممنون
convenient; appropriate; suitable	monaaseb	مناسب
disgusting; abhorrent; repulsive	monzajer konandeh	منزجر کننده
effective	mo'asser	موثر
existing; existent; available	mowjud	موجود

polite; courteous; civil	mo'addab	مودب
sly; harmful; troublesome; crafty	muzi	موذی
successful; prosperous; triumphant	mo'affaq	موفق
temporary; provisional	movaqqati	موقتی
demure; dignified	movaqqar	موقر
kind; affable; compassionate	mehrabaan	مهربان
important; serious; significant	mohemm	مهم
pessimistic; desperate	naa omid	نا امید
ominous	naa khoshaayand	ناخوش آیند
wrong; incorrect	naa dorost	نادرست
unhappy; uncomfortable	naa raahat	ناراحت
dissatisfied; displeased	naa raazi	ناراضی
nice; lovely; tender; kind; delicate	naa zanin	نازنین
unknown; disguised	naa shenaas	ناشناس
unpleasant; unpalatable; distasteful	naa govaar	ناگوار
sudden; unexpected	naa gahaan	ناگهان
unnecessary	naa laazem	نالازم
unpleasant; disagreeable	naa matbu'	نامطبوع
illogical; irrational; unreasonable	naa ma'qul	نامعقول
unclear; unknown; undecided	naa ma'lum	نامعلوم
noble; decent; gentle; aristocratic	najib	نجیب
threadbare	nakh namaa	نخ نما
soft; smooth; fine; lenient	narm	نرم
near; proximate; impending	nazdik	نزدیک
seated	neshasteh	نشسته
unknown	nashenaakhteh	نشناخته
military; martial	nezaami	نظامی
disgusting; loathsome; repugnant	nefrat angiz	نفرت انگیز
precious; exquisite; fine; premium	nafis	نفیس
worried; anxious; uneasy	negaraan	نگران
new; novel; recent; modern	now	نو
shining; bright; sparkling; brilliant	nuraani	نورانی
energising; life-giving	niru bakhsh	نیروبخش
strong; powerful; potent	nirumand	نیرومند
lukewarm	nimeh garm	نیمه گرم
final	nehaa'i	نهائی
necessary; obligatory; compulsory	vaajeb	واجب
clear; plain; obvious; apparent	vaazeh	واضح

real; actual; true; genuine; factual	vaaqe'i	واقعی
frightened; terrified	vahshat zadeh	وحشت زده
frightening; terrifying	vahshatnaak	وحشتناك
wild; savage; fierce; barbarous	vahshi	وحشی
grave; critical; serious	vakhim	وخیم
large; spacious; vast; extensive	vasi'	وسیع
lukewarm; tepid; mild	velarm	ولرم
desolate; destroyed; ruined	veyraan	ویران
adjacent; neighbouring; contiguous	hamjavaar	همجوار
level; smooth; flat; even	hamvaar	هموار
permanent; lasting; perpetual	hamishegi	همیشگی
air (a.); aerial; climatic	havaa'i	هوائی
frightening; terrifying; dreadful	howl naak	هولناك
exciting; stimulating	hayejaan angiz	هیجان انگیز
depressing; discouraging	ya's aavar	یاس آور
monotonous; tedious; wearisome	yek navaakht	یکنواخت

❰❰◆❱❱

Miscellaneous Verbs

افعال متفرقه

to set fire to	aatash zadan	آتش زدن
to catch fire	aatash gereftan	آتش گرفتن
to calm	aaraam kardan	آرام کردن
to calm down	aaraam gereftan	آرام گرفتن
to hope; to wish	aarezu daashtan	آرزو داشتن
to cook (tr.)	aashpazi kardan	آشپزی کردن
to reveal	aashkaar kardan	آشکار کردن
to get ready	aamaadeh shodan	آماده شدن
to prepare	aamadeh kardan	آماده کردن
to come	aamadan	آمدن
to teach; to learn	aamukhtan	آموختن
to sing	aavaz khaandan	آواز خواندن
to bring	aavardan	آوردن
to sigh	aah keshidan	آه کشیدن
to slow down	aahesteh shodan	آهسته شدن
to express (feelings etc.)	ebraaz kardan	ابراز کردن
to disapprove	ebraaz-e naarezaayati kardan	ابراز نارضایتی کردن
to adopt (e.g. an idea)	ettekhaaz kardan	اتخاذ کردن
to happen; to take place	ettefaaq oftaadan	اتفاق افتادن
to iron	otukeshi kardan	اتوکشی کردن
to prove	esbaat kardan	اثبات کردن
to rent out	ejaareh daadan	اجاره دادن
to rent; to hire	ejaareh kardan	اجاره کردن
to give permission	ejaazeh daadan	اجازه دادن
to get permission	ejaazeh gereftan	اجازه گرفتن
to avoid; to eschew	ejtenaab kardan	اجتناب کردن
to respect	ehteraam gozaashtan	احترام گذاشتن
to need	ehtiyaaj daashtan (beh)	(احتیاج داشتن (به
to feel lonely	ehsaas-e tanhaa'i kardan	احساس تنهائی کردن
to feel	ehsaas kardan	احساس کردن
to call back; to produce	ehzaar kardan	احضار کردن
to warn	ekhtaar kardan	اخطار کردن
to manage; to supervise	edaareh kardan	اداره کردن
to continue (intr.)	edaameh peydaa kardan	ادامه پیدا کردن
to continue (tr.)	edaameh daadan	ادامه دادن
to last; to continue	edaameh daashtan	ادامه داشتن

to annoy; to irritate	*aziyat kardan*	اذیت کردن
to present	*eraa'eh kardan*	ارائه کردن
to be of value	*arzesh daashtan*	ارزش داشتن
to assess; to evaluate	*arzyaabi kardan*	ارزیابی کردن
to startle (tr.)	*az jaa paraandan*	از جا پراندن
to startle (intr.)	*az jaa paridan*	از جا پریدن
to begin again	*az sar gereftan*	از سر گرفتن
to get married	*ezdevaaj kardan*	ازدواج کردن
to employ	*estekhdaam kardan*	استخدام کردن
to rest	*esteraahat kardan*	استراحت کردن
to use	*estefaadeh kardan*	استفاده کردن
to vomit	*estefraaq kardan*	استفراغ کردن
to greet; to welcome	*esteqbaal kardan*	استقبال کردن
to masturbate	*estemnaa kardan*	استمناء کردن
to register (one's name)	*esm nevisi kardan*	اسم نویسی کردن
to capture; to imprison	*asir kardan*	اسیر کردن
to make a mistake	*eshtebaah kardan*	اشتباه کردن
to increase; to add	*ezaafeh kardan*	اضافه کردن
to inform	*ettelaa' daadan*	اطلاع دادن
to admit; to confess	*e'teraaf kardan*	اعتراف کردن
to go on strike	*e'tesaab kardan*	اعتصاب کردن
to believe	*e'teqaad daashtan*	اعتقاد داشتن
to announce	*e'laam kardan*	اعلام کردن
to exaggerate	*eqraaq kardan*	اغراق کردن
to increase (tr.)	*afzaayesh daadan*	افزایش دادن
to increase (intr.)	*afzaayesh yaaftan*	افزایش یافتن
to take an examination	*emtehaan daadan*	امتحان دادن
to sign	*emzaa kardan*	امضاء کردن
to hope	*omidvaar budan*	امیدوار بودن
to choose	*entekhaab kardan*	انتخاب کردن
to expect	*entezaar daashtan*	انتظار داشتن
to look forward to	*entezaar keshidan*	انتظار کشیدن
to criticise	*enteqaad kardan*	انتقاد کردن
to carry out	*anjaam daadan*	انجام دادن
to be carried out	*anjaam gereftan*	انجام گرفتن
to throw	*andaakhtan*	انداختن
to weigh; to measure	*andaazeh giri kardan*	اندازه گیری کردن
to stand up	*istaadan*	ایستادن

to lose (i.e. a game)	baakhtan	باختن
to load; to burden	baar kardan	بار کردن
to open (intr.)	baaz shodan	باز شدن
to open (tr.)	baaz kardan	باز کردن
to reflect	baztaab daashtan	بازتاب داشتن
to detain; to imprison	baazdaasht kardan	بازداشت کردن
to be the cause of	baa'es shodan	باعث شدن
to throw up	baalaa aavardan	بالا آوردن
to go up	baalaa raftan	بالا رفتن
to believe (e.g. what someone says)	baavar kardan	باور کردن
to make worse	badtar kardan	بدتر کردن
to pick up	bar daashtan	بر داشتن
to mention; to utter	bar zabaan aavardan	بر زبان آوردن
to approach; to meet	barkhord kardan	برخورد کردن
to take; to carry	bordan	بردن
to shine; to sparkle	barq zadan	برق زدن
to establish; to set up	bar qaraar kardan	برقرار کردن
to return (tr.)	bargardaandan	بر گرداندن
to return; to go back	bargashtan	برگشتن
to inscribe	bar negaashtan	برنگاشتن
to grow up	bozorg shodan	بزرگ شدن
to raise; to bring up	bozorg kardan	بزرگ کردن
to depend	bastegi daashtan	بستگی داشتن
to tie; to fasten	bastan	بستن
to get up	boland shodan	بلند شدن
to pick up (e.g. a prostitute)	boland kardan	بلند کردن
to smell (intr.); to stink	bu daadan	بو دادن
to smell (tr.)	bu keshidan	بو کشیدن
to kiss	busidan	بوسیدن
to ignore	bi e'tenaa'i kardan	بی اعتنائی کردن
to express (e.g. one's feelings)	bayaan kardan	بیان کردن
to wake up (intr.)	bidaar shodan	بیدار شدن
to wake up (tr.)	bidaar kardan	بیدار کردن
to take out	birun bordan	بیرون بردن
to pull out	birun keshidan	بیرون کشیدن
to insure	bimeh kardan	بیمه کردن
to put off; to delay	be ta'viq andaakhtan	به تعویق انداختن
to commit something to memory	be khaater sepordan	به خاطر سپردن

to risk; to put in danger	be khatar andaakhtan	به خطر انداختن
to acquire	be dast aavardan	به دست آوردن
to put down	be zamin gozaashtan	به زمین گذاشتن
to adopt (i.e. a child)	be farzandi qabul kardan	به فرزندی قبول کردن
to occur; to come to mind	be nazar residan	به نظر رسیدن
to bring into existence	be vojud aavardan	به وجود آوردن
to occur; to happen	be voqu' peyvastan	به وقوع پیوستن
to remember; to bring to mind	be yaad aavardan	به یاد آوردن
to stir	beham zadan	بهم زدن
to tear	paareh kardan	پاره کردن
to go too far	paa faraa gozaashtan	پافرا گذاشتن
to come down	paa'in aamadan	پائین آمدن
to bring down	paa'in aavardan	پائین آوردن
to end (tr.)	paayaan daadan	پایان دادن
to end (intr.)	paayaan yaaftan	پایان یافتن
to fill	por kardan	پر کردن
to ask	porsidan	پرسیدن
to fly	parvaaz kardan	پرواز کردن
to nurture; to grow (tr.)	parvardan	پروردن
to nurture	parvaresh daadan	پرورش دادن
to jump	paridan	پریدن
to abstain	parhiz kardan	پرهیز کردن
to save (i.e. money)	pasandaaz kardan	پس انداز کردن
to bring back	pas aavardan	پس آوردن
to give back	pas daadan	پس دادن
to take back	pas gereftan	پس گرفتن
to endorse (i.e. a cheque)	posht nevisi kardan	پشت نویسی کردن
to take refuge	panaah bordan	پناه بردن
to give refuge	panaah daadan	پناه دادن
to have a puncture	panchar daashtan	پنچر داشتن
to hide (intr.)	penhaan shodan	پنهان شدن
to hide (tr.); to conceal	penhaan kardan	پنهان کردن
to ask forgiveness	puzesh talabidan	پوزش طلبیدن
to cover (tr.); to dress (tr.)	pushaandan	پوشاندن
to get dressed; to wear	pushidan	پوشیدن
to get out; to disembark	piyaadeh shodan	پیاده شدن
to set up; to let someone disembark	piyaadeh kardan	پیاده کردن
to screw; to wrap	pichaandan	پیچاندن

to find	peydaa kardan	پیدا کردن
to be victorious	piruz shodan	پیروز شدن
to foresee	pish negari kardan	پیش‌نگری کردن
to forecast; to foresee	pishbini kardan	پیشبینی کردن
to progress	pishraft kardan	پیشرفت کردن
to suggest	pishnehaad kardan	پیشنهاد کردن
to join (intr.)	peyvastan	پیوستن
to spread	pahn kardan	پهن کردن
to date (i.e. to put the date)	taarikh gozaari kardan	تاریخ گذاری کردن
to set up; to establish	ta'sis kardan	تاسیس کردن
to confirm	ta'yid kardan	تایید کردن
to have a fever or temperature	tab daashtan	تب داشتن
to congratulate	tabrik goftan	تبریک گفتن
to stammer	teteh peteh kardan	تته پته کردن
to renew	tajdid kardan	تجدید کردن
to change one's mind	tajdid-e nazar kardan	تجدید نظر کردن
to experience	tajrobe kardan	تجربه کردن
to excite	tahrik kardan	تحریک کردن
to hand over	tahvil daadan	تحویل دادن
to take receipt	tahvil gereftan	تحویل گرفتن
to destroy	takhrib kardan	تخریب کردن
to give discount	takhfif daadan	تخفیف دادن
to empty; to unload	takhliyeh kardan	تخلیه کردن
to think deeply; to deliberate	tadabbor kardan	تدبر کردن
to instruct; to teach	tadris kardan	تدریس کردن
to train	tarbiyat kardan	تربیت کردن
to arrange	tartib daadan	ترتیب دادن
to translate	tarjomeh kardan	ترجمه کردن
to frighten	tarsaandan	ترساندن
to be afraid	tarsidan	ترسیدن
to leave; to give up; to abandon	tark kardan	ترک کردن
to decorate	tazyin kardan	تزیین کردن
to conquer; to subjugate	taskhir kardan	تسخیر کردن
to calm; to deaden pain	taskin daadan	تسکین دادن
to be in command; to have power	tasallot daashtan	تسلط داشتن
to give condolences	tasliyat goftan	تسلیت گفتن
to surrender	taslim shodan	تسلیم شدن
to distinguish	tashkhis daadan	تشخیص دادن

to encourage	tashviq kardan	تشویق کردن
to have an accident (e.g. with a car)	tasaadof kardan	تصادف کردن
to collide	tasaadom kardan	تصادم کردن
to confirm; to certify	tasdiq kardan	تصدیق کردن
to assert	tasrih kardan	تصریح کردن
to decide	tasmim gereftan	تصمیم گرفتن
to compose (i.e. a piece of music)	tasnif kardan	تصنیف کردن
to be surprised	ta'ajob kardan	تعجب کردن
to amend	ta'dil kardan	تعدیل کردن
to describe	ta'rif kardan	تعریف کردن
to pursue; to prosecute	ta'qib kardan	تعقیب کردن
to ponder; to meditate	ta'amoq kardan	تعمق کردن
to repair	ta'mir kardan	تعمیر کردن
to spit	tof kardan	تف کردن
to think deeply	tafakkor kardan	تفکر کردن
to apply; to request	taqaazaa kardan	تقاضا کردن
to be divided	taqsim shodan	تقسیم شدن
to divide	taqsim kardan	تقسیم کردن
to move; to shake	takaan daadan	تکان دادن
to repeat	tekraar kardan	تکرار کردن
to rely	tekyeh daashtan	تکیه داشتن
to heap up	tal anbaar kardan	تل انبار کردن
to waste	talaf kardan	تلف کردن
to telephone	telefon kardan	تلفن کردن
to get in touch	tamaas gereftan	تماس گرفتن
to view; to watch	tamaashaa kardan	تماشا کردن
to finish (intr.)	tamaam shodan	تمام شدن
to finish (tr.)	tamaam kardan	تمام کردن
to extend; to renew	tamdid kardan	تمدید کردن
to clean	tamiz kardan	تمیز کردن
to go fast; to go too far	tond raftan	تند رفتن
to justify	towjih kardan	توجیه کردن
to notice; to pay attention	tavajjoh kardan	توجه کردن
to distribute	towzi' kardan	توزیع کردن
to recommend	towsiyeh kardan	توصیه کردن
to explain	towzih daadan	توضیح دادن
to produce	towlid kardan	تولید کردن
to reproduce (e.g. sexually)	towlid-e mesl kardan	تولید مثل کردن

to threaten	tahdid kardan	تهدید کردن
to insult	tohmat zadan	تهمت زدن
to prepare	tahyeh kardan	تهیه کردن
to register (one's name)	sabt-e naam kardan	ثبت نام کردن
to place; to put s.thing in position	jaa daadan	جا دادن
to succeed (e.g. as king)	jaaneshin shodan	جانشین شدن
to replace	jaaygozin kardan	جایگزین کردن
to compensate	jobraan kardan	جبران کردن
to separate (intr.)	jodaa shodan	جدا شدن
to separate (tr.)	jodaa kardan	جدا کردن
to attract	jazb kardan	جذب کردن
to dare	jor'at kardan	جرات کردن
to dare; to be bold	jesaarat kardan	جسارت کردن
to search	jostoju kardan	جستجو کردن
to wank (sl.)	jalq zadan	جلق زدن
to go forward	jelow raftan	جلو رفتن
to have sexual intercourse	jemaa' kardan	جماع کردن
to tidy up	jam' o jur kardan	جمع و جور کردن
to fight; to wage war	jangidan	جنگیدن
to answer	javaab daadan	جواب دادن
to scream	jiq zadan	جیغ زدن
to print	chaap kardan	چاپ کردن
to be tipped over	chapeh shodan	چپه شدن
to tip over	chapeh kardan	چپه کردن
to nod off; to take a nap	chort zadan	چرت زدن
to turn around; to twist	charkhidan	چرخیدن
to stick (tr.)	chasbaandan	چسباندن
to stick (intr.)	chasbidan	چسبیدن
to ignore; to turn a blind eye	cheshm pushi kardan	چشم پوشی کردن
to snatch	chang zadan	چنگ زدن
to snatch	chang gereftan	چنگ گرفتن
to pick (e.g. a flower)	chidan	چیدن
to overcome; to be dominant	chireh shodan	چیره شدن
to be present; to be ready	haazer shodan	حاضر شدن
to prepare	haazer kardan	حاضر کردن
to talk	harf zadan	حرف زدن
to move; to set off	harekat kardan	حرکت کردن
to be present	hozur daashtan	حضور داشتن

to solve	hall kardan	حل کردن
to carry	haml kardan	حمل کردن
to attack	hamleh kardan	حمله کردن
to have patience	howseleh daashtan	حوصله داشتن
to get bored	howseleh sar raftan	حوصله سر رفتن
to be astonished	heyrat zadeh shodan	حیرت زده شدن
to exit	khaarej shodan	خارج شدن
to point out	khaater neshaan kardan	خاطرنشان کردن
to be extinguished	khaamush shodan	خاموش شدن
to put out (e.g. a light)	khaamush kardan	خاموش کردن
to be embarrassed; to be ashamed	khejaalat keshidan	خجالت کشیدن
to break down; to go bad	kharaab shodan	خراب شدن
to destroy	kharaab kardan	خراب کردن
to scratch	kharaashaandan	خراشاندن
to spend (e.g. money)	kharj kardan	خرج کردن
to shatter	khord kardan	خرد کردن
to snore	khornaas keshidan	خرناس کشیدن
to buy; to go shopping	kharid kardan	خرید کردن
to buy	kharidan	خریدن
to dry	khoshk kardan	خشک کردن
to make happy	khoshnud kardan	خشنود کردن
to choke (intr.)	khafeh shodan	خفه شدن
to choke (tr.); to strangle	khafeh kardan	خفه کردن
to create	khalq kardan	خلق کردن
to smile; to laugh	khandidan	خندیدن
to dream	khaab didan	خواب دیدن
to sleep; to fall asleep	khaabidan	خوابیدن
to want; to desire; to be about to	khaastan	خواستن
to read	khaandan	خواندن
to bump into	khordan (beh)	خوردن (به)
to welcome	khoshaamad goftan	خوشامد گفتن
to imagine	khiyaal kardan	خیال کردن
to stare	khireh shodan	خیره شدن
to enter	daakhel shodan	داخل شدن
to shout	daad zadan	داد زدن
to give	daadan	دادن
to know (a thing)	daanestan	دانستن
to bring out; to take out	dar aavardan	در آوردن

to whisper	dar-e gushi harf zadan	در گوشی حرف زدن
to bring up (a subject)	dar miyaan gozaashtan	در میان گذاشتن
to take into account	dar nazar gereftan	در نظر گرفتن
to sparkle; to shine	derakhshidan	درخشیدن
to study (in general)	dars khaandan	درس خواندن
to teach	dars daadan	درس دادن
to become right	dorost shodan	درست شدن
to make; to put right	dorost kardan	درست کردن
to perceive	dark kardan	درک کردن
to get involved	dargir shodan	درگیر شدن
to tell a lie	doruq goftan	دروغ گفتن
to receive	daryaaft kardan	دریافت کردن
to steal	dozdi kardan	دزدی کردن
to steal	dozdidan	دزدیدن
to wave	dast afshaani kardan	دست افشانی کردن
to tease	dast andaakhtan	دست انداختن
to shake hands	dast daadan	دست دادن
to touch	dast zadan	دست زدن
to invade	dast yaazi kardan	دست یازی کردن
to capture; to arrest	dastgir kardan	دستگیر کردن
to order	dastur daadan	دستور دادن
to argue	da'vaa kardan	دعوا کردن
to invite	da'vat kardan	دعوت کردن
to defend	defaa' kardan	دفاع کردن
to get rid of	dakk kardan	دک کردن
to miss (someone)	deltang budan	دلتنگ بودن
to become discouraged	delsard shodan	دلسرد شدن
to go after; to follow	donbaal raftan	دنبال رفتن
to look for someone	donbaal-e kasi gashtan	دنبال کسی گشتن
to sew	dukhtan	دوختن
to throw away	dur andaakhtan	دور انداختن
to go away	dur raftan	دور رفتن
to take a shower	dush gereftan	دوش گرفتن
to make (someone) run; to keep busy	davaandan	دواندن
to run	davidan	دویدن
to mention	zekr kardan	ذکر کردن
to be satisfied	raazi shodan	راضی شدن
to satisfy	raazi kardan	راضی کردن

to drive (e.g. a car)	raanandegi kardan	رانندگی کردن
to set off	raah oftaadan	راه افتادن
to put in motion; to start up	raah andaakhtan	راه انداختن
to let (someone) in	raah daadan	راه دادن
to walk	raah raftan	راه رفتن
to guide	raahnamaa'i kardan	راهنمائی کردن
to refer	roju' kardan	رجوع کردن
to fail (e.g. an exam)	rad shodan	رد شدن
to reserve	rezerv kardan	رزرو کردن
to reach; to arrive	residan	رسیدن
to see to; to tend to	residan (beh)	رسیدن (به)
to allow; to give one's blessing	rezaayat daadan	رضایت دادن
to behave	raftaar kardan	رفتار کردن
to go	raftan	رفتن
to dance	raqsidan	رقصیدن
to suffer	ranjidan	رنجیدن
to light; to make clear	rowshan kardan	روشن کردن
to copy	runevesht kardan	رونوشت کردن
to pour; to drop	rikhtan	ریختن
to lead	rahbari kardan	رهبری کردن
to hit; to strike	zadan	زدن
to hum	zemzemeh kardan	زمزمه کردن
to live	zendegi kardan	زندگی کردن
to ring	zang zadan	زنگ زدن
to go too far; to go over the top	ziyaadeh ravi kardan	زیاده روی کردن
to burst out laughing	zir-e khandeh zadan	زیر خنده زدن
to question (something)	zir-e so'aal qaraar daadan	زیر سوال قرار دادن
to trip (someone up)	zirpaa'i zadan	زیرپائی زدن
to build; to make	saakhtan	ساختن
to be the cause of	sabab shodan	سبب شدن
to praise	setaayesh kardan	ستایش کردن
to quarrel; to wrangle	setizeh kardan	ستیزه کردن
to have difficulties	sakhti daashtan	سختی داشتن
to give a speech	sokhanraani kardan	سخنرانی کردن
to block the road	sadd-e ma'bar kardan	سد معبر کردن
to blush	sorkh shodan	سرخ شدن
to cough	sorfeh kardan	سرفه کردن
to try	sa'i kardan	سعی کردن

to order (e.g. a book by post)	sefaaresh kardan	سفارش کردن
to travel	safar kardan	سفر کردن
to get on; to embark	savaar shodan	سوار شدن
to ask	so'aal kardan	سوال کردن
to burn (intr.)	sukhtan	سوختن
to burn (tr.)	suzaandan	سوزاندن
to take advantage of; to abuse	su' estefaadeh kardan	سوء استفاده کردن
to include; to comprise	shaamel budan	شامل بودن
to deserve; to be worthy	shaayesteh budan	شایسته بودن
to become	shodan	شدن
to bet	shart bastan	شرط بستن
to take part	sherkat kardan	شرکت کردن
to begin (intr.)	shoru' shodan	شروع شدن
to begin (tr.)	shoru' kardan	شروع کردن
to clean; to wash	shostan	شستن
to doubt	shak bordan	شک بردن
to complain	shekaayat kardan	شکایت کردن
to be defeated	shekast khordan	شکست خوردن
to defeat	shekast daadan	شکست دادن
to break	shekastan	شکستن
to form	shekl daadan	شکل دادن
to dial (a number)	shomaareh gereftan	شماره گرفتن
to count	shomordan	شمردن
to know; to recognise	shenaakhtan	شناختن
to hear	shenidan	شنیدن
to joke	shukhi kardan	شوخی کردن
to desire (sexually)	shahvat varzidan	شهوت ورزیدن
to be exported	saader shodan	صادر شدن
to export	saader kardan	صادر کردن
to talk; to chat	sohbat kardan	صحبت کردن
to make a noise	sedaa daadan	صدا دادن
to make a noise (i.e. be noisy)	sedaa dar aavardan	صدا در آوردن
to call	sedaa zadan	صدا زدن
to spend (e.g. time)	sarf kardan	صرف کردن
to forego	sarf-e nazar kardan	صرف نظر کردن
to ascend	so'ud kardan	صعود کردن
to last; to take time	tul keshidan	طول کشیدن
to appear	zaaher shodan	ظاهر شدن

to develop (e.g. a photograph)	zaaher kardan	ظاهر کردن
to be used to	'aadat daashtan	عادت داشتن
to become accustomed to	'aadat kardan	عادت کردن
to be in love; to love	'aasheq budan	عاشق بودن
to cross (e.g. the road)	'obur kardan	عبور کردن
to hurry	'ajaleh kardan	عجله کردن
to apologise	'ozr khaahi kardan	عذرخواهی کردن
to get married	'arusi kardan	عروسی کردن
to revere; to cherish	'aziz shomordan	عزیز شمردن
to depart	'azimat kardan	عزیمت کردن
to make angry	'asabani kardan	عصبانی شدن
to be a member	'ozv budan	عضو بودن
to sneeze	'atseh keshidan	عطسه کشیدن
to believe; to have an idea	'aqideh daashtan	عقیده داشتن
to take pictures	'aks andaakhtan	عکس انداختن
to film	'aks bardaari kardan	عکس برداری کردن
to like; to be interested	'alaaqeh daashtan	علاقه داشتن
to signal	'alaamat daadan	علامت دادن
to mark (i.e. put a mark on s.thing)	'alaamat gozaari kardan	علامت گذاری کردن
to develop a fault	'eyb peydaa kardan	عیب پیدا کردن
to take by surprise	qaafelgir kardan	غافلگیر کردن
to gossip	qeybat kardan	غیبت کردن
to go bad; to become corrupt	faased shodan	فاسد شدن
to corrupt	faased kardan	فاسد کردن
to swear	fohsh daadan	فحش دادن
to recall (i.e. someone from duty)	faraa khaandan	فرا خواندن
to help escape	faraar daadan	فرار دادن
to escape	faraar kardan	فرار کردن
to forget	faraamush kardan	فراموش کردن
to suppose	farz kardan	فرض کردن
to be different	farq daashtan	فرق داشتن
to sell	forukhtan	فروختن
to shout; to scream	faryaad keshidan	فریاد کشیدن
to think	fekr kardan	فکر کردن
to make understand	fahmaandan	فهماندن
to understand	fahmidan	فهمیدن
to mix up	qaati kardan	قاطی کردن
to accept	qabul kardan	قبول کردن

to walk; to stroll	qadam zadan	قدم زدن
to lend	qarz daadan	قرض دادن
to borrow	qarz gereftan	قرض گرفتن
to cut off	qat' kardan	قطع کردن
to lock	qofl kardan	قفل کردن
to tickle	qelqelak daadan	قلقلک دادن
to disguise	qiyaafeh 'avaz kardan	قیافه عوض کردن
to work	kaar kardan	کار کردن
to put in place	kaar gozaashtan	کار گذاشتن
to direct (e.g. a film)	kaar gardaani kardan	کارگردانی کردن
to copy	kopi kardan	کپی کردن
to become dirty	kasif shodan	کثیف شدن
to dirty	kasif kardan	کثیف کردن
to cultivate	kesht kardan	کشت کردن
to kill	koshtan	کشتن
to discover	kashf kardan	کشف کردن
to struggle; to fight	keshmakesh kardan	کشمکش کردن
to become less	kam shodan	کم شدن
to lessen	kam kardan	کم کردن
to be deficient	kambud daashtan	کمبود داشتن
to help	komak kardan	کمک کردن
to cancel	kansel kardan	کنسل کردن
to try	kushesh kardan	کوشش کردن
to report	gozaaresh daadan	گزارش دادن
to put; to place	gozaashtan	گذاشتن
to pass	gozashtan	گذشتن
to cherish	geraami daashtan	گرامی داشتن
to travel; to go for a walk	gardesh kardan	گردش کردن
to get; to take	gereftan	گرفتن
to warm	garm kardan	گرم کردن
to cry	geryeh kardan	گریه کردن
to choose	gozidan	گزیدن
to broaden; to spread; to extend	gostaresh daadan	گسترش دادن
to talk; to have talks	goftogu kardan	گفتگو کردن
to tell; to say	goftan	گفتن
to listen	gush daadan	گوش دادن
to overflow	labriz shodan	لبریز شدن
to enjoy	lezzat bordan	لذت بردن

to cancel; to annul	laqv kardan	لغو کردن
to deserve; to be worthy of	liyaaqat daashtan	لیاقت داشتن
to squash; to trample	leh kardan	له کردن
to stay; to remain; to resemble	maandan	ماندن
to exchange	mobaadeleh kardan	مبادله کردن
to be sorry	mota'assef budan	متاسف بودن
to be united	mottahed budan	متحد شدن
to consist of; to comprise	motashakkel budan	متشکل بودن
to surprise (someone)	mota'ajjeb kardan	متعجب کردن
to belong to	mota'alleq budan	متعلق بودن
to accuse	mottaham kardan	متهم کردن
to be forced; to have to	majbur shodan	مجبور شدن
to force	majbur kardan	مجبور کردن
to surround	mohaasereh kardan	محاصره کردن
to be deprived	mahrum shodan	محروم شدن
to deprive	mahrum kardan	محروم کردن
to condemn; to sentence	mahkum kardan	محکوم کردن
to ignore	mahal nagozaashtan	محل نگذاشتن
to mix	makhlut kardan	مخلوط کردن
to concern	marbut budan	مربوط بودن
to bother; to annoy; to trouble	mozaahem shodan	مزاحم شدن
to taste	mazeh kardan	مزه کردن
to travel; to go on a journey	mosaaferat kardan	مسافرت کردن
to mock; to belittle	maskhareh kardan	مسخره کردن
to block	masdud kardan	مسدود کردن
to observe	moshaahedeh kardan	مشاهده کردن
to suspect	mashkuk shodan	مشکوک شدن
to consult; to ask advice	mashverat kardan	مشورت کردن
to interview	mosaahebeh kardan	مصاحبه کردن
to use; to consume	masraf kardan	مصرف کردن
to study (e.g. a book)	motaale'eh kardan	مطالعه کردن
to become addicted	mo'taad shodan	معتاد شدن
to introduce	mo'arrefi kardan	معرفی کردن
to reverse; to turn upside down	ma'kus kardan	معکوس کردن
to have meaning	ma'ni daashtan	معنی داشتن
to compare	moqaayeseh kardan	مقایسه کردن
to suck	mekidan	مکیدن
to notice	molaahezeh kardan	ملاحظه کردن

to meet	molaaqaat kardan	ملاقات کردن
to stammer	men men kardan	من من کردن
to wait	montazer shodan	منتظر شدن
to divert; to corrupt	monharef kardan	منحرف کردن
to destroy	monhadem kardan	منهدم کردن
to be careful	movaazeb budan	مواظب بودن
to agree	mo'aafeqat kardan	موافقت کردن
to be successful	mo'affaq shodan	موفق شدن
to disappear	naapadid shodan	ناپدید شدن
to become upset	naaraahat shodan	ناراحت شدن
to upset (someone)	naaraahat kardan	ناراحت کردن
to be ungrateful	naashokri kardan	ناشکری کردن
to moan	naalidan	نالیدن
to be named	naam daashtan	نام داشتن
to name	naamgozaari kardan	نامگذاری کردن
to get a result	natijeh gereftan	نتیجه گرفتن
to exclaim	nedaa dar aavardan	ندا در آوردن
to approach; to get near	nazdik shodan	نزدیک شدن
to show	neshaan daadan	نشان دادن
to sit; to land	neshastan	نشستن
to advise	nasihat kardan	نصیحت کردن
to clean (e.g. the house)	nezaafat kardan	نظافت کردن
to detest	nefrat daashtan	نفرت داشتن
to paint; to draw	naqqaashi kardan	نقاشی کردن
to look	negaah kardan	نگاه کردن
to be worried	negaraan budan	نگران بودن
to become worried	negaraan shodan	نگران شدن
to keep; to hold	negah daashtan	نگه داشتن
to represent	namaayeshgar budan	نمایشگر بودن
to represent	namaayandeh budan	نماینده بودن
to write	neveshtan	نوشتن
to enter; to be imported	vaared shodan	وارد شدن
to import	vaared kardan	وارد کردن
to happen; to occur	vaaqe' shodan	واقع شدن
to pretend	vaanamud kardan	وانمود کردن
to exist	vojud daashtan	وجود داشتن
to join (i.e. s.thing to s.thing else)	vasl kardan	وصل کردن
to endow	vaqf kardan	وقف کردن

to leave alone	*vel kardan*	ول کردن
to sob	*heq heq geryeh kardan*	هق هق گریه کردن
to push	*hol daadan*	هل دادن
to accompany	*hamraahi kardan*	همراهی کردن
to teach	*yaad daadan*	یاد دادن
to learn	*yaad gereftan*	یاد گرفتن

Persian Simple Verbs

افعال ساده فارسی

to adorn; decorate; beautify.	aaraastan (aaraa)	آراستن (آرا)
to hurt; offend; torment; annoy.	aazordan (aazaar)	آزردن (آزار)
to test; try; experiment; examine.	aazmudan (aazmaa)	آزمودن (آزما)
to rest; repose; obtain peace of mind.	aasudan (aasaa)	آسودن (آسا)
to drink; absorb; lap up; drain.	aashaamidan (aashaam)	آشامیدن (آشام)
to get angry, excited or disturbed.	aashoftan (aashub)	آشفتن (آشوب)
to create; initiate; bring into being.	aafaridan (aafarin)	آفریدن (آفرین)
to pollute; contaminate; taint; soil.	aaludan (aalaa)	آلودن (آلا)
to come; become; fit; match; suit.	aamadan (aa)	آمدن (آ)
to forgive; absolve; bless.	aamorzidan (aamorz)	آمرزیدن (آمرز)
to learn; teach; instruct.	aamukhtan (aamuz)	آموختن (آموز)
to mix; mingle; blend; associate.	aamikhtan (aamiz)	آمیختن (آمیز)
to bring; fetch; produce; relate; say.	aavardan (aavar)	آوردن (آور)
to hang; suspend; dangle; put up.	aavikhtan (aaviz)	آویختن (آویز)
to kindle; light; inflame; provoke.	afrukhtan (afruz)	افروختن (افروز)
to increase; add; multiply; enlarge.	afzudan (afzaa)	افزودن (افزا)
to pile up; store; hoard; fill up.	anbaashtan (anbaar)	انباشتن (انبار)
to throw down; throw away; fell.	andaakhtan (andaaz)	انداختن (انداز)
to amass; hoard; save; pile up.	andukhtan (anduz)	اندوختن (اندوز)
to think; reflect; ponder; wonder.	andishidan (andish)	اندیشیدن (اندیش)
to excite; arouse; provoke; inspire.	angikhtan (angiz)	انگیختن (انگیز)
to stand; stop; halt; resist; cease.	istaadan (ist)	ایستادن (ایست)
to lose (a game); to dissipate.	baakhtan (baaz)	باختن (باز)
to rain; pour; fall; shower.	baaridan (baar)	باریدن (بار)
to weave; knit; braid; fabricate.	baaftan (baaf)	بافتن (باف)
to boast; pride oneself; vaunt.	baalidan (baal)	بالیدن (بال)
to give; bestow; pardon; forgive.	bakhshidan (bakhsh)	بخشیدن (بخش)
to suit; become; befit.	baraazidan (baraaz)	برازیدن (براز)
to carry; take; lead; win.	bordan (bar)	بردن (بر)
to cut; sever; tear; separate.	boridan (bor)	بریدن (بر)
to close; fasten; shut; obstruct.	bastan (band)	بستن (بند)
to swallow; gulp; devour; gobble.	bal'idan (bal')	بلعیدن (بلع)
to be; exist.	budan (hast)	بودن (هست)
to kiss	busidan (bus)	بوسیدن (بوس)
to smell; sniff; nose.	bu'idan (bu)	بوئیدن (بو)
to sprinkle; scatter; spray; sow.	paashidan (paash)	پاشیدن (پاش)

to watch; guard; fix one's eyes on.	paa'idan (paa)	پانیدن (پا)
to last (long); be permanent.	paayestan (paa)	پایستن (پا)
to cook; bake; inveigle; persuade.	pokhtan (paz)	پختن (پز)
to accept; receive; admit; approve.	paziroftan (pazir)	پذیرفتن (پذیر)
to scatter; broadcast; disseminate.	paraakandan (paraakan)	پراکندن (پراکن)
to cause to fly; ejaculate.	paraandan (paraan)	پراندن (پران)
to pay; settle; proceed.	pardaakhtan (pardaaz)	پرداختن (پرداز)
to worship; adore; idolize; glorify.	parastidan (parast)	پرستیدن (پرست)
to ask; inquire; question; query.	porsidan (pors)	پرسیدن (پرس)
to bring up; educate; nourish.	parvaraandan (parvaraan)	پروراندن (پروران)
to train; cherish; nurture; develop.	parvardan (parvar)	پروردن (پرور)
to fly; flutter; jump; bounce.	paridan (par)	پریدن (پر)
to abstain; keep away from; refrain.	parhikhtan (parhiz)	پرهیختن (پرهیز)
to investigate; do research; probe.	pazhuhidan (pazhuh)	پژوهیدن (پژوه)
to admire; select; approve of.	pasandidan (pasand)	پسندیدن (پسند)
to fade; wither.	palaasidan (palaas)	پلاسیدن (پلاس)
to hang around; loiter.	pelkidan (pelk)	پلکیدن (پلک)
to suppose; imagine; take for.	pendaashtan (pendaar)	پنداشتن (پندار)
to cause to decay; wear out.	pusaandan (pusaan)	پوساندن (پوسان)
to decay; rot; putrefy; decompose.	pusidan (pus)	پوسیدن (پوس)
to clothe; cover; dress; conceal.	pushaandan (pushaan)	پوشاندن (پوشان)
to wear; dress; put on; cover.	pushidan (push)	پوشیدن (پوش)
to search; seek; inquire about.	pu'idan (pu)	پوئیدن (پو)
to twist; wind; turn; screw; bend.	pichaandan (pichaan)	پیچاندن (پیچان)
to wind; wrap; turn; twist; roll up.	pichidan (pich)	پیچیدن (پیچ)
to embellish; decorate; dress up.	piraastan (piraa)	پیراستن (پیرا)
to traverse; travel; measure; go.	peymudan (peymaa)	پیمودن (پیما)
to join; connect; unite with.	peyvastan (peyvand)	پیوستن (پیوند)
to twist; curl; cause to shine.	taabaandan (taabaan)	تاباندن (تابان)
to shine; glow; radiate; twist; spin.	taabidan (taab)	تابیدن (تاب)
to gallop; rush; invade.	taakhtan (taaz)	تاختن (تاز)
to cause to gallop; cause to rush.	taazaandan (taazaan)	تازاندن (تازان)
to pulsate; beat; palpitate; throb.	tapidan (tap)	تپیدن (تپ)
to shave; scrape; sharpen.	taraashidan (taraash)	تراشیدن (تراش)
to frighten; scare; intimidate; terrify.	tarsaandan (tarsaan)	ترساندن (ترسان)
to fear; be afraid of; dread; feel terror.	tarsidan (tars)	ترسیدن (ترس)
to turn sour; get rancid; ferment.	torshidan (torsh)	ترشیدن (ترش)
to (cause to) burst; crack; explode.	tarkaandan (tarkaan)	ترکاندن (ترکان)

to burst; explode; crack; go off.	*tarkidan (tark)*	ترکیدن (ترک)
to shake; cause to shake; dust off	*takaandan (takaan)*	تکاندن (تکان)
to spin; weave.	*tanidan (tan)*	تنیدن (تن)
to be able to; be permitted to.	*tavaanestan (tavaan)*	توانستن (توان)
to search; seek; find; discover.	*jostan (ju)*	جستن (جو)
(tr.) to move; shake; wag.	*jonbaandan (jonbaan)*	جنباندن (جنبان)
(intr.) to move; shake; wag.	*jonbidan (jonb)*	جنبیدن (جنب)
to fight; wage war; quarrel.	*jangidan (jang)*	جنگیدن (جنگ)
(tr.) to boil; brew; infuse.	*jushaandan (jushaan)*	جوشاندن (جوشان)
(intr.) to boil; bubble; gush; seethe.	*jushidan (jush)*	جوشیدن (جوش)
to chew; gnaw; munch.	*javidan (jav) or jowidan (jow)*	جویدن (جو)
to leap; jump; escape.	*jahidan (jah)*	جهیدن (جه)
to plunder; pillage; ransack; rob.	*chaapidan (chaap)*	چاپیدن (چاپ)
to chill; cool; catch cold.	*chaa'idan (chaa)*	چائیدن (چا)
to cram; jam; stuff; thrust; push into.	*chapaandan (chapaan)*	چپاندن (چپان)
to crowd into; cram into.	*chapidan (chap)*	چپیدن (چپ)
to graze; pasture.	*charaandan (charaan)*	چراندن (چران)
to exceed the due weight; prevail.	*charbidan (charb)*	چربیدن (چرب)
(tr.) to turn; roll; whirl; gyrate; revolve.	*charkhaandan (charkhaan)*	چرخاندن (چرخان)
(intr.) to turn; rotate; spin; revolve.	*charkhidan (charkh)*	چرخیدن (چرخ)
to graze; pasture.	*charidan (char)*	چریدن (چر)
to (cause to) stick; adhere; fasten.	*chasbaandan (chasbaan)*	چسباندن (چسبان)
(intr.) to stick to; adhere; cling.	*chasbidan (chasb)*	چسبیدن (چسب)
to cause to taste; to feed.	*cheshaandan (cheshaan)*	چشاندن (چشان)
to taste; savour; test; experience.	*cheshidan (chesh)*	چشیدن (چش)
to cause to drip or trickle.	*chekaandan (chekaan)*	چکاندن (چکان)
to drip; trickle; leak; fall in drops.	*chekidan (chek)*	چکیدن (چک)
to squeeze; press; wring out.	*chelaandan (chelaan)*	چلاندن (چلان)
to strut; flaunt; parade.	*chamidan (cham)*	چمیدن (چم)
to pick; pluck; cut; pare; arrange.	*chidan (chin)*	چیدن (چین)
to itch; scratch.	*khaaridan (khar)*	خاریدن (خار)
to chew; grind.	*khaa'idan (khaa)*	خائیدن (خا)
to (cause to) scratch; scrape.	*kharaashaandan (kharaashaan)*	خراشاندن (خراشان)
to scratch; scrape; rub against.	*kharaashidan (kharaash)*	خراشیدن (خراش)
to strut; walk gracefully; saunter.	*kharaamidan (kharaam)*	خرامیدن (خرام)
to buy; purchase; acquire.	*kharidan (khar)*	خریدن (خر)
to (cause to) dry; desiccate; drain.	*khoshkaandan (khoshkaan)*	خشکاندن (خشکان)
to become dry; desiccate; wither up.	*khoshkidan (khoshk)*	خشکیدن (خشک)

to sleep; rest; slumber; snooze.	khoftan (khosb)	خفتن(خسب)
to cause to laugh	khandaandan (khandaan)	خنداندن (خندان)
to laugh; smile.	khandidan (khand)	خندیدن (خند)
to cause to sleep; put to bed.	khaabaandan (khaabaan)	خواباندن (خوابان)
to sleep; lie down; run down.	khaabidan (khaab)	خوابیدن (خواب)
to wish; want; intend; request.	khaastan (khaah)	خواستن (خواه)
to read; peruse; sing; study.	khaandan (khaan)	خواندن (خوان)
to cause to eat; feed.	khoraandan (khoraan)	خوراندن (خوران)
to eat; drink; hit against.	khordan (khor)	خوردن (خور)
to cause to rise; raise.	khizaandan (khizaan)	خیزاندن (خیزان)
to rise; get up; elevate.	khizidan (khiz)	خیزیدن (خیز)
to wet; soak; saturate.	khisaandan (khisaan)	خیساندن (خیسان)
to become wet; be soaked.	khisidan (khis)	خیسیدن (خیس)
to give; pay; offer; donate; grant.	daadan (dah)	دادن (ده)
to have; own; hold; retain.	daashtan (daar)	داشتن (دار)
to know (a fact)	daanestan (daan)	دانستن (دان)
to rip; tear to pieces.	daraanidan (daraan)	درانیدن (دران)
to cause to shine; illuminate.	derakhshaandan (derakhsaan)	درخشاندن (درخشان)
to shine; give off light; glow; twinkle.	derakhshidan (derakhsh)	درخشیدن (درخش)
to tear; rip; lacerate; devour.	daridan (dar)	دریدن (در)
to steal; rob; pilfer; kidnap.	dozdidan (dozd)	دزدیدن (دزد)
to blow; breathe upon; infuse; brew.	damidan (dam)	دمیدن (دم)
to cause to run; to give trouble.	davaandan (davaan)	دواندن (دوان)
to sew; tailor; stitch together.	dukhtan (duz)	دوختن (دوز)
to (cause to) milk	dushaandan (dushaan)	دوشاندن (دوشان)
to milk; (tr.) bleed; exploit.	dushidan (dush)	دوشیدن (دوش)
to run; jog; sprint; move fast.	davidan (dav) or dowidan (dow)	دویدن (دو)
to see; visit; experience.	didan (bin)	دیدن (بین)
to drive; pilot; ride; expel; send away.	raandan (raan)	راندن (ران)
to steal; kidnap; hijack.	robudan (robaa)	ربودن (ربا)
to shine; glitter; sparkle.	rakhshidan (rakhsh)	رخشیدن (رخش)
to dye; tinge; colour.	razidan (raz)	رزیدن (رز)
to transport; give a lift; deliver; supply.	resaandan (resaan)	رساندن (رسان)
to escape; be saved; get rid of.	rastan (reh)	رستن (ره)
to grow; spring; sprout.	rostan (ru)	رستن (رو)
to reach; attain; arrive.	residan (res)	رسیدن (رس)
to go; leave; exit; fade; take after.	raftan (rav)	رفتن (رو)
to sweep; wipe.	roftan (rub)	رفتن (روب)

to (cause to) dance; (fig.) to control	raqsaandan (raqsaan)	رقصاندن (رقصان)
to dance	raqsidan (raqs)	رقصیدن (رقص)
to rouse; scare; cause to shy.	ramaandan (ramaan)	رماندن (رمان)
to collapse; cave in; topple over.	rombidan (romb)	رمبیدن (رمب)
to shy; startle; be scared off.	ramidan (ram)	رمیدن (رم)
to offend; annoy; insult; hurt; irritate.	ranjaanidan (ranjaan)	رنجانیدن (رنجان)
to take offence; be hurt.	ranjidan (ranj)	رنجیدن (رنج)
to plane; grate.	randidan (rand)	رندیدن (رند)
(intr.) to grow	ru'idan (ru)	روئیدن (رو)
(tr.) to grow; nurture; raise.	ruyaandan (ruyaan)	رویاندن (رویان)
to pour; spill; scatter; be spilled.	rikhtan (riz)	ریختن (ریز)
(slang) to shit	ridan (rin)	ریدن (رین)
to (cause to) pour; to spill.	rizaanidan (rizaan)	ریزانیدن (ریزان)
to spin (e.g. cloth)	ristan (ris)	ریستن (ریس)
to spin (e.g. cloth)	risidan (ris)	ریسیدن (ریس)
to save; deliver; set free.	rahaandan (rahaan)	رهاندن (رهان)
to be saved; be set free.	rahidan (rah)	رهیدن (ره)
to weep; lament; moan; wail.	zaaridan (zaar)	زاریدن (زار)
to bear; give birth to; deliver.	zaa'idan (zaa)	زائیدن (زا)
to hit; strike; beat; ring.	zadan (zan)	زدن (زن)
to exist; live; subsist.	zistan (zi)	زیستن (زی)
to rub; wear out; make threadbare.	saabidan (saab)	سابیدن (ساب)
to build; construct; make; produce.	saakhtan (saaz)	ساختن (ساز)
to erode; rub; chafe; pulverize.	saa'idan (saa)	سائیدن (سا)
to deposit; pledge; entrust.	sepordan (sepaar)	سپردن (سپار)
to pierce; thrust; (slang) fuck.	sepukhtan (sepuz)	سپوختن (سپوز)
to take; get; obtain.	setaandan (setaan)	ستاندن (ستان)
to praise; eulogize.	setaa'idan (setaa)	ستائیدن (ستا)
to shave; erase; scrape; clean.	setordan (setor)	ستردن (ستر)
to praise; eulogize; extol; commend.	setudan (setaa)	ستودن (ستا)
to sing; compose; versify.	saraayidan (saraa)	سراییدن (سرا)
to cough; (fig.) shell out.	sorfidan (sorf)	سرفیدن (سرف)
to sing; compose; versify.	sorudan (saraa)	سرودن (سرا)
to merit; be worth; suit; match.	sazidan (saz)	سزیدن (سز)
to pierce; bore; puncture; perforate.	softan (sonb)	سفتن (سنب)
to measure; judge; deliberate.	sanjidan (sanj)	سنجیدن (سنج)
(intr.) to burn	sukhtan (suz)	سوختن (سوز)
to (cause to) burn; ignite; set on fire.	suzaandan (suzaan)	سوزاندن (سوزان)

to congeal (e.g. fat or oil)	siridan (sir)	سیریدن (سیر)
(slang) to piss	shaashidan (shaash)	شاشیدن (شاش)
to befit; become; be worthy of.	shaayestan (shaa)	شایستن (شا)
to (cause to) hurry	shetaabaandan (shetaabaan)	شتاباندن (شتابان)
to hurry; to accelerate.	shetaabidan (shetaab)	شتابیدن (شتاب)
to be; become.	shodan (shav)	شدن (شو)
to wash; cleanse	shostan (shu)	شستن (شو)
to split; cleave; slash; tear; unstitch.	shekaaftan (shekaaf)	شکافتن (شکاف)
to break; be broken; crack; violate.	shekastan (shekan)	شکستن (شکن)
to open; bud; bloom; flower.	shekoftan (shekof)	شکفتن (شکف)
to count; compute; reckon; calculate.	shomordan (shomor)	شمردن (شمر)
to know (i.e. a person); recognize.	shenaakhtan (shenaas)	شناختن (شناس)
to make known; introduce; publicize.	shenaasaandan (shenaasaan)	شناساندن (شناسان)
to make s.o. listen or hear.	shenavaandan (shenavaan)	شنواندن (شنوان)
to hear; listen to.	shanidan (shenav)	شنیدن (شنو)
to rebel; mutiny; revolt; rise up.	shuridan (shur)	شوریدن (شور)
to enamour; captivate; charm.	shiftan (shiv)	شیفتن (شیو)
to thrust into; force into; cram in.	tapaandan (tapaan)	طپاندن (طپان)
to throb; beat; palpitate.	tapidan (tap)	طپیدن (طپ)
to call; invite; ask; seek; search.	talabidan (talab)	طلبیدن (طلب)
to scratch; be angry.	qaraashidan (qaraash)	غراشیدن (غراش)
to roar; thunder.	qoronbidan (qoronb)	غرنبیدن (غرنب)
to grumble; roar; growl; rumble.	qorridan (qorr)	غرّیدن (غرّ)
to creep; crawl; lie hidden.	qazhidan (qazh)	غژیدن (غژ)
to (cause to) roll	qaltaanidan (qaltaan)	غلتانیدن (غلتان)
to roll; wallow; tumble.	qaltidan (qalt)	غلتیدن (غلت)
to (cause to) roll	qaltaanidan (qaltaan)	غلطانیدن (غلطان)
to roll; wallow; tumble.	qaltidan (qalt)	غلطیدن (غلط)
to sleep; rest; repose; relax.	qonudan (qanaa)	غنودن (غنا)
to send; despatch; forward.	ferestaadan (ferest)	فرستادن (فرست)
to erode; wear out; tire.	farsudan (farsaa)	فرسودن (فرسا)
to command; order.	farmudan (farmaa)	فرمودن (فرما)
to sell; vend; peddle; betray.	forukhtan (forush)	فروختن (فروش)
to deceive; seduce; cheat; delude.	fariftan (farib)	فریفتن (فریب)
to enchant; bewitch; fascinate.	fasaayidan (fasaa)	فساییدن (فسا)
to press; squeeze; strain; cram.	feshordan (feshaar)	فشردن (فشار)
to make understand; explain.	fahmaandan (fahmaan)	فهماندن (فهمان)
to understand; grasp; comprehend.	fahmidan (fahm)	فهمیدن (فهم)

to snatch, seize; grab.	qaapidan (qaap)	قاپیدن (قاپ)
to make s.o. accept; convince.	qabulaandan (qabulaan)	قبولاندن (قبولان)
to diminish; decrease; lessen.	kaastan (kaah)	کاستن (کاه)
to sow; plant; cultivate.	kaashtan (kaar)	کاشتن (کار)
to diminish; reduce; be reduced.	kaahidan (kaah)	کاهیدن (کاه)
to do; make; perform; render.	kardan (kon)	کردن (کن)
to draw out; prolong; protract.	keshaandan (keshaan)	کشاندن (کشان)
to sow; plant; cultivate; till.	keshtan (kaar)	کشتن (کار)
to kill; murder; slay; extinguish.	koshtan (kosh)	کشتن (کش)
to draw; drag; pull; smoke.	keshidan (kosh)	کشیدن (کش)
to dig; tear off; pluck; root out.	kandan (kan)	کندن (کن)
to pound; mash; hammer; knock.	kubidan (kub)	کوبیدن (کوب)
to try; endeavour; make an effort.	kushidan (kush)	کوشیدن (کوش)
to pound; hammer; knock.	kuftan (kub)	کوفتن (کوب)
(slang) to fuck	gaa'idan (gaa)	گائیدن (گا)
to melt; thaw; liquefy; clarify.	godaakhtan (godaaz	گداختن (گداز)
to put; lay; place; leave; allow.	gozaardan (gozaar)	گذاردن (گذار)
to put; place; permit; allow; admit.	gozaashtan (gozaar)	گذاشتن (گذار)
to pass; cross; overlook; forgive.	gozashtan (gozar)	گذشتن (گذر)
to be inclined; have a tendency for.	geraayidan (geraa)	گراییدن (گرا)
(tr.) to turn around; spin; rotate.	gardaandan (gardaan)	گرداندن (گردان)
(intr.) to turn around; spin; become.	gardidan (gard)	گردیدن (گرد)
to take; seize; receive; obtain; get.	gereftan (gir)	گرفتن (گیر)
to cause to adhere to; make inclined.	gerowaandan (gerowaan)	گرواندن (گروان)
to follow; adhere to; pursue.	gerowidan (geraa)	گرویدن (گرا)
to run away; flee; escape; abscond.	gorikhtan (goriz)	گریختن (گریز)
to cause to escape; alienate.	gorizaandan (gorizaan)	گریزاندن (گریزان)
to weep; cry; wail; sob; whimper.	geristan (gery)	گریستن (گری)
to weep; cry; shed tears.	geryidan (gery)	گریدن (گری)
to perform; put; place; say; pay.	gozaardan (gozaar)	گزاردن (گزار)
to bite; sting; smart; prickle.	gazidan (gaz)	گزیدن (گز)
to choose; select; elect; pick; prefer.	gozidan (gozin)	گزیدن (گزین)
to (cause to) spread; disseminate.	gostaraanidan (gostaraan)	گسترانیدن (گستران)
to spread; diffuse; expand; open.	gostardan (gostar)	گستردن (گستر)
to cut; rupture; sever; tear; end.	gosastan (gosel)	گسستن (گسل)
to cause to tear; rend apart; tear off.	gosalaandan (gosalaan)	گسلاندن (گسلان)
to rotate; revolve; wander; become.	gashtan (gard)	گشتن (گرد)
to open; disclose; resolve; conquer.	goshudan (goshaa)	گشودن (گشا)

to say; tell; relate; speak; declare.	goftan (gu)	گفتن (گو)
to appoint; assign; put to work.	gomaardan (gomaar)	گماردن (گمار)
to appoint; assign; put to work.	gomaashtan (gomaar)	گماشتن (گمار)
to insert; include; cram into.	gonjaandan (gonjaan)	گنجاندن (گنجان)
to be contained; be inserted.	gonjidan (gonj)	گنجیدن (گنج)
to rot; putrefy; decompose; spoil.	gandidan (gand)	گندیدن (گند)
to digest	govaaridan (govaar)	گواریدن (گوار)
to creep; grow; amass.	govaalidan (govaal)	گوالیدن (گوال)
to bark; talk idly; complain.	laa'idan (laa)	لائیدن (لا)
to cause to tremble; shake; vibrate.	larzaandan (larzaan)	لرزاندن (لرزان)
(intr.) to shake; vibrate; shiver.	larzidan (larz)	لرزیدن (لرز)
to cause to slip or stumble	laqzaandan (laqzaan)	لغزاندن (لغزان)
to slip; slide; stumble; blunder.	laqzidan (laqz)	لغزیدن (لغز)
to cause to limp; to nobble.	langaandan (langaan)	لنگاندن (لنگان)
to limp; go lame.	langidan (lang)	لنگیدن (لنگ)
to wriggle; toss and turn; squirm.	lulidan (lul)	لولیدن (لول)
to lick	lisidan (lis)	لیسیدن (لیس)
to be congealed; be coagulated.	maasidan (maas)	ماسیدن (ماس)
to rub; stroke; massage; knead.	maalidan (maal)	مالیدن (مال)
to resemble	maanestan (maan)	مانستن (مان)
to die; pass away; expire; fade out.	mordan (mir)	مردن (میر)
to suck; suckle; absorb.	mekidan (mek)	مکیدن (مک)
to cause to die; kill; mortify.	miraandan (miraan)	میراندن (میران)
to boast of; flaunt.	naazidan (naaz)	نازیدن (ناز)
to groan; moan; whimper; lament.	naalidan (naal)	نالیدن (نال)
to name; call; nominate.	naamidan (naam)	نامیدن (نام)
to seat; implant; settle; suppress.	neshaandan (neshaan)	نشاندن (نشان)
to sit down; reside; settle; be quelled.	neshastan (neshin)	نشستن (نشین)
to reproach; blame; carp; despise.	nekuhidan (nekuh)	نکوهیدن (نکوه)
(arch.) to write	negaaridan (negaar)	نگاریدن (نگار)
to write; paint; draw; portray.	negaashtan (negaar)	نگاشتن (نگار)
(arch.) to look; glance at.	negarestan (negar)	نگرستن (نگار)
(arch.) to look; see; behold.	negaridan (negar)	نگریدن (نگر)
to show; appear; do; perform.	nemudan (namaa)	نمودن (نما)
to caress; pamper; play; sing.	navaakhtan (navaaz)	نواختن (نواز)
(arch.) to swallow without chewing	navaaridan (navaar)	نواریدن (نوار)
to pat; caress; play; strum.	navaazidan (navaaz)	نوازیدن (نواز)
to traverse; fold; roll up.	navardidan (navard)	نوردیدن (نورد)

to cause to drink; to feed	*nushaandan (nushaan)*	نوشاندن (نوشان)
to write; jot down; compose.	*neveshtan (nevis)*	نوشتن (نویس)
to drink; sip.	*nushidan (nush)*	نوشیدن (نوش)
to put; place; establish.	*nahaadan (neh)*	نهادن (نه)
to cultivate; train; work; make.	*varzidan (varz)*	ورزیدن (ورز)
to blow; breeze; gasp; pant.	*vazidan (vaz)*	وزیدن (وز)
to fear; dread; be worried.	*haraasidan (haraas)*	هراسیدن (هراس)
to draw a sword; unsheathe.	*yaakhtan (yaaz)*	یاختن (یاز)
(arch.) to be able; to dare.	*yaarestan (yaar)*	یارستن (یار)
to stretch out; grow; unsheathe.	*yaazidan (yaaz)*	یازیدن (یاز)
to find; obtain; acquire; come upon.	*yaaftan (yaab)*	یافتن (یاب)

530

Other Parts of Speech

قيود و حروف ربط

finally; eventually	aakhar-e sar	آخر سر
there	aanjaa	آنجا
then	aanvaqt	آنوقت
never; not at all	abadan	ابداً
from	az	از
purposefully; on purpose	az dasti	از دستی
on the other hand	az taraf-e digar	از طرف دیگر
as a rule; generally; usually	usulan	اصولاً
now	aknun	اکنون
although	agarcheh	اگرچه
now	alaan	الان
of course; naturally	albatteh	البته
but	ammaa	اما
here	injaa	اینجا
with	baa	با
although	baa inkeh	با اینکه
although	baa vojud-e inkeh	با وجود اینکه
again	baaz ham	باز هم
up; above	baalaa	بالا
worse	badtar	بدتر
without	bedun	بدون
without exception	bedun-e estesnaa	بدون استثنا
undoubtedly	bedun-e shakk	بدون شک
on; against; by	bar	بر
against; opposed to	bar zedd	بر ضد
for	baraayeh	برای
because	baraayeh inkeh	برای اینکه
many; very	besyaar	بسیار
generally	betowr-e kolli	بطور کلی
after	ba'd az	بعد از
afterwards	ba'dan	بعداً
some	ba'zi	بعضی
some of	ba'zi az	بعضی از
sometimes	ba'zi vaqt-haa	بعضی وقت ها
immediately	belaa faaseleh	بلا فاصله
yes	baleh	بلی

531

extremely	bi andaazeh	بی اندازه
extremely	bish az hadd	بیش از حد
more; most	bishtar	بیشتر
between	beyn	بین
to; towards	be	به
enough	be andaaze-ye kaafi	به اندازه کافی
soon	be zudi	به زودی
in other words	be 'ebaarat-e digar	به عبارت دیگر
according to	be qowl	به قول
rarely	be nodrat	به ندرت
in no way; under no circumstances	be hich vajh	به هیچ وجه
better	behtar	بهتر
underneath; below	paa'in	پائین
behind	posht	پشت
in front of; with; at	pish	پیش
next to	pahlu	پهلو
until; as soon as	taa	تا
so that	taa inkeh	تا اینکه
until then; until that time	taa aan vaqt	تا آن وقت
until now	taa behaal	تا بحال
alone; only	tanhaa	تنها
in; inside	tu	تو
in front	jelow	جلو
why	cheraa	چرا
how	chetowr	چطور
how much	cheqadr	چقدر
how many	chand taa	چند تا
because	chun	چون
because	chun ke	چونکه
definitely	hatman	حتماً
even	hattaa	حتی
outside	khaarej	خارج
good; well	khub	خوب
very; many	kheyli	خیلی
inside	daakhel	داخل
constantly; continuously	daa'eman	دائماً
in	dar	در
about; on the subject of	dar baareh	درباره

532

at present	dar haal-e haazer	در حال حاضر
in reality	dar haqiqat	در حقیقت
next to	dar kenaar	در کنار
in the middle of; among; amongst	dar miyaan	در میان
as a result	dar natijeh	در نتیجه
in actual fact; in reality	dar vaaqe'	در واقع
exactly	daqiqan	دقیقاً
again	dobaareh	دوباره
around	dowr	دور
on	ru	رو
opposite; facing	ru-be-ru	روبرو
on the whole	ru-ye ham rafteh	روی هم رفته
quickly	zud	زود
many; lots; a lot of	ziyaad	زیاد
under; underneath	zir	زیر
previously	saabeqan	سابقاً
then	sepas	سپس
moreover; apart from this	'alaaveh bar in	علاوه بر این
despite	'alaa raqm	علی رغم
other than; apart from	qeyr az	غیر از
only	faqat	فقط
as a rule	qaa'edatan	قاعدتاً
before	qabl az	قبل از
previously; before	qablan	قبلاً
completely	kaamelan	کاملاً
generally; on the whole	kollan	کلاً
little by little; gradually	kam kam	کم کم
next to; alongside	kenaar	کنار
sometimes	gaahi	گاهی
apart from this; moreover	gozashteh az in	گذشته از این
although	garcheh	گرچه
unfortunately	mota'assefaaneh	متاسفانه
like	mesl	مثل
especially	makhsusan	مخصوصاً
certainly	mosallaman	مسلماً
usually; normally	ma'mulan	معمولاً
suddenly	naagahaan	ناگهان
as a result	natijatan	نتیجتاً

near	nazdik	نزدیک
relatively	nesbatan	نسبتاً
no	na	نه
neither....nor	na......na	نه ...... نه
really	vaaq'an	واقعاً
in the middle	vasat	وسط
but	vali	ولی
suddenly	yek daf'eh	یک دفعه
never	hargez	هرگز
also	ham	هم
all	hameh	همه
everywhere	hameh jaa	همه جا
still; yet	hanuz	هنوز
never	hich vaqt	هیچ وقت
slowly	yavaash	یواش

to 'come'; to ejaculate	aab aamadan	آب آمدن
insipid; weak (of liquids)	aabaki	آبکی
rubbish; crap	aashqaal	آشغال
bum-boy; queer; homo	obne'i	ابنه ای
to pick up (a woman); to kerb crawl	otu zadan	اتو زدن
sullen; bad-tempered	akhmu	اخمو
to shit oneself from fear	az tars ridan	از ترس ریدن
boasting; showing off; snobbery	efaadeh	افاده
thick; stupid (lit. 'Plato')	aflaatun	افلاطون
to pose; to put on airs and graces	efeh aamadan	افه آمدن
for no reason	alaki	الکی
mad; mental; crazy	amin aabaadi	امین آبادی
quickly; in no time at all	iki saaniyeh	ایکی ثانیه
homo; poofter; queer; fairy; gay; fag	eyvaa khaahar	ای واخواهر
yes, by God; you're too right	ey vaallaah	ای والله
bribe	baaj-e sebil	باج سبیل
cool; neat; ace; great	baa haal	با حال
to throw up	baalaa aavordan	بالا آوردن
shut your mouth!	beband gaala-row	ببند گاله رو!
stupid	babu	ببو
homosexual; paedophile; gay	bacheh baaz	بچه باز
homosexuality	bacheh baazi	بچه بازی
spoilt brat; sissy	bacheh naneh	بچه ننه
shut up; be quiet	bekhaab binam	بخواب بینم!
insult; bad-mouthing; swearing	bad o biraah	بد و بیراه
the boys/girls; the gang	bar o bache-haa	بر و بچه ها
get away!; go on!; you're joking!	boro baabaa	برو بابا!
go to hell!	boro jahannam	برو جهنم!
make-up; 'slap'	bazak	بزک
to put make-up on	bazak kardan	بزک کردن
knees-up; dance; party; rave	bezan o bekub	بزن و بکوب
things; stuff	basaat	بساط
a laugh and a joke	begu bekhand	بگو بخند
argument	begu magu	بگو مگو
to babble	balqur kardan	بلغور کردن
to pick up (a woman)	boland kardan	بلند کردن

to suspect	*bu bordan*	بو بردن
stink; stinker; smelling of shit	*bu gandi*	بو گندی
what do I care?; to hell (with it)	*be tokhmam*	به تخمم
to pick up; to entrap; to catch	*be tur zadan*	به تور زدن
to hell (with it)	*be jahannam*	به جهنم
to sod off	*be chaak zadan*	به چاک زدن
to hell (with it)	*be darrak*	به درّک
to foul up; to screw up; to shame s.o.	*be goh keshidan*	به گه کشیدن
definite; inescapable	*bi boro bargard*	بی برو برگرد
poor thing!	*bichaareh*	بیچاره!
rude; shameless	*bi cheshm o ru*	بی چشم و رو
useless; helpless	*bi dast o paa*	بی دست و پا
useless; futile	*bi khod*	بی خود
excellent; brilliant; mint (lit. 'twenty')	*bist*	بیست
to play with oneself	*bilyaard baazi kardan*	بیلیارد بازی کردن
to bother s.o.	*paa pich shodan*	پا پیچ شدن
barefoot; poor; wretched	*paa pati*	پا پتی
place where one hangs out	*paatoq*	پاتق
pissed; slaughtered; wrecked; old	*paatil*	پاتیل
loudmouth	*paacheh var maalideh*	پاچه ور مالیده
to be willing (sexually)	*paa daadan*	پا دادن
to interrupt; to butt in	*paaraazit andaakhtan*	پارازیت انداختن
useless; coward; sissy	*papeh*	پپه
useless; coward	*pakhmeh*	پخمه
to hurt, annoy or punish s.o.	*pedar dar aavordan*	پدر در آوردن
son-of-a-bitch	*pedar sag*	پدر سگ
sod; bugger; jerk (lit. 'burnt father')	*pedar sukhteh*	پدر سوخته
to talk nonsense	*part o palaa goftan*	پرت و پلا گفتن
rude; shameless	*por ru*	پر رو
to pose; to put on airs	*poz daadan*	پز دادن
hair; fuzz	*pashm*	پشم
good-for-nothing; waster	*pofyuz*	پفیوز
moody; pissed-off	*pakar*	پکر
to take a puff (on a cigarette)	*pok zadan*	پک زدن
to take root; to hang around	*palaas shodan*	پلاس شدن
to go rotten; to hang around	*palaasidan*	پلاسیدن
to hang out; to stroll around	*pelkidan*	پلکیدن
easy; simple	*pish-e paa oftaadeh*	پیش پا افتاده

poo! (said in response to bad smells)	pif	پیف
glass (of alcohol); shot	peyk	پیک
first-rate; great; ace	taap	تاپ
cowpat; cow dung; crap	taapaaleh	تاپاله
to exchange one thing for another	taakht zadan	تاخت زدن
to destroy; to annihilate	taar o maar kardan	تار و مار کردن
to screw (financially or sexually)	tapaandan	تپاندن
fat; fatty	topol	تپل
testicle; balls	tokhm	تخم
crap; useless; shit; pants	tokhmi	تخمی
to have the shits; to mess s.thing up	ter zadan	تر زدن
chic; suited and booted; tarted up	targol vargol	ترگل ورگل
trip; bag; vibe; fashion	terip	تریپ
to screw; to fuck (espec. a virgin)	taqqeh zadan	تقه زدن
faithful; having only one partner	tak par	تک پر
piece (i.e. a woman); girl; totty	tekkeh	تکه
to throw up	tagari zadan	تگری زدن
lazy; idle; good-for-nothing	taneh lash	تنه لش
excellent; brilliant	tup	توپ
to be into something	tu khatt-e chizi budan	تو خط چیزی بودن
nice	tu del boro	تو دل برو
smack in the mouth	tu dahani	تو دهنی
to fuck (lit. 'to put it in')	tush kardan	توش کردن
kid	tuleh	توله
to be into something	tu nakh-e chizi budan	تو نخ چیزی بودن
fashionable; cool	tip	تیپ
to boot out; to kick up the arse	tipaa zadan	تیپا زدن
to aim; to shoot	tir kardan	تیر کردن
pimp	jaakesh	جاکش
to pimp	jaakeshi	جاکشی
to cheat	jer zadan	جر زدن
to rip; to tear	jer daadan	جر دادن
daring; bravery; 'guts'	jorbozeh	جربزه
rubbish; crap (describing speech)	jafang	جفنگ
to sling one's hook; to sod off	jol o palaas jam' kardan	جل و پلاس جمع کردن
to wank	jalq zadan	جلق زدن
prostitute; hooker; whore	jendeh	جنده
s.o. who visits prostitutes	jendeh baaz	جنده باز

consorting with prostitutes	jendeh baazi	جنده بازی
brothel; whorehouse	jendeh khaaneh	جنده خانه
kid (lit. 'chicken')	jujeh	جوجه
hell	jahannam darreh	جهنم دره
pick-pocket	jib bor	جیب بر
quick as a flash	jiringi	جیرینگی
babe; darling	jigar	جیگر
to clear off; to scarper; to play hooky	jim shodan	جیم شدن
to fleece; to rip s.o. off	chaapidan	چاپیدن
liar; lies	chaakhaan	چاخان
fat; fatty	chaaqaalu	چاقالو
to say hello; to pass the time of day	chaaq salaamati kardan	چاق سلامتی کردن
cut-throat; gangster; hood	chaaqu kesh	چاقو کش
to slit (e.g. someone's throat)	chaak	چاك دادن
I'm all yours (lit. "I'm your servant")	chaakeretam	چاکرتم!
to cram; to thrust; to stuff	chapaandan	چپاندن
rubbish; bollocks (said of speech)	chert o pert	چرت و پرت
junkie; shithead	chorti	چرتی
(silent) fart	chos	چس
poser	chos efaadeh	چس افاده
stingy; tight	chos khor	چس خور
to fart (silently)	chos daadan	چس دادن
to pose; to put on airs and graces	chosi aamadan	چسی آمدن
voyeur	cheshm cheraan	چشم چران
to wink	cheshmak zadan	چشمک زدن
to talk about someone; to backbite	choqoli kardan	چغلی کردن
slap	chak	چک
useless; thick; stupid; foolish	cholofti	چلفتی
useless; thick; stupid; dumb	cholman	چلمن
a tiny amount (of money)	chender qaaz (pul)	چندرقاز (پول)
to have a good time	haal kardan	حال کردن
to annoy; to piss s.o. off	haal gereftan	حال گرفتن
to change (one's mood)	haali be haali shodan	حالی به حالی شدن
to understand	haali budan	حالی بودن
horny; randy	hashari	حشری
bribe	haq o hesaab	حق و حساب
sorted; fixed (lit. 'it's sorted')	halleh	حله
animal; monster	heyvaan	حیوان

poor thing!; poor sod!	heyvunaki	حیوونکی !
in love	khaater khaah	خاطرخواه
heroin (lit. 'earth')	khaak	خاک
you stupid jerk; you prat	khaak bar saret	خاک بر سرت!
to gossip or act like an old woman	khaaleh zanak baazi	خاله زنک بازی
to lie; to bullshit	khaali bastan	خالی بستن
lying; bullshitting	khaali bandi	خالی بندی
womaniser	khaanom baaz	خانم باز
madam (i.e. of prostitutes)	khaanom ra'is	خانم رئیس
testicles; balls	khaayeh	خایه
to suck up to someone	khaayeh maali kardan	خایه مالی کردن
plump; fat; podgy; flabby	khepel	خپل
ruined; rotten; fouled up; corrupt	kharaab	خراب
to foul up; to screw up	kharaab kardan	خراب کردن
stinking rich; moneybags	khar pul	خر پول
chaos; confusion; shambles; chaotic	khar tu khar	خر تو خر
drudgery; donkeywork	khar hammaali	خر حمالی
stupid; senile; thick; dumb; dense	khereft	خرفت
well-hung (lit. 'donkey dick')	khar kir	خر کیر
to choke; to shut up	khafeh shodan	خفه شدن
shut up!	khafeh show	خفه شو !
thick; stupid	kheng	خنگ
motherfucker	khaahar kos deh (khaarkosseh)	خواهر کس ده (خواهر کسه)
to raise hell	khun be paa kardan	خون به پا کردن
to be done in; to be wrecked	daaqun shodan	داغون شدن
halves (as in 'to go halves')	daangi	دانگی
lovely; nice	debsh	دبش
to go back on one's word	dabbeh dar aavordan	دبه در آوردن
trip; out and about	dadar	ددر
gadabout; party animal	dadari	ددری
shut your mouth!	dareto bezaar	درتو بذار !
foreplay; non-penetrative sex	darmaali kardan	درمالی کردن
well-matched; made for each other	dar o takhteh	در و تخته
rubbish; crap (said of speech)	dari vari	دری وری
to get rid of s.o	dast be-sar kardan	دست به سر کردن
to unite; to collude; to gang up on	dast be-yeki	دست به یکی
brand new	dast-e avval	دست اول
to die (of loneliness, frustration etc.)	deq kardan	دق کردن

to get rid of (someone)	dak kardan	دك كردن
well done; good for you	damet garm	دمت گرم!
drugs (lit. 'medicine')	davaa	دوا
twosome	dow tarkeh	دو ترکه
smoke; tobacco; narcotics	dud	دود
to catch on slowly	dowzaari dir oftaadan	دوزاری دیر افتادن
willy; cock	dul	دول
arsehole; bastard	dayyus	دیّوث
to be knackered; dog-tired	zelleh shodan	ذله شدن
to be slaughtered	zalil shodan	ذلیل شدن
good-for-nothing asshole	zalil mordeh	ذلیل مرده
to have or get a hard-on	raast kardan	راست کردن
to put in place; to sort out	raast o ris kardan	راست و ریس کردن
weak point	rag-e khaab	رگ خواب
to retreat; to cower	ram kardan	رم کردن
to put one on the spot	ru andaakhtan	رو انداختن
to be beaten	ru dast khordan	رو دست خوردن
chatterbox; windbag	rudeh deraaz	روده دراز
to talk too much	rudeh deraazi kardan	روده درازی کردن
to shit	ridan	ریدن
weakling; sissy	riqu	ریغو
to keep an eye on	zaaq zadan	زاغ زدن
quick-witted	zebr o zerang	زبر و زرنگ
flimsy; cheap; crap	zeperti	زپرتی
collusion; stitch-up	zad o band	زد و بند
fight; scrap	zad o khord	زد و خورد
bullshit	zert o pert	زرت و پرت
to shit one's pants	zard kardan	زرد کردن
to prattle; to talk rubbish	zer zer kardan	زر زر کردن
up yours!	zereshk	زرشک!
oh shit!	zeki	زکی
womaniser	zan baaz	زن باز
mad; crazy; raving; nutter	zanjiri	زنجیری
by force; under duress	zuraki	زورکی
to scare; to put the wind up s.o.	zahr-e cheshm gereftan	زهر چشم گرفتن
insipid; weak (of liquids, tea etc.)	zipu	زیپو
to get rid of; to do away with	ziraab-e kasi-raa zadan	زیر آب کسی را زدن
dosser; vagrant	zir-e pol khaab	زیر پل خواب

to back out of s.thing; to renege	zir-e chizi zadan	زیر چیزی زدن
to pose; to show off	zhest gereftan	ژست گرفتن
collusion; conspiracy	saakht o paakht	ساخت و پاخت
to bribe someone	sebil-e kasi-raa charb kardan	سبیلِ کسی را چرب کردن
carefree; flighty	sar be-havaa	سر به هوا
nuisance; pain in the arse	sar-e khar	سر خر
to cross swords with	sar shaakh shodan	سر شاخ شدن
to trick or deceive s.o.	sar-e kasi-raa shireh maalidan	سر کسی را شیره مالیدن
to chat; to discuss; to debate	sar o kaleh zadan	سر و کله زدن
to find out; to investigate	sar o gush aab daadan	سر و گوش آب دادن
to be on the lookout (for sex)	sar o gush jonbidan	سر و گوش جنبیدن
to sort someone out; to do in	servis kardan	سرویس کردن
dog; bitch	sag	سگ
son of a bitch	sag pedar	سگ پدر
to be wasted (on the wrong person)	sag khor shodan	سگ خور شدن
to work like a dog	sag dow zadan	سگ دو زدن
to do nothing; to waste time	somaaq mekidan	سماق مکیدن
turd	sendeh	سنده
to be shown up; to be shamed	sang-e ru-ye yakh shodan	سنگ روی یخ شدن
quiet and deserted; dead; lifeless	sut o kur	سوت و کور
to let the cat out of the bag	suti dar kardan	سوتی در کردن
to back out of s.thing; to renege	suseh aamadan	سوسه آمدن
quickly; in a jiffy	seh sut	سه سوت
to reveal	seh kardan	سه کردن
to screw	sikh zadan	سیخ زدن
he/she's lost the plot	simaash qaati kardeh	سیماش قاطی کرده
piss	shaash	شاش
shit	shaash-e bozorg	شاش بزرگ
piss-the-bed	shaashu	شاشو
to piss	shaashidan	شاشیدن
angry; annoyed; pissed off	shaaki	شاکی
receiver of stolen goods	sharr khar	شر خر
get lost! ; sod off!	sharreto kam kon	شرتو کم کن !
to talk crap; to talk bollocks	she'r goftan	شعر گفتن
to get hard; to have a hard-on	shaq shodan	شق شدن
glutton	shekamu	شکمو
weak; faint; lethargic	shol o vel	شل و ول
lazy; slob; slovenly; untidy	shelakhteh	شل و پل کردن

wimp; weed; sissy; weakling	sholi babu	شلی ببو
on a high	shangul	شنگول
to be 'up for it'; to be willing (sexually)	shangidan	شنگیدن
loser; tosser	shut	شوت
jungle	shahr-e hert	شهر هرت
to dare; to be brave	shir shodan	شیر شدن
drug den	shireh khaaneh	شیره خانه
junkie; addict	shire'i	شیره ای
naughty; devil	sheytun	شیطون
chic; well-dressed	shik o pik	شیک و پیک
trick; trickery	shileh pileh	شیله پیله
damned; bloody (lit. 'ownerless')	saaheb mordeh	صاحب مرده
to get one over on s.o.	zarb-e shast neshaan daadan	ضرب شست نشان دادن
bald; slaphead	taas	طاس
to evade; to get out of s.thing	tafreh raftan	طفره رفتن
hanger-on; parasite	tofeyli	طفیلی
to hate (to do something)	'aar	عار آمدن
a load (of); lots	'aalameh	عالمه
to moan; to whimper	'ar zadan	عر زدن
moaner; cry-baby	'ar 'aru	عرعرو
love; lovely; great; ace; mint	'eshq	عشق
for the hell of it	'eshq-e laati	عشق لاتی
on a whim	'eshqi	عشقی
flirting (said of women)	'eshveh	عشوه
to flirt; to act coyly (said of women)	'eshveh aamadan	عشوه آمدن
(to cause an) uproar; to kick up a fuss	'alam shangeh (raah andaakhtan)	علم شنگه (راه انداختن)
never; no way	'umran	عمرأ
shit	'an	عن
pig-ugly; minger; minging	'an tarkib	عن ترکیب
snot	'an damaaq	عن دماغ
impotent	'anineh	عنینه
queer; strange; weird	'avazi	عوضی
to be oblivious; to not care	'eyn-e khiyaal nabudan	عین خیال نبودن
to snatch; to grab; to steal	qaap zadan	غاپ زدن
to do nothing; to waste time	qaaz cheraani	غاز چرانی
clever; smart; quick-witted	qebraaq	غبراق
peasant; village idiot	qorbati	غربتی
to moan; to grumble	qor qor kardan	غر غر کردن

to pose; to act like a snob	qompoz dar kardan	غمز در کردن
to disappear; to scarper	qeyb zadan	غیب زدن
to eavesdrop	faalgush istaadan	فالگوش ایستادن
loads; a lot; plentiful	fatt o faraavaan	فت و فراوان
bright; quick-witted	ferz	فرز
to dawdle; to mess about	fes fes kardan	فس فس کردن
tiny; titchy	fesqeli	فسقلی
so-and-so	folaani	فلانی
sharp and quick (lit. 'peppery')	felfeli	فلفلی
whizz-kid	fut-e aab	فوت آب
muddled-up; chaotic; a mess	qaaraashmish	قاراشمیش
mixed-up; jumbled	qaati paati	قاطی پاتی
to get mixed up	qaati shodan	قاطی شدن
to cheat someone; to defraud	qaaleb kardan	قالب کردن
rip-off merchant	qaaltaaq	قالتاق
to stand (s.o.) up	qaal gozaashtan	قال گذاشتن
to show off; to pose	qopi aamadan	قپی آمدن
stubborn	qodd	قد
fuss	qer o fer	قر و فر
appointment	qaraar o madaar	قرار و مدار
many thanks	qorbaan-e shomaa	قربان شما
thanks (informal)	qorbun-e aaqaa	قربون آقا
flighty; flirt; tarty	qerti	قرتی
good-for-nothing asshole	qoramsaaq	قرمساق
cheap; rubbish	qozmit	قزمیت
fake; phony; false; sham	qollaabi	قلابی
roughneck	qolchomaaq	قلچماق
bullying	qoldori	قلدری
sort; kind	qomaash	قماش
flirtatious	qamish	قمیش
ass; arse; bum	qonbol	قنبل
middleman; fixer; broker	kaar chaaq kon	کار چاق کن
work; business	kaar o kaasebi	کار و کاسبی
dosser; vagrant; tramp	kaarton khaab	کارتن خواب
big; thick	kat o koloft	کت و کلفت
to itch (to do something)	kerm daashtan	کرم داشتن
cunt	kos	کس
womaniser (lit. 'cunt-struck')	kos baaz	کس باز

old cunt	kos paareh	کس پاره
fuckwit; stupid cunt; dickhead	kos khol	کس خل
crap; bollocks; tall story	kos-e she'r	کس شعر
fucker; pimp	kos kesh	کس کش
pimping	kos keshi	کس کشی
friends and relatives; folks	kas o kaar	کس و کار
to steal; to pinch; to nick	kesh raftan	کش رفتن
nonsense; rubbish	kashk	کشک
mind your own business!	kashketo besaab	کشکتو بساب !
to be surprised	kaf boridan	کف بریدن
to foam (at the mouth, from talking)	kaf kardan	کف کردن
to get angry; to be pissed off	kofr dar aamadan	کفر در آمدن
to be pissed off	kofri shodan	کفری شدن
to ululate	kal kal kardan	کل کل کردن
to be annoyed; to be pissed off	kalaafeh shodan	کلافه شدن
trickster; cheat; fraud	kolaah bardaar	کلاهبردار
to play a trick	kalak zadan	کلک زدن
to argue; to bicker	kal kal kardan	کل کل کردن
to scrap; to cross swords with	kalenjaar	کلنجار
to fall over	kaleh paa shodan	کله پا شدن
dumb; thick; stupid; ignorant; dense	kaleh khar	کله خر
bigwig; head honcho	kaleh gondeh	کله گنده
to be pissed off; to be annoyed	kenef shodan	کنف شدن
to come down; to give in	kutaah aamadan	کوتاه آمدن
thick; stupid; idiotic	kowdan	کودن
bollocks! sod off!	kuft	کوفت!
arse; ass	kun	کون
bum-boy; queer (lit. 'torn ass')	kun paareh	کون پاره
to give ass; to be passive (in gay sex)	kun daadan	کون دادن
bum-boy	kundeh	کونده
ass-fucker; pimp; paedophile	kun kesh	کون کش
gay (lit. 'ass-fucker')	kun kon	کون کن
lazy	kun goshaad	کون گشاد
queer; bum-boy	kuni	کونی
cock; dick; prick	kir	کیر
dickhead (lit. 'donkey's dick')	kir-e khar	کیر خر
to be fucked up; to suck cock	kir khordan	کیر خوردن
to fuck up; to spoil; to ruin	kir zadan	کیر زدن

awful; crap; minging (lit. 'dick-like')	*kiri*	کیری
shitbag; bag of shite	*kise-ye 'an*	کیسه عن
to enjoy oneself; to have a good time	*keyf kardan*	کیف کردن
to fuck; to screw	*gaa'idan*	گاییدن
mouth; gob	*gaaleh*	گاله
to chat	*gap zadan*	گپ زدن
bully	*gardan koloft*	گردن کلفت
devious (lit. like a wolf)	*gorg*	گرگ
laziness	*goshaad baazi*	گشاد بازی
to be lazy	*goshaad budan*	گشاد بودن
excuse me; pardon my 'French'	*golaab be-ruyetaan*	گلاب به رویتان!
to suddenly appear; to blossom	*gol kardan*	گل کردن
to screw up; to fuck up	*gand zadan*	گند زدن
to cause a stink; to cause a scandal	*gand dar aamadan*	گند در آمدن
scandal; mudslinging	*gand o goh*	گند و گه
big; fat; huge; enormous	*gondeh*	گنده
fart	*guz*	گوز
fart-arse	*guzu*	گوزو
farty	*guzi*	گوزی
to fart	*guzidan*	گوزیدن
chubby; fat	*gushtaalu*	گوشتالو
shit	*goh*	گه
to regret (lit. 'to eat shit')	*goh khordan*	گه خوردن
to foul up; to screw up	*goh zadan*	گه زدن
dog shit	*goh-e sag*	گه سگ
to be dizzy or confused	*goh gijeh gereftan*	گه گیجه گرفتن
shitty	*gohi*	گهی
to get caught; to get stuck	*gir oftaadan*	گیر افتادن
to bother; to annoy	*gir daadan*	گیر دادن
amoral; without etiquette; trashy	*laa obaali*	لا ابالی
(non-penetrative) sex	*laa paa'i kardan*	لا پائی کردن
yob; thug	*laat*	لات
flirting	*laas*	لاس
to flirt	*laas zadan*	لاس زدن
flirty	*laasi*	لاسی
body (lit. 'corpse')	*laash*	لاش
old tart	*laashi*	لاشی
to kiss	*lab daadan*	لب دادن

to go red; to blush	labu shodan	لبو شدن
to beat up; to beat to a pulp; to bash	lat o paar kardan	لت و پار کردن
stubborn; obstinate; pig-headed	laj	لج
obstinacy; stubbornness	laj baazi	لج بازی
to act stubbornly	laj kardan	لج کردن
muck; slime	lajan	لجن
to shame; to disgrace	lajan maal kardan	لجن مال کردن
naked; nude	lokht o pati	لخت و پتی
lazy; slob	lash	لش
laziness; acting the slob	lash baazi	لش بازی
to take too long; to fuss	left daadan	لفت دادن
to string s.thing out; to embellish	left o lo'aab daadan	لفت و لعاب دادن
sponging; sycophancy	left o lis	لفت و لیس
to crave s.thing; to want; to miss	lak zadan	لک زدن
to stuff; to eat like a pig	lombaandan	لمباندن
huge; massive	landahur	لندهور
to throw in the towel	long andaakhtan	لنگ انداختن
mid-day; late in the morning	leng-e zohr	لنگ ظهر
legs; pins	leng o paacheh	لنگ و پاچه
mis-matched (of socks, shoes etc.)	lengeh be-lengeh	لنگه به لنگه
buffoonery; clowing around	lowdegi	لودگی
motherfucker	maadar jendeh	مادر جنده
motherfucker	maadar qahbeh (qahveh)	مادر قحبه (قهوه)
at your service	mokhlesetam	مخلصتم!
toilet; lavatory; loo	mostaraah	مستراح
boobs; tits; breasts	mameh	ممه
profitable; worthwhile	naan o aab daar	نان و آب دار
great; neat; awesome; wicked	vahshatnaak	وحشتناك
to die for s.thing; to crave s.thing	halaak-e chizi budan	هلاك چیزی بودن
to turn up (unexpectedly)	havaar shodan	هوار شدن
to fall in love (at first sight)	havaa'i shodan	هوائی شدن
hurriedly; in a rush	howl howlaki	هول هولکی
voyeur; pervert	hiz	هیز
come on; get a move on; hurry up	ya allaah	یا الله
ass; donkey; idiot	yaabu	یابو
fellow; guy; chap; whatsisname	yaaru	یارو
to waste time explaining to s.o.	yaasin khaandan	یاسین خواندن
crap; no good; pathetic; poor	yakh	یخ

to collar someone	*yakhe-ye kasi-raa gereftan*	یخه کسی را گرفتن
to bait	*yek dasti zadan*	یک دستی زدن
stubborn; pig-headed	*yek dandeh*	یک دنده
suddenly	*yek kaareh*	یک کاره
poor; down-and-out	*yek laa qabaa*	یک لا قبا
to be surprised	*yeke khordan*	یکه خوردن
to argue; to bicker	*yeki be-dow kardan*	یکی بدو کردن
slow; slowly	*yavaash*	یواش
furtively; in secret	*yavaashaki*	یواشکی

Index
of
English Words

The English index includes all of the English words which appear under the individual topics, as well as the nouns, adjectives, verbs and other parts of speech listed in the supplementary sections. To find the Persian equivalent of an English word, simply locate the English word alphabetically and follow the page reference.

adverb 199
adverbial 199
adversity 481
advertisement 106, 178, 309, 447, 479
advertisements 482
advertising 110, 309
advertising, hard 110
advice 106, 491
advice, to ask 519
advise, to 520
adviser 121
advocate, devil's 401
aerial 505
aerobe 34
aeroplane 2, 3, 458
aeroplane, jet 3
aerosol 132
aesthetics 291, 347
affable 337, 504
affair 480
affair, illicit 149
affair, love 149
affairs, administrative 360
affairs, foreign 360
affairs, political 360
affection 487
affiliation, group 415
affirmative 199
affix 201
affixation 287
affliction 481, 490
affluence 418
Afghanistan 87
afraid of, to be 523
afraid, to be 510
after 531
afterbirth 211, 212
afternoon 440
afternoon, late 441
after-shave 343
afterwards 531
again 531, 533
against 531
agate 193
age 140, 339, 440, 441, 485, 486
age, mental 387
age, old 138
agency 123, 492
agency, advertising 106
agency, consular 267
agency, debt collecting 123
agency, news 310
agency, real estate 109, 230
agency, travel 1, 407
agenda 369
agent 118
agent provocateur 380
agent, commission 112
agent, consular 267
agent, customs 123

agent, dehydrating 57
agent, diplomatic 265
agent, estate 409
agent, fixing 57
agent, forwarding 123
agent, oxidizing 57
agent, reducing 57
agent, undercover 104
agent, washing 60
agglutination 282
agglutinative 282, 287
aggressiveness 149
aggressor 319
aggro 104
agile 336
agitated 493
agitation 314, 363, 481
agnostic 349, 401
agnosticism 345, 401
Agnus Dei 391
agora 17
agree, to 520
agreeable 497
agreement 111, 199, 259, 261, 266, 377, 381, 482
agreement, arbitration 111
agreement, bilateral 264
agreement, commercial 122
agreement, written 122
agricultural 501
agriculture 95, 96, 145
agriculturist 146
Ahriman 390
Ahura Mazda 389
aid 480, 489
aid, first 219
aid, foreign 265
aid, legal 105
aide memoire 383
Aids 209
aim 488, 492
aims 320
aims, military 320
air (a.) 3, 505
air 3, 62, 96, 469
air, sea 405
airbase 314
airbed 404
airbus 456
aircraft, passenger 3, 458
airline 2
airmail 1, 255
airport 449
airship 458
aisle 12, 13
alarm 149, 151. 452
alarm, fire 229
alarm, smoke 232
alarm, theft 44, 46
alarmist 366

antigen 210
Antigua and Barbuda 87
anti-hero 293
anti-matter 354
antinomian 396
anti-pollutant 132
anti-pope 396
antireligious 396
anti-Semitism 383
antiserum 210
antispasmodic 217
antithesis 346, 350
antitoxin 210
antler 6
anus 33, 245
anvil 445
anxiety 149, 151, 385, 479
anxious 498, 503, 504
aorta 24, 240
apart from 533
apartheid 358
apartment 229, 447
apartment, furnished 229
apartment, one-roomed 229
apartment, two-bedroomed 229
apathy 385
apathy, political 362
apex (of a triangle) 303
aphid 38
aphorism 285, 293
apogee 19
apolitical 362
apologise, to 517
apostasy 268
apostate 273
apostle 271, 391, 393
apostolic 393
apostrophe 285, 287
apothecary 213, 409
apparatus 353, 484
apparatus, government 369
apparent 504
appeal 97, 98, 365
appeal, court of 100, 104
appear, to 516, 529
appearance 338, 339, 487
appeasement 263, 317
appendicitis 207
appendix (Anat.) 24, 240
appendix (Lit.) 293
appetite 167, 175
apple 185
appliance 238, 239, 277, 279
appliances 237
appliances, household 279
applicant 121
application 248
application, business 84
apply, to 511
appoint, to 529

appointment (to a position) 471
appointment 222, 492
apportionment 364
apposition 199, 287
appreciation 482
apprehension 479
apprentice 129, 474
apprenticeship 128, 129, 474
approach, to 508, 520
appropriate 286, 503
approval 261, 364
approve, to 523
apricot 185
April 42
apron 64
aquamarine 191
aquarium 158
Aquarius 20, 42
aquatic 156
aqueduct 10
aquifer 194
arabesque 18
Arabic 129
arable land 145
arbitration 114, 369, 416
arbitration, ad hoc 262
arbitration, appeal to 112
arc 305, 307
arcade 13, 16, 407, 447
arcade, shopping 408
arch 15
arch, horseshoe 15
arch, lancet 15
archaic 501
archaism 285
archangel 401
archbishop 395
archbishopric 395
archdeacon 395
archdiocese 395
archeologist 471
archery 426
archetype 348
archipelago 188
architect 17, 476
architectural 14
architecture 17, 130
architrave 15
archive 71
archives, consular 260
archives, diplomatic 260
archivist 471, 474
archpriest 395
arduous 503
area 49, 96, 135, 282, 307, 381, 368, 450, 468,
488, 491, 492
area, built-up 49, 450
area, free trade 262, 368
area, industrial 252
area, parking 230

area, penalty 430
area, surface 307
area, voting 368
areas, deprived 252
arena 431
arena, gymnastics 428
arena, sports 428
Argentina 87
argon 51
argot 287
argue, to 514
argument 101, 149, 346, 480, 489
argument from design 346
argument from order 346
argument, circular 345
argument, cosmological 346
argument, first cause 346
argument, ontological 346
Arian 389
Arianism 401
arid 464, 466, 497
aridity 466
Aries 20, 42
aristocracy 359, 418
aristocrat 359
aristocratic 504
aristodemocracy 358
arm 241, 242
arm, upper 241
armadillo 4
armchair 238
Armenia 87
armhole 64
armoured 456
armpit 243
armrest 237, 238
arms, suspension of 314
army 313, 317, 318, 319, 320
aroma 172
aromatherapy 217
aromatic 60
around 533
arouse, to 522
arrange, to 510, 524
arrangement 264, 377, 491
arrangements 482
array 71
arrears 110
arrest 99, 101
arrest, cardiac 209
arrest, to 514
arrhythmia 210
arrival 124, 454, 492
arrivals/departures board 1
arrive, to 515, 525
arrow 483
arsenic 51
arson 97
arsonist 97
art 18

art nouveau 18
art, Byzantine 18
art, Egyptian 18
art, Gothic 18
art, Islamic 18
art, Mesopotamian 18
art, Palaeolithic 18
art, pop 18
art, Romanesque 18
arteriosclerosis 212
artery 30, 243
artery, pulmonary 31
arthritis 222
arthritis, rheumatoid 215
artichoke 225
artichoke, Jerusalem 224
artichoke, prickly 225
article 197, 295, 311
articulator 280
artifice 12, 289
artificial 60, 503
artillery, armoured 314
artist 433, 477
artist, make-up 434
arts, contemporary 18
arts, fine 18, 131
arts, industrial 251
arts, performing 439
as soon as 532
asbestos 53
ascend, to 516
ascent 1, 2
ascetic 347, 349, 395
asceticism 347, 395
ASCII 71
ash 190, 461
ash, mountain 461
ashamed, to be 513
ashram 390
ashtray 233
ask, to 509, 516, 523, 527
asleep 497
asparagus 225
aspect 197, 483
aspen 461
asphalt 297
aspirations 479
aspirin 207
assassination 363
assassination, character 364
assault 98, 100
assembly 379
assembly, constituent 380
assembly, consultative 379
assembly, general 380
assembly, national 380
assembly, people's 379
assembly, representative 380
assembly, senate 379
assembly, unlawful 363

assert, to 511
assess, to 507
assessment 106, 247
assessment, continuous 126
assessment, loss 106
asset(s) 113
asset, capital 113
assets 484
assets and liabilities 113
assets, capital 107
assets, current 113
assets, fixed 113
assets, liquid 113
assets, real 113
assiduous 501
assign, to 529
assignment 127, 129
assimilation 27, 267, 383
assistance 266, 480, 489, 492
assistance, legal 105
assistant 410, 473
assistant, sales 474
ass-licker 337
associate 486
associate, to 522
association 361
association, articles of 117
association, freedom of 358
association, memorandum of 106
assonance 296
assurance 492
assured 503
aster 164
aster, China 163
asterisk 486
asthenosphere 191
asthma 207
astonished, to be 513
astonishment 148, 482
astral 20
astrodome 22
astrolabe 19
astrologer 21
astrology 21
astronaut 21, 474
astronavigation 23
astronomy 21, 129
astrophotography 21
astrophysicist 22
astrophysics 22
asylum seeker 260, 363
asylum seeker, political 260
asylum, economic 260
asylum, political 260, 363
asylum, right of 261, 367
asylum, territorial 363
at 532
atheism 268, 345, 347, 390, 391, 393
atheist 274, 391, 393, 400
athletics 427, 428

atlas, dialect 280
atlas, linguistic 280
atman 401
atmosphere 19, 55, 293, 436, 465
atmospheric 465
atom 51, 56, 351
atomic 356
atomism 345
atonement 398
A-to-Z 49
atrium 11, 12, 28
attaché 259, 267
attaché, commercial 267
attaché, military 267
attaché, press 267
attachment 71
attack 100, 316, 427
attack, air 316
attack, armed 316
attack, counter 429
attack, heart 216
attack, preventive 316
attack, to 513
attacker (Sport) 431
attain, to 525
attempt 103, 489
attendance 484
attendance, church 399
attendant, bath 473
attendant, beach 405
attendant, petrol pump 49
attention 482, 490
attention, to pay 511
attic 229
attorney, power of 124
attract, to 512
attraction 148, 150, 483, 489
attractive 336, 340, 502
attractiveness 148, 150, 484
attributes, the Divine 272, 396
attributive 201
attrition, war of 315
aubergine 224
aubergine, stuffed 170
auburn 69
auction 408
audacity 148, 150, 483
audience 434
audit 112
audit, marketing 120
audition 433, 439
auditor 112
auditorium 434
August 42
aunt, maternal 138
aunt, paternal 140
Australia 87
Austria 87
author 296
author, anonymous 296

beach 133, 403
beads, prayer 269, 392
beak 40
beam 231
bean 225
bean, broad 224
beans, haricot 175
beans, kidney 175
bear (Econ.) 115
bear 5
bear, koala 7
bear, polar 5
bear, to 526
bearable 500
beard 338
bearded 338, 498
beat 324
beat, to 523, 526, 527
beatification 393
beating (of a heart) 422
beatitude 396
Beaufort Scale 468
beautiful 498
beautify, to 522
beauty 338, 483, 485
beaver 6
because 531, 532
become, to 516, 522, 527, 528
bed 211, 237
bed and breakfast 226
bed, bunk 237
bed, double 226
bed, flower 164
bed, fold-up 237
bed, four-poster 237
bed, hospital 209
bed, oyster 156
bed, single 226
bed, to put to 525
bed, travel 237
bedclothes 233, 238
bedding 233, 238
bedroom 229
bedsit 229
bed-sore 209
bedspread 233
bee 37
beech 460, 461, 462
beef 174
beef-burger 176
beehive 39
beehive 49
beekeeping 180
beer 166
beetle 37
beetroot 224
beetroot, boiled 174
befit, to 522, 527
before 533
beggar 450

begin again, to 507
begin, to 516
beginning 479, 480
behave, to 515
behaviour 128, 338, 340, 395
behaviour, criminal 101
behaviour, group 417
behaviour, moral 417
behaviour, political 371
behaviour, social 417
behavourism 283, 347
behind 481, 532
beige 69
being 350, 492
being, absolute 350
being, chain of 347
being, pure 350
being, social 421
Being, Supreme 394
being, unity of 350
Belarus 88
belch 240
belfry 11
Belgium 88
belief 268, 390, 394, 397, 480
believable 494
believe, to 507, 517
believer 400
belittle, to 519
Belize 88
bell 256
bell, alarm 485
belladonna 160
belles-lettres 288, 479
belligerent 319
bellows 445
belly 243
belong to, to 519
beloved 502
below 495, 532
belt 66
belt, ammunition 318, 320
belt, black 430
belt, green 251
belt, safety 2, 48
belt, seat 2, 48
belvedere 16
bench 165, 239
bench, reserve 431
benchmark 84
bend 45, 447
bend, to 523
benediction 393, 400
beneficial 503
beneficiary 114
benefit 123, 486, 488
benefits 490
benign 213
Benin 88
benzene 35

beret 66
berry 460
berthage 118
best 495
best man 153
bestow, to 522
bet 486
bet, to 516
betatron 351
betray, to 527
better 495, 532
betting (e.g. on a horse) 180
between 532
bewildered 496
bewildering 496
bewilderment 484
bewitch, to 527
Bhutan 88
bias 415, 421
biased 341
Bible 398
Bible, Vulgate 398
bibliography 293, 294
bicameralism 382
bicentenary 153
biceps 245
bicycle 453, 456
bid 110
bid, escape 103
bid, sealed 110
bidder 110
bidding 121
bidet 230
big 499
bigger 494
biggest 494
bigotry 415, 416
bikini 67, 405
bilberry 184
bile 29, 31
bilingual 128, 282
bill (Law) 379
bill (restaurant) 172
bill 115, 117, 227, 257, 408, 409
bill, advance 109
bill, banker's 109
bill, clean 109
bill, credit 109
billboard 309
billiards 426
bin, rubbish 233
bin, waste paper 233
binary 77
bindweed 163
binoculars 20, 179, 353, 404
binomial 77, 303
biodegradable 133
bio-engineering 221
biographer 291
biography 291

biologist 30
biology 30, 128, 215
biology, space 20
biophysics 215
biopsy 209
bipartism 382
bipolarity 266
birch 462
birch, silver 462
bird 4, 36, 39
bird of paradise 39
bird, baby 36
bird, humming 40
bird, mynah 40
bird, sea 40
bird-catcher 38
birds, migratory 36
bird-watching 178
biro 256, 332, 343
birth 27, 29, 152
birth, virgin 390
birthmark 340
biscuit 167
bisector 307
bishop 389
bit 73
bitch 6, 336, 339
bite 72
bite, to 528
bit-map 73
bitter 496
bittern 36
bitumen 189, 193
bizarre 500
black 69
black and blue 69
blackberry 184
blackbird 38
blackboard 332
blackhead 212
blackleg 359
blacklist 379
blackmail 97, 367
blackout 218
blacksmith 143, 471
bladder 33, 245
bladder, gall 32, 244
blade, razor 343
blade, shoulder 240
blame 482
blame, to 529
blanket 230
blanket, electric 230
blare 423
blasphemy 398
bleach 59
bleak 158
bleed, to (fig.) 525
bleeding 213
blend (Gram.) 196

blend 479, 490
blend, to 522
bless, to 522
blind 221, 341
blind-man's-buff 178
blindness 221
blindness, colour 214
blinds 234, 238
blister 211
blizzard 465, 468
bloc 260
block of flats 233, 449
block the road, to 515
block, apartment 449
block, concrete 10
block, to 519
blockade 381
bloke 341
blood 28, 213, 242
bloodstone 195
bloom, in 162
bloom, to 527
blooming 162
blossom 162
blossom, pomegranate 164
blouse 63
blow 429, 487
blow, to 525, 530
blowtorch 446
blue 69
blue, navy 69
blue, sky 69
bluebottle 37
blue-tit 37
bluffing 362
blunder 148
blunder, to 529
blurb 288
blush, to 515
boar, wild 7
board, chess 179
board, chopping 276
board, circuit 74
board, ironing 235
board, white 332
boarding 2
boast of, to 529
boast, to 522
boasting 489
boat 404, 457, 458
boat, ferry 457
boat, fishing 158, 404, 458
boat, gravy 277
boat, motor 457
boat, patrol 320
boat, pedal 404
boat, rowing 457
boat, sailing 457
boat, sauce 277
boat, small 456

boat, torpedo 319
bodies, heavenly 19
body 24, 44, 72, 240, 241, 245, 335, 456
body, black 353
bodyguard 476
bodywork 456
bog 93, 96
boil 214, 219, 340
boil, to 524
boiled 496
boiler 229
boiling 55
bold 336
bold, to be 512
boldness 336, 483, 486
Bolivia 88
Bolshevism 362
bolt 231, 445
bomb 314
bombardier 313
bomber (i.e. aircraft) 314
bombing 314
Bonapartism 362
bond 54, 116
bond, bail 102, 118
bond, bank 117
bond, bearer 119
bond, coordinate 54
bond, covalent 54
bond, debenture 116
bond, double 54
bond, government 116
bond, hydrogen 54
bond, indemnity 116
bond, ionic 54
bond, mortgage 116
bond, polar 54
bond, public 116
bondage 481
bondsman 481
bone 24, 166, 208, 240
bone, cheek 240
bone, collar 240
bone, hip 240, 243
bone, shin 240
bone, shoulder 240
bonfire 152
bonnet 48
bonus 110
book 181, 333
book, appointments 332
book, cheque 256, 343, 408
book, exercise 128, 332, 343
book, guide 227
Book, Holy 398
book, invoice 114
book, name and address 343
book, prayer 398
book, receipts 114
book, self-study 129

building (n.) 14, 233, 449, 485
bulb 26, 235
Bulgaria 88
bulimia 209
bull (market) 115
bull 7, 146
bulldozer 456
bullfighting 7
bumblebee 37
bump (in the road) 46, 47, 48
bump into, to 513
bun (i.e. of hair) 341
bunch (of flowers) 161
bunch (of grapes) 185
bunch (of keys) 232
bunch 145
bunches (i.e. of hair) 341
bundle 145
bundle, vascular 28
burbot 158
burden, to 508
bureau de change 257
bureau, weather 464
bureau, writing 239
bureaucracy 362, 370, 414, 416, 417
bureaucratisation 370
bureaucratism 377
burette 53
burial 152
Burkina Faso 88
burn 216
burn, to 516, 526
burner (e.g. Bunsen burner) 55
burner 57, 60
burp 240
burst out laughing, to 515
burst, to 523, 524
Burundi 88
bus 82, 456
bus, address (Comp.) 82
bus, double-decker 447
bus, school 126
bush 93, 160, 184, 460
business 110, 408, 410, 471, 472, 475
businessman 471, 475
busy 499, 503
busy, to keep 514
but 531, 534
butane 53
butcher 410
butcher's 410
butler 471
butter 173
buttercup 162
butterfly 36, 160
buttocks 244
button 64, 77
buttonhole 65
buttress 11
buttress, flying 11

buy, to 513, 524
buyer 113, 408
buying 408
buying and selling 408
buzz 40, 422
buzzard 37
buzzard, black 38
buzzard, honey 38
buzzing 40, 422
by 531
by-election 360
by-law 358
by-product 58, 251
by-products, oil 252
byre 145, 146
C (computer language) 79
cabal 369
Cabalism 397
cabaret 181
cabbage 225
cabbage, stuffed 170
Cabbala 398
cabin, driver's 452
cabinet 377, 383
cabinet, filing 332
cabinet, shadow 377
cabinet, war 318
cable 81
cacography 280
cacophony 284
cadre 377
cadre, political 377
caesarism 382
Caesaropapism 358
café 181, 448, 449
cafeteria 173
cafetiere 234
cage 6, 38
cairngorm 190
cake 174
cake, chocolate 174
cake, cream 174
cake, currant 174
cakes 172
cakes, rice 175
calamity 488
calcium 59
calculate, to 527
calculation 306, 490
calculator 333, 344
calculator, pocket 333
calculus 303
calculus, differential 303
calculus, integral 303
caldarium 16
calendar 43, 332, 343, 440, 441
calendula 162
calf 7, 146, 243
caliph 368
caliphate 270, 368

capture, data 83
capture, to 507, 514
car (of train) 454
car 44, 46, 49, 448, 450, 456, 458
car, armoured 456
car, buffet 453
car, cable 456
car, dining 454
car, estate 456
car, freight 454
car, police 458
car, racing 456
car, second-hand 49
car, sleeping 454
caravan 48, 457
caravanserai 12, 16, 95
carbohydrates 32, 59
carbon 59
carbon monoxide 134
carbonate 59, 193
carburettor 48
carcinogen 216
card, bank 257
card, credit 227, 257, 410
card, identity 140
card, red 430
card, telephone 257
card, yellow 430
cardamom 176
cardboard 299
cardiac 219
cardigan 63
cardinal 398
cardiologist 220, 475
cardiology 218
cardoon 224
cards, game of 182
care, intensive 220
career 472, 474
carefree 494
careful 502
careful, to be 520
carefulness 490
caress, to 529
caretaker 233, 473
cargo 108, 403
cargo, general 108
cargo, return 121
cargo, transport of 249
caricature 294
caries 219
carnation 165
carnival 154
carnivore 32
carnivorous 32
carp 158
carp, freshwater 158
carp, to 529
carpel 160
carpenter 476

carpentry 130
carpet 234, 238
carpet, fitted 235, 239
carriage 124
carried out, to be 507
carrier 113, 122
carrier, aircraft 320, 458
carrot 225
carry out, to 507
carry, to 508, 513, 522
cart 458
cartel 119, 264, 377
cartilage 31, 244
cartoon 181, 437
cartouche 10
cartridge 82, 318
carved 12, 16
carwash 44
caryatid 16
case 197
case, cartridge 314
case, document 333
case, glasses 343
case, lower (letters) 256
case, pencil 333
case, upper 76, 256
casemate 12
cash 123, 491
cashew 184
cashier 474
casino 181
cask 481
casserole 277
cassette 181
cassette, blank 326
Cassiopeia 20
cassiterite 193
cast 288, 433
cast, plaster 211
casting 439
cast-iron 10, 12
castle 16, 94, 95, 449
Castroism 377
casual 339
casualty 47, 48
cat 7
cataclastic 193
catalogue 488
catalyst 59
catapult 319
cataract 207
catastrophe 134, 490
catatonia 385, 387
catch cold, to 524
catch fire, to 506
catcher, oyster 157
catechism 394
categories, Aristotelian 349
categorization 83, 487
category 428, 430

category, semantic 286
category, social 417
catenation 281
caterpillar 39
catfish 158
cathedral 398, 449
cathode 58, 59, 449
Catholic 398
Catholicism 399
cation 59, 62
cattle 94, 144
caucus 365
cauliflower 225
causality 348
causality, principle of universal 345
causative 198
cause 484, 485, 488
cause and effect 348
cause, efficient 348
cause, final 348
cause, first 349
causeway 250
caustic 57
causus belli 317
cautery 213
caution 479
cautious 502
cavalry 317
cave 95, 188
cave in, to 526
caviar 169
cavity 489
CD 79
CD player 238, 323
cease, to 522
ceasefire 313
cedar 461
cedar, Lebanese 461
ceiling 233
ceiling, consumption 249
celandine 164
celebrated 503
celebrity 487
celery 225
celestial 21, 400
celestite 192
celibacy 389
cell 30, 34, 62, 222
cell, dry 52
cell, nerve 35
cell, red blood 35
cell, white blood 35
cellar 14, 232, 233
cellar, salt 279
cellist 323
cello 323
cells, guard 35
cellulose 30, 56
celsius 55
cement 57, 298

cemetery 398, 449
censor 372
censorship 310, 372
census 372
centenary 154, 155
centipede 6, 38
Central African Republic 88
centralism 380
centralization 364
centre 307, 490, 492
centre, community 178
centre, computer 83
centre, detention 98
centre, exhibition 182, 252
centre, music 238
centre, research 248
centre, shopping 407, 411, 447
centre, tourist information 257
centre, town 450
centre, weather 468
centred (justification) 74
centrifuge 59
centrism 380
century 442
ceramic 14
cerebellum 33
cerebrum 24
ceremony 152, 154, 389, 400, 438
ceremony, awards 438
ceremony, closing 155, 438
ceremony, graduation 155
ceremony, opening 155, 252, 438
ceremony, standing on 150
ceremony, wedding 141
certain 496, 501, 503
certainly 533
certainty 479, 492
certificate 120, 490
certificate, birth 140, 257, 344
certificate, debenture 120
certificate, insurance 120
certify, to 511
cervical 215
cervix 30
cession 267
CFCs 134
Chad 89
chafe, to 526
chaffinch 39
chain 56, 344, 486
chain, food 29, 134
chainsaw 444
chair 238
chair, easy 238
chair, electric 102
chair, reclining 238
chairlift 456
chairman 473
chalcedony 192
chalcocite 194

chalcopyrite 194
chalk 59, 194, 299, 333
challenge 369, 430
chamber 10, 11
chamber, gas 97
chamomile 162
champion 429
champion, former 429
championships 431
chance (a.) 495
chance 480, 488
chancel 17
chancellor 374
chandelier 237, 238
change (of players) 426
change 415, 416, 465
change one's mind, to 510
change, catastrophic 369
change, chemical 54
change, cultural 369
change, energy 54
change, oil 45
change, physical 54
change, semantic 282
change, small 407
change, social 369
changeable 468
channel 82, 311
channel, underground water 134
chap 342, 492
chapel 401
chapter 488
character 81, 292, 294, 435, 437, 486
character, main 435
character, secondary or minor 435
characteristic 5, 287
characteristics, secondary sexual 34
characterization 292
charcoal 56
charge (Phys.) 351
charge 97, 258
charge d'affaires 264, 377
charge d'affaires ad interim 264
charge, excess 124
charge, extra 258, 454
charges, collection 124
charges, customs 124
charges, freight 121
charges, postal 258
charisma 365, 483
charm 483, 488
charm, to 527
charming 338
chart 302, 307, 491
chart, bar 85, 307
chart, pie 85, 307
charter 106, 266, 381
charterer 106
Chartism 366
chasm 188

chassis 44, 48, 72
chat, to 516
chateau 16
chauffeur 48
chauvinism 374
chauvinist 336
cheap 493
cheat 102, 340, 341
cheat, to 527
cheating 502
checkers 179
check-in desk 1
checking, error 72
check-out 411
checks and balances 120, 364
cheek 244
cheeky 495
cheer 486
cheerful 494, 497, 498
cheerfulness 484
cheese 168
cheese, Feta 168
cheese, grated 168
cheetah 8
chef 166, 226, 471
chef, head 171, 227
chemicals 135
chemist 213, 472
chemist's, dispensing 408
chemistry 129
chemistry, inorganic 57
chemistry, organic 57
chemistry, physical 57
chemotherapy 217
chemotropism 31
cheque 112, 227, 256, 408
cheque, bounced 112
cheque, crossed 112
cheque, dishonoured 112
cheque, open 112
cheque, post-dated 112
cheque, stale 112
cherish, to 517, 518
cherish, to 523
chernozem 190
cherry 185
cherry, black 184
chert 190, 192
cherubim 400
chervil 224
chess 180
chest 237, 238, 243
chestnut 185
chew, to 524
chiaroscuro 14
chiastolite 194
chic 337, 339, 499
chick 36, 144
chicken 39, 147
chicken, fried 175

climatic 505
climax 288, 433
climax, tragic 433
cling, to 524
clinic 214, 219
clink 422
clinking 422
clip, paper 333
clipboard 74
clippers, nail 344
clipping 199
cloak 65, 66
cloakroom 128
clock 2, 238, 441, 453
clock, alarm 441
clock, grandfather 441
clock, speaking 256
clock, wall 441
clock, water 441
clockmaker 441
clogs 66
cloisters 13
clone 25
clop 423
clopping 423
close (n.) 76
close, to 522
closed 199
closet 234, 237, 238
clot (Med.) 220
clot (sl.) 335, 336
clot, blood 33, 220
cloth, woollen 297
clothe, to 523
clothes 63, 64, 66
clothes, off-the-peg 67
clothes, second-hand 67
clothes, spare 66
clothes, suit of 67
clothes, worn-out 67
clothing 63, 64, 66
cloud 463
cloud, cirrocumulus 463
cloud, cirrus 463
cloud, convective 463
cloud, gas 19
cloud, lenticular 463
cloud, noctilucent 463
cloud, rain 463
cloud, storm 463
cloud, stratocumulus 463
cloud, stratus 464
cloudless 465
cloudlet 463
clouds, high 463
clouds, low 464
clouds, mare's tail 464
clouds, nacreous 464
cloudy 463
clover 162

cloves 173
clown 435
club 178, 425
club, golf 425
club, night 178
club, sports 178
club, youth 181
clumsy 338
clutch 48
coach 430, 456
coagulated, to be 529
coal 56, 133, 191, 298
coalition 259, 361
coarse 298
coarse 497, 498
coarseness 489
coast 95, 134, 188, 404, 405, 467
coastguard 403, 405
coastline 403
coat 4, 8, 63, 66
coat, full-length (female) 67
coat, fur 63
cobalt 59
cobble 192
cobbler 410
cobbler's 410
cobblestone 449
COBOL 82
coccyx 242
cochlea 28
cock-a-doodle-do 39
cockerel 37, 144
cockroach 37
cockscomb 163
cocoa 173
coconut 185
coconut, desiccated 175
cod 157, 158
code 78, 283
code, access 78
code, binary 78
code, character 78
code, city (i.e. part of phone number) 257
code, computer 78
code, error 78
code, instruction 78
code, machine 78
code, post 257
code, social 419
coded-decimal 78
coefficient 304
coercion 358, 485
coexistence, peaceful 267, 320
coffee 173
coffin 152
cognitariat 375
cohabitation 421
coherence 280
cohesion, group 421
coin 257

company 117, 249, 409, 474
company, cooperative 249
company, film 435
company, insurance 117, 409
company, multinational 117, 249
company, parent 117
company, railway 453
company, shipping 117
company, theatre 437
comparative 197
compare, to 519
comparison 490
compartment 454
compartment, freezer 276
compartment, luggage 452
compasses 444
compasses, pair of 332
compassion 491
compassionate 497, 504
compatibility 79
compatibility, hardware 79
compatibility, semantic 284
compensate, to 512
compensation 32, 100, 112, 118, 484
compere 311
competence 281, 488
competence, communicative 281
competence, linguistic 281
competition 26, 115, 181, 249, 428
complain, to 516, 529
complaint 100, 102, 117, 227, 409, 480
complaints (department) 407
complement 199
complete 501
completely 533
completion (of contract) 106, 107
completion 106, 247, 481
complex, industrial 252, 253
complex, inferiority 386, 387
complex, military-industrial 379
complex, Oedipus 387
complex, semantic 287
complex, shopping 411, 450
complex, superiority 385
complexion 336, 338
compliant 503
component 280
compose, to (i.e. a piece of music) 511
compose, to 526, 530
composer 322, 325, 326
composite 14, 190
composition 322, 323, 426, 485
composure 342
compound 54, 287
compound, inorganic 26
compound, organic 26
compounds, iron 54
comprehend, to 527
comprehension 282
compression 85

compression, data 85
comprise, to 516, 519
compromise 372
compromising 498
compulsory 107
compulsory 493, 504
computation 490
compute, to 527
computer 78, 82, 238, 332, 333
computer, central 82
computer, dedicated 82
computer, desktop 82
computer, home 82
computer, laptop 82
computer, notebook 82
computer, office 82
computer, palmtop 82
computer, personal 82, 181
computer, portable 82
computer, super 71
computerese 75
computerization 82
computer-literate 71
computing, mathematical 83
comrade 149
comrades 371
comradeship 149, 371
concave 355, 501
conceal, to 509, 523
concealment 380
conceited 503
concentrate 170
concentrated 58
concentration 58, 482
concept 348, 349, 420
conception, immaculate 389
conceptualism 349
concern, to 519
concert 181
concerto 325
concession 360
conciliation 316, 372
conclusion 481, 484
concord 199, 479
concordance 285, 293
concordat 378
concrete 10, 198, 297
concrete, reinforced 10
concretion 189, 192
concurrence 482
concurrent 306, 308
concussion 217
condemn, to 519
condensation 26, 60, 465, 467
condition 117, 299, 483, 486
conditional 198
conditioner, air 231, 232
conditioning, air 231
conditions 467
conditions, examination 129

condom 211, 219, 344
condor 39
conductivity 353
conductor 56, 324, 353, 354
conductor, lightning 465
cone 35, 306
cone, ice-cream 167
cone, pine 462
cone, traffic 47
confectioner's 407, 409, 410
confederacy 260, 363
conference 265
conference, press 311
conferencing, video 85
confess, to 507
confession 97, 399
confetti 155
confidence 479
confidence, vote of 370
confident 503
confidential 497, 502
configuration 74
confinement, solitary 99, 101
confinement, temporary 98
confirm, to 510, 511
confirmation 110
confiscation 102
conflict 150, 421, 489
conflict, class 364, 421
conflict, cultural 421
conflict, industrial 421
conflict, international 265, 318
conformism 383
conformity 421
confrontation 371
Confucianism 389
confused 499, 502
confusing 493, 502
confusion 481, 487
confusion, mental 385
congeal (e.g. fat or oil), to 527
congealed, to be 529
conglomerate 190
Congo 90
congratulate, to 510
congregation 392
congress 378
congruent 308
conic, improper 306
conifer 462
conjugation 198
conjunct 287
conjunction 197
conjunction, correlative 198
conjunction, subordinating 197
conjunctivitis 222
con-man 99, 103
connect, to 523
connection 1, 138, 139, 452, 453, 479, 485
connections 139

connective 197
connoisseur 489, 492
conquer, to 510, 528
conquest 313, 314, 318, 482
conscience 341, 492
conscience, collective 383
consciousness, black 362
consciousness, class 358, 413
consciousness, false class 358
consciousness, group 413
consciousness, revolutionary 358
consciousness, stream of 290
conscript 317
consecration 392
consecutive 502
consensus 261, 358, 421
consent 115, 371, 482, 485
conservation 133, 135
conservation, energy 133
conservatism 380
conservative 380
Conservative party 367
consignee 120
consignment 106, 121
consist of, to 519
console 82
consonant 282
consonantal 284
consortium 120, 378
consortium, bank 120
conspiracy 365, 483
constant 496, 497
constant proportions, law of 58
constant, Planck's 352
constantly 532
constellation 19
constipation 223
constituency 368
constituent 198
constituent, semantic 284
constitution 359, 376
constitution, written 376
constitutionalism 380
constraint, social 421
construct, to 526
construction 247, 281, 485
consul 265
consulate 265
consulate-general 263
consul-general 263
consult, to 519
consultation 271
consumables 83
consume, to 519
consumer 121
consumption, energy 135
consumption, petrol 49
contained, to be 529
container 276
containment (of Communism) 263

cormorant 38
corn 145, 221
corn on the cob 224
cornea 31
corner 430, 489
cornfield 146
cornflower, blue 163
cornice 13, 16
coronation 152, 363
corporal 317
corporation, multinational 264
corporatism 374
corps 317
corps, consular 267
corps, diplomatic 267
corpse 99
corpus 286
correct 497, 498, 499
correction, error 74
correctness 284, 484
correlative 201
correspondence, diplomatic 266
correspondent 311, 484
correspondent, economic 311
corridor 13, 14, 232
corrosion 189
corrupt, to 517, 520
corrupt, to become 517
corrupted 337
corruption 102, 272, 484
corruption, political 376
cortege (of çars) 154
corundum 192, 194
cosine 302, 306
cosmic 22
cosmogony 349
cosmology 349
cosmonaut 22
cosmopolitanism 261, 366
cosmos 22
cost 119, 124, 227, 253, 258, 488
cost and freight 119
cost, extra 258
cost, operating 124
cost, packaging 124
Costa Rica 90
costly 501
costs 490
costs, shipping 124
costs, travel 124
costume, one-piece swimming 67
costume, swimming 67, 405
cot 237
cottage 146, 234
cotton (a.) 299
cotton (n.) 299
cotyledon 32
couch 238
couchette 452
cough 216

cough, to 515, 526
cough, whooping 216
council 374
council, town 250, 374, 449
councillor 370
counsel 491
counsellor 476
count, to 516, 527
countable 198
counter 256, 408
counter, Geiger 354
counter-culture 375
counter-espionage 264, 375
counterfoil, receipt 112
counter-insurgency 375
counter-intelligence 374
counter-propaganda 375
counter-revolution 374
counter-revolutionary 375
counterscarp 13
counting, vote 370
countless 495
countries, backwarded 265
countries, developing 265
countries, emerging 265
countries, non-aligned 265, 378
country (a.) 93
country 134, 266, 377, 468
country, blend 265
country, forwarding 119
country, home 119
countryside 93, 94, 143, 145
coup d'etat 378
couple 139, 140, 483
couplet 288
courage 483, 484, 486
courageous 498, 499
courgette 225
courier 314
courier, diplomatic 260
course (of treatment) 214
course (Sport) 431
course 128
course, of 531
course, pre-university 128
course, training 473
court 100
court, criminal 100
court, crown 100
court, divorce 100
court, high 100
court, international criminal 263
court, kangaroo 100
court, law 100
court, magistrate's 100
court, revolutionary 100
court, tennis 428
courteous 504
courtesy 479
courthouse 101

current, alternating 353
current, direct 353
current, electric 55
curriculum 414
curry 173
curse 489, 491
cursive 284
cursor 83
curtain 230, 237, 433
curve 307
curve, algebraic 303
curve, normal distribution 33
curve, plane 307
cushion 237
cusp 12
custard 173
custody 98, 99, 140
custody, police 98
custom 292, 485
custom, international 264
customary 499, 503
customer 121, 175, 228, 252, 408, 411
customisation 83
customs (traditions) 413
customs 2, 120, 379, 454
cut 433, 481
cut and paste 73
cut off 501
cut off, to 518
cut, electricity 234
cut, rapid 433
cut, short 47
cut, to 522, 524, 528
cuticle 26
cutlet 173
cutter, paper 333
cutting 162, 481
cuttlefish 157
cyanide 57
cyclamen 160
cycle 56, 290, 294
cycle, carbon 27, 55
cycle, life 30
cycle, menstrual 28, 242
cycle, nitrogen 27, 55
cycle, water 27, 55
cycling 179, 428
cyclist 47, 428
cyclone 465, 466
cyclone, tropical 466
cyclotron 354
cylinder 301
cymbals 324
cynicism 381
cypress 461
Cyrenaicism 400
cyst 215, 219
cystitis 207
cytogenetics 222
cytology 223

cytoplasm 34
czarism 372
Czech Republic 88
dab 158
daddy 137
daffodil 165
dagger 316
dahlia 162
daily (newspaper) 310
dainty 500
dairy 146, 411
daisy 164
daisy, ox-eye 163
damage 100, 113, 132, 217, 463, 484
damage, brain 217
damages 46, 100, 113
damp 468
damson 184
dance 153, 180
dance, to 515, 526
dancer 473
dancer, ballet 435
dancing 180
dandelion 162, 163
danger 113, 133, 484
danger, to put in 509
dangerous 133, 497
dangle, to 522
dare, to 512
daring 483
dark 495
darkness 465, 482
darkroom 11
darling 500
dart 483
darts 178
dash 282, 283
dashboard 46
data 76, 107, 416
data, control 76
data, sense 347
database 72
database, relational 72
date 110, 152, 169, 184, 226, 440, 482, 492
date, acceptance 110
date, delivery 110
date, expiry 110, 115
date, shipment 110
date, to (i.e. to put the date) 510
dating, carbon 59
dative 197
daughter 139
daughter-in-law 139, 140
dawn 441, 467
day 20, 43, 227, 441, 467
day after tomorrow, the 440
day before yesterday, the 440
Day of Judgement 395
day, holy 395
Day, Lord's 395

dermatology 211
dervish 393
descent 2
deschooling 380, 419
describe, to 511
description 282, 289
desert 93, 94, 95, 132, 134, 187, 188
desert, salt 96
deserted 502
deserter 318
deserve, to 516, 519
deserving 502
desiccate, to 524
design 250
design, computer-aided 80
design, set 436
design, system 80
designation 488
designer 474
designer, fashion 474
desirable 503
desire 175, 491
desire, sexual 151
desire, to (sexually) 516
desire, to 513
desired 503
desk 239, 334
desk, check-in 1
desk, information 1, 257, 452
desolate 505
despatch, to 527
desperate 494, 504
despise, to 529
despite 533
despot 368
despotism 359, 368
despotism, Asiatic 359
despotism, oriental 359
dessert 170
de-Stalinization 359
destination 2, 122, 454
destiny 486
destroy, to 510, 513, 520
destroyed 505
destroyer 320
destruction 12, 466
destruction 484
destruction, mutually assured (MAD) 319
details 104, 483
detain, to 508
detection 489
detective 103
detector, mine 319
detention 98, 99
detergent 60, 134, 135
determination 487
determiner 200
determining, divine 398
determinism 346, 348, 375
determinism, economic 365

detest, to 520
detestable 501
detour 47
detritus 190, 192
devaluation 106, 111, 364
develop, to (e.g. a photograph) 517
develop, to 523
developed 248
developer 79
development 248, 365
development, economic 112, 365
development, industrial 248
development, political 365
development, social 415
development, software 79
development, spiritual 391
deviance 413
deviation 413, 280
device 77, 238, 239, 484
device, active 71
device, communications 77
device, peripheral 77
device, storage 71
devices 237, 276
devil 339, 394
devil, Tasmanian 6
Devil, the 268, 396
devilfish 156, 339
devilish 499
Devil-worship 396
devotion 394
devotional 397
devour, to 522, 525
devout 390
dew 161, 467
dexterity 491
diabetes 221
diagnosis 212, 222
diagonal 301, 305, 307
diagram 307, 491
diagram, Venn 307
dial (a number), to 516
dialect 286, 291, 294
dialectic 347
dialectology 286
dialogue 294, 437, 489
dialysis 214
diameter 305
diamond 52, 189
diamonds (in cards) 179
diaper 489
diaphragm 27, 242
diarrhoea 208
diary 290, 332, 343, 440
diatomite 191
diatribe 291
dicotyledons 28
dictator 368, 370
dictatorship 370
dictatorship, constitutional 370

diction 287
diction, poetic 294
dictionary 287, 293, 294, 332, 333
dictionary 488
didacticism 289
die, to 529
die, to cause to 529
dielectric 353
diesel 133, 298
diet 214
diet, balanced 29
difference 148, 479
difference, potential 351
difference, time 440
different 501, 502
different, to be 517
differential 303, 305
differentiation, logarithmic 307
difficult 499, 503
difficulties, to have 515
difficulty 335, 479, 486, 489, 490
diffident 501
diffraction 352
diffractometer 352
diffuse, to 528
diffusion 25, 53, 61, 352, 356
dig, to 528
digest (n.) 289
digest, to 529
digestion 32, 34
digger 456
digit 78, 303, 305, 487
digital 78
digitalis 160
digitised 78
dignified 502, 504
dignity 486
diligent 501
dill 225
dilute 56
dim 501
dimension 10, 480, 481
dimer 56
diminish, to 528
diminutive 197
dimple 241, 336
din 422, 423
dinner 172, 227
diorite 191
diploma 128
diploma, associate 129
diplomacy 262, 370
diplomacy, basic 262
diplomacy, democratic 262
diplomacy, dollar 262
diplomacy, gunboat 373
diplomacy, imperialist 262
diplomacy, Machiavellian 370
diplomacy, open 262
diplomacy, people's 370

diplomacy, preventative 262
diplomacy, secret 262
diplomacy, shirt-sleeve 262
diplomacy, shuttle 262
diplomacy, summit 262
diplomat 262, 370
dipstick 46
direct 454, 503
direct, to (e.g. a film) 518
directing 437, 485
direction 46, 48, 435, 453, 483
direction, stage 435
directions (for use) 256
director (of company) 476
director (stage or screen) 437
director, deputy 474
director, film 437, 475
director, managing 252, 476
director, stage 438
director, theatre 437
directors, board of 253
directory 80, 81, 485
directory, default 80
directory, file 81
directory, telephone 256
dirt 94, 488, 491
dirty, to 518
dirty, to become 518
disability 221
disability, physical 221
disabled 221
disabled person 207
disabled, the 221
disaccharide(s) 28, 56
disadvantage, cycle of 416
disagreeable 504
disagreement 148, 479
disappear, to 520
disappointed 499
disapprove, to 506
disarmament 316, 484
disassociation 387
disaster 488, 490
disaster, air 2
disc, tax 44
discharge 132, 133, 351, 352
disciple 393
discipline 480
discipline, military 313
discipline, party 361
disclose, to 528
disconnection 480
discontinuity 480
discontinuous 200
discount 1, 111, 226, 256
discount, bank 111
discount, cash 111
discount, special 111
discount, trade 111
discouraged 498

division, armoured 319
division, first 427
divisions, local 364
divisor 301
divorce 140, 150, 418
Djibouti 89
do, to 528, 529
dock 247
dockage 118
doctor 210, 472
doctorate 128
doctrinaire 359
doctrine 345, 381, 390
doctrine, act of state 262
doctrine, counterforce 262
document 79, 104, 115, 121, 372, 490
document, source 79
documentary (a.) 294
documentary (film) 311, 437
documentation 49
documents 49, 107
documents, classified 359
documents, confidential 359
documents, diplomatic 259
documents, secret 359
documents, shipping 107
dodecagon 303
dodecahedron 303
dodgy 337
doe 4
dog 6, 145
dog elder (Bot.) 160
dogberry 185
dogfish 157
dogfish, spiny 158
doggerel 292
dogma 369, 375, 393
dogmatism 347, 365, 369
do-it-yourself 445
Doldrums 467
doll 487
dolomite 191
dolphin 5, 156
domain 81
dome (of mosque or church) 450
dome (of mosque) 273
dome 16
dome, salt 194
domesticated 493
domicile 259
dominance 372
dominant, to be 512
Dominica 89
Dominican Republic 89
dominion 266
donate, to 525
donjon 13
donkey 5, 143, 144
door 94, 145, 453
door, car 46

door, front 232
doorman 227, 473
doormat 230, 234
doorstep 230
doorway 232
Doppler effect 351
Doric 14
dormitory 127
dot 491
dot matrix 83
double (doppelganger) 341
double 342
double entendre 290
doubles (tennis etc.) 428
doubt 487
doubt, to 516
doubtful 503
dough 169
doughnut 168
dove 39
dovecote 39
down 495
down payment 408
download 72
downpour 464
downtown 450
dowry 138
doxology 393
Draco 19
draft 109
draft, final 126
draft, first 127
draft, sight 109
drag, to 528
Dragon 19
dragonfly 37
drain, brain 376
drain, to 522, 524
drainpipe 235
drama 290, 438
dramatic 295
dramatis personae 288, 433
dramatist 434
draper 407
drapery 407
draught 468
draughts 179
draughtsman 476
draw 426
draw a sword, to 530
draw out, to 528
draw, goalless 426, 431
draw, to 520, 528, 529
drawee 109
drawer (of cheque) 109
drawer 238
drawers, chest of 238
drawing 12, 13
drawing 491
drawknife 445

dread 149, 151, 482
dread, to 523, 530
dreadful 505
dream 484
dream, the American 371
dream, to 513
dreamer 338
dress 63
dress up, to 523
dress, evening 67
dress, head 65
dress, long 63
dress, modest 270
dress, to 509, 523
dress, woman's 63
dressage 431
dressed, to get 509
dresser, kitchen 239
dressing (Med.) 210, 221
dressing 169
dressing, salad 171
drill 446
drill, electric 446
drill, hand 446
drill, pneumatic 446
drink (alcoholic) 175
drink 176
drink, to 522, 525, 530
drink, to cause to 530
drink, yoghurt 170
drinker 339
drinking 182
drinks, alcoholic 175
drinks, soft 175
drip, intravenous 216
drip, to 524
drive (n.) 180
drive, cassette 82
drive, disk 77
drive, gear 47
drive, hard disk 77
drive, to 515, 525
driver 47, 78, 453
driver, ambulance 473
driver, careless 47
driver, device 77
driver, engine 453
driver, printer 78
driver, taxi 473
driver, train 473
driving 47, 180
driving, careless 47
drizzle 467, 469
droll 503
dromedary 6
drop, to 515
drop-out 336, 413
droppings 38
drops, ear 218
dropsy 208

drought 466, 468
drowsy 497
drug 214
drugs 104, 182, 213
drum 323, 324, 325
drum, bass 324
drummer 324
drumstick 323
drunkard 335, 338, 339
dry 464, 466, 497
dry, to 513, 524
drycleaner's 64, 408
dryer, clothes 232
dryer, tumble 232
dual 197
dual-carriageway 447
dualism 347
dubbing 435
dubious 503
duck 4, 8, 36, 40, 143, 147, 175
duckling 5
ductility 57
dues 118, 112, 251
duet 323
dugong 158
dugout 456
dulcimer 324
dumb 340
dumbo 337
dump, ammunition 313
dump, screen 78
dumping 108
dune, sand 187, 188, 404
dungeon 101
duodenitis 207
duodenum 29
duologue 290
duplex 77
duplicate 480
duration 121, 442, 454, 485, 487, 490
dust 94
dust off, to 524
duster 235
duster, feather 235
duties 251
duties, customs 113, 118
duty 112, 492
duty, probate 120
duty-free 2, 118
duvet 230, 235
dwarf 340
dweller, city/town 449
dweller, mountain 96
dwelling 490
dye, to 525
dyer 473
dyes 56
dyke 193
dynamic 74
dynamics 417

586

dynamics, group 363
dynamics, social 414
dynamite 56
dynasty 368, 486
dysentery 208
dysmenorrhoea 218
dyspnoea 212
eager 503
eagerness 479
eagle 38
ear 32, 244
earache 220
eardrum 241
earlobe 245
early 441
early-riser 339
earnings 250
earring 344
ear-splitting 423, 501
earth 28, 94, 95, 144, 145, 161, 190, 353, 466
earth, the 22, 134
earthenware 298
earthquake 188, 191, 467
earwig 39
ease 485, 488
easel 15
east 467
Easter 154, 397
easy 493, 498
easy going 493
eat, to 525
eat, to cause to 525
eating and drinking 167
eau de cologne 343
eaves 16
eavesdropping 359
ebony 297, 460
eccentric 339
ecclesiastic 399
echo 422
eclipse, lunar 20
eclipse, solar 22
ecologist 134
ecology 134
e-commerce 76, 408
econometrics 107
economic 107, 493
economical 493
economics 107, 126, 360, 480
economics, international 259
economist 107
economy 107, 250, 360, 480
economy, controlled 360
economy, free 360
economy, free market 107
economy, linguistic 284
economy, market 107
economy, mixed 360
economy, money 107
economy, planned 107

economy, political 360
ecosystem 25, 132
ecstasy 148, 150
Ecuador 87
ecumenical 402
ecumenism 392, 415
eczema 208, 211
edge 67, 235, 303, 306
edible 169
editing 85
editing, film 437
editing, sound 436
edition 289, 296, 309
edition, new 309
editor 85, 310, 434, 477
editor, film 472
editor, newspaper 473
editorial 310
editor-in-chief 310
educate, to 523
education 126, 127, 413, 488
education, remedial 126
eel 158
effect 479, 482
effect, Doppler 351
effect, greenhouse 132
effect, piezoelectric 351
effective 503
effector 25
effects, side 221
effects, sound 75, 433
effects, special 434
effects, stage 433
effeminate 338, 498
efficiency 355, 488
efficient 501
efflorescence 57
effluent 135
effort 482, 488
effort, team 426
effort, to make an 528
egalitarianism 380
egg 168
egg, boiled 168
egg, fried 168, 176
egg, scrambled 168
eggcup 276
eggplant 224
eglantine 165
ego 387, 420
egocentric 386
egocentrism 386
egoism 347, 386
Egypt 91
eiderdown 235
ejaculate, to 523
ejaculation, premature 209
ejection (of disk) 73
El Salvador 87
elasticity 355

extractor, fruit juice 276
extradition (of criminals) 259
extra-linguistic 281
extraordinary 339, 496, 500
extraterrestrial 481
extremely 532
extremism 360
extroversion 385
eye 27, 241
eye shadow 344
eye, black 219
eye, naked 20
eyebrow 240
eyelash 245
eyelid 241
eyeliner 344
eyes 336
fable 288
fabricate, to 522
façade 14, 18, 236
face (e.g. of a cube) 301
face 243, 308, 336, 487
face, clock 441
facilities 74, 226
facilities, communication 248
facilities, credit 111
facilities, leisure 226
facilities, new 248
facilities, sports 226
facing 533
fact 383, 484, 491
fact, in actual 533
faction 272, 369, 484, 488
factor 118, 301
factor, bunker adjustment 117
factor, limiting 31
factoring 118
factory 134, 251, 449, 475
factory, tank-building 251
factual 505
fade out, to 529
fade, to 523, 525
faded 498
faeces 33, 220
Fahrenheit (scale) 356
faience 15
fail, to 515
failure 76, 487
failure to pay 118
failure, financial 436
failure, hardware 76
failure, power 81
fainting 218
fair 152, 154, 500
fair, annual 152
fairground 154
fait accompli 375
faith 268, 390
faith 480, 485
faith, age of 397

faith, articles of 389
faith, practical 390
faithful 390
faithfulness 151
falange 376
falangism 376
falcon 36, 38
falcon, royal 38
fall asleep, to 513
fall in drops, to 524
fall, free 353
fall, to 522
fallacy 347, 349
fallacy, logical 349
fallout, radioactive 132
fallow 143
falsificationism 350
fame 487
family (a.) 138
family (n.) 27, 138, 140, 232, 416
family, extended 416
family, man of the 141
family, nuclear 139, 416
family, one-parent 138, 416
famous 341, 503
fan 63, 237
fan, alluvial 189
fanatic 399
fanaticism 364
fancy, passing 151
fang 5
fanlight 231
fantasy 289, 293, 482
faraway 498
fare 405, 452, 454, 457, 489
farm 96, 147
farm, cattle 147
farm, dairy 147
farm, fish 144
farmer 94, 95, 145, 146, 475,
farmer, tenant 146
farmhand 146
farmhouse 94, 144
farming 95, 96, 145
farming, mixed 146
farmyard 144, 147
fascinate, to 527
fascism 376
fashion 67, 486
fast 496
fast, to move 525
fasten, to 508, 522, 524
fasting 271
fat (of meat) 169
fat 27, 336, 496, 501
fatalism 346
fatalist 398
fate 486, 488
father 137
Father Christmas 152

594

frightening 495, 505
frigid 499
frigidity 385, 387
fringe 336
frivolity 486
frivolous 499
frog 6
from 531
front (of a vehicle) 456
front (of building) 236
front 315
front, cold 465
front, in 532
front, national 365
front, occluded 465
front, popular 365
front, united 365
front, warm 465
front, weather 465
frontier 265, 486, 490
frontier, customs 121
frontiers, militarised 319
front of, in 532
frost 464, 469
frost, hoar 467
frostbite 216
fructose 58
fruit 33, 135, 175
fruit and nuts, dried 169
fruit, dried 167
fruit, forbidden 393
fruiterer 411
fuchsia 162, 163
fuchsite 193
fuck, to 526, 528
fuel 48, 57, 134
fuel, diesel 47, 57
fuel, nuclear 353
fugitive 102
fugue 387
fulgurite 191
full 495
full-stop 286, 491
fun 179
function 285, 301
function, algebraic 301
function, exponential 301
function, interpersonal 285
function, logarithmic 301
functional 285
functionalism 349, 419
functionary, international 264
functions, consular 267
fund 124
fund, contingency 124
fund, emergency 124
fund, pension 117
fund, reserve 124
fundamentalism 362, 391
fundamentalism, Islamic 269, 362

fundamentalist 391
fundamentals (of belief) 390
fundamentals of religion, the 268
funfair 181
funicular 457
funnel 404, 445
funny 337, 497, 503
fur 4, 8, 298
furious 493, 497, 500
furnace 276
furnace, blast 59
furnishings 237
furniture 230, 235, 237, 239
furniture, piece of 239
furrow 145
fury 487
fuse 234
fusion 56, 62, 353, 355, 357
fusion, nuclear 357
fuss 486
futility 481
future 132, 440, 471, 493
futurism 10
gaabro 194
Gabon 90
gadfly 37
gaffe 148
gain 351, 352, 486
gains 250
gains, capital 122
gait 339
gaiter 65
galaxy 22
galaxy, elliptical 22
galaxy, irregular 22
galaxy, spiral 22
galaxy, super 19
gale 465
galena 191
gallbladder 32, 244
gallery 10, 11, 18
gallery, art 11, 16, 179, 182, 448, 450
gallop 4
gallop, to 523
gallop, to cause to 523
gallows 99
gallstone 216
galvanized 51
galvanometer 355
Gambia 90
gambling 181
game 72, 178, 425, 430
game, adventure 72
game, arcade 72
game, ball 179
game, computer 72, 178
game, video 72
games 131
Games, Olympic 425
games, war 314

gills 24
ginger 171, 224
gingivitis 207
giraffe 6
girder 483
girdle 66
girdle, pectoral 244
girdle, pelvic 244
girl 139
girl, little 338
girlfriend 149, 179
gist 483
give a lift, to 525
give a speech, to 515
give back, to 509
give birth to, to 526
give condolences, to 510
give discount, to 510
give off light, to 525
give one's blessing, to 515
give permission, to 506
give refuge, to 509
give trouble, to 525
give up, to 510
give, to 513, 522, 525
glacier 188
glad 497, 499
gladiolus 164
gladness 484, 486
glance 491
gland 218
gland, exocrine 218
gland, lachrymal 218
gland, lymph 218
gland, pituitary 31, 222, 244
gland, salivary 218
gland, thyroid 31, 218, 244
glands, adrenal 31, 244
glands, endocrine 31, 218
glasnost 379
glass 57, 134, 279
glass, fibre 297
glass, magnifying 332
glass, stained 15
glass, tea 166, 276
glass, wine 278
glasses 339
glasshouse 162, 235
glassy 193
glaucoma 207
glazier 474
glazing, double 233
glen 94
glider 458
glitch 71
glitter, to 525
glittering 494
globalism 261
globalization 261, 366
globe 333

gloom 482
gloomy 501
glorify, to 523
glorious 502
glory 480
gloss (Lit.) 290
glossary 285, 287, 296
glottis 27
gloves 64
gloves, oven 277
glow, to 523, 525
glow-worm 39
glucose 32, 55, 58
glue 298, 445
glycogen 32
glycol 60
gnat 36
gnaw, to 524
gneiss 192
gnosis 272, 348, 397
Gnostic 390, 397
GNP 112
go after, to 514
go away, to 514
go back, to 508
go bad, to 513, 517
go fast, to 511
go for a walk, to 518
go forward, to 512
go lame, to 529
go off, to 524
go on a journey, to 519
go on strike, to 507
go over the top, to 515
go shopping, to 513
go too far, to 509, 511, 515
go up, to 508
go, to 515, 523, 525
goal 124, 320, 427, 430, 492
goal, equalising 430
goalkeeper 427
goalmouth 427
goalpost 426, 428
goat 4, 143
goatherd 143
gobble, to 522
go-between 123
God 268, 270, 390, 393, 402, 484
God, act of 121
God, belief in 393
God, City of 396
God, Kingdom of 400
God, man of 400
godchild 140
goddaughter 139
goddess 390
godfather 137
God-given 496
godhood 393
godlike 393

grave 154
grave 488, 489, 505
gravedigger 474
gravel 161, 191, 192
graveside 153
graveyard 154, 398, 449
gravitation 353, 355
gravity 22, 353, 483
graze, to 524
grease 56, 298
great 339
great 500, 501
Great Britain 88
great-aunt 138, 140
greatest good, the 347
great-grandchild 140, 141
great-grandfather 137, 138
great-grandmother 140
great-grandson 138
great-uncle 139, 140
Greece 92
green 69
Green Party 133
green, emerald 69
green, olive 69
greenery 161
greenfinch 37
greenfly 38
greengrocer 408
greenhouse 162, 164, 235
greet, to 507
Grenada 90
grenade 319
grey 69
greyhound 6
grid 483, 486
grief 480, 488
grille 13
grin 489
grind, to 524
grinder, coffee 229, 232, 278
grinder, meat 277
grit 193
groan, to 529
grocer 408
grocer's 408
groin 244
groom 147
gross 498, 499
ground 95, 145, 161, 233
ground, dumping 132
ground, grazing 94
grounds (gardens) 160
group 60, 325, 360, 378, 419, 488, 489
group, age 430
group, air 318
group, atomic 355
group, ethnic 378
group, interest 378
group, peer 419

group, pressure 378
group, racial 378
group, social 419
group, theatre 437
grouse 36, 37
grouse, sand 36, 38
grove 93, 94, 164, 185, 460, 461
grove, palm 185, 462
grow up, to 508
grow, to 509, 525, 526, 529, 530
grower, wine 471
growing, flower 160
growl, to 527
growth 29, 114, 214
growth, economic 114, 371
growth, economic 371
growth, primary 29
growth, secondary 29
growth, social 417
growth, spiritual 395
grudge 148, 149
grumble, to 527
grumbling 423
guarantee 117
guarantee, contract 117
guarantee, money-back 111
guarantee, performance 117
guard 453, 454
guard, prison 101, 104
guard, to 523
guardianship 140, 486
Guatemala 90
guava 185
gudgeon 158
guelder-rose 160
guerrilla 315
guerrilla, urban 366
guest 155, 175, 228
guesthouse 96, 226, 227, 228
guidance 485
guide 473, 485
guide, girl 179
guide, spiritual 400
guide, to 515
guide, tour 473
guidebook 227
guild 374
guillotine 104, 333
guilt 99, 385, 482
guilt, sense of 385
Guinea 90
Guinea-Bissau 90
guitar 325
guitar, bass 325
guitarist 325
gulf 187
gully 188
gulp, to 522
gulping 423
gum 244

gum, chewing 166
gun 314
gun, machine 319
gun, sub-machine 319
gunman 314
gurgle 422, (of a baby) 423
gurgling 423
guru 400
gush, to 524
gust (of wind) 469
gut 24
guts 240
gutter 229
guttering 235
guy 341
Guyana 90
gymnasium 129, 428
gymnastics 428
gynaecologist 210
gynaecology 215
gypsum 192
gypsy 340
gyrate, to 524
haberdasher 407
habit 339
habitat 30
Haboob (type of wind) 469
hacker 79
hacking 79
hacksaw 444
haddock 159
hade 194
haematite 195
haematology 213
haemoglobin 34, 62
haemolysis 28, 213
haemophilia 222
haemorrhage 213
haemorrhoids 209
hagiography 292
hail 465
hailstone 466
hailstorm 465
hair 8, 245, 341
hair, long 341
hair, pubic 245
hair, short 341
hairdresser 407, 471
hair-dryer 239
hairnet 64
hairs, root 26
hairspray 343
Haiti 91
haji 392
hajj 392
hake 159
half an hour 442
half, first 431
half, second 431
half-arch 18

half-back 432
half-brother 137
half-life 61, 356
half-marathon 431
halibut 159
halide 62
halite 192
hall 11, 14, 236
hall, concert 323, 448
hall, dance 179
hall, sports 129, 429, 449
hall, town 449
hall, vaulted 10
halls of residence, university 448
hallucination 346, 388
hallway 232, 236
halo (lunar) 466
halo (solar) 465
halo 469
halogen 62
halt 480
halt, to 522
halva 169
ham 171
hamburger 176
hamlet 95
hammer 445
hammer, throwing the 426
hammer, to 528
hammock 405
hamper 486
hand (on a watch or clock) 441
hand 242
hand, on the other 531
hand over, to 510
hand, hour 441
hand, minute 440
hand, second (i.e. on a watch) 440
handbag 66
handball 432
handbook 82
handcuffs 101
handicap 221
handicapped 221
handicapped, mentally 387
handicrafts 129, 250
handkerchief 64, 232, 343
handkerchief, paper 343
handle 232, 277
handling 112
handling, file 81
handsome 337, 497
handwriting 282
handyman 445
hang around, to 523
hang, to 522
hanger, coat 231
hanger-on 341
hanging 100
happen, to 506, 509, 520

happening 479, 485
happiness 149, 484, 486
happy 337, 494, 497, 498, 499
happy, to make 513
harbour 403
hard 298, 499, 503
hardness (of water) 56
hardness 191, 486
hard-pan 191
hardship 486
hardware 249
hare 5
harelip 340
Harmattan (type of wind) 469
harmful 504
harmfulness 134
harmonium 322
harmony 326, 492
harmony, four-part 326
harp 323
harpist 323
harpsichord 326
harpsichordist 326
harsh 497, 498, 499
harshness 484
harvest 93, 143
harvest, grape 93
harvest, wheat 93, 143
harvester, combine 146
hat 66
hat, bowler 66
hat, felt 66
hat, top 66
hatchet 444
hatred 151
haughty 503
haul 121
haulage, road 113
have to, to 519
have, to 525
haven 234
hawk 36, 38
hawk, sparrow 36, 38
hawker 409
hawthorn 161, 460
hay 95, 146, 145
hayloft 146
haystack 144
hazard 133, 484
hazardous 133
hazelnut 173
head (boss) 473
head 201, 243
head, print 85
headband 64, 65
headboard 231
header (in football) 429
header 79
heading 488
headlight 46

headline 311
headmaster 130, 476
headmistress 130
headquarters 490
headquarters, police 449
headrest 46, 47
headscarf 64, 65
healer 214
health (a.) 495
health 212, 216, 414, 481
health, mental 387
healthy 499
heap 144, 146, 483
heap up, to 511
hear, to 516, 527
hear, to make s.o. 527
hearing 99, 243
hearing, preliminary 100
hearing, sense of 27, 242
hearse 458
heart 31, 244
heartbeat 26, 31
heartbeat 26, 31
heartburn 216
hearth 234
heartland 377
hearts (in cards) 179
heat (Sport) 428
heat 55, 135, 355, 466, 468
heat, latent 59, 355
heat, prickly 211
heated 493
heater 230, 237, 238
heater, water 229
heath 93, 94, 95, 187
heating, central 231, 233
heaven 269, 391
Heaven, Kingdom of 400
heaviness 492
heavy 499
Heavy Industries, Ministry of 253
hebephrenia 385, 388
hedge 93, 94, 113, 160, 230
hedgehog 5
hedging 113
hedonism 349
heedful 502
heel 241
heels, stiletto 63
hegemony 372
height 1, 301, 340, 481
heir 141
helicopter 3, 456, 458
helium 62
hell 269
helmet, safety 458
help (file) 78, 81
help 480, 489, 492
help, to 518
hem 65, 67

home 235
Home Office 383
home, holiday 94, 96, 232
home, mobile 456
homeostasis 34, 421
homepage 80
homework 127
homograph 287
homonym 287
homosexual 151, 342
Honduras 91
honest 497
honesty 484, 485
honey 172
honeybee 37
honeymoon 154
honeysuckle 160, 165
honour 479, 480, 486
honourable 493, 502
hood 48
hood, cooker 236, 279
hoof 6
hook 445
hoopoe 37, 40
hoot 40
hooter 44
hooting 40, 423
hope 480
hope, to 506, 507
hopeless 494
hopes 479
hops 145
horde 480
horizon 19, 403
horizontal 301, 493
hormone 34
hormone, sex 34
horn 6, 44, 324, 325
horn, bass 322
horn, French 324, 325
hornstone 192
horrendous 341
horror 151
hors d'oeuvres 168
horse 4, 143
horse and carriage 456
horse chestnut (tree) 461
horse, clothes 65
horse, dark 377
horse-jumping 426
horseradish 224
horseshoe 8
horst 194
horticulture 160
hose, garden 445
hosepipe 162
hospitable 341
hospital 210, 221, 447
hospitality 228, 481
host 155, 175

hostage 103, 378
hostage-taking 103, 378
hostel, youth 94
hostilities 318
Hosts, Lord of 393
hot 466, 501
hotel 96, 227, 228, 450
hotel, four-star 228
hotelier 228
hothouse 235
hour 2, 441
hour, rush 47
hourglass 441
hourly 441
house 232, 235, 237
house, boarding 226
house, commission 122
house, country 232
house, detached 232
house, discount 122
house, hen 147
house, lower 379
house, moving 236
house, opera 323
house, semi-detached 232
house, summer 94, 236
house, upper 379
housewife 139, 233, 473
hovercraft 458
how 532
how many 532
how much 532
howl 422
howling 422
hubcap 48
huge 500, 501
hum, to 515
humanism 345, 390
humanity, crime against 366
humerus 24, 240
humidity 466
humidity, absolute 466
humidity, relative 466
humming 423
humorous 337
humorous 497
humour 484
humour, aqueous 29
humour, good 336
humour, sense of 339
humour, vitreous 29
hump 7
humus 32, 194
hunchback 340
Hungary 91
hunger 174
hunter 95
hunting 95, 180, 429
hurdles 427
hurricane 465

indicator, social 421
indicator, universal 57
indigenous 494
indigo 69
indirect 453
indispensable 499
indisputable 503
individual (n.) 418
individual 140, 292, 339, 486, 499
individuality 486
indoctrination 360
indolent 496
Indonesia 87
induction 345, 351
industrial 250, 499
industrialism 250
industrialist 250, 251, 474
industrialization 250, 418
industries 250
industry 250, 474
industry, aviation 250
industry, car 250
industry, carpet 250
industry, chemical 250
industry, cinema 436
industry, clothing 250
industry, computer 80, 250
industry, farming 250
industry, film 436
industry, food 250
industry, leather 250
industry, nuclear 250
industry, oil 250
industry, petrochemical 250
industry, pharmaceutical 250
industry, shipbuilding 250
industry, space 250
industry, textile 250
industry, transport 250
inequality 420
inertia 355
inexpensive 493
infantry 314
infantry, armoured 314
infantryman 317
infarct 209
infection 217
infection, ear 217
infidel 273, 398
infinite 349, 494
infinitive 199
infinitive, split 199
infinity 301
infix 200
inflame, to 522
inflammation 207, 208
inflatable 500
inflation 111, 365
inflation, galloping 111
inflation, rate of 122, 123

inflection 197, 198
influence 382, 482
influence, sphere of 266, 381
influenza 208
in-focus 17
inform, to 507
informant 100, 280
information 1, 71, 107, 255, 280, 413, 447, 452, 479
information, tourist 447
infrastructure 249, 371
infuse, to 524, 525
inhabitant 95, 449
inhabitants 134
inheritance 137
inhibition, social 415
inhospitable 341
initials 256
initiate, to 522
initiative, strategic defence (SDI) 313
injection 207, 211
injured 47
injury 425, 484
ink 12, 332
inkpad 332
inlaid work 12
inlet 404
inn 96, 227, 228
innumerable 495
inoculation 220
input 85
input, voice 85
input/output (I/O) 85
inquire, to 523
inquiry 97, 98, 481
inquisition 393
inquisitive 340, 501
inquisitiveness 489
insane 498
insanity 485
inscribe, to 508
insect 37
insecticide 37, 133, 144
insectivore 37
insectivorous 37
insemination, artificial 212
insert, to 529
inserted, to be 529
insertion 76
inside 232
insight 481
insinuation 489
insipid 497
insolent 336, 340, 342
insoluble 58
insolvency 118
inspection 44, 109, 247
inspection, certificate of 120
inspector 480
inspector, ticket 452

inspiration, divine 390
inspire, to 522
instability, political 362
installation 84, 248, 252
instant 442, 500
instinct 418
institute 252
institution 253, 382
institution, educational 130
institutionalisation 421
institutions, government 253, 382
instruct, to 510, 522
instruction 77, 127, 482, 484
instructions 256
instructions, forwarding 114
instructor 126, 130, 476
instructor, swimming 476
instrument 324
instrument, musical 322
instrumental 197
instrumentalism 345, 350
instrumentalist 324
instrumentation 324
instruments, brass 324
instruments, percussion 324
instruments, string 324
instruments, wind 324
insufferable 500
insulator 57
insulin 25, 209
insult 148
insult, to 512, 526
insurance 44, 109
insurance, car 44
insurance, cargo 109
insurance, joint 109
insure, to 508
insurgency 374
insurrection 102, 374
intact 499
intaglio 18
integral, improper 301
integration 301, 421
integration, regional 267, 383
integration, social 421
integrity 484
integrity, territorial 261, 364
integument 25, 26
intellect, first 348, 397
intelligence 481
intelligence, artificial 85
intelligent 418, 421, 494
intelligentsia 371, 417
intend, to 525
intense 499
intensifier 197
intensity 488
intensity, electric field 354
intent, criminal 104
intention 488

intention, bad 148, 150
interaction, social 420
interactionism 350, 420
interactionism, symbolic 420
interactive 73
interchange 482
intercom 230
interdependence 267
interest 110, 114, 181, 481
interest, bank 110
interest, compound 114, 303
interest, group 414, 416
interest, places of 179, 448
interest, simple 110
interested, to be 517
interesting 496
interests 490
interests, class 381
interests, national 381
interests, vested 265, 374
interests, vital 266
interference 352
interior 13
Interior, Ministry of the 383
interjection 200
interminable 494
intermission 433, 438, 479
internal 76
internalisation 416
international 260
internationalism 260
Internet 72
interpellation 359
interpretation, semantic 281
interrogation 97, 361
interrogative 200
interrupted 501
intersection 305
interval 433, 438, 441, 479, 488
intervention 262, 265
intervention, armed 316
intervention, humanitarian 262, 369
interventionism 369
interview 420, 476, 490
interview, to 519
intestine 29
intestine, large 29, 243
intestine, small 29, 243
Intifada 361
intimacy 150
intimate (n.) 149
intimidate, to 523
intransitive 199
intrigue 376
introduce, to 519, 527
introduction 295
introspective 496
introversion 386
introvert 338
intrusion 194

jaundice 215, 223
javelin 431
javelin, throwing the 426
jaw 244
jay 37
jazz 323
jealous 496
jealousy 484
jeans 65
jeep 456
Jehova 402
Jehovic 402
Jehovist 402
jellyfish 156, 157, 159, 403, 404
jersey 64
Jesuit 402
Jesuitism 402
Jesus 272
Jesus Christ 397
jet 194, 299
jetty 247, 405
Jew 402
jeweller 408
jeweller's 408
jewellery 343
jewels 190
Jewish 402
jingle 288, 292, 422
jingling 422
jinn 269
Job (the prophet) 268
job 415, 418, 472, 474
jobber, stock 115
jog, to 525
jogging 429
join, to 510, 520, 523
joiner 472
joint 11, 25, 33, 190, 241, 245
joke 483, 489
joke, to 516
jolly 499
Jonah 275
jonquil 163
Jordan 87
Joseph 275
jot down, to 530
jotter 332, 343
joule 56, 353
journal 290, 291, 294, 295, 311
journalese 310
journalism 291, 310
journalism, TV 310
journalist 310, 472, 473
journalist, radio 310
journalistic 310
journey 2, 47, 49, 180, 453, 454, 490
journey, car 180
jovial 494, 498
joy 484, 486
joyful 494, 499

joyous 494, 498
joystick 77
Judah 395
Judaic 402
Judaism 402
Judaism, Orthodox 402
Judaism, Reform 402
Judas tree 460
judge 100, 102, 272, 474
judge, to 526
judgement 100, 103
Judgement, Day of 395
judgement, value 347, 416
judiciary 100
judo 427
jug, milk 277
juggernaut 48
juggler 436
juice, fruit 166
juice, lemon 166
juicer 276
juicer, fruit 277
juicy 499
July 42
jump, to 509, 523, 524
jump, triple 426
junction 45, 448
junction 479
June 42
jungle 93, 133, 144, 187, 460
jungle, law of the 103
junior high 128
junior, office 474
juniper 160, 460, 461
junk, space 19
junta 368
Jupiter 22
jurisprudence 272, 397
jurisprudence, Islamic 102
jurisprudence, principles of 268
jurist (Isl.) 102
jurist 103, 272, 274, 397
juristic 397
juror 102
jury 105
jury, hung 105
jus divinum 398
just 500
justice 102, 272, 375, 418
justice, administration of 100
Justice, Ministry of 105
justice, poetic 293
justification 85
justification, full 74
justified 85
justify, to 511
kangaroo 6
kaolin 193
karate 429
karma 398

lessen, to 518, 528
lesson 128
lesson, driving 46
let (someone) in, to 515
let someone disembark, to 509
letter 182, 295, 483
letter, airmail 258
letter, covering 122
letter, registered 258
letters, capital 76
lettuce 225
leucocyte 220
leukaemia 215
Levanter (type of wind) 464, 466
level 283, 486, 499, 503, 505
levels, subsistence 417
Levite 399
lexicography 285
lexicon 293, 296
liability, absolute 109
liability, admission of 119
liar 338
libel 97
liberal 379
liberalism 379
liberalism, economic 379
liberated 493
liberation 358
Liberia 90
libertarianism 358
liberties, civil 358
libido 151, 487
Libra 23, 42
librarian 475
library 129, 181, 410, 449
library, film 436
library, mobile 457
libretto 288
Libya 91
lice, head 217
licence 112
licence, driving 45, 49, 344
licence, export 110, 251
licence, poetic 293
license 121
lichen 32, 163
lick, to 529
lie down, to 525
lie hidden, to 527
lie, to tell a 514
Liechtenstein 91
lieutenant (army) 317
lieutenant (navy) 320
lieutenant, first 317
lieutenant, second 317
lieutenant-colonel 317
lieutenant-general 317
life 485
life, country 95
life, everlasting 395

life, married 139
life, social 417
lifeboat 405, 457
lifebuoy 403
life-giving 504
lifeguard 405
lifestyle 339
lift (elevator) 226, 229, 230, 407
lift, ski 426
ligament 25, 29, 241, 242
light 23, 231, 237, 356, 485, 491, 499
light, flashing 46
light, red 46
light, tail 46
light, to 515, 522
light, wall 237
lighter, car 48
lighter, cigarette 344
lighthouse 404
lighting 236, 439
lightness 486
lightning 463
lightning, atmospheric 463
lightning, ball 463
lightning, flash of 466
light-polluted 23
lights, funeral 152
lights, northern 20
lights, runway 2
lights, traffic 46
like 533
like, to 517
likeable 498
likelihood 479, 480
likeness 339, 486
lilac 164, 165
lilo 404
lily 163
lily, white 163
lily-of-the-valley 162
limb 240, 335
limb, artificial 208, 217
lime 51, 185, 297
lime, dried 174, 175
lime, slaked 51
limerick 294
limestone 57, 192, 298
limewater 51
limit 483
limit, time 121, 442
limitation, statute of 118
limited sovereignty, doctrine of 369
limitless 494
limonite 195
limp, to 529
limp, to cause to 529
linden 461
line 292, 453
line, assembly 249
line, attacking 427

look, to 520
loop 76
loop, infinite 76
loquacious 495
lorry 48, 457
lorry, articulated 457
lose, to (i.e. a game) 508, 522
loser 425
loss 100, 113, 115, 425, 484
loss, capital 115
loss, hair 215
lot, parking 45, 447
lot of, a 533
lotion, suntan 405
lots 533
loudness 481
loudspeaker 322, 481
lounge, departure 1
louse 38
lovage 225
love 150, 487
love, to 517
love, to be in 517
lovebirds 150
love-lies-bleeding 163
loveliness 485
lovely 501, 504
lover (female) 150
lover (male) 150
lover, film 436
lover, music 323
lovers 150
loving 500
low 322, 495, 501
low-resolution 85
loyalist 383
loyalty, group 421
lozenge 218
LP 324
lucidity 492
luck 480, 486
luck, bad 481
Luddism 368
luggage 1, 226
luggage, excess 1
luggage, hand 1
lukewarm 504, 505
lull 469
lullaby 325
lumbar 219, 220
lumber 460
lumbering 460
lumberyard 460
luminosity 20
lump 218, 219
lunacy 485
lunar 22
lunarnaut 22
lunch 176, 228
lunette 13

lung 241
lungs 29, 31, 243
luscious 502
lust 487
lustre 190
lute 322, 324
Lutheran 399
Lutheranism 399
Luxembourg 90
luxurious 502
lychee 185
lying down 497
lymph 26, 212, 220
lymphoma, Hodgkin's 210
lynx 6
lyre 323
lyric 292
lyrics 325
Macedonia 91
Machiavellianism 379
machicolation 15
machination 483
machine 77, 238, 277, 353, 445
machine, answering 237
machine, fax 256, 332
machine, milking 145
machine, photocopy 332
machine, pinball 181
machine, slot 181
machine, stapling 333
machine, ticket 454
machine, vending 411
machine, washing 239
machine, weighing 54
machine-made 502
machine-readable 83
machinery 252, 446
machinery, industrial 252
mackerel 158
macro 77
macro-linguistics 283
macromolecule 60
macro-sociology 415
mad 338, 387, 498, 500
Madagascar 91
made-to-measure 65
madness 485
Mafia 379
magazine 135, 294, 311
magazine 490
magazine, illustrated 181, 311
maggot 158
magi 400
magic 499
magical 499
magician 436, 474
magistrate 102
magma 195
magnesite 195
magnesium 60

mark 487, 491
mark, exclamation 285
mark, question 285
mark, strawberry 340
mark, to 517
mark, trade 118
marker 333
market 93, 108, 407, 447
market, black 361
market, capital 108
market, consumer 247
market, credit 108
market, currency 247
market, domestic 108
market, foreign 108
market, free 108, 247, 361
market, labour 471
market, mass 309
market, money 108
market, open 108
market, securities 108
market, stock 108, 109
market, wheat 143
marks, distinguishing 339
marksman 314
marl 189
marmalade 175
maroon 69
marriage 137, 139, 141, 152, 413
married 141
married, to get 507, 517
marrow 175, 225
Mars 22
marsh 188
marshal, air chief 317
marshal, air chief 317
marshall (army) 313
Marshall Islands 88
martial 504
martyr 271, 396
martyrdom 154, 271, 396
martyrium 15
martyrolatry 396
martyrology 396
marvel-of-Peru 164
Marxism 379
Marxism, creative 379
Marxism, dogmatic 379
Marxism-Leninism 379
Mary (mother of Jesus) 273
mash, to 528
masher, potato 276
masonry 15
mass 55, 353, 483
mass and energy, conservation of 53, 352
mass, atomic 55, 353
massage 220
massage, to 529
masses 365, 368, 380
massive 501

mast 404
master 487
master, Sufi 269
master's (degree) 129
mastitis 222
masturbate, to 507
mat, place 233
mat, prayer 269, 395
match 425, 426, 428, 430
match, doubles 428
match, final 428
match, first (of two legs) 430
match, friendly 428
match, man of the 431
match, return 430
match, singles 428
match, to 522, 526
matches, preliminary 428
mate 128, 151
material 60, 299
material, dress 63
materialism 349, 379
materialism, dialectical 349, 379
materials 299
materials, raw 252
maternal 140
math 128
mathematician 303
mathematics 128, 303
mathematics, applied 128, 303
mathematics, pure 303
mathnawi 294
mating 144
matriarchy 379
matricide 104
matrimony 413
matrix 83, 306
matrix, dot 83
matter 60, 491
matter, breakdown of 134
matter, conservation of 352
matter, printed 258
matter, waste 134
mattress 237, 238
maturity, date of 110
Mauritania 91
Mauritius 91
mausoleum 10
mauve 69
maverick 364
maxim 293
maximum 302, 483
May 42
mayor 449
Mazdaism 389
Mazdakism 389
Mazdakist 400
meadow 94, 144, 145, 146, 147, 161
meal 227
meal, evening 172

morning, early 441
morning, tomorrow 441
morning-glory 165
Morocco 91
morpheme 197, 200
morphine 221
morphology 198, 284
mortality 419, 420
mortar 279, 316
mortar-shell 316
mortgage 115, 233
mortgage, blanket 115
mortgage, closed-end 115
mortgage, leasehold 115
mortgagee 121
mortgager 114
mortify, to 529
mosaic 17
Moses, Law of 396
mosque 274, 400, 450
mosquito 36
most 532
MOT 47
moth 38
moth, clothes 36
mothballs 235
mother, foster 140
mother, unmarried 140
Mother's Day 153
motherboard 74
mother-in-law (i.e. husband's mother) 140
mother-in-law (i.e. wife's mother) 140
motherly 140
mother-of-pearl 298
motif 18
motion 353
motion, Brownian 55, 353
motion, simple harmonic 353
motion, to put in 515
motionless 494
motive 484
motor 49, 84, 356
motor racing, championship 430
motorbike 458
motorboat 457
motorcycle 458
motorcyclist 49
motorway 44, 48
mould 234
mountain 96, 188
mountaineering 96, 430
mountainous 501
mountainside 188
mourning 153, 272
mouse 8, 83, 84
mouse, field 8
mouse-driven 83
mouse-driver 83
moustache 339
mouth 4, 5, 28, 242

move, house 236
move, to 511, 512, 524
movement 241, 242, 353, 382, 453
movement, Brownian 353
movement, enclosure 383
movement, Green party 366
movement, involuntary 213
movement, labour 366
movement, national liberation 366
movement, non-alignment 261
movement, peasant 366
movement, resistance 383
movement, social 366, 415
movement, urban social 366
Mover, Prime 349, 392, 399
Mozambique 91
Mrs 138
Ms 138
muckraking 360
mucus 28, 33, 212
mud 96, 194
mud-remover (for shoes) 235
mudslinging 379
mudstone 194
mufti 400
mug 173, 278, 279
mulberry 184
mulberry, black 185
mule 6, 143
mullah 274, 400, 476
mullah-ism 400
mullet 156, 157
multi-access 75
multi-cellular 27
multicolour 75
multicoloured 498
multi-functional 249
multimedia 75, 249
multinational (company) 117, 249
multiple 307
multiplication 305
multiply, to 522
multi-programming 75
multi-storey 12
multi-tasking 75
multitude 479
mummy 141
mumps 209, 220
munch, to 524
municipal 499
municipality 449
murder 97, 103
murder, premeditated 103
murder, to 528
murderer 97, 102
murmur 422
murmur, heart 216
murmuring 423
muscle 31, 33, 245
muscle, ciliary 33

muscle, strained 217
muscles, intercostal 31
muscles, suspensory 31
muscles, voluntary 31
muscovite 195
museum 182, 450
mushroom 173, 225
music 130, 325
music, classical 182, 325
music, film 438
music, pop 182, 325
musical 438
musician 325, 326
musicianship 325
music-making 325
musicology 325
musk-rose 164
Muslim 274, 399, 400
muslin 299
mussel 158
mustard 69, 169, 225
mutation 27
mutineer 105
mutiny, to 527
muttering 423
mutton 174
mutualism 34
Myanmar (Burma) 91
myasthenia 216
mysterious 502
mystery 485, 486
mysticism 272, 348, 349
myth 288
nail 245, 446
naïve 337, 338, 498
naked 336, 340
name 84, 137, 196, 255
name, baptismal 401
name, brand 122
name, family 137
name, first 257
name, pet 137, 151, 341
name, to 520, 529
named, to be 520
nameless 495
names, divine 268, 390
Namibia 91
nanny 139, 473
naos 17
nap, to take a 512
nape (of the neck) 241, 244
naphtha 61
nappy 489
narcissus 164, 165
narcolepsy 213
narcotics 104, 220
narration 271
narrative (a.) 290
narrative 290
narrator 290

narrator, omniscient 290
narrow 494
narthex 14
nasturtium 163
nasty 498
nation 377, 381
nation, aggressor 319
nation, debtor 266
nation, host 120, 430
national 381, 503
nationalism 381
nationalism, linguistic 286
nationality 381
nationality, dual 260
nationalization 381
nations, advanced 251
nations, developed 251
nations, developing 251
nations, undeveloped 251
native 493, 494, 502
Nativity 395
natural 132, 134, 500
naturalism 295, 348
naturalization 377
naturally 531
nature 337, 339, 487
naturopathy 217
naughtiness 486
naughty 339, 494, 499
Nauru 91
nausea 213
nave 13
navel 245
navy 252, 320, 405
Nazism 381
near 504, 534
near, to get520
neat 499
neatness 482, 491
nebula 21
nebular 21
necessary 348, 502, 504
necessities 83
neck (meat) 174
neck 191, 244
necklace 344
neckline, low 64
neckline, plunging 64
nectarine 185
need, social 421
need, to 506
needle 445
needs, hierarchy of 414
negative (of photographs) 18
negative 200, 307
negotiable 118
negotiation(s) 252, 265, 380, 419
neighbour 141, 236
neighbourhood 235
neighbouring 505

neither...nor 534
neo-classical 296
neo-classicism 18
neo-colonialism 382
neo-fascism 376
neo-imperialism 360
neologism 286, 296
neo-Marxism 379
neon 61
neo-Platonism 345
neo-realism 439
Nepal 91
nephew (i.e. brother's son) 138
nephew (i.e. sister's son) 138
nephritis 214, 219, 222
nephrology 219
nepotism 362, 472
Neptune 23
nerve 217, 244
nerve, auditory 31
nerve, optic 31
nervous 339, 500
nest 39, 234
Nestorian 401
Nestorianism 400
net 426
net worth, capital 113
net, fishing 156
netball 431
Netherlands 91
netting, side 426
netting, wire 444
nettle, stinging 162
network 80, 304, 486
network, computer 249
network, local area(LAN) 80
network, railway 453
network, transport 249
networking 80
neuralgia 214, 386
neuritis 207, 385
neurobiology 215
neurology 217
neurone 26
neurosis 215, 386
neurosis, obsessional 386
neurosis, traumatic 386
neurosurgery 212
neurotic 386
neutral 55
neutralism 373
neutrality 414
neutrality, treaty of 318
neutralization 55
neutron 61, 356
never 531, 534
new 496, 504
New Zealand 89
newcomer 482
newly-wed (bride) 138

newly-wed (bridegroom) 138
news 132, 178, 479
news, front page 309
news, sports 309
news, television 178
newsagent 409
newsagent's 409
newscaster 309
newsflash 310
newspaper 134, 180, 291, 310, 485
newspaper, daily 310
newsreel 436
newsroom 309
next 494
next to 532, 533
nibbles 168
Nicaragua 91
nice 337, 338, 341, 497, 498, 501, 504
niche 12, 15
niche, prayer 17, 399
nickel 61
nickname 84, 137, 140, 150, 151, 340, 341
niece (i.e. brother's daughter) 139
niece (i.e. sister's daughter) 139
Niger 91
Nigeria 91
night 21, 180, 441, 467
night before last, the 440
night, last 440
night, opening 435
night, tomorrow 441
night, wedding 153
nightcap 65
nightclub 178, 181
nightgown 67
nightingale 36, 38
nightmare 484, 488
night-owl 339
nightshade, woody 163
nihilism 350
nimble 336, 340
nimbostratus 464, 469
nimbus 463
nipple 245
nirvana 401
nitrate 61
nitrification 31, 34
nitrites 61
nitrogen 61
no 534
no confidence, vote of 370
No Smoking 227
Noah 274
nobble, to 529
nobility, the 359
noble 341, 504
nobles 359
nod off, to 512
node 301
nodes, lymph 32

627

olivine 189
Oman 89
omelette 167
ominous 504
omission 483
omnivore 34
omnivorous 34
on 531, 533
on, to get 516
on-board 84
oncology 218
onerous 499
onion 224
onion, spring 224
onions, pickled 168
online 85
only 532, 533
onomatopoeia 288
on-screen 85
ontogeny, linguistic 281
ontology 402
onyx 193
opal 193
open 493, 494
open, to 508, 527, 528
opener, bottle 277
opener, can 277
opener, tin 445
opening 247, 480
opera 178, 322, 433
operation, surgical 218
operations 251, 375
operations, theatre of 317
operative 500
operator, computer 83
operator, telephone 256
operetta 433
ophthalmology 212
opinion 397, 491
opinion, advisory 370
opinion, difference of 148
opinion, freedom of 358
opinion, public 360
opponent 427
opportunism 376
opportunity 442, 488, 492
opportunity, goal scoring 431
opportunity, job 251
opposed to 531
opposite 533
opposition 366, 380
oppression 272, 372, 487
oppressive 495
optative 197
optician 410, 474
optician's 410
optics 356
optics, fibre 74
optimisation 73
optimism 347

optimistic 337
option (to buy) 113
options 82
orange 69, 184
orange, methyl 62
orange, Seville 185
orang-utan 8
orbit 22, 355
orchard 143, 160, 184, 460
orchestra 322, 433
orchid 160
orchitis 207
order 29, 77, 115, 249, 480, 484, 486, 491
order, money 113, 256
order, moral 350
order, new world 266, 382
order, social 420
order, to 514, 516, 527
order, word 200
Orders (of classical architecture) 14
orders, holy 394
ordinary 500, 503
ordinate 305
ordination 400
ore 59, 193, 298
oregano 224
organ 24, 31, 240, 322, 335, 372
organ, female reproductive 240
organ, male reproductive 240
organ, mouth 324
organ, party 359
organ, pipe 322
organic 132, 134
organisation 252
organisation, criminal 101
organisation, non-profit 115
organism 30
organism, indicator 24
organization 372
organization, international 263
organization, non-governmental (NGO) 372
organizations, front 372
organizations, supranational 263
organs, endocrine 240
organs, reproductive 240
oriel 11
orientalism 374
orientation, social 415
origin, certificate of 120
original 493
oriole 39
Orion 19
ornamental 12
ornithologist 36
orogeny 194
orphan 141
orphanage 141
orthodontics 208
orthodox 389, 394
orthoepy 282

parts 251
parts, spare 48, 49
party 152, 155, 182, 367, 484
party of God, the 270
party, birthday 152
party, catch-all 367
party, circumcision 152
party, engagement 152
Party, Green 133
party, Labour 367
party, third 117
pasmolysis 26
pass 426
pass away, to 529
pass, exam 154
pass, mountain 188
pass, to 518, 528
passenger 2, 404, 453, 454
passer-by 448
passing 152, 153, 155
passion 150, 487
passion play, Shi'ite 434
passion, crime of 99
passionate 493, 500
passionflower 160, 163
passive 58, 199, 200
passport 2, 227, 257, 344, 454
passport, diplomatic 265
passport, duty 265
password 82
pasta 175
pastel 16
pastiche 288
pastime 180
pastor 391
pastries 172
pastries, cream-filled 172
pastries, dry 172
pasture 94, 96, 144, 145, 147
pasture, to 524
pat, to 529
patch, knee 65
patella 32, 244
paternal 138
path 93, 95, 161, 485, 487
path, data 83
path, narrow 96
pathogen 25
pathology 207, 221
pathos 289, 291
pathway 95
patience 150, 487
patience, to have 513
patient 499
patio 230
patois 281
patriarch 391
patriarchy 363
patrician 362
patricide 98

patrol 318
patron 12
patronage, political 368
patronymic 286
pattern 18, 305
pattern, cultural 413
pattern, geometric 18, 305
pauperisation 376
pause 483
pavement 447
pavilion 14, 15, 16
paving 233, 449
paw 4
pay, to 523, 525, 528
payment 110, 248, 255
payment, advance 110
payment, warranty of 114
payments, balance of 111, 363
pea, garden 225
pea, green 225
peace 95, 317, 335, 479, 487
peace and quiet 148
peace movement, the 315
peace of mind, to obtain 522
peace, breach of the 382
peace, cold 264
peaceful 493
peach 185
peacock 38
peak 188
peal (of bells) 422
peanut 167, 184
pear 185
pearl 157
peas, black-eyed 175
peas, split 174
peasant 94, 145
peat 190
pebble 95, 161, 192, 404
peculiarity 492
pedal 45
pedalfer 190
peddle, to 527
peddler, street 448
pedestrian 48, 449
pediment 15
peel 184
peel, lemon 168
peeler 276
peg, coat 231
Pegasus 19
pegmatite 189
pejorative 280
Pelagianism 391
pelican 40
pelvis 244
pen 332, 333, 343
pen, felt-tip 333
pen, fountain 332
pen, light 81

penalty (football) 426
penalty (Isl.) 99
penalty 99, 103
penalty, death 100, 104
pencil 333, 344
pencil, propelling 333
pendant 343
pendentive 11
pendulum 351
penguin 4, 36
peninsula 188
penis 24, 240
penitentiary 104
penknife 444
pen-name 281, 288, 289
pennyroyal 160
pensioner 141
pentagon 301
Pentateuch 398
pentathlon 426
peony 163
people 141, 368, 380
people, young 138
pepper 173, 225
pepper, chilli 225
pepper, stuffed 170
pepsin 25
peptide 25, 53
perceive, to 514
percentage 60, 303
perch 40, 158
percolator, coffee 234
percussion 325
perestroika 363
perfect (tense) 198
perfect 501
perfection 349
perforate, to 526
perform, to 528, 529
performance 285, 322, 433
performance, linguistic 285
performer 326, 438, 439
performing 439
perfume 172, 344
perfumer 409
perfumery 409
peridot 191
perigee 20
perihelion 20
peril 484
perimeter 301
period (punctuation) 286
period 28, 56, 121, 128, 353, 370, 440, 441,
442, 485, 490, 491
period, delivery 114
period, gestation 28
period, grace 108
period, incubation 214
period, payback 114
periodical 293, 311, 490

peripheral 75
periphrasis 290
perishable 118
peristalsis 27, 213
peritonitis 208, 210, 222
perjury 102
permanent 497, 505
permanent, to be 523
permeability 190, 356
permission, to get 506
permit 97, 112, 121
permit, fishing 94
permit, hunting 93
permit, residence 366
permit, to 528
permit, work 471
permitted 270, 273
permitted to, to be 524
permutation 302
peroxide 53
peroxide, hydrogen 51
perpendicular (n.) 303
perpetual 505
Persian 129
persimmon 185
person 137, 140, 198, 335, 339, 486
person, per 227
person, retired 137
personal 497, 499
personalism 347
personality 339, 418
personality 486
personality, authoritarian 374
personality, bureaucratic 374
personality, international 264
perspective 416
perspective 483
perspective, liberationist 417
perspicacity 481
persuade, to 523
Peru 88
peruse, to 525
pessimism 346
pessimistic 336, 504
pest 24
pesticide 24, 132, 134, 143, 145
pestle 277
pet 5
petal 164
petition 100
petrochemical 53
petroglyph 284
petrol 44, 53, 132, 297
petunia 162
pewter 54, 299
phalangitis 207
Pharaoh 272
pharmacist 213
pharmacology 127, 213
pharmacopoeia 219

pharmacy 213, 408
pharynx 32
phase 58, 354, 490
phatic 284
pheasant 38
phenol 58
phenomenalism 346
phenomenology 385, 414
phenotype 29
Philippines 90
philology 283, 294
philosopher 348, 393
philosophical 348
philosophy 129, 348
philosophy, Islamic 272, 348, 397
philosophy, peripatetic 348
phlebitis 214
phlegm 213
phloem 24
phlox 163
phobia 211, 385, 388
phobic 388
phone, mobile 343, 344
phoneme 286
phonemics 287
phonetic 280
phonetics 280
phonological 287
phonologist 286
phonology 286
phosphate 58
phosphorous 58
photo-booth 257
photo-emission 355
photograph 181, 234, 487
photograph, passport 257
photographer 474
photography 181
photography, director of 438
photosynthesis 31, 58
phototropism 34
phrase 199, 487
phrase, prepositional 199
phylum 30
physician 210, 472
physics 129, 355
physics, applied 129
physics, nuclear 355
physiology 218
physiotherapist 212, 475
physiotherapy 212
pianist 322
piano 322
piazza 17
piccolo 322
pick up, to (e.g. a prostitute) 508
pick, to (e.g. a flower) 512
pick, to 524, 528
pickaxe 445
picketing 381

pickle 168
pickle, mixed 168
pick-me-up 213
pick-pocket 99
picnic 93, 179, 403
picture 12, 231, 234, 237, 482, 487
pictures, to take 517
picturesque 497
piece (of music) 325
pier 12, 14, 403
pierce, to 526
piety 391, 392, 394
pig 5, 144
pigeon 39
pigeon, carrier 39
pigeon, fantailed 39
pigeon, homing 39
pigeon, rock 39
piglet 143
pigskin 297
pigsty 144
pike 156
pilaster 14
pile 144, 146, 483
pile up, to 522
piles (Med.) 209
pile-up 45
pilfer, to 525
pilfering 101
pilgrim (to Mecca) 392
pilgrim 395
pilgrimage (to Mecca) 392
pilgrimage 395
pilgrimage, place of 271
pill 218
pill, birth-control 218
pillage, to 524
pillar 11, 13, 14, 486
Pillars of Islam, the 268
pillow 230, 235
pillowcase 233
pilot 2, 472
pilot, to 525
pimple 212, 338, 340
pin 445
pin, drawing 444
pin, hair 344
pin, rolling 278, 279
pin, safety 445
pinball (machine) 181
pincers 446
pine (tree) 462
pine, spruce 461
pineapple 184
pink 69
pinnacle 11, 16
pins and needles 216
pioneer 482
pip (in fruit) 185
pipe 235

pipe, hose 162
pipeline 249
pipeline, gas 249
pipette 53
piracy (Comp.) 79
piracy, software 77
Pisces 20, 42
piss, to 527
pistachio 167, 184
pistil 164
pistol 314
pitch (Sport) 431
pitch 354
pitchblende 189
pitiable 498
pitiful 498
pity 148, 149
pizza 168
place 431, 448, 450, 483, 490
place, first 431
place, to 512, 518, 528, 530
place, to put in 518
place, watering 4
placenta 27, 212
placing (i.e. of the ball) 427
plagiarism 290
plague 217
plaice 156
plain (Geog.) 94, 95
plain 187, 498, 504
plait 341
plan 1, 247, 454, 491
plan, development 362
plan, economic 109
plan, five-year 247
plan, route 44
plane 304, 445
plane, bedding 189
plane, cleavage 191
plane, fighter 320
plane, to 526
plane, war 320
planet 21
planetarium 22
planetary 21
planetoid 21
plankton 26
planner, daily 332
planning 247, 362
planning, development 247
planning, economic 109
planning, environmental 414
planning, family 212
planning, military 362
planning, social 414
planning, town and country 132
planning, urban 414
plant 164
plant, flowering 164
plant, house 164

plant, to 528
plantation 94, 146, 185, 461, 462
plants 135
plasma 26, 28, 352
plaster 16, 299
plastic 53, 297
plate 167, 276, 277
plate, dessert 276, 277
plate, dinner 277
plate, registration 45
plateau 95, 188
platelet 32
platform (in election) 362
platform 435, 453
platform, floating 247
platinum 53, 297
Platonism 345
play 295, 425, 438
play on words 294
play, morality 295
play, mystery 295
play, passion 295
play, shadow 435
play, stage 182, 295, 438
play, to 529
player 326, 425, 433, 439
player, handball 432
player, horn 325
player, record 235
player, soccer 429
player, trumpet 324
player, volleyball 431
playground 127, 180
playing (Mus.) 324, 326
playing 178, 425
playschool 130
playtime 128
playwright 434, 439
plea 97
pleasant 337, 338, 494, 497
pleased 498
pleasing 503
pleasurable 502
pleasure 484, 489
pleat 63, 64
plebiscite 267, 383
plectrum 325
pledge 123
pledge, to 526
pledgee 124
pledger 124
Pleiades 19
plenipotentiary, minister 267
pleonasm 282
pleura 32
pleurisy 214
pliers 444
plot (of land) 95
plot 434, 483
plot, main 434

plotter, graph 78
plough 145
plough, snow 468
ploughing 145
ploughman 145
plover 39
pluck 483
pluck, to 524, 528
plug, spark 48
plum 184
plum, egg 184
plum, wild 185
plum, yellow 184
plumber 475
plumule 29
plunder, to 524
plunger 446
pluperfect 199
plural 197
pluralism 349, 416, 419
pluralism, political 377
plurality 349
plus 301
Pluto 19
plutocracy 367
plutonium 53
plywood 297
pneumonia 214, 217
PO box 257
poaching 95
pocket 64
pocketknife 444
pod, seed 161
podium 14
podium, winners' 428
podsol 189
poem, couplet 294
poem, lyric 293
poem, prose 292
poet 292
poetaster 292
poetic 292
poetry 129, 292
pogrom 377, 390
point 425, 491
point of view 295, 346
point out, to 513
point, boiling 61, 356
point, curie 356
point, dew 466, 469
point, freezing 356, 469
point, information 257
point, melting 61
point, power 230
point, starting 491
point, triple 356
point, weak 341
pointed 496
pointer 71
pointillism 18

pointless 495
poison 56, 134, 135, 215
poisoning 221
Poland 91
polarization 355, 377
pole 22, 58, 355, 483
pole, telegraph 93
poles, galactic 22
pole-vaulting 426
police 45, 49, 97, 104, 363
police, chief of 101
police, motorcycle 45
police, secret 98, 363
police, traffic 45
policeman 97, 98, 447, 450
policy 368, 373
policy holder, insurance 113
policy, 'big stick' 263, 373
policy, bipartisan foreign 263
policy, criminal 373
policy, domestic 373
policy, dynamic 373
policy, economic 109, 116
policy, fiscal 116
policy, foreign 263, 373
policy, insurance 44, 98, 110
policy, open door 263, 373
policy-maker 373
polio 218
polished 494
polite 335, 341, 494, 504
politeness 479
political 374
politician 373, 474
politicisation 374
politics 373, 417, 418, 486
politics, ABC of 360
politics, international 263
politics, linkage 373
politics, power 263
poll 382
poll, opinion 418
poll, public opinion 382
pollen 32, 162
pollination 32, 162
pollutant 135
pollute, to 522
polluted 132
pollution 24, 132
pollution, air 447
pollution, light 135
pollution, sound 134
polo 427
polo, water 431
poly-alphabetic 282
polyandry 416
polycentrism 366
polyester 53
polyether 53
polygamy 138, 269, 270, 415, 416

practical 500
practices, restrictive 418
practitioner, general (GP) 210
pragmatism 345, 349, 375
praise 486
praise, to 515, 526
pram 457
prat 337
prawn 159
prawns 175
praxis 377
prayer 270, 274, 393, 400, 401
prayer, afternoon 274
prayer, canonical 272, 274, 401
prayer, congregational 274
prayer, late evening 274
prayer, mid-day 274
prayer, morning 274
prayer, night 274
Prayer, the Lord's 393
preacher 401
precaution 479
precedent 485
precession 19
pre-Christian 391
precious 504
precipice 187
precipitate 54, 56
precipitation 464
precipitation, annual 468
precise 497
precursor 482
pre-dated 110
predator 28, 31
predatory 28, 31
predestinarian 398
predestination 398
predicate 198, 199
pre-eternity 389
preface 289, 290, 295
prefer, to 528
preference 480, 490
prefix 197
pregnancy 24, 27
pregnancy, ectopic 207
prehistory, linguistic 283
pre-judgement 414
prejudice 148, 364, 414, 415
prelapsarian 391
preliminary 493
premature 215
premises 349
premises, consular 259
premium 504
premium, insurance 113
pre-molar 242
preoccupation 489
preoccupied 503
prepaid, charges 124
preparations 482

prepare, to 506, 512
preposition 197
pre-programmed 74
presbyter 391
presbyterate 391
Presbyterianism 399
prescription 221
presence 484, 492
presence, constructive 261
present 154, 155, 496
present, at 533
present, the 440
present, to 507
present, to be 512
presenter 311, 475
presenter, news 311
presenter, weather 477
preservation 133
president 371
press, freedom of the 309, 358
press, the 311
press, to 524, 527
pressure 48, 58, 354
pressure, atmospheric 468
pressure, blood 218
pressure, group 376
pressure, low 468
pressure, ridge of high 469
pressure, ridge of low 469
pressure, social 418
prestige 368
prestige 479
pretend, to 520
preterite 199
pretty 337, 497, 501
prevail, to 524
prevalence 487
prevention 211
preview 309, 434
previous 498
previously 533
prey 6
prey, bird of 36
price 119, 227, 248, 255, 257, 410, 488
price, buying 119
price, cost 119
price, fixed 119, 227, 410
price, invoice 119
price, maximum 227
price, minimum 227
price, offering 119
price, retail 119
price, sale 119
price, standard 119
price, wholesale 119
prices, bargain 410
prices, competitive 251
prices, reduced 410
prickle, to 528
pride 150, 480, 489

prohibited 270, 503
project, development 248
prolapse 211
proletariat 363
proletariat, dictatorship of the 359
proletariat, lumpen 379
prologue 289, 294, 295
prolong, to 528
Promised Land, the 395
promotion 472
prompt 74
prompter 435
pronominal 199
pronoun 198
pronoun, demonstrative 198
pronoun, possessive 198
pronoun, relative 198
pronunciation 281
proof 101, 347
propaganda 363
propaganda, international cultural 260
propane 53
propeller 2
proper 497
properties 303
property 55, 416, 419, 420
property, private 379
property, stolen 104
prophecy, self-fulfilling 415
prophet 269, 271, 391
prophethood 271, 401
prophylaxis 211
proposition 348
props 439
proscribed 503
prose (n.) 295
prosecute, to 511
prosecution 98, 100
prosecution, criminal 98
prosecution, the 100
prosecutor, public 100
proselytising (Isl.) 270
prosody 293
prosperity 488
prosperous 501, 504
prosthetics 212
prostitute 474
prostrate 497
prostration (in prayer) 271
protagonist 292
protection 133, 480, 482, 486
protection, data 76
protection, diplomatic 262
protectorate 363, 377
protein 25, 53
protest 359, 480
Protestant 391
Protestantism 391
protocol 364
proton 352

protoplasm 26
prototype 74
protract, to 528
proud 503
prove, to 506
proverb 285, 293, 479
providence, divine 400
province 93
provisional 504
provisions 122
provocation 314, 363
provoke, to 522
provost 395
proximate 504
prudence 479
prudent 502
prune 184, 185
psalmodist 401
psalmody 401
psalms 400
pseudonym 280, 281, 288, 289
pseudo-poet 292
psoriasis 213
psyche 485
psychiatrist 386, 473
psychiatry 128, 214, 386
psychoanalysis 215, 387
psychoanalysis, Freudian 387
psychoanalyst 387
psychobiological 386
psychobiology, developmental 386
psychodynamics 386
psychogenic 386
psycholinguistics 386
psychological 387
psychologist 386, 473
psychologist, criminal 101
psychology 128, 215, 386, 417
psychology, behavioural 386
psychology, body-centred 386
psychology, collective 371
psychology, ego 387
psychology, group 417
psychology, individual 387
psychology, space 20
psychometrics 386
psychopath 386
psychopathic 386
psychopathology 385, 413
psychopathy 385, 386
psychosexual 387
psychosis 386
psychosis, manic depressive 386
psychotherapy 214
pub 182, 411
public 500
publication 295, 311
public-domain (PD) 71
publicity 179, 482
publicize, to 527

quelled, to be 529
query 481
query, to 523
question (something) , to 515
question 135, 196, 373, 481, 486
question, indirect 196
question, rhetorical 196, 288
question, to 523
questioning 97
questionnaire 414
questionnaire, census 421
queue 409, 449
quick 340, 499
quickly 533
quicksand 187
quid pro quo 260
quiet 337, 486, 493, 496, 499, 501
quietism 372
quilt 235
quince 184
quintet 323
quintuplets 138
quits 503
quorum 367
quota 117
quotation 491
quotient 301
rabbi 393
rabbinical 393
rabbit 5
rabble 375
rabies 222
race 420, 427, 431
race, arms 319, 380
racecourse 8
racing, dog 429
racing, Formula 1 425
racing, horse 4, 425
racism 382
racist 341
rack, coat 237
rack, draining 276
rack, luggage 44, 452
rack, towel 235
racket (noise) 422
racket 428
racoon 5
radar 2
radian 303
radiate, to 523
radiation 133, 352
radiation, atomic 133
radiation, solar 19
radiation, ultraviolet 54, 352
radiator 232, 238
radical 370
radicle 29
radio 180, 238, 310
radio, car 47
radio, clock 238

radioactivity 54, 133, 353
radiobiology 210
radiograph 210
radiology 210
radio-opaque 356
radiotherapy 208, 210
radish 224
radius 30, 243, 304
raffia 298
raffle 154
raft 404
rage 487
rags 67
raid 316
rail (fence) 235
rail 453
railing 96
railway 453
railway, double-track 453
railway, underground 448, 450
railwayman 454
rain 132, 160, 464
rain, acid 132
rain, to 522
rainbow 467, 468
raincoat 63
raindrop 468
rainfall 464, 467
rainforest, tropical 133
rainstorm 465
rainy 464
raise (in wages) 471
raise, to 508, 525, 526
rake 445
rally (of party members) 358
ram 6, 145
Ramadan 271
ramble 181
rambling 93, 180
rancour 150
range 486
range, mountain 188
rank 316, 490
rank, taxi 447, 452
ranking 428
ranking, social 417
ranking, world 428
ransack, to 524
rape 98, 148
rapid 499
rapist 98
rapprochement 261
rare 501
rarely 532
raspberry 184
rat 5, 8
rate 122, 255, 258, 488, 491
rate, annual consumption 252
rate, average purchasing 123
rate, bank 122

relationship 139, 149, 141, 347
relatively 534
relatives 139, 140
relatives, blood 139
relatives, close 139
relatives, distant 139
relativism 350
relativism, cultural 420
relativity 356
relax, to 527
relaxation 178
relaxed 335, 338
relay 425
release, press 309
relegation 428
reliance 479
relief 11, 148, 149
religion 270, 394, 399, 417, 485
religion, Biblical 394
religion, natural 394
religion, philosophy of 348, 397
religion, sociology of 392
religiosity 394
religious 394, 498, 502
relish 169
rely, to 511
remain, to 519
remainder 108, 109, 480
remains 480, 481
remedy 214, 217
remember, to 509
remembrance 155, 483
reminder 492
remission 219
remittance 124
remnant 480
remnants 481
remorse 482
removal (e.g. of organ) 214
removal 485
Renaissance 13, 291
renal 219
rend apart, to 528
render, to 528
renew, to 510, 511
renewal 269
renewer (of Islam) 273
renowned 503
rent 106, 230, 489
rent out, to 506
rent, to 506
rental 489
rental fee, telephone line 255
renting 230
repagination 80
repair, to 511
reparations 264
repatriation 361
repayments 247
repeat (programme) 309

repeat, to 511
repentance 269, 392
repentant 495
repercussion 480
repetition 289
replace, to 512
reply 256
report 104, 130, 251, 311
report, special 311
report, to 518
report, weather 468
reporter 311, 484
repose 479
repose, to 522, 527
represent, to 520
representation, diplomatic 261
representation, proportional 382
representative 123, 382, 431, 476
representative, commercial 123
representative, permanent 267
repression 372
reprint 309
reprisal 261, 314
reproach, to 529
reproduce, to (e.g. sexually) 511
reproduction 25, 27
reproduction, asexual 27
reproduction, sexual 27
reproduction, vegetative 27
reptile 5
republic 366
republic, banana 261, 366
republic, democratic 366
republic, Islamic 366
republic, people's democratic 366
republicanism 366
repugnant 504
repulsive 498, 503
reputable 493
request, to 511, 525
requiem 400
requiescat 393
requisite 502
re-route 83
rescue 104
research 126, 248
research, market 309
research, philosophical 346
research, social 414
research, to do 523
researcher 126, 472
resemble, to 519, 529
resentment 150
reservation 1, 2, 226, 452, 453
reservation, seat 452
reserve 428
reserve, capital 114
reserve, to 515
reserved (e.g. seat) 498
reserved 337, 496, 501

reserves, oil 249
reshuffle, cabinet 363
reside, to 529
residence 226, 480, 490
residence, summer 96, 232
resident 228
resident, hotel 227
resident, local 447
resident, minister 267
residue 56
resignation 471
resin, acrylic 15
resist, to 522
resistance 355
resistance, active 380
resistance, non-violent 380
resistance, passive 381
resistivity 355
re-sit (i.e. an exam) 127
resolution (e.g. UN resolution) 377
resolution 482, 487, 488
resolution, display 85
resolution, print 77
resolve, to 528
resonance 352
resort, coastal 403
resourceful 340
resources, human 252
resources, national 252
resources, natural 135
resources, water 252
respect 479
respect, to 506
respected 502
respectful 495
respiration 27, 28, 54, 241, 482
respiration, artificial 212
respite 488
response 31, 34, 256, 483
responsibility, international 266
responsibility, ministerial 380
responsible 503
rest 178, 479, 488
rest and relaxation 319
rest, to 507, 522, 525, 527
restaurant 170, 227, 409, 449, 453
restaurant, station 452
restless 495
restoration 17
restrictions, trade 119
restrictive 196
result 130, 431, 479
result, as a 533
result, to get a 520
resumption 479
resurrection 394, 400
retail 113
retailer 408
retailer's 408
retain, to 525

retaliation 313
retardation, mental 385
retardation, psychomotor 387
retarded, mentally 385
retina 27, 30
retirement 152, 414
retribution, law of (Isl.) 103, 398
retrieval, data 72
retrogression 481
return 255, 481
return, rate of 122
return, to 508
re-usable 73
reveal, to 506
revelation 401
revelation, divine 401
revenge 148
revenue, inland 114
revenues 250
revere, to 517
reverence 479
reverse 487
reverse, to 519
review 295
review, film 311
review, literary 296
review, theatre 311
revisionism 363
revocation 481
revolt 103, 358, 377
revolt, to 527
revolution 97, 22, 361, 413, 480
revolution, bourgeois 361
revolution, commercial 361
revolution, cultural 361
revolution, export of 374
revolution, Green 361
revolution, industrial 361
revolution, Islamic 268, 361
revolution, permanent 361
revolution, political 361
revolution, social 413
revolution, socialist 361
revolution, technological 361
revolutionary 97, 361, 480
revolve, to 524, 528
revolver 105, 320
revue 295
reward 99, 256, 481
rhetoric 288, 292
rheumatism 215
rheumatology 215
rhinoceros 7
rhinology 210
rhizome 29, 30
rhombus 306
rhubarb 185
rhyme 293, 488
rhyme, nursery 292, 324, 325
rhyolite 194

roof 10, 11, 230
roof, sun 45
roof, thatched 93
roofer 471
room 10, 226, 229, 237
room, computer 126
room, dining 227, 229
room, double 226
room, family 226
room, fitting 407
room, guest 229
room, janitor's 229
room, living 229
room, prayer 401
room, rented 229
room, shower 229
room, single 226
room, sitting 229
room, study 126
room, utility 229
room, visual 97
room, waiting 208, 452
root 29, 161, 198, 200, 304, 461
root out, to 528
root, cube 304, 306
root, simple 304
root, square 302, 304
rope 298, 445
rosary 392
rose 163
rose, corn 163
rose, Damascus 163, 164
rose, hundred-leafed 163
rose, red 163
rose, tea 163
rose, yellow 163
rosebud 164
rosemary 224
rosewater 174
rot, to 523, 529
rotate, to 524, 528
rotation 20, 302, 353
rotation, crop 32, 146
rotten 495, 501
rouge 343
rough 298, 497, 498
roughage 29
roughness 484
round 428, 501
round, final 428
round, preliminary 431
round, third 428
roundabout 46
roundel 15
rouse, to 526
route 49
row, death 98
rowan 461
rowdy 336
rowing 429

royalism 372
royalties 309, 311
rub against, to 524
rub, to 526, 529
rubber 60, 299
rubber, foam 297
rubbish 132, 229
rubella 215
rubric 488
ruby 195
rudder 404
rude 336, 338, 340, 495, 497
rudeness 150, 481
rug 234, 238
rug, prayer 271
rugby 428
ruin 484
ruined 505
ruins 13, 94
rule 199, 305, 367, 488
rule, as a 531, 533
rule, cannon shot 264
rule, home 367
rule, majority 367
ruler 332, 366, 472
ruler, horizontal 76
rules 419
ruling 100
rumble 423
rumble, to 527
rumbling 423
rumour 374
rumourmonger 374
rumpus 423
run 78
run away, to 528
run down, to 525
run, test 78
run, to 514, 525
run, to cause to 525
runner 428
runner-up 431
running 427
running, cross-country 427
running, long-distance 427
running, middle-distance 427
runway 1
runway, temporary 1
rupture, to 528
rural 145, 498
ruse 484
rush, to 523
rush, to cause to 523
rushing (of water) 422
Russia 89
Russian 128
rustle 422
rustling 422
rutabaga 225
ruthlessness 481

saw, compass 444
saw, coping 444
saw, crosscut 444
saw, hand 444
sawfish 156
saxophone 324
say, to 518, 522, 528, 529
saying 285, 288, 293, 479
scabies 212, 220
scaffolding 445
scale 156, 322, 325, 490
scale, arithmetic 304
scale, binary 303
scale, Celsius 355
scale, social 420
scale, wage 476
scales 54, 157, 231, 237
scallop 156
scalloped 16
scan 74
scandal, political 371
scanner 74, 255, 332
scanner, flatbed 74
scanning 74
scansion 289
scapegoat 372
scapula 24
scar 212, 241, 243, 335
scarce 501
scare, to 523, 526
scarecrow 146
scared off, to be 526
scarf 65
scarlet 69
scatter, to 522, 523, 526
scatter-brained 337
scattering 352
scenario 435
scene 293, 436
scene, first 436
scenery 490
scent 162
scepticism 348, 487
schedule, tariff 112
scheming 99, 101
schist 193
schizophrenia 208, 215, 386
schizophrenic 386
scholar 338
scholar, learned 271
scholars, Muslim 397
scholars, religious 272
school (of thought) 345, 349, 381
school 130, 450
school, art 10
school, boarding 130
school, church 399
school, driving 49
school, girls' 130
school, grade 128

school, high 128
school, middle (9-13) 128
school, political 381
school, primary 128
school, private 130
school, reform 100
school, secondary 128
school, state 130
schoolboy 127
schoolgirl 128
schoolyard 127
schooner 457
sciatica 216
science, behavioural 387
Science, Christian 397
science, computer 80, 129
science, political 129, 375, 418
science, space 21
science, speech 285
science, veterinary 127
sciences 129
sciences, natural 129
sciences, social 129, 418
scientists 133
scintillation 354
scissors 333, 445
sclerosis 212
sclerosis, multiple 218
sclerotic 30
scoliosis 219
scoop 310
scooter, motor 458
score 130, 322, 427, 431, 484
score, film 438
scorer, goal 430
scorer, leading goal 426
scoring, goal 430
Scorpio 21, 42
scout 179, 316
scrape, to 523, 524, 526
scraping (sound) 423
scratch 213, 242
scratch, to 513, 524, 527
scratching (sound) 423
scream 422, 423
scream, to 512, 517
screeching 423
screen 73, 13, 231, 232, 238, 433, 482
screen, folding 238
screen, rood 13
screen, split 73
screening 207, 438
screw 444
screw, lag 444
screw, set 444
screw, to 509, 523
screwdriver 444
script, film 293, 437
script, play 437
scriptwriter 437

scriptwriting 437
scrofula 213
scrolling 80
scrounger 339, 341
scud 467
scuffle 104
sculpting 11
sculpture 11, 12, 17
scutch 444
sea (a.) 156
sea 133, 187, 404
sea lion 6
sea, law of the 262
seafood 156
seagull 40, 405
seahorse 156
seal 6, 157
seaman 404
seaplane 458
search 75, 99
search and replace 75, 86
search, global 75
search, to 512, 523, 524, 527
seas, freedom of the 259
seasickness 404
seaside 405
season 43, 441, 442, 468, 488
season, festive 154
season, mating 145
season, sale 410
season, slack (i.e. tourist trade) 404
seasonal 468
seasoned 501
seasoning 169
seat 238, 453
seat, reserved 2
seat, safe 368
seat, to 529
seated 504
seaweed 405
secateurs 162, 445
secession 361
second (e.g. sixty seconds) 440
secondary 500
secrecy 380
secret 485, 486, 499, 502
secretariat 262
secretary 369, 476
secretary-general 262
sect 272, 376, 397, 399, 418, 484, 488
sectarianism 397
section 288, 293, 449, 481, 483, 488
section, Caesarian 218
section, conic 305
sector 72, 305
sector, agricultural 247
sector, bad 81
sector, economic 109
sector, private 247, 361
sector, public 247

sector, social 414
secular 375, 390, 393, 399
secularisation 375, 394, 417
secularism 365, 394
securities 108
securities, bearer 108
securities, gilt-edged 108
securities, government 108
security 360, 480
security, collective 260
security, international 259
security, national 360
security, social 363, 413
sedative 207, 213, 221
sedition 364, 376
seduce, to 527
seductive 338, 342
see to, to 515
See, Holy 390
see, to 525
seed 26, 143, 144, 145, 161
seeds, melon 168
seeds, pumpkin 168
seeds, sunflower 168
seedsman 143
seeing 241
seek, to 523, 524, 527
seeker, asylum 260
seethe, to 524
segment 488
segment 81, 288, 301, 305
segmentation 196
segregation 363, 364
seize, to 528
select, to 523, 528
selection 480, 489
selection, natural 32
self 416, 420, 491
self, social 416
self-absorbed 337
self-aggrandizement 149
self-alienation 148
self-assurance 335
self-awareness 149, 337
self-belief 149
self-confidence 148, 480
self-conscious 337
self-consciousness 149
self-control 149
self-criticism 149
self-deception 149
self-defence, anticipatory 316
self-dependence 149
self-destruction 149
self-determination 368
self-determination, right of 261, 367
self-doubt 149
self-evident 346
self-government 367
self-hatred 148

self-image 149
self-interest 382
selfish 337
selfishness 149
self-knowledge 149
self-love 149
self-portrait 13
self-preservation 367
self-protection 380
self-respect 148, 150
self-sacrificing 493
self-sufficiency 249, 368
self-taught 127, 337
self-worship 347
sell, hard 110
sell, to 517, 527
seller 118
seller, antique 409, 474
seller, bird 36
seller, book 410
seller, cigarette 409
seller, newspaper 449
seller, shoe 411
seller, stamp 408
seller, toy 407
seller, watch 409
sellotape 446
semanteme 286
semantic 286
semanticist 286
semantics 286
sememe 287
semen 245
semester 130
semi-aquatic 159
semi-circle 307
semi-colon 286
semi-conductor 61, 356
semi-final 428
seminary 17
seminary, theological 273
semiotics 295
send away, to 525
send, to 527
sender 118, 257
sending 255
sending off 425
Senegal 89
senility 217
seniority 471
sensation 479, 484
sensationalism 345
sense 484, 490
sense, common 339, 348
senses, five 242
sensitive 337
sensitivity 213
sensor, image 77
sentence (Law) 100
sentence 127, 197, 282, 483

sentence, complex 197
sentence, death 100
sentence, to 519
sentenced 104
sentiment 479, 487
sentiment, public 358
sentimental 493
sentry 320
sepal 162
separate, to 512, 522
separation 55
separatism 365
separatist 365
sepsis 217
September 42
septicaemia 217
Septuagint 402
sequel 310
sequence 74, 303, 435
sequencing 74
sequin 63
sergeant 318
sergeant first class 313
sergeant-major 313
serial 79, 180, 310
series 79, 180, 310, 486
series, electrochemical 56
series, geometric 304
series, homologous 54
serious 336, 496, 504, 505
sermon 270, 290
serum 213
serum, blood 216
servant 472
servant, civil 377, 475
serve (tennis, badminton etc.) 428
server 76
service 456, 484
service, annual 47
service, intelligence 372
service, military 316, 317, 320, 368
service, social 416
serviceman 320
services 256
services, after-sale 46
services, armed 320
services, emergency 100, 255
services, postal 256
servitude 481
session 358
session, secret 365
set 306, 436
set fire to, to 506
set free, to 526
set free, to be 526
set off, to 512, 515
set on fire, to 526
set up, to 508, 509, 510
set, character 83
set, ordinate 306

651

shop, barber's 407, 408, 409
shop, carpet 410
shop, chemist's 213
shop, cigarette 409
shop, clothes 407, 411
shop, coffee 449
shop, computer 410
shop, computer software 411
shop, dairy food 411
shop, electrical goods 410
shop, fast food 410
shop, florist's 164
shop, fruit 411
shop, furniture 411
shop, gift 410
shop, greetings card 410
shop, hardware 410
shop, health 410
shop, kebab 410
shop, leather 408
shop, musical instruments 410
shop, paint 409
shop, pastry 409
shop, pet 5
shop, record 409
shop, second hand goods 409
shop, shoe 411
shop, sock 408
shop, sports 410
shop, tie 410
shop, video 411
shop, wine 407, 411
shopkeeper 408, 411, 473
shopkeeping 409
shopper 408
shopping 179, 408
shopping, electronic 76
shore 404, 405
short 340, 501
shortage 120, 488, 489
shortcut 47, 485
shortened 501
shorts 65
shorts, cycling 65
short-sighted 341
short-term 120
shot (in football, rugby etc.) 429
shot 438
shot, closing 438
shot, long 438
shot, opening 438
shot, putting the 426
shot, swerving 429
shot-putter 426
shot-putting 431
shoulder 243
shoulder, hard 48
shout 422, 488
shout, to 513, 517
show 182, 491

show, fashion 67
show, flower 165
show, musical 438
show, sound and light 182
show, to 520, 529
shower 232, 467
shower, sudden 467
shower, to 522
shower, to take a 514
showers, scattered 467
showroom, car 49, 411
shrew 8
shrimp 159
shrimps 175
shrine 17
shrub 161, 164
shrubbery 161
shut, to 522
shuttle 3
shuttle, space 21, 456, 457
shy 337, 496, 501
shy, to 526
shyness 149, 484
sick 210
sickle 144
sickness 210, 221
sickness and diarrhoea 219
sickness, air 1
sickness, sleeping 214, 222
side 96, 241, 305, 308
sideboard 237, 239
sideburns 337
sidewalk 447
Sierra Leone 89
sieve 277
sigh 422
sigh, to 506
sighing 422
sight 241
sight, long 28
sight, sense of 27, 242
sight, short 34
sights 448
sign 221, 309, 448, 487, 491
sign, plus 305
sign, to 507
sign, traffic 45, 48
signal 487
signal, digital 84
signal, to 517
signatory 107
signature 107, 255
significance 480
significant 504
signpost 93
Sikh 396
Sikhism 394
silence 486
silent 496, 499
silica 193

solo (instrumental) 323
solo (vocal) 323
soloist (instrumental) 323
soloist (vocal) 323
Solomon 271
Solomon Islands 88
solubility 55
solute 60
solution 33, 60, 133, 303, 485
solution, aqueous 60
solution, saturated 60
solution, supersaturated 60
solve, to 513
solvent 55
Somalia 89
some 531
some of 531
sometimes 531, 533
sommelier 227
son 138
song 288, 289, 322, 323
song, love 323
song, religious 395
songwriter 323
song-writing 322
sonic 80
son-in-law 139
sonnet 291
soon 532
sophistry 347
soprano 324
sore, cold 211
sorrel 224
sorrow 150, 480, 488
sorry 495, 500
sorry, to be 519
sort 491
soul 401, 485, 491
sound (a.) 80
sound (healthy) 499
sound 354, 422, 423, 436, 487
sound, cracking 422
soundproofing 234
soundtrack 434
soup 171
soup, barley 171
soup, chicken 171
sour, to turn 523
source 95, 479
source, data 84
sources, secondary data 420
south 465
South Africa 87
South Korea 90
south-east 465
south-west 465
souvenir 409, 492
sovereign 362
sovereignty 366
sovereignty, national 366

sovereignty, people's 366
soviet 373, 374
sow 5
sow, to 522, 528
space 22, 80, 483, 488
space, back 73
space, loading 118
space, parking 45, 447
space, social 418
spacebar 80, 82
spacecraft 21
spaceport 19
spaceship 22, 457, 458
spacing, line 80
spacious 505
spade 403, 444
spades (in cards) 179
Spain 87
span 490
spanner 444
spar, Iceland 189
spark 483
sparkle, to 508, 514, 525
sparkling 504
sparkplug 48
sparrow 39
spasm 220
spatula 278
speak, to 529
speaker (in parliament) 371
speaker 73
speakers, internal 73
special 493, 502
specialist 220, 252, 489
specialist, eye 212
specialist, heart
speciality 492
species 34, 489, 491
specific 502
specifications 83
spectator 426, 434, 482
spectators 434
spectrometer, mass 354
spectrometry 354
spectrum 354
spectrum, absorption 354
spectrum, visible 354
speech 153, 284, 285, 382, 483, 486, 489
speech, direct 285
speech, indirect 200
speed 2, 21, 47, 304, 353, 453
speedboat 404, 457
speeding 45, 47
speedometer 47
spell, cold 466
spell, warm 466
spell-check 72
spelling 126, 280
spelling, phonetic 280
spend, to (e.g. money) 513

spend, to (e.g. time) 516
sperm 24, 34
sphere 306
sphincter 34
spices 166
spick and span 495
spicy 496
spider 38
spies, den of
spill, to 526
spilled, to 526
spin 351, 353
spin, to 523, 524, 526, 528
spina bifida 208
spinach 224
spin-dryer 239
spine 241
spinel 194
spines (of hedgehog) 5
spinster 138
spiracle 30
spire 447
spirit 338, 395, 401, 485
Spirit, Holy 395
spirits 172
spirits, methylated 51
spiritual 395, 398, 400
spiritualism 395
spiritualist 395
spiritualistic 395
spit, roasting 277
spit, to 511
splash 423
splashing 423
spleen 31, 243
splenitis 222
split 150
split, to 527
spoil, to 529
spoils, war 318
spondylitis 222
sponge 229
sponge, bath 229, 235
spoon 173
spoon, dessert 278
spoon, soup 278
Spoonerism 280
spore 34
sport 131, 431
sportsman 431
sportsman, professional 477
sportswoman 431
sportswoman, professional 477
spot (Med.) 212, 337, 338
spot, beauty 337
spot, blind 34
spot, penalty 431
spouse 141
sprain 214
spray, deodorant 132

spray, throat 208
spray, to 522
spraying, crop 145
spread 487
spread, to 510, 518, 528
spreadsheet 72
spring (of water) 94
spring 41, 187, 445
spring, to 525
sprinkle, to 522
sprinkler 160
sprint 427
sprint, to 525
sprite 80
sprout, Brussels 225
sprout, to 525
spruce, red 462
spruce, white 461
sputtering (of an engine) 422
spy 99, 365
spy-hole 233
squabble 490
squadron 318
squall 465
square (i.e. to the power of 2) 302
square 17, 302, 306, 307, 450
square, set 333
squash (drink) 172
squash, to 519
squawk 38
squawking 38
squeak 422
squeaking 422
squeeze, to 524, 527
squeezer, lemon 276
squelching 423
squid 158
squinch 16
squint 220
squirm, to 529
squirrel 6
squirrel, flying 6
Sri Lanka 89
St. Elmo's Fire 463
St. Kitts and Nevis 89
St. Lucia 89
St. Vincent and the Grenadines 89
St. Vitus dance 213
stabbing 99
stability, economic 365
stability, political 365
stable 6, 496
stadium, sports 182, 431, 450
staff 318
staff, editorial 311
staff, general 317
staff, teaching 129
stage (of a journey) 96
stage 436, 490
stage manager, assistant 434

stellar 19
stem 30, 196, 198
stenosis 209
stepbrother 137, 139
stepfather 137, 140, 141
stepladder 446
stepmother 139, 140, 141
steppe 187
steps 230
stereo, personal 182
stereotype 370, 489
sternum 27, 240
steroids 208
stew 169
steward 2
steward, air 476
stewardess 2
stewardess, air 476
stewpot 277
stick 94
stick, ski 427
stick, to 512, 524
stick, walking 64, 66, 94
sticker 481
still 465, 493, 494, 496, 534
stillness 486
stills 436
stimulating 505
stimulus 25
sting 215
sting, insect 222
sting, to 528
stink, to 508
stir, to 509
stitch (from running) 219
stitch together, to 525
stitches 209
stock (of goods) 122
stock 116
Stock Exchange, Tehran 248
stock, active 116
stock, authorized 116
stock, bonus 116
stock, capital 116
stock, classified 116
stock, debenture 117
stock, fully-paid 116
stock, goods in 122
stock, guaranteed 116
stock, inactive 116
stock, voting 116
stockings, nylon 64
stockpiles, nuclear 316
stocks 116
stolon 30
stoma 29
stomach 33, 245
stomach-turning 341
stone (in fruit) 185
stone 95, 161, 192, 193, 404

stone, kidney 216
stone, pumice 233, 298
stone, semi-precious 192
stone-carving 15
stonecutter 474
stonemason 15, 474
stones, precious 190, 192
stool 233
stop (n.) 452, 480, 483
stop, bus 447
stop, emergency 45
stop, to 522
stopover 1, 452, 483
stoppage (of trade) 122
stopwatch 441
storage 123
storage, data 78
storage, primary 75
store 143, 230
store, department 410, 449
store, food 407
store, general 408
store, to 522
storeman 471
storeroom 276
storey 15, 227, 409
stork 39
storm 465
storm, ice 469
stormy 500
story 290, 293, 310, 434
story, fairy 290
story, love 290, 434
story, serialised 179
story, short 290
storyteller 181
story-writing 179
stove 276
stowaway 490
straight 498, 503
strain, to 527
strait 187
strange 500
strangeness 148
stranger 488
strangle, to 513
strap, shoulder 63
strata, social 419
stratagem 484
strategy 313, 314, 359
strategy, military 316
stratification 283
stratification, ethnic 419
stratification, social 419
stratocumulus (cloud) 463
stratum 191
stratus (cloud) 464
straw 146, 299
straw, drinking 176
strawberry 184

success 426, 488
successful 501, 504
successful, to be 520
succession, law of state 262
successive 502
succulent 499
suck, to 519, 529
suckle, to 529
sucrose 57, 61
Sudan 89
sudden 504
suddenly 533, 534
suede 297
suffer, to 515
suffix 197
Sufi 272, 396
Sufism 269, 392
sugar 57
suggest, to 510
suicide 416
suicide, egoistic 416
suit (n.) 66
suit, morning 67
suit, space 22
suit, to 522, 526
suit, track 66
suitable 503
suitcase 2, 227
sulky 335
sullen 335
sulphate 57
sulphide 57
sulphide, hydrogen 62
sulphur 60, 299
sultan 372
sultanas 173
sultanate 372
sum 121, 302, 306, 489, 490
sumac 171
summary 483
summary, news 310
summer 41, 465
summit 188
sumptuous 502
sun 20, 161, 466
sunbathing 403
sunburn 207, 403
Sunday 42
sundial 441
sunflower 162
sunglasses 404
sunken 501
sunna (of the Prophet Muhammad) 396
Sunni 396
Sunnis 390
Sunnism 269
Sunnite 271
sunny 463, 493
sunshade 404
sunshine 463

sunspot 22
sunstroke 403
superb 500
superconductivity 355
supercooling 355
superficial 339
superhighway, information 71
superior 503
supermarket 410
supernova 19
superpower 358
superpowers 259
superpowers, new 259
superscript 72
superstructure 371
supervise, to 506
supervision 486
supervisor, doctoral 126
supervisor, school 130
Supper, Last 396, 397
supplement 454
suppletion 196
supplication 401
supplies, office 333
supply and demand 118, 250
supply, to 525
supporter 383, 432
supporter, government 383
suppose, to 517, 523
suppress, to 529
surcharge 120, 124
sure 503
surety 102
surface 304, 308, 486
surgeon 212, 472
surgeon, veterinary 472
surgery 212, 472
surgery, brain 212
surgery, doctor's 221, 411
surgery, heart 212
surgery, plastic 212, 241
surgery, reconstructive 212
surgery, thoracic 212
Surinam 89
surname 137, 257
surplus 485
surplus, economic 107
surprise 482
surprise, to 519
surprise, to take by 517
surprised, to be 511
surprising 495
surrealism 15, 292, 293
surrender 314
surrender, to 510
surrender, unconditional 314
surround, to 519
survey 109, 414
survey, market 109, 247
survey, pilot 414

661

tab, auto 72
tab, centred 72
tab, decimal 72
tab, left-aligned 72
tab, right-aligned 72
table (i.e. league or medals) 427
table 239, 279, 302, 334, 483, 488, 491
table(s), multiplication 302
table, astronomical 20
table, bedside 239
table, coffee 238, 239
table, dressing 239
table, periodic 55
table, round 381
table, small 238
table, water 192
table, work 334
table, writing 239, 334
tablecloth 170, 233, 278
tablet 218
tablet, sleeping 218
tableware 278
tabloid 310
tabulation 72, 75
taciturn 501
tackle, fishing 156
tactics 426
tactics, delaying 425
tadpole 156, 158
taekwando 426
tagmeme 200
tail 5, 37
tail, shirt 64
tailcoat 67
tailor 408, 472
tailor, to 525
tails 66
taint, to 522
Taiwan 88
Tajikistan 88
take after, to 525
take for, to 523
take out, to 508, 513
take part, to 516
take place, to 506
take, to 508, 518, 522, 526, 528
take-off 1
talc 193
tale 293
tale, morality 290
talent 335
talented 494
talk 486, 489, 490
talk idly, to 529
talk, to 512, 516, 518
talkative 495
talks 252, 265, 380
talks, to have 518
tall 340, 494, 501
talons 37

tamarind 168, 184
tambour 323
tambourine 323
tame 493
tangent 302, 307
tangerine 185
tank (fish) 158
tank 314, 456
tank, petrol 44
tank, think 380
tanker 458
Tanzania 88
Taoism 392, 393
Taoist 391, 393
tap 233
tape 85, 182
tape, blank 326
tape, magnetic 85
tape, red 364, 377
tapestry 15
taping 324
target 124, 320
targets, economic 106
tariff 111, 226
tariff, customs 111
tarmac 297
tarragon 224
task 81, 129
Tasmanian devil 6
Tasmanian wolf 7
taste 172, 292
taste, sense of 27, 242
taste, to 519, 524
tasty 502
tatami 12
tattoo 337
Taurus 42
tautology 282, 290, 296
tavern 182, 411
tax 104, 120, 135, 257
tax, income 121
tax, inheritance 120
tax, value-added (VAT) 120
taxes 104, 120, 489
taxi 1, 448, 452, 456
taxi, air 456
taxonomy 285
tea 169
tea, afternoon 172
teabags 174
teaboy 471, 474
teach, to 506, 510, 514, 521, 522
teacher 126, 130, 476
teaching 126, 127, 130, 482
teacup 276, 278
tea-house 448
teak 461
team, away 427
team, home 427
team, national 426

teapot 278
tear (i.e. from crying) 335
tear 63, 481
tear off, to 528
tear to pieces, to 525
tear, to 509, 522, 525, 527, 528
tear, to cause to 528
teargas 318
tea-rose 163
tea-rose, hybrid 162
tease, to 514
teaspoon 278
tea-strainer 276
teat 8
technical 81, 500
technique 251, 289, 293
technique, airbrush 17
technique, management 418
technocracy 376, 418
technocrat 376
techno-diplomacy 364
technology 248, 251, 415, 418
technology, information (IT) 74, 127
tedious 505
teenager 141
teeth 28
teeth, false 242, 338
teeth, milk 28
telecommunications 83
Telecommunications, Ministry of 253
telegram 256
telegraph 256
teleology 348
telephone 179, 226, 237, 256, 332
telephone, cordless 237
telephone, mobile 237
telephone, to 511
telescope 19, 353, 403
telescope, radio 19
television 226, 231, 237
television, closed circuit 74
television, satellite 309
tell, to 518, 529
teller, fortune 181
temper 484, 487
tempera 13
temperament 337, 484
temperature 55, 133, 353, 466, 468
temperature and pressure, standard 353
temperature, absolute 55
temperature, high 211
temperature, Kelvin 56
temperature, room 56
temperature/pressure, normal (NTP) 354
tempering 52
tempestuous 500
template 71
temple 17, 243, 400
temple, fire 389
temporal 441

temporary 504
Ten Commandments 394
tenant 230, 235
tench 156
tend to, to 515
tendency 482, 491
tendency for, to have a 528
tendency, criminal 103
tender 121, 122, 504
tender, legal 110
tenderness 150, 151
tenders, appeal for 114
tendon 27, 241
tennis, table 426
tenor 323
tense 198, 284, 441
tense, future 198
tense, past 198, 199
tense, past narrative 199
tense, perfect 199
tense, present 198
tension 314
tension, nervous 218
tension, revolutionary 365
tension, social 415
tent 94
tepid 505
term (of office) 370
term (school or university) 127, 130
term 479
terminal 1, 73
termite 40
terms and conditions 118
terms, credit 117
terracotta 14, 16, 298
terrible 341
terrified 505
terrify, to 523
terrifying 505
territories, non-self governing 263
territories, overseas 263
territory 263
territory, abandoned 263
terror 151, 482
terror, balance of 266
terror, to feel 523
terrorism 98, 364
terrorism, international 261
terrorism, state 364
terrorist 98, 364
terry-towelling 297
terylene 54
test 127, 207
test, blood 207
test, driving 44
test, flame 51
test, psychological 385
test, skin 207
test, to 522, 524
test, urine 207

testa 26
Testament, New 390, 397
Testament, Old 397
testicle 241, 242
testicles 25
testimony 102
testis 25
test-tube baby 209
tetanus 219
tetrahedron 55, 302
text (book) 129
text 286, 294
texture 12, 14
texture, soil 26
Thailand 88
thankful 503
thanks 482
thanksgiving 486
thaw 469
thaw, to 528
theatre 179, 434, 438, 448
theatre, children's 434
theatre, operating 208
theatre-in-the-round 434
theatrical 295, 434, 438, 439
theatricality 434
theatrics 438
theft 101
theft, car 47
theft, petty 101
theism 347, 393
theme 289, 434
theme, main 434
then 531, 533
theocracy 367, 394, 400
theology 273, 397, 398
theology, Biblical 390
theology, Islamic 397
theorem, Pythagoras's 305
theory 350, 491
theory, 'end of history' 267
theory, 'end of ideology' 382
theory, conspiracy 382
theory, domino 267
theory, fault 382
theory, game 382
theory, kinetic 61
theory, learning 388
theory, music 323
theory, political 382
theory, quantum 356
theory, risk 267
theory, social 420
theory, virtue 350
therapeutics 214
there 531
thermal (a.) 55, 59
thermal (n.) 466
thermodynamics 352
thermometer 55, 466

thermometer, wet-bulb 466
thermostat 54
thesis 289, 346, 350
thesis, doctoral 127
thesis, dominant ideology 364
thick 340
thicket 93, 94, 164, 460, 461
thickness 305, 489
thief 101
thieves, den of 101
thigh 242
thin 340, 502
thing 483, 487
think deeply, to 510, 511
think, to 517, 522
third-person (narrative) 292
thirst 168
this-worldly 390
thorax 31
thorn 94, 161
thorough 501
thought 488
thought, political 376
thoughtful 335
thoughtless 494
thread 299
threadbare 504
threadbare, to make 526
threat, nuclear 315
threaten, to 512
three-dimensional 304
thrift 250
thriller 180, 437
thriving 501
throat 244
throat, sore 220
throb, to 523, 527
thrombosis 211, 220
thrombus 220
Throne, the Divine 397
throng 479, 480
throw away, to 514, 522
throw down, to 522
throw up, to 508
throw, to 507
thrush 36, 209
thrust into, to 527
thrust, to 524, 526
thug, knife-wielding 99
thumb 243
thumbtack 444
thunder 466
thunder and lightning 466
thunder, rumble of 423
thunder, to 527
thunderbolt 467
thunderclap 463
thundercloud 463
thunderstorm 465
Thursday 42

urn, tea 277
urology 209
Ursa Major 20
Ursa Minor 20
Uruguay 87
usage 81, 285
use 81, 248, 488
use, office 81
use, to 507, 519
used to, to be 517
useful 503
usefulness 479
useless 495
uselessness 481
user 81
user-friendly 81, 83
usher 472, 473
usual 500, 503
usually 531, 533
usury 123, 271
utensil 279
utensils 276
utensils, cooking 276
utensils, kitchen 279
uterus 30, 243
uterus, cancer of 215
utilitarianism 348, 376
utilitarianism, negative 348
utility 488
utopia 358
utter, to 508
utterance 286
Uzbekistan 87
vacation, summer 127
vaccination 222
vaccine 222
vacuole 32, 34
vacuum 20, 55, 353
vade-mecum 290
vagina 33, 240, 245
vain 503
valency 57, 62
validity 418
valley 94, 187
valuables 230, 235, 344
value 106, 305, 307, 479, 488
value, capitalized 106
value, commercial 106
value, customs 106
value, export 247
value, face 106
value, nominal 106
value, social 413
value, surrender 106
value, to be of 507
valve 28, 47
van 96, 147, 450, 458
Van der Waals' forces 61
van, breakdown 49, 458
vanadium 62

vanilla 176
Vanuatu 91
vapour 53, 352, 480
variable 468
variable, global 83
variant 287
variation 34
variegated 498
variety 491
various 501, 502
varnish, nail 344
vase 164, 235
vast 495, 505
Vatican City 91
vault 14
vaunt, to 522
veal 174
vector 301, 352
Vedanta 401
Vedantism 397
vegetables 134, 161, 171, 224
vehicle 46, 249, 448, 450, 456
vehicle, armoured 316
vehicle, goods 458
vehicle, space 23
veil 64, 67, 269
vein 29, 30, 191, 242
vein, jugular 216, 243
vein, pulmonary 30
veins, varicose 222
velocity 304
velocity, relative 304
velvet 299
vena cava 25
vend, to 527
vendor 118
vendor, street 449
venereology 220
Venezuela 91
vengeance 150
venison 174
venom 6
vent, air 236
ventilation 231, 236
ventricle 31
ventriloquism 436
ventriloquist 436
Venus fly-trap 164
veranda 230, 235
verb 199
verb, auxiliary 199
verb, irregular 199
verb, phrasal 199
verbena 163
verdict 100
verdure 161
verge 48
verifiable 348
vernacular 291
verse (of Koran) 268

willow, weeping 460
willpower 491
wilting 26
win (n.) 425, 426
win, to 522
wind 464
wind, prevailing 464
wind, solar 19
wind, to 523
windless 465
windmill 143
window 73, 231
window, active 74
window, dormer 11
window, lancet 11
window, rose 11
window, shop 411
window, ticket 454
winds, easterly 464
winds, northerly 464
winds, southerly 464
winds, westerly 464
windscreen, back 48
windscreen, front 48
windy 464
wine 172
wine-coloured 69
wing 1, 36, 427
wing, left 366, 427
wing, right 366, 427
wink 483
winner 425, 429
winner, award 433
winner, Oscar 433
winter 41, 467
wipe, to 525
wiper, board 332
wipers, windscreen 44
wire 298
wire, barbed 95, 445
wish, to 506, 525
wistaria 164
wit 336, 489
with 531, 532
wither, to 523
withering 26
without 531
witness 101, 104
witticism 489
woe 488
woeful 500
wolf 7
wolf, Tasmanian 7
wolframite 195
woman, country 95
woman, old 138
woman, unmarried 139
woman, young 139
wonder 150, 482
wonder, to 522

wonderful 339
wood (forest) 144
wood 17, 27, 93, 94, 133, 298, 460
woodbine 165
woodcut 10
woodcutter 460
woodlouse 37
woodpecker 37
woodpigeon 39
woodsman 472
woodwork 130
wool 4, 297
wool, cotton 211, 297
woollens 67
word 199, 200, 483, 489
word processor, dedicated 334
work 81, 129, 355, 377, 474
work, flower 164
work, social 419
work, team 429
work, to 518, 530
work, to put to 529
work, voluntary 475
workbench 446
worker 475
worker, construction 475
worker, dairy 146
worker, factory 475
worker, hard 335
worker, industrial 251
worker, metal 474
worker, office 475
worker, post office 475
worker, skilled 475
worker, social 419, 476
worker, steel 475
workers 251
workforce 477
workplace 475
works, collected 294
workshop 251, 445, 450, 475
workstation 72, 230, 237, 332
worktable 334
work-to-rule 377
world 133
World Wide Web (WWW) 85
World, First 261
World, Fourth 261
world, free 261
world, invisible 397
World, Second 261
World, Third 261, 366
world, visible 397
worldly 393
worldview 347
worm 7, 39, 162, 219
worn-out 495, 500, 501
worried 498, 504
worried, to be 520, 530
worried, to become 520

675

Lightning Source UK Ltd.
Milton Keynes UK
UKOW06f2107060913

216720UK00008B/151/P

9 780415 567800